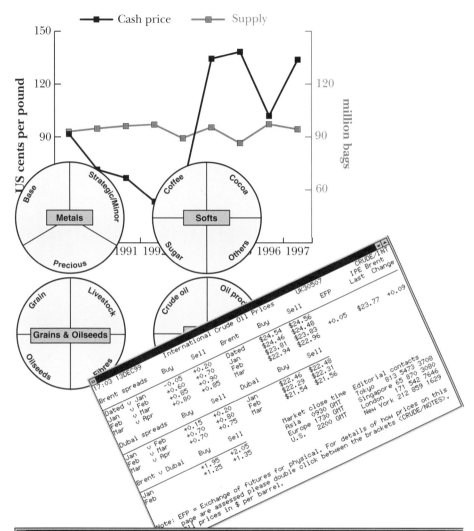

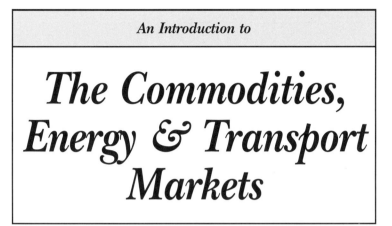

An Introduction to

The Commodities, Energy & Transport Markets

John Wiley & Sons (Asia) Pte Ltd

Singapore   New York   Chichester
Brisbane   Toronto   Weinheim

Other titles in the series

An Introduction to Technical Analysis *0-471-83127-1*
An Introduction to Derivatives *0-471-83176-X*
An Introduction to Foreign Exchange & Money Markets *0-471-83128-X*
An Introduction to Equity Markets *0-471-83171-9*
An Introduction to Bond Markets *0-471-83174-3*

You can get more information about the other titles in the series from the Reuters Financial Training series companion web site at *http://www.wiley-rft.reuters.com.*

Acknowledgments

The publishers and Reuters Limited would like to thank the following people for their invaluable assistance in this book:

William Slatyer of International Commodities Services Pty. Ltd. for his thorough review of the book and constructive feedback.

Dr. Keith A. Rogers of Training and Learning Design who wrote, designed and produced the original version of the book.

Numa Financial Systems Ltd for use of their Directory of Futures & Options Exchanges at the back of this book.

Other Wiley Editorial Offices
John Wiley & Sons, Inc., 605 Third Avenue, New York, NY 10158-0012, USA
John Wiley & Sons Ltd, Baffins Lane, Chichester, West Sussex PO19
1UD, England
John Wiley & Sons (Canada) Ltd, 22 Worcester Road, Rexdale,
Ontario M9W 1L1, Canada
John Wiley & Sons Australia Ltd, 33 Park Road (PO Box 1226), Milton,
Queensland 4064, Australia
Wiley-VCH, Pappelallee 3, 69469 Weinheim, Germany

Library of Congress Cataloging-in-Publication Data
An introduction to the commodities, energy & transport markets.
        p.   cm. — (The Reuters financial training series)
    Includes bibliographical references.
    ISBN 0-471-83150-6
    1. Commodity exchanges.   2. Energy industries — Finance.   3. Transportation
    — Finance.   4. Stocks.   I. Title: Commodities, energy & transport markets.
    II. Title: Commodities, energy, and transport markets.   III. Reuters ltd.
    IV. Series.
HG6046.I484   2000
332.64'4 — dc21   00-024648

ISBN 0-471-83150-6

Typeset in 10/12 point New Baskerville
Printed in Singapore by Craft Print Pte Ltd
10 9 8 7 6 5 4 3 2 1

An Introduction to

The Commodities, Energy & Transport Markets

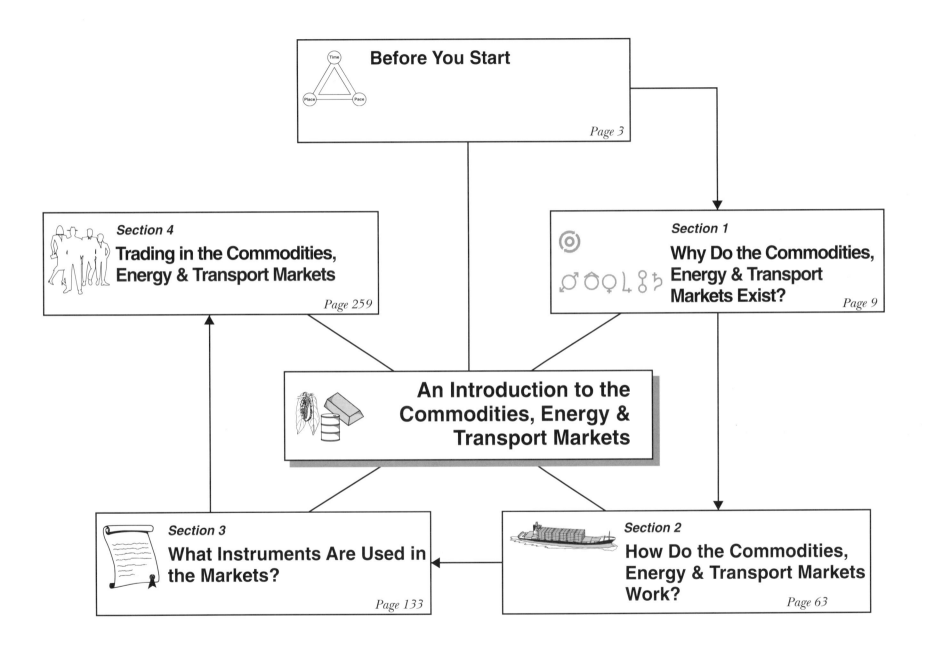

Before You Start

Page 3

Section 4

Trading in the Commodities, Energy & Transport Markets

Page 259

Section 1

Why Do the Commodities, Energy & Transport Markets Exist?

Page 9

An Introduction to the Commodities, Energy & Transport Markets

Section 3

What Instruments Are Used in the Markets?

Page 133

Section 2

How Do the Commodities, Energy & Transport Markets Work?

Page 63

Contents

Who Should Use This Book?

This book is designed to provide an overview of the commodities, energy and transport markets for a variety of readers: salespeople, support and operations staff, trainers, managers or investors who want to learn more about the markets to refine their investing strategies. Also, anyone beginning an in-depth study of the markets will find this book to be a very useful primer.

Despite the complexity of the financial markets, more and more people need a working knowledge of what the basic instruments are and how the markets are structured, for for professional and personal pursuits. Such readers will find this book to be helpful as it provides not only the fundamental definitions, but also exercises and examples to make markets more accessible.

This book will take you through the basics of the commodities, energy and transport markets, from what the instruments are and why the markets exist, to whom the market players are, to how the markets are structured and regulated and how information is used. By the time you have completed this book, you should be able to participate in these markets in an informed fashion.

An Introduction to the Commodities, Energy and Transport Markets is one in the Reuters Financial Training series, designed to provide readers with an overall understanding of the financial markets. Other titles cover equities, bonds, derivatives, technical analysis, and foreign exchange and money markets.

What Will You Find in This Book?

This book provides a new approach to gaining some basic familiarity with the essential concepts of the commodities, energy and transport markets. The book is written in a very accessible style with jargon kept to a minimum, but with market language clearly explained.

Most importantly, the book includes a range of materials to help you reinforce what you are learning. Each section offers a solid explanation of basic concepts, followed by actual examples for the reader to work through. Additional exercises and quick quizzes enable the reader to further enhance learning. To enable the reader to better understand how market players use financial data, screens from Reuters electronic information services are provided. Finally, each section concludes with a graphic overview – a visual outline – of what has been covered for quick yet thorough review, and ends with a listing of additional reference materials.

> In addition, the **RFT Web Site** has been created as this book series' companion web site, where additional quiz questions, updated screens and other information may be found. You can find this web site at:
>
> **http://www.wiley-rft.reuters.com**

This text frequently references UK and US exchanges and organisations. For the specifics of markets throughout the world, the reader is advised to refer directly to organisations in the Further Resources listings, and to exchanges around the world, whose contact information is provided at the back of the book.

How Is This Book Organised?

This book contains the following sections:

Before You Start

This section!

Why Do the Commodities, Energy and Transport Markets Exist?

This section covers the history and purpose of the markets.

How Do the Commodities, Energy and Transport Markets Work?

This section explains operation or "mechanics" of the market and addresses market "jargon" and conventions.

What Instruments Are Used in the Markets?

This section provides a brief overview of all the instruments used in the markets. Each instrument is defined and accompanied by sample screens from Reuters' electronic information services to illustrate how information is provided to market players via data terminals.

Trading in the Commodities, Energy and Transport Markets

This section describes market players and their trading techniques, as well as an overview of how these markets are regulated.

Throughout the book you will find that important terms or concepts are shown in **bold**, for example, **forward market**. You will also find that activities included to enhance your learning are indicated by the following icons:

 This indicates the definition of a term that you must know and understand to master the material.

 This means stop and think about the point being made. You may also want to jot a few words in the box provided.

 This indicates an activity for you to do. It is usually something written – for example, a definition, notes, or a calculation.

 This is the answer or response to an activity and it usually follows the activity or is close to it.

 This indicates the main points of the section.

 This indicates questions for you to answer to help you to review the material. The answers are also provided.

 This indicates the one-page summary that provides a quick overview of the entire section. This page serves as an excellent study tool.

Additional reference material is listed in **Further Resources** at the end of each section.

How to Use This Book

Before you start using this book, decide what you want from the material. If you are using it as part of your work, discuss with your manager how she will help by giving time for study and giving you feedback and support. Although your learning style is unique to you, you will find that your learning is much more effective if you allocate reasonable sized periods of time for study. The most effective learning period is about 30 minutes – so use this as a basis. If you try to fit your learning into odd moments in a busy schedule you will not get the best from the materials or yourself. You might like to schedule learning periods into your day just as you would business meetings.

Remember that the most effective learning is an interactive process and requires more than just reading the text. The exercises in this book make you think through the material you have just read and then apply your understanding through basic activities. Take time to do the exercises. This old Chinese saying sums up this concept:

> I hear and I forget
> I see and I remember
> I do and I understand

Try to make sure your study is uninterrupted. This probably means that your workplace is not a good environment! You will need to find both the time and place where you can study – you may have access to a quiet room at work, you may have a room at home, you may need to use a library.

This section of the book should take about two hours of study time. You may not take as long as this or you may take a little longer – remember your learning is individual to you.

Cargoes

Dirty British coaster with salt-caked smoke stack,
Butting through the Channel in the mad March days,
With a cargo of Tyne coal,
Road-rail, pig-lead,
Firewood, iron-ware, and cheap tin trays.

John Masefield

Introduction

The commodities, energy and transport markets are closely related. **Commodities** are the basic raw materials which provide people with food; oil for heating, power and gasoline (energy); and materials for manufacturing. Without the worldwide shipping and cargo markets, these commodities would not be transported from producer to consumer. Thus, these markets exist to make commodities available. And in doing so, they provide another trading arena for market players.

Fluctuations in the commodities, energy and transport markets also affect the debt, equities, foreign exchange and money markets. For example, the cost of raw materials is a key to forecasting inflation rates – which affect interest rates – which in turn affect the bond and equity markets.

This section introduces each of the three markets and covers the following:

- An introduction to the concept of supply and demand in commodities markets and the importance of weather

- An introduction to commodities markets and the major types of commodities traded

- How the energy markets operate for oil, natural gas and electricity

- The importance of dry and wet cargoes in the shipping markets and the emerging air cargo market

Before moving on, try the activity opposite to check your current understanding of the markets mentioned above. No specific answers are given as the following text covers all you will need to know.

 Before moving on, what do you think comprise the major commodity and energy markets? List any commodities, energy products or transport areas you think are important.

Supply, Demand and the Weather

Within the different markets, the market players all need as much information as possible in order to buy and sell commodities, crude oil and energy products or to charter vessels for cargoes to their best advantage. The players are all seeking the most favourable prices or contract conditions. But how are such prices or contract conditions determined?

Provided a market is operating freely, the price of a commodity, product or service is a good indicator of the **demand** for it. By allowing prices to move freely the markets tend to match the **supply** of the commodity, product or service to the demand. A marketplace acts therefore as a pivot point in balancing supply and demand as shown in the diagram below.

If supply exceeds demand, then prices fall and eventually production output or service provision falls. The result is that demand exceeds supply. This effect causes prices to rise which in turn causes production output or service provision to rise until a balance point is achieved between supply and demand.

Prices of commodities, products and services can vary in both the short and long term based on a wide variety of factors including the following:

- Weather
- Political/international events
- Availability and cost of labour
- Availability of domestic/international resources
- Production/processing demands

Weather

Weather conditions, especially unusual ones, are a major consideration for agricultural commodities. Adverse weather conditions during the planting, growing and harvesting periods for a crop can have dramatic effects on cash and futures prices for the commodity in the short term. Weather conditions are also important in the long term for commodities involving long periods before being sold, for example, crops involving plantations reaching maturity, livestock development etc.

A good example of the importance of weather is the phenomenon known as El Nino. This phenomenon originates in the South Pacific Ocean and occurs every three to five years. In 1997 El Nino was considered to be the strongest this century. El Nino affects worldwide weather causing drought and flood conditions that are either atypical or exaggerated for a particular region. Both crop and mineral ore production are affected by such adverse weather conditions.

The availability of news on the weather and its potential effects on crop and other yields is therefore very important to market players.

Political/International Events

Events such as international wars and action taken by individual governments in an international context can quickly affect the markets. The prices of commodities and their availability can change dramatically within a very short period of time. For example, within a few weeks of the start of the Arab-Israeli conflict in 1973, the international price of oil had risen by 320%.

The availability of news on political events and their potential effects on the supply of commodities, crude oil etc are therefore very important to market players.

International news services publish market information in the daily newspapers of major cities, and the majority of market players subscribe to electronic news services such as Reuters. Brokers also often supply their clients with news second-hand.

The Reuters screens below show weather updates.

```
13:45  RTRS-***GLANCE - Grains,oilseeds,livestock 1345 GMT***
13:42  WSC-China weather update
13:32  RTRS-WEATHE
13:05  WSC-World We   13:45  13 Oct  RTRS-***GLANCE - Grains,oilseeds,livestock 1345 GMT***
13:02  RTRS-Philippin  --------------------------------------------------------------
13:00  RTRS-Potentia
12:53  RTRS-CSCE co     To access news and prices click on the codes in brackets
12:48  RTRS-Mild har      or type code and hit the news key (f9) for [] itens
12:22  RTRS-Philippin                 or enter for <> items
12:02  WSC-Argentina
12:01  WSC-Brazil Sur
12:01  WSC-South Afr * RUSSIA SEARCHES FOR SOLUTIONS TO WINTER FOOD SHORTAGES
11:58  RTRS-Indian SI * FOCUS-Russia seeks to avert food crisis        [nMY1300717]
11:55  WSC-Brazil Cof * Russia has not asked for food aid - Dep PM Kulik [nMB1300605]
10:24  RTRS-***GLAN  * Russia prepares to abolish higher VAT rate on food[nMY1300362]
10:23  RTRS-***GLAN  * Slovakia plans 70pct wheat import tariff -agency  [nK1305692]
14:46  Headlines Olde
                        WEATHER FAVOURS HARVEST IN U.S. MIDWEST
                      * Mild harvest weather continues in U.S. Midwest   [nN13280096]
                      * Potential showers late this week in U.S. Plains  [nN13284736]

13:42  WSC-China weather update
13:05  WSC-World Weather Daybook          DRLD PHYSICAL MARKET
12:02  WSC-Argentina Summary          an $55 nln wheat import        [nSP320699]
12:01  WSC-Brazil Summary             ice outside tenders--trade[nJAK000327]
12:01  WSC-South African Summary      4,000 tonnes U.S. soy       [nRTR050455]
11:55  WSC-Brazil Coffee Weather Update tender 108,000T U.S. corn  [nRTR050454]
```

```
11:55  13 Oct  WSC-Brazil Coffee Weather Update
As of 11:55 GMT, 13 OCT 1998
 FROM: WEATHER SERVICES CORP. TUESDAY 13-OCT-1998  07:54 AM EDT
 BRAZIL COFFEE/CITRUS/COTTON...A FEW THUNDERSTORMS IN MINAS
 GERAIS. TEMPERATURES NEAR TO BELOW NORMAL.
 COFFEE/CITRUS/COTTON FORECAST...MOSTLY DRY CONDITIONS ARE
 EXPECTED THROUGH THURSDAY. TEMPERATURES TRENDING WARMER.
 CHANCE OF SCATTERED SHOWERS AND THUNDERSTORMS FRIDAY-
 SATURDAY.
 COFFEE PROSPECTS
  GENERALLY FAVORABLE CONDITIONS FOR THE FLOWERING TREES IN
 BRAZIL.
  FAVORABLE CONDITIONS FOR THE DEVELOPING AND MATURING CROP IN
 CENTRAL AMERICA AND MEXICO. HOWEVER SEVERE DROUGHT
 CONDITIONS EARLIER IN THE YEAR CAUSED SIGNIFICANT, IRREVERSIBLE
 CROP LOSSES ESPECIALLY IN THE LOWER ELEVATIONS. THE EARLY
 HARVEST WILL BE GETTING UNDERWAY THIS MONTH.
  GENERALLY FAVORABLE CONDITIONS FOR THE HARVEST IN COLOMBIA.
  INCREASED RAINFALL THROUGH IVORY COAST DURING SEPTEMBER AND
 OCTOBER FAVORS DEVELOPING CROPS.
  MOSTLY FAVORABLE CONDITIONS FOR COFFEE TREES IN SOUTHERN
 INDONESIA.
```

The Reuters screen below provides updates on labour negotiations affecting mining.

```
09:13  29 Dec  DIARY - World metals/mining labour contracts
   The following diary covers current labour contract expiries, negotiations and industrial
action at metals mines, refineries and smelters worldwide, compiled from recent Reuter
news reports and updated to Dec 29.
   New or amended entries are denoted by a double asterisk (**).
   Output figures per annum unless specified otherwise.
   If you have any comments or suggestions, please call London Commodities Desk on
+44 171 542 7726.

   LATEST LABOUR DISPUTES/NEGOTIATIONS
   _____

   SOUTH AFRICA
   **Dec 29 - National Union of Mineworkers entered seventh day of strike action at mines
and smelters of Anglo American Platinum Corp (Amplats) <AMSJ.J>.
   Mediation talks to settle wage dispute will resume Dec 30 after nearly 12 hours of
negotiations on Dec 28 failed to bring solution -industry sources.
   Amplats had group output of 1.89 million oz of refined platinum in the year to June 30,
1998 - or nearly 40 percent of global supply.
   MEXICO
   **Dec 28 - Labour Minister intervenes in bid to settle six-week-old strike at Grupo
Mexico's <GMEXICOB.MX> Cananea mine -company.
   Negotiations continued as Cananea workers' union threatened to strike at all 22
companies owned by Grupo Mexico, among the 12 biggest copper producers in the world.
   Next talks will be held at the Labour Ministry on January 4.
   Strike started in protest over change in company productivity bonus policy.
   Analysts have said the copper giant has sufficient inventories for keeping smelter
operations running for another month and a half before any impact of the strike may be
felt.
   Grupo Mexico has forecast its total copper production in 1998 at 420,000 to 440,000
tonnes, a rise of up to 16 percent from its output in 1997.
   UNITED STATES
   **Dec 28 - Kaiser Aluminum Corp <KLU.N> will meet representatives of United
Steelworkers of America January 7 -spokesman.
   Kaiser submitted new proposal to union December 17, calling for contract expiry on
September 30, 2003, a $1,000 ratification bonus, a $3.13 per hour average wage increase,
along with the elimination of antiquated work rules. This would result in the elimination of
approximately 700 jobs.
```

Availability of Domestic/International Resources

The supply of minerals and energy can be affected by the opening of new mines and sources of supply becoming available, as well as the closure of existing mines and wells. For example, any increase in the amount of oil allowed for sale by Iraq after the Gulf War has caused drops in oil prices. The price of copper rose in 1999 when copper miner BHP closed its North American mining operation.

Availability and Cost of Labour

Many crop commodities require large labour forces for planting, growing and harvesting. For example, much of the worldwide coffee supply is still harvested by hand and the number of people involved with coffee production is estimated to be some 20 million in 40 different countries, demonstrating that the availability and cost of labour is very important. The transport of commodities is also important when considering the availability and cost of labour. For example, a dock strike can severely affect the cash and future prices of commodities.

Production/Processing Demands

Varying production/processing demands may influence prices – consider the following two examples.

1. Sugar and Wheat

The worldwide demand for these commodities is relatively stable on a monthly basis, that is, consumers consume bread and products containing sugar on a regular basis throughout the year. However, the supply of sugar and wheat is very much dependent on the harvest yields of these commodities and on the stocks held by governments and consumers. This means there is a situation of constant demand but of variable supply. The following chart shows the relationship between prices of raw sugar and stocks available worldwide for the period 1992/93 to 1997/98...

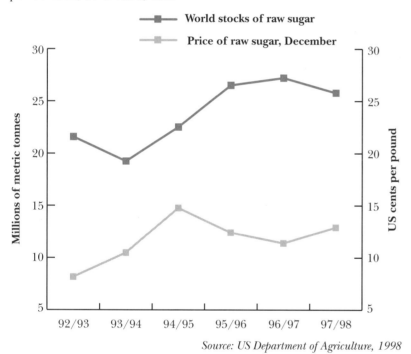

Source: US Department of Agriculture, 1998

This chart shows that in broad terms as stock levels rise, prices fall and vice versa.

2. Aluminium

The worldwide demand for this metal, on an annual basis, is somewhat variable. However, the supply of the metal is relatively constant and stable. In general the warehouse stocks of metals held by the London Metal Exchange are used as a global barometer of supply and demand. The Reuters Graphics chart below illustrates the relationship between prices and available stocks.

These charts illustrate the principals of supply and demand. As the demand for a commodity increases and the supply or stocks fall, then prices rise and vice versa.

In a book this size it is not possible to cover in detail the supply and demand issues and pricing fluctuations for every type of commodity, product or service. However, before moving on to the introductions to each of the markets covered, you may find the following case studies useful. These brief studies provide you with some background information to the commodity, product or service and how the weather and other factors can affect prices.

Case Study One

Here are a few facts about this well known commodity. Do you know what it is?

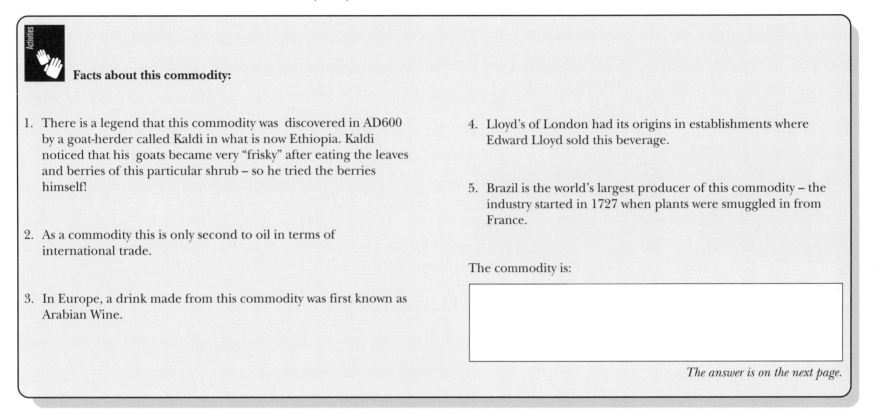

Activities

Facts about this commodity:

1. There is a legend that this commodity was discovered in AD600 by a goat-herder called Kaldi in what is now Ethiopia. Kaldi noticed that his goats became very "frisky" after eating the leaves and berries of this particular shrub – so he tried the berries himself!

2. As a commodity this is only second to oil in terms of international trade.

3. In Europe, a drink made from this commodity was first known as Arabian Wine.

4. Lloyd's of London had its origins in establishments where Edward Lloyd sold this beverage.

5. Brazil is the world's largest producer of this commodity – the industry started in 1727 when plants were smuggled in from France.

The commodity is:

The answer is on the next page.

You probably guessed that the commodity is **Coffee**.

The Plant

Coffee is a tropical, evergreen bush shrub or small tree growing to a height of ten metres. It is the coffee **bean** that consumers buy and this comes from the fruit of the plant – the **cherry** – which is red in colour when ripe – hence its name. The cherry contains two seeds or beans. Coffee is an unusual plant in that cherries at different stages of ripeness can be found on the same branch. This means that most coffee is still picked by hand.

Berries in various stages of ripeness on the same bush

A ripe berry with its two seeds

Source: The International Coffee Organisation

Types of Coffee

There are two main types of coffee produced:

- Arabica

- Robusta

Arabica coffee accounts for about 70% of world production. The two main producers of this coffee are Brazil and Colombia – the beans are often called **Brazils** and **Colombian Milds** respectively. Arabica beans from other countries are usually termed **Other Milds**. Although most of this coffee comes from Latin and South America a small quantity is still produced in East Africa – where it was first discovered. Most Arabica coffee is roasted and ground for use as a beverage.

Robusta coffee accounts for the remaining 30% or so of world production. Robusta beans are usually smaller than Arabica and have a less aromatic aroma. Robusta coffee is grown mainly in West Africa, Vietnam, Indonesia and a small amount in Brazil. Most Robusta coffee is used in soluble products such as "instant coffee".

In general, both types of coffee are most productive under the following conditions:

- 3–4 years after planting. The plants can continue to bear cherries for up to 30 years.

- Within the temperature range 23°C–28°C. Arabica plants will tolerate cooler conditions but frost will kill both species.

- An annual rainfall of 1.5–2.0 metres. For plantations receiving less than 1.0 metre of rain per annum, an irrigation system is required.

Most Arabica cherries take 6 to 8 months to ripen whereas the time for Robusta cherries is longer – 9 to 11 months. There is usually only one harvest for coffee and the period depends on the geographical zone where the coffee is being grown. In the northern hemisphere the harvest period is between September and March; in the southern hemisphere the harvest is in April or May.

During its development, the coffee plant and its cherries are susceptible to damage by the following:

- **Leaf rust** is a fungus ultimately causing large black spots on the plant's leaves which then fall off. Untreated an infected plant will die. Arabica coffee plants are prone to this disease, whereas Robusta plants are more resistant.

- **Berry borer** is an insect which, as its name implies, bores into the cherry and damages the beans. Both species are susceptible to this pest.

Processing Coffee

After harvesting, the cherries can be processed in one of two ways:

- The **dry method**. This is the traditional method where the cherries are left to dry in the sun before the beans are removed. If it rains or the temperature drops the cherries must be protected, otherwise they will be damaged and the yield of beans will be affected.

- The **wet method**. In this case the cherries are fermented in water and soaked for up to 48 hours.

Depending on the processing method used, the beans are then removed, sorted and graded. The **green** beans as they are known are then exported in **60 kilogram bags**.

1. Approximately 600,000 Arabica beans are needed to fill a 60 kg bag of coffee.

2. Approximately 4,000 Arabica beans are needed to produce 500 g of roasted coffee.

Coffee Statistics and Prices

The **International Coffee Organisation (ICO)** is a body representing the interests of most of the coffee-producing countries. The ICO pulishes market statistics and cash prices, some of which is available on electronic information services.

Below is a Reuters screen showing various producers' coffee prices.

ONCOFFEE	COFFEE PHYSICALS							
Commodity	Del.Date	Last		Srce	Terms	Loc	Ccy	Units
COMPOSITE 79	SPOT	↓ 94.10	-3.84	ICO	EXD Index	-	USc	LBS
15 DAY AVERAGE	SPOT	↑ 94.72	+0.17	ICO	EXD Index	-	USc	LBS
NEW YORK ARA	SPOT	↓ 104.54	-5.13	ICO	EXD Index	-	USc	LBS
BREMEN/HMBG	SPOT	↓ 115.36	-5.10	ICO	EXD Index	-	USc	LBS
COL ARABICA	SPOT	↓ 113.00	-5.25	ICO	EXD Index	-	USc	LBS
BRAZIL/OTHER	SPOT	↓ 90.25	-3.00	ICO	EXD Index	-	USc	LBS
AVERAGE ARABICA	SPOT	↓ 107.25	-5.12	ICO	EXD Index	-	USc	LBS
15DAY ARABICA	SPOT	↑ 109.40	+0.04	ICO	EXD Index	-	USc	LBS
NEW YORK ROBUSTA	SPOT	↓ 81.50	-2.50	ICO	EXD Index	-	USc	LBS
LEHARVE/MAR	SPOT	↓ 80.12	-2.62	ICO	EXD Index	-	USc	LBS
AVGE ROBUSTA	SPOT	↓ 80.95	-2.55	ICO	EXD Index	-	USc	LBS
15DAY ROBUSTA	SPOT	↑ 80.03	+0.30	ICO	EXD Index	-	USc	LBS
OTHER DIFFS	SPOT	↓ 26.85	-0.24	ICO	EXD Index	-	USc	LBS
SANTOS NO 4	SPOT	↓ 91.40	-5.10	RTRS	CIF NYC	BRA	USc	LBS
COL MAMS	SPOT	↓ 114.40	-5.10	RTRS	CIF NYC	COL	USc	LBS
EL SALVADOR	SPOT	↓ 107.40	-5.10	RTRS	CIF NYC	SAL	USc	LBS
MEXICAN	SPOT	↑ 106.50	0	RTRS	CIF NYC	MEX	USc	LBS
GUAT PME WSH	SPOT	↓ 107.40	-5.10	RTRS	CIF NYC	GUA	USc	LBS

The bar chart below shows the 1997 monthly prices for the ICO composite price for coffee, that is, a weighted average of Arabica and Robusta prices.

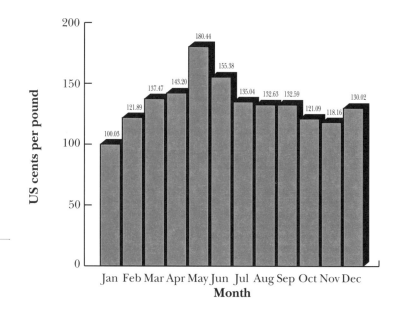

Source: ICO Coffee Statistics: December 1997. Published June 1998.

The chart shows that there were considerable price fluctuations over the year which were caused by basic changes in supply and demand. In the first six months of the year, prices rose due to a number of factors. There had been a reduction in exports by producers, port strikes in Colombia, the possibility of reduced crop yields in Brazil and the possible effects of El Nino.

The following charts, also taken from ICO data, show price fluctuations over the period 1989 – 1997.

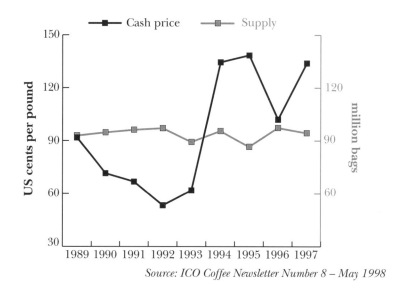

Source: ICO Coffee Newsletter Number 8 – May 1998

The chart above shows ICO composite cash prices in US cents per pound and supply figures in terms of million bags. In general the chart shows that as supply increases prices fall and that as supply decreases prices rise.

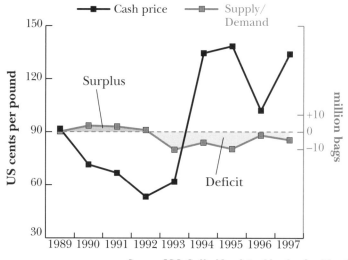

Source: ICO Coffee Newsletter Number 8 – May 1998

The second chart shows a similar picture when the ICO composite cash prices are compared with the **difference** between the supply and demand – the worldwide stock – on an annual basis. As can be seen, an overall surplus brings a price fall; an overall deficit causes prices to rise.

In summary, the price of coffee is affected by a number of factors including the following:

- Weather conditions
- Pests and disease
- Harvesting methods
- Internal governmental controls on prices, quotas etc
- World export quotas

Who Is Affected by Prices?
Within the market place there are a number of market players who are affected by price fluctuations, including the following:

- **Producers**. In some developing countries coffee is grown by large numbers of farmers who each cultivate a small plot of land. In these countries there is often a state marketing board which handles the export of the coffee on behalf of the small farmers.

- **Commodity houses**. In this case traders buy coffee from the exporting country, assume the risk of transportation and sell the coffee to consumers in their own domestic market.

- **European and United States roasters**. These consumers buy green beans to blend and roast for domestic and export markets.

- **Speculators**. Fund managers and institutional investment specialists are making increased use of coffee futures and options instruments to take both short- and long-term positions.

The importance of weather news may be obvious but what kind of other news will the market players be interested in? The following screens provides news stories from various coffee growing countries about different issues affecting the coffee markets.

In Colombia, a dry spell caused by El Nino severely damaged bean quality. The 1996/97 harvest was the worst in nine years.

REUTERS NEWS

01/10/97 COLOMBIA: DISSIDENT COLOMBIAN *COFFEE* GROWERS WARN OF *EL NINO*.

BOGOTA, Oct 1 (Reuter) - A group of dissident Colombian *coffee* growers has accused industry chiefs of covering up the true impact of the *El Nino* weather phenomenon on the quality and volume of the *coffee* crop.
The Unidad Cafetera Nacional (UCN), a loosely-woven independent organization of growers, said the recent dry spell caused by *El Nino* had severely damaged the quality of beans.
The powerful National *Coffee* Growers' Federation, however, said it is too early to tell what the effect of the weather pattern may be.
"The federation is not only hiding the scale of the problem but is overlooking problems in bean quality," Aurelio Suarez, the new UCN leader, told Reuters in a phone interview.
He said that 36,00 acres (15,000 hectares) of a total 156,000 acres (65,000 hectares) in central Risaralda province, Colombia's sixth largest *coffee*-producing area, had already been hit by the drought, which was particularly severe in July and August.
He said it took 242 pounds (110 kg) of *coffee* cherries, compared to the normal volume of just 132 pounds (60 kg), to make just 25 pounds (11.36 kg) of parchment *coffee*.
But after a meeting at the start of this week, federation chief Jorge Cardenas warned against panic.
He put the total harvest for the 1996/97 *coffee* year, which ended Sept. 30, at about 10.7 million 60-kg bags, up from the previous best estimate of 10.5 million bags. That figure is still subject to revision.
Even at 10.7 million bags, it will be worst harvest in nine years and a hefty drop from the 12.9 million bags harvested in the 1995/96 *coffee* year.
Cardenas forecast production in the first quarter of the 1997/98 cycle, which has just begun, would be between a healthy 4.5 million and 4.7 million bags -- up from the 3.6 million bags in the same period of 1996/97.
Expert agro-climatologists working at the federation's CENICAFE research center said last week that "near normal" rains had returned to the central and southwest *coffee*-growing region and that the impact of 50 percent lower-than-normal rainfall in July and August had been minimal.
They said the main harvest, which accounts for about 60 percent of Colombia's total crop and peaks in November and December, was unlikely to be affected.
They added that the dry spell had helped the flowering of trees that will bear beans for next March's so-called Mitaca harvest, which provides about 40 percent of total output.
"The impact of *El Nino* on the *coffee* industry cannot be calculated as yet. Until now the flowering for the Mitaca period has been normal."

Why Do the Commodities, Energy & Transport Markets Exist?

The Honduran Coffee Institute reported that up to 380,000 bags of coffee were smuggled out of the country in 1997.

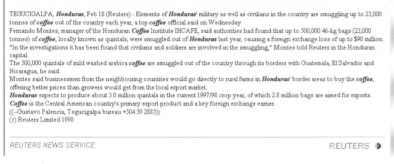

REUTERS NEWS

18/02/98 HONDURAS: HONDURAN MILITARY ACCUSED OF COFFEE SMUGGLING.

TEGUCIGALPA, Honduras, Feb 18 (Reuters) - Elements of Honduras' military as well as civilians in the country are smuggling up to 23,000 tonnes of coffee out of the country each year, a top coffee official said on Wednesday.
Fernando Montes, manager of the Honduran Coffee Institute IHCAFE, said authorities had found that up to 500,000 46-kg bags (23,000 tonnes) of coffee, locally known as quintals, were smuggled out of Honduras last year, causing a foreign exchange loss of up to $90 million.
"In the investigations it has been found that civilians and soldiers are involved in the smuggling," Montes told Reuters in the Honduran capital.
The 500,000 quintals of mild washed arabica coffee are smuggled out of the country through its borders with Guatemala, El Salvador and Nicaragua, he said.
Montes said businessmen from the neighbouring countries would go directly to rural farms in Honduras' border areas to buy the coffee, offering better prices than growers would get from the local export market.
Honduras expects to produce about 3.0 million quintals in the current 1997/98 crop year, of which 2.8 million bags are aimed for exports.
Coffee is the Central American country's primary export product and a key foreign exchange earner.
((--Gustavo Palencia, Tegucigalpa bureau +504 39 2885))
(c) Reuters Limited 1998

REUTERS NEWS SERVICE   REUTERS

In Tanzania the heavy rains linked to El Nino destroyed early coffee plant flowers and led to widespread berry disease and leaf rust.

REUTERS NEWS

19/02/98 TANZANIA: RAINS DAMAGE 1998/99 NORTHERN TANZANIA ARABICAS.

By Mark Dodd
DAR ES SALAAM, Feb 19 (Reuters) - Continuing heavy rains in northern Tanzania's Kilimanjaro region will cause a fall in output of the premier mild washed arabica coffee for 1998/99 (Oct/Sept), a senior industry official said on Thursday.
Leslie Omari, managing director of the state-run Tanzania Coffee Board (TCB) told Reuters that heavy rains blamed on the El Nino weather phenomenon had destroyed early flowers and led to widespread Coffee Berry Disease (CBD) and Leaf Rust.
"We have had continuous rains especially in the mountains and this has affected the flowering," Omari told Reuters by telephone from the northern coffee town of Moshi.
"The flowers have aborted to a considerable extent in the uplands. For the flowers that have survived and made it to the coffee berry stage, CBD is rampant and taking its toll.
"The effect of El Nino for 1998/99 in the north is a concern," Omari added.
Omari stressed that coffee production in southern Tanzania remained unaffected. "The area in the south will come out in a very good way -- there's no problems," he said.
He said total Tanzanian coffee production for 1997/98 season would now fall below 40,000 tonnes of clean coffee.
"It will be slightly below forty (thousand tonnes) -- thirty eight or thirty nine but definitely below forty," he said.
Omari posted coffee export earnings from October 1997 to January 1998 at around $69.64 million.
From a production peak of 55,160 tonnes between 1981-85, production for 1996/97 fell to around 43,000 tonnes worth some $95 million.
Traders said last week that production in Tanzania could fall to as low as 34,000 tonnes because of heavy rain damage.
Coffee is Tanzania's most important commodity crop. About half of Tanzania's total coffee exports are sent to Europe with Germany alone accounting for 30 percent.
Japan is also a major customer but only for the famed Kilimanjaro-grown arabica, Omari said. "Their (Japan) main taste is for coffee from the north."
In the key southern regions of Mbeya and Ruvuma, arabica production for 1997/98 was forecast at 16,000 tonnes but the harvest exceeded that figure by more than 1,000 tonnes.
Omari said Kilimanjaro coffee farmers were battling desperate odds to contain the spread of leaf rust and CBD because continuing rains were washing away the chemicals.
"Spraying against leaf rust and CBD has to be done with chemicals which stick to the leaves. Blue copper has to be made to stick to the

A Reuters poll of 14 US and European commodity analysts puts the 1998/99 Brazilian crop at an average of 36.2 million bags.

REUTERS NEWS

22/05/98 UK: POLL-BRAZIL 98/99 COFFEE CROP SEEN AT 36.2 MLN BAGS.

LONDON, May 22 (Reuters) - World coffee prices will take a downward path in the coming months under pressure from a huge Brazilian 1998/99 crop of 36.2 million 60-kg bags, according to a Reuters poll on Friday.
From Monday to Thursday, Reuters asked 14 U.S. and European analysts and traders for their views on the size of Brazil's coming crop and price expectations for the rest of 1998.
On average, they forecast the crop from the world's number one grower at 36.2 million bags. This would be sharply up from 20-28 million in 1997/98.
The median prediction for the crop was 36.0 million. The high and the low were 39.5 million and 33.5 million respectively while the mode prediction, the most cited often, was 35.0 million.
An update of the official Brazilian government estimate was due to released in the first week of June. In January the government put the 1998/99 crop at 31.17 million against 18.86 million.
The U.S Department of Agriculture was also expected to release its first estimate of the Brazilian 1998/99 crop in June. Barring crop-damaging frost in Brazil this year, the analysts and traders expect prices to take a dip, with arabicas falling to 122 U.S. cents a lb at end-December from 124 cents at end-September.
Robustas will fall to $1,775 a tonne from $1,895.
They were however divided on world consumption outlook for calendar 1998 over 1997, with views ranging from 4.0 percent down to 2.1 percent up. ((Jalil Hamid, London newsroom +44 171 542 4985, fax +44 171 542 8077, london.commodities.desk@reuters.com))
(C) Reuters Limited 1998.

REUTERS NEWS SERVICE   REUTERS

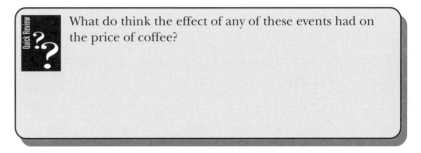

Quick Review

What do think the effect of any of these events had on the price of coffee?

As a world commodity, coffee is second only to oil in importance in international trade. It is the world's most popular beverage – over 400 billion cups are drunk each year!

Case Study Two

Here are a few facts about this well known commodity. Do you know what it is?

Facts about this commodity:

1. This metal takes its name from the miners in Saxony 250 years ago who called it 'Old Nick's Copper' because they thought the ore was 'bewitched'.

2. This metal was used for Swiss 20 centime coins in 1881. This was the first time a pure base metal had been used as a coinage metal.

3. The oxide of this metal is used to colour the glass of Champagne bottles its distinctive green.

4. As a catalyst, this metal is used in the production of about one-third of all worldwide edible fats and oils.

5. Up until 1905 the largest source of this metal was an island in the South Pacific – New Caledonia – a French penal colony from 1863 – 1897.

The metal is:

The answer is on the next page.

You may have guessed that the metal is **Nickel**.

The History of Nickel

Nickel is one of the less well-known base metals traded on the London Metal Exchange (LME.) It takes its name from the Saxony miners who found nickel ore in association with copper ore – which is what they were really looking for. Unfortunately the presence of the nickel ore produced a brittle slag-like material when refined. Being rather superstitious, the miners thought that their misfortune was due to Old Nick's or Satan's gnomes who had bewitched the ore. Hence the original name for the metal was Old Nick's Copper – **Kupfernickel**.

In 1751 the Swedish chemist Cronstedt extracted and identified nickel for the first time from an ore containing niccolite (Nickel Arsenide). Having established that the metal was a new element, Kupfer was dropped from its name – hence nickel.

The pure metal is silvery-white in colour, hard and tough – it is harder than Iron and like this metal has some magnetic properties. nickel is also very corrosion- and stain-resistant.

Pure Nickel as pellets and briquette

Source: The International Nickel Company (Inco)

Uses of Nickel

Nickel is mainly used in association with other metals to produce a variety of alloys which have stain-, corrosion- or heat-resistant properties. The vast majority of nickel produced annually is used in the production of the iron alloy stainless steel. Trading in nickel is closely linked to the fortunes of the stainless steel industry.

Nickel metal is used as a catalyst in a number of important food processing industries such as in the production of edible fats and oils. With the increasing focus on reducing world pollution from vehicle emissions, Nickel is finding an increasing use in the production of a variety of different types of batteries for electric vehicles.

The chart below shows worldwide usage of nickel in 1998 – over 65% was used in the production of stainless steel.

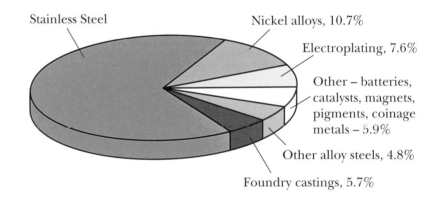

Source: AME Mineral Economics – Strategic Studies: Nickel 1998

Production of Nickel

In 1997 the world production of Nickel was 1,080,000 metric tons with a market value of approximately $7 billion, which is much less than for copper or aluminium. The chart below indicates the main producers of nickel for 1997.

Country	Metric tons
Russia	230,000
Canada	182,000
New Caledonia	157,000
Australia	120,000
Other	391,000
Total	**1,080,000**

Source: US Geological Survey: Nickel 1997.

Not all nickel is refined from newly mined nickel ore. There is a large market for recycling base metals from scrap sources. For example, in the US, of the 150,000 tons of nickel consumed in 1997, it was estimated that 72,000 tons was recovered from scrap – mainly stainless steel.

In 1997 it was estimated that the world reserves and stocks of nickel stood at 40,000,000 metric tons.

What do you think the effect of having such a large world stockpile of nickel had on prices in 1997?

The Reuters graphics screen below displays a line chart of the weekly closing prices for the 3-month LME Nickel contract prices (the dotted line displays stock prices).

During 1997 the world supply of nickel exceeded demand and the price of nickel fell to 1994 levels. Speculators sold holdings as a result of financial problems in East Asia and large amounts of nickel and scrap stainless steel reached the markets from Russia. In 1999, metal analysts predicted that the oversupply of nickel would continue for another four to five years.

As the world production figures on the previous page show, Canada is the second largest producer of nickel. Where does all this nickel come from?

In 1883 the Canadian Pacific Railway discovered an area rich in minerals in a North Ontario wilderness now called the Sudbury basin. By 1886 the Canadian Copper Company had been formed to mine copper ore, which it shipped to be refined in the US and Wales. However, just as the miners in Saxony had found, some of the copper ore also contained nickel which was difficult to separate. In 1891 the Orford Copper Company developed a method of separation and in 1902 the two copper companies merged to become the International Nickel Company (Inco).

In 1993 nickel/copper/cobalt deposits were found in a remote area of Labrador known as Voisey's Bay. Inco plans to make Voisey's Bay the largest nickel smelting and refining complex outside Russia; however, there have been some delays to the project. Before moving on, review the Reuters Business Briefing at right to check developments on this project. Reuters electronic service provides information from industry sources, as well as from Reuters own journalism services. This project was still delayed at the time this book went to press.

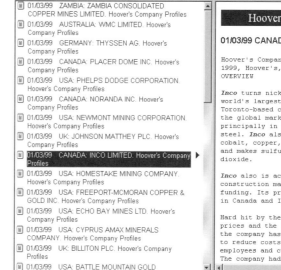

Hoover's Company Profiles

01/03/99 CANADA: *INCO* LIMITED.

Hoover's Company Profiles, Copyright (C), 1999, Hoover's, Inc., Austin, Tx. OVERVIEW

Inco turns nickel into gold. One of the world's largest nickel producers, the Toronto-based company claims about 27% of the global market for the metal, used principally in the manufacture of stainless steel. *Inco* also mines and processes cobalt, copper, gold, silver, and platinum, and makes sulfuric acid and liquid sulfur dioxide.

Inco also is active in metals reclamation, construction materials, and venture capital funding. Its primary mining operations are in Canada and Indonesia.

Hard hit by the collapse of world nickel prices and the financial crisis in Asia, the company has restructured its operations to reduce costs, including laying off 1,000 employees and closing four Canadian mines. The company had banked on beginning

REUTERS NEWS

17/02/99 CANADA: LABRADOR INUIT ADD TO DOUBTS ABOUT *VOISEY*'S BAY MINE.

By Paul Simao
TORONTO, Feb 17 (Reuters) - Nickel giant Inco Ltd. was dealt another blow on Wednesday when a key Native Canadian group withdrew tentative support for development of the stalled C$43-billion *Voisey*'s Bay project in Labrador, Newfoundland.
The Labrador Inuit Association (LIA), which represents 5,000 Native Canadians in the barren territory bordering northeastern Quebec, said it would not flash the green light for the project until a comprehensive land claims agreement had been negotiated.
The group had agreed to a tentative land claims agreement with the Canadian and Newfoundland governments in late December, which would have allowed work to proceed at *Voisey*'s Bay while a final agreement was negotiated.
Inuit representatives said environmental concerns and the current impasse between Inco and Newfoundland had made it impossible to negotiate native rights at *Voisey*'s Bay into the framework of December's deal.
"With all those uncertainties we couldn't negotiate the content and the detail of the *Voisey*'s Bay chapter in the agreement in principle," said Toby Andersen, land claims director for the association.
"The Inuit position is that we need a final agreement that includes the *Voisey*'s Bay chapter," said Andersen, who added the group had not closed the door on further negotiations.
Dealing with Native groups in Labrador has been one of the

Nickel Production and the Weather

Look at the map below showing the location of Sudbury and also notice the River Saint Lawrence/Seaway, the main channel used by ships in the export of nickel ore from Sudbury. Due to the very cold winters in northern Canada, the Seaway can be unnavigable between mid-December and early April because of freezing.

It is therefore very important that market players consider the approach of winter in Canada. An early freeze can mean cargo trapped for up to four months!

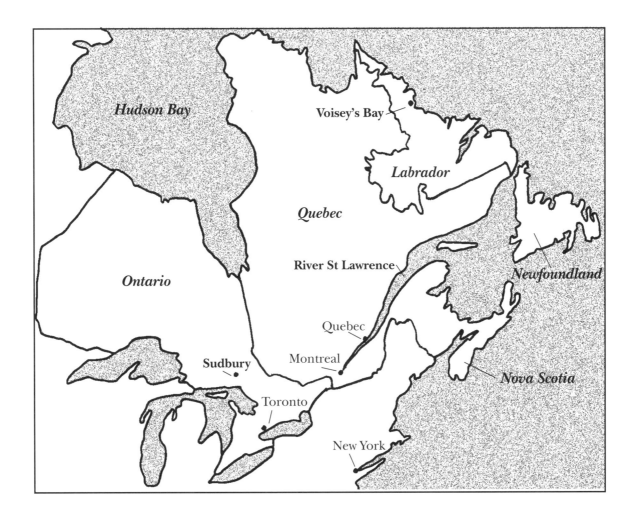

The Reuters screens below display international news about metals projects and production.

```
NIC/DIARY                    Nickel
    The following diary lists new projects, planned expansions and expected
closures at nickel mines, refineries and smelters, compiled from recent Reuters
news reports and updated to October 20.
    New or amended entries are marked with two asterisks (**). If you have any
comments or suggestions, please call London Commodities Desk on +44 171 542
2935, e-mail london.commodities.desk@reuters.com
    Next update due on October 27.

-----------------------------------------------------------------------
For advice on how to print this type of display, please scroll to the base of
the window.
-----------------------------------------------------------------------

    1998
    ONTARIO/INDONESIA - Restructuring of Inco Ltd operations and extended
shutdown of Ontario division will cut nickel production to 425 mln lb from
planned 440 mln. Ontario divisions cut by 20,000 t to 80,000.

    1998
    CHINA - Jinchuan Non-Ferrous Co, country's largest nickel smelter, planning
to cut output due to weak demand. Output 36,000 t nickel in 1997.

    1998
    NEW CALEDONIA/FRANCE - Eramet to produce 57,000 t nickel, up four pct from
1997 but 2-3,000 t below capacity. Had initially planned 58,000 t in 1998,
reached first qtr rate of 60,000 t/yr.
```

```
08:46  RTRS-***GLANCE - Metals news at 0845 GMT***
11:09  Headlines Older than 24 Hours Not Available (0)
```

```
08:46  27 Oct  RTRS-***GLANCE - Metals news at 0845 GMT***

         To access news and prices click on the codes in brackets
          or type code and hit the news key (f9) for [] items
                        or enter for <> items
-----------------------------------------------------------------------
 -S.KOREA SEEKS ALUMINIUM, JAPAN SEPT COPPER CABLE ORDERS FALL
* S.Korea says seeks 15,000 tonnes of aluminium       [nSE0002425]
* Japan Sept copper cable shipments, orders slide       [nT62996]
* Japan Sept aluminium mill output, shipments down      [nT49980]
* INSIGHT - Copper and aluminium expected to fall     [nL27323486]
* LME base metals bounce seen set by Asia zone rise [nSYD207817]
* FEATURE - Metals trade drinks to a cheerless futur[nL26170245]
* Brazil posts record aluminium recycle rate in H1   [nN26204915]
* Inco to produce less nickel than planned in 1998   [nN26223405]

 CORPORATE--BILLITON RAISES OFFER FOR NICKEL PRODUCER QNI
* Billiton lifts QNI<QNI.AX> offer to A$1.05 a share  [nSYA7406]
* QNI<QNI.AX>tops turnover as Billiton beefs ups bid[nSYD201637]
* Tinah<TINS.JK> sees '98 net more than double 1997  [nJK000075]
* Homestake <HM.N> reports US$182.2 mln Q3 loss      [nSYD209645]
* Lepanto <LC.PS> to borrow $30 mln for gold project [nMN005515]
* Normandy <NDY.AX> sees steady H1 profit result     [nSYD203887]
* Inco says still negotiating price for alloys unit  [nN26578387]
* Soquinich to take Chile copper project bids in Nov[nN26211879]

 PRECIOUS/MARKETS--PRECIOUS METALS TRADE SEEN SLOW
* INSIGHT - Precious metals seen stable, trade slow  [nL27335318]
* Gold and silver barely softer early in Europe      [nL27430964]
```

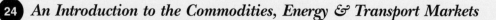

Case Study Three

This example is not a commodity but it is a subject that affects everybody's life and lifestyle. Do you know what it is?

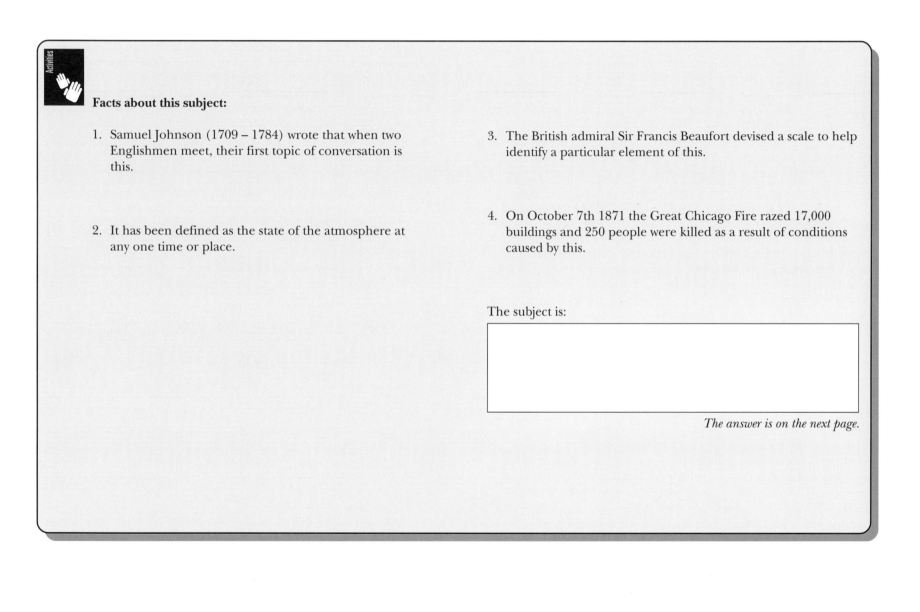

Facts about this subject:

1. Samuel Johnson (1709 – 1784) wrote that when two Englishmen meet, their first topic of conversation is this.

2. It has been defined as the state of the atmosphere at any one time or place.

3. The British admiral Sir Francis Beaufort devised a scale to help identify a particular element of this.

4. On October 7th 1871 the Great Chicago Fire razed 17,000 buildings and 250 people were killed as a result of conditions caused by this.

The subject is:

The answer is on the next page.

Why Do the Commodities, Energy & Transport Markets Exist?

You may have guessed that the subject is the **weather**. The Beaufort Scale is used to define wind velocity. The destruction of the Great Chicago Fire was caused by winds fanning the flames over a tinder dry environment following a severe drought.

Weather and the Derivatives Markets

The importance of weather concerning commodities has already been discussed. You also need to be aware of the origin and importance of derivative instruments such as futures, options and swaps for commodities and energy products in general. The *Introduction to Derivatives* book in this series, ISBN 0-471-83176-X, for more detail information. Most commodity and energy instruments have a trading unit of an underlying physical commodity such as crude oil, coffee, sugar, corn, cattle etc.

In the early 1990s the **Chicago Board of Trade (CBOT)** introduced futures and options contracts on catastrophe insurance with trading units based on US national or regional loss indices provided by the Property Claim Services (PCS). More recently, CBOT introduced US Corn Yield Insurance futures and options contracts for national and certain state yield estimates. The underlying instrument for these contracts is the estimate for corn published by the US Department of Agriculture (USDA), during the growing/harvest season.

More recently **weather derivatives** have been introduced into the OTC markets. The underlying instrument is a weather index or variable. In particular, option contracts are available for specific locations and calendar periods based on Heating Degree Days (HDD) or Cooling Degree Days (CDD).

These weather options provide hedging instruments for market players such as energy producers and consumers who have weather-related risks. For example, an energy producer in the US may be expecting a hot summer requiring a high cooling demand for air-conditioning etc. If the temperatures fall, then cooling demand falls, resulting in a loss of revenue for the energy producer. The producer would like to protect this risk and these recently introduced weather options provide a hedging strategy.

Options such as floors and **caps** are written using a strike which is based on a temperature index such as HDD or CDD. Once written and bought, weather options are used and exercised like any other type of OTC option.

In September 1999, the **Chicago Mercantile Exchange (CME)** initiated trading of futures and options on futures contracts for temperature-related weather derivatives. These HDD and CDD futures contracts will use indexes for four US cities, Atlanta, Chicago, Cincinnati and New York. The HDD and CDD futures contracts have a trading size of $100 times the CME HDD index and $100 times the CME CDD Index – the index values are based on cumulative monthly HDDs and CDDs.

For the CME Index futures contracts:

- A **Heating Degree Day** occurs when the average temperature is **below** 65° Fahrenheit

- A **Cooling Degree Day** occurs when the average temperature is **above** 65° Fahrenheit

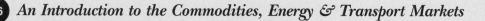

These Reuters screens provide HDD and CDD information for Boston and other North American cities.

```
RZWTHR/BOS                                                        16:01 14Feb
                            Boston Weather

FORECAST      Sun 14Feb Mon 15Feb Tue 16Feb Wed 17Feb Thu 18Feb Fri 19Feb Sat 20Feb
Tmp Max/Min    34/24     37/20     44/28     42/32     39/32     40/27     40/31
Tmp Average    28        29        35        37        35        34        35
Nrn Max/Min    36/24     37/25     37/25     37/25     37/25     37/25     38/25
Nrn Average    30        31        31        31        31        31        32
DprtFronNrn    -2        -2        +4        +6        +4        +3        +3
HDD/CDD        37/0      36/0      30/0      28/0      30/0      31/0      30/0
Effect HDD     42        40        32        31        34        33        33
Wthr Code      PCLD      SUN       SUN       RAIN      SNOW      PCLD      PCLD
Sky Cover %    50        10        30        90        100       30        60
Heat Index     39        40        46        47        44        44        45
Dew Point      13        12        21        30        27        22        28
Wind Sp/Dir    13/N      12/NW     8/W       11/W      12/N      8/W       10/W

OBSERVED      13 Feb    Past 7Days  Past 30Days
Tmp Max/Min    45/34     44/31       42/29
Tmp Average    37        37          35
DprtFronNrn    +7        +8          +5
HDD/CDD        28/0      191/0       892/0
Nrn HDD/CDD    35/0      245/0       1050/0
Precip (in)    0.22      0.23        3.81
Precip DFN     0.10      -0.61       0.12

Speedguide <NAPOWER>   Weather Guide <WTHR/GUIDE>        Source: WSC
```

```
WTHRNA                            NA CITIES WTHR

The following index provides access to North American city tabular weather data.
To access information double-click on codes in < >.

City Weather - Provides seven day forecast information for each North
               American city.
NERC Weather - Provides five day forecast information for all cities
               within a given NERC region.

        CITY              CITY WEATHER      NERC WEATHER
        ====              ============      ============
    AKRON-CANTON  OH      <WTHR/CAK>        <WTHRECAR>
    ALBANY        NY      <WTHR/ALB>        <WTHRNPCC>
    ALBUQUERQUE   NM      <WTHR/ABQ>        <WTHRWSCCS>
    ATLANTA       GA      <WTHR/ATL>        <WTHRSERC>
    AUSTIN        TX      <WTHR/AUS>        <WTHRERCOT>
    BALTIMORE     MD      <WTHR/BWI>        <WTHRMAAC>
    BILLINGS      MT      <WTHR/BIL>        <WTHRWSCCN>
    BIRMINGHAM    AL      <WTHR/BHM>        <WTHRSERC>
    BISMARCK      ND      <WTHR/BIS>        <WTHRMAPP>
    BOISE         ID      <WTHR/BOI>        <WTHRWSCCN>
    BOSTON        MA      <WTHR/BOS>        <WTHRNPCC>
    BUFFALO       NY      <WTHR/BUF>        <WTHRNPCC>
    BURLINGTON    VT      <WTHR/BTV>        <WTHRNPCC>
    CALGARY       AB      <WTHR/YYC>        <WTHRWSCCN>
    CASPER        WY      <WTHR/CPR>        <WTHRWSCCN>
```

```
WTHRNPCC          Five Day Weather Forecasts - NPCC WEATHER     Source: WSC
          ==> DOUBLE CLICK ON EACH CITY FOR ADDITIONAL DATA <==  16:01 14Feb
          For explanatory information double click on <WTHR/GUIDE>
              Sun 14Feb      Mon 15Feb      Tue 16Feb      Wed 17Feb      Thu 18Feb
           Max/Min  DFN   Max/Min  DFN   Max/Min  DFN   Max/Min  DFN   Max/Min  DFN
           HDD/CDD  %SC   HDD/CDD  %SC   HDD/CDD  %SC   HDD/CDD  %SC   HDD/CDD  %SC
ALBANY  NY  24/13   -5     34/7    -3     41/19    6     37/26    7     35/24    5
            47/     40     44/     10     35/      10    34/      90    36/      90
BOSTON  MA  34/24   -2     37/20   -2     44/28    4     42/32    6     39/32    4
            37/     50     36/     10     30/      30    28/      90    30/      100
BUFFALO NY  28/11   -3     39/22    7     42/30    12    37/34    11    34/30    7
            44/     10     34/     50     29/      100   30/      100   34/      100
BURLINGTON VT 20/8  -4     31/4           36/17    8     32/22    8     31/20    7
            51/     40     47/            39/      10    39/      90    40/      90
CONCORD NH  27/21    2     35/10          40/17    6     35/21    6     35/21    5
            42/     30     43/            37/      30    37/      60    38/      90
HALIFAX NS  32/30    4     32/25    1     38/24    4     40/29    7     39/32    8
            34/     100    37/     90     34/      40    31/      80    30/      100
HARTFORD CT 29/20   -4     38/10   -4     44/19    4     41/29    6     38/28    4
            42/     10     41/            33/      30    31/      100   33/      90
MONTREAL QE 17/7    -4     29/5           34/17    8     28/21    7     29/18    6
            53/     10     48/            40/      30    41/      90    42/      90
NEW YORK NY 35/23   -5     45/27    2     48/30    6     42/35    5     45/33    5
            37/     10     30/     30     26/      50    27/      90    27/      40
OTTAWA  ON  18/3    -3     29/-1          32/18    10    28/23    9     28/14    6
            54/            50/     30     40/      80    41/      100   44/      100
```

Why Do the Commodities, Energy & Transport Markets Exist?

Weights and Measures

The weights and measures used in the commodities, energy and transport markets are a confusing mixture of Anglo-Saxon, Imperial, Metric and US standards. For example, troy weights used for the precious metals silver and gold date back to the Middle Ages. Metric tons are a comparatively modern invention combining metric with imperial weights.

The following tables on weights and capacities may help – particularly when you look at futures contracts.

Tons

Term	Pounds,lbs		Kilograms,kg
One **ton** or **long ton**	2240	which is	1016.05
One **short** or **US ton**	2000	which is	907.19
One **metric ton** or **tonne**	2204.6	which is	1000.00

Imperial Weights

Weight	Abbrev.		Weight	Abbrev.
16 ounces	16oz	is	1 pound	1lb
14 pounds	14lb	is	1 stone	
112 pounds	112lb	is	1 hundredweight	1 cwt
20 hundredweight	20cwt	is	1 ton (2240lbs)	

US Weights

Weight	Abbrev.		Weight	Abbrev.
16 ounces	16oz	is	1 pound	1lb
100 pounds	100lb	is	1 hundredweight	1 cwt
20 hundredweight	20cwt	is	1 ton (2000lbs)	

Capacity

Measure		Equivalent
1 Imperial gallon	is	4.546 litres
1 US gallon	is	3.785 litres = 0.83 Imperial gallons
1 Barrel (1 bl)	is	36 Imperial gallons = 42 US gallons
1 Tonne oil	is	approx. 7.3 – 7.4 barrels of crude oil depending on the specific gravity of the oil
1 Bushel (1bu)	is	8 Imperial gallons = 36.4 litres **or** 8 US gallons = 30.3 litres Bushels are used for corn, liquids, fruit etc. The weight of a bushel therefore varies according to the commodity.

One troy ounce is approximately 1.1 Imperial ounces = 31.1035g

28 *An Introduction to the Commodities, Energy & Transport Markets*

REUTERS

You can even use electronic services to assist with conversions. These Reuters screens provide weight, volume and temperature conversion factors.

```
CONVERSION AND LOOK-UP TABLES - REUTERS SPEED GUIDE          CONVERSION1
This guide provides details of Conversion Factors and Look-up Tables.  To access
the table specified, double-click on the page code shown in < > brackets.


=TABLES=====================================================================
Weight Conversion Factors...............................................<CONVERT1>
Volume Conversion Factors...............................................<CONVERT2>
Energy Volume to Weight Conversaion Factors.............................<CONVERT3>
Energy Volume to MMBTU Conversion Factors...............................<CONVERT4>
Stowage Conparison Tables - SG 1.000 to 0.904/API 10 to 25..............<CONVERT5>
Stowage Conparison Tables - SG 0.898 to 0.820/API 26 to 41..............<CONVERT6>
Stowage Conparison Tables - SG 0.816 to 0.746/API 42 to 58..............<CONVERT7>
Stowage Conparison Tables - SG 0.742 to 0.685/API 59 to 75..............<CONVERT8>
Marine Speed and Distance tables - Fron Caribbeans and US Gulf..........<CONVERT9>
Marine Speed and Distance tables - Fron Arabian Gulf....................<CONVERT10>
Marine Speed and Distance tables - Fron Eastern Mediteranean............<CONVERT11>
Temperature Conversion Look-up Table - Fahrenheit to Celsius............<CONVERT12>
Hours and Minutes as Decinals of a Day Look-up table....................<CONVERT13>



=============================================================================
Shipping Guide <SHIPPING>      Energy Guide <ENERGY>      Connodity Guide<COMMOD>
   Lost? Selective Access?..<USER/HELP>     Reuters Phone Support...<PHONE/HELP>
```

```
WEIGHT CONVERSION FACTORS - REUTERS SPEED GUIDE                      CONVERT1
In the following tables each figure represents the number of units in the row
(down the left hand side) in one unit of the column (along the top of the table)
e.g. 42 US Gallons - 1 barrel
============TROY OZ============POUNDS===========SHORT TON==========LONG TON=====
Troy Oz          -            14.583          29,167.00         32,667.00
Pounds      0.068571             -             2,000.00          2,240.00
Cwt         0.00061224       0.0089286           17.857            20.00
Short Ton   0.000034286      0.00050000             -              1.12
Long Ton    0.000030612      0.00044643          0.89286            -
Gran        31.103           453.59            907,180        1,016,000.00
Kg          0.031103         0.45359             907.18         1,016.00
Tonne       0.000031103      0.00045359          0.90718        1.01605
============CWT================GRAM==============KG================TONNE========
Troy Oz 1,633.30              0.032151            32.151         32,150.77
Pounds    112.00             0.0022046            2.2046          2,204.64
Cwt          -               0.000019684         0.019684        19.684
Short Ton 0.056000           0.0000011023        0.0011023       1.1023
```

```
VOLUME CONVERSION FACTORS - REUTERS SPEED GUIDE                     CONVERT2
In the following tables each figure represents the number of units in the row
(down the left hand side) in one unit of the column (along the top of the table)
e.g. 3.7854 Litres =1 US Gallon and 42 US Gallons = 1 Barrel.
============UKG================USG===============CU FT========BUSHELS===
UK Gallon       -             0.83268           6.2289        7.7517
US Gallon    1.2009              -               7.4805        9.3094
CU Ft        0.16054          0.13368             -            1.2445
Bushels      0.12900          0.10742           0.80355          -
Barrels      0.028594         0.023810          0.17811        0.22165
Litres       4.5461           3.7854            28.317         35.240
Hectolitres  0.045461         0.037854          0.28317        0.35240
Cubic Metres 0.0045461        0.0037854         0.028317       0.035240
============BARRELS============LITRES===========HECTOLITRES====CUBIC METERS=
UK Gallon    37.9726          0.21997           21.997         219.97
US Gallon    42.000           0.26417           26.417         264.17
Cu Ft        5.61459          0.035314          3.5314         35.314
```

```
FAHRENHEIT TO CELSIUS APPROXIMATIONS LOOK=UP TABLE                   CONVERT12
 ××××××××××××××××××××××××××××××××××××××××××××××××××××××××××××××××××××××××××
 ×    F =  C ×  F = C  ×F =  C × F =  C ×  F =   C ×  F =  C  ×  F =  C  ×
 × =10  =23 ×   9  =13 × 28  =2 × 47   8 × 66   19 × 85    29 × 130   54 ×
 ×  =9  =23 ×  10  =12 × 29  =2 × 48   9 × 67   19 × 86    30 × 140   60 ×
 ×  =8  =22 ×  11  =12 × 30  =1 × 49   9 × 68   20 × 87    31 × 150   66 ×
 ×  =7  =22 ×  12  =11 × 31  =1 × 50  10 × 69   21 × 88    31 × 160   71 ×
 ×  =6  =21 ×  13  =11 × 32   0 × 51  11 × 70   21 × 89    32 × 170   77 ×
 ×  =5  =21 ×  14  =10 × 33   1 × 52  11 × 71   22 × 90    32 × 175   79 ×
 ×  =4  =20 ×  15   =9 × 34   1 × 53  12 × 72   22 × 91    33 × 180   82 ×
 ×  =3  =19 ×  16   =9 × 35   2 × 54  12 × 73   23 × 92    33 × 190   88 ×
 ×  =2  =19 ×  17   =8 × 36   2 × 55  13 × 74   23 × 93    34 × 200   93 ×
 ×  =1  =18 ×  18   =8 × 37   3 × 56  13 × 75   24 × 94    34 × 210   99 ×
 ×   0  =18 ×  19   =7 × 38   3 × 57  14 × 76   24 × 95    35 × 220  104 ×
 ×   1  =17 ×  20   =7 × 39   4 × 58  14 × 77   25 × 96    36 × 225  107 ×
 ×   2  =17 ×  21   =6 × 40   4 × 59  15 × 78   26 × 97    36 × 230  110 ×
 ×   3  =16 ×  22   =6 × 41   5 × 60  16 × 79   26 × 98    37 × 240  116 ×
 ×   4  =15 ×  23   =5 × 42   6 × 61  16 × 80   27 × 99    37 × 250  121 ×
 ×   5  =15 ×  24   =4 × 43   6 × 62  17 × 81   27 × 100   38 × 260  127 ×
 ×   6  =14 ×  25   =4 × 44   7 × 63  17 × 82   28 × 110   43 × 270  132 ×
 ×   7  =14 ×  26   =3 × 45   7 × 64  18 × 83   28 × 120   49 × 280  138 ×
 ×   8  =13 ×  27   =3 × 46   8 × 65  18 × 84   29 × 125   52 × 290  143 ×
 ××××××××××××××××××××××××××××××××××××××××××××××××××××××××××××××××××××××××××
Commodities <COMMOD>      Energy <ENERGY>              Shipping <SHIPPING>
Menu Page    <CONVERSION1>
```

Why Do the Commodities, Energy & Transport Markets Exist?

Your notes

Commodities Markets

What Are the Commodities Markets?

Commodity markets deal with the buying and selling of raw materials – commodities. These markets are among the oldest traded and the concept of trading **forward** started here, that is, buying and selling a product for delivery at a **future** date.

There are two basic ways in which commodity trading can take place:

- **Physical markets,** or **Over-The-Counter (OTC)** market, are those in which traders buy and sell the actual commodity and settle the deal in cash – this is why these markets are sometimes known as the **cash markets**. Typically trading takes place over the telephone and occasionally in sale rooms or at auction. Trades are non-standardised and each deal is individuall negotiated for an individual commodity.

- **Exchange based** or **Paper markets** are those in which **exchanges** provide facilities for trading commodities contracts. These contracts have standardised terms and conditions and the exchange acts as the counterparty between buyers and sellers.

What are hard and agricultural commodities?

- **Hard** commodities are materials such as non-ferrous metals, including copper, lead, tin, nickel, aluminium and zinc, and precious metals, including gold, silver, palladium and platinum.

- **Agricultural** commodities include materials such as coffee, cocoa, sugar, grain, soya, corn, rubber and cotton.

How Do the Physical Markets Work?

The terms and conditions of OTC spot and forward contracts are individually negotiated but typically cover the following for the commodity being traded:

- Quality
- Quantity
- Delivery location
- Delivery terms, for example "CIF" or "FOB" – these terms are explained in *Section 2*
- Settlement details
- Price

Settlement Details

For **spot** transactions the settlement period is usually between 1 and 45 days depending on the market conventions for a particular commodity. For some commodities the period is two days which is the same as used in the foreign exchange and money markets.

For **forward** transactions the settlement period is determined by the agreed date in the future.

Price

As these OTC transactions are private, how do market players know the value of a particular commodity which is vital for their trade negotiations? Reuters (as well as other reporting services) reporters and editorial desks assess market values, which involves a lot of hard effort, from conversations with traders, brokers and other sources. To derive a cash quote, a Reuters reporter will contact typically more than five key players in the market to find out the prices at which they are trading. The reporter then has to use his or her experience and judgement to ascertain which quotes are accurate – traders may be quoting book prices in an effort to influence published market prices.

It is also worth noting that the time of day can make significant differences in determining a quotation. This means that reporters from different organisations may and often do have different views on the value of a commodity at a specific time.

Why Do the Commodities, Energy & Transport Markets Exist?

Most cash market prices are updated once or twice a day – the frequency is somewhat dependent on the liquidity of the market. For example, Brent crude oil prices are updated in near real-time by a link with futures prices and differentials whereas less liquid markets such as that for European Liquefied Petroleum Gas (LPG) are updated only once per week.

Look at the following article about a Reuters reporter's day written by William Hardy of the London Energy Newsroom:

An energy reporter's day is a day spent on the phone: gossiping, cajoling, flattering, delving, broking information and sorting out the truth from the half-truths.

The bulk of the world's physical oil trade – tankers sold in and out of refineries - is done by a small club of traders, most of them in London.

Prices may be related to futures contracts, but the real price of the oil that actually makes the world work only goes public as a result of hard journalistic graft. Reporters have to sort out the good information from the misleading or useless. That requires a sound understanding of not only market mechanics but the personalities of traders and some idea of their underlying motivations.

Some traders will at times attempt to influence a reporter's view on a market either by outright mis-information or more often by obscuring certain details of a reported deal. An energy reporter is constantly on guard for this and continuously looking for clues to the "fair" value of specific crude oils or products in his patch.

Traders don't have to speak to us - they'd rather be making money. So contacts are forged through respect as the reporter becomes part of the information machine that runs this highly secretive market.

Through constant contact with the market, price tables for everything from super unleaded gasoline to the sludgiest crude are updated throughout the day and reports written at regular intervals.

Regular futures reports covering the International Petroleum Exchange (IPE) Brent crude and gas oil contracts, in-depth coverage of the esoteric swaps market and a daily technical insight piece complete the groundwork covered each day.

The day stretches from 7.30 am when the bureau opens until 8.30 pm when the last futures report is filed after the IPE closes.

With that daily workload whirring in the background reporters roam their markets chasing stories - refinery fires, strikes and storms that disrupt the market and move prices.

On top of these are the big stories - the machinations of the OPEC oil sheikhs, the faltering Russian economy and the tussle between oil and its rival energy sources.

So by the time the day ends, the energy reporter may have spoken to anyone from the man on a North Sea oil platform to the oil minister of Gabon and all points in between.

Tendering

Within some commodities markets, offers to buy or sell a commodity may be made by request or by **tender**. These tenders are usually made by national organisations and are most common in the global agricultural and oil markets.

A tender is typically issued in writing with a reasonable lead time to a list of traders and potential suppliers. Very often trading companies must establish a relationship with the tendering company or country to gain position on the list of companies that are issued with the tender, the so-called "short list". Some tenders are public, meaning anyone is invited to present and offer. The tendering process gives the issuing organisation an opportunity to review price offers for their requested specification etc. from a range of suppliers.

Tenders may be used to buy or to sell commodities. For instance, the Indian Oil Company (IOC) typically tenders for companies to supply them with refined oil products or crude oil to meet their needs while Vietnam typically uses tenders to sell their crude oil production.

Petroleum tenders are most common in Asia and the Middle East. Tender results are reported by the news sources, in commodity categories such as crude oil and grains. The Reuters sources below show news headlines and tender prices.

```
09:17  17 Mar  RTRS-Taiwan MFIG buys 54,000T of U.S. corn
09:16  17 Mar  RTRS-TAIWAN FEED GROUP BUYS 54,000 TONNES OF U.S. CORN AT TENDER -
               TRADERS
22:20  16 Mar  RTRS-CCC details 711,400 T wheat tender results
15:33  16 Mar  RTRS-CCC flour
15:18  16 Mar  RTRS-Pakistan    09:16  17 Mar  RTRS-TAIWAN FEED GROUP BUYS 54,000 TONNES OF U.S. CORN AT
10:20  16 Mar  RTRS-Taiwan M                   TENDER - TRADERS
09:44  16 Mar  RTRS-Taiwan b    09:17  17 Mar  RTRS-Taiwan MFIG buys 54,000T of U.S. corn
15:08  15 Mar  RTRS-Union Pac
13:29  15 Mar  RTRS-CCC expo    TAIPEI, March 17 (Reuters) - Taiwan's Members Feed Industry Group bought a 54,000-
16:12  12 Mar  RTRS-EU publis   tonne shipment of U.S. corn at a tender on Wednesday, traders said.
13:47  12 Mar  RTRS-CCC expo    The shipment was bought on a cost-and-freight basis from grain supplier Cargill, traders
13:39  12 Mar  RTRS-CCC rice    said.
09:25  12 Mar  RTRS-Taiwan to   The feed group's main buyers are Taiwan's Formosa Oilseed <1225.TW>, Fomau Cereal,
09:18  12 Mar  RTRS-TAKE A L    Morn Sun Feed Mill and Shin Tai Industry.
08:58  12 Mar  RTRS-Date of n
08:25  12 Mar  RTRS-EU adds 5      Details for the tender are as follows:
17:59  11 Mar  RTRS-EU to hold  Tonnage   Date/Location                 Prices/Futures
17:00  11 Mar  RTRS-EU agrees             U.S. Gulf   Pacific N.W.
16:26  11 Mar  RTRS-TABLE-EU    54,000    May 11-25   May 26-June 9   61.47 US cents/May
13:11  11 Mar  RTRS-CCC expo       Reuters Terminal users can see Asian grain, oilseed/meal
10:55  11 Mar  RTRS-Austrians   prices by double clicking on:
10:38  11 Mar  RTRS-UK trade    <GRAIN/ASIA1> Thailand, Malaysia, Indonesia, Japan, S.Korea
08:14  11 Mar  RTRS-S.Korean    <GRAIN/ASIA2> Taiwan, China, India, Philippines
                                <GRAIN/ASIA3> Rice in Thailand, India, Vietnam, Pakistan
11:15  17 Mar  RTRS-DIARY - Vegetable oils/oilseeds tenders, results                2508-0204,
11:13  17 Mar  RTRS-DIARY - Grain tenders and results
11:15  17 Mar  RTRS-DIARY - Vegetable oils/oilseeds tenders, results
11:13  17 Mar  RTRS-DIARY - Grain tenders and results
09:47  16 Mar  RTR
02:33  15 Mar  RTR   11:13  17 Mar  RTRS-DIARY - Grain tenders and results
04:21  12 Mar  RTR   This diary gives grain tender announcements, results and cancellations, and
23:30  10 Mar  RTR   other grain buying background news and talk, updated to March 17.
09:32  09 Mar  RTR   .
10:55  02 Mar  RTR   FORTHCOMING BUYING TENDERS
04:38  01 Mar  RTR   COUNTRY      GRAIN        AMOUNT    DATE      OTHER DETAILS/COMMENT
17:15  25 Feb  RTR   Bangladesh   rice         40,000    Apr 12    ship within 30 days of signing
09:10  25 Feb  RTR   Bangladesh   rice         40,000    Apr 7     ship within 30 days of signing
20:03  22 Feb  RTR   Sri Lanka    hard wheat   50,000    Mar 26    Apr/May shipment
10:52  19 Feb  RTR   Sri Lanka    soft wheat   50,000    Mar 26    Apr/May shipment
                     Guatenala    US corn      20,100    Mar 23    Apr 10/30 shipment, CCC
                     Ghana        US wheat     12,000    Mar 22    Mar 31/Apr 15 shipment, CCC
                     Cape Verde   US corn       5,000    Mar 22    Mar 31/Apr 15 shipment, CCC
                     Israel       feed wheat   10,000    Mar 17    Apr 20/May 10 shipment
                     Israel       feed barley  10,000    Mar 17    Apr 20/May 10 shipment
                     Sri Lanka    hard wheat   30,000    Mar 16    Apr arr
                     Bangladesh   wheat        60,000    Mar 16    May del, EU food aid
                     Sonalia      naize         7,500    Mar 16    Apr ship, EU food aid, WFP
                     Syria        rice         12,000    Mar 9     result Mar 18, Apr ship GEZA

                     FORTHCOMING SELLING TENDERS
                     .
                     TENDERS CANCELLED/PASSED/POSTPONED
                     S.Korea      US corn      52,500    Mar 17    high prices, Jul 30 arr, KOCOPIA
                     .
                     BUYING TENDER RESULTS
                     S.Korea      US corn      52,500    Mar 17    $109.78-110.38, Aug 10 arr
                     Taiwan       corn         54,000    Mar 17    61.47 US cents/May, May/Jun ship
                     S.Korea      US corn      52,500    Mar 16    $108.98-109.58 C&F, May 15 arr
                     Taiwan       US corn     105,800    Mar 16    $128.80-164.20, Apr/May del
                     S.Korea      US corn      52,000    Mar 16    $109.40-110.20 C&F May 15 arr
```

How Do Commodity Exchanges Work?

In general, futures contracts and options on futures contracts are traded in **pits** scattered across the exchange floor which are designated for a particular commodity at a particular time of day. The trading is then carried out **open outcry** – to the casual observer the process may appear chaotic and colourful.

Depending on membership rules participants are **brokers** or **traders** acting on behalf of clients and **locals** acting on their own behalf. Participants have to buy or rent a seat on an exchange in order to participate. The pits are ringed by broker's booths in contact with their front offices which receive client instructions. These instructions are passed to traders in the pit who bid between each other in open outcry. This type of dealing system allows three things to happen:

- They allow commodity trading under guaranteed conditions

- They allow price transparency to all market participants

- They offer a means of protection against sharp changes in prices, known as **hedging**. Hedging is explained in more detail later.

However, more recently **electronic trading** on exchanges has gained in importance. Most exchanges have now implemented some form of electronic trading system and it is likely that open outcry may disappear in the long term from some exchanges.

Examples of exchanges dealing in commodities are as follows:

- **London Metal Exchange (LME)**
- **London International Financial Futures and Options Exchange (LIFFE)**
- **New York Coffee Sugar and Cocoa Exchange (NYCSCE)**
- **Chicago Board of Trade (CBOT)**
- **Commodity Exchange of New York (COMEX) – a part of the New York Mercantile Exchange (NYMEX)**
- **Tokyo Commodity Exchange**

Why Do the Commodities, Energy & Transport Markets Exist?

Who Uses the Exchanges?

Exchanges meet the needs of:

- Physical traders who need to take physical delivery of a commodity
- Farmers, producers, consumers and merchants who must take or make delivery at some time in the future and who need to hedge their price risk
- Speculators wishing to take advantage of the high volatility and leverage of margin trading

Why Are There Futures Markets?

The futures market was created for those who need and use commodities. Commodities prices are unpredictable and are dependent on factors such as weather conditions, crop diseases, political events, strikes by workers etc. Most businesses which produce or use commodities trade in the spot market and use the futures market as a protection against the risk of price volatility. A futures contract can be defined as:

> A firm contractual agreement between a buyer and seller for a specified asset on a fixed date in the future. The contract price will vary according to the market place, but it is fixed when the trade is made. The contract also has a standard specification so both parties know what is being traded.

One of the first examples of futures trading was in 17th century Japan where landlords collecting a share of the rice harvest as rent found weather and other conditions too unpredictable. So the landlords who needed cash, shipped the rice for storage in city warehouses. They then sold warehouse receipts – rice tickets – which gave the holder the right to receive a certain amount of rice, of a certain quality, at a future date. The landlords received a steady income and merchants had a steady supply of rice plus an opportunity to profit by selling the tickets.

Other early examples of futures contracts involving commodities were Dutch whalers, Maine potato growers and cotton importers in Liverpool.

The "timeline" below illustrates when various exchanges were established.

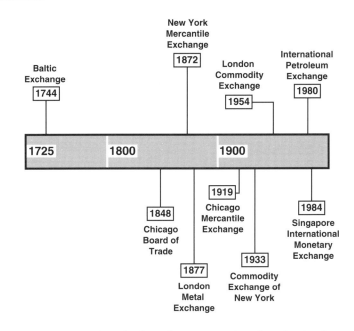

The futures contract is a deal made now to take place in the future. When it is used as a **hedge** against a physical position it is, in effect, an insurance policy locking in prices against changes. Futures contracts are rarely used to take a physical position – nearly 98% of futures are **closed out (cancelled)** before the delivery date. More recently, Exchange of Futures for Physicals (EFPs) contracts are gaining in use – these instruments are explained later in *Section 3*.

There are two terms associated with buying and selling futures contracts that you need to understand. These are:

- **Go long**. This is when you **buy** a particular contract and expect the price to rise prior to contract expiry. So you make a profit when you sell at a higher price than when you bought the contract.

- **Go short**. This is when you **sell** a particular contract and expect to make a profit when you buy back the contract prior to expiry at a lower price than when you sold.

Types of Commodities

Though commodities are often divided into two main types – hard and agriculturals – this book will refer to three broad categories:

- **Metals** which includes base, precious and strategic/minor

- **Softs** which includes coffee, cocoa, sugar, rubber, pepper, tea and citrus fruits

- **Grains and Oilseeds** which includes cereals, fibres, meal, livestock, soya and oilseeds

Within each of these categories are important commodities described in greater depth later. For the moment the commodities of importance are classified as follows:

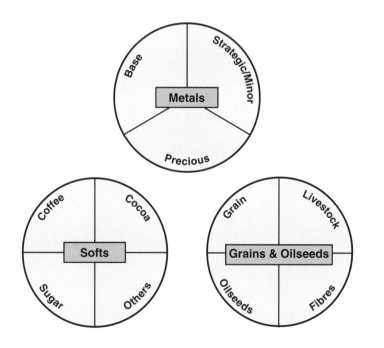

Metals

The metals markets are divided into the following three main areas:

Base metals The original meaning of a base metal was one that dulls or tarnishes when in contact with the air at ordinary atmospheric temperatures. Base metals contain no iron and include the major non-ferrous metals of copper, aluminium, zinc, lead, tin and nickel. The chief market place for these metals is the **London Metal Exchange (LME)**. Stocks delivered on LME contracts are held under warrant in LME warehouses.

Strategic/ minor metals Strategic metals are produced as a by-product of base metal ore mining and include metals such as antimony, bismuth, gallium, vanadium, silicon and selenium. Many of these metals are used in the semi-conductor industry. Minor metals include many other metals such as cobalt, cadmium and chromium and some minerals such as talc, barytes and fluorspar, which are used commercially. Strategic and minor metals are traded as physical markets mainly by way of direct trade agreements between producer and consumer. For example, Sumitomo of Japan markets titanium directly to end-users in the automotive, aerospace and weapons industries where it is used in the manufacture of certain types of steel alloys. Key consumers of strategic and minor metals are the electrical, pharmaceutical, aerospace and automotive industries.

Precious metals These include the traditional coinage metals of silver and gold together with the rare metals of platinum and palladium which are used in automotive catalysts for pollution control. Most silver is obtained as a by-product of base metal mining and its price is affected by the price of these metals. Although gold is no longer the international currency standard, its price is still influenced by the equity and debt markets. Generally gold prices are more influenced by political and economic factors rather than by levels of consumption.

Why Do the Commodities, Energy & Transport Markets Exist?

Before moving on refer to the Reuters screens below to find out more about the metals markets only.

Below is the Commodities Speed Guide page, from which you can access Quick Summary Guides or Market Sector Guides, as shown at right.

```
COMMODITIES - REUTERS SPEED GUIDE                                    COMMOD
To access information double-click in < >.  For more guidance see <USER/HELP>
=QUICK SUMMARY GUIDES================  =MARKET SECTOR GUIDES=================
Base/Minor/Strategic Metals.<METAL/SUM>  Base, Minor & Strategic Metals.<METAL1>
Fibres.......................<FIBRE/SUM>  Fibres.........................<FIBRE1>
Grains, Soy & Oils...........<GRAIN/SUM>  Grains, Soy & Oils.............<GRAIN1>
Meals & Livestocks............<MEAL/SUM>  Meals & Livestocks..............<MEAL1>
Precious Metals...........<PRECIOUS/SUM>  Precious Metals............<PRECIOUS1>
Softs........................<SOFT/SUM>   Softs..........................<SOFT1>

=OTHER COMMODITY GUIDES==============  =RELATED GUIDES=====================
Commodity Specialist Data<COMMOD/SPEC1>   Global Futures/Options........<FUTURES>
All Commodity News.......<COMMOD/NEWS1>   Free Cross Market Data.....<CROSS/MKT1>
Cash Market Specifications.<COMMSPECSA>   News Cross Reference Pages..<NEWSXREF1>
CPC Grains/Oilseeds............<CPCBDTA>  Conversion Rates...........<CONVERT1>-4
CPC Veg.Oils/Oilseeds.........<CPCBDUA>   Volatilities..................<VOL/1>
CFTC Guide................<CFTCGUIDE>     RIC Rules Guide.............<RULES1>-7
Commod Price Info Ref...<RATESXREF1>-25   Shipping Information.........<SHIPPING>
                                          J.P. Morgan RiskMetrics........<RISK/1>
=DATA NOTIFICATIONS & ALERTS===========
Scheduled Data Notifications..<CHANGES>
Service Alerts................<ALERT>

What's New? <COMMOD/INFO>         Event Diary [DIARY]      Main Guide <REUTERS>
    Lost? Selective Access.<USER/HELP>       Reuters Phone Support.<PHONE/HELP>
```

```
BASE AND MINOR METALS - REUTERS SPEED GUIDE SUMMARY             METAL/SUM
This is the Base & Minor Metal overview,for a complete guide see page <METAL1>

=BASE METALS INDEX PAGES=============  =NEWS & ANALYSIS======================
Base Metals Index.............<METAL1>   All Metals News...................[MTL]
Metals Cash/Producer Prices<BASE/CASH1>  Base Metals News..................[MET]
Futures Prices.............<BASE/FUT1>   London Metals Report............[MET/L]
Options Prices.............<BASE/OPT1>   Latest Copper Report............[COP/]
All base metals news......<METAL/NEWS1>  COMEX Copper Report.............[COP/X]
=KEY MARKET PRICES==================    COMEX Delivery Notices.........[MET/XD]
LME Market Prices/Stocks........<RING:>  COMEX Stocks...................[MET/XS]
COMEX Copper..................<O#HG:>    NYMEX Stocks...................[MET/NS]
LME Copper Outrights/Spreads..<O#MCU:>   Minor Metals Report............[MET/M]
LME Aluminiun Outrights/Spreads<O#MAL:>  All Other Reports................[C/R]
Tokyo
LME                                      REUTERS SPEED GUIDE             METAL1
LME N  This is the main index page for all Base and Minor Metals
LME L
LME A  =BASE METALS INDEX PAGES=============  =NEWS & ANALYSIS=================
Minor  Key codes quick summary.....<METAL/SUM>  Metals News...............[MTL]
Woger  Cash/Producer Prices.....<BASE/CASH1>-2  Base Metals News..........[MET]
=====  Base Metal Futures.........<BASE/FUT1>   Base Metals Insight..[INSI-MET]
Main   Base Metal Options.........<BASE/OPT1>   COMEX Copper Report.....[COP/X]
Lost?                                           COMEX Copper Vol/Open Int.[COP/VOLO]
       =LONDON METAL EXCHANGE==============     COMEX Delivery Notices..[MET/XD]
       Prices/Stocks composite......<RING=>     COMEX/NYMEX Stocks.....<MTXU>-X
       Top Level Index...........<LME/INDEX>    ...Base Metals (logical)...<O#CMX-BASE>
       LME Brokers Index........<LME/BROKER1>   ...Prec Metals (logical)...<O#CMX-PREC>
       Contract Details.........<LME/FUTEX1>    Minor Metals Report.....[MET/M]
```

```
PRECIOUS METALS - REUTERS SPEED GUIDE SUMMARY          PRECIOUS/SUM
To access information double-click in <> or [ ].For more guidance see<USER/HELP>

=KEY MARKET PRICES===================   =NEWS AND ANALYSIS===================
Spot Gold....................<XAU=>      All Metal News...................[MTL]
Spot Silver..................<XAG=>      All precious reports......<METAL/NEWS3>
Spot Platinum................<XPT=>      NYMEX Stocks...............[MET/NS]
Spot Palladium...............<XPD=>      Survey of analyst's predictions<POLL16>
Gold Contributions...........<O#XAU=>    Gold/Precious Metals.............[GOL]
Silver                                   Gold Mining
Plati  PRECIOUS METALS - REUTERS SPEED GUIDE                        PRECIOUS1
Palla  To access information double-click in <> or [ ].For more guidance see<USER/HELP>
Comex
Comex  =PRECIOUS METALS INDEX PAGES===========   =NEWS AND ANALYSIS SUMMARY=======
Comex  Cash Precious Metals...<PRECIOUS/CASH1>    All Metal News...............[MTL]
Comex  Precious Futures........<PRECIOUS/FUT1>    All precious reports......<METAL/NEWS4>
       Precious Options.......<PRECIOUS/OPT1>     NYMEX Stocks...............[MET/NS]
=GOLD  Precious Swaps........<PRECIOUS/SWAP1>     Gold/Precious Metals.........[GOL]
Bull   Precious Metals Summary..<PRECIOUS/SUM>    Gold Mining..................[GDM]
Baird  Precious Volatilities...<PRECIOUS/VOL1>    Commodity News...............[C/]
Compa  Physical Gold............<GOLD/CASH1>      Commodity Market Report......[C/R]
Quest  Gold Futures.............<GOLD/FUT1>       Weather Services Index.......[WSC]
=====  Gold Options.............<GOLD/OPT1>       Survey of analyst's predictions<POLL16>
Commo  Gold Forward/Lending..........<GOFO=>
   Lo  Physical Silver..........<SILVER/CASH1>    =CROSS MARKET==================
       Silver Futures...........<SILVER/FUT1>     Cross Market Package.......<CROSS/MKT1>
       Silver Options...........<SILVER/OPT1>     Foreign Exchange Rates..........<FX=S>
       London Bullion Market Assoc....<LBMA01>   World Cross Rates...........<WX=X>

                                                  Weight Conversion Factors..<CONVERT1>-2

       Commodities Index<COMMOD>                               Metal Index<METAL1>
          Lost?Selective Access?...<USER/HELP>   Reuters Phone Support...<PHONE/HELP>
```

Softs

In common with all commodity markets the prices of softs are subject to:

- Supply and demand fluctuations
- Adverse weather conditions
- Stock piles
- Harvest forecasts
- Transport costs
- Government programmes and subsidies

The most important soft commodities traded worldwide are:

- Coffee
- Cocoa
- Sugar

There are smaller markets for rubber, orange juice, tea and pepper.

Most trading in softs involves the underlying physical market place with a wide range of players including roasters, refiners, processors, distributors and traders. There are also futures markets in the major soft commodities on exchanges such as LIFFE, NYCSCE and MATIF.

Information on the major soft commodities is available from electronic news services such as Reuters. You will also find short items concerning commodity prices in the relevant section of financial papers such as the *Financial Times* and *The Wall Street Journal*.

Why not see what today's commodity item is about in the *Financial Times* ?

The Reuters screens below show world summary prices and spreads for several softs.

Grains and Oilseeds

The most important agricultural commodities traded worldwide in this category are:

- **Grains**. These include wheat, barley, corn (maize in the US), rice and oats.

- **Oilseeds**. This group includes the seeds that produce edible oils, oils for livestock feeds or oils for industrial use. Seeds of importance worldwide are soybean, rapeseed, palm kernel and flaxseed – the latter is used to produce linseed oil. This group also includes meals and fertilizers.

- **Livestock**. These markets are concerned with both live animals and meat products, for example, frozen pork bellies. This group also includes dairy products such as milk and cheese.

- **Fibres**. These markets include wool, cotton and silk.

Most trading in these commodities takes place in the spot or cash markets and it is sometimes difficult to obtain accurate prices as contracts are direct between producer and consumer. The prices of these agriculturals are subject to the same factors as for softs but in addition growth cycles have to be taken into account – for example, a pig takes four years to mature, cereals take time to grow etc.

These major agriculturals are traded on futures exchanges such as:

- **London International Financial Futures and Options Exchange (LIFFE)**
- **Chicago Mercantile Exchange (CME)**
- **Chicago Board of Trade (CBOT)**
- **Tokyo Grain Exchange (TGE)**
- **Sydney Futures Exchange (SFE)**

The Reuters screens below show the grains, soy and oils summary page and a cereals index page.

```
GRAINS - REUTERS SPEED GUIDE                               GRAIN/SUM
This is the Grain, Oilseed and Meals, Livestock and Fibre overview, for a
complete guide see <GRAIN1>.
=SECTOR INDEX PAGES==================   =KEY MARKET PRICES Contd==============
Cereal Index.................<CEREAL1>   MGE White Wheat...............<O#NW:>
Fibre Index...................<FIBRE1>   MIDAM Corn....................<O#XC:>
Livestock Index...........<LIVESTOCK1>   MIDAM Soybean.................<O#XS:>
Meal Index.....................<MEAL1>   MIDAM Wheat ..................<O#XW:>
Oilseed Index...............<OILSEED1>   Tokyo Corn...................<O#JCR:>
                                         Tokyo Soybean................<O#JAS:>
=KEY MARKET PRICES==================     Tokyo Red Beans..............<O#JRB:>
Chicago Corn...................<O#C:>    Winnipeg Canola..............<O#RS:>
Chicago Oats...................<O#O:>    Winnipeg Flaxseed............<O#WF:>
Chicago Soybeans...............<O#S:>
Chicago Soybean Meal..........<O#SM:>    =NEWS & ANALYSIS=====================
Chicago Soybean Oil...........<O#BO:>    All Grains/Oilseeds News..........[GRO]
Chicago Wheat..................<O#W:>    Grain market reports....<GRAIN/NEWS1>-8
Kansas Board of Trade Wheat...<O#KW:>    Grains Diary...............[GRO/DIARY]
MATIF DEM Rapeseed..........<O#COM:>     CFTC Commitments of Traders...<1CFTC>-4
MATIF USD Rapeseed..........<O#COD:>     Foreign Exchange Rates.........<FX=S>
MATIF FRF Rapeseed..........<O#COF:>     Stock Indices..............<O#.INDEX>
MGE Spring Wheat.............<O#MW:>     World Cross Rates.............<WX=X>
=====================================================================
What's New   <COMMOD/INFO>   Main Index   <REUTER> Commodities Index  <COMMOD>
Lost
```

```
CEREAL - REUTERS SPEED GUIDE                               CEREAL1
To access information double-click in <> or [ ].For more guidance see<USER/HELP>
Please see <GRAIN/CASH1>-4 for new logical displays of data.

=WHEAT INDEX PAGES===================   =OATS INDEX PAGES====================
Physical By region........<WHEAT/CASH1>   Physical By region.........<OATS/CASH1>
Futures By Instrument......<WHEAT/FUT1>   Futures By Instrument.......<OATS/FUT1>
Option By Future...........<WHEAT/OPT1>   Option By Future............<OATS/OPT1>

=BARLEY INDEX PAGES==================   =RICE INDEX PAGES====================
Physical By region.......<BARLEY/CASH1>   Physical By region.........<RICE/CASH1>
Futures By Instrument.....<BARLEY/FUT1>   Futures by Instrument.......<RICE/FUT1>
Option By Future..........<BARLEY/OPT1>   Option By Future............<RICE/OPT1>

=CORN INDEX PAGES====================   =NEWS & ANALYSIS=====================
Physical By region.........<CORN/CASH1>   All Grains News...................[GRA]
Futures By Instrument.......<CORN/FUT1>   Grain Derivative News........[GRO-DRV]
Option By Future...........<CORN/OPT1>   Weather Service Index...........[WSCC]
                                         Foreign Exchange Rates..........<FX=X>
                                         World Cross Rates..............<WX=X>
                                         Stock Indices...............<O#.INDEX>
Questions/Comments: Contact your local Help Desk - see <PHONE/HELP> for details
=====================================================================
Main Index...<REUTER>                          Grains Index Page...<GRAIN1>
Lost? Selective access?...<USER/HELP>   Reuters Phone Support...<PHONE/HELP>
```

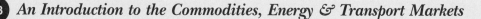

Energy Markets

Why Do the Energy Markets Exist?

Energy is an essential commodity for basic living requirements as well as for providing the power required for industrialised economies. The types of energy used have to some extent depended on their discovery and availability. For example, coal was a very important source of energy in the nineteenth century. In 1886 the Coal Exchange was built in Cardiff, Wales – then the largest coal exporting city in the world. It was said that on the Coal Exchange trading floor a millionaire was only an arm length's distance away in any direction.

An impression of the Coal Exchange in 1886

From the beginning of the twentieth century, oil became increasingly more important as the major world source of energy. More recently, natural gas has had a significant affect on energy supply and usage. With the deregulation of worldwide power generation markets as well as environmental pressures, there is an interesting balance of energy sources and requirements facing the markets. The chart below shows the total energy primary supply by source for 1996 – the latest figures available.

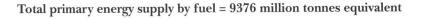

Total primary energy supply by fuel = 9376 million tonnes equivalent

Oil 35.3%
Combustible Renewables & Waste 11.1%
Natural Gas 20.2%
Coal 24%
Nuclear 6.7%
Hydroelectric, 2.3%
Other (Geothermal, Solar etc), 0.4%

Source: OECD Statistics 1999

Although oil is the most important energy market in terms of the value of worldwide trade and as a source of energy, markets for other energy sources and generation are increasing in importance. The below broad categories are used in this book:

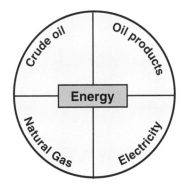

The energy markets considered here are as follows:

- Oil
- Natural Gas
- Electricity
- Other

Oil Markets

The consumption of oil as a source of energy has risen steadily from the turn of the century. Oil is now the major source of energy worldwide with increasing use in Far Eastern and Eastern European developing countries.

In 1959 the Organisation of the Petroleum Exporting Countries (OPEC) was formed as a direct result of the low oil prices being offered by the major oil companies – the once so-called 'Seven Sisters':

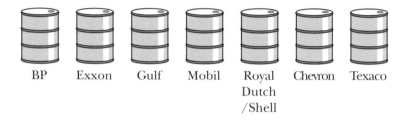

| BP | Exxon | Gulf | Mobil | Royal Dutch /Shell | Chevron | Texaco |

The oil companies had lowered the price of oil to $1.76 a barrel and they continued to dominate the oil markets up to the early 1970s. The Seven Sisters controlled 80% of exploration through refining to retail marketing. Only about 5% of oil production was traded and until 1971 the international price was very stable and there was a balance between supply and demand. The oil companies wielded both political and economic power based on their large profits.

In 1973 there was an oil crisis brought about by the Arab-Israeli conflict during which time Arab states imposed an oil embargo on countries supporting Israel – the US and Holland. This had an immediate effect of raising the price of oil from $2.50 to $8 a barrel.

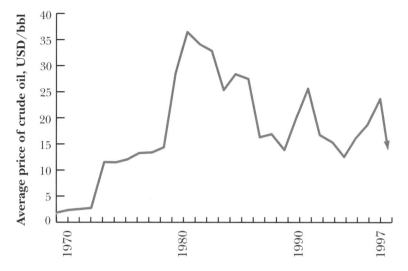

Source: US Department of Energy – Energy Information Administration 1998

In 1979 -1980 there was a second crisis precipitated by the revolution in Iran which was followed by the Iran -Iraq war. Japanese industry, which was entirely dependent on imported oil, paid up to $42 a barrel – a record high which has not been equalled since.

The result of these two crises within a decade resulted in sensitive and volatile spot market trading between producers and refiners. It also brought about forward and futures markets.

The invasion of Kuwait by Iraq in 1990 and the subsequent war lasting until 1991 resulted once again in very high prices. The anticipation of reduced supplies and panic buying sent prices almost up to $42 a barrel again – jet fuel increased in cost by 155%.

The OPEC countries – Iran, Iraq, UAE, Saudi Arabia, Kuwait, Qatar, Libya, Nigeria, Algeria, Gabon, Venezuela, Ecuador and Indonesia – control about 75% of the world oil reserves. The Gulf states combined own about 60% and from the above paragraph it is probably obvious that oil prices are very sensitive to events in the Gulf!

However, oil prices are also sensitive to many other factors including:

- Disasters such as the *Piper Alpha* platform catastrophe in the North Sea and the *Exxon Valdez* tanker oil spill in Alaska

- Industrial relations disputes in oil producing/refining countries

- OPEC statements resulting from their regular meetings

- Seasonal factors where refineries produce more gasoline in the late winter/early spring or heating oil in the late summer/early autumn

- Absolute price levels. If oil prices are high then consumers reduce their driving and flying commitments and energy providers switch to cheaper energy sources such as coal or natural gas for power generation.

Toward the end of 1999, OPEC announced that its members would continue to cut crude oil production, which would put pressure on prices, in the knowledge that non-OPEC producers' production and reserves are declining. As OPEC countries hold the bulk of world reserves in the next decade or so they are expected to continue to have an important role in the markets.

It is not only the price of crude oil which has changed radically since the creation of the Seven Sisters. Between 1998 and 1999, several of the major oil companies have either merged – Exxon and Mobil – BP and Amoco – or reorganised, as with Royal Dutch/Shell, to cope with changes in world economies and declining prices in the oil markets.

The Reuters screens below show the summary of the OPEC Price Basket average prices and then detail about the OPEC countries' crude oil production output.

```
OPEC PRICE BASKET                                         OPEC/BASKET

   WEEKLY AVERAGES    --   2ND WK OCT     vs    1ST WK OCT
                            $13.32              $13.96
   MONTHLY AVERAGES   --    SEP       AUG       JULY
                           $12.91    $11.89    $12.06
   QUARTERLY AVERAGES --    Q398      Q298      Q198
                           $12.33    $12.46    $13.35
   YEARLY AVERAGES    --    1998×     1997      1996
                           $12.73    $18.68    $20.29
   ×Year to Oct 8  All prices in dollars per barrel
   The OPEC basket conprises Algeria's Saharan Blend, Indonesia's Minas,
 Nigeria's Bonny Light, Saudi Arabia's Arabian Light, Dubai of the United Arab
 Enirates, Venezuela's Tia Juana and Mexico's Isthnus crude.
```

```
11:04 07OCT98          REUTERS OPEC PRODUCTION SURVEY      UK99999       OPEC/SURVEY
 (MLN BPD)
                 SEP       AUG       JUL     APR1 QUOTA  JULY 1 QUOTA
 ALGERIA         0.80      0.80      0.81      0.818      0.788
 INDONESIA       1.36      1.35      1.35      1.310      1.280
 IRAN            3.43      3.45(R)   3.60      3.483      3.318
 IRAQ            2.49      2.47      2.38       --         --
 KUWAIT          1.98      2.01      2.02      2.080      1.980
 LIBYA           1.35      1.35      1.35      1.373      1.323
 NIGERIA         2.00      1.87      2.10      2.133      2.033
 QATAR           0.63      0.63      0.67      0.670      0.640
 S.ARABIA        7.85      7.95      8.15      8.448      8.023
 UAE             2.15      2.18      2.25      2.257      2.157
 VENEZUELA       2.98      3.00      3.04      3.170      2.845

 TOTAL          27.02     27.06(R)  27.72    ×25.742    ×24.387


      Figures in nillions of barrels a day. Saudi Arabia and Kuwait
      include Neutral Zone. ×Total excludes Iraq.
       × Total includes March nonthly estinate for Iraq
```

Up until the oil crises of the 1970s, contracts had been bought and sold for fixed terms. This system worked well in periods of stable prices, however, when prices are volatile losses and profits can be very large.

Example

A Very Large Crude Carrier (VLCC) has a cargo of 250,000 tons of crude oil. This represents 1,825,000 barrels of oil. If the price of a barrel of oil is $21 then the cargo is worth $38,325,000. During the course of a trading day the price of a barrel of oil can fluctuate by ±$1 which means that the value of the cargo fluctuates by ±$1,825,000!

The Spot Markets

Although crude oil is an international commodity with well developed spot markets, quite a lot of crude oil is delivered from producers to refiners under supply agreements based on **posted** or **official prices**. Supply agreements tend to be written for one month to a year with renewal provisions.

Oil companies cannot always predict their exact requirements under supply agreements – they sometimes have a shortfall; sometimes a surplus. The **open** or **spot markets** are where the oil companies balance their requirements.

The informal **Over-The-Counter (OTC)** spot markets have developed around the major refining centres of the world which are used as standard delivery locations for trading – these centres are not necessarily where the actual market exists. For example, there are OTC markets using Cushing (Oklahoma), St. James (Louisiana), New York Harbour, Rotterdam, Singapore and Tokyo.

The spot markets are well established and use marker or benchmark crude oils such as North Sea Brent Blend, West Texas Intermediate (WTI) and Dubai for pricing in the underlying physical markets and for the forward and futures markets.

The growth of spot trading has established an effective market mechanism and the need for reporting the activity and deals concluded. Organisations such as Platt's, Petroleum Argus, London Oil Reports and Reuters provide price reporting services.

There is still some resistance from oil producers to spot market trading – Saudi Arabia does not permit any of its crudes to be traded on the spot market.

It is important to remember that the spot market in crude oil is the single, largest physical commodity traded worldwide in terms of value.

Official Selling Price (OSP)

In many oil producing countries a national oil company is responsible for the sale of crude oil. Buyers usually contract to purchase an agreed amount of crude oil over an agreed period of time for a price determined by a standard formula – this formula sets the **Official Selling Price**. The formula may be based typically on a benchmark such as Dated Brent, or an average of benchmarks, to which a **differential** is applied. The differential is generally changed on a monthly basis and the benchmark price is often taken as the Platt's published price.

One contract area that buyers need to establish is that of the date used to set the cargo price. This date could be the loading date, a specific number of days after loading or the unloading date. Since the price movement among these dates can be significant, it is to both the buyer's and seller's interests that the date used to set the cargo price is known and agreed.

Electronic news services such as Reuters provide detailed information about pricing. These Reuters screens show the Energy Speed Guide, an outline of data available, with the Crude Cash Speed Guide following. Specific pages of detail for Brent forward pricing, and other suppliers of crude follow.

```
O#BRENT              BRENT
Name     Delivery  Buy  Sell   Time  Date  Prev.Close    Terms      Source  API  Sulphur
BRENT    Dtd      +9.95/+9.97  11:14 15FEB +9.96/+9.98   FOB SVOE   EUR     38.3
BRENT    Mar      10.30/10.32  11:14 15FEB 10.31/10.33   FOB SVOE   EUR     38.3
BRENT    Apr      10.48/10.50  11:14 15FEB 10.49/10.51   FOB SVOE   EUR     38.3
BRENT    May      10.69/10.71  11:14 15FEB 10.72/10.74   FOB SVOE   EUR     38.3
```

```
ENERGY 2000 - REUTERS SPEED GUIDE                                        ENERGY
To access information, double-click on the code in <> or [].

=KEY PAGE DISPLAYS=====================    =CASH PRODUCTS BY REGION=============
Composite DISPLAYS .......<ENERGY/COMP>    Asia...................<ASIA/PRODUCT1>
                                           Europe/Africa/Gulf......<EURO/PRODUCT1>
=DATA BY MARKET=======================      Africa................<AFRICA/PRODUCT1>
Futures Index............<ENERGY/FUT1>     Gulf..................<GULF/PRODUCT1>
Futures Spreads........<ENERGY/SPREAD1>    North America.......<AMERICAS/PRODUCT1>
Options Index............<ENERGY/OPT1>
Cash Crude Index..............<CRUDE/1>    =MISCELLANEOUS========================
Cash Product Index.........<PRODUCT/1>     FX quotes for Energy............<FX=S>
Energy Swaps.........<ENERGY/SWAPS1>       US Equities (delayed)...........<QIIU>-Z
Natural Gas Index............<NATGAS1>     Typical Conversion factors...<CONVERT3>
Netbacks and Refining........<NETBACKS>    Energy Statistics......<ENERGY/STATS1>
Electricity .............<ELECTRICITY>     Energy Cash Specifications...<ENGSPECA>
                                           Energy Specialist data...<ENERGY/SPEC1>
=NEWS and ANALYSIS===================       Energy Contacts......<ENERGY/CONTACTS>
```

```
CRUDE CASH - REUTERS SPEED GUIDE                                        CRUDE/1
           Double click on the codes in the <> or [] brackets

=BY REGION Displays===================     =CRUDE TYPE Displays==================
All Crude oils..................<O#C->     KEY CASH AND FUTURES CRUDE.....<CRDWLD>
Asian crude.......<O#C-A>.<CRUDE/ASIA1>    All Brent........<O#BRENT> or <O#BRT->
European crude....<O#C-E>.<CRUDE/EURO1>    Brent / Dubai forwards .....<CRUDE/INT>
N.America crude...........<O#C-N>          " (non-fee liable).......<CRUDE/INTL>
US West Coast ................<O#C-WC>     Regional Brent/Dubai .......<CRUDE/TS1>
Malaysian crudes .............<O#C-MY>     Brent Swaps.............<O#BRT-SWAP>
Indonesian crudes ............<O#C-ID>     Brent CFD's...............<O#BRT-CFD>
                                           All Dubai...................<O#DUB->
=NEWS and STATISTICS==================      All WTI...................<O#WT->
Crude related news and reports....[CRU]
Crude market reports..<ENERGY/REPORTS2>    =CRUDE Differentials==================
Official selling prices....<CRUDE/OSP1>    European Brent and Dubai ...<O#BRT-DIF>
OPEC basket ..............<OPEC/BASKET>    US Crudes + Brent & Dubai ..<O#C-DIF-N>
OPEC output Estimates.....<OPEC/SURVEY>    Asian Crude ................<O#C-DIF-A>
US GC Crude oil postings .......<PPIG>
US WC Crude oil postings ......<PPHN>      =INDIVIDUAL RICS BY INSTRUMENT========
Canadian crude postings...<PPJA>.<PPHO>    Cash Spot Crudes .......<CRUDE/CASH1>-3
                                           Cash Forward Crudes........<CRUDE/FWD1>

=====================================================================
Main Index..<REUTERS>    Commodities Index..<COMMOD>    Energy Index..<ENERGY>
Lost?Selective Access?..<USER/HELP>      Reuters Phone Support..<PHONE/HELP>
```

```
13:01 03JUN98                OIL PRICES              UK30507         CRUDE/OSP1
Crude oil - official selling prices

    This series of Reuter pages (CRUDE/OSP1 to CRUDE/OSP9) gives details of the
official selling prices of crude oil. A list of the various countries covered
in this series is given below. To access individual pages either double-click
between <> brackets or type in the page code and hit return.

    If you have any questions about this series of pages plase contact Reuters
London energy desk. Tel: 0171 542 4984

Country          Current prices

Saudi Arabia     <CRUDE/OSP2>
Nigeria          <CRUDE/OSP3>
Mexico           <CRUDE/OSP9>
Iraq             <CRUDE/OSP4>
Iran             <CRUDE/OSP5>
Kuwait
Libya
Egypt

Note: Th
Reuter p
```

```
22:10 14FEB99                OIL PRICES              UK30507         CRUDE/OSP3
Nigerian crude oil prices. All prices in $ per barrel.

Nigerian crude oil    Dated Brent +  Differential  = Price
                                        Feb
Bonny Light           $9.97       +    +0.20        =  $10.17
Bonny Medium          $9.97       +    -0.10        =  $9.87
Brass River           $9.97       +    +0.25        =  $10.22
Escravos              $9.97       +    +0.15        =  $10.12
Forcados              $9.97       +    +0.10        =  $10.07
Pennington            $9.97       +    +0.45        =  $10.42
Qua Iboe              $9.97       +    +0.20        =  $10.17
```

```
22:11 14FEB99                OIL PRICES              UK30507         CRUDE/OSP2
Saudi Arabia crude oil prices. All prices in $ per barrel fob Ras Tanura.
                      -----------Feb----------
Asia                  Reference crude price  +Differential=Saudi price
Arab Light            Oman/Dubai    $9.56  +  -0.15  =  $9.41
Arab Medium           Oman/Dubai    $9.56  +  -0.60  =  $8.96
Arab Heavy            Oman/Dubai    $9.56  +  -1.05  =  $8.51
Berri Extra Lt        Oman/Dubai    $9.56  +  +0.15  =  $9.71
Arab Super Lt         Oman/Dubai    $9.56  +  +0.80  =  $10.36

Europe
Arab Light            Dated Brent   $9.97  +  -1.55  =  $8.42
Arab Medium           Dated Brent   $9.97  +  -2.15  =  $7.82
Arab Heavy            Dated Brent   $9.97  +  -2.65  =  $7.32
Berri Extra Lt        Dated Brent   $9.97  +  -1.05  =  $8.92

U.S.
Arab Light            WTI           $11.88 +  -3.00  =  $8.88
Arab Medium           WTI           $11.88 +  -4.30  =  $7.58
Arab Heavy            WTI           $11.88 +  -5.05  =  $6.83
Berri Extra Lt        WTI           $11.88 +  -2.35  =  $9.53

Note: Saudi crude oil prices are calculated by adding differentials to the
regional reference crude prices. If you have any questions about this page
please call Reuters energy editorial on 0171 542 4984.
```

Forward Markets

Brent Blend monthly oil production is mostly allocated to the organisations owning the production rights – the equity holders. The oil is allocated in 500,000 barrel (±10%) lots or cargoes for a specific 3-day loading period or window. The equity holders are allocated cargoes once per month. Typically 30 - 40 cargoes are scheduled for loading each month.

The standard contracts used for trading forward Brent stipulate that the seller must give 15 days notice of a 3-day loading window to the buyer. Cargoes loading within the 15-day period are referred to as **Dated Brent** while the forward cargoes are termed **15-day Brent**.

With the increased volatility of the markets, market players used a forward pricing structure as a method of tying their deal prices into price reports. For example, a deal might be concluded today for a cargo of oil in ten days time and the price would be linked to the price reported by Platt's on the day of lifting the contract. The **forward market** is an OTC physical market in which contracts are individually negotiated between two parties which fix the price of a forward supply of oil. The contracts are not cleared through a central clearing house so there is no counterparty or payment/performance risk protection.

Therefore, traders will hold a daily portfolio of sales and purchases of 15-day Brent contracts across a range of prices which they use to match customer requirements or trade on their own account.

The 15-day Brent forward contracts proved successful instruments and by the late 1980s, other OTC instruments based on them – such as spreads and swaps – were introduced.

Below is a Reuters screen listing the Global Cash Forward Crude Oil Instruments available, with detail of forward Brent and Dubai prices for the 1st Forward month for delivery in Europe.

```
GLOBAL CASH FORWARD INSTRUMENT - REUTERS SPEED GUIDE          CRUDE/FWD1
To access information, double click on the code in <> or [] brackets.

=CRUDE FORWARDS=====================   =CRUDE FORWARDS Cont================
Brent 1st Fwd Mth Asia.......<BRT-1M-A>  Dubai 2nd Fwd Mth U.S........<DUB-2M-N>
Brent 2nd Fwd Mth Asia.......<BRT-2M-A>  Murban 1st Fwd Diff........<MUR-1Madn->
Brent 3rd Fwd Mth Asia.......<BRT-3M-A>  Murban 2nd Fwd Diff........<MUR-2Madn->
Brent 1st Fwd Mth Europe.....<BRT-1M-E>  Oman 1st Fwd Mth Asia.......<OMA-1M-A>
Brent 2nd Fwd Mth Europe.....<BRT-2M-E>  Oman 2nd Fwd Mth Asia.......<OMA-2M-A>
Brent 3rd Fwd Mth Europe.....<BRT-3M-E>  Oman MPM 1st Fwd Mth Diff.<OMA-1Mpn-A>
Brent 1st Fwd Mth U.S........<BRT-1M-N>  Oman MPM 2nd Fwd Mth Diff.<OMA-2Mpn-A>
Brent 2nd Fwd Mth U.S........<BRT-2M-N>
Brent 3rd Fwd Mth U.S........<BRT-3M-N>
Dubai 1st Fwd Mth Asia......<DUB-1M-A>   =See Also==========================
Dubai 2nd Fwd Mth Asia......<DUB-2M-A>   Brent Swaps, Europe ........<O#BRT-SWAP>
Dubai 3rd Fwd Mth Asia......<DUB-3M-A>   Brent CFDs, Europe .........<O#BRT-CFD>
Dubai 1st Fwd Mth Europe....<DUB-1M-E>   Brent Differentials, Europe.<O#BRT-DIF>
Dubai 2nd Fwd Mth Europe....<DUB-2M-E>   US Crude Differentials......<O#C-DIF-N>
Dubai 3rd Fwd Mth Europe....<DUB-3M-E>   Asian Crude Differentials...<O#C-DIF-A>
Dubai 1st Fwd Mth U.S.......<DUB-1M-N>

Questions/Comments: Contact your local Help Desk - see <PHONE/HELP> for details.
================================================================
Energy Index <ENERGY>  Cash Crude Index <CRUDE/I>  A-Z Listings <CRUDE/CASH1>-3
    Lost? Selective Access?..<USER/HELP>    Reuters Phone Support..<PHONE/HELP>
```

```
BRT-1M-E     BRENT    1M       29OCT98
             Close at 1730GMT    11:08

Terms Loc         Buy      Sell
FOB   EUR  Sul.Voe 12.55    12.57
Delivery          Previous Day's
Nov               12.40    12.42
API/Spec Spec Grav Size     Units
38.3     0.833    500KB     D/B
Spec       Bbl/Ton
           7.565
```

```
DUB-1M-E     DUBAI    1M       29OCT98
             Close at 1730GMT    11:07

Terms Loc         Buy      Sell
FOB   EUR  A/G     12.83    12.85
Delivery          Previous Day's
Dec               12.60    12.62
API/Spec Spec Grav Size     Units
31.8     0.867    Size      D/B
Spec       Bbl/Ton
           7.275
```

Futures Markets

The end of price stability in the oil markets meant that market players needed to find ways of hedging against price risk other than using the OTC forward markets. This situation provided a prime opportunity for exchange traded futures contracts.

The **New York Mercantile Exchange (NYMEX)** was the first exchange to commence futures trading in 1978 with a Heating Oil (HO) contract. Now NYMEX offers contracts for light sweet crude oil and NY Harbour gasoline. NYMEX is the world's largest exchange for energy futures and options on futures contracts.

The **International Petroleum Exchange (IPE)** is the second largest futures exchange offering contracts for Brent Crude oil and Gasoil (GO) – this is the equivalent of NYMEX's Heating Oil. The Brent Crude oil contract is unique in that it is for cash settlement rather than physical delivery.

The Reuters screens below show real-time NYMEX and IPE futures prices, and a comparison of crude spot prices with exchange traded futures prices.

```
OILOIL                        IPE - NYMEX Futures                      11:50
Brent Last  Net  Bid   Ask   Vol   Sprd Brt/WTI WTI   Last   Net  High  Low   Sprd
APR9↓ 992  -13   991   993   2567  -0.19  1.46  MAR9↓11.27 -0.10 11.39 11.26 -0.11
MAY9↓ 1011 -13  1010  1012   1203  -0.21  1.44  APR9↑11.39 -0.09 11.48 11.37 -0.17
JUN9↑ 1032 -11  1030  1033    923  -0.24  1.38  MAY9↑11.55 -0.09 11.65 11.53 -0.15
JUL9↓ 1056  -6  1049            96  -0.22  1.34  JUN9↓11.70 -0.08 11.80 11.70 -0.20
AUG9↓ 1078                      26  -0.15  1.27  JUL9↓11.90 -0.02 11.90 11.90 -0.15
SEP9↓ 1093                      95  -0.15  1.25  AUG9↓12.05 -0.01 12.05 12.05 -0.13
Gasoil Last Net Bid   Ask    Vol   Sprd Gsl/HO Heat  Last   Net  High  Low   Sprd
MAR9↑ 9125      9100  9125   1380  -0.50 -0.27  MAR9↓ 2940  -12  2965  2940  -0.62
APR9↓ 9175 -50  9175  9225    285  -1.75 -0.74  APR9↓ 3002   -9  3020  3002  -0.71
MAY9↓ 9350 -75  9375  9400    180  -2.50 -0.89  MAY9↑ 3094  +18  3097  3075  -0.66
JUN9↓ 9600 -75  9625  9650     28  -2.75 -0.75  JUN9↓ 3140   -1  3140  3140  -0.90
JUL9↓ 9875 -50  9850           113  -2.75 -0.77  JUL9                           -0.90
AUG9↑10150 -50 10125 10175    225  -2.25 -0.79  AUG9                           -0.95
Unld Swap FOB ARA                                Unld  Last   Net  High  Low   Sprd
Mar        109.00     0                          MAR9↓ 3270  -22  3290  3270  -3.40
Apr        117.00     0                          APR9↓ 3600  -13  3620  3600  -1.30
GBP  1.6339  1.6344      EUR  1.1258 1.1266      MAY9                           -0.91
JPY  118.47  118.52      CHF  1.4182 1.4192      JUN9                           -0.70
XAU  285.20  285.70      XAG  5.38   5.41        JUL9                          = = =
Help:<ENERGY>  Other key pages:<OILOOK><NYMOIL><IPEOIL><OILARB><OILSPD><CRDWLD>
     Platt's logical/historical data add-on now expanded. See <O#PLATTS>
```

```
CRDWLD                        World Crudes                            11:29
IPE/    Last  Net  Bid   Ask   Spread NYM/   Last       High  Low
APR9   ↓1043        1043  1044  +1.53  MAR9  $11.88 +0.03 12.07 11.85
MAY9   ↑1062  -1    1060         +1.47  APR9  $11.96 ↑0.03 12.12 11.95
JUN9   ↑1080  -5                 +1.41  MAY9  $12.09 +0.03 12.23 12.05
GBP  1.6291/ 01     JPY  114.55/.65     CHF  1.4167/ 77   EUR  1.1261/ 66
        Platt's logical/historical data add-on now expanded. See <O#PLATTS>
Crude    Deliv              Time  Diff     Deliv             Time
BRENT    Dtd       9.95/ 9.97 11:14 Brent    Dtd/Mar -0.36/-0.34 00:00
BRENT    Mar      10.30/10.32 11:14 Brent    Mar/Apr -0.20/-0.16 00:00
BRENT    Apr      10.48/10.50 11:14 Brent    Apr/May -0.22/-0.20 00:00
BRENT    May      10.69/10.71 11:14 Brent    May/Jun -0.22/-0.18 00:00
BONNY LT           9.75/ 9.77 11:14 BONNY LT         -0.30/-0.10 11:14
FLOTTA L           9.05/ 9.07 11:14 FLOTTA           -0.95/-0.85 11:14
FORTIES            9.85/ 9.87 11:14 Forties          -0.15/-0.05 11:14
EKOFISK            9.78/ 9.80 11:14 Ekofisk          -0.22/-0.12 11:14
STATFJOR           9.90/ 9.92 11:14 STATFJORD        -0.10/      11:14
N/A                                 ES SIDER         +0.20/+0.30 12:59
DUBAI    Mar       9.55/ 9.57 11:14 Dubai    Mar/Apr -0.25/-0.15 00:00
DUBAI    Apr       9.75/ 9.77 11:14 Dubai    Apr/May -0.20/-0.14 09:17
DUBAI    May       9.92/ 9.94 11:14 Dubai    May/Jun -0.19/-0.14 09:17
OMAN     MAR       9.57/ 9.67 05:40 OMAN/MPM MAR     +0.10/+0.15 05:40
OMAN     APR       9.66/ 9.76 05:40 OMAN/MPM APR          /+0.10 05:40
MURBAN   MAR      10.26/10.36 05:40 MURBAN   MAR     +0.18/+0.23 05:40
MINAS    FEB      10.40/11.60 05:24 MINAS DifFEB     +0.50/      05:24
TAPIS    MAR      11.05/11.15 05:24 TAPIS DifMAR     +0.35/      05:24
WTI               11.87/11.93 18:07                      /       :
```

Natural Gas Markets

Natural Gas is a colourless, highly flammable **hydrocarbon** mixture of gases originating from the decomposition of organic matter or formation of fossil fuels such as coal and oil. Natural gas has been produced from marshy grounds or swamps for centuries and gave rise to its older name of **Marsh** or **Swamp** gas. From early times, miners have known of the explosive nature of a mixture of natural gas and air. Coal miners of the eighteenth and nineteenth centuries using lamps with naked flames were well aware of the dangers – they called the gas **Firedamp**. In 1815 the English scientist Sir Humphry Davy invented a lamp that allowed miners to work much more safely underground. The following quote is taken from a chemistry book of 1857 by George Wilson.

A Davy Lamp

To prevent accidents in coal-pits, Sir Humphry Davy devised a very ingenious lamp, which goes by the name of the Davy or Safety Lamp, and is intended to furnish the miner with a source of light which shall have no power to kindle fire-damp.

More recently, huge natural gas pockets have been found in association with crude oil deposits, where it is found above the oil. The natural gas has been formed in much the same way as the oil by the action of heat and pressure on organic matter over millions of years. Natural gas in association with crude oil is now the major source of this type of energy. In cases where the natural gas cannot be easily extracted and transported, it is burnt or flared off at the well head.

Source: Reuters

Natural gas is a mixture of hydrocarbon gases – gases which contain **only** the elements carbon and hydrogen – together with small amounts of other gases such as carbon dioxide (CO_2), nitrogen (N_2), and hydrogen sulphide (H_2S). Hydrogen sulphide is commonly called rotten-egg smell but the human nose can detect levels of this gas as low as 0.3 parts per million in air – you do not need much of this gas to know that it is there! The principal component of natural gas is **Methane, CH_4**, but the percentage amount of methane varies from 70–90+ % depending on its extraction location. The table below indicates the typical composition of natural gas from New South Wales, Australia.

Component	%
Methane, CH_4	**91.0**
Ethane, C_2H_6	4.7
Propane, C_3H_8	1.0
Butane, C_4H_{10}	0.3
Carbon Dioxide, CO_2	2.4
Nitrogen, N_2	0.4
Other	0.2
Total	100

Source: Gas Technology Services, Victoria, Australia 1998

The major world producers of natural gas in 1997 are indicated in the chart below:

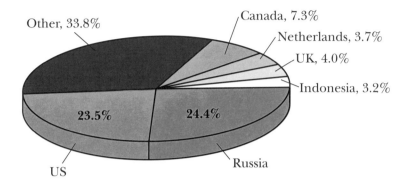

Source: OECD Statistics 1999

The table below indicates the typical composition of dry natural gas from Victoria, Australia.

Component	%
Methane, CH_4	**96.23**
Ethane, C_2H_6	1.34
Propane, C_3H_8	0.04
Butane, C_4H_{10}	0.05
Carbon Dioxide, CO_2	0.35
Nitrogen, N_2	1.78
Other	0.21
Total	100

Source: Gas Technology Services, Victoria, Australia 1998

Extracted natural gas is termed **wet** as in most cases it needs to be refined to produce the **dry** gas suitable for transportation. In the refinement process the less volatile hydrocarbons such as propane and butane and other gases are removed. The remaining dry gas is almost pure methane and is transported via pipelines or liquefied at low temperatures and transported in pressurised **Liquefied Natural Gas (LNG)** containers on specially designed ships. The less volatile gases such as propane and butane, which are produced in large quantities, are also liquefied and known as **Liquefied Petroleum Gas (LPG)**. LPG is also stored in pressurised containers and transported on specially designed ships. LPG is marketed in many countries as a domestic and industrial fuel.

Since the 1970s and 1980s the importance of natural gas as an energy source has increased. This has been for three main reasons:

1. Natural gas is seen as a cleaner, more environmentally friendly energy source for power generation. The amount of pollutants, such as sulphur dioxide and nitrogen oxide gases, produced during combustion is significantly less than from oil.

2. The fluctuating availability of crude oil supplies.

3. The deregulation of nationalised or regional power industries in countries such as the US and UK.

Since the early 1990s the combination of these factors has helped to establish natural gas markets in which power producers, marketers and power consumers are all now subject to price fluctuations for which they need risk management tools. The development of the natural gas market in Europe provides a good example to illustrate the growth and development of this market sector.

In 1996, 419 billion cubic metres (bcm) of natural gas were used in Europe mainly to generate power. It is estimated that by the year 2010 the annual requirement will rise to 612 bcm. The expansion of the European market is likely to continue, particularly taking into account the following developments:

- The deregulation of the UK gas supply industry between 1992–96 allowed access to the national pipeline distribution network for new suppliers. The combination of this factor together with a surplus of gas meant that gas could be bought and sold much more freely.

- The opening of the 235 km Interconnector gas pipeline between Bacton, England and Zeebrugge, Belgium. Thi pipeline means that UK North Sea gas can now be delivered directly to the European markets.

- The introduction of the EU Gas Directive which will allow gas consumers to buy their supplies in competitive markets rather from state monopolies.

Although OTC contacts for gas supplies for 1 month up to 3 years forward have been available since early 1994, the International Petroleum Exchange (IPE) launched an exchange traded natural gas futures contract in 1997. The IPE contract has a lot size of 1000 therms – a therm is a measure of the heating value of the gas supplied – and a minimum trade size of 5 lots for a contract month. This means that gas is delivered for 5000 therms of heating value **daily** during the contract month and contract delivery is at the National Balancing Point (NBP).

In the US, the New York Mercantile Exchange (NYMEX) introduced natural gas futures contracts at a much earlier date than the IPE – in 1990. It is also interesting to note that the NYMEX contracts have a trading unit of 10,000 million British Thermal Units (mmBTU) whereas in the UK the therm is used for the heating value of gas supplied! To compare the contracts you need to know:

$$1 \text{ therm} = 100,000 \text{ BTU}$$

Natural gas market information is available on the electronic news services. This Reuters Speed Guide show the array of available instruments, with specific detail on the UK market.

```
NATURAL GAS - REUTERS SPEED GUIDE                              NATGAS1
To access information double click on the code in the <> or [].

=KEY PRICE CHAINS=====================  =DERIVATIVES and MISCELLANEOUS=========
NYMEX Henry Hub Natural Gas ....<O#NG:>  AECO C Hub Spot Gas Daily Prc Idx<ALTA>
NYMEX Pernian Natural Gas ......<O#NP:>  AECO Hub-Alberta..........<NG-AECO-ALB>
KCBT Natural Gas Futures .......<O#KG:>  Natural Gas Clearinghouse........<PPIC>
IPE UK Natural Gas Futures....<O#NGLN:>  Nat Gas vs. No.2 and No.6 .......<PPIN>
IPE UK Natural Gas Daily......<O#NGLD:>
US Natural Gas -daily prices...<O#NG-N>  Natural Gas Strips and Spreads...<PIJQ>
Canadian Natural Gas - weekly.<O#NG-CA>
BTU -daily Nat Gas prices ...<O#NG-BTU>  =EUROPEAN NAT GAS=====================
                                         UK Natural Gas Prices ........<O#NG-GB>
=INDIVIDUAL INSTRUMENT RICs BY========   PH Energy Analysis Index.....<EURGAS01>
Field Gate...................<NATGAS2>   PH Energy UK Spot Prices.....<EURGAS02>
Export                       <NATGAS2>   PH Energy European Prices    <EURGAS04>
```

```
O#NG-GB              UK NATURAL GAS
Connodity         Del.Date      Last        Srce    Terms       Loc  Ccy Units  Date
NG NBP 24HR       24 HR      B↓  9.50  A9.90  RTRS  Nat Bal Pnt. NBP  GBp       12FEB99
NG NBP MthBal     BAL. FEB   B↑  9.50  A9.80  RTRS  Nat Bal Pnt. NBP  GBp       12FEB99
NG NBP Mth 1      MAR        B↓  9.40  A9.45  RTRS  Nat Bal Pnt. NBP  GBp       12FEB99
NG NBP Mth2       APR        B↓  9.20  A9.25  RTRS  Nat Bal Pnt. NBP  GBp       12FEB99
NG NBP Mth3       MAY        B↓  9.15  A9.25  RTRS  Nat Bal Pnt. NBP  GBp       12FEB99
NG NBP 1Qtr       2Q99       B↓  9.15  A9.18  RTRS  Nat Bal Pnt. NBP  GBp       12FEB99
NG NBP 2Qtr       3Q99       B↓  9.02  A9.05  RTRS  Nat Bal Pnt. NBP  GBp       12FEB99
NG NBP 3Qtr       4Q99       B↓  12.40 A12.45 RTRS  Nat Bal Pnt. NBP  GBp       12FEB99
NG NBP 4Qtr
NB NBP 5Qtr
NG NBP Year
NG StFergus Mbal
NG StFergus 24HR
NG StFergus Mth1
NG StFergus Mth2
```

```
10:34 08FEB99      PH ENERGY ANALYSIS              UK42219      EURGAS02
UK SPOT PRICE TABLE  05 FEB 1999
Terminal:
                       NBP        Bacton      St Fergus
DAY AHEAD             9.837       9.887        9.687
WEEKEND              9.550       9.600        9.400
BALANCE OF MONTH     9.537       9.587        9.387
MAR                  9.450       9.550        8.950
APR                  9.312       9.412        8.812
MAY                  9.212       9.312        0.712
JUN                  9.125       9.225        8.625
JUL                  9.012       9.112        8.512
AUG                  9.000       9.100        8.500
Q4'99               12.687      12.787       12.187
Q1'00               14.687      14.787       14.137
Q2'00               10.000      10.050        9.500
Q3'00                9.750       9.850        9.500
Q4'00               12.712      12.812       12.112
OCT '99 1 YEAR      11.787      11.887       11.212
OCT '00 1 YEAR      11.887      11.987       11.287
OCT '01 1 YEAR      12.400      12.500       11.775

UK Short tern market prices (all prices in pence per thern )
( 1 Thern = 100.000 British Thermal units)
```

Electricity Markets

It is hard to imagine how many world economies would survive without electricity. Its availability is essential for both domestic and industrial use. In the US, retail electricity sales are in excess of $200 billion per year. The relative share of these sales is shown in the chart below.

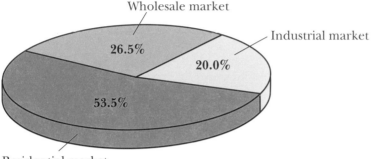

Source: CBOT Electricity Futures and Options Contracts Publication

In many countries electricity has been supplied traditionally by large suppliers, often nationalised or public industries, at regulated prices on a **regional** basis. In other words, if you lived in a particular power generating utility region, that was the company who supplied your electricity. Since the early 1980s there have been a number of major changes taking place to affect the electricity supply industries in many countries. Wholesale power markets have been established and developed depending on the following factors, in part at least:

- **Deregulation**. It is now the case that in many countries in Europe and in regions of the US that domestic and industrial customers can now choose their electricity supplier. Access to national transmission grid systems is now possible for a variety of power-generating organisations and more importantly to power marketers – buyers and sellers of wholesale electricity as a commodity.

- **Price competition**. The price of this commodity depends on the fuel or energy source used for generation. For example, power can be generated not only using Natural Gas, coal, oil or nuclear sources, but also from renewable sources such as hydroelectric schemes, solar panels, wind generators and geothermal sources. The price is also subject to seasonal supply demands.

- **Technological advances**. Improvements in power generation and distribution.

The combination of all these factors means that there is now a significant market risk associated with the generation of electricity. As in other commodity markets, the producers and consumers may need to hedge their relative positions while power marketers buy and sell for profit.

Active cash or spot markets together with derivative markets have been established and developed in a number of countries. It is now possible to buy and sell wholesale power in advance for later delivery and hedge or speculate on positions using futures and options on futures contracts just as for other commodities.

In 1996 NYMEX launched two electricity futures contracts to provide risk management instruments for the power industry in the western US. One contract was based on delivery of energy at the California/Oregon border and the other contract was for delivery at the Palo Verde switchyard in Arizona. Since the introduction of these first electricity futures, NYMEX has added contracts for the Cinergy and Entergy regional transmission systems. Options on these futures contracts are also available.

Why Do the Commodities, Energy & Transport Markets Exist?

Electricity futures and options on futures contracts are now traded on a number of exchanges worldwide, including the following:

- **New York Mercantile Exchange (NYMEX)**
- **Chicago Board of Trade (CBOT)**
- **New Zealand Futures and Options Exchange (NZFOE)**
- **Sydney Futures Exchange (SFE)**
- **Scandinavian NordPool**

It is worth noting that different exchanges use different contract sizes. For example, NYMEX contracts are for 736 Mega Watt Hours (Mwh) of power delivered over a monthly period. CBOT contracts are for 1,680 Mwh and the SFE contracts are for 500 Mwh.

These Reuters screens provide access to news about electricity, with a specific access screen for the North American market, by region. Index pages are also given for Norway and Australia.

```
ELECTRICITY - REUTERS SPEED GUIDE                        ELECTRICITY
To access information, double click on the codes in the <> or [] brackets.

=Regional Guides======================   =Related Guides=================
North American Power ........<NAPOWER>*  Natural Gas.................<NATGAS1>
Norway/Sweden...............<NORDPOOL>   Cross Markets data ........<CROSS/MKT1>
Finland.....................<FI/ELEX>
New Zealand ................<NZMEINDEX>
Australia...................<AUEMINDEX>

=NEWS and ANALYSIS====
Energy News..........
Electricity news ....
Natural Gas news ....
North American power
Energy Weather.......
US Electricity futures
Nordic Power News....

*NAPOWER requires RT D
  to check which versi
========================
Energy Index  <ENERGY
  Lost?Selective Acce
```

```
NAPOWER    North American Power
                                               [BORDER]

                                               [NEWS]

              MAPP        NPCC                  [PRICES]
   WSCC
                                MAAC
                            ECAR               [WEATHER]
                     MAIN
               SPP          SERC
                                               [STATS]
          ERCOT

Take a look at Power Deals Done - Click on <PWR/TRADES>
```

```
                AUSTRALIAN ELECTRICITY MARKET                    AUEMINDEX

=NEWS INFORMATION=====================  =*ENERGYBANKLINK SPECIALIST SERVICE====
Australian News..............[AU].[AUF] Index Page...............<AUELEC01>-3
International Energy News...........[E] Elect Spot Price Forecast....<AUELEC46>
International Utilities News......[ELG] 2 Way Ref Forward Pricing....<AUELEC04>
International Gas News...........[NGS]  Retail Deals Done..........<AUELEC379>
Aust Elect Market News.....[AU AND FI G] Individual Participants.....<AUELEC170>
Aust Weather News..........[AU AND WEA] Latest Wholesales Deals.....<AUELEC302>
                                        On the Grapevine...........<AUELEC14B>
=AUSTRALIAN PRICES==================    Generator Sell Fwrd Pricing.<AUELEC09>
**SFE NSW Elec Futures........<O#2YNE:> Ban Daily Price Overview....<AUELEC159>
                                                                  .<AUELEC15B>
                                                                  .<AUELEC200>
                                                                  .<AUELEC300>
                                                                  .<AUELEC180>
                                                                  ..<AUELEC0B>
                                                                  ..<AUELEC06>
                                                                  ..<AUELEC07>
                                                                  ..<AUELEC2B1>
                                                                  ..<AUELEC140>
                                                                  ..<AUELEC150>
                                                                  ..<AUELEC378>

                                                                  <AUEMINDEY>
```

```
NORDPOOL ASA INDEX PAGE                                        NORDPOOL
Vollsveien 13B, Postboks 373, 1324 Lysaker          Tel:  +47 67 528 000
Official trading hours: Monday - Friday  10:00-15:00 After market: 15:00-15:30

===============FIXINGS===============   ==========CONTRACT DETAILS==========
                                        Base Power: 00:00 Mon - 24:00 Sun(168h)
System Average................<.NPXSYS> Weeks:      4 to 7 weeks are traded
Oslo Average..................<.NPXOSL> Blocks:     Trading period from the
Stockholm Average.............<.NPXSTO>             last week listed to the
System Fixings  (01-24h).<O#SYSFIX=NPX>             first season (27-52 weeks
Oslo Fixings    (01-24h).<O#OSLFIX=NPX>             ahead)
Stkhln Fixings  (01-24h).<O#STOFIX=NPX> Seasons:    Traded from last block
                                                    (27-52 weeks) to three
                                                    years ahead, minimum four
===============FUTURES===============                seasons and maximum of six
Weekly Futures................<O#NPW:>
Block Futures.................<O#NPB:>  Expiry Day: Friday or the last market
Season Futures................<O#NPS:>              day in the week of delivery
                                        Last Price: Last price within bid/ask
===============FORWARDS==============                spread when closed or an
Winter 1/Summer/Winter 2.......<O#NPF:>              average of bid/ask.
                                        On expiry:  Volume weighted last price
Trading unit: kr/MWh                    Sys price:  Hour weighted average of
                                                    the powerprice in the 24
                                                    hour market (day market)
========Questions/Comments: call the NDM Team in Stockholm +46-8-700 1141======
```

Other Energy Markets

The importance of coal as an energy source in the nineteenth century has already been mentioned. More recently, as a result of deregulation in worldwide power generation and economic factors, OTC derivative contracts are being traded – the first coal swaps were arranged by the broker TFS in 1998.

During 1999, both NYMEX and SFE were considering developing and introducing exchange traded coal futures contracts. As of publication, the contracts had not yet been launched.

| 15:26 | RTRS-London coal/ore fixtures |
| 11:05 | PRN-Barrett Resources Announces Signing of Coal Bed Methane Bill
<BARC.0> |

O#CO- Spot Coal Prices

Commodity	Del.Date	Last	Srce	Terms	Loc
CENTRAL APPALACH	within 90	23.95	CDLY	12,500	CSXB
CENTRAL APPALACH	within 90	22.75	CDLY	12,500	CSXB
CENTRAL APPALACH	within 90	21.95	CDLY	12,500	CSXB
CENTRAL APPALACH	within 90	26.00	CDLY	12,000	BSAN
CENTRAL APPALACH	within 90	22.90	CDLY	12,000	BSAN
CENTRAL APPALACH	outside 90	23.95	CDLY	12,500	CSXB
CENTRAL APPALACH	outside 90	22.75	CDLY	12,500	CSXB
CENTRAL APPALACH	outside 90	21.95	CDLY	12,500	CSXB
CENTRAL APPALACH	outside 90	26.00	CDLY	12,000	BSAN
CENTRAL APPALACH	outside 90	22.70	CDLY	12,000	BSAN
POWDER RIV BASIN	outside 90	3.60	CDLY	8,400	MINE
POWDER RIV BASIN	within 90	3.60	CDLY	8,400	MINE
POWDER RIV BASIN	outside 90	4.80	CDLY	8,800	MINE
POWDER RIV BASIN	within 90	4.80	CDLY	8,800	MINE
COLORADO-UTAH	FOB MINE	12.00	CDLY	11,100	GRB
COLORADO-UTAH	FOB MINE	15.80	CDLY	11,700	UINU
COLORADO-UTAH	FOB MINE	13.00	CDLY	11,700	UINC
ILLINOIS BASIN	FOB BARGE	19.50	CDLY	11,200	ORVR
ILLINOIS BASIN	FOB MINE	17.75	CDLY	11,200	ILIN
ILLINOIS BASIN	FOB MINE	22.85	CDLY	11,500	ILIN
ILLINOIS BASIN	FOB MINE	16.70	CDLY	11,000	ILIN
PITTSBURGH SEAM	FOB MINE	23.35	CDLY	13,000	MINE
PITTSBURGH SEAM	FOB MINE	21.85	CDLY	13,000	MINE
PITTSBURGH SEAM	FOB MINE	19.00	CDLY	12,500	MINE
6,000 kcal/kg	CIF ARA	29.50	CDLY	6,000	NAR

Another interesting development in the energy markets is the **Carbon Dioxide Emissions Trading Programme**, proposed by the IPE for exchange traded futures contracts.

Carbon dioxide, CO_2, is the natural product of metabolism when oxygen and food are converted into energy and carbon dioxide. Fortunately, plants containing the green compound chlorophyll in their leaves use carbon dioxide for their growth and produce oxygen. This balance of carbon dioxide production and usage has been upset by the activities of mankind. The combustion of fossil fuels such as natural gas, oil and coal to produce energy also produces large amounts of carbon dioxide. If this factor is combined with the global trend to deforestation, then the build up of carbon dioxide is inevitable unless checked.

The result of the increased atmospheric levels of carbon dioxide and other pollutant gases is a warming effect on the planet – the so-called **greenhouse** effect. The proposed IPE programme is a way to help prevent this effect becoming worse and reduce the global problem. In effect, the producers of carbon dioxide would need to hold permits governing the amount of CO_2 they were allowed to produce. If a producer of CO_2 could reduce emissions for any reason, for example, by using improved processing techniques, then the unused portion of their permit could be sold or leased to other producers who were over their permitted levels. The IPE programme proposes a secondary market in exchange traded futures contracts, valid for a month, which would provide producers with a risk management instrument and help control CO_2 emissions.

A similar programme for sulphur dioxide, SO_2 emissions is currently operated by CBOT in the US. Sulphur dioxide is a pollutant gas associated with acid-rain which is produced when fossil fuels containing sulphur compounds, such as oil and coal, are combusted.

Transport Markets

There are two transport markets which will be considered briefly here. These are:

- Shipping bulk markets
- Air cargo markets

Shipping Bulk Markets

Why Do the Shipping Markets Exist?

Ships have been used for the bulk transport of commodities around the world from ancient times. Today there are four basic reasons why shipping markets exist:

- The supply and demand for commodities

- Most commodities are not produced where there are needed and therefore need to be transported

- There are differentials between commodity prices which provide an opportunity for arbitrage

- Economic factors affecting governments, producers and consumers

The majority of commodities shipped today involve **wet** cargoes using tankers and **dry** cargoes using bulk carriers. Four commodities – crude oil, coal, iron ore and grain – account for about two-thirds of all seaborne trade. The remainder are a variety of agricultural products, minor ores, timber, rubber, fibres, chemicals, heavy plant and machinery, cars, steel and consumer goods. The chart below indicates the world tonnages shipped in 1996 in millions of tons (mt).

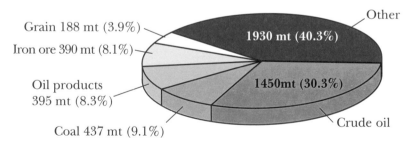

Grain 188 mt (3.9%)
Iron ore 390 mt (8.1%)
Oil products 395 mt (8.3%)
Coal 437 mt (9.1%)
Other 1930 mt (40.3%)
Crude oil 1450mt (30.3%)

Source: Norges Rederiforbund, World Seaborne Trade 1998

There are usually three parties associated with the shipping market who are described in greater detail later. In brief, the **ship owner** and the **charterer** (the cargo owner) are brought together by a **shipbroker** who acts as an intermediary to negotiate the **fixture** of a vessel with a cargo.

The Reuters screens below provide shipping news.

```
SHIPPING  - REUTERS SPEED GUIDE                          SHIPPING
Welcome to the Shipping Speed Guide.  On the following pages you will find
Shipping Infonation. To access information, double click in the <> or [] bracket

=SHIPPING NEWS========================   =CROSS MARKET INFORMATION=============
Shipping Service News.............[SHG]   Cross Market Rates/Prices..<CROSS/MKT1>
Shipping Topic Codes......<SHIP/CODES>    Money/Forex Reports......<MONEY/NEWS1>*
Shipping Glance............[GLANCE/SHP]   Debt Reports..............<DEBT/NEWS2>*
Port/Waterways Info..
Market Reports.......   16:38  RTRS-G7 ministers to work on calming markets-Clinton
All Energy News......   16:15  RTRS-CBOT soybeans up early on Russia talk, deliveries
Energy Reports.......   16:15  RTRS-Swelling sea stocks depress oil outlook-report
Refinery Maintenance    16:10  RTRS-TAKE A LOOK-G7 statement on global fin system
All Commodities News    16:10  RTRS-London timecharter fixtures
Metal Market Reports.   16:06  RTRS-FOCUS-G7 unveils sweeping financial reform plan
Grains/Oilseeds Repor   16:03  RTRS-Draft U.S. aid deal for Russia Nov 2 -reports
Softs Market Reports    16:01  RTRS-CORRECTED - CBOT soy products called to open higher
Shipping
Sports Di    16:10  30 Oct  RTRS-London timecharter fixtures
Sports Ne      LONDON, Oct 30 (Reuters) - Lowlands Grace - (built 1991) 149,518 dwt del
General N    Kaohsiung end Nov 12 months trading option of further 12 months $10,700/$13,000
             daily respectively Deiulemar.
=========      Georgios M - (built 1982) 148,629 dwt del Dunkirk Nov trip via Brazil redel Far East
Data Noti    approx. $6,500 daily CNR.
  Lost?         National Prosperity - (built 1995) 75,100 dwt del Sakaide Nov 5/10 trip U.S.
             Gulf/Atlantic $9,000 daily Japanese charterers.
                CSK Eminence - (built 1997) 73,606 dwt del Rotterdam Nov 15/30 trip 12 months
             trading with option of further 12 months $7,350/$8,350 daily respectively Navios
             (reported)
                Lucky Bulker - (built 1977) 71,740 dwt 14 on 45.5 plus 3 del Fancheng in direct
             continuation early Nov trip west Australia r/v $5,800 daily Noble Chartering.
                Imperial - (built 1989) 68,676 dwt 13 on 36 del retroactive sailing South Korea end
             Oct trip via Nopac redel Bin Qasim $8,000 daily ETA.
                Grischuna - (built 1987) 64,400 dwt 13 on 28 del Osaka in direct continuation Nov
             10/15 trip via Long Beach redel Japan $7,150 daily Navix.
                Wadi Alarab - (built 1995) 64,214 dwt 13.5 on 32 plus 0.5 del Richards Bay mid Nov
             trip Continent $6,750 plus $90,000 bb daily Safmarine.
                Northern Light - (built 1981) 64,592 dwt 13.5 on 38 plus 2 del north China mid Nov
             trip via west Australia redel passing Muscat outbound or Red Sea $7,000 daily Pan
             Ocean.
                Pacific Mercury - (built 1996) 49,016 dwt 14 on 31.1 del Tubarao mid Nov trip one
             or three laden legs redel Atlantic or Far East $8,200 daily Tschudi and Eitzen.
                Theotoko - (built 1983) 37,612 dwt del Puerto Cabello spot trip via Aruba redel U.S.
             Atlantic coast $7,000 daily Bulkshipping.
```

Dry Bulk Cargoes – The Baltic Exchange

This Baltic Exchange is the only international shipping exchange in the world. Its origins can be traced to the London coffee houses of the eighteenth century where ship owners and merchants met to fix vessels. Foremost among the coffee houses were the Jerusalem Coffee House and the Virginia & Maryland Coffee House – the latter becoming known as the Virginia & Baltick Coffee House on 24th May 1744. By 1900 this coffee house had become the Baltic Mercantile & Shipping Exchange.

Although the Baltic Exchange still maintains a floor for members to meet and trade, most fixing of ships is carried out between members from their offices. Today, the exchange's main role is concerned now with the proper regulation of the market and member transactions. The Baltic Exchange motto *Our Word Our Bond* is still appropriate today.

The Baltic Exchange is primarily concerned with fixing worldwide dry bulk cargoes such as coal, iron ore, grain, steel, minerals etc. The **Baltic Freight Index (BFI)** comprises a basket of 11 major, international **dry** cargo routes by Baltic brokers on a daily basis. This index is a measure of the cost of the international ocean transport of major dry bulk commodities.

The **Baltic Exchange Freight Futures Exchange (BIFFEX)** was established in 1985 to provide exchange traded instruments for shipowners and charterers to hedge their risks in the dry cargo market. BIFFEX freight futures are traded on LIFFE and, as with other index, contracts they are cash settled.

The Reuters screens below include a summary of shipping indices. Detail for BIFFEX futures is also shown.

```
SHIPPING 2000 - REUTERS SPEED GUIDE                              BIFFEX
To access information double-click in the <> or [] brackets.

=BIFFEX INDICES=====================    =HANDY & TANKER INDICES===============
Baltic Index..................<BIFFEX1>  Baltic Handy Index.............<.BAHA>
Baltic Freight................<.BAFI>    BHI Continent - Far East......<.BACFI>
BOF US Hampton Road-ARA........<.BFHA>   BHI Japan - N. Pacific.........<.BAJAI>
BOF Japan - S. Korea..........<.BFJP>    BHI Singapore - Continent......<.BAACI>
BOF Montreal - Rotterdam.......<.BFMR>   BHI Continent - NS Atlantic....<.BACAI>
BOF SKAW......................<.BFTA>    BIT ME Gulf - Japan............<.BAGJI>
BOF KAW Gult - FE.............<.BFSE>    BIT W. Africa - US Gulf........<.BAAGI>
BOF US Gulf - ARA.............<.BFGA>    BIT W. Africa - USAC...........<.BAAUI>
BOF US Gulf - Japan...........<.BFGJ>    BIT North Sea - Continent......<.BANCI>
BOF US N.Pacific - Japan.......<.BFPJ>   BIT Caribbean - US Gulf........<.BACGI>
BOF Vancouver -                          BIT CPP/UNL ME Gulf - Japan....<.BACJI>
    San Diego - Rotterdam......<.BFVR>   BIT CPP/UNL Continent - USAC...<.BACUI>
                                         BIT CPP/UNL Continent to USAC..<.BACCI>
=BIFFEX FUTURES=====================     BIT ME Gulf to Continent.......<.BAGEI>
Ocean Freight Contracts........<O#BOF:>  BIT ME Gulf to Singapore.......<.BAGSI>
Nearest Month Contact Quote.....<BOFc1>  BIT Kuwait-Singapore(Crude/DPP)<.BAKSI>
```

```
BALTIC OCEAN FREIGHT INDEX COMPONENTS   BIFFEX                    BIFFEX1
TITLE                               RATE     INDEX   PR.RATE  PR.INDEX
-----                               ----     -----   -------  --------
BALTIC FREIGHT INDEX                          825                 821
USG/ARA 55000 LIGHT GRAIN 10 PC     10.058   1.108   9.992       1.101
SKAW-P T/A R/V 3MLN CFT G-O-C 10 PC  6700     885    6564         867
USG/S.JAPAN 54000 HVY GRAIN 10 PC   15.117   1.094   15.142      1.096
SKAW-P VIA USG/F.EAST 3MLN CFT G-O-C 10 PC 7018  856  6986       852
USNP/S.JAPAN 54000 HVY GRAIN 10 PC   8.992   1.018   8.983       1.017
JAPAN-SK T/P R/V 3MLN CFT G-O-C 10 PC 3968    503    3911         496
HRDS NOT BALT/ROTTERDAM 110000 COAL 7.5 PC 3.400 0.698 3.408     0.700
JAPAN-SK/SKAW-P VIA USWC 3MLN CFT GC P. 10 P 4300  492  4279      489
TUBARAO/ROTTERDAM 150000 IRON ORE 7.5 PC 3.357 0.665 3.358      0.665
TUBARAO/BEILUN-BAOSHAN 140000 IRON ORE 7.5 P 4.864 0.688 4.857  0.687
R.BAY/ROTTERDAM 140000 COAL 7.5 PC   4.150   0.783   4.136       0.780

ABBREVIATIONS : HVY GRAIN - HEAVY GRAIN, SORGHUM & SOYA  P.COKE - PETROLEUM COKE
                MOP       - MURIATE OF POTASH            HRDS   - HAMPTON ROADS
                USG       - U.S. GULF                    USNP   - U.S. N PACIFIC
                USWC      - U.S. WEST COAST              SK     - SOUTH KOREA
                R.BAY     - RICHARDS BAY                 PHOS   - PHOSPHATE
                BALT      - BALTIMORE                     ARA    - ANTW-ROTT-AMST
                VANC      - VANCOUVER                     P      - PASSERO
                T/A       - TRANS-ATLANTIC               T/P    - TRANS-PACIFIC
                R/V       - ROUND VOYAGE                  MLN    - MILLION
```

```
O#BOF:           OCEAN FRGHT       LIF/    GBp
Index  825                              Tot.V   39    Tot.OI  2421
Mth    Last  Last1 Net  Bid   Ask   PrvSet Open High Low Volume Op.Int Sett
FEB9  ↑836   835   -4   830   845    840   835  836  835   15    195
MAR9  ↑900   895   -3         910    903   895  900  885   10    209
APR9  ↑945   945   -5   925   950    950   940  945  940   14    1010
JUL9                    800   850    840                          602
OCT9                    930          950                          373
JAN0                                 940                           28
APR0                    945          970                            4
JUL0                    840          840
```

Wet Cargoes – Reuters Tanker Industry Index (RTII)

This service was launched in 1996 to introduce accurate and unbiased data for the tanker industry. Rate assessments are made daily on nine tanker freight routes based on the average values from contributing tanker owners, oil companies, oil traders and tanker brokers.

The index values are used by the industry for a number of purposes. These include:

- Settlement prices for tanker freight swaps

- Pricing physical intercompany freight movements

- Calculation of crude and product netbacks

You may be unfamiliar with some of the terms used here such as tanker freight swaps and netbacks, but they are explained in later sections.

The Reuters Tanker Industry Index, is shown at right.

```
Reuters Tanker Industry Index                          RTII1
Contents Page
---------------------------------------------------------------------

Double click on the bracketed page code below to access the page

<RTII2>          List of Contributors and Applicable West Routes

<RTII4>          List of Contributors and Applicable East Routes

<RTII6>          Index Basis

<RTII8>          Christmas/New Year period Index

<RTII9>          Reuters Tanker Industry Index (West routes)

<RTII10>         Reuters Tanker Industry Index (East routes)

<MJLF11> **NEW** MJLF Market Snapshot Contents Page

[HOL/DIARY]      World Holidays


For further information on RTII contact Reuters on Fax (+44) 171-542-7522 or
          Reuters Mail =RTII.REUTERS.LON or e-mail john.cohen@reuters.com
```

```
Reuters Tanker Industry Index                          RTII9
         DAILY INDEX RATES FOR 27OCT98      Contributions received 28OCT98
ROUTES                       SIZE     WS RATE   PREV WKG DAY   RIC NAMES
W.AFRICA-US GULF           260,000     56.43      55.00      <TI-WAF-USG-VL>
W.AFRICA-USAC              130,000     73.75      73.75      <TI-WAF-USAC-SU>
CARIBS-U.S. GULF            70,000    125.00     124.69      <TI-CAR-USG-AF>
CARIBS-USAC (FUEL OIL)      50,000    113.75     113.75      <TI-CAR-USAC-FO>
CARIBS-USAC (CLEAN)         30,000    179.38     161.00      <TI-CAR-USAC-CL>
AG-U.S. GULF               280,000     52.10      52.17      <TI-AG-USG-VL>
W.AFRICA SPREAD - VLCC/SUEZMAX         17.32      18.75
=========================================================================

                                    New contributors welcomed on all routes -
Contact Reuters for details - Tel: (44) 171 542-7471/Fax: (44) 171 542-7522
-------------------------------AVERAGES----------------------------------
ROUTES                       SIZE   22-26OCT98  10-27OCT98   28SEP-27OCT98
W.AFRICA-US GULF           260,000    55.23       55.07        54.03
W.AFRICA-USAC              130,000    76.17       76.73        74.85
CARIBS-U.S. GULF            70,000   130.90      121.82       119.62
CARIBS-USAC (FUEL OIL)      50,000   114.41      112.30       112.43
CARIBS-USAC (CLEAN)         30,000   177.02      178.06       178.58
AG-U.S. GULF               280,000    51.04       51.58        51.67
W.AFRICA SPREAD - VLCC/SUEZMAX        20.94       21.66        20.82

<RTII1> for Menu                       <RTII8> for historic monthly averages
```

```
Reuters Tanker Industry Index                          RTII10
FAR EAST ROUTES - DAILY INDEX RATES FOR 28OCT98 - Contributions received 28OCT98
ROUTES                     SIZE     WS RATE   PREV WKG DAY   RIC NAMES
AG-JAPAN/KOREA (NHC)     250,000     59.08      59.25      <TI-AG-JPN-VL>
INDO-JAPAN (NHC)          80,000     78.60      79.75      <TI-INDO-JPN-80>
AG-JAPAN (CL/UL)          55,000    142.08     142.81      <TI-AG-JPN-CL>
```

Air Cargo Markets

Why Do the Air Cargo Markets Exist?

Although shipping dominates the transport markets in terms of tonnage and international trade value, there is still a need to quickly transport certain goods and materials around the world. The air cargo markets serve these needs where airlines and charter companies provide the cargo space for forwarders and shippers.

Reuters Air Cargo Service (RACS) is an on-line Internet product providing market players with constantly updated availability, rates for air freight transport and news relevant to the industry. The service allows subscribers to match shipments with cargo space availability on aircraft.

 Using the Internet browser of your choice enter **www.racs.com** to locate the Home page. From here you can navigate to pages of interest. The examples here show pages a subscriber to the service would see.

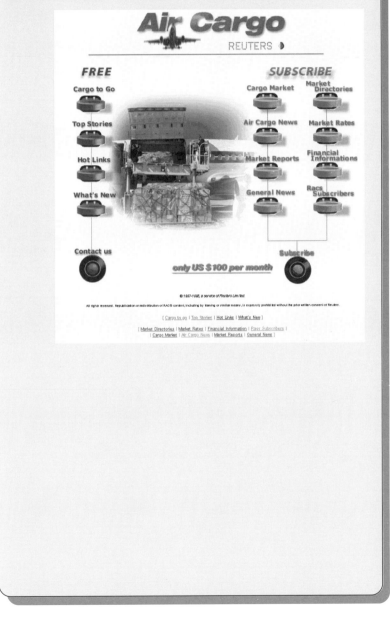

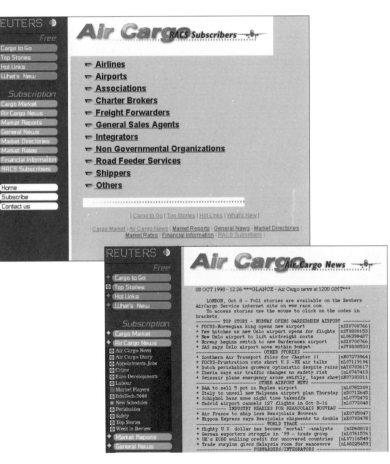

Why Do the Commodities, Energy & Transport Markets Exist?

Summary

You have now finished the first section of the book and you should have a clear understanding of the following:

- Supply and demand

- The importance of weather

- Weights and measures

- The different types of commodities markets and the major types of commodities traded

- How the energy markets operate for oil, natural gas and electricity

- The importance of dry and wet cargoes in the shipping markets and the emerging air cargo market

As a check on your understanding, try the Quick Quiz Questions on the opposite page. You may also find the Overview section to be a helpful learning tool.

The Reuteres screens below show information for commodities, specifically, the Softs Specification page and the Colombia-Coffee Specifications page.

```
                                                            COMMSPECSD
                 =====Softs Specification Page Index=====

=============Coffee=============          =============Rubber============
ICA/ICO       <M111>-<M117>          AIRT          <M221>-<M226>
NewYork       <M122>-<M126>          Indonesia     <M231>-<M243>
Brazil        <M132>-<M136>          NewYork       <M251>-<M256>
Colombia      <M143>-<M144>          RAS           <M264>-<M275>
Kenya         <M151>-<M154>          Thailand      <M284>-<M313>
Brenen        <M161>-<M166>          Malaysia      <M325>-<M346>
Indonesian    <M171>-<M173>          Africa        <AFRIK06>
Africa        <AFRIK05>

=============Sugar=============          =============Pepper===========
All Sugar     <M358>-<M367>          All Pepper    <M193>-<M199>

=============Cocoa=============          =============Tea==============
ICCA          <M177>                 Calcutta      <M381>-<M391>
New York      <M178>-<M184>          Colonbo       <M398>-<M417>
Africa        <AFRIK04>              Bangladesh    <M423>-<M425>
                                     Kenya         <M466>-<M476>
                                     London        <M484>-<M512>
Previo
```

```
                                                                M143
                    Colombia-Coffee Specifications
                    ------------------------------

CONTRACT: Colombia Green 1      <COFCO-GRN1-CO>
Connodity.........Coffee             Unit..............70 Kg
Origin............Colombia           Currency..........USD
Pricing Terns......CIF               Specification......Green 1
Location..........Ports in Colombia
Source...........Reuters
Additional Information: Quoted Daily.


CONTRACT: Colombia Soluble      <COFCO-SOL-CO>
Connodity.........Coffee             Unit..............70 Kg
Origin............Colombia           Currency..........USD
Pricing Terns......CIF               Specification......Soluble
Location..........Ports in Colombia
Source...........Reuters
Additional Information: Quoted Daily.


                         Colobia-coffee continues on <M144>
For nain index page of physical price specifications double-click: <COMMSPECSA>
```

Quick Quiz Questions

1. What are the basic ways in which commodities/energy trading can take place?

2. What is a base metal and which are traded on the London Metal Exchange (LME)?

3. What is a futures contract?

4. What do the terms to "go long" and to "go short" mean in the commodities markets?

5. Name the three commodities categories used in this book and give examples of each.

6. What contracts are traded on NYMEX and IPE?

7. Besides shipowners and shipbrokers, who else is interested in shipping information?

You can check your answers on page 59.

Overview

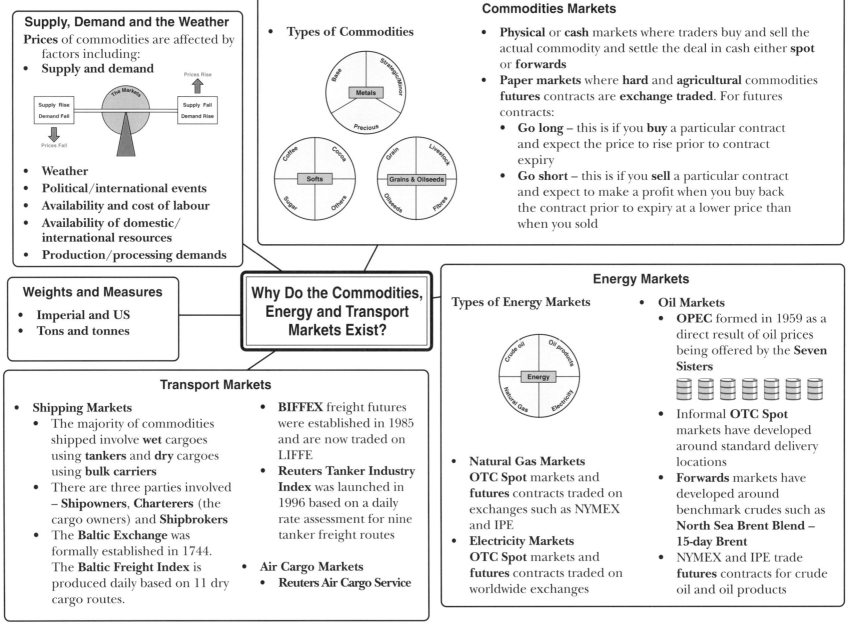

Supply, Demand and the Weather

Prices of commodities are affected by factors including:

- **Supply and demand**

Supply Rise / Demand Fall → Prices Fall

Supply Fall / Demand Rise → Prices Rise

The Markets

- **Weather**
- **Political/international events**
- **Availability and cost of labour**
- **Availability of domestic/international resources**
- **Production/processing demands**

Weights and Measures

- **Imperial and US**
- **Tons and tonnes**

Why Do the Commodities, Energy and Transport Markets Exist?

Commodities Markets

- Types of Commodities

  Metals — Base, Strategic/Minor, Precious

  Softs — Coffee, Cocoa, Sugar, Others

  Grains & Oilseeds — Grain, Livestock, Oilseeds, Fibres

- **Physical** or **cash** markets where traders buy and sell the actual commodity and settle the deal in cash either **spot** or **forwards**
- **Paper markets** where **hard** and **agricultural** commodities **futures** contracts are **exchange traded**. For futures contracts:
  - **Go long** – this is if you **buy** a particular contract and expect the price to rise prior to contract expiry
  - **Go short** – this is if you **sell** a particular contract and expect to make a profit when you buy back the contract prior to expiry at a lower price than when you sold

Energy Markets

Types of Energy Markets

Energy — Crude oil, Oil products, Natural Gas, Electricity

- **Natural Gas Markets**
  OTC Spot markets and **futures** contracts traded on exchanges such as NYMEX and IPE
- **Electricity Markets**
  OTC Spot markets and **futures** contracts traded on worldwide exchanges

- **Oil Markets**
  - **OPEC** formed in 1959 as a direct result of oil prices being offered by the **Seven Sisters**
  - Informal **OTC Spot** markets have developed around standard delivery locations
  - **Forwards** markets have developed around benchmark crudes such as **North Sea Brent Blend – 15-day Brent**
  - NYMEX and IPE trade **futures** contracts for crude oil and oil products

Transport Markets

- **Shipping Markets**
  - The majority of commodities shipped involve **wet** cargoes using **tankers** and **dry** cargoes using **bulk carriers**
  - There are three parties involved – **Shipowners**, **Charterers** (the cargo owners) and **Shipbrokers**
  - The **Baltic Exchange** was formally established in 1744. The **Baltic Freight Index** is produced daily based on 11 dry cargo routes.

- **BIFFEX** freight futures were established in 1985 and are now traded on LIFFE
- **Reuters Tanker Industry Index** was launched in 1996 based on a daily rate assessment for nine tanker freight routes

- **Air Cargo Markets**
  - **Reuters Air Cargo Service**

Quick Quiz Answers

1. *What are the basic ways in which commodities/energy trading take place?*

   The **spot/physical** markets are where traders buy and sell the actual commodity and settle at an agreed date. The **Exchange** driven paper markets are where terms and conditions are standardised and traders enter into contracts for delivery of a commodity at a future date.

2. *What is a base metal and which are traded on the London Metal Exchange (LME)?*

   A base metal originally referred to a metal that tarnishes in air but is now taken to mean a non-ferrous metal. Copper, Nickel, Aluminium (and Aluminium Alloy), Tin, Lead and Zinc are base metals traded on the LME.

3. *What is a futures contract?*

   This is a legally binding commitment to buy or sell a specific amount of a product of a given quantity and quality at a predetermined time in the future on an exchange.

4. *What do the terms to "go long" and to "go short" mean in the commodities markets?*

   Go long is when you **buy** a particular commodity contract and expect the price to rise prior to the contract expiry.
   Go short is when you **sell** a particular commodity contract and expect the price to fall prior to the contract expiry. This allows you to profit by buying back the commodity at the lower price.

5. *Name the three commodities categories used in this book and give examples of each.*

   Metals: Base metals, for example, copper, tin, lead
   Strategic metals, for example, cobalt, silicon
   Precious metals, for example, gold, platinum

   Softs: Cocoa, Coffee, Sugar, Rubber

   Grains & Oilseeds: Wheat, barley, corn, soybean, livestock, fibres

6. *What contracts are traded on NYMEX and IPE?*

   Futures contracts for energy products including Gasoil, Crude light, Heating oil and Brent crude.

7. *Besides shipowners and shipbrokers, who else is interested in shipping information?*

   All commodities and energy traders who have to transport goods between buyers and sellers. Nearly all commodities/ energy products have to be transported from point of origin to point of consumption.

Further Resources

Books

The CRB Commodity Year 1999
Commodity Research Bureau, John Wiley & Sons, Inc., 1999
ISBN   0 471 32704 2

Getting Started in Futures
Todd Lofton, John Wiley & Sons, Inc., 3rd Edition 1997
ISBN   0 471 17759 8

All About Commodities
Russell Wasendorf and Thomas McCafferty, Probus, 1993
ISBN   1 557 38459 2

**Reuters Glossary of International Economic & Financial Terms
(3rd edition)** Longman, 1994
ISBN   0 582 24871-X

World Energy Outlook 1998
International Energy Agency
ISBN   92-64-16185-6

Booklets

Chicago Mercantile Exchange
• How to get started trading CME commodities

International Petroleum Exchange
• An introduction to the IPE

New York Mercantile Exchange
• An Illustrated History of the New York Mercantile Exchange
  1872–1997

London Metal Exchange
• Profile

Chicago Board of Trade
• Weather and the Soybean Market
• Weather and the Corn Market
• Weather and the Wheat Market

International Energy Agency
• The Evolving Renewable Energy Market (IEA/REWP)

Internet

RFT Web Site
• **http://www.wiley.rft.reuters.com**
This is the series' companion web site where additional quiz
questions, updated screens and other information can be found.

Commodities Research Bureau
• **http://www.crbindex.com**

Organisation for Economic Co-operation and Development (OECD)
• **http://www.oecd.org**

Numa Financial Systems
• **http://www.numa.com**

International Energy Agency
• **http://www.iea.org**

AME Mineral Economics
• **http://www.ame.com.an**

United States Geological Survey
• **http://www.usgs.gov**

Energy Information Administration
• **http://www.eia.doe.gov**

Reuters Air Cargo Service
• **http://www.racs.com**

Norwegian Shipowners' Association
• **http://www.rediri.no**

Exchanges

Refer to the back of this book for a listing of worldwide exchanges'
contact information and web sites.

This section of the book should take between 3.5 and 4.5 hours of study time. You may not take as long as this or you may take a little longer – remember your learning is individual to you.

Everyman is the maker of his own fortune.

Sir Richard Steele (1672–1729)

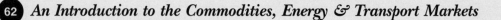

Introduction

This section deals with the some of the important aspects of how the commodities, energy and transport markets operate. In a book of this size it is not possible to cover every aspect of every commodity and market. Therefore, to provide as broad a view as possible, this section concentrates on the following:

- The different ways delivery or settlement may take place in the commodities and energy futures markets – both in the physical and derivatives markets. The most important methods used include:

    - Spot, cash and physical settlement and delivery
    - In store/Ex store
    - Free On Board (FOB)
    - Cost-Insurance-Freight (CIF)
    - Free Along Side (FAS)
    - Alternative Delivery Procedures (ADPs)
    - Exchange of Futures for Physicals (EFPs) for exchange traded futures contracts

- Descriptions of the ways each of the commodity, energy and shipping markets work. In the case of the commodities and energy markets, the description is mainly concerned with the production and uses of the important metals, softs, grains and oilseeds and energy products rather than how different market exchanges operate. This particular aspect is covered later in *Section 4: Trading in the Commodities, Energy and Transport Markets*. For the shipping markets, the description is concerned with the types of business, types of vessel, types of charter and the associated vessel fixings and Worldscale rates.

Before moving on, write down what you think the difference is, if any, between spot, cash and physical transactions and how they are used.

Delivery/Settlement Methods

Spot, Cash and Physical Settlement and Delivery

Spot Transactions

Spot transactions are those carried out "**on the spot**". They are OTC transactions widely used in the commodities and energy markets, although in some cases the deals take place in an auction or sales room. A spot transaction takes place immediately. Both sides agree upon amount, price, delivery location and date and settlement occurs between one day and a month from the trade date. On the settlement date the seller receives payment and the buyer takes ownership of the commodity.

For example, the OTC spot market for gold is very similar to that for foreign exchange markets – prompt delivery two business days after the trade date. Market makers display their latest bid and offer quotes using providers such as Reuters. However, it is important to note that these quotes are only **indications** of prices – a client will need to contact the market maker for a firm quote. The final price agreed will depend on the client's credit rating, size of the order etc.

The Reuters screen below shows market maker contributed prices for gold.

```
O#XAU=                      GOLD
RIC            Bid/Ask    Contributor  Loc Srce Deal  Time  High    Low

XAU=        ↓  289.30/9.80 AIG INTL     GWH AIGG AIGG 15:03 290.45  289.10

XAU=DEUN    ↓  322.20/2.70 DEUTSCHE BK  NYC DBIN DBGS 15:25
XAU=AIGG    ↓  289.30/9.80 AIG INTL     GWH AIGG AIGG 15:03
XAU=RNBN    ↓  289.40/9.90 REPUBLIC NAT NYC RNBG RNBA 15:02
XAU=CSNY    ↑  289.60/0.10 CR SUISSE    NYC CSSG CSGD 15:02
XAU=JPMO    ↑  298.10/8.60 MORGAN GTY   NYC MGTY MGTN 14:23
XAU=ARON    ↑  290.20/0.60 J ARON       LON JAUK JAUK 12:29
XAU=NMRL    ↓  289.85/0.35 ROTHSCHILD   LON NMRB NMRB 12:41
XAU=MIDL    ↓  289.80/0.30 S MONTAGU    LON SMBU SMBL 12:33
XAU=RNBL    ↑  290.30/0.70 REPUBLIC     LON RNBL RNBL 12:18
XAU=MANL    ↓  290.35/0.75 SCOTIAMOCATA LON MANG MNGL 12:22
XAU=DRBF    ↑  290.15/0.65 DRESDNER     FFT DRE2 DRGF 12:18
XAU=DMGA    ↓  289.10/9.60 DEUTSCHE     GFX DBGO DBAU 01:44
XAU=RVTB    ↓  285.00/5.40 VNESHTORG    MOW RVTB VTBX 12:02
XAU=AIGL    ↑  290.00/0.50 AIG INTL     LON AIGB AIGB 09:43
XAU=BBML    ↓  289.95/0.35 BARCLAYS     WLD BARS BBPM 11:26
XAU=SBCH    ↓  289.25/9.65 UBS AG WDR   HKG UBSP UBSP 07:22
XAU=CSBM    ↓  289.40/9.80 CR SUISSE    MEL CSBM CSMA 05:30
XAU=AMKS    ↑  289.55/0.05 M.K.S FIN    SYD AMKS MKSA 06:15
```

In the oil markets, spot transactions for Dated Brent, for example, refer to a specific, date-identified cargo.

Physical Settlement
Describes a market where the contractual agreement is for the buyer to physically take delivery of a commodity.

Cash Settlement
A contract that is settled in cash.

Exchange traded futures commodities and energy contracts provide examples of physical and cash settlement if the contracts are not closed out and allowed to expire. In most cases if the contract is allowed to expire, then one of two conditions usually applies:

1. The buyer of the contract takes **physical delivery** of the commodity. For example the buyer will take delivery of 25 tonnes of copper which has been stored in a warehouse, 500,000 barrels of oil from a VLCC (Very Large Crude Carrier) or 736 Mwh of electricity delivered over the next month.

2. The buyer of the contract settles in **cash** using a physical price index which is agreed – the settlement being calculated on the difference between the contract price index value and that at expiry. The index may be calculated and published by the exchange as for crude oil contracts on the IPE, or an index may be produced by an independent organisation such as Platt's.

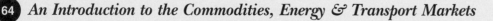

Most exchanges publish **Official Settlement** bid and offer prices which are used for daily margin payments and contract settlement on expiry. These settlement prices are for cash but are also used by market players in the spot markets to price contracts. However, in most cases they are used as a price guide only. On the LME both bid and offer Official Cash and Forward prices are published and it is not uncommon for spot transactions to use these prices for the contract conditions. For example:

Contract Details	Meaning
To be priced on the Official LME Copper Cash settlement price for 5th November 1998.	The contract price is the Official LME Copper Cash **offer** price set on 5th November 1998.
To be priced on a premium of $5.00 over the Official LME Lead Cash settlement price for the period 2nd–6th November 1998.	The contract price is the **average** Official LME Lead Cash **offer** price for the 5 day period **plus** $5.00.

As with all OTC markets there are disadvantages in the spot commodity and energy markets which include the following:

- The **lack of contract transparency**. Although Official or Index prices are published, these only act as guides for the spot markets.

- The **cost** and **time** involved in setting up a trade. In many cases brokers are used who match buyer and seller requirements.

- **Creditworthiness** of counterparty. Both sides of a trade have to be convinced that payment/delivery will take place on the due date.

- Possibility of **default** in a volatile market place.

- **Price risk** associated with a volatile market.

The Reuters screen below show LME Daily Offical Prices for various metals.

```
O#LME-OFFCL     LME       Daily Official Prices                      12FEB99
                Cash           3 Month       15 Month      27 Month   Settlement
Copper        1446.0/1447.0  1476.0/1477.0  1550.0/1560.0  1595.0/1605.0  1447.0
(STG Eq.)      889.75/        908.93/
Tin           5210/5215      5180/5185      5135/5145                   5215
Lead          529.50/530.00  526.00/527.00  517.00/522.00              530.0
(STG Eq.)      325.89/        324.31/
Zinc          1032.0/1033.0  1048.0/1048.5  1083.0/1088.0  1120.0/1125.0  1033.0
Aluminiun     1192.0/1193.0  1215.5/1216.0  1295.0/1300.0  1357.0/1362.0  1193.0
Nickel        4550/4555
Al.Alloy      1029.0/1031.0
Settlement Rates - GBP ↑1.63
```

```
1906 LME DAILY OFFICIAL PRICES - 13 FEB 1999                          MTLE
              CASH        3 MTHS     15 MTHS     27 MTHS    SETT
COPPER     1446.0/47.0 1476.0/77.0 1550.0/60.0 1595.0/05.0 1447.0
(STG EQ)    889.75      908.93
TIN        5210/5215   5180/5185   5135/5145        /       5215
LEAD       529.50/0.00 526.00/7.00 517.00/2.00      /       530.0
(STG EQ)    325.89      324.31
ZINC       1032.0/33.0 1048.0/48.5 1083.0/88.0 1120.0/25.0 1033.0
ALUMINUM   1192.0/93.0 1215.5/16.0 1295.0/00.0 1357.0/62.0 1193.0
NICKEL     4550/4555   4625/4630   4865/4885   5065/5085   4555
AL.ALLOY   1029.0/31.0 1052.0/53.0 1130.0/50.0      /       1031.0
SETTLE - GBP  1.6263   DEM  1.7385   JPY  114.53   EUR 1.1250
Prompt Dates : Cash - 17/02/99      15Mth - 17/05/00
               3Mth - 14/05/99      27Mth - 16/05/01
```

Prompt dates are shown here. The prompt date is the delivery date for a contract, versus the date on which the contract price is quoted.

```
1640 LME DAILY UNOFFICIAL PRICES                                    MTLF
              CASH        3 MTHS     15 MTHS     27 MTHS
COPPER     1443.0/44.0 1472.0/73.0 1545.0/55.0 1590.0/00.0
TIN        5180/5185   5155/5160   5110/5120
LEAD       520.00/1.00 517.00/8.00 520.00/5.00
ZINC       1026.0/27.0 1041.0/42.0 1078.0/83.0 1115.0/20.0
ALUMINUM   1191.5/92.5 1215.0/16.0 1295.0/00.0 1358.0/63.0
NICKEL     4550/4560   4620/4630   4860/4880   5060/5080
AL.ALLOY   1033.0/38.0 1055.0/60.0 1135.0/55.0

                    12 FEB 1999
```

In Store/Ex Store

In Store

This is the simplest form of physical delivery and is often used for base metals, cocoa and coffee. The seller is responsible for delivery of the commodity to an agreed warehouse. As with all physical deals the quality, quantity, delivery location etc of the commodity are negotiated on a contract by contract basis. Where the contract is linked to a futures contract, the commodity is delivered to an exchange approved warehouse and the commodity must be "**on warrant**" before it can be traded. The commodity must fulfil the exchange quantity and quality contract specifications. These specifications have to be fulfilled by the seller **prior** to the buyer paying for the commodity. The following table indicates the types of issues involved with the quantity and quality of commodities.

Quantity	Quality
The weight of individual bags of coffee or cocoa, or metal ingots will be noted on the warrant or separate weight note. With grain the storekeeper warrants the exact quantity.	The quality of the commodity must be determined prior to delivery. Metals are required to be produced by listed manufacturers whose brands conform to international or government approved standards, for example, BSI/ISO.
Delivering exact contract weights for commodities is not normally possible so contracts specify tolerances within which delivery must conform. Price adjustments are made between buyer and seller to compensate for any minor differences, usually at a standard rate dependent on the commodity.	Commodities such as coffee and cocoa are graded by the exchange warehouse. Samples are taken from the lots by the storekeeper and graded by a panel of experts. A grading certificate is issued by the exchange warehouse containing any premiums/discounts for excellent/poor quality that are attached to the lot for delivery. It is the responsibility of the seller to have the commodity graded prior to delivery and at his cost.

If everything is in order, the warehouse issues a warrant identifying the lot. This warrant is a bearer document and is therefore valuable. When the lot is traded, the original warrant owner is cancelled and ownership of the commodity transfers to the buyer together with the warrant. The lot can now be shipped for delivery if required or placed back on warrant in the warehouse – the new buyer is now responsible for storage costs. If the new owner does place the lot on warrant, then delivery has taken place without the commodity even moving!

The difference between "on warrant" and "on cancelled warrant" stocks held in a warehouse can be used to assess the amount of true market trading.

Ex Store

This is identical to In Store except that the seller has to pre-pay the storekeeper for loading onto the buyer's transport. This is used for cocoa and grain delivered in the UK.

Grain samples are drawn on delivery to the buyer's transport for analysis and grading by an independent analyst.

In all physical deliveries the seller delivers the required documents, that is, grading certificates, warrants, weight notes etc to the nominated party for the transaction, for example, bank or exchange clearing house. Once delivered, payment is arranged and the documents are exchanged for cash from the buyer.

Free On Board (FOB)

FOB is concerned with the loading and shipping of bulk commodities, such as gasoil, raw and white sugar, soybean meal and potatoes, that can be poured into a vessel. In essence, FOB means that once the goods have passed over a ship's rail at the named port of shipment, the seller has fulfilled its obligations. The buyer then bears all costs and risks for loss or damage to the goods. FOB also requires that the seller clears the goods for export. FOB deliveries can take a long time to complete – up to 2 months sometimes.

Buyers must be aware that normal shipment quantities of the commodity will not necessarily be delivered in any one port **but** it is still the buyer's responsibility to take delivery.

As loading takes place, samples are taken from the commodity and analysed by independent supervisors. These supervisors also weigh the commodity to be shipped, using weighbridges, weighed hoppers or calculations from the density of the samples and volume loaded using the following formula:

Weight = Density x Volume

Once the commodity is loaded onto the vessel the cargo becomes the **buyer's responsibility**.

The responsibilities of buyers and sellers are summarised in the table below:

Buyer	Seller
Within the delivery time the buyer has to provide a suitable vessel and notify the seller of the vessel's description and estimated time of arrival.	Within the delivery time the seller is required to bring the commodity to a port or warehouse specified by the contract.
The time within which a delivery must take place depends on the commodity. The buyer can normally choose when to take delivery since he has to provide the vessel.	The cost of loading lies with the seller. Long delays may result in a claim for costs by the buyer.

A **Bill of lading** for a vessel acts in much the same way as a warrant for goods in a warehouse. The ship's master issues a Bill of lading which is the document title for the commodity that he has on board. It is also a valuable document as it can be sold or transferred and entitles the holder to receive the commodity when the vessel reaches its destination.

The Bill of lading together with the sample analyses are presented by the seller to the buyer's bank or clearing house for payment. Ownership of the cargo passes to the buyer when he pays for and collects the documents from the bank or clearing house. On reaching the vessel's destination the ship's master will release the cargo when the Bill of lading is presented.

Cost-Insurance-Freight (CIF)

This refers to a sale in which the buyer pays a unit price which includes the FOB value **plus** all costs of insurance and transportation. In effect this means that the seller delivers to the buyer.

In many cases, CIF delivery means that the buyer accepts the quality and quantity of the commodity or energy product at the loading point rather than paying at the unloading port for the delivery. However, it is a negotiable contract condition and the quality and quantity are accepted by the buyer on discharge of the cargo.

The seller must provide insurance for the cargo although the risk and the title for the commodity are transferred to the buyer at the loading port. A variation of CIF is where the terms are just for Cost and Freight with **no** insurance – this is abbreviated to **C+F** or **CFR**.

So the next time you see the terms FOB and CIF, you will now have an idea what the delivery conditions involve. Look at the Reuters screen below under the **Location** column.

```
OHGL-E          GASOLINE - EUR     For product specifications click on <ENGSPECB>
Name      Spec1 Location Delivery  Buy       Sell      Time  Date  PreviousDay    Size  Misc
Premium   UNL   CIF NWE  PROMPT    140.00/143.00       14:09 06NOV 141.00/144.00 CARGO
Premium   UNL   FOB NWE  PROMPT    130.00/133.00       14:09 06NOV 131.00/134.00 CARGO
Prem 98   98 RON CIF NWE PROMPT    155/160             14:09 06NOV 156/    161  CARGO
Prem 98   98 RON FOB NWE PROMPT    139/143             14:09 06NOV 140/    144  CARGO
Regular   UNL   CIF NWE  PROMPT    130.00/133.00       14:09 06NOV 131.00/134.00 CARGO
Regular   UNL   FOB NWE  PROMPT    121.00/125.00       14:09 06NOV 122.00/126.00 CARGO
Premium   UNL   FOB ARA  PROMPT    137.00/140.00       13:53 06NOV 137.00/140.00 BARGE
Premium   UNL   FOB ARA  NOV 16-30 134.00/136.00       13:53 06NOV 138.00/149.00 BARGE
Premium   UNL   FOB ARA  Nov       135.50/0            13:25 06NOV 137.75/203.00 BARGE Swap
Premium   UNL   FOB ARA  Dec       134.00/0            13:28 06NOV 136.00/202.50 BARGE Swap
Premium   UNL   FOB ARA  Jan       136.00/0            13:29 06NOV 138.00/201.00 BARGE Swap
Premium   UNL   FOB ARA  Feb       139.00/0            13:29 06NOV 141.00/201.00 BARGE Swap
Premium   UNL   FOB ARA  1Q99      139.19/0            15:17 06NOV 140.28/203.00 BARGE Swap
Premium   UNL   FOB ARA  2Q99      150.94/0            15:04 06NOV 151.77/207.00 BARGE Swap
Prem 98   98 RON FOB ARA           154/157             13:53 06NOV 154/    157  BARGE
Regular   UNL   FOB ARA  PROMPT    129.00/132.00       13:53 06NOV 139.00/132.00 BARGE
Regular   UNL   FOB ARA  NOV 16-30 130.00/133.00       13:53 06NOV 130.00/133.00 BARGE
MTBE            FOB ARA            218/220             13:53 06NOV 218/    220  BARGE
Premium   UNL   CIF MED  PROMPT    144.00/150.00       08:42 06NOV 144.00/150.00 CARGO
Premium   UNL   FOB MED  PROMPT    136.00/142.00       08:42 06NOV 136.00/142.00 CARGO
```

In the screen you should also now understand the meaning of **Prompt** in the **Delivery** column and **Cargo** and **Barge** in the **Size** column. However, under the Location column you may not be aware of the regional codes that are used. These are explained in the table below:

Code	Region
A	All Asia
ARA	Amsterdam – Rotterdam – Antwerp region
C	All Canada
E	All Europe
G3	Group 3 – Central US region
LA	Los Angeles
MC	Mid Continent region
MED	Mediterranean
N	All North America
NWE	Northwest Europe
NYH	New York Harbour
PNW	Pacific Northwest
R/H	Rotterdam – Hamburg
SF	San Francisco
SIN	Singapore
TYO	Tokyo
UK	United Kingdom
USG	US Gulf Coast

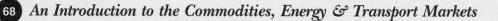

Free Along Side (FAS)

This is very similar to FOB except that the seller's responsibilities cease when the commodity is brought alongside the vessel. In other words the seller is not responsible for loading the commodity onto the vessel.

For both FOB and FAS the contract should specify who is responsible for goods/services tax, import duty, local taxes and any other commodity or location-related costs. Disputes in FOB and FAS matters are referred to arbitration, which is normally run by an exchange.

Alternative Delivery Procedures (ADPs)

These are allowed on some exchanges. In principle they allow for delivery conditions specified in a contract to be altered provided both buyer and seller agree. Both parties may agree to a commodity delivery of a different standard, to a different location and by a different method than that originally specified.

Example

In a gasoil delivery, the original contract called for delivery FOB by barges in the Amsterdam–Rotterdam–Antwerp (ARA) area to be paid in USD. The buyer and seller subsequently agreed for delivery in road tankers at various UK destinations and the contract to be paid in GBP.

The standard conditions of a futures contract have thus been altered resulting in a physical contract with the subsequent loss of the clearing house guarantees.

Exchange of Futures for Physicals (EFPs)

On exchanges such as the IPE and NYMEX it is possible to exchange a position in the futures markets with an equivalent position in the physical markets – hence the term. The exchange may be a straight forward reversal of positions or counterparties may establish equal and opposite positions to each other in the cash and futures markets. On some exchanges such as NYMEX the commodity delivered does not necessarily have to conform to the contract specification in all terms. EFPs are described in more detail in Section Three of this text.

A Few Examples of Delivery/Settlement Methods

Delivery/Settlement	Commodity	Delivery To/From
Cash settlement	Brent Crude oil BIFFEX	
In store/Ex store	Cocoa Coffee Wheat Barley LME metals	UK/NWE UK/NWE UK/NWE UK/NWE Worldwide warehouses
FOB	Raw sugar White sugar Potatoes Gasoil Unleaded gasoline Crude oil	Worldwide Worldwide UK ARA ARA Worldwide
CIF	Unleaded gasoline Raw sugar Pepper Cocoa Coconut Oil	ARA UK R/H UK Rotterdam

You may also come across other delivery terms such as **EXW – Ex-works**. In this case the seller makes goods available at his premises ready for collection by the buyer. The buyer is responsible for loading the goods onto his vehicles, clearing the goods for export and for costs and risks in taking the goods from the seller to their destination.

Metals

Within the description of commodities used in this book are three categories of metals:

- Base metals

- Strategic and minor metals

- Precious metals

For each category, the most important of the metals is described in terms of production, use and consumption. Before moving on, try the activity opposite.

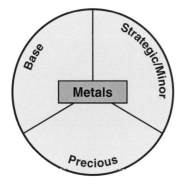

1. Do you know what metals use pigs and sows?

2. What part of the world do you think Tin Straights comes from?

3. Why is mercury sold in flasks?

The answers can be found on pages 73 and 74.

Base Metals

Within the commodities markets there is a huge global market for trading base metals. In particular, six base metals are actively traded on exchanges including the **London Metal Exchange (LME)** which was founded in 1877 and is the oldest and largest worldwide metal exchange. The metals traded on the LME – Copper, Nickel, Tin, Lead, Zinc and Aluminium – all have symbols to identify them, which are shown below:

Aluminium   Zinc   Copper   Tin   Nickel   Lead

The LME trades forward contracts but it is not the only exchange trading base metals. Although a small exchange compared with the LME, the Shenzhen Metal Exchange in China also trades most of the base metals. Other exchanges trade only a single base metal – these exchanges include:

- **COMEX, a division of NYMEX**, where copper futures are traded

- **Tokyo Commodity Exchange (TCE)**, where aluminium futures are traded

- **Kuala Lumpur Commodity Exchange**, where tin futures are traded

COMEX is an important exchange for trading copper futures in the US. It was founded in 1933 when four commodity exchanges in New York combined activities to form the Commodity Exchange Inc. (COMEX). In 1994 NYMEX and COMEX merged to become the world's largest physical commodity futures exchange.

Before moving on to the descriptions of the base metals in terms of production, use and consumption, it is important to recognise that not all base metals consumed are derived from **primary** sources such as ores and minerals. Depending on the particular metal, a considerable amount of "pure" metal comes from **recycled** or **scrap** sources.

The Importance of Scrap or Recycled Metals

With world resources diminishing, the international scrap metal markets are becoming increasingly more important. For example, in 1996 it was estimated that approximately 40% of the world copper consumption came from scrap sources. Some metal refiners in Europe and China now rely almost exclusively on scrap as their primary source for feed metal.

Scrap prices are interdependent with standard grade base metal prices – standard grade is of a lower purity, for example, 97%, than Grade A or premium grades which are usually 99+%. If there is a downturn in base metal cash prices, then this usually results in scrap famines. The reason is simple – scrap merchants who bought in high do not want to sell low and take a loss. This means that the scrap merchants hold onto their stocks until base metal cash prices improve. The result is that consumers of scrap for feed have to use standard grade or even premium grade metal. In general this generates an increase in base metal prices and scrap becomes an attractive feed once again. It is another example of the principles of supply and demand operating in the markets.

In 1992 the LME introduced a contract for recycled aluminium – Aluminium Alloy – in its belief that recycled metals would become increasing more important. This contract has proved quite popular, particularly within the motor vehicle industry. The symbol used to identify this metal on the LME is shown below.

Aluminium Alloy

Precise data about the amount of recycled metal used in the worldwide production of primary grade materials is difficult to obtain; however, the US Geological Survey (USGS) does provide US data detailing the amount of scrap from "old sources" used in production compared with the amount of metal consumed. Old sources of scrap typically include recycled household goods, motor vehicle parts etc – they do not include scrap from manufacturing plants, refiners, smelters etc which also provide scrap. The 1998 levels of usage of old scrap for the base metals are shown in the table below:

Metal	Old Scrap Supply as % of Consumption	Major Sources
Copper	14.0	Domestic electrical services and components
Aluminium	20.0	Used beverage cans
Nickel	35.0	Stainless steel items
Lead	64.0	Spent lead-acid batteries
Tin	15.2	De-tinning items
Zinc	7.0	Brass and galvanised iron

Source: USGS Mineral Commodity Summaries, January 1999

The Reuters screens below display cash and scrap base metal prices.

```
15:54 06NOV98    EURO BASE METALS PHYSICAL PRICE QUOTE UK99999         BASE/EU1
         Latest quotes as a premium/discount to LME in $/tonne unless stated:
Metal     Location                        Latest      Previous   Last chg
Copper    Rotterdam    Chilean            +20/25      +20/30     04/11/98
Copper    Rotterdam    Grade A            +15/20      +15/25     06/11/98
Copper    Rotterdam    Standard           -5/+5       -10/+10    06/11/98
Copper    UK           Grade A            +20/25      25/30      06/11/98
Copper    Italy        Grade A            +20/30      +15/25     06/11/98
Copper    Hamburg      Grade A            +15/20      +20/30     06/11/98
Aluminiun Rotterdam    Russian A7E        +18/23      +20/25     06/11/98
Aluminiun Rotterdam    Russian A6         +10/20      +15/25     06/11/98
Aluminiun Rotterdam    Russian A5         0/+5        +5/15      06/11/98
Aluminiun Rotterdam    Russian A0         -5/-10      +5/-5      06/11/98
Aluminiun Rotterdam    Western duty-unpaid +25/35     +30/35     06/11/98
Aluminiun Rotterdam    Western duty-paid  +90/100     +95/100    06/11/98
Tin       Rotterdam    Chinese            +50/70      +60/70     06/11/98
Tin       Rotterdam    Malaysian          +20/35      +35/50     06/11/98
Tin       Rotterdam    Indonesian         +50/60N     +50/60     06/10/98
Zinc      Rotterdam    SHG duty-paid      +50/60      +55/65     06/10/98
```

```
16:57 06NOV98    EURO SCRAP METALS PRICE QUOTE         UK30507        BASE/EU2
            Latest quotes, per tonne, delivered consumer works
Grade            Location   Currency  Latest          Previous    Last change
Cu Millberry     N.Europe   dlrs      1,550/1,580     1,530/1,550  04/11/98
Cu Millberry     UK         stg       920/950         915/935      04/11/98
Cu Berry         N.Europe   dlrs      1,490/1,520     1,450/1,480  04/11/98
Cu Birch/cliff   N.Europe   dlrs      1,320/1,360     1,300/1,340  04/11/98
Cu Candy         N.Europe   dlrs      1,350/1,390     1,380/1,420  04/11/98
Brass Honey      N.Europe   dlrs      870/900         850/880      06/11/98
Brass Ocean      N.Europe   dlrs      600/640         660/710      06/11/98
Al Taint/Tabor   N.Europe   dlrs      760/800         750/790      06/10/98
Al Taboo         N.Europe   dlrs      860/910         850/900      06/10/98
Al UBC           N.Europe   dlrs      950/990         990/1,030    06/10/98
Al Tabloid       N.Europe   dlrs      1,200/1,250     1,140/1,190  06/10/98
Al Tense         N.Europe   dlrs      760/800         780/820      06/10/98
Lead Racks       UK         stg       240/250         245/255      06/11/98
Lead Rains       UK         stg       60/65           60/65        06/11/98
Zinc Saves       UK         stg       400/430         450/470      06/11/98
Zinc Score       UK         stg       300/320         350/370      06/11/98
Nickel Burly     N.Europe   dlrs      3,800/3,840     3,800/3,870  06/10/98
Cupronickel 70/30 N.Europe  dlrs      1,990/2,090     1,800/1,900  06/10/98
St. Steel Ultra  UK         stg       140/150         150/160      06/11/98
St. Steel Sabot  UK         stg       210/230         220/240      06/1104B
```

News service reporters gather physical metal prices from the markets and either quote these as outright prices or as a spread against LME prices.

```
LME ------Officials 06-NOV-1998---- Stocks ---
          Cash        3 Months      09-NOV-1998
CU  1615.0/1616.0  1642.0/1643.0    465625
SN  5610/5620      5530/5535        7465
PB  488.50/489.00  498.00/499.00    110375
ZN  962.5/963.0    980.5/981.0      342275
AL  1296.0/1296.5  1317.0/1317.5    526275
NI  4295/4300      4355/4360        60402
AA  1092.0/1094.0  1121.0/1122.0    86580
```

Official LME prices from a Reuters page.

Base Metals	Copper, Cu	Aluminium, Al & Aluminium Alloy, AA	Zinc, Zn
Discovery 	Copper is a reddish-coloured, easily worked metal which has been used since ancient times. The Egyptians used it and it was in use in Britain before the Romans arrived. In 1900 most of the world's copper was smelted in Swansea.	This light, shiny, corrosion resistant metal was first isolated in 1827. This late discovery date was partly due to the unavailability of very large amounts of electricity required for its production and processing. When it was first discovered it was a rare metal – Napoleon III had cutlery made from aluminium to impress his guests.	Zinc is a dullish-looking metal which was known by the Chinese in the 16th century. The metal was in production in Europe by the 1740s – the first commercial zinc smelting was carried out in 1743, in Bristol. Zinc is commonly mined in association with lead.
Uses	Copper is an excellent conductor of electricity through wires and cables, thus, its major use, almost 50% of output, is in the electrical and telecommunications industries. It is also used in the construction industry for cladding and piping and for producing alloys such as **brass** and **bronze**.	Aluminium's good electrical conductivity, corrosion resistance and alloying properties means it is used extensively in motor vehicle and aerospace production and in the construction industry, for example, in the manufacture of window frames. It is also widely used in the packaging industry in cans and as foil.	Zinc is characterised by its resistance to corrosion and about 50% of zinc production is used to produce **galvanised** steel. Its other major use is in the production of alloys for die-casting. Zinc alloys with copper to produce **brass**. Zinc is also used to produce **bronze** and alloys which are used in the motor vehicle, domestic and electrical appliance industries.
Annual Production (mmt = million metric tonnes)	New or primary = 11.9 mmt Supplied as: Cathodes and wirebars	New or primary = 22.2 mmt Supplied as: Ingots, T-bars and sows	New or primary = 7.8 mmt Supplied as: Slabs, plates and ingots
Exchange Markets	LME, COMEX, Shanghai, and Shenzhen.	LME, Shanghai, and Shenzhen and TCE.	LME and Shenzhen.
Countries of Origin	US, Chile, Canada, Peru, Australia, Indonesia and Russia.	US, Russia, Canada, Australia, Brazil, China and Norway.	Canada, Australia, China, Peru, US.
Major Consumers	Major industrialised countries – US, Japan, Europe, USSR		
Major Influences on Price	• Stocks • Strikes • Production costs • Technology • Economic situation of country of origin		

Base metals	Lead, Pb	Tin, Sn	Nickel, Ni
Discovery	Lead is a dullish-black looking metal which is easy to beat into sheets or melt and pour into molds. It has been used since Roman times for sanitation and plumbing pipes etc. Its symbol Pb comes from its Latin name – plumbum. Unfortunately lead and its compounds are very toxic!	Tin is a shiny metal which has been used from very early times to alloy with other metals. **Bronze** and **pewter** are both alloys of tin. Britain has produced tin from ancient times – by the 1800s one-third of the world's tin supplies came from the Cornish tin mines.	Centuries ago German miners encountered nickel ores in their search for copper. The miners considered the ore bewitched and ascribed it to "Old Nick". This became known as **Kupfernickel** – "Old Nick's copper". The nickel ore was regarded as a problem and it was not until 1751 that the shiny metal was first isolated.
Uses	Because of its great resistance to corrosion lead has been used as a roofing material for centuries. Lead alloys were traditionally used in printing for type setting – the strips of lead placed between rows of type gave rise to the term "leading". Lead compounds were also used in gasoline as an engine 'anti-knocking' agent. The major use for lead now is in the manufacture of batteries.	The best known use for tin is in the production of food cans where steel was tin-plated to prevent corrosion. Although tin cans have largely been replaced tin-plating is still used. Tin is also used in the production of metal alloys and in the manufacture of chemicals such as pesticides and fungicides. Tin compounds are still used in the packaging industry, for example, in "crystal" plastics.	Nickel is used in the production of stainless steel and other steel alloys as it has extra hard strength, a high melting point and is very resistant to corrosion. Nickel alloys have also been used for coinage. A Ni/Cu alloy was first used for coins in 1850 in Switzerland – this alloy is known as **German Silver**. **Electro Plated Nickel Silver (EPNS)** is a Cu/Ni/Zn alloy which contains no silver but is silver plated to look like silver!
Annual Production (mmt = million metric tonnes)	New or primary = 3.1 mmt Supplied as: Pigs	New or primary = 0.22 mmt Supplied as: Ingots and slabs	New or primary = 1.17 mmt Supplied as: Cathodes , briquettes & pellets
Exchange Markets	LME and Shenzhen.	LME, Kuala Lumpur and Shenzhen.	LME and Shenzhen.
Countries of Origin	Australia, China, US, Peru and Canada.	China, Indonesia, Peru, Brazil and Bolivia.	Russia, Canada, New Caledonia, Australia and Indonesia.
Major Consumers	Major industrialised countries – US, Japan, Europe, USSR		
Major Influences on Price	• Stocks • Strikes • Production costs • Technology • Economic situation of country of origin		

Strategic and Minor Metals

These are all metals or metalloids (semi-metals) which are produced and used in smaller quantities than base metals. Typically metals in this category are used for specialist alloys, in the electronics industries and for chemicals and pigments.

The Reuters screen below shows a list of the strategic and minor metals covered by Reuters.

The production, use and consumption details for two strategic/minor metals below provide a brief overview of one metal with which you may be familiar – mercury – and one not so familiar but nonetheless very important in the manufacture of TVs and photocopiers – selenium. Before moving on, look below at the cash prices of the minor metals which Platt's supplies to news services such as Reuters.

```
STRATEGIC CASH                                    STRATEGIC/CASH1
To Access information double-click in the <> brackets.
=KEY PRICES=========================  =KEY PRICES Cont=====================
European Prices.......<STRATEGIC/EU1>-3  Mang.Ferro 75/76%-LON...<MNG-FERRO-LON>
Chinese/Japanese strat<STRATEGIC/ASIA1>  Manganese 99.7%-LON..........<MNG-LON>
All Strategic Metals..........<O#MINOR>  Mercury Flask-LON.......<MER-FLASK-LON>
Arsenic 99.0%-LON.............<ARS-LON>  Molyb.Oxide 57%-LON....<MLY-OXIDE-LON>
Antinony 99.6%-LON............<ANT-LON>  Molybdenum Ferro-LON....<MLY-FERRO-LON>
Bisnuth 99.99%-LON............<BIS-LON>  Ruthenium-LON...............<RUTH-LON>
Cadniun 99.9%-LON.......<CAD-99.99-LON>  Seleniun 99.5%-LON..........<SELE-LON>
Cadniun 99.95%-LON......<CAD-99.95-LON>  Sil.Lumps 98.5%..............<SIL-LON>
Chrone Mtl 99.0%-LON..........<CRO-LON>  Silicon Fer.75%-LON....<SIL-FERRO-LON>
Cobalt Ing 99.3%-LON.....<COB-ING-LON>   Tantalite 30/35%-LON.........<TANT-LON>
Cobalt Cathodes-LON.....<COB-CATH-LON>   Titaniun Sponge-LON....<TIT-SPONGE-LON>
Cobalt-PAR..................<COB-PAR>    Tungst.Fe.80/85%-LON....<TUN-FERRO-LON>
Galliun Ing 99.9%-LON....<GALL-ING-LON>  Van.Pentox 98%-LON.......<VAN-PENT-LON>
Gern.Diox 99.9%-LON.....<GERM-DIOX-LON>  Vanadiun Fe.80%-LON.....<VAN-FERRO-LON>
Gernaniun-LON..............<GERM-LON>    Wolfranite 65%-LON.........<WMITE-LON>
Indiun Ing 99.97%-LON.....<IND-ING-LON>
                                         Foreign Exchange Rates..........<FX=S>
                                         World Cross Rates...............<WX=X>
Questions/Conments: contact your local Help Desk - see <PHONE/HELP> for details

Base Sumnary....<METAL/SUM> Main Index....<COMMOD> Strategic Metals.<STRATEGIC1>
  Lost? Selective Access?..<USER/HELP>    Reuters Phone Support...<PHONE/HELP>
```

```
O#MINOR           MINOR METALS
Connodity     Del.Date      Last             Srce    Terns     Loc  Ccy Units
Antinony 99.65  SPOT      B↓  1270  A1350     RTRS      ROT     ANY  USD TONNE
Antinony 99.85  SPOT      B↓  1370  A1470     RTRS      ROT     ANY  USD TONNE
Arsenic         SPOT      B↓   0.4  A0.5      RTRS  WHS ROT     ANY  USD LBS
Bisnuth         SPOT      B↓   2.8  A3        RTRS  WHS ROT     ANY  USD LBS
Cadniun 99.99   SPOT      B↓  0.13  A0.18     RTRS  WHS ROT     ANY  USD LBS
Cadniun 99.95   SPOT      B↓  0.13  A0.18     RTRS  WHS ROT     ANY  USD LBS
Chrone, El. Deg SPOT      B↑     9  A10       RTRS  WHS ROT     RUS  USD LBS
Chrone El. Std  SPOT      B      4  A5        RTRS  WHS ROT     ANY  USD LBS
Fe Chrone,HiCarb SPOT     B↓  0.36  A0.4      RTRS  WHS ROT     RUS  USD LBS
Fe Chrone,LoCarb Spot     B↓  0.68  A0.72     RTRS  WHS ROT     RUS  USD LBS
Chrone, Al. CH  SPOT      B↓  5100  A5300     RTRS  WHS ROT     CHN  USD TONNE
Chrone, Al. RU  SPOT      B↓  5100  A5300     RTRS  WHS ROT     RUS  USD TONNE
Cobalt (RU) Ing SPOT      B↓    14  A15       RTRS  WHS ROT     RUS  USD LBS
Cobalt Cathodes SPOT      B↓  16.5  A17.5     RTRS  WHS ROT     AFR  USD LBS
Cobalt (ZCCM C) SPOT      B↓    16  A17       RTRS  WHS ROT     ZAR  USD LBS
Galliun Ingots  SPOT      B↑   420  A460      RTRS  WHS ROT     ANY  USD KG
Gernaniun. Diox SPOT      B↓   830  A870      RTRS  WHS ROT     ANY  USD KG
Gernaniun 50ohn SPOT      B↓  1200  A1250     RTRS  WHS ROT     ANY  USD KG
```

```
O#MET-MIN=PLT       Minor Metals
Connodity       Last            Srce    Terns   Loc  Ccy Units
Antinony 99.65%  1250   1300    Platt   Weekly  HK   USD TONNE
Antinony NY Dlr    68     78    Platt   Weekly  USA  USc LBS
Bisnuth NY Dlr   3.15   3.65    Platt   Weekly  USA  USD LBS
Cadniun NY Dlr   0.19   0.26    Platt   Weekly  USA  USD LBS
Indiun Arconiun                 Platt   Weekly  USA  USc OZS
Indiun Ind Corp   855           Platt   Weekly  USA  USc OZS
Indiun NY Dealer  235    270    Platt   Weekly  USA  USD KG
Merc US Donestic  164    185    Platt   Weekly  USA  USD
Mercury Free Mkt  135    145    Platt   Weekly  Intl USD
Seleniun MW Dlr   1.9    2.4    Platt   Weekly  USA  USD LBS
```

Minor Metals	Mercury, Hg	Selenium, Se
Discovery 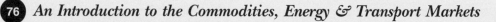	Mercury or **Quicksilver** has been known since ancient times and was known as **Hydrargyrum** or 'silver water' by the Romans. It is the only metal which is a **liquid** under normal conditions – hence it is sold in flasks. Mercury has been mined at Almaden, Spain since Roman times and the appalling conditions under which the metal was extracted by slaves are well documented. A slave would rarely survive more than three years in the mines. The mineral **Cinnabar**, Mercury sulphide, occurs naturally and when crushed is used as the pigment **vermillion**.	Selenium is a metalloid or semi-metal. It was first discovered as a red powder by-product of copper extraction in 1818 by the Swedish chemist J.J. Berzelius. The element can also be extracted as a grey metal. Selenium takes its name from the Greek word for moon – selene. It seems to have come by its name because it was similar to the element Tellurium which had been named after the earth.
Uses	The medicinal uses of mercury in treating venereal and other diseases have been known for centuries. In the seventeenth and eighteenth centuries patients drank daily doses of an ounce or so of the liquid metal to help cure them of syphilis. Sometimes the treatment worked but unfortunately mercury is also quite toxic – particularly as a vapour. The eccentric behaviour of the **Mad Hatter** in *Alice Through the Looking Glass* by Lewis Carrol is typical of the effects of mercury poisoning. The saying "Mad as a Hatter" comes from the trade of hatters who used felt which had been impregnated with a mercury compound to prevent mold growth. The felt would be steamed and shaped and during this time the hatters would breathe in vapours containing the mercury compound. Over a period of time the hatters first exhibited eccentric behaviour and then went mad. Mercury is used for scientific instruments such as thermometers and barometers. Until recently mercury amalgams (alloys with other metals) have been used in dentistry although its use is now declining. Mercury fulminate is used as a detonator as it is very shock sensitive.	The most useful property of the metallic form of selenium is its photoconductivity – on illumination with white light the element's electrical conductivity increases more than 1000 fold. This property is used in a variety of semiconductor, photoelectric and photosensitive devices such as alarms, safety systems and more importantly for TVs and photocopiers. Selenium is also used in the glass and ceramic industries – selenium produces a ruby coloured glass which was traditionally achieved using gold in the process. It is also used as a trace element in health products and livestock feeds, because of reputedly promoting resistance to disease.
Annual Production	New or primary = 2,600tonnes	New or primary = 1,660 tonnes
Countries of Origin	Spain, Kyrgystan and Algeria.	Japan, Canada, US and Belgium.

Before moving on, review the Reuters screens on this page for prices and specifications of mercury and selenium.

```
STRATEGIC CASH                                                STRATEGIC/CASH1
To Access information double-click in the <> brackets.
=KEY PRICES===========================    =KEY PRICES Cont=====================
European Prices.......<STRATEGIC/EU1>-3    Mang.Ferro 75/76%-LON...<MNG-FERRO-LON>
Chinese/Japanese strat<STRATEGIC/ASIA1>    Manganese 99.7%-LON..........<MNG-LON>
All Strategic Metals..........<O#MINOR>    Mercury Flask-LON......<MER-FLASK-LON>
Arsenic 99.0%-LON.............<ARS-LON>    Molyb.Oxide 57%-LON.....<MLY-OXIDE-LON>
Antinony 99.6%-LON............<ANT-LON>    Molybdenun Ferro-LON....<MLY-FERRO-LON>
Bisnuth 99.99%-LON............<BIS-LON>    Rutheniun-LON...............<RUTH-LON>
Cadnium 99.9%-LON......<CAD-99.99-LON>     Seleniun 99.5%-LON..........<SELE-LON>
Cadnium 99.95%-LON.....<CAD-99.95-LON>     Sil.Lunps 98.5%..............<SIL-LON>
Chrone Mtl 99.0%-LON..........<CRO-LON>    Silicon Fer.75%-LON.....<SIL-FERRO-LON>
Cobalt Ing 99.3%-LON.....<COB-ING-LON>     Tantalite 30/35%-LON........<TANT-LON>
Cobalt Cathodes-LON......<COB-CATH-LON>    Titaniun Sponge-LON....<TIT-SPONGE-LON>
Cobalt-PAR...................<COB-PAR>     Tungst.Fe.80/85%-LON....<TUN-FERRO-LON>
Galliun Ing 99.9%-LON....<GALL-ING-LON>    Van.Pentox 98%-LON......<VAN-PENT-LON>
Gern.Diox 99.9%-LON.....<GERM-DIOX-LON>    Vanadiun Fe.80%-LON.....<VAN-FERRO-LON>
Germaniun-LON................<GERM-LON>    Wolfranite 65%-LON..........<WMITE-LON>
Indiun Ing 99.97%-LON....<IND-ING-LON>
                                           Foreign Exchange Rates..........<FX=S>
                                           World Cross Rates...............<WX=X>
Questions/Conments: contact your local Help Desk - see <PHONE/HELP> for details
===============================================================================
Base Sunmary....<METAL/SUM> Main Index....<COMMOD> Strategic Metals.<STRATEGIC1>
   Lost? Selective Access?..<USER/HELP>    Reuters Phone Support...<PHONE/HELP>
```

```
MER-FLASK-LON      Mercury Flask   Currency -        USD      04NOV98
                   Strategic Metals Lot.Size -    76 LBS      11:44
   Last             Source   Terns 1    Basis      For   :
 B↑140    A150      RTRS     WHS                    info  :
 B↑140    A150      Mkt.Loc  Terns 2    Bas.Mnth   see   :
 B↑140    A150      ANY      ROT                    <M945>:
 Cls:02NOV98        Yr.High  Spec 1     Bas.Loc
 145.00             170      Daily
 Del.Date           Yr.Low   Spec 2     Status
 SPOT               95       99.99%
```

```
                                                                         M945
MMTA Product Norn for: Mercury
~~~~~~~~~~~~~~~~~~~~~~~~~~~~~~~~~
The General Notes & Consolidated Regulations are part of this Product Norn.
1. Origin            :    In Sellers option
2. Tariff No.        :    2805 4010
3. Quality           :    Hg 99.99% nin. Prine Virgin production.
                          No other elenents specified.
4. Forn              :    Free flowing.
5. Packing           :    Original producer's intact iron/steel flasks,
                          each containing 34.5 kilos net. Other than
                          Chinese, where each flask is to be packed in
                          it's own outer protective wooden case, flasks
                          can be supplied with or without additional
                          packing - with any nunber to a case.
                          Regardless whether packed or not, all flasks
                          are to be standing in an upright position and
                          all flat or all round bottoned per release.
6. Lot size          :    50 flasks, with nil tolerance.
7. Documentation     :    Standard documentation, as per MMTA Consolidated
                          Regulations.

contd...<M946>
```

```
SELE-LON           Seleniun        Currency -        USD      04NOV98
                   Strategic Metals Lot.Size -     1 LBS      11:44
   Last             Source   Terns 1    Basis      For   :
 B↑1.2    A1.5      RTRS     WHS                    info  :
 B↑1.2    A1.5      Mkt.Loc  Terns 2    Bas.Mnth   see   :
 B↑1.2    A1.5      ANY      ROT                    <M956>:
 Cls:02NOV98        Yr.High  Spec 1     Bas.Loc
 1.35               4.40     Daily
 Del.Date           Yr.Low   Spec 2     Status
 SPOT               1.5      99.50%
```

```
                                                                         M956
MMTA Product Norn for: Seleniun
~~~~~~~~~~~~~~~~~~~~~~~~~~~~~~~~~
The General Notes & Consolidated Regulations are part of this Product Norn.
1. Origin            :    In Sellers option, excluding Mexico/Russia/
                          C.I.S./forner Yugoslavia/Bulgaria & Chile.
2. Tariff No.        :    2804 9000
3. Quality           :    Se 99.50% nin.
                          No other elenents specified.
4. Forn              :    Powder, ninus 200 nesh.
5. Packing           :    Original producer's packing, in accordance with
                          the IMDG code and RID & ADR Rules. Packages
                          should be clearly narked and labelled in
                          accordance with IMDG & CHIPS (UK) regulations.
6. Lot size          :    500 kilos (+/- 2%) & tolerance
7. Documentation     :    Standard documentation, as per MMTA Consolidated
                          Regulations.
8. Weighing/sampling :    As per MMTA Consolidated Regulations.
9. Other             :

contd...<M957>
```

Precious Metals

These metals include gold, silver and the platinum group metals which have traditionally been important in the financial markets as a haven for money in a financial crisis, for coins and in jewellery manufacture.

Gold and Silver

Most gold and silver traded internationally is cleared by members of the **London Bullion Market Association (LBMA)**. There are two types of LBMA member – market makers from bullion houses and ordinary members. The bullion houses act both as brokers and as primary dealers acting on their own account. In December 1997, British Invisibles estimated that some 43.7 million troy ounces of gold worth $12.7 billion and 396 million troy ounces of Silver worth $2.3 billion were cleared **daily** in London.

London fixes the spot price of gold twice a day and the spot Silver price only once. The gold price is fixed by a small number of LBMA market makers – but how are these fixes made? The spot gold fixing rates occur at 12.00 and 15.00 GMT and the spot rate is used to price OTC physical contracts and mark-to-market open cash market forward contracts. The spot gold fixing rates are used by banks to establish their lending rates and are shown on the Reuters page below.

```
1210              LONDON INTERBANK FORWARD BULLION RATES              GOFO
                  ~~~~~~~~~~~~~~~~~~~~~~~~~~~~~~~~~~~~~~~~

=×=  Loco London Gold, Most Recent Lending Rates (v.USD)  =×=
=×=  TIME CONTRIBUTOR          RATE    11am MEAN - 15FEB  =×=
=×=  1012 DeutscheBk     1 M  4.25   1 M  4.16           =×=
=×=  1012 DeutscheBk     2 M  4.20   2 M  4.14           =×=
=×=  1012 DeutscheBk     3 M  4.15   3 M  4.13           =×=
=×=  1012 DeutscheBk     6 M  4.00   6 M  3.99           =×=
=×=  1012 DeutscheBk    12 M  3.60  12 M  3.58           =×=

                ----- REAL-TIME COMPOSITE SUMMARY -----
TIME  CONTRIBUTOR        1 M   2 M   3 M   6 M   12 M  |
~~~~  ~~~~~~~~~~~        ~~~   ~~~   ~~~   ~~~   ~~~~   |
1240  AIG INTL                                        | Gold Spot, USD OZ
0923  BARCLAYS BANK PLC 4.15  4.10  4.05  3.95  3.55  | =================
0855  CHASE             4.20  4.15  4.15  3.90  3.55  | 1210   289.70/20
0845  CSFB LONDON       4.15  4.10  4.10  4.00  3.60  |
1012  DEUTSCHE LONDON   4.25  4.20  4.15  4.00  3.60  |
1156  J ARON            4.15  4.15  4.15  4.00  3.55  | London Fixings
1559  MIDLAND BANK PLC                                | =================
1122  MORGAN GUARANTY   4.15  4.10  4.10  4.00  3.55  |  AM : 290.05
1159  N M ROTHSCHILD    4.15  4.15  4.15  4.00  3.65  |  PM :
1506  REPUBLIC NAT'L BK                               |
1044  SCOTIAMOCATTA     4.15  4.15  4.15  4.00  3.65  |
0806  U B S             4.15  4.15  4.15  4.00  3.60  |
```

The process of fixing may seem a little unusual in today's electronic marketplace, but illustrates how significant the role of individual market players still is.

The fixing market makers meet in a wood-panelled room at merchant banker and bullion house N.M. Rothchilds. The meeting of this small group is chaired by a representative of N.M. Rothchilds who starts the fixing process by suggesting a price for Gold in USD per ounce based on the most recent market quotation. Each of the other bullion house representatives contacts his trading room using a direct line and then specifies if there is an interest in buying or selling a number of 400 troy ounce gold bars at this price. But how do the representatives indicate interest?

Each representative has a small Union Jack flag attached to a piece of wood. To indicate their interest to the group, a representative raises the flag and says, for example, 'Rothchilds is a buyer of 10 bars'.

If the proposed fix price is $291 per troy ounce, then this represents a value of 400 ounces/bar x 10 bars x $291/bar = $1,164,000. The representative then lowers the flag and each of the other representatives declares their interest on an open outcry basis using his or her flag.

Once all the representatives have indicated their interest, the chairman totals the number of bars on the buy and sell sides. If the numbers on both sides are equal, then the chairman announces **'fix'** and the price is fixed. The chairman also informs the meeting of the current USD/GBP exchange rate at the time of the fix.

If the number of bars on the buy and sell sides do not match, then the chairman suggests a different price level and the process restarts. Market makers can alter their position but must raise their flags and say **"flag"** before they are allowed to change. Although most fixes take place within 20 minutes the chairman can, at his discretion, fix the price if a number of hours have passed and the number of bars on the buy side is no more or less than 15 on the sell side.

Below is a Reuters screen showing the LBMA Index page – listing all pertinent names and details connected with the LBMA – and the LBMA Market Makers page.

After 3.00 P.M., the gold fixing price – as well as fundamental gold information from various countries – is available on electronic news services such as Reuters.

```
15:07 17AUG98    The London Bullion Market Association UK14137        LBMA01
                 6 FREDERICK'S PLACE, LONDON EC2R 8BT
                 TEL: 0171-796 3067 FAX: 0171-796 4345
                 E-MAIL: nail@lbma.org.uk
Chairman: Mr Peter Fava, Midland Bank Plc
Vice Chairman: Mr Martin Stokes, Morgan Guaranty Trust Company
Chief Executive and Company Secretary: Mr Chris Elston
Public Relations Manager: Ms Susanne Capano
-INDEX-
  Brief History ...........................<LBMA02>
  Functions ...............................<LBMA03>
  Membership ..............................<LBMA04>
  Committees ..............................<LBMA05>-<LBMA06>
  Market Makers ...........................<LBMA07>
  Value Dates for 1998.....................<LBMA08>
  Recent Changes to the Good Delivery Lists..<LBMA09>
  Clearing Statistics Overview.............<LBMA11>
  Clearing Turnover........................<LBMA13>
-PRICES-
  LBMA Gold Lending Rates.................<GOFO=> or <O#GOFO=>
  Market-Maker Prices.....................GOFO=XXXX (where XXXX is your
                                          contributor ID. See <LBMA07>)
  Gold Fixing.............................<XAUFIX=>
  Silver Fixing...........................<XAGFIX=>
  Implied Mid-Market Gold Interest Rates..<O#LGLR=> or <LGLR>
```

```
11:52 04SEP98    The London Bullion Market Association UK14137        LBMA07
MARKET MAKERS

* denotes Clearing Member
# denotes Gold Fixing Member
+ denotes Silver Fixing Member

MEMBERS' NAMES                         GOFO Market
                                       Maker Rates    Contributor ID
AIG International Limited...........................<O#GOFO=AIGL>    AIGL
J Aron & Company(Bullion)...........................<O#GOFO=AROL>   AROL
The Bank of Nova Scotia-ScotiaMocatta *#+...........<O#GOFO=MANL>
Barclays Bank Plc...................................<O#GOFO=BBML>   BBML
The Chase Manhattan Bank............................<O#GOFO=CHEL>   CHEL
Credit Suisse First Boston, London Branch *........<O#GOFO=CSCS>   CSCS
Deutsche Bank AG *#+................................<O#GOFO=DBBL>   DBBL
Midland Bank Plc, (trading as HSBC Midland) *#+.....<O#GOFO=MIDL>   HSBC
Morgan Guaranty Trust Company of New York *.........<O#GOFO=JPML>   JPML
N M Rothschild & Sons Limited *#....................<O#GOFO=NMRL>   NMRL
Republic National Bank of New York *#...............<O#GOFO=RBNL>   RBN
Union Bank of Switzerland *.........................<O#GOFO=PADB>   PADB


                                                Main Index <LBMA01>
```

```
XAUFIX=          London Gold Fix   Currency -        USD      09NOV98
                 AM & PM Fix       Lot.Size -      1 OZS       15:09

    Last                    Source    Terms 1    Basis     Fixing:
 ↓292.05    -1.25          RTRS      LON                   times :
  0          0             Mkt.Loc   Terms 2    Bas.Mnth   LON AM:12.00
 ↓292.40    -0.90          LON       LOCO                  LON PM:15.00
Cls:06NOV98                Yr.High   Spec 1     Bas.Loc
 293.30                    302.35    99.99%
Del.Date                   Yr.Low    Spec 2     Status
SPOT                       273.40
```

```
XAGFIX=          London Silver    Currency -        USc      09NOV98
                 PM Fix.          Lot.Size -      500 OZS     12:04

    Last                    Source    Terms 1    Basis     Fixing:
 ↓499.50    -4.00          RTRS      LON                   times :
  0          0             Mkt.Loc   Terms 2    Bas.Mnth   LON PM:12.15
  0          0             LON       LOCO                          :
Cls:06NOV98                Yr.High   Spec 1     Bas.Loc
 503.50                    583.25    99.90%
Del.Date                   Yr.Low    Spec 2     Status
SPOT                       422.35
```

```
JAPAN:GOLD IMPORTS                                          GOLD/JP1

                      Sep-98    Aug-98    Sep-97
Gold
Total (in tonnes)      5.51      3.50      7.17
Mth/Mth pct change    57.40    -20.89     78.37
Yr/Yr pct change     -23.13    -12.89
Run total (cal. yr)   46.60     41.09     92.56

Major Supplier
Australia              3.53      1.00      1.55
South Africa           0.00      0.00      1.58
Switzerland            0.71      0.24      1.95
South Korea            0.03      0.00      0.70
```

Japan is one market providing fundamental gold data.

How Do the Commodities, Energy & Transport Markets Work?

Platinum Group Metals

These metals often occur in association with each other and are therefore often mined and extracted together. These metals are only produced in small quantities and usually command a high price. The group of metals includes the following:

- Platinum, Pt
- Palladium, Pd
- Rhodium, Rh
- Ruthenium, Ru
- Iridium, Ir
- Osmium, Os

Platinum, palladium and rhodium are mainly used in the manufacture of catalytic converters to help remove nitrous oxide gas emissions from vehicle exhausts. As these metals in general are very hard, highly resistant to corrosion and have high melting points, they are used for specialist applications. For example, iridium is used for certain types of spark plug electrodes, osmium and ruthenium are used to tip fountain pen nibs and osmium is used in certain types of electroplating. Gold containing up to 20% palladium is sometimes used in jewellery and described as **white gold**.

It is difficult to obtain world production data for metals other than platinum and palladium. However the United States Geological Survey (USGS) reported that in 1998 the following quantities of the platinum group metals were imported into the US.

Metal	Tonnes
Platinum, Pt	82.0
Palladium, Pd	151.0
Rhodium, Rh	8.6
Ruthenium, Ru	10.2
Iridium, Ir	1.0
Osmium, Os	.75

Cash and Platt's prices – as well as fundamental information about the platinum group metals in various countries – is available on Reuters and other electronic news services.

Precious Metals	Gold, Au	Silver, Ag
Discovery	Gold is a yellow-coloured, shiny metal which has been known and prized since ancient times. It is resistant to corrosion and tarnishing and has been used for jewellery, coins, dishes, bowls, plates and eating utensils for centuries. It has long been a symbol of wealth. The 1840s and 1850s saw the gold-rushes of California and Australia. In 1873 the South African Transvaal gold-fields were opened and the Klondike rush of 1897 established Canada and Alaska as gold producers.	Silver is a shiny metal which is an excellent conductor of heat and electricity. It has been known since ancient times when it was discovered as a by-product of base metal mining. The "queen of metals" was used for jewellery coins, bowls etc and again as a symbol of wealth. To be born "with a silver spoon in one's mouth" was an old expression indicating the high cost of silver cutlery. Silver was mined near Aberystwyth at the Gogerddan mines in the 1660s and provided its owner with an annual profit of £25,000.
Uses	Gold is a reserve asset in international financial affairs and has played a special role in international foreign exchange and investment in the past. The historical associations of gold with the markets are many, for example, Gilts. Gold also has kept its real value in times of economic crisis, war etc. Vast stocks of gold are held by all major economies – the legendary US Fort Knox holdings are the world's largest. In the late 1990s, some of the world's central banks and the International Monetary Fund (IMF) depressed world gold prices by divesting large amounts of gold from their reserves. Gold is used in the manufacture of jewellery and scientific instruments. Smaller amounts are used for electrical and electronic components, coins, medals and dentistry.	Most silver produced is used in the photographic, jewellery and electronic industries. It is also used in the manufacture of modern batteries. Silver is considered to be the "poor man's gold" as an investment but governments and investors hold large quantities of silver bullion, coins and art-objects to hedge the markets. The legendary American investor Warren Buffet, bought huge quantities of silver in 1998. "Challenge" cups and trophies have traditionally been made of silver. In the early nineteenth century a Birmingham pub had a silver cup known as the "Fine Slapper". Anyone committing a breach of good manners had to drink a slapper of ale – 3 pints!
Annual Production	New or primary = 2,400 metric tonnes = 77.16 million troy ounces	New or primary = 16,200 metric tonnes = 520.84 million troy ounces
Exchange Markets	London Bullion Market and COMEX. There are spot markets in London, New York and Zurich and futures markets in New York and Tokyo.	London Bullion Market and COMEX. The markets are orientated about futures contracts.
Countries of Origin	South Africa is the largest producer – about 65%. Other producers include US, Australia, Canada and Russia.	Mexico, Peru, US, Canada and Australia.
Major Consumers		US (largest consumer), Japan, Western Europe
Major Influences on Price	• Hoarding • Government • Production problems	• Economic factors • Currency stability

Precious Metals	Platinum, Pt	Palladium, Pd
Discovery	Native platinum was discovered in Peru in 1735 by the Spanish and called Platina del Pinto – little silver of the River Pinto. At the time platinum had little commercial value – even in 1874 its market price was only £1.25 per Troy ounce. The silver-white metal is soft and ductile which means it can be drawn into wires easily. It is also extremely resistant to corrosion and chemical attack.	Palladium is an even more precious metal than Platinum. It is a grey-white, very ductile and easily worked metal. It was discovered in 1803 and is named after the planet – Pallas. Its properties are very similar to those of platinum.
Uses	Most platinum is used for jewellery and for catalysts, both in the industrial chemical processing industry and in automobile emission systems to combat vehicle pollution. Platinum is also used to a small extent in scientific instruments.	Palladium is used in the electrical, dental and catalyst manufacturing industries, consuming about 90% of the annual supply of palladium. An alloy of gold and palladium is known as white gold – because of its colour – and is used for expensive jewellery.
Annual Production	New or primary = 155,000 kg = 155 metric tonnes	New or primary = 125,000 kg = 125 metric tonnes
Exchange Markets	NYMEX, Tokyo Commodity Exchange (TCE) and Mid America Commodity Exchange (MACE).	NYMEX.
Countries of Origin	South Africa is the largest producer – about 80%. Other producers include Russia, Canada and US.	Canada and US.
Major Consumers	Japan and the US for catalysts used in motor vehicles.	Japan and the US for catalysts used in motor vehicles.
Major Influences on Price	• Hoarding • Government • Production problems • Economic factors • Currency stability	

The Reuters screens on this page comprise the European Strategic Metals Physical Price Quotations.

```
EUROPEAN STRATEGIC METALS PHYSICAL PRICE QUOTATIONS          STRATEGIC/EU1
Prices valid at:12Feb99
Metal               Current    Previous   Date of   Logical          Spec
Name                Price      Price      Change    RIC              Page
~~~~~               ~~~~~~~    ~~~~~~~~   ~~~~~~~    ~~~~~~~          ~~~~

Antinony Metal 99.65  1400/1480  1380/1480  28Jan99  <ANT-LON>        <M901>
Antinony Metal 99.85  1600/1700  1500/1700  28Jan99  <ANT-HG-LON>     <M903>
Arsenic               0.4/0.48   0.4/0.48   28Jan99  <ARS-LON>        <M905>
Bismuth               2.8/3.1    2.8/3.1    09Feb99  <BIS-LON>        <M906>
Cadnium 99.95         0.2/0.25   0.18/0.25  09Feb99  <CAD-99.95-LON>  <M907>
Cadnium 99.99         0.25/0.35  0.21/0.35  09Feb99  <CAD-99.99-LON>  <M907>
Chrone, Al. CH        4300/4500  4400/4600  12Feb99  <CRO-ALUM-CHINA> <M908>
Chrone, Al. RU x99    4300/4500  4400/4600  12Feb99  <CRO-ALUM-RU>    <M911>
Chrone, El. Degassed  9/10       8/10       19Mar98  <CRO-LON>        <M913>
Chrone, El. Standard  4/5        3/5        19Mar98  <CRO-EL-RU>      <M915>
Fe Chrone, Hi Carbon  0.32/0.35  0.33/0.35  09Feb99  <FECRO-HC-RU>    -
Fe Chrone, Lo Carbon  0.64/0.68  0.64/0.68  09Feb99  <FECRO-LC-RU>    -
Cobalt Cathodes 99.8  19/21      18.5/21    09Feb99  <COB-CATH-LON>   <M919>
Cobalt (ZCCM C) 99.6  17/19      14/19      29Jan99  <COB-99.6-ZA>    <M928>
Cobalt (RU) Ing 99.3  16.5/18    8.25/9.25  29Jan99  <COB-ING-LON>    <M923>
Gallium Ingots
Germaniun 50ohn/cn
Germaniun Diox 99.99

More...<STRATEGIC/EU2>
```

```
EUROPEAN STRATEGIC METALS PHYSICAL PRICE QUOTATIONS          STRATEGIC/EU2
Prices valid at:12Feb99
Metal               Current    Previous   Date of   Logical          Spec
Name                Price      Price      Change    RIC              Page
~~~~~               ~~~~~~~    ~~~~~~~~   ~~~~~~~    ~~~~~~~          ~~~~

Indiun                180/200    185/215    05Jan99  <IND-ING-LON>    <M941>
Iridiun               385/415    375/415    08Feb99  <IRID-LON>       <M947>
Magnesiun 99.9 China  1900/2000  1950/2000  22Jan99  <MGN-CHINA>      <M942>
Magnesiun 99.9 RU     2250/2350  2300/2350  14Jan99  <MGN-RU>         <M942>
Magnesiun 99.9 Uk     2200/2300  2225/2300  14Jan99  <MGN-UA>         <M942>
Manganese Electro 99. 1080/1140  1070/1140  07Jan99  <MNG-LON>        <M944>
Manganese Ferro (HC)  420/430    430/430    06Nov98  <MNG-FERRO-LON>  <M778>
Mercury Flask         135/145    135/145    14Jan99  <MER-FLASK-LON>  <M945>
Molyb Mo3 - Western   3/3.2      2.9/3.2    09Feb99  <MLY-OXIDE-LON>  <M969>
Molyb MoO3 - Chinese  2.9/3.1    2.7/3.1    09Feb99  <MLY-CH57-LON>   <M964>
Molyb Fe 65 Western   7.8/8.2    7.4/8.2    04Feb99  <MLY-FERRO-LON>  <M968>
Molyb Fe 60 Chinese   7.7/8.1    7.6/8.1    09Feb99  <MLY-F60-LON>    -
Rhodiun               865/900    865/900    01Feb99  <RHOD-LON>       <M952>
Ruthenium             39/42      39/42      15Dec98  <RUTH-LON>       <M954>
Seleniun              1.5/1.8    1.4/1.8    14Jan99  <SELE-LON>       <M956>
Silicon Metal Lunps
Silicon Fe 75 Russian
Tantalite

More...<STRATEGIC/EU3>
```

```
EUROPEAN STRATEGIC METALS PHYSICAL PRICE QUOTATIONS          STRATEGIC/EU3
Prices valid at:12Feb99
Metal               Current    Previous   Date of   Logical          Spec
Name                Price      Price      Change    RIC              Page
~~~~~               ~~~~~~~    ~~~~~~~~   ~~~~~~~    ~~~~~~~          ~~~~

Titaniun Sponge 99.6  6.6/7      6.8/7      23Jul98  <TIT-SPONGE-LON> <M788>
Titaniun Ferro        2/2.4      2/2.4      09Feb99  <TIT-FERRO-LON>  <M977>
Tungstate APT         49/52      50/52      16Dec98  <APT-CHINA>      -
Tungsten Ferro        5.9/6.2    5.7/6.2    10Dec98  <TUN-FERRO-LON>  <M973>
Vanadiun Fe 80 (T2)   12.5/13.25 12.5/13.25 09Feb99  <VAN-FERRO-LON>  <M982>
Vanadiun Fe 50 (T1)   12/12.2    12.5/12.2  07Jan99  <VAN-F50-RU>     <M979>
Vanadiun Pentox       2.4/2.6    2.6/2.6    04Feb99  <VAN-PENT-LON>   <M791>
Wolfranite            40/45      39/45      19Mar98  <WMITE-LON>      <M792>

Prev...<STRATEGIC/EU2>   Full RIC Listing...<OHMINOR>   Metals Index...<METAL1>
```

How Do the Commodities, Energy & Transport Markets Work?

Softs

The most important of the soft commodities products traded internationally are Coffee, Cocoa and Sugar. The other softs covered in this text include the following:

- Rubber

- Tea

- Pepper

- Citrus and tropical fruits

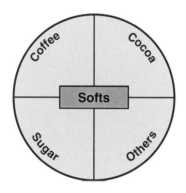

Cash and Futures Contracts Prices

The cash prices quoted for softs by news services are either official prices, prices supplied by contributors or prices obtained by reporters who are in constant communication with their contacts in the markets. As in other commodity markets these cash prices should be used as indicative values only.

Futures contracts prices are a reflection of the cash markets and prices for softs can be found on the news services.

The Reuters screens below show the sequence of screens leading to robusta coffee futures prices.

```
O#SOFTS-FUT        SOFTS FUTURES    Exchange
RIC                Contract         ID
O#COCCHN           Cocoa Futures    RCT/
O#COFCHN           Coffee Futures   RCT/
O#OJCHN            Orange Futures   RCT/
O#POTCHN           Potato Futures   RCT/
O#SUGCHN           Sugar Futures    RCT/
O#RUBCHN           Rubber Futures   RCT/
```

```
O#COFCHN               Coffee Futures  Exchange
RIC                    Contract        ID
O#KC:                  COFFEE          CSC/
O#LKD:                 ROBUSTA COFFEE $ LIF/
O#KB:                  BRZL COFFEE     CSC/
O#CFC:                 COFFEE          BMF/
O#CFR:                 COF ROBUSTA     BMF/
O#SKD:                 SICOM COFF      SIC/
O#JAC:                 TOKYO ARABICA     /
O#JRC:                 TOKYO ROBUSTA     /
```

```
O#LKD:          ROBUSTA COFFEE $ LIF/    USD
                                    Tot.V  5974      Tot.OI  44077
Mth   Last  Last1 Net  Bid   Ask  PrvSet Open High Low  Volume Op.Int Sett
NOV8 12040  2040  -85  2025  2035 2125   2115 2115 2025  412   5345
JAN9 11670  1671  -55  1668  1670 1725   1720 1725 1665  3725  24960
MAR9 11626  1628  -44  1623  1627 1670   1670 1670 1624  1181  8710
MAY9 11606  1608  -40  1600  1610 1646   1645 1647 1605  656   3565
JUL9                              1592   1631                  991
SEP9                              1580   1616                  276
NOV9                                     1596                  230
```

Each commodity in the softs markets is now described in a little more detail covering production, countries of origin, consumption and some of the more interesting statistics about these plantation crops.

84 *An Introduction to the Commodities, Energy & Transport Markets*

REUTERS

Coffee, Cocoa and Sugar

These are the three major softs traded worldwide and to put their importance into perspective the following statistics have been taken from a variety of sources. Following these charts are brief descriptions of each of the major markets. For each of these softs there is an international organisation that publishes official or index prices on a daily basis. These organisations are as follows:

- **International Coffee Organisation (ICO)**
- **International Cocoa Organisation (ICCO)**
- **International Sugar Organisation (ISO)**

Coffee

This chart shows the world supply of types of coffee for the period 1996/97.

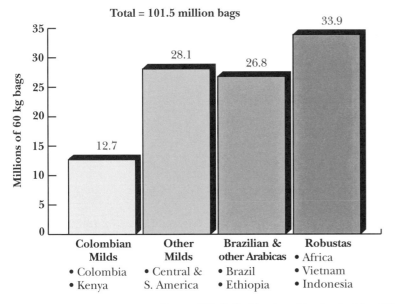

Source: ICO Coffee Newsletter Number 8 – May 1998

Cocoa

This chart shows the ICCO daily price average in USD/tonne for the period 1991–1998.

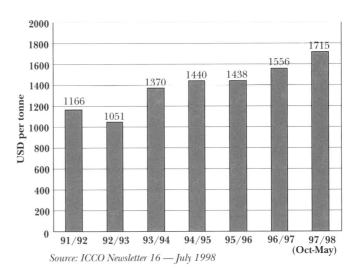

Source: ICCO Newsletter 16 — July 1998

Sugar

This chart shows the world production of sugar for the period 1992–2000 in million metric tonnes.

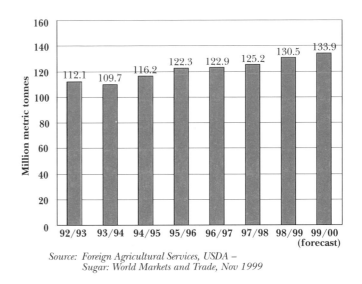

Source: Foreign Agricultural Services, USDA –
Sugar: World Markets and Trade, Nov 1999

How Do the Commodities, Energy & Transport Markets Work?

Softs	Coffee	Coffee Markets
Production  Coffee "cherries"	Coffee beans, or seeds, grow on evergreen bushes up to 10 metres high. Coffee bushes originated in Ethiopia/Africa but are now grown in some 80 different countries. When ripe, the beans are 15–18 mm long, red in colour and are known as "cherries". There are two main types of coffee: **arabica** and **robusta**, each requiring different growing conditions. **Arabicas** grow best at 600–2000 metres above sea-level in sub-tropical to temperate climates and are cultivated mostly in Brazil and Colombia. **Robustas** grow in tropical rain forest conditions up to 800 metres altitude and are cultivated mainly in Africa and Indonesia. Once the beans are harvested they can be processed in two ways. In Brazil and Ethiopia the beans are sun-dried either before or after being separated from the outer cherry shell. These beans are known as "hard" or "unwashed". With wet processing the cherries are soaked in water, the beans separated and finally dried. This process results in "soft" or "mild" coffee. Coffee is harvested somewhere in the world almost every month of the year. For example: Brazil — Apr–Sept Ivory Coast — Nov–Apr Colombia — Oct–Mar Angola — May–Sept	Arabica beans about 70% of the world markets and Robusta 30%. Brazil has nearly 30% of the global export coffee market. Coffee-producing countries such as Brazil and Colombia have special government-owned or -controlled agencies to regulate the market. Although the preference is for arabica beans, robusta coffee production is gaining in importance as the demand for instant coffee increases. Most physical trading takes place in New York, London, Hamburg and Rotterdam. Arabica futures and options are traded on the New York Coffee, Sugar and Cocoa Exchange (NYCSCE), while robusta futures and options are traded on LIFFE. Arabica and robusta futures are available from BM&F and MATIF trades futures in robusta. The **International Coffee Organisation (ICO)** publishes daily and 15 day average prices for arabica and robusta coffees.
Countries of Origin	Brazil, Colombia, Ivory Coast, Tanzania, Kenya and Angola.	**Consumers** — Europe and the US are the major consumers accounting for about 60% of world coffee imports.
Major Influences on Price	• Weather, for example, frost • Stock levels • Crop forecasts • Economic statistics • Plant disease • Industrial relations	**Market size** — 97.3 million 60 kg bags = 5.84 million metric tonnes 1997

REUTERS :)

Softs	Cocoa	Cocoa Markets
Production 	Cocoa beans grow in large pods on the cocoa, or cacao, tree. Each pod has from 20–0 beans, or seeds, about 2.5cm long. A mature tree may bear 60–70 pods annually. After harvesting the pods are split and the beans removed. They are then left a few days before drying, cleaning and roasting. Once harvested and roasted the beans are exported. The next step in the production process is grinding the roasted beans. Grinding is carried out by large corporations or processors and yields a paste called **chocolate liquor**. This liquor is then pressed to produce **cocoa butter** and **cocoa powder**. The major use of the butter and powder is in chocolate confectionery products. The Ivory Coast – Ghana and Nigeria – is the largest producer of cocoa. The majority of the crop is harvested in the "main crop" period October to March. The remaining is harvested in the "mid crop" period of May to July. The growing tendency is for cocoa-producing countries to process a larger share of their production thus reducing the amount of beans available for export.	Cocoa prices are most influenced by prospective or actual changes in supply. Both the nature of the commodity and terrain where it is grown make it difficult to estimate production levels accurately. The market is therefore very sensitive to reports of disease, adverse industrial relations etc. The **International Cocoa Organisation (ICCO)** publishes daily prices based on the London and New York markets. Futures and options on cocoa are traded on both LIFFE and NYCSCE. Kuala Lumpur trades futures in cocoa.

Countries of Origin	Ghana, Nigeria, Brazil, Malaysia and Indonesia.	**Consumers**	The developed world, in particular the US and Europe, account for most consumption of the crop.
Major Influences on Price	• Weather, for example, frost • Stock levels • Crop forecasts • Economic statistics • Plant disease • Industrial relations	**Market size**	2.72 million metric tonnes 1997

How Do the Commodities, Energy & Transport Markets Work?

Softs	Sugar	Sugar Markets
Production 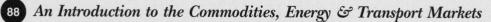	The world's sugar supplies come from two sources. **Sugar cane** is a giant grass with canes growing from 3–8 metres tall and 2.5–5 cm in diameter. Sugar cane is grown in warm, moist, tropical or sub-tropical climates and is the main source of sugar. **Sugar beet** is a type of root vegetable which is similar in appearance to a parsnip. It is grown in temperate or cold climates, mostly in the Northern hemisphere. With sugar cane, the growing and processing of the crop is highly integrated. The output, **raw sugar**, is then delivered to separate refineries, which produce refined sugar products. Sugar beet is grown in rotation with other crops and the type of sugar produced is **refined** or **white sugar**. The by-product of sugar refining is **molasses**. The majority of sugar traded is raw sugar – about 75% of the world's annual production. The harvesting period varies widely for sugar cane, usually taking place between autumn and early summer. Sugar beet is harvested mainly in the autumn. Sugar demand is seasonal with the highest requirements during the summer months when sugar is used in soft drinks, canning and preserving.	Only about 15% of the world sugar production is traded on the open market. The remainder is either consumed in the country of origin where many governments subsidise both output and consumption or it is sold at cheap rates under special trade agreements. However, the amount available on the free market is still significant. Small changes in the availability of sugar result in dramatic changes in world prices. The **International Sugar Organisation (ISO)** publishes average prices for raws in London and New York. Futures and options are traded for both raw and white sugar on both LIFFE and NYCSCE. On LIFFE the No: 5 contract is for White Sugar futures and options whilst the No: 7 contract is for Raw Sugar futures only. Both MATIF and NYCSCE trade futures in White sugar; NYCSCE and the Tokyo Grain Exchange trade futures in Raw Sugar.

Countries of Origin	Cane – Cuba, Brazil, Australia, Mexico, Philippines and India. Beet – Russia, France, Germany, Poland and the US.	**Consumers**	Russia, Europe, India and the US.
Major Influences on Price	• Weather, for example, frost • Stock levels • Crop forecasts • Economic statistics • Plant disease • Industrial relations	**Market size**	123 million metric tonnes 1997

REUTERS :::

Before moving on, review the Reuters screens on this page showing global news and pricing for coffee, cocoa and sugar.

```
COFFEE - REUTERS SPEED GUIDE                                COFFEE/CASH1
To access information double-click in <> or [ ].For nore guidance see<USER/HELP>

=PHYSICAL COFFEE CONTRACTS=============    =NEWS AND ANALYSIS====================
African Coffee Prices...<O#COFFEE-AFR>     Coffee News.......................[COF]
Arabica Coffee Prices...<O#COFFEE-ARA>     Softs News........................[SOF]
Brazilian Coffee Prices..<O#COFFEE-BR>     All Commodities News................[C]
Brenen Coffee Prices.....<O#COFFEE-BRE>    Latest Coffee Report.............[COF/]
Colombian Coffee Prices...<O#COFFEE-CO>    New York Coffee Report..........[COF/N]
Global Coffee Cash Prices....<O#COFFEE>    London Coffee Report............[COF/L]
ICO Coffee Prices........<O#COFFEE-ICO>    F.O.Licht Coffee Report.....[LICHT-COF]
Indonesian Coffee Prices..<O#COFFEE-ID>    All Other Reports.................[C/R]
New York Coffee Prices...<O#COFFEE-NYC>    WSC Coffee Weather..............<WSAA>
Robusta Coffee Prices...<O#COFFEE-ROB>     Political/Economic News........[NEWS]
S.American Coffee.........<O#COFFEE-S>     Sport News........................[SPO]
Linwood Coorg Coffee, India...<LINWOOD>
Asia Coffee inc.IND &VIET<COFFEE/ASIA1>
Brazil
```

```
O#COFFEE              COFFEE PHYSICALS
Connodity        Del.Date    Last            Srce   Terms   Loc  Ccy Units
KENYA TT         SPOT     L ↑ 111.00 H 157.00 RTRS  FOB NAI  KEN  USD KG50
KENYA C          SPOT     L ↑ 132.00 H 144.00 RTRS  FOB NAI  KEN  USD KG50
KENYA AB         SPOT     L ↓ 118.00 H 167.00 RTRS  FOB NAI  KEN  USD KG50
KENYA E          SPOT     L ↑ 155.00 H 168.00 RTRS  FOB NAI  KEN  USD KG50
KENYA PB         SPOT     L ↑ 134.00 H 163.00 RTRS  FOB NAI  KEN  USD KG50
KENYA AA         SPOT     L ↑ 141.00 H 181.00 RTRS  FOB NAI  KEN  USD KG50
KENYA MISC       SPOT     L ↓ 26.00 H 154.00 RTRS   FOB NAI  KEN  USD KG50
BRAZIL           SPOT     ↑ 117.00  +16.00    RTRS  FOB BRE  BRA  USD KG50
COLOMBIAN EXELSO SPOT     ↑ 133.00  +9.00     RTRS  FOB BRE  COL  USD KG50
SALVADOR SHG     SPOT     ↑ 135.00  +18.00    RTRS  FOB BRE  SAL  USD KG50
GUATEMALA HB     SPOT     ↑ 132.00  +9.00     RTRS  FOB BRE  GUA  USD KG50
COST RICA        SPOT     ↑ 136.00  +12.00    RTRS  FOB BRE  COS  USD KG50
KENYA AB         SPOT     ↑ 165.00  +7.00     RTRS  FOB BRE  KEN  USD KG50
ZAIRE            SPOT                         RTRS  FOB BRE  ZAI  USD KG50
Vietnam G-2      SPOT     ↓ 74.50   -15.00    RTRS  CIF BRE  VN   USD KG50
Indonesian EK-1  SPOT       0        0        RTRS  CIF BRE  ID   USD KG50
MEDAN 4B                    0        0        ICE   FOB JKT  ID   USc
PALEMBUNG 4B     DEC      ↑ 177.00  +2.00     ICE   FOB JKT  ID   USc KG
LAMPUNG 4B       DEC      ↑ 176.00  +2.00     ICE   FOB JKT  ID   USc KG
SURABAYA 4B      DEC      ↑ 177.00  +2.00     ICE   FOB JKT  ID   USc KG
SURABAYA 1                  0        0        ICE   FOB JKT  ID   USc KG
```

```
COCOA - REUTERS SPEED GUIDE                                 COCOA/CASH1
To access information double-click in <> or [ ].For nore guidance see<USER/HELP>

=PHYSICAL COCOA ========================    =NEWS AND ANALYSIS===================
Indonesian&Malasyain Cocoa<COCOA/ASIA1>     Cocoa News........................[COC]
European Cocoa.............<COCOA/EU1>      Softs News........................[SOF]
Ghana Cocoa...............<O#COCOA-GH>      All Commodities News................[C]
ICCO Cocoa................<O#COCOA-ICCO>
New York Cocoa............<O#COCOA-NYC>     Latest Cocoa Report.............[COC/]
                                            London Cocoa Report............[COC/L]
Cocoa Market Overview........<O#COCOA>      New York Cocoa Report..........[COC/N]
                                            Ghana Cocoa....................[COC/G]
=CROSS MARKET FOCUS===============          Bahia Cocoa....................[COC/B]
Foreign
World
Stock
Cross M
```

```
O#COCOA            COCOA PHYSICALS
Connodity       Del.Date   Last            Srce      Terms   Loc  Ccy Units
DAILY (SDR)     SPOT    ↓1134.88  -21.45   ICCO      LON     -    XDR TONNE
DAILY (USD)     SPOT    ↓1590.52  -30.25   ICCO      LON     -    USD TONNE
IvCst G.Fern    SPOT    ↓1681.00  -6.00    US ME EXD US       CI  USD TONNE
Brazil Bahia    SPOT    ↓1662.00  -6.00    US ME EXD US       BRA USD TONNE
Rep.Don Sanchez SPOT    ↓1534.00  -6.00    US ME EXD US       DOM USD TONNE
Indo. Sulawesi  SPOT    ↓1464.00  -6.00    US ME EXD US       ID  USD TONNE
Ecuador Arriba  SPOT    ↓1874.00  -6.00    US ME EXD US       ECU USD TONNE
Malaysia Stand  SPOT    ↓1496.00  -6.00    US ME EXD US       MY  USD TONNE
Ecuador Liquor  SPOT    ↓2310.00  -10.00   US ME EXD US       ECU USD TONNE
Brazil Liquor   SPOT    ↓2334.00  -10.00   US ME EXD US       BRA USD TONNE
Africa Butter   SPOT    ↓3750.00  -15.00   US ME EXD US       -   USD TONNE
                SPOT    ↓3750.00  -15.00   US ME EXD US       BRA USD TONNE
Misc. Natcake   SPOT    ↓ 730.00  -3.00    US ME EXD US       -   USD TONNE
GHANA DIFF-S    SPOT    ↓ 85.00   0        RTRS      CIF UK   GHA GBP TONNE
GHANA DIFF-1    OCT/DEC ↑ 65.00   0        RTRS      CIF UK   GHA GBP TONNE
GHANA DIFF-2    NOV/JAN ↓ 35.00   0        RTRS      CIF UK   GHA GBP TONNE
GHANA DIFF-3    DEC/FEB ↓ 35.00   0        RTRS      CIF UK   GHA GBP TONNE
```

```
SUGAR - REUTERS SPEED GUIDE                                 SUGAR/CASH1
To access information double-click in <> or [ ].For nore guidance see<USER/HELP>

=SUGAR=============================== ==    =NEWS AND ANALYSIS===================
European Sugar Prices......<O#SUGAR-EU>     Sugar News........................[SUG]
Global Sugar Cash Prices......<O#SUGAR>     All Softs News....................[SOF]
London Sugar Prices....<O#SUGAR-LON>       All Commodities News................[C]
Ukranian Nat. Exch. Assoc....<CHEMON2>
Thai Sugar preniums and Chinese cash       Latest Sugar Report.............[SUG/]
prices...................<SUGAR/ASIA1>      New York Sugar Report..........[SUG/N]
European Sugar..............<SUGAR/EU1>
Sugar Mill and Refinery................     F.O.Licht Sugar Report......[LICHT-SUG]
Projects.
```

```
O#SUGAR             SUGAR PHYSICALS
Connodity        Del.Date   Last           Srce   Terms       Loc  Ccy Units
ISA DAILY SUGAR  SPOT    ↓  7.99  -0.08    ISO    FOB LON     -    USc LBS
ISA 15 DAY AVGE  SPOT    ↑  7.74  +0.01    ISO    FOB LON     -    USc LBS
WORLD 11         SPOT    ↓  8.43  -0.06    RTRS   FOB NYC     -    USc LBS
WORLD 11 AVG     SPOT    ↓  7.90  -0.01    RTRS   FOB NYC     -    USc LBS
Daily Indicator  SPOT    ↓ 118.00 -1.10    LIFFE  UK  UK      -    GBP TONNE
LON FOB White    SPOT    ↓ 231.80 -4.00    LIFFE  FOB UK      ANY  USD TONNE
LON CIF Raw      SPOT    ↓ 196.00 -1.80    LIFFE  CIF UK      -    USD TONNE
LON FOB Equiv    SPOT    ↓ 175.00 -1.80    LIFFE  FOB UK      -    USD TONNE
Freight Carib/UK SPOT    ↑  21.00  0       LIFFE       -      -    USD TONNE
USD Daily        SPOT    ↓ 233.00 -3.00    RTRS   FOB PAR     ANY  USD TONNE
FRF Daily        SPOT    ↓1312.0  -3.0     RTRS   FOB PAR     ANY  FRF TONNE
EU CANE          SPOT    ↑  16.20  0       EC     EUinport    ANY  XEU KG
EU BEET SUGAR    SPOT    ↑  16.20  0       EC     LON EUinport ANY XEU KG
EU WHITE         SPOT    ↑  19.18 +1.68    EC     EUinport    ANY  XEU KG
EU CANE DUTY     SPOT    ↓  8.30   0       EC     EUinport    ANY  XEU KG
EU BEET DUTY     SPOT    ↓  8.07   0       EC     EUinport    ANY  XEU KG
EU WHITE DUTY    SPOT    ↓  11.53 -1.18    EC     EUinport    ANY  XEU KG
```

Rubber

Natural rubber is produced throughout SE Asia by tapping the bark of a number of different species of trees for latex. The three largest producing countries are Thailand, Indonesia and Malaysia. In 1996 the world production of natural rubber was 6.34 million metric tonnes and the world consumption of natural rubber was approximately 39% of all natural and synthetic rubber products. About 70% of the world consumption of natural rubber is used in the manufacture of vehicle tires. Most natural rubber is traded using privately negotiated deals – over 80% of rubber production comes from small farms of two hectares or less. There are important trading centres in Singapore and Indonesia. Futures contracts on Rubber are traded on the Singapore International Commodity Exchange (SICOM) and the TCE.

Synthetic rubber is derived from petroleum and alcohol sources and represents the remaining 61% of world production. Synthetic rubber is both manufactured and consumed in the US, Europe and Russia predominantly in the production of vehicle tires. International organisations such as the Association of International Rubber Traders (AIRT) and the International Natural Rubber Organisation (INRO) publish spot and average rubber prices. The chart below shows the average daily market indicator price published by INRO for the period 1990–1997.

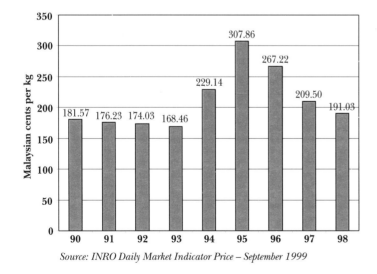

Source: INRO Daily Market Indicator Price – September 1999

The Reuters screens below are the Rubber Speed Guide, an index of rubber-related news items, and a page detailing A.I.R.T. Rubber prices.

```
RUBBER - REUTERS SPEED GUIDE                          RUBBER/CASH1
To access information double-click in <> or [ ].For more guidance see<USER/HELP>

=RUBBER=============================   =NEWS AND ANALYSIS==================
AIRT Price Chain........<O#RUBBER-AIRT>   Rubber News....................[RUB]
ICE Rubber, Noon........<O#RUBBER-IDNN>   Softs News.....................[SOF]
ICE Rubber, Close.......<O#RUBBER-IDCL>   All Commodities News.............[C]
Indonesian Rubber.......<O#RUBBER-ID>     Latest Rubber Report..........[RUB/]
Malaysian Rubber........<O#RUBBER-MY>     Singapore Report.............[RUB/L]
NY Rubber Prices........<O#RUBBER-NYC>    Malaysian Report.............[RUB/M]
RSS1 Rubber.............<O#RUBBER-RSS1>   Tokyo Report.................[RUB/T]
RSS2 Rubber.............<O#RUBBER-RSS2>   Kobe Report..................[RUB/K]
RSS3 Rubber.............<O#RUBBER-RSS3>   Kobe Exchange Commentary.....<KRECO>
Singapore Rubber........<O#RUBBER-RAS>    Colombo Report...............[RUB/O]
SIR20 Rubber...........<O#RUBBER-SIR20>   All Other Reports.............[C/R]
TSR20 Rubber...........<O#RUBBER-TSR20>   WSC Weather Report..........<WTHR>
Thailand Rubber........<O#RUBBER-THAI>    Political/Economic News......[NEWS]
                                          Sport News...................[SPO]




Questions/Comments: Contact your local Help Desk - see <PHONE/HELP> for details
=================================================================
Softs Index<SOFT1>       Rubber Index<RUBBER1>      Rubber Futures<RUBBER/FUT1>
   Lost?Selective Access?...<USER/HELP>    Reuters Phone Support...<PHONE/HELP>
```

```
O#RUBBER-AIRT          A.I.R.T. RUBBER
Commodity       Del.Date      Last        Srce   Terms    Loc  Ccy Units
RSS1 OFFICIAL    DEC      B↓  49.00  A50.00  AIRT  CIF LON  Mult GBp  KG
RSS2 OFFICIAL    DEC      B↓  48.50  A49.50  AIRT  CIF LON  Mult GBp  KG
RSS3 OFFICIAL    DEC      B↓  47.50  A48.50  AIRT  CIF LON  Mult GBp  KG
RSS1-1 OFFICIAL  JAN      B↓  49.50  A50.50  AIRT  CIF LON  Mult GBp  KG
INRA RSS1 MKTIND DEC      ↓   50.00  0       AIRT  CIF EUR  ANY  GBp  KG
INRA RSS3 MKTIND DEC      ↓   48.50  0       AIRT  CIF EUR  ANY  GBp  KG
INRA TSR20MKTIND DEC      ↑   41.25  0       AIRT  CIF EUR  MY/I GBp  KG
INRO INDICATOR   SPOT     ↓  179.60  -0.32   INRO  KUL      ANY  MYc  KG
INRO AVERAGE     SPOT     ↓  178.81  0       INRO  KUL      ANY  MYc  KG
SRILANKA SOLE CR DEC      ↓  144.00  0       RTRS  LON      GBp  KG
```

Tea

Tea is an evergreen tropical plant that is grown mainly on the Indian sub-continent, in East Africa and in China. Tea is a physical crop and is grown on estates – often as large as 100 hectares – and on smallholdings – as small as 0.5 hectares – as bushes are approximately one metre high and spaced in rows for easy picking, which is still done mostly by hand. The beverage is made from the leaves and leaf buds which are plucked every 7–14 days. An experienced tea plucker can harvest 30–35 kg of leaves in a day which will produce 7.5–9.0 kg of processed **black tea**. This means that the leaves have been allowed to ferment before they are dried and cut. Most tea is a blend of leaves – up to 35 different varieties can be mixed together for the quality, character and taste required.

Tea trading takes place by auction in Mombasa, Calcutta and Jakarta, where tea is bought and distributed via brokers to the international markets. Tea was first auctioned in England on a regular basis by the East India Company in the City of London in 1687 and by 1706 dedicated tea auctions were held quarterly. The last tea auction in London was held on 29th June 1998. Why? The majority of tea trading now takes place directly between plantations and the four larger tea blenders – Twinings, Brooke Bond, Lipton and Lyons. This factor, combined with an increase in trading via the Internet, meant that it was no longer economical to hold auctions in London.

An early London Tea auction: Courtesy the Tea Council

These Reuters screens show the Speed Guide for Tea, with detailed price information about Kenya tea.

```
TEA - REUTERS SPEED GUIDE                                           TEA1
To access information double-click in <> or [ ].For more guidance see<USER/HELP>

=TEA CASH - KEY DISPLAYS===============  =TEA CASH CONTRACTS BY LOCATION========
Calcutta...................<O#TEA-CCU>   Calcutta...................<TEA/CASH1>
Colombo....................<O#TEA-CMB>   Colombo....................<TEA/CASH2>
CTC Broken.................<O#TEA-CTCBRK> Kenya......................<TEA/CASH5>
CTC Fannings...............<O#TEA-CTCFAN>
CTC........................<O#TEA-CTC>   =NEWS AND ANALYSIS==================
Dooars.....................<O#TEA-DOOARS> All Commodities News...............[C]
Dust.......................<O#TEA-DUST>  All Softs News..................[SOF]
Kenya......................<O#TEA-KE>
```

```
O#TEA-KE              KENYA TEA
Commodity      Del.Date      Last          Srce    Terms    Loc  Ccy Units
BEST BP1       SPOT        ↑ 2.22  +0.02    RTRS  AUC NBO    MANY USD  KG
BEST PF1       SPOT        ↑ 2.10  +0.07    RTRS  AUC NBO    MANY USD  KG
BEST PDUST     SPOT        ↑ 2.31  +0.01    RTRS  AUC NBO    MANY USD  KG
BEST DUST      SPOT        ↓ 2.33  -0.07    RTRS  AUC NBO    MANY USD  KG
GOOD BP1
GOOD PF1
GOOD PDUST
GOOD DUST 1
GOOD/MED BP1
GOOD/MED PF1
GD/MED P DUS
GD/MED DUST1
MEDIUM BP1
MEDIUM PF1
MEDIUM PDUST
MEDIUM DUST1
LOWER BP1      SPOT
LOWER PF1      SPOT
LOWER PDUST    SPOT
LOWER DUST 1   SPOT
```

```
TEABP1-BEST-KE      BEST BP1         Currency -        USD      02NOV98
                    Kenya TeaAuction Lot.Size -     1 KG        15:20

   Last                  Source   Terms 1   Basis    For  :
 ↑2.22      +0.02        RTRS     AUC                 info :
 ↓2.20       0           Mkt.Loc  Terms 2   Bas.Mnth see  :
 ↓2.20      -0.05        MANY     NBO                 <M466>:
Cls:26OCT98             Yr.High  Spec 1    Bas.Loc
 2.20                   3.45     Weekly
Del.Date               Yr.Low   Spec 2    Status
SPOT                   1.60     BP1
```

```
                                                                    M466
               Kenya Tea Auction-Specifications
               --------------------------------
CONTRACT: Best BP1
Commodity..........Tea              <TEABP1-BEST-KE>
Origin.............Multi*           Unit...............KG
Pricing Terms......Auction          Currency...........USD
Delivery Location..Nairobi, Kenya
Source.............Reuters

CONTRACT: Best PF1
Commodity..........Tea              <TEAPF11-BEST-KE>
Origin.............Multi*           Unit...............KG
Pricing Terms......Auction          Currency...........USD
Delivery Location..Nairobi, Kenya
Source.............Reuters

Additional information for both contracts: Quoted weekly.
* Multi Origin: Kenya, Tanzania, Uganda, Zaire and Rwanda.

                                         Tea continues on <M467>
For main index page of physical price specifications double-click:<COMMSPECSA>
```

Pepper

The spice **black pepper** is more commonly known as just "pepper". The commodity is in fact the plant's fruits, or **peppercorns**, which grow on vines. When ripe the corns are yellowish-red in colour and about 5mm in diameter. Black pepper is produced by boiling the peppercorns in water and then drying them in the sun.

White pepper is produced by removing the outer part of the peppercorn.

Pepper is also a physical market with trading taking place in London and Singapore.

This Reuters screens shows global pepper physical prices.

```
O#PEPPER               PEPPER PHYSICALS
Commodity          Del.Date    Last              Srce   Terms    Loc  Ccy Units
PEP SARAWAK FAQ    SPOT        ↓6900.00   0       RTRS   CIF R/H  MY   USD TONNE
PEP SARAWAK W SP   NOV/DEC     ↓6600.00   0       RTRS   CIF R/H  MY   USD TONNE
PEP MUNTOK FAQ     SPOT        ↓6900.00   0       RTRS   CIF R/H  ID   USD TONNE
PEP MUNTOK W SH    NOV/DEC     ↓6600.00   0       RTRS   CIF R/H  ID   USD TONNE
PEP SARAWAK SPEC   SPOT        ↑5100.00   0       RTRS   CIF R/H  MY   USD TONNE
PEP SARAWAK B SH   NOV/DEC     ↓4950.00   0       RTRS   CIF R/H  MY   USD TONNE
PEP BRAZIL GRD 1   SPOT        ↓5000.00   0       RTRS   CIF R/H  BRA  USD TONNE
PEP BRAZIL SHIP    NOV/DEC     ↓4750.00   0       RTRS   CIF R/H  BRA  USD TONNE
PEP INDIA SHIP     NOV/DEC     ↓4950.00   0       RTRS   CIF R/H  IND  USD TONNE
PEP MUNTOK         /100        ↑1050.00   0       RTRS   FOB SIN  ID   SGD KG100
PEP SARAWAK        /100        ↑1047.50   0       RTRS   FOB SIN  MY   SGD KG100
PEP SARAWAK SPEC   /100        ↓ 760.00   0       RTRS   FOB SIN  MY   SGD KG100
PEP SARAWAK ASTA   /100        ↓ 850.00   0       RTRS   FOB SIN  MY   SGD KG100
```

Citrus and Tropical Fruits
Orange Juice

New York is the largest location for orange juice trading. The physical market is dominated by the US and Brazil – the world's leading orange fruit growers.

These Reuters screens show orange juice futures prices.

```
ORANGE JUICE FUTURES - REUTERS SPEED GUIDE                          OJ/FUT1
To access information double-click in <> or [ ].For more guidance see<USER/HELP>

=ORANGE JUICE CONTRACT CODE============   =NEWS AND ANALYSIS====================
New York Orange Juice..........<O#OJ:>    All Commodities News...............[C]
NY Internonth Spreads..........<O#OJ=R>   All Softs News..................[SOF]
Navelina/Navel (Newhall).....<O#NAVEL:>   Orange Juice News.................[ORJ]
Valencia Late................<O#VLATE:>   FCOJ Futures Report..............[ORJ/]
Mandarina Clementina.........<O#CLEME:>   FCOJ Movement..................[ORJ/M]

RIC Rules Guide.............<RULES1>-7    =CROSS MARKET=========================
                                          Cross Market Package.......<CROSS/MKT1>
                                          Global Futures & Options......<FUTURES>
                                          Foreign Exchange Rates.........<FX=S>
                                          World Cross Rates.............<WX=X>

                                          For Tropical Fruits see.....<TROPICAL1>
```

```
O#OJ:            NYC/     FROZEN OJ       USc
Ques Mth  Last             Bid    Ask    Size    Open 1   High    Low    Time
==== JAN9  S121.10  +1.75                  /      L119.00  121.40  119.40 19.19
Conn MAR9  S123.10  +1.95                  /      T121.90  123.50  121.50 19.19
Lo   MAY9  S124.85  +2.00   124.80  24.90  /      B123.10  125.00  124.50 19.19
     JUL9  S126.45  +2.20   126.40  26.50  /      T125.50  125.50  125.50 19.20
     SEP9  S126.45  +1.70   126.40  26.50  /      T126.00  126.00  125.75 19.20
     NOV9  S126.00  +1.15   125.95  26.00  /      A126.75  126.75  125.00 19.21
     JAN0  S126.50  +1.35   126.40  26.60  /      A127.50                 19.22
     MAR0  S127.00  +1.55   126.90  27.10  /      A128.00                 19.22
     MAY0  S127.00  +1.25   126.90  27.10  /                              19.22
     JUL0                                  /                              :
     SEP0                                  /                              :
```

Tropical Fruits

Consumption of tropical and exotic fruits such as bananas, mangoes, passion fruit etc is increasing in Europe. The West African Domestic Service (WADS) produces information for both producers and consumers to check market prices and quantities of these commodities.

The Reuters screens on these pages shows WADS prices for bananas and pineapples.

```
TROPICAL FRUIT - REUTERS SPEED GUIDE                        TROPICAL1
To access information double-click in <> or [ ].For more guidance see<USER/HELP>

=TROPICAL FRUIT ======================   =TROPICAL FRUIT REPORTS (cont)=========
Avocado Prices.................<WADS57>  Pepper.......................<PEPPER1>
Banana Prices (Import).........<WADS54>  IZMIR Raisins and Sultanas......<IZMIR>
Banana Prices (Wholesale)...<WADS54>-55  Futures on Oranges (NAVEL).<VLC/FUTEX1>
Banana Volumes.................<WADS51>
Mango Prices...................<WADS57>  =NEWS AND ANALYSIS====================
Pineapple Prices (Import)......<WADS52>  All Reuters Commodities News........[C]
Pineapple Prices (Wholesale)...<WADS53>  All Softs News....................[SOF]
Pineapple Volumes..............<WADS51>  Commodity News Directory..........[C/]
Latest Fruits Reports.........<AFRIK10>  Commodity Market Rpt Directory....[C/R]
                                         Weather News Headlines..........[WEA]
=Herbs & Spices Index=================    Weather Services Index..........<WTHR>
Pepper,Cloves,chilies.........<AFRIK18>  Political/Economic News.........[NEWS]
=Dried Fruits=========================   Sports News.....................[SPO]
Raisins, Apricots,Alonond.....<AFRIK17>
=Essential Oils=======================
Citronella, Geranium, Vetiver.<AFRIK19>


Questions/Comments: Contact your local Help Desk - see <PHONE/HELP> for details
================================================================================
Commodities Index<COMMOD>       Softs Index<SOFT1>        Grain Index<GRAIN1>
```

```
                    REUTER AFRICALINK                        WADS54
BANANE Location -  Condition ----  ----- Origine  Size- Fr/Kg  var.  +bas +haut
27Nov  Marseille   quai/wagon dep.  Côte d'Ivoire Extra  4.20 -0.30  4.20  4.20
27Nov  Marseille   quai/wagon dep.  Côte d'Ivoire Cat.1  3.70 -0.30  3.70  3.70
27Nov  Marseille   quai/wagon dep.      Cameroun  Extra  4.22 -0.25  4.22  4.22
27Nov  Marseille   quai/wagon dep.      Cameroun  Cat.1  3.73 -0.11  3.73  3.73

02Dec  Dieppe/Lhv  quai/wagon dep.       Afrique  Extra  4.15 +0.35  4.10  4.20
02Dec  Dieppe/Lhv  quai/wagon dep.       Afrique  Cat.1  3.70 +0.45  3.70  3.70
19Nov  Dieppe/Lhv  quai/wagon dep.       Afrique  Cat.2    NC          NC    NC
02Dec  Dieppe/Lhv  quai/wagon dep.    Guadeloupe  Extra  3.85 +0.35  3.50  4.20
02Dec  Dieppe/Lhv  quai/wagon dep.    Guadeloupe  Cat.1  3.35 +0.30  3.00  3.70
02Dec  Dieppe/Lhv  quai/wagon dep.    Martinique  Extra  4.10 +0.45  4.00  4.20
02Dec  Dieppe/Lhv  quai/wagon dep.    Martinique  Cat.1  3.60 +0.50  3.50  3.70

02Dec  Rungis      gros/bateau           Afrique  Extra  5.80      =  5.50  6.00
02Dec  Rungis      gros/bateau           Afrique  Cat.1  5.30      =  5.00  5.50
02Dec  Rungis      gros/bateau          Dom.Tom   Extra  5.80      =  5.50  6.00
02Dec  Rungis      gros/bateau          Dom.Tom   Cat.1  5.30      =  5.00  5.50

02Dec  Nantes      gros/bateau    Côte d'Ivoire  Extra  5.60 +0.10  5.50  5.80
02Dec  Nantes      gros/bateau    Côte d'Ivoire  Cat.1  4.90 +0.30  4.80  5.20
02Dec  Nantes      gros/bateau          Cameroun Extra  5.60 +0.10  5.50  5.80
02Dec  Nantes      gros/bateau          Cameroun Cat.1  4.90 +0.30  4.50  5.00
```

```
                    REUTER AFRICALINK                        WADS53
ANANAS Location -  Condition ----  ----- Origine  Size- Fr/Kg  var.  +bas +haut
02Dec  Nantes      gros/bateau    Côte d'Ivoire cal.B   5.00 -0.50  4.50  5.50
05Nov  Nantes      gros/bateau    Côte d'Ivoire cal.C   5.70      =  5.50  6.00
01Dec  Avignon     gros/bateau    Côte d'Ivoire cal.B   5.50 -0.50  5.50  5.50
01Dec  Avignon     gros/bateau    Côte d'Ivoire cal.C   5.00      =  5.00  5.00
19Nov  Toulouse    gros/par avion Côte d'Ivoire cal.B  13.50      = 13.50 13.50
02Dec  Toulouse    gros/bateau    Côte d'Ivoire cal.B   5.50      =  5.00  6.00

02Dec  Lille       gros/par avion Côte d'Ivoire cal.B   4.00      =  3.20  4.30
02Dec  Lille       gros/bateau    Côte d'Ivoire cal.B   3.80 +0.10  3.50  4.00

02Dec  Lyon        gros/par avion       Afrique cal.A  12.00      = 11.50 12.50
02Dec  Lyon        gros/bateau          Afrique cal.A   5.00      =  4.80  5.20
02Dec  Lyon        gros/par avion       Afrique cal.B  12.50      = 12.00 13.00
02Dec  Lyon        gros/bateau          Afrique cal.B   5.50      =  5.00  6.00
02Dec  Lyon        gros/par avion       Afrique cal.C  11.50      = 11.00 12.00
02Dec  Lyon        gros/bateau          Afrique cal.C   4.50      =  4.00  5.00

02Dec  Bordeaux    gros/par avion Côte d'Ivoire cal.A  13.50      = 13.50 14.00
02Dec  Bordeaux    gros/bateau    Côte d'Ivoire cal.B   6.00      =  6.00  6.10
02Dec  Marseille   gros/bateau    Côte d'Ivoire cal.B   5.30      =  5.00  5.50
02Dec  Nice        gros/bateau    Côte d'Ivoire cal.B   5.30      =  5.00  5.50
01Dec  Angers      gros/par bateau Côte d'Ivoire cal.B  7.50 +1.60  6.50  7.60
```

Your notes

Grains and Oilseeds

This is a large group of commodities covering a wide range of crops and animals. In a book of this size it is not possible to cover every commodity but the most important types are briefly covered to give you an overview of this large market sector. The commodity groups covered include the following:

- Grains: Coarse grains, wheat and rice

- Oilseeds

- Livestock

- Other agriculturals

Cash and Futures Contracts Prices

The cash prices quoted for grains and oilseeds on the various news services are either official prices, prices supplied by contributors or prices obtained by reporters who are in constant communication with their contacts in the markets. As in other commodity markets these cash prices should be used as indicative values only.

Grain quotes are also made as **flat** or **straight** prices or as **basis** quotes. The basis is the difference between the price quoted for a specific location and the price at the central market or futures price.

Other factors which may also affect grain prices include:

- Weather
- Transport costs. In the US, grain is generally moved by road, rail, lake barge and then sea. For each stage there is a transport charge.
- Subsidies from government programmes

Futures contracts prices are a reflection of the cash markets and prices for grains and oilseeds can be found on the Reuters screens to the right.

The Reuters screens below show wheat futures prices on various exchanges.

O#COMMOD-FUT	COMMODITY FUTURE	Exchange
RIC	Contract	ID
O#BASE-FUT	BASE METAL FUT.	RCT/
O#FIBRES-FUT	FIBRES FUTURES	RCT/
O#FINANCIAL-FUT	FINANCIAL FUTURE	/
O#FREIGHT-FUT	FREIGHT FUTURES	RCT/
O#GRAINS-FUT	GRAINS FUTURES	RCT/
O#LIVESTOCK-FUT	LIVESTOCK FUTURE	RCT/
O#OILSEEDS-FUT	OILSEEDS FUTURES	RCT/
O#PRECIOUS-FUT	PRECIOUS FUTURES	RCT/
O#SOFTS-FUT	SOFTS FUTURES	RCT/

O#GRAINS-FUT	GRAINS FUTURES	Exchange
RIC	Contract	ID
O#BARCHN	Barley Futures	RCT/
O#CORCHN	Corn Futures	RCT/
O#FERTCHN	Fert Futures	RCT/
O#OATCHN	Oat Futures	RCT/
O#POTCHN	Potato Futures	RCT/
O#RICCHN	Rice Futures	RCT/
O#WHECHN	Wheat Futures	RCT/

O#WHECHN	Wheat Futures	Exchange
RIC	Contract	ID
O#W:	WHEAT	CBT/
O#KW:	WHEAT	KBT/
O#LWB:	LDN WHEAT B	LIF/
O#XW:	WHEAT	MAC/
O#MW:	SPRING WT	MGE/
O#NW:	WHITE WHEAT	MGE/
O#SWW:	WHITE WHEAT	SCE/
O#WW:	DOM FD WHT	WPG/
O#CWT:	CZCE WHEAT	ZHC/
O#DWT:	DCE WHEAT	DLC/
O#MOW:	WHEAT 60000 FUT	/
O#YWH:	WHEAT FUTURES	SFE/
O#WE:	AON EUROCAN	CME/
O#BL2:	MIL. WHEAT FRF	MAT/
O#KJ:	EURO CANADA	CME/

Grains

Grains trading is a complex market comprising a small number of dominant companies who compete with hundreds of small traders and state concerns such as Russia's Exportkhleb, the Australian and Canadian Wheat Boards and the US Department of Agriculture.

The types of grain traded on physical and exchange markets together with approximate world production figures for 1996/97, in million metric tonnes (mmt) are given in the table below:

Grain	Types	mmt
Coarse grain "Feed grains" (Source: IGC)	Corn (maize), barley, oats, grain sorghum (milo), rye, millet	916
Wheat (Source: IGC)	Spring, Winter, Red, White, Soft, Hard, Durum	373
Rice (Source: FAS)	Long grain, short grain, brown, white, paddy, aromatic, sweet	583
Oilseeds (Source: FAS)	Soybean, cottonseed, peanuts, sunflower seeds, rapeseeds, oil palm, copra (coconut)	259

Sources: *International Grains Council (IGC)*
Foreign Agricultural Service (FAS)
US Department of Agriculture

The top ten producers of coarse grains for the period 1996 – 1998 are shown in the chart below – the amounts shown are ammt annual averages for the three-year period.

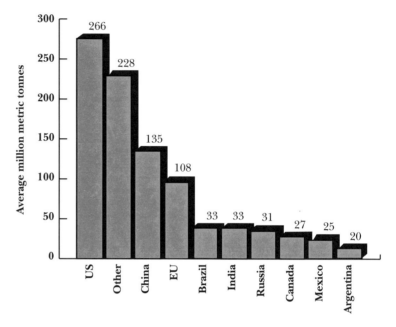

Source: IGC Grain Market Report – Nov 25, 1999

During the same period 1996–1998 the world production of grain by type, in ammt annual average, are shown in the chart below.

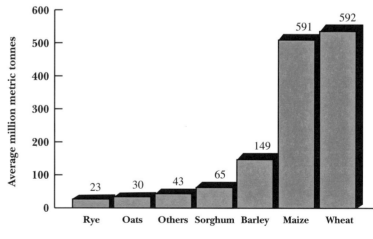

Source: IGC Grain Market Report – Nov 25, 1999

Coarse Grains

Most coarse grain production is fed to livestock and poultry. This fact is related to the worldwide consumption of meat – as this rises so too does the consumption of grains such as barley and corn.

Corn, or maize, is the only principal grain native to the Americas and was introduced into Europe by Christopher Columbus on his return from discovering the New World. In the US more acres are planted with corn than any other crop. Although the US produces a huge amount of corn, it is mainly used as a livestock feed as its nutritional value is not as high as for cereals such as wheat.

Rye is grown in Europe, Asia and North America where the climate and soil are unsuitable for other crops. It is the only cereal crop other than wheat used for making bread.

Sorghum is grown in hot and arid regions as it is resistant to drought conditions. Sorghum varieties such as milo and millet are used to grind into meal to make a type of porridge or flatbread.

Some barley is used in the malting and brewing industries.

The Reuters screen at right show various statistics about maize and barley provided by the International Grains Council.

```
13:08 29OCT98        INTERNATIONAL GRAINS COUNCIL      UK30507    IGC/MAIZE/SD1
INTERNATIONAL GRAINS COUNCIL

MAIZE SUPPLY/DISAPPEARANCE IN MAJOR EXPORTING COUNTRIES    (Sep 28  estimates)
1998/99 (million tonnes)
                  Argentina  China      EC       S.Africa  USA
                  (Mar/Feb)  (Oct/Sep) (Oct/Sep) (May/Apr)(Sep/Aug)
Opening Stocks       0.5       ---       5.3       2.5     33.2
Production          19.3      122.0     35.3       7.5    247.5
Inports            ---         0.5       2.2       0.2      0.3
Total Supplies      19.8      ---       42.8      10.2    281.0

Domestic use         5.5      123.0     38.5       7.1    195.6


Exports             13.5       4.0       0.5       1.5     41.9
Closing Stocks       0.8      ---        3.8       1.6     43.5
```

```
13:06 29OCT98        INTERNATIONAL GRAINS COUNCIL      UK30507    IGC/BARLEY/IMP1
IGC World Inports of Barley.
(Million tonnes)                    -----Forecast 1998-----
                          1997/98    previous      current
 Country/Region             ----    ---------    ---------
EUROPE                      1.0        0.7          0.7
Poland                      0.2        0.2          0.2
Others                      0.8        0.5          0.5
CIS and BALTICS             0.1        0.1          0.1
Baltic States               -          -
CIS                         0.1        0.1          0.1
Russia                      -          -            -
Other CIS                   0.1        0.1          0.1

N & C AMERICA               1.1        1.0          1.0
USA                         0.9        0.7          0.7
Others                      0.2        0.3          0.3

SOUTH AMERICA               0.5        0.5          0.5
Brazil                      0.2        0.3          0.3
Oth
```

```
13:07 29OCT98        INTERNATIONAL GRAINS COUNCIL      UK30507    IGC/BARLEY/EXP1
IGC World Exports of Barley.                    More on <IGC/BARLEY/EXP2>
(Million tonnes)                    -----Forecast 1998-----
                          1997/98    previous      current
 Country/Region             ----    ---------    ---------
Australia                   2.5        2.7          2.7
of which
Feed                        1.3        1.2          1.2
Malting                     1.2        1.5          1.5

Canada                      2.4        2.0          1.5
of which
Feed                        0.9        0.4          0.2
Malting                     1.5        1.6          1.3

EC                          2.7        5.5          6.0
USA                         1.5        0.9          0.9
of which
Feed                        1.3        0.7          0.7
Malting                     0.2        0.2          0.2

Ukraine                     0.5        0.3          0.3
Syria                       0.2        0.3          0.3
Turkey                      0.8        1.0          1.0
Others                      2.7        1.7          1.8
```

Wheat

Wheat is a versatile grain and the market is quite complex, as different types of wheat have different uses and markets. Wheat is basically categorised by growing season and protein content, which is the dominant factor in wheat value. The wheat's protein content is measured by its **gluten** content; the higher the gluten content, the richer and longer lasting the flour obtained by milling the wheat.

Growing Season	Planted	Harvested
Spring Wheat **White Wheat** **Durum**	Spring	Autumn
Winter	Autumn	Early summer

Although spring wheat ranks highest for protein content, varieties of wheat are often blended for specific customer requirements.

Gluten Content	%	Example	Main Use
Soft	8–11	Soft Red Winter	Pastries
Hard	11–18	Hard Red Winter	Bread

Hard varieties are usually grown in dry climates, whereas the Soft varieties grow best in humid conditions. Hard and Soft types of wheat flour are used in bread making and pastries, whereas Durum wheat is milled to produce semolina flour for pasta.

In the milling process, approximately 72% of the grain is recovered as flour. The remainder is known as **bran**, which is used in cereals, and **middlings** which is used for livestock feed.

In 1998 the world production of wheat was estimated to be 585.3 mmt. The following chart shows wheat production by region.

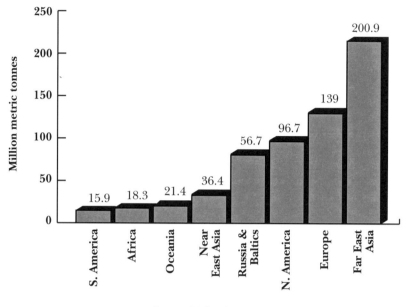

Source: IGC – Grain Market Report – Nov 25, 1999

The following chart shows the supply of wheat varieties for the US in 1998/99 in million tons of grain.

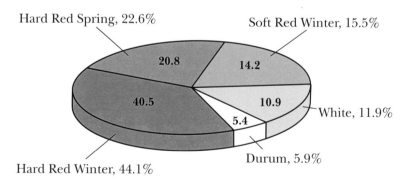

Source: IGC – Grain Market Report – Nov 25, 1999

You can learn more about wheat from IGC statistics, as shown on the Reuters screens below.

```
09:25 11SEP98    Reuters Speed Guide - Wheat Index    UK30507         WHEAT
To access information double-click within <> or [ ] below.
===========================WHEAT MARKETS BY REGION=========================
 <WHEAT/AM> - Americas      <WHEAT/EU> - Europe      <WHEAT/AS> - Asia

           <WHEAT/AU> - Australia         <WHEAT/AF> - Africa

==KEY FUTURES CODES-GLOBAL=============   --KEY CASH/PHYSICAL CODES-GLOBAL======
CBOT Wheat......................<O#W:>    CPC Global FOB Summary......<CPCBDTB>-D
KCBOT Wheat.....................<O#KW:>   EU Wheat export prices.....<O#WHEAT-FR>
LIFFE Wheat.....................<O#LWB:>  CWB Posted prices..........<O#WHEAT-CA>
MGE Durum Wheat.................<O#DW:>   US Gulf FOB/CIF basis<O#WHEAT-BASIS-US>
MGE Spring Wheat................<O#MW:>   US Pacific Wheat Proces..<O#WHEAT-PORT>
MGE White Wheat.................<O#NW:>   Argentine export prices.......[GRO/ARG]
NCE Domestic Feed Wheat.........<O#WW:>   Ocean Freight rates........<CPCBDTY>-Z
                                          EU Wheat price summary<O#WHEAT-FRONT-E>
=============================MAIN MARKET NEWS==============================
 All Wheat Headlines..[WHEAT]  All Grains news....[GRA]  All USDA data...[USDA]
 Grain summary...[GLANCE/GRO]  All Meal news.....[MEAL]  Weather..........[WEA]
 Grain
```

```
13:09 29OCT98      INTERNATIONAL GRAINS COUNCIL     UK30507    IGC/WHEAT/PROD1
IGC World Production of Wheat, Including DURUM.
(Millions/tonnes)                        -----Forecast 1998-----
                       Est 1997          Previous        Current
                       ----              ----------      ---------
Country/Region
Europe                 129.9             139.4           138.6
Bulgaria               3.3               3.3             3.3
Czech Republic         3.6               4.0             3.9
E.C.                   94.7              104.9           104.0
Denmark                5.0               5.1             5.1
France                 33.9              39.9            39.9
Germany                19.8              20.4            20.1
Greece                 2.0               2.2             2.2
Italy                  6.8               8.3             8.3
Spain                  4.6               5.0             5.0
Sweden                 2.1               2.4             2.4
UK                     15.0              16.1            15.5
E.C. Others            5.6               5.5             5.5
Hungary                5.3               5.0             5.0
Poland                 8.2               9.0             9.2
Romania                7.2               5.3             5.3
Slovakia               1.9               1.8             1.8
Yugoslavia (FR)        2.9               3.0             3.0
Others                 2.7               3.1             3.1
                                         More on <IGC/WHEAT/PROD2>
```

Rice

The world production of rice is almost exclusively consumed by humans – over 95% of the crop. As harvested, **Paddy** or **Rough** rice kernels have an outer **hull** or **husk** which must be removed before the cereal is cooked. If the kernels have had only the hull removed, then the rice is termed **brown**. The brown colour comes from the presence of **bran** layers which are rich in minerals and the vitamin thiamine – a lack of these gives rise to the disease known as **beriberi**. Rice which has the husk and bran removed is termed **white**. White rice can also be **polished** using glucose and talc in the milling process.

The top five world rice exporting countries as of mid-1999 in million metric tonnes are shown in the chart below.

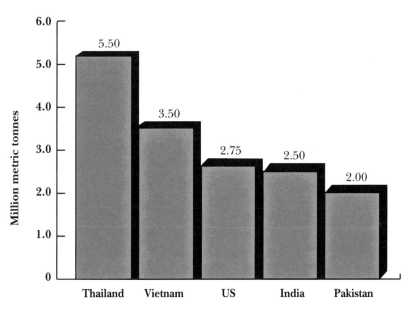

Source: Foreign Agricultural Service, USDA – World Rice Production and Trade Tables 1999

Oilseeds

Oilseeds are produced almost exclusively for two products which are obtained by crushing the seeds:

- **Meal** for high protein livestock feed supplements

- **Oils** for edible consumption and for industrial use in paints and plastics

The world output of oilseeds in mmt for 1997/98 is shown in the chart below:

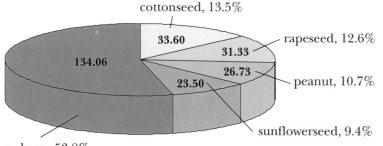

cottonseed, 13.5%

33.60

rapeseed, 12.6%

31.33

26.73

134.06

23.50

peanut, 10.7%

sunflowerseed, 9.4%

soybean, 53.8%

Source: Foreign Agricultural Service, USDA – Major Oilseeds: World Supply and Distribution 1999

Soybean production accounts for over 50% of the world output for oilseeds and the US is the dominant producer – some 63 mmt per annum.

In general, crushing oilseeds produces fairly consistent and reliable amounts of products, for example, each bushel of soybeans (60 lbs) yields 47 – 48 lbs of meal/hulls and 11 lbs of oil. This means that the worldwide production of edible soybean oil is some 20 mmt per annum.

Soybean pods

Because the ratio of products to soybeans crushed is so predictable market players use the **crush margin** to hedge positions. The crush margin is the profit margin calculated by subtracting the cost of soybeans from the sum of soybean oil and meal prices.

Crush margin = (Price of Soybean oil + Price of Soybean meal) – Cost of Soybeans

Market players such as soybean processors hedge their positions to lock in prices using the spread or margin between prices for CBOT futures contracts. The hedge involves the simultaneous:

- Sale of CBOT Soybean futures
- Purchase of CBOT Soybean oil and Soybean meal futures

The Reuters screens below show soybean crush margins.

```
O#CRUSH=R        REU/    Crush spreads     USc  Status CLS
Mth          Last   Net.Ch   Close    Open     High    Low  Time
MAR9/MAR9  ↑+14.84  +1.08   +13.76  +16.51   +17.71  +11.70 19:14
MAY9/MAY9  ↑+15.03  +0.70   +14.33  +16.44   +17.49  +12.69 19:14
JUL9/JUL9  ↓+13.89  -1.19   +15.08  +14.36   +16.01  +11.98 19:14
AUG9/AUG9  ↓+16.74  -0.06   +16.80  +16.10   +19.05  +11.85 19:14
SEP9/SEP9  ↓+17.85  -1.29   +19.14  +18.26   +20.70  +16.85 19:14
JAN0/JAN0
MAR0/MAR0
MAY0/MAY0
JUL0/JUL0
JUL1/JUL1
```

```
19:56  08 Mar  RTRS-CBOT soybean futures crush margins
17:11  08 Mar  RTRS-U.S. soybean crush seen waning due to poor margins
14:17  08 Mar  RTRS-TAKE A LOOK-WCE canola crush calculator <CRUSHPI 1>
21:26  05 Mar  RTRS-Soccer-Beierle scores hat-trick as Duisburg crush Rostock
20:08  05 Mar  RTRS-CBOT soybean futures crush margins
14:03  05 Mar  RTRS-TAKE A LOOK-WCE canola crush calculator <CRUSHPL1>
13:42  05 Mar  RTRS-U.S. weekly soybean crush - NOPA
```

```
19:56  08 Mar  CBOT soybean futures crush margins
    Chicago, March 8 (Reuters) -Based on CBOT settlements, in
cents/bu (1 bu soybeans=11 lbs oil, 44 lbs meal, 4 lbs hulls).
    Contract        Margin          Change
    Mar-99          16.74  up        3.34
    May-99          15.64  up        1.75
    Jul-99          14.01  up        0.89
    Aug-99          16.38  up        0.57
    Sep-99          18.85  up        0.81
    Oct/Nov-99      16.49  up        0.93
    Dec/Nov-99      27.05  up        1.37
    Jan-00          21.03  dn        1.00
    ((Chicago commodities desk(312)408-8720, chicago.commods.newsroom@reuters.com))

Monday, 8 March 1999 19:56:49
ENDS [nN08502018]
```

How Do the Commodities, Energy & Transport Markets Work?

Another important oilseed that is crushed for its oil is Canola. This is a genetic variation of rapeseed developed by plant breeders in the early 1970's in Canada. This oilseed was developed specifically to produce an edible oil low in saturated fat levels – approximately 7% of canola oil is saturated fat. Oils low in saturated fats are considered to be beneficial in human diets and for the prevention of heart disease.

On crushing, canola yields about 40% oil and the remainder is used as a high protein livestock feed. In Canada, canola oil has to meet stringent government quality standards before being used in food products.

It is possible to calculate a crush margin for canola oilseed and it is also possible to calculate a profit margin of soybean oil and soybean meal prices over the price of Canola oilseed. In Canada Canola futures are traded on the **Winnipeg Commodity Exchange (WCE)** where processors hedge their positions by selling WCE Canola futures and buying CBOT Soybean oil and CBOT Soybean meal futures.

The Reuters screens opposite show real-time canola crush margin prices. Canola crush margins can be calculated in various currencies from some electronic services such as Reuters.

```
Reuters Crush Profit Margin Calculator                          CRUSHPL1
Real Time.                                            02-MAR-1999 14:20

CBOT Soybean Oil    CBOT Soybean  Meal   WCE Canola Seed       Crush Margin
   <O#BO:>             <O#SM:>            <O#RS:>
Mnth  Last   +/-   | Mnth Last   +/-   | Mnth Last   +/-   | CAD/T  DEM/T   JPY/T
----  ----  -----  | ---- ----  -----  | ---- ----  ----- | -----  -----  -------
MAR9  17.70        | MAR9 124.9 26.4   | MAR9 318.0 5.7    |  7.77   9.14   616.35
MAY9  17.99 -0.05  | MAY9 128.4  1.0   | MAY9 314.5 6.4    | 17.63  20.75  1398.92
JUL9  17.63 18.61  | JUL9 126.9 33.1   | JUL9 313.5 5.9    | 12.74  14.99  1010.72
AUG9  18.20        | AUG9 126.0 34.7   | AUG9 307.1 5.1    | 26.16  30.79  2075.63
SEP9  18.54        | SEP9 129.0        | SEP9 299.5 4.4    | 40.44  47.60  3208.84
OCT9  18.40        | OCT9 130.0        | SFP9 299.5 4.4    | 39.26  46.22  3115.60
DEC9  18.60 19.25  | DEC9 132.0        | NOV9 303.0 4.8    | 39.86  46.92  3162.90
JAN0  18.50        | JAN0 138.5  2.1   | JAN0 307.0 4.0    | 39.10  46.03  3102.59
MAR0  18.69        | MAR0 143.5  3.5   |                   | 41.18  48.47  3267.39

1 Minute Currency Rates:    Bid      Offer     Mid
-----------------------     ---      -----     ---        -------------------
CAD to the USD-           1.5224    1.5234   1.5229     | For more details of |
JPY to the CAD-            79.30     79.40    79.35     | the formula used in |
DEM to the CAD-          1.1766    1.1777   1.1772      | this calculation,   |
                                                        | see page <CRUSHCALC>|
Please note that all Crush Margin currency conversions are based on the Mid
point for the relevant currency shown above.
```

```
Reuters Crush Profit Margin Calculator                          CRUSHCALC
Calculation

STEP 1
 CBOT Soyoil × 22.04625 = Conversion to USD/T, X1
 X1 × 0.4 = 40% Oil produced when crushing beans, Y1
 Y1 × USD/CAD conversion nid point = CAD/T Oil produced in CAD, Z1

STEP 2
 CBOT Soymeal×2204.625/2000 = Conversion to USD/T, X2
 X2 × 0.6 = 60% Meal produced when crushing beans, Y2
 Y2 × 0.7 = Market Correction of 70%, Y2a
 Y2a × USD/CAD conversion nid point = CAD/T Meal produced in CAD, Z2

STEP 3
 40% Oil,Z1 + 60% Meal,Z2 (with correction) = Sum of products, X3
 X3 - WCE Canola Seed price,X4 = Crush Margin in CAD/T

STEP 4
 Crush Margin CAD/T × CAD/DEM conversion nid point = Crush Margin in DEM/T
 Crush Margin CAD/T × CAD/JPY conversion nid point = Crush Margin in JPY/T
```

Livestock

Livestock production and trading is a long-term industry tied to rising international living standards. Meat production is also tied to grain production and its use in livestock feeds. Meat production is also seasonal and cyclical. This means livestock breed and pasture best at certain times – breeding cycles range from 12 years for cattle to four years for pigs.

In the US, cash meat trading is supported by futures markets at the CME – the main players being the meat packing organisations. The futures and options contracts available on the CME are for:

- Live cattle – steers with an average weight of 1050–1250 lb
- Feeder cattle – steers with an average weight of 700–799 lb
- Live hog – pigs with an average weight of 230–260 lb
- Frozen pork bellies – this means bacon!

Some of the world production figures for pork and beef/veal are shown in the table below:

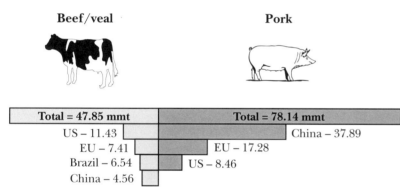

Beef/veal	**Pork**
Total = 47.85 mmt	**Total = 78.14 mmt**
US – 11.43	China – 37.89
EU – 7.41	EU – 17.28
Brazil – 6.54	US – 8.46
China – 4.56	

Source: Foreign Agricultural Service, USDA – Livestock Report 1999

It is important to recognise that these production figures are not export figures. For example, in 1998 Australia produced 1.86 mmt of beef/veal and exported 1.24 mmt – over 66% of production. However, the US produced 11.43 mmt of beef/veal but exported only 1.37 mmt – about 12% of production.

You will also find dairy products and shrimp among commodities classifications. The Reuters screens below show futures contract prices and nows for milk, butter and cheese, and for tiger shrimp traded on the MGE.

```
DAIRY - REUTERS SPEED GUIDE                                      DAIRY1
To access information double-click in <> or [ ].For more guidance see<USER/HELP>

=DAIRY FUTURES========================   =DAIRY OPTIONS=======================
CME Fluid Milk.................<O#DA:>   CSC Cheddar Cheese..................EZ
CME Butter.....................<O#DB:>
CSC Cheddar Cheese.............<O#EZ:>
CSC Non-fat Dry Milk...........<O#MU:>   =RULES GUIDE TO CONSTRUCT A RIC=======
CSC Milk Grade A...............<O#MI:>   How to construct an Option...<RULES1>-7

=DAIRY BY COUNTRY====================    =CROSS MARKET========================
Turkish Dairy Products......<TR/DAIRY1>  Cross Market Package.......<CROSS/MKT1>
                                         Global Futures & Options......<FUTURES>
Questions/Commen
================                         ============
Main Commodities
  Lost? Selectiv
```

```
14:12  05 Mar  Weekly dairy products prices - USDA
        WASHINGTON, March 5 (Reuters) - The following is the weekly dairy products
prices report issued by the U.S. Department of Agriculture on Friday:

                         Dairy Product Prices Mixed

Cheddar Cheese prices received for US 40 pound Blocks averaged $1.30 per
pound for the week ending February 27. The price per pound decreased 0.5
cents from the previous week. The price for US 500 pound Barrels
averaged $1.27 per pound, an increase of 0.8 cents per pound from the
previous week.

Butter prices received for 25 kilogram and 68 pound boxes meeting USDA
Grade AA standards averaged $1.32 per pound for the week ending February
27. The price per pound increased 3.7 cents from the previous week.

Nonfat Dry Milk prices received for bag, tote and tanker sales meeting
USDA Extra Grade or USPH Grade A standards averaged $1.03 per pound for
the week ending February 27. The price per pound decreased 0.8 cents
from the previous week and is the seventh consecutive week of price
decline.
```

```
14:49  02 Mar  Ecuador shrimp exports grew 2.8 pct in January
  QUITO, Ecuador, March 2 (Reuters) - Ecuadorean shrimp exports rose 2.8 percent to 8,266 tonnes
in January from 8,037 tonnes in January 1998, the official shrimp monitoring agency said Tuesday.
  The agency said Ecuador's export earnings from shrimp fell to $55.5 million in January from $63.5
million in January 1998.
  Shrimp is Ecuador's second-biggest export after bananas. Ecuador is the world's sixth largest
producer of shrimp.
  In 1998, Ecuador exported 113,484 tonnes of shrimp worth $844 million.
  ((Gustavo Oviedo, Quito Newsroom, 5932 431753 x114, quito.newsroom@reuters.com))

Tuesday, 2 March 1999 14:49:05
ENDS [nN02150011]
```

Other Agriculturals

Potatoes are by tradition one of the most volatile of the commodities. The major markets for human consumption have increased considerably but prices are still influenced significantly by weather, perishability and storage.

It was the volatility of potatoes in the USA that caused the government to ban trading in potato futures, until they were introduced in 1996 by a division, SPUD$_{SM}$, of the NYCE. Potato futures trading on NYCE and in Europe on MATIF, LIFFE and EOE is still relatively inactive.

On the CME, Random Length Lumber (Timber) futures and options contracts are available for lengths of timber between 8 and 20 feet, 2 inches by 4 inches, from species of spruce-pine-fir trees.

As you will probably have noticed there are a large number of grains and oilseeds that are traded. Within a particular commodity, for example wheat, there is a range of varieties available. Look at the Reuters screens at right for contract specifications for some of the most important grains, oilseeds, vegetable and fish oils traded.

```
08:26 09SEP98   Reuters Speed Guide - Oilseeds Index  UK30507        OILSEEDS
To access information double-click within <> or [ ] below
========================OILSEEDS MARKETS BY REGION========================
<OILSEEDS/AM> - Americas      <OILSEEDS/EU> - Europe      <OILSEEDS/AS> - Asia

                          <OILSEEDS/AU> - Australia


==KEY-SEED FUTURES===============     ==KEY-OILS FUTURES===============
CBOT Soybean..............<O#S:>      US Fats.........................<O#FATS-US>
US Soy Summary..........<O#SOY-US>    CBOT Soybean Oil................<O#BO:>
EU Soybeans Prices..<O#SOYBEAN-E>     European Rapeoil prices.......<O#RAPEOIL-E>
EU Rape summary.....<O#RAPESUM-E>
Shanghai Soybeans........<O#SSB:>     ==KEY-FEED FUTURES===============
Tokyo Soybeans..........<O#JAS:>      US Feeds........................<O#FEED-US>
                                      CBOT Soybean Meal...............<O#SM:>
                                      EU Rapemeal prices........<O#RAPEMEAL-E>
```

```
OILSEEDS/AM                    American Seeds
To access information double-click in <> or [] below.
                    OILSEEDS SPECIFICATIONS
                    -----------------------
Palm....................<S431>-<S434>   Tapioka....................<S252>
Millet..................<S566>          Coconut Oil................<S417>
Rape.................<S166>-<S16B>       Fish Oil...............<S345>-<S347>
Soybean.............<S217>-<S249>       Palm Oil...............<S431>-<S434>
Soymeal.............<S733>-<S741>       Rape Oil...............<S166>-<S16B>
Sunflower...........<S495>-<S512>       Soy Oil................<S222>-<S223>
Ta
```

```
                                                                  S217
                    Soy Specifications
                    ------------------

CONTRACT:AR Soybean P1-6   <IMSYB-AR-P1>-6
Commodity.........Soybean              Unit...............Tonne
Origin............Argentine            Currency..........USD
Pricing Terms......CIF                 Moisture Content...max 14%
Delivery Location..Rotterdam
Source............Reuters
Additional Information: Quoted daily
```

```
OILSEEDS/EU                    European Seeds
To access information double-click in <> or [] below. Some news reports are not
                    EUROPEAN VEG OILS PRICES/TRADES
                    -------------------------------
European veg oils trades.<VEGTRADES/EU>   R'dam veg oils stocks..<VEGOILSTX/EU01>
Dutch soyoil.............<VEGOILS/EU01>   Dutch/EU rapeoil........<VEGOILS/EU02>
Sunoil any origin........<VEGOILS/EU03>   Sunoil EU...............<VEGOILS/EU04>
Groundnutoil any origin..<VEGOILS/EU05>   Linseed oil any origin..<VEGOILS/EU06>
Crude palm oil cif.......<VEGOILS/EU07>   BD palm oil cif.........<VEGOILS/EU08>
RBD palm oil fob.........<VEGOILS/EU09>   RBD Palm olein fob......<VEGOILS/EU11>
Palm stearin fob.........<VEGOILS/EU12>   Coconut oil cif.........<VEGOILS/EU13>
Palmkernel oil Mal/Indo..<VEGOILS/EU14>   Palmkernel oil Indon....<VEGOILS/EU15>
Palmkernel oil Dutch.....<VEGOILS/EU16>   Tung oil any origin.....<VEGOILS/EU17>
Castoroil any origin.....<VEGOILS/EU18>   Fatty acid distillate...<VEGOILS/EU19>

                    EUROPEAN IMPORTED SEED PRICES
                    -----------------------------
U.S. soybeans............<EUROBEANS01>   Brazilian soybeans......<EUROBEANS02>
Argentine soybeans.......<EUROBEANS03>   Philippine copra........<EUROBEANS04>

                    EUROPEAN FEEDS PRICES & MEAL TRADES
                    -----------------------------------
Soymeal pellets Brazil....<EUROFEED01>   Soymeal pellets Argentine..<EUROFEED02>
Soymeal EU high protein...<EUROFEED03>   Soymeal EU 44/7............<EUROFEED04>
Soymeal U.S...............<EUROFEED05>   Soymeal U.S. high protein..<EUROFEED06>
Cornglutenfeed pellets....<EUROFEED07>   Citruspulp pellets.........<EUROFEED08>
Sunmeal pellets Argentine.<EUROFEED09>   Sunmeal pellets EU.........<EUROFEED11>
Feed peas Canadian........<EUROFEED12>   Rapemeal EU................<EUROFEED13>
Tapioca...................<EUROFEED14>   Palmkernel expellers.......<EUROFEED15>
Copra expeller pellets....<EUROFEED16>   Copra extraction pellets...<EUROFEED17>
European Meal trades....<MEALTRADES/EU>
```

How Do the Commodities, Energy & Transport Markets Work?

The Reuters screens on this page show information about the wheat markets.

```
09:51 16NOV98    Reuters Speed Guide - Grain Index    UK30507      GRAIN
To access information double-click in <> or [] below. Some news reports are not
published on a daily basis but are accessed via Newsyear 2000. This product is
an integral part of Commodities & Energy 3000 Pro. Please call your local
Reuters office. Should you require further info. about this product.<PHONE/HELP>

            =========| MAJOR GRAIN MARKETS |==========
**GRAINS BY REGION**                  **GRAIN & ASSOCIATED MARKET NEWS**
WHEAT By region.......<WHEAT>         * All Grain market news.........[GRA]
                                      * All Commodity market news.......[C]
CORN By region.<MAIZE>/<CORN>         * All Shipping market news......[SHP]
                                      * Weather information...........[WEA]
BARLEY By region.....<BARLEY>         * USDA Market Information......[USDA]
                                      * Intern. Grain Council....<IGCWORLD>
RICE By region.........<RICE>         * Reuters market summary.[GLANCE/GRO]
                                      * CPC Grains data...........<CPCBDUA>
OTHER By region.<GRAIN/OTHER>         * Reuters Grain tender diary..[GRA/T]
                                      * USDA World Agri. report.... <WASDE>
                                      * UK Delvd Grain trades.....[GRA/UTR]
        Currency Spot rates.........<FX=S>   Currency Cross rate............<WX=X>
                        <OILSEEDS>  <LIVESTOCK>
==========================================================================
What's New <COMMOD/INFO>   Grain News Index<COMMOD/NEWS3>   Grain News <GRAIN2>
   Lost?Selective Access?...<USER/HELP>   Reuters Phone Support...<PHONE/HELP>
```

```
09:25 11SEP98    Reuters Speed Guide - Wheat Index    UK30507      WHEAT
To access information double-click within <> or [ ] below.
===================WHEAT MARKETS BY REGION===========================
   <WHEAT/AM> - Americas     <WHEAT/EU> - Europe     <WHEAT/AS> - Asia

        <WHEAT/AU> - Australia      <WHEAT/AF> - Africa

==KEY FUTURES CODES-GLOBAL============   ==KEY CASH/PHYSICAL CODES-GLOBAL======
CBOT Wheat.....................<O#W:>    CPC Global FOB Summary......<CPCBDTB>-D
KCBOT Wheat....................<O#KW:>   EU Wheat export prices.....<O#WHEAT-FR>
LIFFE Wheat....................<O#LWB:>  CWB Posted prices..........<O#WHEAT-CA>
MGE Durum Wheat................<O#DW:>   US Gulf FOB/CIF basis<O#WHEAT-BASIS-US>
MGE Spring Wheat...............<O#MW:>   US Pacific Wheat Proces..<O#WHEAT-PORT>
MGE White Wheat................<O#NW:>   Argentine export prices.......[GRO/ARG]
NCE Domestic Feed Wheat........<O#WW:>   Ocean Freight rates........<CPCBDTY>-Z
                                         EU Wheat price summary<O#WHEAT-FRONT-E>
==================================MAIN MARKET NEWS========================
All Wheat Headlines..[WHEAT]  All Grains news....[GRA]  All USDA data...[USDA]
Grain summary...[GLANCE/GRO]  All Meal news.....[MEAL]  Weather.........[WEA]
Grain tender diary...[GRA/T]  USDA World Stats.<WASDE>  IGC Reports [IGCINDEX]
      <MAIZE>  <BARLEY>  <RICE>  <GRAIN>  <OILSEEDS>  <LIVESTOCK>
```

```
WHEAT/AM                       American Wheat

        =========| AMERICAS- KEY CASH/PHYSICAL CODES |==========
US Basis Wheat....<O#WHEAT-BASIS-US>   US Durum Wheat..........<O#DURUM-US>
All US Wheat Data.......<O#WHEAT-US-1>  US Hard Wheat........<O#WHEAT-HARD-US>
Alphabetically..........<O#WHEAT-US-2>  US Soft Wheat........<O#WHEAT-SOFT-US>
Sorted..................<O#WHEAT-US-3>  US Spring Wheat.....<O#WHEAT-SPRNG-US>
........................<O#WHEAT-US-4>  US Winter Wheat.....<O#WHEAT-WNTER-US>
                                        US Wheat Exports....<O#WHEAT-EXPRT-US>

        =========| GRAINS NEWS |==========   =========| WEATHER |==========
= Global Grain News............[GRA]=  = Global Weather News.....[WEA] =
= Grains News Summary.....[GLANCE/GRO]=  = Rice Global Weather..<WSDG-P> =
= Grains Derivative News...[GRA-DRV]=  = WSC Weather Reports.....[WSC] =
= World Grain Tender Diary.....[GRA/T]=  = Grain Weather news..[GRO-WEA] =
```

```
O#WHEAT-US-1              American Wheat-1
Commodity       Del.Date      Last          Srce    Terms   Loc  Ccy Units
Amarillo HRW    Spot       ↓    3.04   -0.03  CFSA  Sto AMAR  US   USD BSH
1AtlnSpring13.5% Spot      ↑  264.70   +0.60  CWB   Sto ATLN  CAN  CAD TONNE
1AtlnSpringExStr Spot                         CWB   Sto ATLN  CAN  CAD TONNE
2AtlnSpringExStr Spot                         CWB   Sto ATLN  CAN  CAD TONNE
1HRW Texas SthPl          B↑  3.4675  A3.527  USDA  FOB TEX   US   USD BSH
US National Avg Spot       ↑    5.86   +0.11  USDA  AVG US    US   USD BSH
Wheat ARG Fix-BA Spot      ↓  108.0    -2.5   RTRS  AVG BA    ARG  USD TONNE
Wheat ARG Fix-BB Spot      ↓  110.0    -0.7   RTRS  AVG BB    ARG  USD TONNE
Billing HRW 12%           ↑    3.02   +0.02  RTRS  DLV BILL  US   USD BSH
Billing Spring14 Spot                         RTRS  DLV BILL  US   USD BSH
Baltimore SRW   Spot       ↓    2.66   -0.04  CFSA  Sto BLTM  US   USD BSH
Baltimore SWW   Spot       ↓    2.51   -0.04  CFSA  Sto BLTM  US   USD BSH
Catoosa HRW     Cash            0       0    RTRS  DLV OKLA  US   USD BSH
Chicago SRW Term Spot      ↓    2.43   -0.01  CFSA  Sto CHGO  US   USD BSH
Cincnti SRW Term Spot      ↓    2.52   -0.05  CFSA  Sto CIN   US   USD BSH
Colby HRW HighPl Cash           0       0    RTRS  DLV KANS  US   USD BSH
CooleCity HRW 12 Spot                         RTRS  DLV COOL  US   USD BSH
CooleC.Spring 14 Spot      ↓    3.87   -0.01  RTRS  DLV COOL  US   USD BSH
Coole City White Spot      ↑    2.65   +0.02  RTRS  DLV COOL  US   USD BSH
```

The Reuters screens on this page show the Livestock Index and prices specifically for the US beef and pork spot markets.

```
08:35 06NOV98    Reuters Speed Guide - Livestock Index UK30507          LIVESTOCK
To access information double-click within <> or [ ] below.
=====================LIVESTOCK MARKETS BY REGION=============================
 <LIVESTOCK/AM> - America    <LIVESTOCK/EU> - Europe      <LIVESTOCK/AS> - Asia

                       <LIVESTOCK/AU> - Australia

==KEY FUTURES CODES-GLOBAL=============== ==KEY CASH PRICES-GLOBAL============
CME Live Cattle.................<O#LC:>  US Cattle Prices........<O#CATTLE-US>
CME Feeder Cattle...............<O#FC:>  UK Smithfield Meat Market..<MEAT/GB1>
ATA Live Pigs..................<O#ALP:>  US Hogs and Pork Prices...<O#HOGS-US>
MIDAM Live Cattle..............<O#XL:>
USD Denominated Live Cattle....<O#BOI:>
USD Denominated Feeder Cattle..<O#BZR:>

==============================MAIN MARKET NEWS==============================
Livestock News....................[LIV]   Cattle markets...............[CATTLE]
Hog markets......................[HOGS]   Livestock weather...........[LIV-WEA]
Livestock News........<LIVESTOCK/NEWS1>   IGC Reports................<IGCINDEX>

      <MAIZE>  <BARLEY>  <RICE>  <GRAIN>  <OILSEEDS>  <LIVESTOCK>
============================================================================
What's New <COMMOD/INFO>  Grain News Index <GRAIN/NEWS1>  Sector Index <COMMODS>
   Lost? Selective access? <USER/HELP>   Reuters Phone Support <PHONE/HELP>
```

```
O#CATTLE-US          CATTLE/BEEF US
Commodity        Del.Date      Last            Srce   Terms    Loc  Ccy Units
BOX BEEF CHC LWT SPOT       ↓  98.56   -0.41   USDA  FOB USA   USA  USD CWT
BOX BEEF CHC HWT SPOT       ↓  97.82   -0.29   USDA  FOB USA   USA  USD CWT
BOX BEEF SEL LWT SPOT       ↓  91.77   -0.58   USDA  FOB USA   USA  USD CWT
BOX BEEF SEL HWT SPOT       ↓  90.25   -0.72   USDA  FOB USA   USA  USD CWT
BOX RIB CHC LWT  SPOT       ↓ 169.22   -1.25   USDA  FOB USA   USA  USD CWT
BOX RIB CHC HWT  SPOT       ↑ 176.57   +2.72   USDA  FOB USA   USA  USD CWT
BOX RIB SEL LWT  SPOT       ↓ 153.84   -1.56   USDA  FOB USA   USA  USD CWT
BOX RIB SEL HWT  SPOT       ↓ 154.14   -0.46   USDA  FOB USA   USA  USD CWT
BOX CHK CHC LWT  SPOT       ↓  66.41   -0.55   USDA  FOB USA   USA  USD CWT
BOX CHK CHC HWT  SPOT       ↓  63.01   -0.72   USDA  FOB USA   USA  USD CWT
BOX CHK SEL LWT  SPOT       ↓  67.55   -1.13   USDA  FOB USA   USA  USD CWT
BOX CHK SEL HWT  SPOT       ↓  63.71   -0.98   USDA  FOB USA   USA  USD CWT
BOX RND CHC LWT  SPOT       ↓  82.60   -0.76   USDA  FOB USA   USA  USD CWT
BOX RND CHC HWT  SPOT       ↓  82.60   -0.76   USDA  FOB USA   USA  USD CWT
BOX RND SEL LWT  SPOT       ↓  81.65   -0.19   USDA  FOB USA   USA  USD CWT
BOX RND SEL HWT  SPOT       ↓  81.65   -0.19   USDA  FOB USA   USA  USD CWT
BOX LOIN CHC LWT SPOT       ↑ 158.18   +1.08   USDA  FOB USA   USA  USD CWT
BOX LOIN CHC HWT SPOT       ↓ 155.58   -0.14   USDA  FOB USA   USA  USD CWT
BOX LOIN SEL LWT SPOT       ↑ 133.78   +0.39   USDA  FOB USA   USA  USD CWT
BOX LOIN SEL HWT SPOT       ↓ 131.75   -1.10   USDA  FOB USA   USA  USD CWT
```

```
O#HOGS-US            HOGS/PORK US
Commodity        Del.Date      Last            Srce   Terms    Loc  Ccy Units
HOT CARCASS NC   SPOT       ↓   23.51  -1.66   NCDA  DLV NC    NC   USD CWT
LIVE SOW FYV NC  SPOT       ↓   17.00  -3.00   NCDA  DLV NC    FYV  USD CWT
LIVE SOW WLC NC  SPOT            0       0      NCDA  DLV NC    WLC  USD CWT
LIVE SOW RWL NC  SPOT            0       0      NCDA  DLV NC    RWL  USD CWT
LIVE SOW SPC NC  SPOT            0       0      NCDA  DLV NC    SPC  USD CWT
HOG 45-46% M/STH SPOT     B↓   18.50  A22.99   USDA  DLV MSUS  MSUS USD CWT
HOG 47-48% M/STH SPOT     B↓   19.50  A24.83   USDA  DLV MSUS  MSUS USD CWT
HOG 49-50% M/STH SPOT     B↓   20.50  A26.79   USDA  DLV MSUS  MSUS USD CWT
HOG 51-52% M/STH SPOT     B↓   22.80  A27.77   USDA  DLV MSUS  MSUS USD CWT
HOG 53-54% M/STH SPOT     B↓   23.80  A29.73   USDA  DLV MSUS  MSUS USD CWT
HOG 45-46% ECBLT SPOT     B↑   11.75  A23.32   USDA  DLV ECUS  ECUS USD CWT
HOG 47-48% ECBLT SPOT     B↑   15.25  A24.13   USDA  DLV ECUS  ECUS USD CWT
HOG 49-50% ECBLT SPOT     B↑   17.25  A24.69   USDA  DLV ECUS  ECUS USD CWT
HOG 51-52% ECBLT SPOT     B↑   19.25  A25.90   USDA  DLV ECUS  ECUS USD CWT
HOG 53-54% ECBLT SPOT     B↑   20.40  A27.15   USDA  DLV ECUS  ECUS USD CWT
HOG 45-46% WCBLT SPOT     B↑   12.50  A23.99   USDA  DLV WCUS  WCUS USD CWT
HOG 47-48% WCBLT SPOT     B↑   16.00  A24.68   USDA  DLV WCUS  WCUS USD CWT
HOG 49-50% WCBLT SPOT     B↑   18.00  A26.50   USDA  DLV WCUS  WCUS USD CWT
HOG 51-52% WCBLT SPOT     B↑   20.00  A27.98   USDA  DLV WCUS  WCUS USD CWT
HOG 53-54% WCBLT SPOT     B↑   24.00  A28.98   USDA  DLV WCUS  WCUS USD CWT
```

How Do the Commodities, Energy & Transport Markets Work?

The Reuters screens on this page show information about the maize, corn, barley, rice and other grain markets.

```
09:51 16NOV98    Reuters Speed Guide - Grain Index    UK30507         GRAIN
To access information double-click in <> or [] below. Some news reports are not
published on a daily basis but are accessed via Newsyear 2000. This product is
an integral part of Commodities & Energy 3000 Pro. Please call your local
Reuters office. Should you require further info. about this product.<PHONE/HELP>
=======================================================================
            ==========| MAJOR GRAIN MARKETS |==========
  **GRAINS BY REGION**              **GRAIN & ASSOCIATED MARKET NEWS**
WHEAT By region.......<WHEAT>        * All Grain market news.........[GRA]
                                     * All Commodity market news.......[C]
CORN By region.<MAIZE>/<CORN>        * All Shipping market news......[SHP]
                                     * Weather information...........[WEA]
BARLEY By region.....<BARLEY>        * USDA Market information......[USDA]
                                     * Intern. Grain Council....<IGCWORLD>
RICE By region........<RICE>         * Reuters market summary.[GLANCE/GRO]
                                     * CPC Grains data..........<CPCBDUA>
OTHER By region.<GRAIN/OTHER>        * Reuters Grain tender diary..[GRA/T]
                                     * USDA World Agri. report....<WASDE>
```

```
13:42 02DEC98    Reuters Speed Guide - Corn Index    UK30507          CORN
To access information double-click within <> or [] below
=========================CORN MARKETS BY REGION========================

 <CORN/AM> - America      <CORN/AS> - Asia        <CORN/AU> - Australia
            <CORN/EU> - Europe        <CORN/AF> - Africa

==KEY FUTURES CODES-GLOBAL=============    ==KEY CASH/PHYSICAL CODES===========
CBOT Corn.....................<O#C:>   European Corn/Maize prices..<O#MAIZE-E>
Beijing Corn..................<O#BCN:>   US Corn prices.............<O#CORN-US>
BCE Corn......................<O#BCC:>   Argentine Grain prices.....<O#GRAIN-AR>
MIDAM Corn....................<O#XC:>    EU Grain Tariffs.....<O#GRAIN-TARIFF-E>
DCE Corn......................<O#DCN:>
KCE Corn......................<O#JKC:>


============================MAIN MARKET NEWS===========================
All Corn Headlines....[CORN]  All Grains news....[GRA]  All USDA data...[USDA]
Grain summary...[GLANCE/GRO]  All Meal news.....[MEAL]  Weather..........[WEA]
                         USDA World Stats.<WASDE>
          <MAIZE>  <BARLEY>  <RICE>  <GRAIN>  <OILSEEDS>  <LIVESTOCK>

What's New <COMMOD/INFO>  Grain News Index <GRAIN/NEWS1>  Sector Index <COMMODS>
     Lost? Selective access? <USER/HELP>   Reuters Phone Support <PHONE/HELP>
```

```
14:11 11SEP98    Reuters Speed Guide - Barley Index    UK30507      BARLEY
To access information double-click within <> or [] below
========================BARLEY MARKETS BY REGION=======================

  <BARLEY/AM> - Americas     <BARLEY/EU> - Europe    <BARLEY/AS> - Asia

          <BARLEY/AU> - Australia     <BARLEY/AF11> - Africa

=FUTURES CONTRACTS====================    =PHYSICAL BARLEY===================
Minneapolis Grain Exch - Barley.<O#FG:>   US Barley.................<O#BARLEY-US>
Winnepeg CE Western Barley......<O#AB:>   Winnipeg Cash Grain............<GNEP>
CCFE of Hainan - Barley.........<O#HBL:>  European Barley..........<O#BARLEY-E>
Shanghai CE Barley..........   ..<O#SBL:>  French Onic Barley Est....<ONIC/BARLEY>
Shenyang CE Barley..............<O#YBL:>  Home Grown Cereals Authority...<HGCD>-E
Budapest CE - Feed Barley.....<O#BCWB:>
Liffe Barley...................<O#LBA:>

===========================MAIN MARKET NEWS============================
All Rice Headlines..[BARLEY]  All Grains news....[GRA]  All USDA data...[USDA]
```

```
14:16 11SEP98    Reuters Speed Guide - Rice Index    UK30507         RICE
To access information double-click within <> or [] below
=========================RICE MARKETS BY REGION========================

 <RICE/AM> - Americas      <RICE/AS> - Asia        <RICE/AU> - Australia

          <RICE/EU> - Europe        <RICE/AF> - Africa

==KEY FUTURES CODES-GLOBAL=============    ==KEY CASH/PHYSICAL CODES===========
CBOT Rough Rice.................<O#RR:>   Bangkok Rice Offered Prices....<RCQG>-J
CZCE Rough Rice................<O#CRD:>   Bangkok Rice Association Prices........
GUFE Long Grain Rice...........<O#URC:>   Display....................<O#RICE-TH>
Shanghai Rice..................<O#SRD:>   US Rice New display........<O#RICE-US>
Shanghai Long Grain Rice.......<O#SRC:>

===========================MAIN MARKET NEWS============================
All Rice Headlines..[RICE]  All Grains news....[GRA]  All USDA data...[USDA]
```

```
GRAIN/OTHER                          Other Grains
To access information double-click in <> or [] below. Some news reports are not

         ############# AMERICAS CASH & FUTURES MARKET #############

   US MARKET DATA                            LATIN AMERICA MARKET DATA
   --------------                            -------------------------
US Cotton..............<O#COTTON-US>   Argentine gen. grain prices..<O#GRAIN-AR>
US Oats.................<O#OATS-US>   Argentine Grain Exports.....<O#EXPORT-AR>
US Rye..................<O#RYE-US>    Argentine Cash grain..............<GRAE>
US Sorghun..............<O#SORGHUM-US>  Argentine Export Prices..........<GBRA>-D
US Sorghun Prices..............<GNET>        CANADA MARKET DATA
Chicago Oats...................<O#O:>        ------------------
MIDAM Oats.....................<O#XO:>   Winnipeg Oats...................<O#WO:>



         ############# EUROPEAN DATA AND NEWS #############
EU Grain Tariffs.....<O#GRAIN-TARIFF-E>  Cereal Forw.Exp Refund........<GRRB>-F
EU Grain Exp.Tenders Result......<GRHJ>  Cereal/Grain Exp Ref..........<GRGA>-FL
EU Grain Inport Levels.........<GREE>-F  Cumulative Grain Exp.Limits......<GRHN>
EU Grain Tender Bids............<GRHH>   French Grain Prices...........<GRPE>-H
EU Intervent.Grain Sale Result...<GRHL>  UK Seeds Prices................<OVLE>
EU Imported Grains............<GRGA>-GG  Liverpool Cotton..........<O#COTTON-E>
```

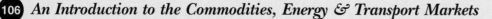

Energy

Petroleum and Products

The word petroleum is derived from the Latin for rock and oil – *petra* and *oleum*. Petroleum is also frequently referred to as "oil" – the terms are synonymous in many cases. Petroleum is extracted from the earth's crust as a brown to black liquid known as **crude oil**. It is normal to find **natural gas** in association with crude oil – an important source of energy in its own right.

Petroleum is formed over millions of years by the compression of dead aquatic plants and animals mixed with mud and sand in layered deposits. Gradually the mud and sand formed sedimentary rock and the organic material formed petroleum in the rock structures.

Crude oils vary greatly in their composition, viscosity (thickness), specific gravity (density) and colour. They are generally named after the production field with which they are associated, for example, Brent and West Texas Intermediate (WTI).

There are seven major oil-producing regions, included on the map opposite:

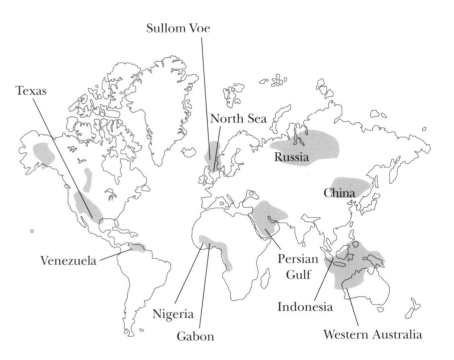

- Russia and China

- The Middle East

- North America (US and Canada)

- Latin America (Central and South America)

- Africa

- Western Europe (Mainly in the North Sea)

- Far East and Australasia

Types of Crude Oil

The main use of crude oil is that it can be fractionally distilled or **cracked** into refined products such as **gasoline** or **petrol**, diesel fuel, fuel oil etc, which comprise the major world energy products. If you do not know what all these terms mean don't worry, the next section explains them in detail.

Crude oils are categorised using the **American Petroleum Institute (API)** grading system based on specific gravity. The specific gravity of a liquid is a measure of how heavy a chosen volume of liquid is compared with the same volume of water. In the API system water is API10 and, for example, Arabian Light crude is API34 which means that this crude oil is lighter than water.

The **sulphur** content of a crude oil is also important.

- **Sweet** crude oils have a relatively **low** sulphur content, a high specific gravity and can be refined into lighter, high value products such as gasoline.

- **Sour** crude oils have a relatively **high** sulphur content, a lower specific gravity and produce a greater proportion of heavy fuel oils and tar on refining.

There are two important crude oils produced that are significant for futures contracts, although in production terms, combined, they only account for 3% of world production. These are:

Brent

Brent crude oil acts as the **benchmark** against which other crudes are priced, in particular those from the North Sea, West African and Mediterranean fields. Brent crude is a blend of crude oils from the Brent and Ninian systems which is carried via pipelines to the **Sullom Voe** oil terminal in the Shetland Islands. Brent is a light, sweet crude that is now past its peak in terms of production.

Loading takes place at Sullom Voe with a minimum of 500,000 barrels, so the terminal is geared for VLCC and ULCC (Ultra Large)tankers.

Loading has to take place to a vessel which has been nominated 7 days prior to the first loading date, within 3 consecutive days. This type of spot cargo is known as **Dated Brent**. Below are Brent prices as shown on a Reuters screen.

O#BRENT		BRENT							
Name	Delivery	Buy Sell	Time	Date	Prev.Close	Terms	Source	API	Sulphur
BRENT	Dtd	+9.95/+9.97	11:14	15FEB	+9.96/+9.98	FOB SVOE	EUR	38.3	
BRENT	Mar	10.30/10.32	11:14	15FEB	10.31/10.33	FOB SVOE	EUR	38.3	
BRENT	Apr	10.48/10.50	11:14	15FEB	10.49/10.51	FOB SVOE	EUR	38.3	
BRENT	May	10.69/10.71	11:14	15FEB	10.72/10.74	FOB SVOE	EUR	38.3	

In the spot markets, counterparties will often buy a cargo that is not necessarily Brent crude oil but is priced at a premium or discount to the published Dated Brent price. It is therefore important to know the **differentials** in these prices. The Reuters screen below shows Brent differential prices.

O#BRT-DIF		Brent Diffs							
Name	Delivery	Buy Sell	Time	Date	Prev.Close	Terms	Source	API	Sulphur
Brent	Dtd/Dec	-0.97/-0.77	14:35	10NOV	-1.05/-0.95	FOB DIFF	SVoe	38.3	0.833
Brent	Dec/Jan	-0.38/-0.36	08:10	10NOV	-0.73/-0.68	FOB DIFF	SVoe	38.3	0.833
Brent	Jan/Feb	-0.30/-0.27	08:10	10NOV	-0.35/-0.31	FOB DIFF	SVoe	38.3	0.833
Brent	Feb/Mar	-0.24/-0.21	08:10	10NOV	-0.26/-0.24	FOB DIFF	SVoe	38.3	0.833
Brt/Dub	Dec	+0.30/+0.35	10:20	06NOV	+0.30/+0.35	FOB Spread			
Brt/Dub	Jan	+0.20/+0.25	08:09	10NOV	+0.25/+0.35	FOB Spread			
Dubai	Dec/Jan	-0.10/+0.10	08:10	10NOV	+0.10/+0.20	FOB DIFF	A/G	31.8	
Dubai	Jan/Feb	+0.08/+0.13	08:10	10NOV	+0.03/+0.07	FOB DIFF	A/G	31.8	
Dubai	Feb/Mar	-0.05/0	08:10	10NOV	/+0.07	FOB DIFF	A/G	31.8	
BONNY LT		/+0.05	14:47	10NOV	/+0.05	FOB DIFF	Nig	35.0	
CARTNNA	DATED	-0.80/-0.82	14:47	10NOV	-0.80/-0.82	FOB DIFF	Nig		
Ekofisk		-0.05/+0.05	14:47	10NOV	-0.05/+0.05	FOB DIFF	Tees	39.3	
FLOTTA		-0.85/-0.75	14:47	10NOV	-0.85/-0.75	FOB DIFF	Flot	36.0	
FORCADOS		+0.05/+0.10	14:47	10NOV	+0.05/+0.10	FOB DIFF	Nig	29.4	
Forties		-0.05/	14:47	10NOV	-0.05/	FOB DIFF	HiPt	39.3	
IRAN HVY		-1.75/-1.55	14:47	10NOV	-1.75/-1.55	FOB DIFF	A/G	30.8	
KIRKUK	DATED	-1.45/-1.25	14:47	10NOV	-1.45/-1.25	FOB DIFF	MED		
OSEBERG		-0.05/	14:47	10NOV	-0.05/	FOB DIFF	Stur	34.8	
QUA IBOE	DATED	/+0.05	14:47	10NOV	/+0.05	FOB DIFF	Nig		
Sahara B		+0.05/+0.15	14:47	10NOV	+0.05/+0.15	FOB DIFF			
Siberian		-0.10/	14:47	10NOV	-0.10/	FOB DIFF			
STATFJOR		-0.15/-0.10	14:47	10NOV	-0.15/-0.10	FOB DIFF	PLAT	38.3	
Urals/Br	DTD	-0.60/-0.45	14:47	10NOV	-0.60/-0.45	CIF DIFF	MED	32.0	
URALS NW	DATED	-0.60/-0.50	14:47	10NOV	-0.60/-0.50	CIF DIFF	NWE		

Crude oils are the raw material for conversion into products which can be used by consumers, for example, LPG, gasoline (petrol) and jet fuel (kerosene). The conversion process is called **refining** and takes place in complex chemical plants – refineries – which may or not be close to the actual production site of the crude oil. The refining process is described next.

However, many traders prefer using the 15-day Brent forwards market prices because there is greater liquidity in this market and so it is easier to hedge a cargo. If one party wishes to use a Dated Brent price and the other a forward price, then the differential between the prices is important. This type of arrangement is known as a **Contract For Difference (CFD);** this differential in prices is available on Reuters.

```
O#BRT-CFD          Brent CFD's
Delivery    Basis        Buy   Sell  Time  Date      Previous Day
NOV 09-13 vs.DEC Brent  -0.97 -0.95 18:12 09NOV98   -0.81 -0.79
NOV 16-20 vs.JAN Brent  -0.91 -0.87 12:40 10NOV98   -0.92 -0.95
NOV 23-27 vs.JAN Brent  -0.71 -0.68 12:40 10NOV98   -0.75 -0.72
NOV 31-04 vs.JAN Brent  -0.68 -0.64 12:40 10NOV98   -0.70 -0.68
          vs.  Brent              12:01 08JAN98   -0.49 -0.45
          vs.  Brent              10:15 29DEC97
          vs.  Brent              10:15 29DEC97
```

West Texas Intermediate (WTI)

WTI describes a variety of crudes which meet a certain specification – it is not a single type of crude. The main delivery point of WTI is Cushing, Oklahoma where it is delivered by pipeline. US law prevents the export of WTI or any other US crude with the exception of crude from Cook Inlet, Alaska. The NYMEX Light Sweet Crude futures contract, formally known as WTI, is the largest energy futures contract traded in terms of value and volume.

WTI is used as a benchmark for other North American crude oils which are priced at a differential to WTI in the same way as Brent is used in Europe.

The Reuters screens below shows WTT prices and the differentials for WTI versus other crude oils.

```
O#WT-                WTI PRICES
Name     Delivery  Buy   Sell   Time  Date  Prev.Close   Terms       Source API  Sulphur
WTI                13.36/13.42 21:30 09NOV 13.89/13.96 FOB CUSHING  US   39.6 0.827
WTI                13.58/13.63 21:15 09NOV 14.06/14.11 FOB CUSHING  US   39.6 0.827
WTC-Pp   Spot      +2.35/+2.37 14:31 09NOV +2.35/+2.37 PP  CUSHING  US   39.6 0.827
WTI-Midl           13.02/13.05 21:30 09NOV 13.58/13.60 FOB MIDLAND  US   39.6 0.827
Cush-Mid Spot      -0.37/-0.34 21:29 09NOV -0.35/-0.33 FOB DIFF     US   39.6 0.827
WTS                11.69/11.74 21:30 09NOV 12.25/12.30 FOB MIDLAND  US   34.1 0.863
WTI-WTS  Spot      -1.70/-1.65 21:29 09NOV -1.68/-1.63 FOB DIFF     US   34.1
```

```
O#C-DIF-N            CRUDE DIFFS - US
Name     Delivery  Buy   Sell   Time  Date  Prev.Close   Terms       Source API  Sulphur
Cush-Mid Spot      -0.29/-0.26 19:45 12FEB -0.24/-0.21 FOB DIFF     US   39.6 0.002
WTI-LLS  Spot      -0.57/-0.53 15:23 12FEB -0.57/-0.54 FOB DIFF     US   34.7 0.003
WTI-HLS  Spot      -0.82/-0.78 14:36 12FEB -0.82/-0.78 FOB DIFF     US   31.6 0.003
WTI-WTS  Spot      -1.30/-1.25 19:47 12FEB -1.22/-1.17 FOB DIFF     US   34.1 0.016
WTI-EUGI Spot      -1.15/-1.05 14:36 12FEB -1.15/-1.05 FOB DIFF     US   30.0 0.016
WTC-Pp   Spot      +2.52/+2.54 15:20 12FEB +2.51/+2.53 PP  CUSHING  US   39.6 0.002
WTI-BRT1 Feb          /        05:03 15FEB    /        FOB DIFF     US   38.3
WTI-BRT2 Mar      +1.50/       11:50 15FEB +1.47/      FOB DIFF     US   38.3

BRT-BRT1 Mar/Apr  -0.20/-0.16 00:00 15FEB -0.20/-0.16 FOB DIFF     US   38.3
BRT-BRT2 Apr/May  -0.22/-0.20 00:00 15FEB -0.22/-0.20 FOB DIFF     US   38.3
BRT-BRT3 May/Jun  -0.22/-0.18 00:00 15FEB -0.22/-0.18 FOB DIFF     US   38.3
BRT-DUB1 Mar      +0.70/+0.80 00:00 15FEB +0.70/+0.80 FOB DIFF     US   31.8
BRT-DUB2 Apr      +0.40/+0.50 00:00 15FEB +0.40/+0.50 FOB DIFF     US   31.8
DUB-DUB1 Mar/Apr  -0.25/-0.15 00:00 15FEB -0.25/-0.15 FOB DIFF     US   31.8
DUB-DUB2 Apr/May  -0.20/-0.17 00:00 15FEB -0.20/-0.17 FOB DIFF     US   31.8
DUB-DUB3 May/Jun  -0.19/-0.16 00:00 15FEB -0.19/-0.16 FOB DIFF     US   31.8
Line 63  FEB/FEB  -2.20/-2.10 22:02 12FEB -2.20/-2.10 WTI DIFF     US   30.0 0.01
ANS USWC FEB/FEB  -1.63/-1.53 22:02 12FEB -1.63/-1.53 WTI DIFF     US   27.9 0.011
ANS Diff FEB/FEB      /       22:02 12FEB     /       WTI DIFF     US   27.9 0.011
WilnngP+ Spot     +0.50/+0.60 22:02 12FEB +0.50/+0.60 PP  POSTING+ US   18.4 0.015
KernRvP+ Spot         /+0.10  22:02 12FEB     /+0.10  PP  POSTING+ US   13.4 0.012
```

The Refining Process

The refining process can be broken down into four stages which will each be described briefly:

1. Gas separation
2. Fractional distillation
3. Cracking
4. Extraction and treatment processes

Gas Separation

This usually takes place at the well-head where most natural gas is separated from the crude oil before it is piped or transported to the refinery.

Fractional Distillation (topping)

When crude oil is heated in a large container the lightest and most volatile products evaporate first and the heaviest products last. If the vapours are cooled then they condense in the opposite order, that is, heaviest first. This process of evaporation and condensation is called distillation and in the refinery distillation is carried out in tall cylindrical columns. Different refining fractions are obtained by placing trays at various levels to collect the condensing vapours as they ascend the column. Condensing liquids fall back towards the bottom of the column.

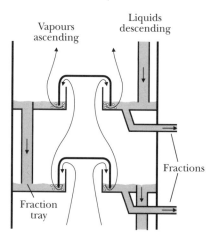

Vapours ascending / Liquids descending / Fractions / Fraction tray

This entire process is called fractional distillation. When crude oil is fractionally distilled under atmospheric conditions the process yields the more volatile fractions of gasoline, kerosene, gasoil and diesel. If the products of this distillation are further fractionally distilled under vacuum, the process yields the heavier products of lubricating oils, paraffin waxes, fuel oils and bitumen.

There are four basic components resulting from the distillation process – the proportion varies depending on the quality of crude oil. The various percentage components and the products from the fractional distillation of light and heavy crudes are shown in the table below:

Component	Light	Heavy	Products
Gases	5%	5%	Propane Butane
Spirits	20%	15%	Gasoline (petrol) Naphtha
Distillates	35%	25%	Kerosene (paraffin) Jet fuel Gasoils Heating oils for industry Diesel
Residues	40%	55%	Fuels Bitumen

Cracking

The market demand for the lighter products such as gasoline far outweighs the amount obtained by simple fractional distillation. Therefore some of the heavier crude components are cracked to produce lighter products. Cracking can be carried out either by subjecting the components to heat and pressure in the presence of a catalyst.

Extraction and Treatment Processes

Impurities in crude oil such as sulphur have to be removed in the refining process. Therefore sweet crude oils are more valuable than sour oils as not so much processing is required.

The whole refining process is illustrated in the simplified diagram below:

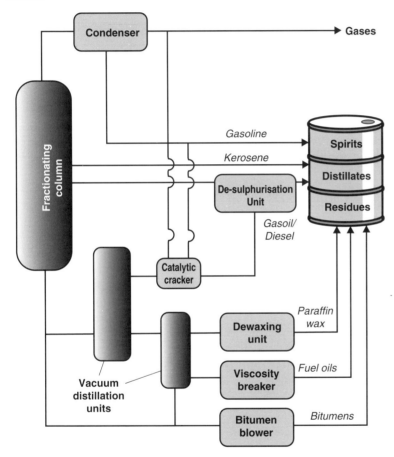

The Reuters screens below show gasoline, jet and LPG spot prices.

```
O#GL-            GASOLINE
Name    Loc  Delivery    Buy    Sell   C Units  Terms          Spec 1 Spec 2
Premium NWE  PROMPT    135.00 138.00   D/T     CIF            UNL    95 RON
Premium NWE  PROMPT    125.00 128.00   D/T     FOB            UNL    95 RON
Pren 98 NWE  PROMPT    150    155      D/T     CIF            98 RON
Pren 98 NWE  PROMPT    134    138      D/T     FOB            98 RON
Regular NWE  PROMPT    125.00 127.00   D/T     CIF            UNL    91 RON
Regular NWE  PROMPT    115.00 117.00   D/T     FOB            UNL    91 RON
Premium ARA  PROMPT    129.00 131.00   D/T     FOB            UNL    95 RON
Premium ARA  NOV 16-30 130.00 131.00   D/T     FOB            UNL    95 RON
Premium ARA  Nov       130.00 0        D/T     FOB Swap       UNL
```

```
O#JET-            JET
Name     Loc  Delivery    Buy    Sell   C Units Terms          Spec 1 Spec 2
JET FUEL NWE  PROMPT    124.00 126.00   D/T     CIF
JET FUEL NWE  PROMPT    116.00 118.00   D/T     FOB
JET      ARA  PROMPT    122.00 124.00   D/T     FOB
JET      MED  PROMPT    120.00 123.00   D/T     FOB
JET/KERO AG   PROMPT     13.75  14.00   D/B     FOB
JET/KERO SING PROMPT     15.00  15.10   D/B     FOB            DPK    0.8
JET/KERO TYO  PROMPT     16.20  16.40   D/B     C+F            A1     0.8
JET      USG  PROMPT     38.25  38.50   C/GAL   FOB USGulf
JET      USG  NOV 11-20  37.75  38.00   C/GAL   FOB USGulf
```

```
O#LPG-            LPG
Name     Loc  Delivery    Buy    Sell   C Units  Terms         Spec 1 Spec 2
BUTANE   NWE  PROMPT    170.00 180.00   D/T     CIF N SEA
BUTANE   NWE  PROMPT    160.00 170.00   D/T     FOB N SEA
PROPANE  NWE  PROMPT    190.00 195.00   D/T     CIF N SEA
PROPANE  NWE  PROMPT    182.00 185.00   D/T     FOB N SEA
BUTANE   MED  PROMPT    185.00 190.00   D/T     CIF
PROPANE  MED  PROMPT    190.00 195.00   D/T     CIF
BUTANE   AG   PROMPT    218.00 220.00   D/T     FOB
PROPANE  AG   PROMPT    183.00 185.00 N D/T     FOB
BUTANE   TYO  PROMPT    190.00 196.00   D/T     C+F
PROPANE  TYO  PROMPT    180.00 195.00 N D/T     C+F
BUTANE   USG  PROMPT     31.50  32.00   C/GAL   FOB MtBlvieu
ETHANE   USG  PROMPT     18.00  18.50   C/GAL   FOB MtBlvieu
ISOBUT   USG  PROMPT     31.00  31.50   C/GAL   FOB MtBlvieu
ETHMIX   USG  PROMPT     18.25  18.75   C/GAL   FOB MtBlvieu
NATGASOL USG  PROMPT     33.50  34.00   C/GAL   FOB MtBlvieu
PROPANE  USG  PROMPT     25.50  25.75   C/GAL   FOB MtBlvieu
BUTANE   USMC PROMPT     29.25  29.75   C/GAL   FOB Conway
ETHANE   USMC PROMPT     16.00  16.50   C/GAL   FOB Conway
ISOBUT   USMC PROMPT     31.25  31.50   C/GAL   FOB Conway
NATGASOL USMC PROMPT     31.75  32.25   C/GAL   FOB Conway
PROPANE  USMC PROMPT     24.25  24.50   C/GAL   FOB Conway
BUTANE   CAN  PROMPT     29.00  29.50   C/GAL   FOB Sarnia
BUTANE   CAN  PROMPT     20.75  21.25   C/GAL   FOB Ednonton F BUT
ISOBUT   CAN  PROMPT     28.00  28.50   C/GAL   FOB Sarnia
PROPANE  CAN  PROMPT     17.75  18.25   C/GAL   FOB Ednonton
```

How Do the Commodities, Energy & Transport Markets Work?

Energy Products

The table below indicates the various products and some of their uses.

	Product	Uses
Gases	**Propane and butane or LPG (LPG)**	These gases provide a valuable feedstock for the chemicals and plastics industries where they are used, for example, in the production of solvents, aerosols, polyethylene and polystyrene. The gases are compressed to produce Liquefied Petroleum Gas (LPG) which is used as a domestic and industrial fuel.
Spirits	**Gasoline or Mogas (GL)**	Motor Gasoline (Mogas) or petrol is a blend with different grades based on **octane rating**. This rating is measured using the **Research Octane Number (RON)** and indicates the resistance of petrol to pre-ignite or "knock" in an engine – the higher the rating the better the fuel burns. Most Mogas is now divided into Regular and Premium grades. Petrol used to have Tetraethyl lead (TEL) added to prevent "knocking". On combustion TEL releases toxic lead fumes into the atmosphere. With modern developments in engine technology, **unleaded gasoline** is gradually replacing the leaded grades.
	Naphtha (NAF)	This is also used for gasoline production by processing and blending. It is also used as a chemical feedstock for the production of Benzene-Toluene-Xylene (BTX) which are used in the manufacture of nylon, polyesters, dyes and polyurethanes.
Distillates	**Kerosene, Jet fuel and Jet-kero (JET)**	Kerosene or **paraffin** is used as a heating fuel in Asia and for lamps. Jet fuel is basically the same as kerosene but has to meet rigid quality specifications.
	Gasoil (GO), Heating oil (HO) and Diesel (DL)	These are basically the same product only differing in the exact specification for their particular use in diesel engines and as industrial oils in large furnaces. You may also see reference to Marine Gasoil (MGO) and Marine Diesel Oil (MDO).
Residues	**Fuel oil (FO)** **Residual Oil (FO)** **Bunker Fuel (BK)**	These comprise heating oils, heavy diesel and heavy industrial fuels for industry, shipping and power generation. Bunker fuel is the name given to the fuel used in marine engines and comes from the days when ships were powered by coal which was stored in bunkers.
	Bitumen **Asphalt**	This is the "tar" residue which is used in road building and the construction industry.

The Reuters screens below provide more detail about crude oil and product production for the US and European markets.

```
O#API-STATS      Exchange   API STATISTICS
RIC              ID         Contract
O#API-FLASH      /          KEY API STATS
O#PADD1-API      /          PADD1-API
O#PADD2-API      /          PADD2-API
O#PADD3-API      /          PADD3-API
O#PADD4-API      /          PADD4-API
O#PADD5-API      /          PADD5-API
O#LPG-API        /          LPG-API
O#MOGAS-API      /          MOGAS-API
O#DST-API        /          DST-API
O#JET-API        /          JET-API
O#UNFIN-API      /          UNFIN-API
O#RESID-API      /          RESID-API
O#CRUDE-API      /          CRUDE-API
O#REF-API        /          REF-API
```

```
O#API-FLASH           KEY API STATS
Commodity        Last            Srce   Terms   Loc   Ccy Units Date
CRUDE STOCK      ↓ 325966  -7426  API                 US          09FEB99
TTL DST STOCK    ↑ 148323  +72    API                 US          09FEB99
GAS STOCK        ↑ 228543  +4119  API                 US          09FEB99
NPH JET STOCK    ↑    39   +1     API                 US          09FEB99
JET KERO STOCK   ↓ 45036   -1668  API                 US          09FEB99
CRUDE RUNS       ↑ 14412   +189   API                 US          09FEB99
PCT CAP OPERATED ↑  93.1   +0.9   API                 US          09FEB99

CRUDE STOCK PD1  ↓ 14426   -118   API                 PD1         09FEB99
DST STOCK PD1    ↓ 66417   -1144  API                 PD1         09FEB99
GAS STOCK PD1    ↑ 67505   +2352  API                 PD1         09FEB99
NPH JET STK PD1      0     0      API                 PD1         30APR96
JET KERO STK PD1 ↓ 11272   -511   API                 PD1         09FEB99
CRUDE RUNS PD1   ↑  1640   +56    API                 PD1         09FEB99
PCT CAP OP PD1   ↑ 100.8   +3.3   API                 PD1         09FEB99

CRUDE STOCK PD2  ↓ 68103   -2045  API                 PD2         09FEB99
DST STOCK PD2    ↑ 35599   +952   API                 PD2         09FEB99
GAS STOCK PD2    ↑ 62131   +3407  API                 PD2         09FEB99
NPH JET STK PD2      0     0      API                 PD2         24JUN97
JET KERO STK PD2 ↓  9002   -154   API                 PD2         09FEB99
CRUDE RUNS PD2   ↑  3300   +8     API                 PD2         09FEB99
PCT CAP OP PD2   ↓  95.6   -0.6   API                 PD2         09FEB99
```

```
PRODUS                    US PRODUCTS
NO 2 HT OIL            High  Low  Spread    UNLEAD GAS              High Low
DEC8 ↓3760   +15  3785 3710   3.50    DEC8 ↑4110  +30   4125 4060
JAN9 ↓3880   -1   3905 3845   2.85    JAN9 ↓4165  +14   4180 4130
           US Gulf        NY Harbor        Mid Cont       Los Angeles
Product   <O#P-USG>       <O#P-NYH>       <O#P-MC>        <O#P-LA>
Propane   25.50/25.75        /           24.25/24.50          /
Regular   35.35/35.60    39.10/39.35     39.10/39.35     47.00/48.00
Premiun   38.15/38.60    42.85/43.10     42.10/42.60     52.50/53.50
No2/Dsl   34.90/35.10    36.60/36.85     40.60/40.85     42.50/43.50
Jet       38.60/38.85    43.20/43.60     42.10/42.60     42.00/43.00
Resid1%   10.50/11.00    11.25/11.50         /           79.00/81.00
Resid3%    9.75/10.00    10.25/10.50         /           75.00/77.00
```

```
PRODEUR                European Products Overview
              Last   Chg   Bid   Ask   Vol                    Last  Chg  Bid   Ask   Vol
GAS OIL NOV8  ↑10700 -125 10675 10700  8969  BRENT CRUDE DEC8↑ 1196  +6  1197 1199 13248
GAS OIL DEC8  ↑11050 -250 11050 11075 11486  BRENT CRUDE JAN9↑ 1230  +4  1230 1232 11034
                 FOB NWE         CIF NWE         FOB MED          CIF MED          FOB ARA
               10NOV 12:39     10NOV 12:39     10NOV 15:30      10NOV 15:30      10NOV 14:14
Premiun UNL    125.00/128.00   135.00/138.00   132.00/138.00    140.00/146.00   129.00/131.00
Regular UNL    115.00/117.00   125.00/127.00        /                /          121.00/124.00
NAPHTHA             /          131.00/134.00   120.00/122.00    130.00/133.00   135.00/137.00
JET FUEL       116.00/118.00   124.00/126.00   120.00/123.00         /          122.00/124.00
Gas Oil FOD     98.00/101.00   105.50/107.25    98.00/101.00    106.00/109.00   107.00/108.00
Gas Oil RUSSIA      /          105.00/109.00        /           105.00/108.00        /
Diesel C GERMAN     /          114.50/116.50   109/112          117/120        115.00/116.00
FUEL OIL 1.0%S  63.00/65.00     71.00/73.00     62.00/64.00      70.00/73.00     70.00/72.00
FUEL OIL 3.5%S  50.00/52.00     57.00/59.00     53.00/55.00      61.00/63.00     59.00/61.00
SRFO    0.7%S   70.00/72.00     78.00/80.00         /            66/69               /

    Help: <ENERGY>  Other displays: <OILOIL><NYMOIL><IPEOIL><OILARB><OILSPD><PRODUS>
```

How Do the Commodities, Energy & Transport Markets Work?

The Reuters screens below show the Speed Guide index for energy specifications, with a particular example of mogas (motor gasoline) in Europe.

```
ENERGY SPECIFICATION DETAILS - REUTERS SPEED GUIDE              ENGSPECA
Specifications of Spot Price Assessments - INDEX

=EUROPEAN PRODUCTS====================  =AMERICAN PRODUCTS====================
Mogas......................<ENGSPECB>  Mogas......................<ENGSPECM>
Naphtha....................<ENGSPECC>  Jet........................<ENGSPECN>
Jet & Gasoil...............<ENGSPECD>  Heating Oil / Diesel.......<ENGSPECO>
Fuel-Cracked...............<ENGSPECE>  Residual Fuel..............<ENGSPECP>
Fuel-Straight Run..........<ENGSPECF>  MTBE / RFG.................<ENGSPECQ>

=ASIAN PRODUCTS=======================  =OTHERS==============================
Mogas......................<ENGSPECH>  Bunker Fuels...............<ENGSPECT>
Naphtha....................<ENGSPECI>
Jet & Kerosene.............<ENGSPECJ>  =FUTURES=============================
Gasoil.....................<ENGSPECK>  IPE Futures...............<IPE/FUTEX1>
Fueloil....................<ENGSPECL>  Nymex Futures.............<NYM/FUTEX1>

=CRUD
Bren  ENERGY SPECIFICATION DETAILS - REUTERS SPEED GUIDE           ENGSPECB
      Products Specifications - Europe

Ques  GASOLINE    <O#GL-E> <O#PU-ARA-S>
====  ========
Main  SUPER PREMIUM 98 UNLEADED
   L  Octane = 98 RON, 88 MON, Specific Gravity = 0.755 g/ml
      Sulphur Max 500 ppm, Benzene Max 1%
      Reid Vapour Pressure
          Summer (1/4 through 30/9)  0.45-0.70 Bar
          Winter (1/10 through 31/3) 0.60-0.90 Bar

      PREMIUM UNLEADED, NWE CARGO and ARA BARGE = (GERMAN GRADE)
      Octane = 95 RON, 85 MON, Specific Gravity = 0.755 g/ml

      REGULAR UNLEADED
       Octane = 91 RON, 82.5 MON, Specific Gravity = 0.745 g/ml

      PREMIUM 0.15 G/L - ***DISCONTINUED For NWE, MED and ARA from April 22 1996.
      Octane = 97-98 RON, 86-88 MON, Specific Gravity = 0.755 g/ml
      RVP (Reid Vapour Pressure) varies seasonally by country

      =================================================================
      Other Specs <ENGSPECA>     US Mogas <ENGSPECM>     Asian Mogas <ENGSPECH>
        Lost? Selective Access?..<USER/HELP>   Reuters Phone Support..<PHONE/HELP>
```

Netbacks

The concept behind a netback is to assign a **value** to a particular crude rather than a straightforward cost. The value of a barrel of crude is dependent on its quality and on the worth of the refined products.

To calculate a netback the following data and costs must be known:

- The yield of products from the specific crude and refinery
- The local market price for each of the products
- The refinery costs
- The cost of transporting the oil

The revenue from products can therefore be derived from the respective yields and market prices. Some refineries can only top or distil whereas others can crack to produce more valuable products.

Reuters uses two types of refining scenarios:

- Topping
- Cracking

REUTERS

The Reuters screens below illustrate netbacks for crudes in Europe and North America.

```
ENERGY NETBACKS - REUTERS SPEED GUIDE                              NETBACKS
To access information, double-click on the code in < > or [ ] brackets.

=NETBACK PAGE DISPLAYS================     =*NETBACK RIC TILES===================
NorthWest Europe (ARA).......<NETBACKA>    European (ARA & Med).............<NB-E>
Mediterranean................<NETBACKB>    Asian (Singapore)...............<NB-A>
Singapore....................<NETBACKC>    US (Gulf, Mid Cont & LA).......<NB-N>
US Gulf coast................<NETBACKD>
US Mid Continent.............<NETBACKE>    =MISCELLANEOUS======================
US West Coast(Los Angeles)...<NETBACKF>    Explanation of Calculations.<NETBACKT>
                                           List of Products used....<NETBACKX>
=REFINERY MAINTENANCE REPORTS=========     Representative routes ...<NETBACKZ>
European refinery maintenance...[REF/E]
```

```
NB-E              NETBACK SUMMARY   Netbacks Europe
Crude             Loc  Delivery Spot    Top    Crack  Freight   Time    API
ARAB LT MED NB    MED  SPOT     8.90    9.47   10.70            18:08   32.7
ES SIDER MED NB   MED  SPOT             10.08  11.24            16:54   36.9
FORCADOS MED NB   MED  SPOT     9.62    8.67   11.76            17:32   29.4
IRAN LT MED NB    MED  SPOT     9.97    9.02   10.58            17:31   34.0
KUWAIT MED NB     MED  SPOT             9.38   10.19            17:10   31.1
URALS CIF MED NB  MED  SPOT     9.27    9.60   10.67            17:32   32.0
ARAB LT NWE NB    NWE  SPOT     8.90    9.50   10.43    0.51    18:08   32.7
BONNY LT NWE NB   NWE  SPOT     9.77    10.79  11.62            17:42   36.7
```

```
NB-N              NETBACK SUMMARY   Netbacks NA
Crude             Loc   Delivery Spot   Top    Crack  Freight  Time   API
BONNY LT USG NB   USG   SPOT            10.04  11.20    1.25   21:32  36.7
WTI MIDL USG NB   USG   SPOT    11.63   9.98   11.71    1.05   21:32  39.6
ARAB LT USG NB    USG   SPOT    8.90    8.18   10.11    1.46   21:32  32.7
BRENT FWD USG NB  USG   SPOT    9.97    10.03  11.49    0.72   21:32  38.3
ISTHMUS USG NB    USG   SPOT            9.49   11.15    0.42   21:32  34.1
WTS USG NB        USG   SPOT    10.63   9.38   10.74    0.50   21:32  32.4
LLS USG NB        USG   SPOT    11.35   10.51  12.11    0.50   21:32  40.0
MAYA USG NB       USG   SPOT            7.40   8.29            21:32  22.1
MARS USG NB       USG   SPOT            9.27   10.58           21:32  31.0
WTI MIDL MC NB    USMC  SPOT    11.90   10.81  12.46           21:32  39.6
LLS MC NB         USMC  SPOT    11.35   11.17  12.33           21:32  40.0
MAYA MC NB        USMC  SPOT            7.36   8.23            21:32  22.1
ISTHMUS MC NB     USMC  SPOT            9.78   11.41           21:32  34.1
ANS CIF WC NB     USWC  SPOT    10.32   10.18  13.15           09:22  26.6
MINAS WC NB       USWC  SPOT    11.00   10.96  11.50           09:22  35.3
KERN RIV WC NB    USWC  SPOT    7.04    8.40   11.29           09:22  12.6
TAPIS WC NB       USWC  SPOT    11.30   13.52  14.79           09:22  46.3
WILMINGTON WC NB  USWC  SPOT    7.78    9.43   11.84           09:22  19.4
OMAN WC NB        USWC  SPOT    9.61    9.82   13.71           09:22  35.3
```

Refineries are very large, complex chemical plants that need regular, scheduled maintenance. There are times when refineries shut down due to accidents, mechanical failures etc. Whenever a refinery is shutdown, for whatever reason, it is termed a **turnaround**. Refineries can plan for scheduled turnarounds and stockpile products; however, unscheduled turnarounds requiring lengthy repairs can have severe financial consequences for both refinery owners and consumers. Refinery Maintenance Reports are shown on the Reuters screens below.

```
17:04  08 Feb  DIARY-Europe/Med/Africa Refinery 1999 Maintenance
    (Updates Italy, all Agip)
    LONDON, Feb 8(Reuters) - The following is a list of
maintenance plans compiled through a survey of European oil
refiners and analysts and will be updated as information becomes
available.
    Some refiners declined to confirm information about
shutdowns or would only partially confirm the data.
    All data refers to 1999 unless otherwise stated
    (* = Confirmed by company).
REFINERY      LOCATION      UNIT/DATE              CAPACITY BPD
ALGERIA (total capacity approx 483,000 bpd)
Sonatrach    Skikda                                335,000
             Alger                                 60,500
             Arzew                                 56,000
AUSTRIA (total capacity approx 210,000 bpd)
OMV          Schwechat   no information            210,000
BELGIUM (total capacity approx 639,000 bpd)
BRC          Antwer
Esso         Antwer
Petrofina    Antwer
Nynas        Antwer
BULGARIA (total c
*Nefotchin   Bourg
*Plana       Pleve
CROATIA (total ca
INA          Sisak
```

```
23:25  10 Feb  DIARY-U.S. Midwest Refinery Shutdowns - Clark
    Summary of U.S. Midwest refinery operations.
(Capacity in '000 bpd)
Company, location        Unit Capacity    Shutdown period
-------------------------------------------------------------
BP-AMOCO: Toledo, OH     CDU     160      Mar:6-wk maintenance
CITGO: Lemont, IL        FCC     65       Dec 29-Jan 18.
CLARK: Lima, OH          CDU     170      1Q, 4Q: major t/rnd
FARMLAND: Coffeyville, KS FCC    30       Mid-Feb for 2-3 wks.
GARY-WILLIAMS ENERGY CORP: Wynnewood, OK
                         cat cracker 18   Jan 19-Jan 24.
UDS: Ardmore, OK         CDU     77       Feb- cuts 10-pct
     Alma, MI            CDU     46            "
SUNOCO: Toledo, OH       CDU     140      Feb: cuts 25 kbpd
-------------------------------------------------------------

    The following list details Midwest refineries and their
main operating units and processing capacities, with outages
and operational problems listed for 1999.
    "*" indicates maintenance or outage confirmed by company.
    "+" denotes company, market or other sources.
    The list is compiled on a "best efforts" basis using market
sources where the company does not confirm and may not be
definitive.
COMPANY, LOCATION, REFINERY DETAILS
-------------------------------------------------------------
-----BP-AMOCO OIL CO
    1) WHITING, IN
    - Crude distillation:    410,000 bpd
    - Vacuum distillation:   228,000 bpd
    - Fluid cat cracking:    149,200 bpd
```

Profit margins are used as a key indicator of productivity levels of refineries. A refinery profit margin is calculated by subtracting the cost of crude oil and other operating costs from the value of the products produced – the Gross Product Value (GPV).

Profit margin = GPV – (cost of crude oil + operating costs)

The GPV is calculated by adding the revenues generated from fixed percentages of the refined products at four refining centres worldwide. The profit margins calculated are therefore only approximations and do not reflect the profitability of any particular refinery. Also the margins do not change with season.

You can use an electronic service such as Reuters to find out the recent profit margins for the four refining centres. The first Reuters screen at right shows Refinery Profit Margins, the next shows the yields used at the four centres and the last shows how costs are calculated.

```
12:19 10NOV98      Refinery Profit Margins           UK30507      REF/MARGIN1
                  US Gulf Coast    Rotterdam       Mediterranean   Singapore

$/barrel          Brent  WTI      Brent  Brent     Urals  Urals    Dubai  Dubai
                  crack  crack    crack  hydro     crack  hydro    crack  hydro

09-Nov Close      1.51  -0.60     2.37   1.66      2.19   1.23     1.44   0.79

Average
Last 5 days       1.61  -0.43     2.28   1.52      2.12   1.15     1.25   0.50
Last 15 days      1.77  -0.02     2.22   1.46      2.26   1.30     1.22   0.39

Oct-98            1.78   0.38     1.93   1.19      2.16   1.23     1.25   0.40
Sep-98            0.84  -0.38     1.17   0.35      0.89  -0.15     0.31  -0.47
Aug-98            0.75  -0.25     1.52   0.65      1.14   0.09    -0.15  -1.52
Jul-98            2.06   0.55     2.54   1.72      2.39   1.26     1.01  -0.81
Jun-98            2.68   1.56     2.48   1.73      3.18   2.37     1.47  -0.34
May-98            1.54   1.58     1.47   0.63      1.73   0.74     2.01   0.14
Mar-98            1.29   0.03     2.25   1.42      2.22   1.20     2.20   0.52
Feb-98            1.34   0.10     2.35   1.34      1.95   0.65     1.75  -0.48
```

```
09:52 17MAR97          REFINERY PROFIT MARGINS       UK30507   REFINERY/MARGIN3
The table below details the yields of various refined oil products used to
calculate refinery profit margins.

              US Gulf Coast    Rotterdam       Mediterranean   Singapore

              Brent  WTI      Brent  Brent     Urals  Urals    Dubai  Dubai
              crack  crack    crack  hydro     crack  hydro    crack  hydro

Gasoline      49.24  51.79    28.56  17.00     25.22  12.84    26.56  11.91
Naphtha                        9.08   6.49      8.88   6.68     7.41   5.14
Jet/kerosene   2.62   2.62     8.88   9.39      4.40   8.60     3.96   9.90
Gas oil       29.69  30.04    37.45  35.98     36.81  30.60    38.55  24.38
1 pct fuel    16.56  13.51    14.36  28.41      9.54  19.95
3.5 pct fuel                                   13.97  19.19    22.25  46.15

Total         98.11  97.96    98.32  97.27     98.82  97.86    98.72  97.48
```

```
08:43 09OCT98        Refinery Profit Margins         UK30507      REF/MARGIN4
The table below details the Reuter Instrument Codes or RICs for oil prices used
in calculating refinery profit margins. To see the underlying prices double
click on the codes between <> brackets. To see weight to volume conversions
please double click on <REFINERY/MARGIN5>.

              US Gulf Coast    Rotterdam       Mediterranean    Singapore

              Brent  WTI      Brent  Brent     Urals  Urals     Dubai  Dubai
              crack  crack    crack  hydro     crack  hydro     crack  hydro

Gasoline      <RU-USG>         <PU-ARA>        <PU-F-MED>        <GL95-SIN>
Naphtha                        <NAF-ARA>       <NAF-F-MED>       <NAF-SIN>
Jet/kerosene  <JET-USG>        <JET-ARA>       <JET-F-MED>       <JET-SIN>
Gas oil       <HO-USG>         <GO-E-ARA>      <GO-FE-MED>       <GO-SIN>
1 pct fuel    <FO1-L-USG>      <LFO-ARA>       <LFO-F-MED>
3.5 pct fuel                                   <HFO-F-MED>       <FO380-SIN>
Crude oil     <BRT-N> <WTC->        <BRT-E>    <URL-E>           <DUB-1M-A>
Freight       <DFRT-UKC-TA-S> <DFRT-INT-UKC>                     <DFRT-ME-SIN>
Fixed costs   $0.50  $0.50    $0.40  $0.30     $0.40  $0.30      $0.35  $0.25
Other costs   0.45   0.60     0.81   0.81      0.41   0.41       0.10   0.10

Note: Fixed costs reflect refinery operating costs in $ per barrel. Other costs
reflect insurance, ocean loss and credit in percentage of crude oil price.
Other costs also include pipeline cost $0.60 for WTI refined on US Gulf coast.
```

Reuters news service provides a glossary of energy terms for its users, as illustrated below.

Your notes

```
ENERGY TERMS AND ABBREVIATIONS                              ENERGY/TERMS1
Typical Terms and Abbreviations

ADNOC:  Abu Dhabi National Oil Company
AGA:    American Gas Association (a trade group representing companies
        in the U.S. natgas industry)
AG:     Arab Gulf
ALEP:   Arab Light Equivalent Price. Used as a measure of the relative
        worths of different crude oils
ANS:    Alaskan North Slope Crude oil
API:    American Petroleum Institute: Often refers to the API scale of  measure
        for Gravity
APPI:   Asian Petroleum Price Index - commonly used to price Asian  crudes
ARA:    Amsterdam-Rotterdam-Antwerp region
ARB:    A term used by futures traders for the spread between a crude  oil and
        one or more products
Avails: Availability's
AV:     Average
AVG:    Average
Barge:  Oil carrying vessel of up to 50,000 barrel capacity, mostly  employed
        on lakes and rivers
Batch:  A measured amount of oil in a pipeline.
```

```
ENERGY TERMS AND ABBREVIATIONS                              ENERGY/TERMS9
ULCC:   Ultra Large Crude Carrier
UNL:    Unleaded Gasoline
USG:    United States Gulf Coast
USWC:   United States West Coast
VAN:    Vanadium: A heavy metal found in fuel oil and an undesirable impurity
VLCC:   Very Large Crude Carrier
WS:     World Scale: An index of freight rates between various ports
WTI:    West Texas Internediate Crude oil
WTS:    West Texas Sour Crude oil
YIELD:  The relative quantities of various products than can be obtained from a
        crude at a refinery.


        Main Guide <REUTERS>
```

Shipping

Types of Business

Although the Baltic Exchange is the only centralised market for fixing vessels, its importance has been much reduced with the improved international communications systems and services offered by organisations such as Reuters. There are now major shipping centres located worldwide including London, New York, Los Angeles, Tokyo, Paris, Rotterdam, Oslo and Singapore.

Three types of business are transacted at these centres:

- **Tankers**. This market is focused on chartering **dirty** (crude oil) and **clean** (refined oil products) tankers for the movement of these commodities in **bulk**. If the oil is in barrels then it would be a dry cargo. This market also includes specialist tankers for the transport of chemicals, vegetable oils and gases.

- **Dry cargo**. This type deals with almost every other type of cargo, for example, container ships, bulk carriers, ore carriers etc. Some ships operating in this market are flexible in their construction so that they can be used as Ore, Bulk and Oil (OBO) carriers.

- **Sale and Purchase**. There is a large market in "second-hand" ships in which vessels change ownership but remain trading. Allied with this market are "scrap" dealings in which vessels are bought for their scrap value only.

Types of Vessels

There are a number of different types of vessel used or that can be chartered depending on the cargo to be transported. The major types are briefly described here.

Tankers

These vessels are designed to carry liquid cargoes, usually crude oil or its products, which are pumped directly into the vessel's holds. These comprise self-contained tanks with dividers, to stop the cargo shifting; expansion tanks, to allow cargoes to expand in hot weather; and liquid-tight covers.

The size of tankers is measured in two main ways:

1. **Dead Weight Tonnage (Dwt)**. This is the most usual method and represents the cargo and fuel (bunker) carrying capacity of the vessel.

2. **Displacement**. This is a measure based on the tonnage of water displaced which is the sum of the cargo plus vessel weights.

Tankers range from 1,000 tonnes unladen up to 300,000 tonnes unladen for a **Very Large Crude Carrier (VLCC)** and up to 550,000 tonnes for the largest **Ultra Large Crude Carrier (ULCC)**, the *Jahre Viking*.

Unladen tonnages for tankers		
Coasters Chems, Veg. Oil etc	**Clean/Dirty** Oil products	**Crude oil**
1,000 – 30,000	15,000 – 70,000	30,000 – 500,000
		VLCC = 200 – 299,000 ULCC = >300,000

Today's tanker is on average 15 years old and in recent times there has been a move away from U and VLCCs. The reasons for this include a surplus of worldwide tanker tonnage, a move away from Gulf crude oil in the 1980s and the possible environmental effects of oil spillages from such large vessels.

Container Vessels

These have been in use since the 1970s – some can accommodate up to 3000 containers. They offer rapid loading and unloading and are very flexible in the types of cargoes transported.

Tramp Steamers and Coastal Vessels

The tramp steamer or general trader is designed with large holds to carry bulk commodities such as ore, grain, timber etc. There are large fleets of tramp steamers operating off the coasts of Asia, the US and continental Europe.

Ore, Bulk and Oil Carriers (OBOs)

Tankers shipping crude oil between production site and refinery tend to make the return journey empty – in ballast. This is obviously a waste of resources and certain vessels have been converted to carry ore and bulk cargoes on the return trip.

This allows a much more economic and profitable use of the vessel.

LNG Carriers

The transportation of highly volatile **Liquefied Natural Gas (LNG)** has meant that special vessels have had to be built which will keep the cargo under pressure and at a temperature of minus 161°C. These vessels are characterised by their large spherical insulated tanks.

RoRo vessels

These vessels are in common use on ferry routes providing a rapid Roll-On-Roll-Off system for the transportation of commodities.

The Charter Party

On the exchange floor a vessel is fixed and the contract terms are agreed by word of mouth. This contractural pledge is epitomised in the Baltic Exchange motto – *Our word is our bond*. However, the contract is made legally binding using a written contract that is signed by both parties. This document is known as a **charter party** and comes from the Latin *carta partita* meaning 'divided paper'.

The charter party must be in hard copy. Standard charter party contracts for voyage and time charters exist having names such as Texacovoy and Essotime.

Types of Charter

There are a number of ways a vessel can be fixed for a particular charter which have implications for the costs of transporting and delivering a commodity. The types of charter described briefly here cover:

- Time charter by demise
- Time charter non-demise
- Single voyage charter
- Consecutive voyage charter
- Tonnage exchange

Time Charter by Demise

A **demise** or **bareboat** charter is one in which the shipowner simply provides a vessel of the type required. The charterer provides or covers the cargo, bunker (fuel), port fees, crew and all other associated costs such as food, insurance etc.

The term **bunker** refers to the slow burning fuel oil used by ships for propulsion, heating and electricity generation. Bunker costs can represent up to 60% of the operating cost of a vessel. There are numerous ports around the world offering bunkering – refuelling – facilities. It is worth remembering that a U/VLCC may use up to 90 tonnes of fuel per day.

A bareboat charter is usually for a specified period of time – 5 years or more is common. A time charter by demise means that the charterer effectively operates the vessel as his own.

Time Charter Non-Demise

In this case the charterer takes the vessel for a fixed period ranging anywhere from a few weeks to 5 years. The ship owner effectively operates the vessel and charges the charterer on a cost per day or cost per dead weight tonne per month basis.

Single Voyage Charter

This is the most common type of charter for a one-way voyage between specified ports for a specified cargo. Once the charterer gets the cargo to port the rate paid pays all the vessel costs and normally includes 72 hours for loading and discharging the cargo. This time allocated for loading and discharging a vessel is known as **laytime**. Any delay beyond the allocated time is charged at a per tonne basis and is known as **demurrage**. These demurrage charges can be a considerable sum for long delays involving large vessels.

Consecutive Voyage Charter

In this type of fixture the shipowner undertakes to conduct a series of continuous voyages for the charterer. The speed and fuel consumption of the vessel are not guaranteed and the charterer has to pay for the fuel costs on an on-going basis.

Tonnage Exchange

Ship operators may exchange vessels for logistical reasons. The transaction does not necessarily involve the exchange of funds although this may be taken into account if there are significant differences in vessel sizes and operating costs.

Contract for Affreightment

This may also be known as a **lump-sum** contract. An owner agrees to perform a given number of voyages to carry a specified amount of cargo for a given rate, usually between two locations and within a defined period. The contract does not always specify the vessel by name. For a charterer who simply wants to transport a cargo within a certain timescale this type of contract offers a degree of security without the risk of a time charter which may not be fully utilised.

Tanker Fixtures and Worldscale

The rate for a single voyage tanker charter is either as a cost/metric tonne of cargo or is based on a **Worldscale (WS)** rate. The WS rate is a benchmark, or reference rate which both the charterer and shipowner can use to independently arrive at an agreed rate for the fixture. The **standard rate**, WS100, is based on a 'standard vessel' which is a 75,000 tonne tanker and is also known as the WS **flat** rate. If applied the WS100 or flat rate gives the specific cost of a cargo based on a per tonne rate. Smaller vessels with lower operating costs and greater flexibility trade at a higher rate. In times of tonnage shortage or surplus owners may quote at greater than or less than WS100 respectively. The WS rates are published in book form which also includes demurrage rates, canal fees and discharge fees.

Example

A 50,000 tonne naphtha cargo is to be transported from Yanbu on the Red Sea to Rotterdam at a rate of WS120. The vessel will use the Suez Canal and discharge the cargo at Rotterdam. Both these latter activities will involve additional fees as specified in the Worldscale book. For fee calculations for using the Suez Canal the ship's net tonnage is 21,000 metric tonnes (mt).

Cargo costs		Worldscale $/mt
Yanbu – Rotterdam rate	=	7.49
Rotterdam discharge differential	=	0.49
		7.98
Agreed rate WS120. (7.98 x 120%)	=	9.58
Yanbu fixed differential to be added	=	0.27
Total per tonne of cargo	=	9.85

Worldscale cost = 50,000 x 9.85 = $492,500

Suez Canal costs		Costs, $
Lump sum	=	140,500
21,000 x $3.72	=	78,120
Total Suez Canal costs	=	**218,620**

Total cost of voyage

Worldscale cost	=	492,500
Suez Canal cost	=	218,620
Total voyage cost	=	**711,120**
Cost per tonne of naphtha cargo=		**14.22**

The Reuters screen below shows Worldscale Market Rates.

```
                                                      TANKER/RATE1
17-Mar-99
ROUTE              WS RATE    $/TONNE    VESSEL    SIZE
MidEast-West        58.00      9.20      Dty       250
MidEast-Japan       67.00      7.13      Dty       250
MidEast-Spore       65.00      4.24      Dty       250
Mideast-USG         56.50      9.29      Dty       280
WAF-USG-260K        65.00      5.70      Dty       260
WAF-USG-130K        87.50      7.67      Dty       130
NSea-USAC-250K      70.00      4.94      Dty       250
NSea-USAC-130K      92.50      6.53      Dty       130
Inter UK/Cont       97.50      3.58      Dty        80
Caribs-USAC        157.50      6.35      Dty        70
Cross Med-130k      90.00      3.09      Dty       130
Cross Med-80K       95.00      3.26      Dty        80
Indo-Japan          97.50      5.79      Dty        80
Inter UK/Cont      200.00      7.80      FO         25
Cross Med          200.00      7.56      FO         25
Caribs-USAC        115.00      4.63      FO         50
Mideast-Japan      110.00     12.20      Cln        55
Inter UK/Cont      250.00      7.15      Cln        20
Caribs-USAC        175.00      7.00      Cln        30
Mideast/Jpn (FO)   100.00     11.09      FO         80
```

How Do the Commodities, Energy & Transport Markets Work?

Vessel Position, Fixtures and Enquiries

One of the key activities of ship brokers is to monitor ship positions around the world. This vital information is by its nature confidential and is not reported directly by Reuters. Communications services assist in this area with the ability to act as a messaging system.

Reuters reports fixtures on ships chartered and enquiries on cargoes awaiting vessels from a series of broker reports as shown on this page.

Reports on freight

Report on sugar

```
19:50  12 Feb  CSCE sugar ends quietly up ahead of holiday
   NEW YORK, Feb 12 (Reuters) - CSCE world sugar futures
closed modestly higher Friday as a light burst of local buying
late in the day lifted raws off their session lows in subdued
dealings in front of a holiday weekend, trading sources said.
   Key March rose 0.08 to settle at 6.75 cents a lb as it
ranged from 6.80-6.62 cents. May went up 0.09 to 6.64 cents and
back months were 0.04 to 0.11 cent firmer.
   The market ended on a quiet note after a turbulent week
which saw sugar prices carve out fresh 11-year lows, with the
key March contract sinking Thursday to a fresh low of 6.51
cents.
   The CSCE sugar market will be closed Monday for the U.S.
President's Day holiday. Business will resume on Tuesday.
   "It was so nixed the market just zigzagged ainlessly
throughout the day," a sugar broker for a New York-based
investment house said.
   Early trade buying boosted raws to their session peaks
before profit-taking and producer pricing slowly chipped away
at market gains, floor sources and sugar dealers said.
   Selling by small speculators pressed March sugar down to
the low for the day of 6.62 cents, but local buying allowed the
market to recover as it moved into positive territory, they
said.
   "We got back up when the selling ran out at the bottom,"
another dealer said.
   Options expiration passed quietly in the market. Dealers
said it seems a lot of 7.00 cent puts will be exercised.
   Market participants paid little heed to the decision by the
U.S. Senate to acquit President Bill Clinton of impeachment
```

Report on grain

```
20:04  12 Feb  WCE canola futures end mixed, flax mostly up
   WINNIPEG, Feb 12 (Reuters) - Winnipeg Commodity Exchange canola prices ended
mixed after posting contract lows in the nearby March and May positions, traders
said.
   On Friday, canola was weighed down by commercial selling and late hedge
pressure while new crop months were supported by commercial buying, especially
the November contract, an oilseeds trader said.
   The market had a "general bearish sentiment," a trader said, citing the slide in
Chicago Board of Trade soybean futures as another bearish factor.
   Spread activity dominated most of the volume, traders said.
   Flax futures languished until a bout of late afternoon commercial buying pushed up
prices at the close, a trader said. Volume was light.
   March canola firmed $0.10 at $347.00 a tonne and May canola lost $1.80 at $345.20.
March flax rose $3.00 at $313.50 a tonne.
   Western barley futures were mixed. Commission houses and commercials rolled
over their March positions into the May ahead of first notice day on February 26, a
grains trader said.
   In feed wheat, "we continued to see commercial selling coupled with commission
house short covering. We also saw the March positions switching over into the
May," the trader said.
   March western barley was up $0.30 at $117.80 and March feed wheat was off $0.20
at $144.20.
   There were no trades in peas and oats.
   ((All values quoted in Canadian dollars/tonne except feed peas and oats.)
   ((Doris Frankel, Chicago commodities desk(312)408-8720,
chicago.commods.newsroom@reuters.com))

Friday, 12 February 1999 20:04:51
ENDS [nN12502064]
```

```
17:51  12 Feb  RTRS-Ldn freight - Atlantic panamaxes see improvement
13:37  12 Feb  RTRS-Ldn freight - Atlantic panamaxes firmer
17:19  11 Feb  RTRS-Ldn freight - Panamaxes steady Baltic indices
16:20  10 Feb  RTRS-Ldn freight - Baltic indices gain on firmer grain
16:54  09 Feb  RTRS-Ldn freight - Baltic indices gain on active fixing
16:54  08 Feb  RTRS-Ldn freight - Panamax business aids Baltic indices
17:46  05 Feb  RTRS-Ldn freight - Rising panamax demand boosts indices
15:57  03 Feb  RTRS-London freight - Atlantic grain stirs
17:16  02 Feb  RTRS-London freight - Conditions remained unfavourable
16:18  01 Feb  RTRS-London freight - BFI eases, panamaxes weaken
```

```
17:51  12 Feb  Ldn freight - Atlantic panamaxes see improvement
   LONDON, Feb 12 (Reuters) - Improved conditions for panamaxes in the Atlantic
pushed the Baltic Freight Index (BFI) up five points to 812 and the Baltic Panamax
Index up nine points to 790, brokers said.
   The most striking feature of the dry cargo freight market at the end of the week
was the strength of demand for handy-size tonnage in Brazil and Argentina for grain
and to a lesser extent sugar charterers.
   GRAIN - Baumarine completed its fixture of Full Comfort for 54,000 tonnes heavy
grain U.S. Gulf/Taiwan for Feb 25/March 5 at a firmer $14.90, equivalent to about 25
cents more than a U.S. Gulf/Japan no combo fixture. Reports that Andre had fixed
similar business to Taiwan with Navios tonnage at $15 could not be confirmed.
   Little evidence was seen of trans-Atlantic trade from the U.S. Gulf although Cereol
was reported to have booked 45,000 tonnes grain to the Continent on private terms.
   Toepfer fixed Adventure 1 1.5 million cubic feet up river Plate/France on prompt
dates at rates estimated by brokers to be between $17.50 and $18 basis 53 feet and
nine days purposes.
   Transcatalana fixed Top Wing for aqbout 36,000 tonnes grain basis 56 feet up river
Plate/Spanish Mediterranean for end Feb at a lumpsum equivalent of $15.50 basis 10
days, in addition to Adriana 38,000 dwt delivery recalada end Feb trip Spain at a
much firmer $6,000 daily plus $60,000 ballast bonus.
   Fresh grain enquiry included:.
   NSAC - 54,000 tonnes heavy grain U.S. Gulf/Japan or Taiwan March 20/30.
   Dreyfus - 10/15,000 tonnes grain basis 55 feet U.S. Gulf/Glasgow Feb/March.
   Andre - 21,000 tonnes wheat U.S. Gulf/Tema Feb 20/27.
   Andre - 27,000 tonnes wheat Nopac/Hodeidah or Aden Feb 22/March 3.
   Andre - 10,000 tonnes wheat Riga/Israel Feb 15/20.
   Toepfer - 11,600/12,100 tonnes corn Koper/Libya 15/20 Feb.
   Tradigrain - 25,000 tonnes wheat Hamburg/Algeria Feb 15/19.
   MINERALS - The caper market remained in the doldrums especially in the Far
```

 REUTERS

Example – Dirty Fixtures/Enquiries

1. Using the Reuters screens provided here, a typical fixture contains information as follows:

Front Fighter   130   End3 WAFR/USG   W85   CNR

Translated this means that the vessel is the Front Fighter, 130,000 metric tonnes, chartered from West Africa to the US Gulf Coast, at a Worldscale rate of 85, loading for the end of March to a charterer who has not been reported in this case – CNR.

You can check the Worldscale rate on the Reuters system; the Fixture reports a rate of W = 85 whereas the reported rate is for W = 87.5.

```
                                                    TANKER/RATE1
17-Mar-99
ROUTE               WS RATE    $/TONNE    VESSEL    SIZE
MidEast-West         58.00      9.20       Dty       250
MidEast-Japan        67.00      7.13       Dty       250
MidEast-Spore        65.00      4.24       Dty       250
Mideast-USG          56.50      9.29       Dty       280
WAF-USG-260K         65.00      5.70       Dty       260
WAF-USG-130K         87.50      7.67       Dty       130
NSea-USAC-250K       70.00      4.94       Dty       250
NSea-USAC-130K       92.50      6.53       Dty       130
Inter UK/Cont        97.50      3.58       Dty        80
Caribs-USAC         157.50      6.35       Dty        70
Cross Med-130k       90.00      3.09       Dty       130
Cross Med-80K        95.00      3.26       Dty        80
Indo-Japan           97.50      5.79       Dty        80
Inter UK/Cont       200.00      7.80       FO         25
Cross Med           200.00      7.56       FO         25
Caribs-USAC         115.00      4.63       FO         50
Mideast-Japan       110.00     12.20       Cln        55
Inter UK/Cont       250.00      7.15       Cln        20
Caribs-USAC         175.00      7.00       Cln        30
Mideast/Jpn (FO)    100.00     11.09       FO         80
```

```
14:21  16 Mar  Dirty tanker fixtures - March 16
  LONDON, March 16 (Reuters) -
-MIDEAST GULF-
PHOENIX TRADER    260   5/4  MIDEAST/THAILAND   W57.5         STENTEX
IKARIA            260   3/4  MIDEAST/SAFR UKC   W60/57/54.5   SHELL
-MED/BLACK SEA-
ALANDIA FORCE     130  11/4  AL BAQR/CHINA      RN      SINOCHEM-RPTD
KRONVIKEN         135  25/3  CEYHAN/UKC MED     W87.5   KODIAK-RCNT
GLEN ROY          130  26/3  CEYHAN/OPTS        RNR           ADDAX
RABIGH BAY 3      129  27/3  SKERIR/ITALY       W80             ERG
SKS TYNE  (COND)   80  31/3  BEJAIA/BRAZIL      RNR           PBRAS
NSEA CHASER (NA)   60  21/3  SICILY/USGULF      W110     VITOL-RCNT
-WEST AFRICA-
STENA CONCORDIA   256  28/3  WAFR/S.AFRICA      W68.75       ARCADIA
DOHA              255   5/4  WAFR/TAIWAN        W42.55           CPC
PRINCESS SUSANA   130  27/3  WAFR/SPAIN         RNR      CEPSA-RCNT
MALIBU            130   3/4  FORCADOS/EAST      W67.5      TRAFIGURA
TBN               130   2/4  ZAFIRO/WEST        W85            MOBIL
FRONT FIGHTER     130  END3  WAFR/USG           W85              CNR
-WESTERN HEMISPHERE-
PROSPECT           80   -/3  NSEA/UKC           W105          NAVION
ALANDIA PRINCE     78  24/3  FLOTTA/UKC         W97.5        STENTEX
K.STANKOV  (GO)    69  22/3  VPILS/UKC-USAC     W95/85        BP-FLD
NSEA DOWELL (UMS)  63  29/3  PEMBROKE/USAC      W110      TEXACO-FLD
SIBOHELLE  (COND)  61  30/3  KAARSTOE/USGULF    W115        NAVION M
MARLIN (UMS)       60   1/4  CONT/USAC          W105         CARGILL
```

2. Fixture information can vary and may give an indication to market conditions. For example this fixture:

K Stankov (GO) 69 22/3 Vpils/UKC–USAC WS95/85 BP-FLD

Translated this means that the vessel is the Komandarn Stankov which last carried a clean cargo of Gasoil. The 69,000 metric tonne vessel is now taking a dirty cargo of crude oil. It is likely that in this case that the market in clean cargoes is poor which has caused the owners to transfer the vessel to trading in the dirty market. The cargo is to be loaded on the 22nd March at the port of Ventspils (ex-Soviet Baltic Sea), for delivery to the UK to Continent range or US Atlantic Coast at a Worldscale rate of 95 for UKC or 85 for USAC and the charterer is British Petroleum. However, the code FLD means that the fixture failed. Vessels are generally fixed "on subjects" which leaves the charterer an agreed amount of time to check the vessel dimensions and timing at the loading and discharge ports. Fixtures can fail if the vessel details are found to be unacceptable – as in this case.

Example – Clean Fixtures/Enquiries

1. Using the Reuters screen provided here – which is updated weekly
   – usually on a Friday – you can see that a typical fixture will
   contain information displayed as follows:

Palva 39 (GO) 10-12/3   UK/CONT W125   Cargill

Translated this means the vessel Palva has contracted to load
39,000 tons of Gasoil, loading 10–12th March, at a port in the UK, for
discharge at a port on the Continent, for a Worldscale rate of 125, to
charterers Cargill.

```
19:30  05 Mar  Clean tanker fixtures/enquiries MARCH 05
    LONDON, March 5 (Reuters) -
 - UK/CONT -
   PALVA      39 (GO)    10-12/3      UK/CONT     W125    CARGILL
   VIRGO      28 (GO)    12           UK/CONT     W170    KERISHI
   ARCADIA    27         06           UK/CONT     W180    IPCO
   - CARIBS -
   EVROS      40.6       15           Brazil      W137.50 P'BRAS


Friday, 5 March 1999 19:30:53
ENDS [nG05536230]
```

Summary

You have now finished the second section of the book and you should have a clear understanding of the following:

- The different ways delivery or settlement may take place in the commodities and energy futures markets

- The production and uses of the important metals, softs, grains and oilseeds for the commodities markets

- The production and uses of energy products for the energy markets

- The types of business, types of vessel, types of charter and the associated vessel fixings and Worldscale rates in the shipping markets

As a check on your understanding, try the Quick Quiz Questions on the next page. You may also find the Overview section to be a helpful learning tool.

Your notes

How Do the Commodities, Energy & Transport Markets Work?

Quick Quiz Questions

1. What do CIF and FOB stand for?

2. Which precious metals have futures contracts traded on worldwide exchanges?

3. How is wheat categorised?

4. Why do you think livestock information is included in the grains and oilseed market sector?

5. How are crude oils categorised?

6. What does an oil products trader trade as opposed to a crude oil trader?

7. What are netbacks?

8. Who are the principal players in the shipping markets?

You can check your answers on page 128.

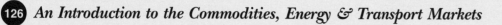

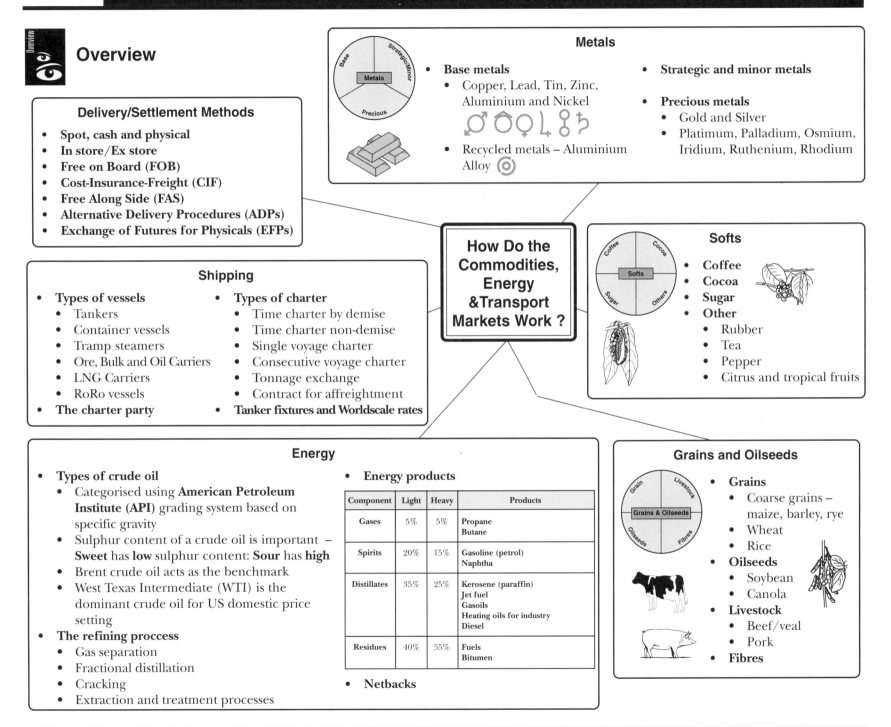

Overview

Delivery/Settlement Methods

- **Spot, cash and physical**
- **In store/Ex store**
- **Free on Board (FOB)**
- **Cost-Insurance-Freight (CIF)**
- **Free Along Side (FAS)**
- **Alternative Delivery Procedures (ADPs)**
- **Exchange of Futures for Physicals (EFPs)**

Metals

- **Base metals**
  - Copper, Lead, Tin, Zinc, Aluminium and Nickel
  - Recycled metals – Aluminium Alloy
- **Strategic and minor metals**
- **Precious metals**
  - Gold and Silver
  - Platinum, Palladium, Osmium, Iridium, Ruthenium, Rhodium

How Do the Commodities, Energy &Transport Markets Work ?

Shipping

- **Types of vessels**
  - Tankers
  - Container vessels
  - Tramp steamers
  - Ore, Bulk and Oil Carriers
  - LNG Carriers
  - RoRo vessels
- **The charter party**
- **Types of charter**
  - Time charter by demise
  - Time charter non-demise
  - Single voyage charter
  - Consecutive voyage charter
  - Tonnage exchange
  - Contract for affreightment
- **Tanker fixtures and Worldscale rates**

Softs

- **Coffee**
- **Cocoa**
- **Sugar**
- **Other**
  - Rubber
  - Tea
  - Pepper
  - Citrus and tropical fruits

Energy

- **Types of crude oil**
  - Categorised using **American Petroleum Institute (API)** grading system based on specific gravity
  - Sulphur content of a crude oil is important – **Sweet** has **low** sulphur content: **Sour** has **high**
  - Brent crude oil acts as the benchmark
  - West Texas Intermediate (WTI) is the dominant crude oil for US domestic price setting
- **The refining proccess**
  - Gas separation
  - Fractional distillation
  - Cracking
  - Extraction and treatment processes

- **Energy products**

Component	Light	Heavy	Products
Gases	5%	5%	Propane Butane
Spirits	20%	15%	Gasoline (petrol) Naphtha
Distillates	35%	25%	Kerosene (paraffin) Jet fuel Gasoils Heating oils for industry Diesel
Residues	40%	55%	Fuels Bitumen

- **Netbacks**

Grains and Oilseeds

- **Grains**
  - Coarse grains – maize, barley, rye
  - Wheat
  - Rice
- **Oilseeds**
  - Soybean
  - Canola
- **Livestock**
  - Beef/veal
  - Pork
- **Fibres**

How Do the Commodities, Energy & Transport Markets Work?

Quick Quiz Answers

1. *What do CIF and FOB stand for?*

   CIF: Cost-Insurance-Freight.
   FOB: Free on Board.
   If you cannot remember the difference between these two delivery methods, look at pages 67 and 68 where they are described.

2. *Which precious metals have futures contracts traded on worldwide exchanges?*

   Gold and silver are traded on a number of worldwide exchanges such as CBOT, NYMEX, TCE and MACE, whereas platinum and palladium are traded mainly on NYMEX.

3. *How is wheat categorised?*

   Wheat is categorised by **growing season**, for example, spring, winter, and **protein content**, for example, hard and soft.

4. *Why do you think livestock information is included in the grains and oilseed market sector?*

   This is because grains are a principal ingredient in animal feed thus affecting the cost of maintaining livestock. This in turn affects livestock prices when the animals are sold.

5. *How are crude oils categorised?*

   Using the **American Petroleum Institute (API)** grading system. This system is based on the specific gravity of the crude oil compared with that of water.

6. *What does an oil products trader trade as opposed to a crude oil trader?*

   An oil products trader trades one or more of the many energy products which are derived from refining crude oil, for example, jet fuel, gasoline, propane, butane, naphtha etc.

7. *What are netbacks?*

   The concept underlying netbacks is in the assignment of a value to a particular crude oil which depends on its quality and on the worth of the refined products which can be obtained from it.

8. *Who are the principal players in the shipping markets?*

   Shipowners, charterers who are normally cargo owners, and shipbrokers. These players were described in Section 1.

REUTERS

Further Resources

Books

The International Cocoa Trade
Robin David, John Wiley & Sons, Inc. 1997
ISBN 0 471 19055 1

The International Sugar Trade
A.C. Hannah and Donald Spence, John Wiley & Sons, Inc., 1997

Getting Started in Futures
Todd Copton, John Wiley & Sons, Inc., 3rd Edition 1997
ISBN 0 471 17759 8

All About Commodities
Russell Wasendorf and Thomas McCafferty, Probus, 1993
ISBN 1 557 38459 2

Reuters Glossary of International Economic & Financial Terms
(3rd edition) Longman, 1994
ISBN 0 582 24871 X

Booklets

International Petroleum Exchange
• Brent Crude... the international benchmark

New York Mercantile Exchange
• NYMEX Energy Complex
• NYMEX Metals Complex
• Glossary

London Metal Exchange
• Profile

Internet

RFT Web Site
• **http://www.wiley.rft.reuters.com**
This is the series' companion web site where additional quiz questions, updated screens and other information can be found.

US Geological Survey
• **http://minerals.er.usgs.gov./pub/commodity**

International Coffee Organisation
• **http://www.ico.org**

International Cocoa Organisation
• **http://www.icco.org**

Tea Council
• **http://www.teacouncil.co.uk**

International Natural Rubber Organisation
• **http://www.inro.com.my/inro**

International Grains Council
• **http://www.igc.org.uk**

US Department of Agriculture, Foreign Agricultural Service
• **http://www.fas.usda.gov**

Exchanges

Refer to the back of this book for a listing of worldwide exchanges' contact information and web sites.

Your notes

This section of the book should take between 3.5 and 4.5 hours of study time. You may not take as long as this or you may take a little longer – remember your learning is individual to you.

What money is better bestowed than that of a man thinking of his future?

William Makepeace Thackeray (1811–1863)

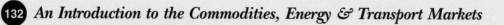

Introduction

As you have learned thus far, the commodities, energy and transport markets are diverse and have widely differing historical origins. For some markets, the instruments and methods of trading have been established for a hundred years or more, for example, in the shipping markets and trading on the London Metal Exchange. In other cases, the instruments and markets are relatively new, for example, exchange traded electricity futures contracts.

Within the commodities, energy and transport markets, there is a great variety of both OTC and exchange traded instruments you need to know about and understand. This section classifies the instruments to provide a broad overview of the types of instruments and how they are used by buyers and sellers in the market places. If you need to know more about derivatives in general, then you may find it useful to refer to the *Introduction to Derivatives* (ISBN 0-471-83127-1) in this series.

Before moving on, try the activity opposite.

How many different types of commodities, energy and transport markets instruments do you already know something about? Write your list here.

What Instruments Are Used in the Markets?

Commodities, Energy and Transport Markets Instruments

Although the following diagram places the instruments used in the three markets into a simple classification, it is important to remember that the markets and market players are different. The classification used here is based on the following:

- Spot, cash and physical delivery contracts

- Forward contracts

- Derivatives

There are a number of derivatives available which are derived from underlying commodity and energy contracts. There are also a number of derivative instruments which are based on an index or index price. For these instruments the contracts are **cash settled** as it is not possible to deliver an index.

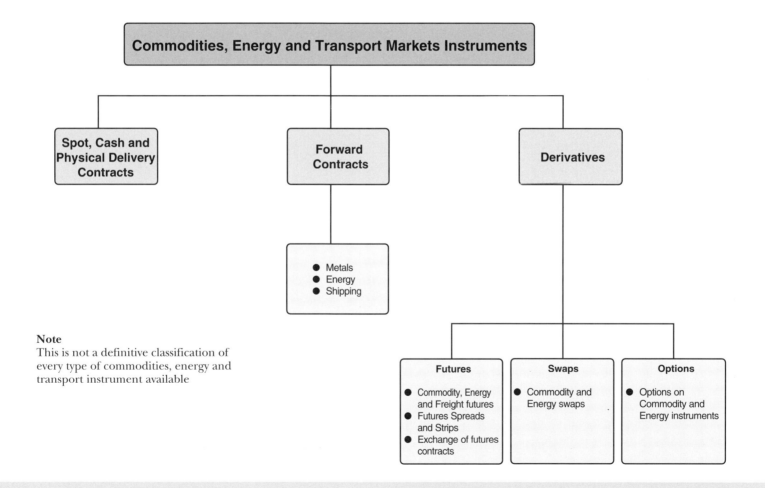

Note
This is not a definitive classification of every type of commodities, energy and transport instrument available

REUTERS :::

Spot, Cash and Physical Delivery Contracts

As have already been mentioned, spot contracts in the commodity and energy markets are privately negotiated Over-The-Counter (OTC) transactions that take place between a buyer and a seller. In some cases a broker is involved as an intermediary in the transaction. Spot settlement dates depend on the conventions of the market involved and may range from 1 to 45 days – it is important that both parties are clear about the contract terms and conditions. Spot transactions involve credit risk to the counterparties. Any redress for failure to comply with a contract has to be taken using the normal business practice and the laws of the state land or country designated in the contract. For example, redress under a contract specifying UK law mould be sought in the UK civil Courts.

Reported data on spot transactions is difficult to obtain as by their very nature these transactions are private; however, official prices for commodities such as crude oil, coffee, cocoa and sugar are published by their representative organisations such as OPEC, ICO, ICCO and ISO. It is important to remember that these are only **indication** or **guide** prices.

Spot transactions and official prices are important both in the physical markets and for pricing forward and futures contracts. Forward and exchange traded futures contracts either use **physical** or **cash settlement** for delivery as the underlying instrument on contract expiry.

> **Definitions**
>
> A **spot contract** is a privately negotiated OTC transaction which takes place between a buyer and a seller. Prompt delivery is usually between 1 and 45 business days after the trade date.
>
> A **cash contract** is settled in cash using one of the following as the basis for the settlement:
>
> - A physical price index – for example, Platt's Crude Oil price
> - An official price – for example, an ICO Coffee price
> - A price fixed by an exchange – for example, the LME, Base Metal Cash Settlement prices. On the LME Prompt delivery is usually for 2 business days after the contract expiry date.
>
> A **physical delivery contract** means that the buyer of the contract will take **actual** delivery of the commodity.

What Instruments Are Used in the Markets?

Trends in spot and official prices are important to the markets from the viewpoint of market players such as producers/consumers and investors speculating in the commodity markets. The World Bank has produced monthly commodity price data for a number of years as a simple sheet. This sheet is known as the **Pink Sheet** as originally the data was printed on pink paper. The data produced summarises the annual, quarterly and monthly average prices of a broad range of softs, grains, metals and energy commodities with prices taken from a wide range of sources.

Pink sheets can be downloaded from the World Bank's Internet website at: **www.worldbank.org/prospects/pinksheets**

In addition to straightforward spot prices there are a number of **Commodity Indices** that are used as benchmarks for investment performance in the markets. These commodity indices are used in much the same way as indices such as the FTSE 100 and S&P 500 are used in the equities markets. Commodity indices are of two types and are calculated as either arithmetic or geometric averages:

- **Composite indices** such as the **Goldman Sachs Commodity Index (GSCI)** are weighted averages of a range of commodities from different market sectors

- **Specific indices** such as the **IPE Crude Oil Index** deal with a single commodity

For example, the GSCI is an arithmetic average, in US dollars, of the weightings of 22 commodities based on their production quantities. The commodities comprise nine metals, four energy products and nine agricultural products. For the GSCI the spot index is a measure of the price levels of nearby commodity prices whereas the total return index is the return accrued from investing in fully collateralised nearby futures contracts.

Most commodity indices have been devised and developed by banks or data providers such as Reuters. The following chart indicates some of the more important composite indices available and the method of calculating the average.

Commodity Index	Arithmetic average	Geometric average
JP Morgan Commodity Index	✔	
Goldman Sachs Commodity Index	✔	
Commodity Research Bureau Index (Knight Ridder)		✔
Energy & Metals Index (Merrill Lynch)		✔
Reuters Commodity Index	✔	

Commodity	Unit	Annual averages Jan-Dec 1997	Jan-Dec 1998	Jan-Nov 1999	Quarterly averages Jul-Sep 1998	Oct-Dec 1998	Jan-Mar 1999	Apr-Jun 1999	Jul-Sep 1999	Monthly averages Sep 1999	Oct 1999	Nov 1999
Energy												
Coal, Australia	$/mt	35.10	29.23	26.00	27.76	26.43	26.10	26.10	26.10	26.10	25.60	25.50
Coal, US	$/mt	36.39	34.38	33.18	34.04	33.50	33.50	33.17	33.00	33.00	33.00	33.00
Crude oil, average spot	a/ $/bbl	19.17	13.07	17.43	13.01	11.85	11.79	16.10	20.65	22.70	21.95	24.16
Crude oil, Brent	a/ $/bbl	19.09	12.72	17.10	12.42	11.09	11.24	15.40	20.54	22.40	21.95	24.59
Crude oil, Dubai	a/ $/bbl	18.10	12.12	16.58	12.41	11.56	11.07	15.26	19.69	21.84	21.26	23.05
Crude oil, West Texas Int.	a/ $/bbl	20.33	14.35	18.62	14.16	12.90	13.05	17.66	21.73	23.86	22.64	24.85
Natural gas, Europe	$/mmbtu	2.74	2.42	2.08	2.37	2.15	1.99	1.89	2.09	2.20	2.47	2.51
Natural gas, US	$/mmbtu	2.48	2.09	2.26	2.01	1.91	1.81	2.23	2.55	2.54	2.72	2.36
Non-Energy Commodities												
Agriculture												
Beverages												
Cocoa	b/ ¢/kg	161.9	167.6	115.5	169.5	159.1	139.4	113.6	105.7	106.1	102.2	92.2
Coffee, arabica	b/ ¢/kg	416.8	298.1	224.9	259.2	252.4	238.0	235.5	198.8	185.9	207.7	250.0
Coffee, robusta	b/ ¢/kg	173.6	182.3	149.0	173.5	179.7	172.7	149.1	135.4	131.3	129.0	139.0
Tea, Calcutta auctions	b/ ¢/kg	214.5	216.5	207.9	214.5	190.0	162.3	223.4	224.9	221.0	230.6	224.6
Tea, Colombo auctions	b/ ¢/kg	202.0	207.5	163.5	197.3	181.4	160.3	145.9	170.7	183.9	186.6	181.8
Tea, Mombasa auctions	b/ ¢/kg	201.5	189.9	179.9	171.2	164.6	180.3	175.1	176.9	197.8	199.5	162.3
Food												
Fats and Oils												
Coconut oil	b/ $/mt	656.8	657.9	740.1	662.0	740.3	736.0	832.3	681.3	704.0	690.0	702.5
Copra	$/mt	433.8	411.1	464.0	404.7	459.3	457.7	521.3	433.7	421.0	430.0	436.3
Groundnut meal	$/mt	221.0	116.2	n.a.	108.0	105.0	102.3	n.a.	n.a.	n.a.	n.a.	n.a.
Groundnut oil	b/ $/mt	1,010.4	909.4	785.2	862.7	857.7	808.0	755.7	781.7	797.0	804.0	797.0
Palm oil	b/ $/mt	545.8	671.1	445.1	691.9	679.3	563.3	458.7	353.7	388.0	381.0	388.0
Palmkernel oil	$/mt	651.8	686.7	695.3	694.3	741.0	704.7	729.0	656.7	710.0	684.0	693.8
Soybean meal	b/ $/mt	275.8	170.3	150.5	149.0	160.7	145.7	140.0	152.3	167.0	173.0	168.3
Soybean oil	b/ $/mt	564.8	625.9	432.7	606.3	606.3	492.3	476.7	406.3	411.0	401.0	000.0
Soybeans	b/ $/mt	295.4	243.3	201.8	224.3	229.0	210.3	200.0	196.3	207.0	203.0	196.8
Grains												
Maize	b/ $/mt	117.1	102.0	90.5	91.6	96.5	95.9	93.4	85.4	86.5	85.8	85.4
Rice, Thai, 5%	b/ $/mt	303.5	304.2	249.8	322.3	282.2	278.7	244.5	244.3	229.3	217.0	228.0
Rice, Thai, 25%	$/mt	257.1	259.9	217.9	273.7	257.7	239.6	211.6	217.9	202.5	190.3	199.2
Rice, Thai, 35%	$/mt	246.8	249.7	212.2	262.1	251.6	232.9	205.9	212.7	197.8	186.0	194.0
Rice,Thai, A1.Special	$/mt	210.4	213.0	196.0	225.6	238.5	214.2	189.5	201.1	184.5	169.8	172.0
Sorghum	$/mt	109.6	98.0	84.7	90.5	90.0	90.9	87.6	79.5	80.0	78.4	79.4
Wheat, Canada	$/mt	181.4	162.9	151.7	153.0	164.7	160.7	148.2	148.2	150.1	147.6	149.5
Wheat, US, HRW	b/ $/mt	159.5	126.1	112.9	111.6	127.7	119.9	112.8	109.2	113.2	108.1	108.8
Wheat, US, SRW	$/mt	143.7	111.5	96.7	95.3	109.0	99.5	96.4	93.4	102.1	98.7	96.9
Other Food												
Bananas	b/ $/mt	502.7	491.6	425.8	456.5	520.1	479.3	444.0	406.4	395.5	299.0	395.3
Beef	b/ ¢/kg	185.5	172.6	183.3	166.7	168.2	177.1	175.6	192.5	190.7	186.6	193.9
Fishmeal	$/mt	606.3	661.9	390.7	670.3	601.3	453.3	343.3	389.3	382.0	399.0	401.0
Lamb	¢/kg	339.2	275.0	261.0	251.1	264.2	247.0	263.2	267.1	268.0	272.2	266.6
Oranges	b/ $/mt	459.0	442.4	448.9	516.3	415.1	420.3	458.6	474.8	471.9	518.0	358.1
Shrimp	¢/kg	1,612	1,579	1,458	1,574	1,427	1,413	1,470	1,485	1,452	1,444	1,488
Sugar, EU, domestic	b/ ¢/kg	62.72	59.75	59.19	58.59	60.88	59.72	58.78	58.55	59.35	60.61	59.35
Sugar, US, domestic	b/ ¢/kg	48.36	48.64	47.29	49.10	48.27	49.45	49.88	47.01	44.36	42.84	38.36
Sugar, world	b/ ¢/kg	25.06	19.67	13.87	17.92	17.34	15.40	12.63	13.06	14.70	14.88	14.35
Raw Materials												
Timber												
Logs, Cameroon	$/cum	284.8	296.4	266.4	279.4	295.9	282.3	255.3	247.2	n.a.	269.3	307.5
Logs, Malaysia	b/ $/cum	238.3	162.4	186.0	140.7	162.0	175.3	178.4	195.9	202.8	198.4	198.6
Plywood	¢/sheet	485.0	376.1	437.3	344.3	395.2	426.4	429.9	440.3	455.5	462.4	458.0
Sawnwood, Cameroon	$/cum	563.6	526.3	451.7	519.2	532.0	461.5	424.4	441.8	456.2	481.4	504.6
Sawnwood, Malaysia	b/ $/cum	664.5	484.2	597.0	465.5	519.8	544.3	582.8	632.9	643.4	643.4	643.4
Woodpulp	$/mt	556.5	508.4	498.0	507.5	458.3	447.6	491.5	521.2	544.6	548.7	548.7
Other Raw Materials												
Cotton	b/ ¢/kg	174.8	144.5	118.9	150.2	127.5	123.9	129.4	113.8	109.1	104.6	101.9
Jute	$/mt	304.6	258.0	274.2	260.0	270.0	250.0	260.0	295.0	305.0	301.0	300.0
Rubber, Malaysia	b/ ¢/kg	101.8	72.2	62.6	68.0	70.6	68.0	59.7	55.6	54.2	64.7	74.1
Rubber, US	¢/kg	121.6	89.5	80.4	86.1	87.0	83.7	77.5	74.6	75.7	83.3	94.0
Rubber, Singapore	¢/kg	101.0	70.9	61.8	68.3	69.0	65.5	59.9	55.9	56.9	64.7	70.9
Sisal	$/mt	776.6	820.8	703.5	850.0	850.0	779.2	731.7	647.5	612.5	628.0	635.0
Wool	¢/kg	430.3	338.3	304.6	313.0	307.2	301.4	307.8	309.0	300.6	300.6	295.0

Source: The World Bank Pink Sheet, December 1999

REUTERS

The Reuters screen below shows the Commodity and Energy Market Indices, with detailed screens for the Reuters. Commodity Index and the GSCI Total Return.

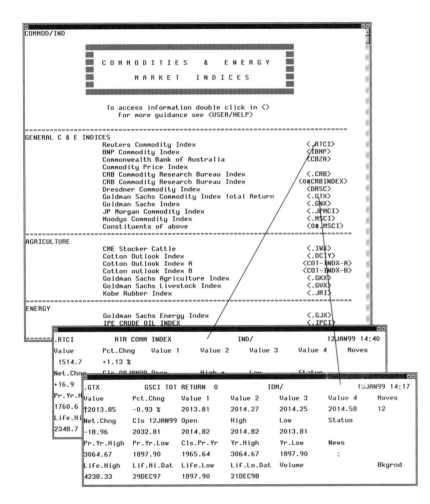

Who Uses Spot, Cash and Physical Delivery Contracts?

Metals

In general the key market players in the base metal markets are mining corporations, merchants – including scrap dealers – and organisations involved in processing the metals. Strategic and minor metals are traded almost exclusively directly between producer and consumer. For example, titanium produced by Sumitomo or Kobe Steel, both of Japan, supply the metal directly to worldwide producers in the automobile and aircraft industries. The precious metal gold market is very similar to the international foreign exchange markets – spot trading is worldwide and carries on 24 hours a day. Silver trading is also important and is used by fund managers to hedge and speculate for profit from arbitrage opportunities in the gold/silver spread ratios or prices.

Softs

For commodities such as coffee, cocoa, sugar, tea and rubber, most physical trading takes place between producers and consumers directly or between traders/brokers and consumers. In the case of tea and rubber, privately negotiated deals between plantation owners and a small number of manufacturers accounts for most of the commodity production. For example, most of the world supply of rubber is bought by the three largest tyre manufacturers in the world – Goodyear, Michelin and Bridgestone.

Grains and Oilseeds

The worldwide grain markets involve many market players from farmers via shippers, railroads, brokers to end users such as bakers, millers and food processors. This means that spot grain prices may sometimes be difficult to obtain. When spot prices are available they may be quoted in one of two ways:

- **Flat or straight prices**, for example, $3.15 per bushel

- **Basis quotes**, for example, ¢15 under CBOT December wheat

What Instruments Are Used in the Markets?

It is important to recognise that grains such as wheat and rice are used mainly for human consumption, whereas coarse grain such as maize and barley are used mainly as a feed for livestock and poultry. Oilseeds are produced by crushing crops such as soybeans and are used for livestock feed supplements and to produce oils for edible and industrial use.

Energy

Within the oil markets there are two important types of spot markets involving risk for different market players. These markets are:

- **Crude oil markets** where variations in the **absolute** spot price affect the oil producers. Spot transactions such as Dated Brent were described earlier in this book.

- **Energy product markets** where the **differential** between such products as gasoline, naphtha, heating oil, jet fuel, and feedstocks such as ethane and propane, affect the activities of oil refiners.

The worldwide deregulation of electricity markets has lead to the recent development of local OTC spot markets centred on large capacity distribution hubs. These spot markets are quite active but as the commodity in this case is not storable there can be considerable price volatility caused by transmission problems, seasonal and unforeseen weather conditions, holidays etc. Much of the cash trading in electricity is therefore in the forward markets – one-day ahead or more.

Spot, Cash and Physical Delivery Contracts

- A **spot contract** is a privately negotiated OTC transaction for prompt delivery which is usually between 1 and 45 business days after the trade date

- A **cash contract** is settled in cash using a physical price index, official price or exchange fixed price for prompt delivery which is usually between 1 and 45 business days after the trade date

- A **physical delivery contract** means that the buyer must take actual delivery of the commodity according to the terms of the contract

REUTERS

This and the five pages that follow provide Reuters screens to illustrate what type of information from a news service a market player uses to aid in conducting transactions.

The Reuters screens on this page show the Reuters Speed Guide, with specific detail for European Sugar spot prices and the LIFFE No. 5 White Sugar FOB in London with contract details.

```
SUGAR - REUTERS SPEED GUIDE                                    SUGAR/CASH1
To access information double-click in <> or [ ].For more guidance see<USER/HELP>

=SUGAR=================================    =NEWS AND ANALYSIS=====================
European Sugar Prices......<O#SUGAR-EU>    Sugar News.......................[SUG]
Global Sugar Cash Prices......<O#SUGAR>    All Softs News...................[SOF]
London Sugar Prices.......<O#SUGAR-LON>    All Commodities News...............[C]
Ukranian Nat. Exch. Assoc.....<CHEMON2>
Thai Sugar premiums and Chinese cash       Latest Sugar Report..............[SUG/]
 prices...................<SUGAR/ASIA1>    New York Sugar Report..........[SUG/N]
European Sugar.............<SUGAR/EU1>
Sugar Mill and Refinery..............      F.O.Licht Sugar Report......[LICHT-SUG]
Projects...............<SUG/REFINE0 >      F.O.Licht Estimates..............<FOLO>
                                           WSC Sugar Weather...............<WSAQ>

                                           All Other Reports...............[C/R]

                                           Political/Economic News.........[NEWS]
                                           Sports News.....................[SPO]



Questions/Comments: Contact your local Help Desk - see <PHONE/HELP> for details
==================================================================================
Sugar Index<SUGAR1>       Sugar Futures<SUGAR/FUT1>       Sugar Options<SUGAR/OPT1>
     Lost?Selective Access?...<USER/HELP>   Reuters Phone Support...<PHONE/HELP>
```

```
O#SUGAR-EU            EUROPEAN SUGAR
Commodity      Del.Date      Last           Srce  Terms   Loc  Ccy Units Date   Time
Daily Indicator  SPOT     ↓ 128.60   -4.40  LIFFE UK  UK    -   GBP TONNE 13JAN99 12:07
LON FOB White    SPOT     ↓ 251.30   -3.20  LIFFE FOB UK   ANY  USD TONNE 13JAN99 12:07
LON CIF Raw      SPOT     ↓ 212.10   -4.00  LIFFE CIF UK    -   USD TONNE 13JAN99 12:07
LON FOB Equiv    SPOT     ↓ 191.10   -4.00  LIFFE FOB UK    -   USD TONNE 13JAN99 12:07
Freight Carib/UK SPOT       21.00     0     LIFFE     -     -   USD TONNE 13JAN99 12:07
USD Daily        SPOT     ↓ 251.8    -3.2   RTRS  FOB PAR  ANY  USD TONNE 13JAN99 11:44
FRF Daily        SPOT     ↓ 1413.0  -42.0   RTRS  FOB PAR  ANY  FRF TONNE 13JAN99 11:44
```

```
SUG5-FOB-LON      LON FOB White   Currency -        USD      13JAN99
                  Sugar LON Daily Lot.Size -        1 TONNE  12:07

   Last                 Source   Terms 1  Basis   For  :
 ↓251.30   -3.20        LIFFE    FOB              info :
 ↑254.50    0           Mkt.Loc  Terms 2  Bas.Mnth see  :
 ↑254.50   +1.50        ANY      UK               <M361>
Cls:12JAN99             Yr.High  Spec 1   Bas.Loc
 254.50                 482.00   DAILY
Del.Date                Yr.Low   Spec 2   Status
SPOT                    209.80   WHITE
```

```
                                                                    M361
                        Sugar Specifications
                        --------------------

London Daily Indicator       <SUG4-IND-LON>
Commodity.........Sugar              Unit...............Tonne
Origin............N/A                Currency..........GBP
Pricing Terms......CIF               Quality...........Raw
Delivery Location..UK
Source............LIFFE
Additional Information: Quoted daily.


FOB White London             <SUG5-FOB-LON>
Commodity.........Sugar              Unit...............lbs
Origin............N/A                Currency..........USD
Pricing Terms......FOB               Quality...........White
Delivery Location..UK
Source............LIFFE
Additional Information: Quoted daily.
```

What Instruments Are Used in the Markets?

The Reuters screens on this page show the Wheat Speed Guide, including cash prices and contract details.

```
WHEAT - REUTERS SPEED GUIDE                                    WHEAT/CASH2
For all new displays within the Grains/Oilseeds markets, see <GRAIN/CASH1>-4
For Page Based Wheat data see <WHEAT/CASH3>.

=AUSTRALIAN WHEAT PHYSICAL PRICES======  =EUROPEAN WHEAT PHYSICAL PRICES contd==
Australian Wheat ..........<O#WHEAT-AU>   Turkish Wheat...............<TR/WHEAT1>
                                          Ukranian Nat. Exch. Assoc.....<CHEMON2>
=ARGENTINE GRAIN PRICES================   CPC EU Cash Grains.........<CPCBDTU>-X
General Grain prices.......<O#GRAIN-AR>
Argentine Grain Exports...<O#EXPORT-AR>     =CPC MARKET INFORMATION===============
CPC Argentine Grains..........<CPCBDTT>   CPC World Wheat prices and comment.....
                                          ...............................<CPCBDTB>-D
=EUROPEAN WHEAT PHYSICAL PRICES========   World Grain Tenders..........<CPCBDTL>
European Wheat..............<O#WHEAT-E>    World Grain Sales...........<CPCBDTM>
European Wheat Summary<O#WHEAT-FRONT-E>   Ocean Freight Rates.........<CPCBDTY>-Z
EU Grain Tariffs.....<O#GRAIN-TARIFF-E>   CPC Index Page...............<CPCBDTA>
Specific French Ports......<O#WHEAT-FR>
French Wheat Production..<WHE/PROD/FR1>   =COMMODITY MARKET NEWS================
French Wheat Yields......<WHE/YLDS/FR1>   Commodities News Guide...<COMMOD/NEWS1>
French Wheat Area........<WHE/AREA/FR1>
EU Calculator...............<EUWHE-VAL>
French Onic Wheat Estimates<ONIC/WHEAT>   Previous page.............<WHEAT/CASH1>

Cereals Index  <CEREAL1>   Wheat Futures<WHEAT/FUT1>   Wheat Options<WHEAT/OPT1>
Lost? Selective access? <USER/HELP>       Reuters Phone Support <PHONE/HELP>
```

```
O#WHEAT-AU             Australian Wheat
Commodity        Del.Date        Last          Srce    Terms   Loc Ccy Units Date   Time
Standard Wht P1  Jan        ↓ 157.50  -2.00    RTRS  FOB EcAU  AUS USD TONNE 13JAN99 04:58
Standard Hard P1 Jan        ↓ 168.50  -2.00    RTRS  FOB EcAU  AUS USD TONNE 13JAN99 04:58
Prm Hard 13% P1  Jan        ↓ 174.50  -2.00    RTRS  FOB EcAU  AUS USD TONNE 13JAN99 04:58
Prm Hard 14% P1  Jan        ↓ 202.50  -0.50    RTRS  FOB EcAU  AUS USD TONNE 13JAN99 04:58
Standard Wht P2  Feb        ↓ 158.50  -2.00    RTRS  FOB EcAU  AUS USD TONNE 13JAN99 04:58
Standard Hard P2 Feb        ↓ 169.50  -2.00    RTRS  FOB EcAU  AUS USD TONNE 13JAN99 04:58
Prm Hard 13% P2  Feb        ↓ 175.50  -2.00    RTRS  FOB EcAU  AUS USD TONNE 13JAN99 04:58
Prm Hard 14% P2  Feb        ↓ 203.50  -0.50    RTRS  FOB EcAU  AUS USD TONNE 13JAN99 04:58
Standard Wht P3  Mar        ↓ 159.50  -2.00    RTRS  FOB EcAU  AUS USD TONNE 13JAN99 04:58
Standard Hard P3 Mar        ↓ 170.50  -2.00    RTRS  FOB EcAU  AUS USD TONNE 13JAN99 04:58
Prm Hard 13% P3  Mar        ↓ 176.50  -2.00    RTRS  FOB EcAU  AUS USD TONNE 13JAN99 04:58
Prm Hard 14% P3  Mar        ↓ 204.50  -0.50    RTRS  FOB EcAU  AUS USD TONNE 13JAN99 04:58
Standard Wht P4  Apr        ↓ 161.00  -2.00    RTRS  FOB EcAU  AUS USD TONNE 13JAN99 04:58
Standard Hard P4 Apr        ↓ 172.00  -2.00    RTRS  FOB EcAU  AUS USD TONNE 13JAN99 04:58
Prm Hard 13% P4  Apr        ↓ 178.00  -2.00    RTRS  FOB EcAU  AUS USD TONNE 13JAN99 04:58
Prm Hard 14% P4  Apr        ↓ 206.00  -0.50    RTRS  FOB EcAU  AUS USD TONNE 13JAN99 04:58
Standard Wht P5  May        ↓ 162.50  -2.00    RTRS  FOB EcAU  AUS USD TONNE 13JAN99 04:58
Standard Hard P5 May        ↓ 173.50  -2.00    RTRS  FOB EcAU  AUS USD TONNE 13JAN99 04:58
Prm Hard 13% P5  May        ↓ 179.50  -2.00    RTRS  FOB EcAU  AUS USD TONNE 13JAN99 04:58
Prm Hard 14% P5  May        ↓ 207.50  -0.50    RTRS  FOB EcAU  AUS USD TONNE 13JAN99 04:58
Standard Wht P6  June       ↓ 164.00  -2.00    RTRS  FOB EcAU  AUS USD TONNE 13JAN99 04:58
Standard Hard P6 June       ↓ 175.00  -2.00    RTRS  FOB EcAU  AUS USD TONNE 13JAN99 04:58
Prm Hard 13% P6  June       ↓ 181.00  -2.00    RTRS  FOB EcAU  AUS USD TONNE 13JAN99 04:58
Prm Hard 14% P6  June       ↓ 209.00  -0.50    RTRS  FOB EcAU  AUS USD TONNE 13JAN99 04:58
```

```
EXW-AUSTHD-P1    Standard Hard P1 Currency -        USD
                 Australian Wheat Lot.Size -        TONNE

  Last                 Source    Terms 1   Basis    For  :
 ↓168.50    -2.00      RTRS      FOB       Info :
 ↓170.50     0         Mkt.Loc   Terms 2   Bas.Mnth see  :
 ↓170.50    -2.00      AUS       EcAU               <S257>
Cls:12JAN99            Yr.High   Spec 1    Bas.Loc
170.50                 306.50    Daily
Del.Date               Yr.Low    Spec 2    Status
Jan                    168       11.5%
```

```
                                                                        S257
                          Wheat Specifications
                          --------------------

CONTRACT:Standard Hard P1-6    <EXW-AUSTHD-P1>-6
Commodity..........Wheat                    Protein Content....min11.5%
Origin.............Australia                Moisture Content...max 12%
Delivery Point.....FOB; East Coast Australia
Unit...............Tonne
Currency...........USD
Additional Information: Quoted daily


CONTRACT:N. Spring 14-P1,2-4   <IMW-USNS14-P1>-4
Commodity..........Wheat                    Protein Content....14%
Origin.............US;N.Spring              Moisture Content...max 13%
Delivery Point.....1 FOB,2-3 CIF; Rtdm      Hagberg............300 secs
Unit...............Tonne
Currency...........USD
Additional Information: Quoted daily
```

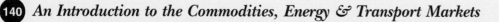

REUTERS :::

On the LME, the **Official** benchmark cash prices for each metal are published on a metal-by-metal basis 10 minutes after the end of the second morning ring session for each metal. These Official LME cash prices are displayed on a number of different Reuters pages as shown here.

While both pages below show final monthly settlement prices, the bottom page also shows the range of prices (bid/ask) that resulted in the settlement price. This page also shows the bid/ask prices for future contracts.

```
0#LME-OFFCL      LME      Daily Official Prices
                 Cash           3 Month         15 Month         27 Month      Settlement
Copper      1446.5 /1447.0  1472.0 /1473.0  1560.0 /1570.0  1615.0 /1625.0   1447.0
(STG Eq.)   874.16 /        891.54 /
Tin         5060   /5065    5060   /5065    5030   /5040                      5065
Lead        487.00 /487.50  489.50 /490.00  520.00 /525.00                    487.5
(STG Eq.)   294.51 /        296.57 /
Zinc        913.0  /913.5   933.0  /933.5   992.0  /997.0   1035.0 /1040.0    913.5
Aluminium   1231.0 /1231.5  1237.5 /1238.0  1323.0 /1328.0  1387.0 /1392.0    1231.5
Nickel      4350   /4355    4420   /4430    4650   /4670    4855   /4875      4355
Al.Alloy    1037.0 /1038.0  1063.0 /1065.0  1135.0 /1155.0                    1038.0
Settlement Rates - GBP ↑1.6553  DEM ↓1.6672   JPY ↑112.09       13:15
```

```
LONDON METAL EXCHANGE    OFFICIAL MONTHLY SETTLEMENT PRICES        SETTLME

DATE:    CU       CS       SN       PB     PS      ZN      AL       NI      AA
DEC98  1473.57  881.83  5257.62  501.26  299.96  959.19 1249.41  3881.1 1046.91
NOV98  1573.95  947.48  5478.33  494.17  297.48  967.12 1295.29  4135.2 1084.26
OCT98  1586.39  936.00  5432.05  492.82  290.77  940.48 1304.41  3875.0 1114.18
SEP98  1647.64  980.36  5485.68  520.16  309.50 1000.36 1342.66  4105.6 1154.05
AUG98  1620.93  993.44  5691.50  536.70  328.96 1029.80 1311.25  4084.0 1148.90
JUL98  1651.04 1004.33  5653.70  546.20  332.24 1040.26 1309.57  4328.9 1245.04
JUN98  1660.52 1006.15  5970.00  528.32  320.11 1009.82 1307.59  4478.6 1226.02
MAY98  1732.53 1058.14  5874.74  543.47  332.00 1061.11 1365.13  5023.1 1265.26
APR98  1800.90 1077.27  5714.75  572.65  342.59 1096.95 1418.60  5396.7 1285.50
MAR98  1747.98 1052.00  5476.82  559.82  336.86 1047.64 1438.02  5398.8 1271.59
FEB98  1664.80 1015.45  5242.50  516.38  314.95 1044.00 1465.95  5389.5 1291.60
JAN98  1688.45 1032.55  5206.25  531.58  325.16 1097.20 1486.10  5494.50 1330.88

FOR CURRENT MONTHS DAILY OFFICIAL PRICES DOUBLE CLICK ON:
      <SETTMCU01> <SETTMCS01> <SETTMSN01> <SETTMPB01>  <SETTMPS01>
      <SETTMZN01> <SETTMAL01> <SETTMNI01>  <SETTMAA01>
```

```
1403 LME DAILY OFFICIAL PRICES - 13 JAN 1999                     MTLE
             CASH          3 MTHS        15 MTHS      27 MTHS    SETT
COPPER     1446.5/47.0  1472.0/73.0  1560.0/70.0  1615.0/25.0  1447.0
(STG EQ)     874.16       891.54
TIN        5060/5065    5060/5065    5030/5040         /       5065
LEAD       487.00/7.50  489.50/0.00  520.00/5.00       /       487.5
(STG EQ)     294.51       296.57
ZINC       913.0/13.5   933.0/33.5   992.0/97.0   1035.0/40.0  913.5
ALUMINUM   1231.0/31.5  1237.5/38.0  1323.0/28.0  1387.0/92.0  1231.5
NICKEL     4350/4355    4420/4430    4650/4670    4855/4875    4355
AL.ALLOY   1037.0/38.0  1063.0/65.0  1135.0/55.0               1038.0
SETTLE - GBP  1.6553    DEM  1.6672    JPY  112.09    EUR 1.1732
Prompt Dates : Cash - 15/01/99      15Mth - 19/04/00
                    3Mth - 13/04/99       27Mth - 18/04/01
```

```
LONDON METAL EXCHANGE - MONTHLY AVERAGES                    SETTLME1
MONTH : DECEMBER 1998
                  COPPER       TIN      LEAD    ZINC  ALUMINUM   NICKEL  AL.ALLOY

CASH  MID        1473.24    5254.52    500.82  958.82  1249.06  3878.21  1045.29
      BID        1472.90    5251.43    500.38  958.45  1248.71  3875.24  1043.67
      SETT       1473.57    5257.62    501.26  959.19  1249.40  3881.21  1046.90

3MTH  MID        1502.38    5249.05    480.58  977.44  1258.56  3947.26  1075.99
      BID        1501.95    5246.43    480.14  977.07  1258.21  3944.05  1075.00
      ASK        1502.81    5251.67    481.02  977.81  1258.90  3950.48  1076.98

15MTH MID        1584.05    5195.48    507.26 1037.69  1344.83  4171.67  1162.62
      BID        1579.05    5190.48    504.76 1035.19  1342.33  4161.67  1152.62
      ASK        1589.05    5200.48    509.76 1040.19  1347.33  4181.67  1172.62

27MTH MID        1626.19                       1081.64  1410.07  4371.90
      BID        1621.19                       1079.14  1407.57  4361.90
      ASK        1631.19                       1084.14  1412.57  4381.90
```

These pages show daily metal prices for cash and future transactions. The top page results by calling up the LME on the Reuters terminal, the bottom page results from a Reuters reporting service. The bottom page also shows prompt dates.

What Instruments Are Used in the Markets?

Various Reuters web sites offer clients helpful information about metals markets. The website at www.commods.reuters.com makes available a wide range of data about the commodities markets. Interested market players can gain free access to real-time market data about the energy and shipping markets for a 14-day trial period at www.reuters.inform.

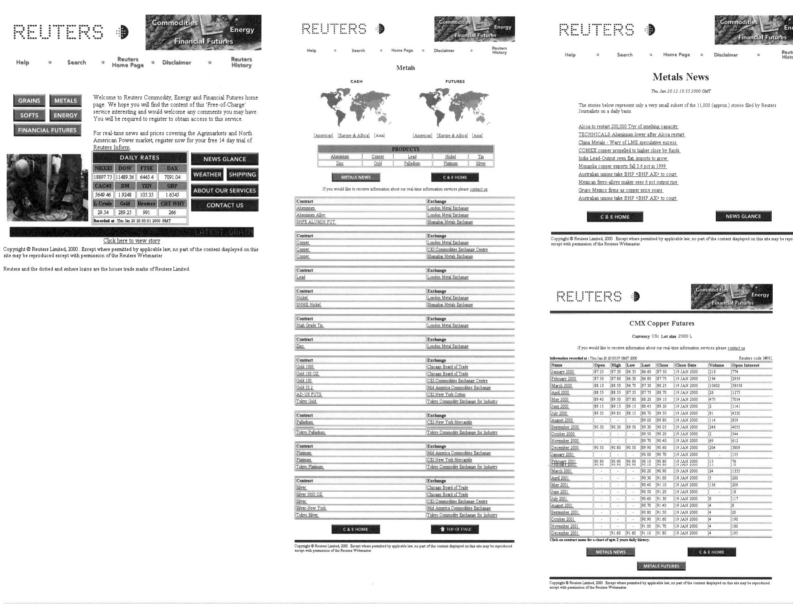

These Reuters screens show detailed information about Crude Oil Official Selling Prices in the U.S., Europe and Asia, as well as global averages. Reuters also provides data from the U.S. Energy Information Administration (EIA)

```
13:01 03JUN98          OIL PRICES          UK30507          CRUDE/OSP1
Crude oil - official selling prices

  This series of Reuter pages (CRUDE/OSP1 to CRUDE/OSP9) gives details of the
official selling prices of crude oil. A list of the various countries covered
in this series is given below. To access individual pages either double-click
between <> brackets or type in the page code and hit return.

  If you have any questions about this series of pages plase contact Reuters
London energy desk. Tel: 0171 542 4984

Country          Current prices

Saudi Arabia     <CRUDE/OSP2>
Nigeria          <CRUDE/OSP3>
Mexico           <CRUDE/OSP9>
Iraq             <CRUDE/OSP4>
Iran             <CRUDE/OSP5>
Kuwait           <CRUDE/OSP6>
Libya            <CRUDE/OSP7>
Egypt            <CRUDE/OSP8>


Note: The official selling prices of all crude oils are calculated using
Reuter prices.
```

```
17:03 13DEC99     International Crude Oil Prices     UK30507      CRUDE/INT
                                                                  IPE Brent
Brent spreads   Buy    Sell   Brent    Buy      Sell    EFP    Last  Change

Dated  v Jan   -0.05  +0.20   Dated   $24.54  $24.56
Jan    v Feb   +0.60  +0.70   Jan     $24.46  $24.48
Feb    v Mar   +0.85  +0.90   Feb     $23.81  $23.83  +0.05  $23.77  +0.09
Mar    v Apr   +0.80  +0.85   Mar     $22.94  $22.96

Dubai spreads   Buy    Sell   Dubai    Buy      Sell

Jan    v Feb   +0.15  +0.20   Jan     $22.46  $22.48
Feb    v Mar   +0.70  +0.80   Feb     $22.29  $22.31
Mar    v Apr   +0.70  +0.75   Mar     $21.54  $21.56

Brent v Dubai   Buy    Sell
                                Market close time   Editorial contacts
Jan            +1.95  +2.05     Asia   0930 GMT     Tokyo     813 5473 3708
Feb            +1.25  +1.35     Europe 1730 GMT     Singapore 65 870 3080
                                U.S.   2200 GMT     London    171 542 7646
                                                    New York  212 859 1629

Note: EFP = Exchange of futures for physical. For details of how prices on this
      page are assessed please double click between the brackets <CRUDE/NOTES>.
      All prices in $ per barrel.
```

```
EIA/STATS
     U.S. Petroleum Balance Sheet, 4 Weeks Ending 10/30/98

                                                    Cumulative
                              Four Week Averages    Daily Averages
                                  Ending              302 Days
Petroleum Supply                           %    ----------------  %
(Thousand Barrels per Day)  10/30/98 10/30/97 Chg   1998   1997   Chg
--------------------------------------------------------------------
Crude Oil Supply
Domestic Production (1) ........ E6,411   6,467  -0.9  E6,394  6,442  -0.7
Net Imports (Incl SPR) (2) ..... 8,195    8,775  -6.6   8,421  8,153   3.3
  Gross Imports (Excl SPR) ..... 8,300    8,927  -7.0   8,553  8,266   3.5
  SPR Imports .................      0        0    --       0      0    --
  Exports .....................   E105      152 -30.9    E131    112  17.0
SPR Stocks W/D or Added ........      0        0    --       0      8    --
Other Stocks W/D or Added ......   -637     -393    --    -101   -104    --
Product Supplied and Losses ....     E0        0    --      E0     -3    --
Unaccounted-for Crude Oil (3)...    -33        5    --     137    131    --

Crude Oil Input to Refineries... 13,935   14,854  -6.2  14,851  14,629  1.5


Other Supply
Natural Gas Liquids Prod. (6)... E1,766   1,989 -11.2  E1,944  1,948  -0.2
Other Liquids New Supply .......   E208      167  24.6    E183    220 -16.8
Crude Oil Product Supplied .....     E0        0   0.0      E0      3 -100.0
```

```
EIA/STATS
     U.S. Petroleum Balance Sheet, 4 Weeks Ending 10/30/98

Methodology:
Monthly world oil supply and demand figures are interpolated from figures
published by the US Energy Information Administration (EIA). Each month the EIA
publishes a "Short Term Energy Outlook" which includes a table of "International
Petroleum Supply and Demand: Mid World Oil Price Case". This table contains
quarterly forecasts which are basis for Reuters monthly forecasts on pages
EIA/STATS3. The EIA's four quarterly figures are taken as the niddle month of
the quarter. (i.e. 1st quarter = February, 3rd quarter = August). Other months
are then interpolated. The average monthly figure each year is always within
50,000 barrels per day (bpd) of the annual EIA figure. See below:

Year         EIA forecast          Reuters forecast         Error < 0.05
1999 Demand     73.21                 73.20                    0.01
     Supply     74.04                 74.03                    0.01
1998 Demand     74.17                 74.14                    0.03
     Supply     74.88                 74.86                    0.02
1997 Demand     75.95                 75.92                    0.03
     Supply     76.07                 76.05                    0.02
```

Forward Contracts

A **forward contract** is a cash transaction in which the buyer and the seller agree upon delivery of a specified quality and quantity of commodity at a specified future date. A price may be agreed upon in advance or at the time of delivery.

It is important to remember that forward contracts are OTC transactions which involve credit risk to both counterparties as in the spot markets.

Forward contracts are not usually traded on exchanges as they are drawn up privately and not transparent since they do not need to be reported. However, as you will see, the benchmark base metals contracts on the LME are forward contracts which are traded on the exchange floor. There are other interesting forward contracts in the energy and shipping markets which you should also know something about and understand.

When a forward contact is made it has no value – payment is only made at the agreed contract date in the future. In the forward markets there are two terms commonly used:

- If the spot price is at a **premium** to the forward price, then the market is described as in **backwardation**

- If the spot price is at a **discount** to the forward price, then the market is described as in **contango**

But how are forward prices determined? In principle a forward price is calculated as the spot price at the time of the trade plus a **cost of carry**. Depending on the commodity this cost of carry takes into account factors such as storage, insurance, transport etc.

Forward price = Spot or cash price + cost of carry

Although there are similarities in trading in the financial and commodity markets, it is important to recognise that there are also great differences. For example, if the forward price of oil is high, buying a tanker cargo of oil on the spot market with a view to selling it in the future may seem an attractive investment. However, how will you fund this position, where will you store the oil, how much will storage and insurance cost, and if the markets reverse what will you do with several thousand barrels of oil?

In general, commodity markets are much more susceptible to supply and demand volatility. For example, harvests can be affected by weather and natural disasters and consumption of materials can be affected by rapid technological changes, manufacturing process and political events. It is also the case that many commodity markets use instruments to trade directly between producers and consumers rather than provide opportunities for hedging and speculation.

However, within the commodity markets there are established forward contracts for base metals, oil and electricity, and Forward Freight Agreements (FFAs) are used in the shipping markets.

Who Uses Forward Contracts?

London Metal Exchange Base Metal Contracts

Although these are contracts traded on an exchange with some degree of transparency, the contracts are for 3 months where market players can take positions for any business day out to 3 months forward. This is a similar situation to that found in the OTC Forward foreign exchange. Why are the contracts 3 months forward? Historically, three months was the time it took for shipments of metals from South America to reach London.

The most important contracts traded on the LME are the 3-month forward contracts for copper, tin, zinc, lead, nickel, aluminium and aluminium alloy. These contracts are **rolling** contracts. This means that the contracts have fixed delivery dates **exactly three months forward** from the trade date. Ultimately the LME is a physical market whereby all contracts involve the actual delivery or receipt of metal on the contract delivery date. However, most contracts are closed out in a similar way to futures contracts and delivery does not take place.

Using forward contracts allows market players to trade future positions either side of the 3-month price as **outright prices** or as **spreads** relative to the 3-month price. By adding or subtracting the spreads relating to the 3-month prices, a trader is able to calculate the outright or broken-date price for any delivery date necessary. This facility is a distinct advantage over futures contracts which have fixed delivery dates.

The Reuters screen at right is the Forwards and Spreads page. Below is an explanation of how to read the screen; the table below gives the abbreviations used for the various metals.

xx	Metal
CU	Copper
AL	Aluminium
AA	Aluminium Alloy
NI	Nickel
ZN	Zinc
SN	Tin
PB	Lead

O#MCU:	COPPER		LME/	USD	Total Stock 610000			
Mth	Last		Bid	Ask	Time	Open	High Low	Evaluation
CASH	T ↓1438.00	RING	1438.0	1439.0	RING 12:45	1438.0	1438.0 1438.0	E 1457.25
3MT	M 1469.5	CLRS	1469.0	1470.0	CLRS 16:20	1487.5	B1489.0A1457.0	E 1485.00
Mth	Last		Bid	Ask	Time	Last 2	Last 3	Evaluation
C-3M	T c28.00	RING	c28.0	c27.8	RING 16:10	M 28	M 27.5	P -27.75
FEB9-3M	M 18	RING	c18.5	c18.0	RING 15:34	M 18.25	M 9.375	P -17.75
MAR9-3M	M 8.25	WOLF	c8.5	c8.0	WOLF 13:49	M 8.25	M 8.25	P -8.00
APR9-3M	C			:		C	C	
C-FEB9	M 9.5	RING	c9.8	c9.5	RING 15:30	C	M 9.9	
FEB-MAR	T c9.75	RING	c9.8	c9.5	RING 16:13	T c9.75	M 9.75	
MAR-APR	C			:		C	C	
3M-MAY9	M 8.25	MGAA	c8.8	c8.3	RING 16:11	M 8.5	M 8	P -8.25
3M-JUN9	M 16	MGAA	c17.0	c15.5	RING 15:31	M 16.5	M 15.5	P -15.75
3M-JUL9	M 25	MGAA	c26.0	c24.5	RING 15:31	M 25.5	M 24.5	P -24.75
3M-AUG9	M 32	MGAA	c33.0	c31.0	MGAA 14:04	M 32.5	M 33	P -32.50
3M-SEP9	M 40	MGAA	c41.0	c39.0	MGAA 14:04	M 40.5	M 40.5	P -40.25
3M-OCT9	M 49	MGAA	c50.0	c48.0	MGAA 14:04	M 49.5	M 49	P -49.00
3M-NOV9	M 56	MGAA	c57.0	c55.0	MGAA 14:04	M 56.5	M 56.5	P -56.25
3M-DEC9	M 63	RING	c65.0	c64.0	RING 15:31	M 64.5	M 63.5	P -63.50
3M-JANO	M 75	MGAA	c78.0	c72.0	MGAA 14:04	M 71.5	M 70.5	P -70.50

Each line represents the most recent quote from the exchange floor and gives the ID of the market member

The **first line** is the outright quotation for the **CASH** price. (This price is updated infrequently during the day and a more accurate value is calculated adding the **C–3M spread** – third line – to the **3MT outright price** – second line – check the **Calculations** box opposite.)

The **second line** is the 3-month outright forward price – **3MT**.

These lines display spreads relative to the 3-month price. If the spread is **prior to or within** the 3-month period this is denoted by the future month **followed** by **3M**. For example, **FEB9-3M** is the February 99 to the 3-month date spread. Spreads **beyond** the 3-month date **start** with **3M**. For example, **3M-APR99** is the 3-month date to April 99 spread. LME spread contracts are a mixture of forwards and future month dates where the future month code, for example, FEB99, refers to the **3rd Wednesday** of that month. A **3-month forward** price rolls forward on a daily basis so a 3-month contract is always three months forward from the trade date. A **3rd future month** is the 3rd Wednesday of the 3rd month from the current month. For example, if the date is 30th September 1998:

3rd Future month date   =   16th December 1998
3-month forward date   =   30th December 1998

So the 3rd Future month – 3-month forward spread is the spread between 16th December and 30th December 1998.

O#MCU:	COPPER		LME/	USD	Total
Mth	Last		Bid	Ask	Time
CASH	T ↓1438.00	RING	1438.0	1439.0	RING 12:45
3MT	M 1469.5	CLRS	1469.0	1470.0	CLRS 16:20
Mth	Last		Bid	Ask	Time
C-3M	T c28.00	RING	c28.0	c27.8	RING 16:10
FEB9-3M	M 18	RING	c18.5	c18.0	RING 15:34
MAR9-3M	M 8.25	WOLF	c8.5	c8.0	WOLF 13:49
APR9-3M	C			:	
C-FEB9	M 9.5	RING	c9.8	c9.5	RING 15:30
FEB-MAR	T c9.75	RING	c9.8	c9.5	RING 16:13
MAR-APR	C			:	
3M-MAY9	M 8.25	MGAA	c8.8	c8.3	RING 16:11
3M-JUN9	M 16	MGAA	c17.0	c15.5	RING 15:31
3M-JUL9	M 25	MGAA	c26.0	c24.5	RING 15:31
3M-AUG9	M 32	MGAA	c33.0	c31.0	MGAA 14:04

Calculations

To calculate broken date prices using spreads you need to know if the market is in **contango (c)** or in **backwardation (b)**.

- If it is a **c** market, then spreads are **subtracted** from the **3MT** price if the date is **prior** to 3-month date, and **added otherwise**
- If it is a **b** market, then spreads are **added** to the **3MT** price if the date is **prior** to 3-month date, and **subtracted otherwise**

What Instruments Are Used in the Markets?

Using a news service such as Reuters, it is also possible to display all market members quotes for a particular contract – outright or spread. A green strip display identifies the most recent quote for the contract taken from those currently available from market members.

As a user of this service, you would display a green strip page for any spread by either double-clicking on the contract in the left hand column in the previous page or by typing in the precise RIC and pressing F3. The RICs can be constructed as follows:

1. Type in the **Metal Code, Mxx**
2. If the spread date is **prior** to the 3-month date, type in **3 - Month code + Year**
3. If the spread date is **after** the 3-month date, type in **Month code + Year - 3**

Examples: **MCU3-J9** displays the spread quote for 3 MT to April 99 for Copper

MCUF9-3 displays the spread quote for Jan 99 to 3MT for Copper

Type in **MCU0-3** and press **F3** to see the Copper Cash to 3-month forward spread.

Month	Code	Month	Code
Jan	F	Jul	N
Feb	G	Aug	Q
Mar	H	Sep	U
Apr	J	Oct	V
May	K	Nov	X
Jun	M	Dec	Z

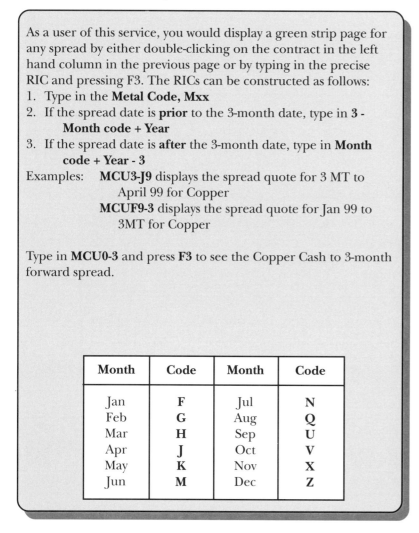

```
20JAN99  LME /      3MONTH    COPPER    Prev Cls    1485.0
Last Trade M  1469.5  M  1469.5        Official Vol    67017

          Most  Recent  LME  Member  Quote
          CLRS      1469.0 / 1470.0     16:20

AMTL  1463.0 - 1467.0   15:23  BARC  1461.0 - 1465.0   15:08
N/A                            BRAN  1464.0 - 1467.0   15:51
FMAT  1464.0 - 1467.0   15:57  CLRS  1469.0 - 1470.0   16:20
CARR  1482.0 - 1485.0   08:19  DSML       -              :
EDFM  1465.0 - 1466.0   13:30  ARON  1466.0 - 1470.0   16:04
LBCL       -             :     MAQR  1488.0 - 1491.0   04:12
MERL       -             :     MGAA  1469.0 - 1470.0   16:15
MDTL       -             :     MBUA  1465.0 - 1469.0   16:05
MOCC  1465.0 - 1469.0   16:04  BACH  1464.0 - 1468.0   14:40
BHHK  1488.0 - 1491.0   06:35  REFO       -           11:51
WOLF  1469.0 - 1470.0   16:15  SOGM  1465.0 - 1469.0   13:44
SBNK  1465.0 - 1470.0   16:07  SDUK  1467.0 - 1472.0   16:09
TRIL       -           11:44
```

```
O#MCU:      COPPER          LME/    USD         Total
Mth       Last          Bid      Ask         Time
CASH    T ↓1438.00  RING  1438.0  1439.0  RING 12:45
3MT     M  1469.5   CLRS  1469.0  1470.0  CLRS 16:20
Mth       Last          Bid      Ask         Time
C-3M    T c28.00    RING c28.0   c27.8   RING 16:10
FEB9-3M M  18       RING c18.5   c18.0   RING 15:34
MAR9-3M M  8.25     WOLF c8.5    c8.0    WOLF 13:49
```

Double-click here or type in MCU0-3 + F3

```
20JAN99  LME /      C-3M      COPPER    Prev Cls    27.8
Last Trade T c28.00    M  28          Official Vol

          Most  Recent  LME  Member  Quote
          TRIL      -28.5 / -27.5     13:05

AMTL  -28.2 - -27.3    :     BARC       -              :
N/A                          BRAN  -28.0 - -27.0       :
FMAT       -           :     CLRS  -28.0 - -27.0    08:17
CARR       -           :     DSML       -              :
EDFM  -28.0 - -27.0  08:52   ARON  -26.5 - -25.0       :
LBCL       -           :     MAQR       -              :
MERL       -           :     MGAA  -28.0 - -27.0    12:05
MDTL       -           :     MBUA  -30.0 - -29.0
MOCC  -28.0 - -27.0  09:32   BACH  -29.0 - -27.5    09:10
BHHK  -28.5 - -26.5    :     REFO  -28.0 - -26.0    07:27
WOLF  -28.0 - -27.0    :     SOGM  -26.0 - -25.0       :
SBNK  -28.0 - -26.0  08:24   SDUK       -              :
TRIL  -28.5 - -27.5  13:05
```

REUTERS

Energy Markets

In the energy markets there are informal forward markets in gasoline, gas oil, naphtha and heavy fuel oil.

The 15-day Brent market is the largest and most important crude oil forward market worldwide. The Brent forward contract gives 15 days notice to the buyer to take delivery of a cargo at Sullom Voe during a nominated 3-day loading period.

This forward market was introduced by some of the larger oil companies and refiners to try to ensure producers could buy/sell oil for future delivery and refiners could help hedge risk.

Although the 15-day Brent contract has standardised terms and conditions its method of trading involves a number of unique features which are summarised in the chart below.

Term	Description
Daisy-chain	This is where A sells a cargo to B, B sells the same cargo to C, C sells the same cargo to D and so on. In financial terms a daisy-chain is only as strong as the weakest link. On volatile days up to 60 buyers and sellers can be involved in a single daisy-chain.
Book-out	This is an agreement between a number of market players in a daisy-chain who agree to cancel their contracts with each other in return for a cash settlement of any difference between the contract price and an agreed reference price.

Term	Description
Five-o'clocked	This term describes the process whereby any cargo involved in forward contracts that have **not** been booked-out are passed on to other market players. For example, A has a contract for physical delivery but has sold the cargo to B in the 15-day market. A serves a 15-day notice of delivery on B who in turn can sell the contract to C and serve a notice of delivery and so on. This process can continue until 17.00 London time on the last day on which the 15-day notice can be served. The market player left with the notice of delivery at this time is said to have been five-o'clocked and becomes the physical owner of the cargo.

Within the 15-day Brent market, financial exposure between counterparties is strictly controlled. Major market players operate a system of agreed credit limits or performance bonds.

Many crude oil traders prefer the 15-day forward markets for pricing contracts because it is quite liquid. If however, one party insists on using Dated (spot) Brent prices as the benchmark, then the other party can still use 15-day Brent prices as a **differential**. These instruments are known as **Contracts For Difference (CFDs)**. The latest Brent CFD prices are available via Reuters as shown below:

```
O#BRT-CFD              Brent CFD's
Delivery     Basis         Buy    Sell   Time   Date     PreviousDay
JAN 18-22 vs.MAR Brent    +0.05  +0.07  11:35  13JAN99  +0.05  +0.09
JAN 25-29 vs.MAR Brent    -0.03  +0.02  11:35  13JAN99  +0.03  +0.05
FEB 01-05 vs.MAR Brent    -0.16  -0.14  11:36  13JAN99  -0.16  -0.12
FEB 08-12 vs.MAR Brent    -0.18  -0.14  18:54  12JAN99  -0.14  -0.10
          vs.    Brent                  12:01  08JAN98  -0.49  -0.45
          vs.    Brent                  10:15  29DEC97
          vs.    Brent                  10:15  29DEC97
```

What Instruments Are Used in the Markets?

Within the more recently established electricity markets much of the cash trading is in the **day-ahead** or forward markets. In Europe the Norwegian/Swedish Nord Pool exchange has introduced two types of contracts as follows:

- **Forward contracts** for standardised physical contracts for hourly power during the next 24 hour period. These contracts are traded on a daily basis for delivery next day and are similar to OTC traded contracts.

- **Futures contracts** which are cash settled

Below is the Reuters screen displaying the Nordpool ASA Index page with forward prices.

```
NORDPOOL ASA INDEX PAGE                              NORDPOOL
Vollsveien 13B, Postboks 373, 1324 Lysaker    Tel:  +47 67 528 000
Official trading hours: Monday - Friday  10:00-15:00 After market: 15:00-15:30

===============FIXINGS===============   ===========CONTRACT DETAILS===========
                                        Base Power: 00:00 Mon - 24:00 Sun(168h)
System Average...............<.NPXSYS>  Weeks:      4 to 7 weeks are traded
Oslo Average.................<.NPXOSL>  Blocks:     Trading period from the
Stockholm Average............<.NPXSTO>              last week listed to the
System Fixings (01-24h).<O#SYSFIX=NPX>              first season (27-52 weeks
Oslo Fixings   (01-24h).<O#OSLFIX=NPX>              ahead)
Stkhln Fixings (01-24h).<O#STOFIX=NPX>  Seasons:    Traded from last block
                                                    (27-52 weeks) to three
===============FUTURES===============               years ahead, minimum four
Weekly Futures...............<O#NPW:>               seasons and maximum of six
Block Futures................<O#NPB:>   Expiry Day: Friday or the last market
Season Futures...............<O#NPS:>               day in the week of delivery
                                        Last Price: Last price within bid/ask
===============FORWARDS===============              spread when closed or an
Winter 1/Summer/Winter 2.....<O#NPF:>               average of bid/ask.
                                        On expiry:  Volume weighted last price
Trading unit:  kr/MWh                   Sys price:  Hour weighted average of
                                                    the powerprice in the 24
                                                    hour market (day market)
========Questions/Comments: call the NDM Team in Stockholm +46-8-700 1141=======
```

```
O#NPF:          NPX FORWARDS       /  NOK
Mth   Last Net.Ch Bid   Ask   Settle Open High  Low  Volume Op.Int Time
S099 ↓102.75 -0.75 102.00 103.00      103.00 103.00 102.75 20000 26440 08:28
V299          135.25 138.00                              31300 14:26
V100          150.25 152.50                              17870 14:27
S000          119.00 121.15                              12000 10:36
YR01 ↑148.75 +0.75 148.00 148.95  148.25 148.75 148.25  5000  8180 10:17
V101          159.50 162.00                               3690 12:25
V200          150.00 152.50                              14450 13:02
YR00          138.25 139.00                              13740 14:29
S001          129.10 132.00                                980 07:26
V201          159.50 162.00                               2230 12:26
```

More recently, developments in the energy markets particularly in the UK have seen the introduction of OTC Electricity Forward Agreements (EFAs). These agreements are paper swaps settled against the wholesale pool market purchase price. EFAs are based on standard terms and are typically sold for volumes of 20 to 50 MWH. The main periods traded are six-month blocks, summer and winter and years starting in April or October. There are three main types of agreement:

- **Baseload** which is for continuous day and night load

- **Peak** which covers the period 7.00 am to 7.00 pm on weekdays

- **Loadshape 44** which is a specific combination of Baseload and Peak

In early 1999 the market was relatively illiquid but proposed reforms in the UK pool are expected to create a more active market by April 2001. The Reuters screen below shows prices for EFAs in the UK.

```
EL/GB
UK electricity forward agreement (EFA) prices
Updated: 11 Feb 1999 1850 GMT

Time period          Baseload        Loadshape 44     Peak
                     Buy/Sell        Buy/Sell         Buy/Sell

February             34.00/36.00     N/A              N/A
March                26.00/28.00     N/A              N/A

Summer               19.00/19.20     20.70/20.90      25.50/25.70
Winter               32.30/32.90     37.05/37.55      49.00/51.00
Annual Apr 1999      25.80/25.95     28.95/29.15      N/A
Annual Oct 1999      26.10/26.20     N/A              N/A
2 yrs from Apr 99    25.35/25.75     N/A              N/A

All prices in UK pounds per megawatt hour (MWh)

Explanatory notes:
1. Electricity forward agreements are paper swaps set
purchase price of the Electricity Pool of England and Wales.
2. Summer runs from 1 April to 30 September
3. Winter runs from 1 October to 31 March
4. Annual is the calendar year starting on 1 April or 1 October
5. Baseload is continuous demand day and night.
6. Peak represents consumption between 7am and 7pm on weekdays.
7. Loadshape 44 represents 20 megawatts of baseload and 20 megawatts of peak.
```

Shipping Contracts

The shipping industry is responsible for transporting a high proportion of commodities and raw materials around the world. The industry basically comprises two market sectors whose activities, in general, are controlled by brokers. The market sectors are described as follows:

- **Dry sector** involving dry bulk cargoes which is dominated by shipowners

- **Wet sector** involving the transport of liquid cargoes by tanker and which is dominated by customers such as oil companies, oil traders etc

The diverse requirements of these sectors, combined with established practices in the OTC markets, have not encouraged an active derivatives market for shipping.

In 1985 the Baltic Exchange introduced the **Baltic Freight Index (BFI)** for dry cargoes. This index is a weighted average of a group of panelists' assessments of spot dry cargo and time charter rates for specified routes and cargoes which is produced daily. In the same year the **Baltic International Freight Futures Exchange (BIFFEX)** was established to trade a futures contract for hedging dry bulk freight risk and exposure which was cash settled. This contract, is still traded, currently as a LIFFE contract. Since the introduction of the BIFFEX futures contract the volume of trading and its liquidity in the market has not been high.

In the case of wet cargoes, attempts have been made by a number of organisations such as the Baltic Exchange and Reuters to establish an index that reflects the value of tanker freights. In order for a contract to be cash settled an agreed index needs to be used for prices at the trade and delivery dates. At present no single index has been accepted by the industry. However, the **Worldwide Tanker Nominal Freight Scale – Worldscale (WS)** – is used almost universally to determine tanker freight rates. WS rates are also based on specified routes and cargoes.

More recently market players in the shipping industry have recognised the need to hedge cargoes and OTC contracts have been developed to match the particular needs of buyers and sellers. In 1991, **Forward Freight Agreements (FFAs)** for dry cargoes were introduced as cash settled OTC contracts based on the BFI routes. The contract does not involve a ship but is a binding fixture which is cash settled. Counterparties may vary the terms of a dry cargo FFA to suit their needs. Tanker FFAs are now traded that are cash settled OTC instruments based on WS rates. These Tanker FFAs are also known as **Tanker Swap Agreements**.

> **Definitions**
>
> A **Forward Freight Agreement** is a contract between buyer and seller for an agreed freight or hire rate, for a specific cargo or type of vessel, for an agreed BFI rate, for an agreed rate in the future against the relevant index route rate.
>
> A **Tanker FFA** is a contract to fix a wet freight rate on a predetermined route, at or over a mutually agreed time

In June 1997 a number of organisations such as SSY Futures, GNI/ Howe Robinson and Cargill Investor Services joined the FFA Brokers Association which could in the future act similarly to the way International Swap and Derivatives Association (ISDA) operates in the financial markets.

Forward Contracts in the Market Place

This section deals with a number of important ways in which forward contracts are used to hedge positions. The examples that follow are specifically concerned with the base metals and shipping markets.

LME Base Metal Contracts as Hedges

Hedging in the base metals markets has the same underlying principles as in any other commodity or financial market. Market players need to lock-in prices that will be paid or received at a future date. As has been mentioned previously, forward contracts involve no capital outlay as they are settled on the prompt date. However, once a trade has been made the **London Clearing House (LCH)** takes on the role of buyer to the seller and vice versa – counterparty to both sides of the trade. In order to cover the market risk, the LCH requires **margin payments** to be made which may be as cash or other types of collateral.

As with most derivative contracts, few LME contracts are physically delivered – over 95% of forward contracts are closed out before the due contract expiry date. There are a number of reasons why the buyer of a forward contract may wish to hedge but not wish to take physical delivery. Some of the more important reasons include the following:

- The metal the buyer is trading may not be in a form deliverable on the LME

- The metal the buyer is trading may not be of an approved brand or type of production on the LME

- The metal the buyer is trading may not be of an approved grade

- The delivery and storage costs using a LME warehouse may be high

There are two basic types of hedge used by market players in the base metal markets. These are:

- The **price fix hedge**

- The **offset hedge**

Price Fix Hedge

This type of hedge is used by a buyer or seller to lock-in an attractive forward price level for a base metal traded on the LME. Market players use this type of hedge to remove any market place volatility by fixing the price of buying or selling raw materials at the same time as allowing them to make a profit on their activities.

Example

It is 20th January 1999 and a refiner has an excess production of 60 tonnes of 99.8% primary grade Nickel. As yet the refiner has no buyer for this metal but sees that the forward prices of Nickel are above his production costs. If he can sell the Nickel in the future he stands to make a profit.

The refiner contacts his LME market member to sell 10 lots of Nickel – each contract lot is 6 tonnes – for delivery in one month. The forward price for 1-month delivery on 2th February is 4316 USD/tonne.

As the contract delivery date approaches the refiner manages to sell the 60 tonnes of Nickel to a stainless steel manufacturer. The refiner sells the Nickel on 18th February at the prevailing LME cash price which has fallen to 4300 USD/tonne.

At the same time the refiner instructs the LME market member to buy back the forward contract at the current cash settlement price of 4300 USD/tonne. The timing is fortunate as the forward position needs to be closed out to allow for prompt delivery two business days ahead of the contract date.

The outcome is summarised here:

Physical	LME
20th January Refiner has excess 60 tonnes of Nickel	**20th January** Refiner sells 10 lots Nickel on LME for delivery 20th February @ 4316 USD/tonne
18th February Refiner sells 60 tonnes Nickel to buyer – Cash settlement price @ 4300 USD/tonne	**18th February** Refiner buys 10 lots Nickel on LME for delivery 20th February Cash settlement price @ 4300 USD/tonne
Profit/loss = +4300 USD/t	**Profit/loss** = +4316 –4300 +16 USD/t
Overall profit to refiner = 4300 + 16 = **4316 USD/tonne**	

Physical	LME
20th January Refiner has excess 60 tonnes of Nickel	**20th January** Refiner sells 10 lots Nickel on LME for delivery 20th February @ 4316 USD/tonne
18th February Refiner sells 60 tonnes Nickel to buyer – Cash settlement price @ 4340 USD/tonne	**18th February** Refiner buys 10 lots Nickel on LME for delivery 20th February Cash settlement price @ 4340 USD/tonne
Profit/loss = +4340 USD/t	**Profit/loss** = +4316 –4340 –24 USD/t
Overall profit to refiner = 4340 – 24 = **4316 USD/tonne**	

Now supposing the market had reversed in the 1-month period and the case price of Nickel had risen to 4340 USD/tonne. The situation is summarised opposite.

The summaries here show that there is no difference to the refiner's profit whether the nickel prices rise or fall once the hedge has been locked-in. This example illustrates the fundamental nature of a hedge transaction – it is designed to protect exposure not for speculation. The refiner has avoided losses but has also forfeited the chance to make extra profits.

The example here is also very simple and clear-cut which is not usually the situation in the real world. No exchange or broker fees have been included and the refiner has timed the whole transaction to perfection.

Using the principle of the price fix hedge it would be possible for the refiner to hedge a position for the next 12 months, for example, if he expected a monthly over production. The refiner would buy and sell contracts on a monthly basis and thus fix an average price for his nickel for the next year.

This price fix hedge will allow the refiner to establish a stable price for the year assuming that there are no variations in tonnage requirements, that production capacity is maintained and that production costs remain constant.

Offset Hedge

This type of hedge uses a LME forward contract to protect a market player from the risks involved in a physical transaction. In this case it is important to know if the market is in contango or backwardation at the time of the hedge as this affects the potential for profit.

Example

It is 20th January 1998 and a galvanised steel producer agrees to sell state plate to a shipbuilder which will require 200 tonnes of zinc. The shipbuilder needs the plate in six weeks time and the contract is based on today's cash LME price of 923 USD/tonne plus production costs and profit. The production lead in time is two weeks which means that the producer needs the zinc in four weeks time. The producer can do one of the following at this stage:

1. Buy the zinc today in the physical market and store it for 4 weeks. This would incur an immediate physical cost and possibly warehouse costs.

2. Wait 4 weeks and buy the zinc on the physical market. The risk is that the price of zinc may have increased which represents a loss of profit to the producer. Some producers operate a surcharge policy thus avoiding this possibility but most customers prefer a fixed price contract. If the price of zinc falls in this period, then the producer can earn extra profit but this is a risk.

3. Hedge the transaction using a LME forward zinc contract. This is what the producer decides to do.

On the 20th January the cash Zinc price is 923 USD/tonne and the 1-month forward contract price is 918 USD/tonne. This means that the market is 5 USD/tonne backwardation. The hedge transaction is summarised as follows when the cash price for Zinc is 930 USD/tonne on 18th February – a price rise on the day the forward contract is sold for prompt delivery 20th February.

Physical	LME
20th January Producer sells 200 tonnes of Zinc used in plate production @ 923 USD/tonne	**20th January** Producer buys 8 lots Zinc (200 tonnes) for delivery 20th February @ 918 USD/tonne
18th February Producer buys 200 tonnes of Zinc for plate production – Cash settlement price @ 930 USD/tonne	**18th February** Producer sells 8 lots of Zinc for delivery 20th February – Cash settlement price @ 930 USD/tonne
Profit/loss = +923 −930 −7 USD/t	**Profit/loss** = +930 −918 +12 USD/t
Overall profit to refiner = −7 + 12 = **5 USD/tonne**	

The overall profit to the producer is 5 USD/tonne which is the same as the backwardation value. Had the producer not hedged the position then he would have made a **loss** of 7 USD/tonne on the position. The purchase of the zinc would have reduced his overall profit on the deal.

In the case of a contango market at the time of the deal with the shipbuilder and when future prices fall the offset hedge can still be effective. On the 20th January the cash Zinc price is 923 USD/tonne and the 1-month forward contract price is 928 USD/tonne. This means that the market is 5 USD/tonne contango. The hedge transaction is summarised as follows when the cash price for Zinc is 920 USD/tonne on 18th February – a price fall on the day the forward contract is sold for prompt delivery 20th February.

Physical	LME
20th January Producer sells 200 tonnes of Zinc used in plate production @ 923 USD/tonne	**20th January** Producer buys 8 lots Zinc (200 tonnes) for delivery 20th February @ 928 USD/tonne
18th February Producer buys 200 tonnes of Zinc for plate production – Cash settlement price @ 920 USD/tonne	**18th February** Producer sells 8 lots of Zinc for delivery 20th February – Cash settlement price @ 920 USD/tonne
Profit/loss = +923 −920 +3 USD/t	**Profit/loss** = −928 +920 −8 USD/t
Overall loss to refiner = +3 − 8 = −5 USD/tonne	

The overall loss to the producer is known and is the value of the contango market – 5 USD/tonne. In this case had the producer not hedged the position the profit on the deal would have been 3 USD/tonne – the difference between buying and selling in the physical market.

The producer has used the offset hedge to eliminate the risk of a rising market, accepted a known loss and forfeited the opportunity for extra profit.

Your notes

What Instruments Are Used in the Markets?

Forward Freight Agreements (FFAs)

OTC FFAs are negotiated by a broker between buyers and sellers in a very similar way to fixing cargoes. A FFA is a cash settled **paper trade** based on a freight or hire rate for a particular cargo size, usually for a specific BFI route for an agreed contract date.

The cash settlement is the difference between the agreed FFA price and the settlement price, for example, the average rate for the BFI route for the last 5 business days.

Although standard FFA documentation is used by brokers, variations are sometimes introduced by buyers/sellers according to their specific requirements.

Example – Buying a FFA to hedge a cargo

It is June 1998 and a coal trader in the US is close to agreeing a CIF sale to a purchaser in Germany for August shipment. The cargo is for 110,000 mt and the current market rate on BFI Route 7 (110,000mt coal Hampton Roads to ARA) is $3.82/mt. The trader has calculated that if the freight costs exceed $4.00/mt, then there will be little profit in the deal. The trader fears that prices will rise over the summer. In order to hedge his position the trader contacts a broker with instructions to buy a FFA for BFI Route 7. The broker finds an owner who has an opposite view to that of the trader and thinks that summer prices will fall. After negotiations the parties agree the following terms:

- Route 7   Hampton Roads to ARA

- Cargo size   110,000 mt

- Price agreed $3.78/mt

- Settlement date   Average last 5 business days of July 1998

At the time of fixing the cargo the trader is proven to be correct and the cost of freight for BFI Route 7 is $4.05/mt.

However, the FFA contract means that the trader receives:

BFI Route 7 Settlement price	=	$4.05/mt
FFA agreed price	=	$3.78/mt
Difference	=	$0.27/mt

Trader receives 110,000 x 0.27 = $29,7000

The trader has therefore protected himself from the price rise in the freight market by using the FFA to hedge.

REUTERS

Forward Contracts

- A **forward contract** is a cash transaction in which the buyer and the seller agree upon delivery of a specified quality and quantity of commodity at a specified future date. A price may be agreed upon in advance or at the time of delivery.

- **Forward price = Spot or cash price + cost of carry**

- If the spot price is at a **premium** to the forward price, then the market is described as in **backwardation**

- If the spot price is at a **discount** to the forward price, then the market is described as in **contango**

- Base metal contracts on the London metal Exchange are 3-month **rolling** forward contracts – their delivery dates are fixed **exactly three months forward** from the trade date

- The **15-day Brent** market is the largest and most important crude oil forward market worldwide

- **Forward Freight Agreements (FFAs)** for dry cargoes are cash settled OTC contracts based on **Baltic Freight Index (BFI)** routes

The Reuters screens on this page show the Brent Closing Prices for Dated and Forward contracts for three forward months – for the U.S., Europe and Asia, as well as the global averages. Also shown are the Dubai Closing Prices.

```
02:04  20JAN99              Brent Closing Prices        UK30507          BRENT/CLS
       -----United States-----   --------Europe--------   ----------Asia---------
       Dated Feb   Mar   Apr    Dated Feb   Mar   Apr    Dated Feb   Mar   Apr
19Jan  10.94 11.05 10.84 10.91  11.19 11.30 11.09 11.18  10.95 11.00 10.83 10.97
15Jan  10.97 11.02 10.85 10.99  10.81 10.93 10.78 10.91  10.95 11.00 10.83 10.97
14Jan  11.04 11.09 10.96 11.09  10.97 11.02 10.85 10.99  11.09 11.14 10.97 11.11
13Jan  11.06 11.11 11.00 11.15  11.10 11.15 11.02 11.15  11.28 11.33 11.14 11.29
12Jan  11.37 11.45 11.31 11.40  10.90 10.95 10.91 11.09  11.37 11.45 11.31 11.40
11Jan  12.03 12.11 11.92 11.98  11.78 11.86 11.67 11.76  11.98 12.06 11.87 11.94
       Dated Jan   Feb   Mar    Dated Jan   Feb   Mar    Dated Jan   Feb   Mar
08Jan  11.65 11.98 11.80 11.65  12.07 12.15 11.99 12.05  11.99 12.14 11.98 12.08
07Jan  11.35 11.62 11.46 11.34  11.70 12.03 11.85 11.73  11.45 11.76 11.60 11.48
06Jan  11.23 11.53 11.48 11.45  11.08 11.49 11.33 11.24  11.28 11.58 11.53 11.50

       -------------------Global average of all three regions------------------
       Dated  1-nth 2-nth 3-nth          Dated  1-nth 2-nth 3-nth
Avg 98 12.45  13.01 13.28 13.56   4Q98   11.16  11.49 11.80 12.04
Dec     9.87  10.22 10.36 10.57   3Q98   12.53  12.89 13.13 13.41
Nov    10.99  11.46 11.84 12.14   2Q98   13.31  13.78 14.07 14.43
Oct    12.61  12.78 13.21 13.40   1Q98   14.07  14.43 14.72 15.00
Sep    13.54  13.83 13.89 14.13   4Q97   18.67  18.65 18.72 18.75
Aug    11.93  12.25 12.47 12.76   1997   19.18  19.41 19.40 19.38
Jul    12.11  12.59 13.02 13.34   1996   20.64  20.75 20.15 19.57
Jun    12.03  12.84 13.49 13.96   1995   17.03  17.17 16.92 16.74
May    14.33  14.52 14.39 14.66   1994   15.78  15.93 15.79 15.73
```

```
17:03  13DEC99         International Crude Oil Prices      UK30507        CRUDE/INT
                                                                         IPE Brent
Brent spreads     Buy     Sell    Brent    Buy     Sell    EFP     Last   Change

Dated v Jan      -0.05   +0.20    Dated   $24.54  $24.56
Jan   v Feb      +0.60   +0.70    Jan     $24.46  $24.48
Feb   v Mar      +0.85   +0.90    Feb     $23.81  $23.83   +0.05   $23.77  +0.09
Mar   v Apr      +0.80   +0.85    Mar     $22.94  $22.96

Dubai spreads     Buy     Sell    Dubai    Buy     Sell

Jan   v Feb      +0.15   +0.20    Jan     $22.46  $22.48
Feb   v Mar      +0.70   +0.80    Feb     $22.29  $22.31
Mar   v Apr      +0.70   +0.75    Mar     $21.54  $21.56

Brent v Dubai     Buy     Sell
                                  Market close time   Editorial contacts
Jan              +1.95   +2.05    Asia    0930 GMT    Tokyo     813 5473 3708
Feb              +1.25   +1.35    Europe  1730 GMT    Singapore 65 870 3080
                                  U.S.    2200 GMT    London    171 542 7646
                                                      New York  212 859 1629

Note: EFP = Exchange of futures for physical. For details of how prices on this
      page are assessed please double click between the brackets <CRUDE/NOTES>.
      All prices in $ per barrel.
```

What Instruments Are Used in the Markets?

These Reuters screens illustrate how to use the news service to both gain relevant data about forwards contracts, and input data to price a contract.

Here is the **LME Metals Calculator** with the **3 Month Cross-currency Display** showing the contract prices for the 7 LME traded metals in USD and up to 4 other currencies. The FX spot rates and forward points are shown together with the 3 month forward date.

By entering **Metal, Bid/Ask, Currency** and **Date** data, you can calculate outright prices for a forward date. See the prices and spread to 3 months in the **Outright Forward Prices** display.

Finally, you can display a **forward curve** for a selected metal in the **Forwards** display. The curve data is calculated from live spreads and outright prices from all quoted dates and those based on Last Night Settlement Prices.

What Are Derivatives?

Although futures contracts for commodities have been offered by exchanges from the mid-nineteenth century, since the 1970s the financial and commodities markets have been subject to the effects of dramatic worldwide regulatory and economic changes, political events, wars etc. These events, combined with technological improvements in communications, have produced much more volatile commodity, energy and transport markets. The need for hedging against risk and the opportunities for speculation have increased and helped establish the derivatives markets and ensured their importance.

If you need an overview of futures derivatives or you need to remind yourself about derivatives in general, then you may find it useful to refer to the *Introduction to Derivatives* book (ISBN 0-471-83176-X), at this stage.

Within the commodities, energy and transport markets the following derivatives are traded on exchanges and OTC:

- Futures contracts
  - Commodities, energy and freight futures contracts
  - Futures spreads and strips

- Swaps
  - Commodity and energy swaps

- Options
  - Options on commodity and energy instruments

A **commodity, energy or freight futures contract** is a firm contractual agreement between a buyer and seller for a specified asset on a fixed date in the future. The contract price will vary according to the market place but it is fixed when the trade is made. The contract also has a standard specification so both parties know exactly what is being traded.

The definition refers to a "specified asset", but what exactly is this?

The types of asset for which commodity and energy futures contracts exist are summarised in the chart below. The only shipping or freight market futures contract currently traded on an exchange is for a contract on the Baltic Freight Index on LIFFE.

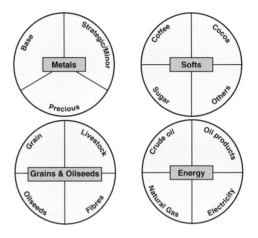

An exchange traded futures contract has the following characteristics:

- A **standardised specification** in terms of unit of trading, trading cycle of contract months, delivery days, quotation, minimum price movement etc

- The **opportunity to trade** the instrument and offset the original contract with an equal and opposite trade. Very few contracts, less than 2%, reach maturity

- A **public market** in that prices for contracts are freely available. Trading takes place open outcry on an exchange floor and prices are published on exchange indicator boards, in the financial press and by providers such as Reuters.

- Once a trade has been made a **clearing house** acts as the counterparty to both sides of the trade. The contract is not directly between buyer and seller. The clearing house takes on the credit risk should a counterparty default. This is important because it means anyone can have access to the markets provided they have the required creditworthiness

by the clearing house – in this way large organisations have no advantage over smaller organisations or investors.

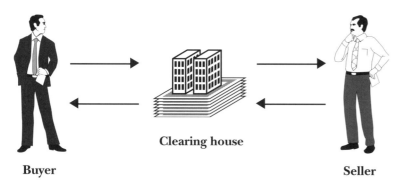

Buyer   **Clearing house**   **Seller**

When a futures contract is agreed, the full contract price is not paid at that time. Instead, **both** counterparties make an initial "good faith" or **margin** payment to the clearing house. This **initial margin** or deposit is usually only 5-10% of the total contract value – different exchanges and contracts require different initial margins. The fact that both counterparties deposit initial margin assures the integrity of the contract.

Once a contract has been purchased, it can be sold and closed at any time prior to the settlement date. With this in mind a futures contract is **marked-to-market** on a daily basis. This means the contract value is calculated at the close of exchange trading every day it is open.

All profits and losses are credited to or debited from the counterparties' clearing house accounts daily. Any profits can be withdrawn but if the losses are such that the initial margin is depleted, then extra margin – variation margin – is required by the clearing house.

This system of maintaining margin ensures the loser can bear any losses and that winners are credited with their gains. A futures margin payment is in effect a performance pledge that each of the counterparties' obligations will be met. Trading on margin is an example of **gearing** or **leverage**. Leverage allows market players to make larger trades than could otherwise be afforded. Small margins can generate large profits but equally large losses can also be made!

Example

An investor buys a NYCSCE Sugar 11 futures contract at 8.50¢/lb. The contract trading unit is for 112,000 lbs which means the contract value is 112,000 x 8.50 = $9,520.00. The buyer sells the contract when the futures price reaches 10.00¢/lb. The contract is now worth $11,200.00 representing a profit of $1,680.00 to the investor. At the start of the contract the initial margin payment required was $1,000.00. When the position was closed out this margin was returned to the investor. The return on the margin payment – the leverage – is therefore 1680 ÷ 1000 x 100% = **168%**.

Problems in the commodity markets may occur because sellers of futures have a limited amount of asset to protect whereas buyers may purchase a number of contracts on margin for short-term trading. For example, if a buyer is required to pay a $1000 margin on a futures contract, this is equivalent to buying $10–20,000 of commodity or financial asset if the contract expires.

As the expiry date of the contract approaches the futures price will equal the current spot price and so the differential is not very large. This is why the vast majority, 95%, of futures contracts are closed out before the contract reaches the agreed expiry date.

Before moving on have a look at the following activity...

Use the space here to write down any thoughts you may have concerning the following question.

What are the differences between forward and futures contracts and the way they are used?

No specific answer is given as it is covered in the following text.

The distinctions between forward and futures contracts are summarised in the chart below. However, the main difference is that a **forward contract** is an **OTC** agreement between a buyer and a seller, whereas a **futures contract** is a **traded on an exchange**.

Futures Contracts	Forwards Contracts
• Are traded on the floor of an exchange	• Are **not** traded on the floor of an exchange – OTC
• Use a clearing house which provides protection for both parties	• Are private and are negotiated between the parties with no exchange guarantees
• Require a margin to be paid	• Involve no margin payments
• Are used for hedging and speculating	• Are used for hedging and physical delivery
• Are standardised and published	• Are dependent on the negotiated contract conditions
• Are transparent – futures contracts are reported by the exchange	• Are not transparent as there is no reporting requirement – they are private deals

Exchange Contracts

There are many worldwide exchanges trading commodity and energy futures contracts both using open outcry on exchange floors and using electronic trading. Obtaining data for all the worldwide exchanges for the number of futures contracts traded and the number of contracts settled by delivery or cash settlement, in a consistent format, is difficult. However, in the US the CFTC do provide this data on an annual basis for contracts traded on US exchanges only. The following charts indicate the numbers of contracts traded and delivered for commodity and energy products for the period 1991–1998.

Contracts Traded in Millions

Year	Grain	Oilseed Products	Livestock Products	Other Agric.	Energy/ Wood	Metals
1991	16.58	19.84	6.93	9.49	31.85	13.87
1992	17.55	18.59	6.43	9.41	38.42	12.22
1993	16.01	20.74	5.77	10.75	42.84	15.20
1994	19.97	20.99	6.14	12.32	50.46	18.23
1995	21.09	20.69	6.24	12.74	47.94	17.39
1996	30.22	25.59	7.05	12.02	46.89	16.94
1997	25.51	27.13	7.55	13.19	51.51	17.09
1998	26.14	26.85	7.36	14.04	61.71	17.04

Contracts Delivered in Thousands

Year	Grain	Oilseed Products	Livestock Products	Other Agric.	Energy/ Wood	Metals
1991	70.0	184.4	13.4	39.4	42.7	146.2
1992	64.2	177.0	14.3	48.3	55.7	133.0
1993	48.6	179.3	11.7	56.8	62.7	184.6
1994	76.7	88.74	8.4	44.4	78.1	189.5
1995	70.5	158.0	12.9	60.6	75.2	157.3
1996	38.2	172.4	13.4	39.4	87.8	132.5
1997	36.6	148.7	29.7	38.0	119.5	130.0
1998	131.4	116.4	42.2	31.8	129.6	163.1

Source: CFTC Annual Report 1998

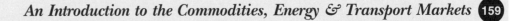

What Instruments Are Used in the Markets?

The CFTC data also shows that for all futures contracts in 1997, including financial instruments and currencies, only 8.5% of contracts were settled by delivery or cash.

There are a number of ways you can find out about exchanges and the derivative contracts they trade using an electronic information system such as Reuters.

Displayed at right is the Global Exchanges Speed Guide, followed by specific data for German exchanges. Then look at the screen for the WTB Warenterminboerse Hannover Exchange for information about the new exchange. Also shown below are screens that would lead you to detailed information about specific contracts.

```
GLOBAL EXCHANGES - REUTERS SPEED GUIDE                          EXCHANGES
Detailed below is a list of Exchange Guides by country.

=EXCHANGES BY COUNTRY==================   =EXCHANGES BY COUNTRY Cont===========
AFRICAN Countries..........<AFR/EXCH1>    MIDDLE EASTERN Countries.....<ME/EXCH1>
ASIAN Countries............<ASIA/EXCH1>   Netherlands..................<NL/EXCH1>
Australia....................<AU/EXCH1>   New Zealand..................<NZ/EXCH1>
Austria......................<AT/EXCH1>   Norway.......................<NO/EXCH1>
Belgium......................<BE/EXCH1>   Portugal.....................<PT/EXCH1>
Canada.......................<CA/EXCH1>   Sweden.......................<SE/EXCH1>
Denmark......................<DK/EXCH1>   Spain........................<ES/EXCH1>
EASTERN EUROPEAN Countries..<EEU/EXCH1>   Switzerland..................<CH/EXCH1>
Finland......................<FI/EXCH1>   Turkey.......................<TR/EXCH1>
France.......................<FR/EXCH1>   United Kingdom...............<GB/EXCH1>
Germany......................<DE/EXCH1>   United States................<US/EXCH1>
Greece.......................<GR/EXCH1>
Iceland......................<IS/EXCH1>   For Data Health Coverage.<DATAHEALTH/1>
```

```
O#COMMOD-FUT      COMMODITY FUTURE  Exchange
RIC               Contract          ID
O#BASE-FUT        BASE METAL FUT.   RCT/
O#FIBRES-FUT      FIBRES FUTURES    RCT/
O#FINANCIAL-FUT   FINANCIAL FUTURE    /
O#FREIGHT-FUT     FREIGHT FUTURES   RCT/
O#GRAINS-FUT      GRAINS FUTURES    RCT/
O#LIVESTOCK-FUT   LIVESTOCK FUTURE  RCT/
O#OILSEEDS-FUT    OILSEEDS FUTURES  RCT/
O#PRECIOUS-FUT    PRECIOUS FUTURES  RCT/
O#SOFTS-FUT       SOFTS FUTURES     RCT/
```

```
GERMAN EXCHANGE INFORMATION - REUTERS SPEED GUIDE              DE/EXCH1
Welcome to the German Exchanges Information Guide.  Detailed on the following
pages, is Information for all German Exchanges.
-------------------------------------------------------------------------
Berliner Börse..............................................<DE/EXCH2>
Frankfurter Wertpapierbörse.................................<DE/EXCH3>
Hanseatische Wertpapierbörse................................<DE/EXCH4>
Bayerische Börse............................................<DE/EXCH5>
Baden-Württembergische Wertpapierbörse zu Stuttgart.........<DE/EXCH6>
Rheinisch-Westfälische Börse zu Düsseldorf..................<DE/EXCH7>
Brener Wertpapierbörse......................................<DE/EXCH8>
Niedersächsische Börse zu Hannover..........................<DE/EXCH9>
Eurex Deutschland..........................................<DE/EXCH10>
XETRA Exchange Electronic Trading..........................<DE/EXCH11>
WTB Warenterminboerse Hannover.............................<DE/EXCH12>

The following Guides may also be of interest to you when looking at Exchange
data.
German Futures Guide......................................<DE/FUTEX1>
```

```
O#ENERGY-FUT      ENERGY FUTURES    Exchange
RIC               Contract          ID
O#CRUDE-FUT       Crude Oil         RCT/
O#ELECTRIC-FUT    Electricity       RCT/
O#NATGAS-FUT      Natural Gas       RCT/
O#PRODUCTS-FUT    Products          RCT/
```

```
                                                              DE/EXCH12
Detailed on <DE/EXCH1> - <DE/EXCH12>   is Information for all German Exchanges.

EXCHANGE NAME.       Warenterminboerse Hannover (WTB)

ADDRESS:             Prinzenstrasse 17
                     30159
                     Hanover , Germany


PHONE:               0511/ 30159-0

INTERNET:            www.wtb-hannover.de

TRADING HOURS:       Monday to Friday:      09:55am to 3.25pm Live Hog Future
                                            10:00am to 3:30pm Potato Future


EXCHANGE MNEMONIC: HCE        EXCHANGE ID:


========================================================================
Main Index <REUTERS> German Equties <DE/EQUITY> German Futures <DE/FUTEX1>
Lost? <USER/HELP> Reuters Phone Support <PHONE/HELP>  Page back<DE/EXCH11>
```

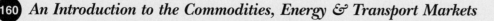

Typical Contract Specifications

Futures contracts specifications vary depending on the underlying commodity, energy product or freight index and from exchange to exchange. Exchanges publish details of their contracts in printed form, on the Internet and via information providers such as Reuters. Have a look at the following contract specifications which are taken from a variety of sources.

BACKGROUND
FEATURES OF THE CONTRACT
CONTRACT SPECIFICATION

DELIVERY MECHANISM
CLEARING AND REGULATION
DOWNLOAD THIS CONTRACT

BRENT CRUDE FUTURES: Contract specification

Date of launch
23 June 1988.

Trading hours
Open 10:02 Close 20:13 (local time).

Unit of trading
One or more lots of 1,000 net barrels (42,000 US gallons) of Brent crude oil.

Specification
Current pipeline export quality Brent blend as supplied at Sullom Voe.

Quotation
The contract price is in US dollars and cents per barrel.

The contract price is in US dollars and cents per barrel.

Minimum price fluctuation
One cent per barrel, equivalent to a tick value of $10.

Maximum daily price fluctuation
There are no limits.

Daily margin
All open contracts are marked-to-market daily.

Trading period
Twelve consecutive months then quarterly out to a maximum twenty-four months and then half yearly out to a maximum thirty-six months.

Position limits
There are no limits to the size of position.

◀ TO FEATURES OF THE CONTRACT   TO DELIVERY MECHANISM ▶

Reviewed on 23 Dec 1999

New York Mercantile Exchange
NYMEX/COMEX. Two divisions, one marketplace.

| description | contract specifications | current month index calculations | | links to price reporting services | historical index calculations | | download entire series | holiday schedule | request information |

NYMEX Division

Middle East Sour Crude Oil Futures and Options Contract Specifications

Trading Unit: 1,000 barrels.

Price Quotation: U.S Dollars and cents per barrel.

Minimum Price Fluctuation: $.01 per barrel.

Maximum Price Fluctuation: Futures: $15.00 per barrel ($15,000 per contract) for the first two contract months. Initial back month limits of $1.50 per barrel rise to $3.00 per barrel if the previous day's settlement price in any back month is at the $1.50 limit. In the event of a $7.50 per barrel move in either of the first two contract months, back month limits are expanded to $7.50 per barrel from the limit in place in the direction of the move. Options: No price limits.

Last Trading Day: The final Exchange business day of the month preceding the delivery month.

Delivery: Cash settlement based on normal export quality Dubai crude oil delivered free on board at the Fateh Terminal in Dubai and Oman crude oil delivered FOB at the Mina Al Fahal terminal in Oman.

New York Mercantile Exchange
NYMEX/COMEX. Two divisions, one marketplace.

| futures and options home | contract specifications | | request information |

Coal Futures and Options Contract Specifications

Trading Unit
Futures: 37,200 million British thermal units (MMBtus) of coal.
Options: One NYMEX Division coal futures contract.

Trading Hours
To be determined.

Trading Months
Futures: 18 consecutive months.
Options: To be determined.

Price Quotations
Futures and options: U.S. dollars and cents per MMBtu.

Minimum Price Fluctuation
Futures and options: $.001 per MMBtu ($37.20 per contract).

Maximum Price Fluctuation
Futures: Maximum daily price fluctuation in all but the first two months shall be $0.10 per MMBtu above or below the preceding day's settlement price. If the market settles at $0.10 above or below the previous day's settlement price, the maximum permissible fluctuation in either direction for all months during the next business session shall be $0.20. The expanded limit shall remain in effect until there are two trading days in which no month settles at the expanded limit.
In the closest two months of trading, the maximum daily price fluctuation will be $1.00, applied in two stages.
Options: No price limits.

Last Trading Day
Futures: Trading terminates on the fourth business day prior to the first day of the delivery month.
Options: Expiration occurs on the business day preceding the futures contract termination.

Exercise of Options
By a clearing member to the Exchange clearinghouse not later than 5:30 P.M., or 45 minutes after the underlying futures settlement price is posted, whichever is later, on any day up to and including options expiration.

Options Strike Prices
Twenty strike prices in increments of $0.01 per MMBtu above and below the at-the-money strike price, and the next 10 strike prices in increments of $0.05 above the highest and below the lowest one-cent increment. The at-the-money strike price is closest to the previous day's futures settlement price.

Contract Delivery Unit
The seller shall deliver 1,550 tons of coal per contract. A loading tolerance of 60 tons or 2%, whichever is greater, over the total number of contracts delivered is permitted. The MMBtus of coal is determined by multiplying the weight of the coal by the heat content of the coal as determined by testing procedures.

Delivery Location
At a delivery facility on the Ohio River between Milepost 306 and 317, or on the Big Sandy River. There will be a discount of $.004 per MMBtu below the final settlement price for any delivery to a terminal on the Big Sandy River.

Heat Content
Minimum of 12,000 Btus per pound, gross calorific value, with an analysis tolerance of 250 Btus per pound.

Ash Content
Maximum of 13.5% by weight with no analysis tolerance.

Sulfur Content
Maximum of 1.0%, measured by weight or in pounds of sulfur dioxide per MMBtu, with analysis tolerance of .05%.

Moisture Content
Surface or inherent moisture at a maximum of 10% by weight with no analysis tolerance.

Volatile Matter
Minimum of 30% gas or vapor products exclusive of moisture given off by combustion of the coal — with no analysis tolerance.

Hardness/Grindability
Minimum 41 Hardgrove Index with three point analysis tolerance below. Hardness measures how difficult it is to pulverize coal for injection into the boiler flame.

Size
Three inches topsize, nominal, with a maximum of 55% passing one-quarter-inch-square wire cloth sieve or smaller, to be determined on the basis of the primary cutter of the mechanical sampling system.

Exchange of Futures for, or in Connection with, Physicals (EFP)
The buyer or seller may exchange a futures position for a physical position of equal quantity/quality by submitting a notice to the Exchange. EFPs may be used either to initiate or liquidate a futures position. The EFP deadline is 10 A.M. (Eastern prevailing time) on the first business day following termination of trading.

Position Limits
5,000 contracts for all months combined, but not to exceed 3,500 in any one month or 200 in the last three days of trading in the spot month.

July 8, 1999

What Instruments Are Used in the Markets?

The following examples of commodity and energy futures contracts are taken from exchange published details which are available in printed form or on the Internet in many cases.

CME
Frozen Pork Bellies Futures

Trading unit	40,000 lbs USDA inspected pork bellies
Price quote	$ per hundred pounds or cents per pound
Minimum price fluctuation (Tick)	.025 = $10.00/tick 2.5¢/100 lbs or .025¢/lb
Daily price limit	2.00 = $800.00 $2.00/100 lbs 2.0¢/lb
Contract months	Feb, Mar, May, July, Aug
Trading hours (Chicago time)	9.10am–1.00pm Last day 9.10am–12.00pm
Last day of trading	The business day immediately preceding the last 5 business days of the contract month
Delivery days	Any business day of the contract month
Delivery points	Consult CME for list of current warehouses.

- This is the standard contract size
- The futures price is quoted as either $/100 lbs or ¢/lb
- This is smallest amount a contract can change value and the tick size
- This is the maximum daily allowable amount a futures price may advance or decline in any one day's trading session
- This is the trading cycle of contract months
- Exchange trading hours – open out-cry.
- This is the last day and time trading can take place
- This is the day contracts are settled
- The locations specified for physical delivery

COMEX (NYMEX)
Copper High-Grade Futures

Trading unit	25,000 lbs
Price quote	Cents per pound
Minimum price fluctuation (Tick)	.05¢/lb
Initial price limit	20¢/lb
Contract months	Current calendar month and next 23 consecutive calendar months
Trading hours (NY time)	8.10am–2.00pm
Last day of trading	The third last business day of the maturing delivery month
Delivery days	First business day of delivery month and last delivery day is last business day of month
Delivery points	High-grade Copper from an exchange warehouse in the US.

- This is the standard contract size
- The futures price is quoted as ¢/lb
- This is smallest amount a contract can change value and the tick size
- This is the maximum based on the preceding day's settlement price
- This is the trading cycle of contract months
- Exchange trading hours – open out-cry.
- This is the last day and time trading can take place
- This is the day contracts are settled
- The locations specified for physical delivery – delivery must be on a domestic basis

LIFFE
Robusta Coffee Futures

Contract unit	5 metric tonnes
Price basis	US dollars per tonne in an exchange nominated warehouse
Tick size	1 US dollar per tonne
Origins tenderable	A variety of worldwide locations
Delivery months	Jan, Mar, May, July, Sept, Nov
Tender period	The seller may submit a tender to the Clearing House up to 12.00 hours on any market day in the delivery month and, in respect of each sale contract that remains open at cessation of trading for that month shall be bound to do so no later than 14.30 hours on the last market day in that month
Cessation of trading	At 12.30 on the last business day of the delivery month
Trading hours	09.45–12.30 14.15–17.00

This is the standard contract size

London, Home Counties, Bristol, Felixstowe, Hull, Amsterdam, Rotterdam, Le Havre, Antwerp, Hamburg, Bremen, Barcelona, Trieste, New York, New Orleans

Angola, Brazilian Conillon, Cameroon Central African Republic, Ecuador, Ghana, Guinea, India, Indonesia, Cote d'Ivoire, Liberia, Malagasy Republic, Nigeria, Philippines, Republic of Zaire, Sierra Leone, Tanzania, Thailand, Togo, Trinidad, Uganda, Vietnam

All times quoted are London times

IPE
Brent Crude Oil Futures

Unit of trading	One or more lots of 1000 net barrels (42,000 US galls) of Brent crude oil
Specification	Current pipeline export quality Brent blend as supplied at Sullom Voe
Quotation	US $ and ¢ per barrel
Min. price fluctuation	One cent/barrel is equivalent to a tick value of $10.00
Max. daily price fluct.	No limits
Trading period	Twelve consecutive months following the contract month
Delivery/ settlement basis	In cash against the Brent Index price for the last trading day of the futures contract
Trading hours	10.02–20.13

This is the standard contract size

The Brent Index is produced by the IPE and is the weighted average of the prices of all confirmed 15-day Brent deals throughout the trading day for the appropriate trading month.

The daily Brent Index price for every day is published the day after cessation of trading at 12.00 noon local time.

What Instruments Are Used in the Markets?

You can use an electronic information service such as Reuters to find out about contract specifications. Suppose you need to know the specification for CBOT Corn futures contracts...

Below is a Reuters screen showing the Global Futures and Options Exchanges speed guide, with screens to the right giving specific detail about CBOT corn futures contracts.

```
US FUTURES AND OPTIONS EXCHANGES SPEED GUIDE                    US/FUTEX1
Welcome to the US Futures and Options Exchange Guide. To access information
double-click in the <> brackets
This guide lists details of all contracts traded on the following exchanges,
as well as general information about the individual exchanges:

=FUTURES AND OPTIONS EXCHANGES================================================
CBOT × Chicago Board of Trade:
CBOT Futures - Interest Rate.........................................<CBT/FUTEX1>
CBOT Futures - Equity Index..........................................<CBT/FUTEX2>
CBOT Futures - Agricultural..........................................<CBT/FUTEX3>
CBOT Futures - Metals & Others.......................................<CBT/FUTEX4>
CME × Chicago Mercantile Exchange:
CME Futures - Currencies.............................................<CME/FUTEX1>
CME Futures - Currencies.............................................<CME/FUTEX2>
CME Futures - Currencies.............................................<CME/FUTEX3>
CME Futures - Interest Rates.........................................<CME/FUTEX4>
CME Futures - Interest Rates.........................................<CME/FUTEX5>
CME Futures - Stock Indices..........................................<CME/FUTEX6>
CME Futures - Agricultural & Others...........................<CME/FUTEX7>-8

RIC Rules Guide.............<RULES1>-7  USD Conversion Factors...<U$/FACTOR1>-9
==============================================================================
Main Guide<REUTERS>  U.S<UNITEDSTATES> Futures<FUTURES>  More Futures<US/FUTEX2>
   Lost? Selective Access...<USER/HELP>    Reuters Phone Support<PHONE/HELP>
```

```
GLOBAL FUTURES AND OPTIONS EXCHANGES - REUTERS SPEED GUIDE          FUTURES
Welcome to the GLOBAL FUTURES GUIDE. This Guide lists Futures Contract Codes,
Contract Details and all associated exchange information. To access information
double click on the code in < > or [ ]. For more guidance see <USER/HELP>.

=COUNTRY FUTURES GUIDES===============  =COUNTRY FUTURES GUIDES Cont===========
All LATAM Futures/Options<LATAM/FUTEX1>  Malaysian Futures/Options...<MY/FUTEX1>
Australian Futures.........<AU/FUTEX1>   Netherlands Futures/Options.<NL/FUTEX1>
Austria Futures............<AT/FUTEX1>   New Zealand Futures........<NZ/FUTEX1>
Belgium Futures............<BE/FUTEX1>   Norway Futures/Options......<NO/FUTEX1>
Canadian Futures/Options...<CA/FUTEX1>   Poland Futures.............<PL/FUTEX1>
Chinese Futures............<CN/FUTEX1>   Portugal Futures/Options...<PT/FUTEX1>
Dennark Futures............<DK/FUTEX1>   Singapore Futures/Options...<SG/FUTEX1>
Finland Futures/Options.....<FI/FUTEX1>  South African Futures.......<ZA/FUTEX1>
French Futures/Options......<FR/FUTEX1>  Spanish Futures/Options.....<ES/FUTEX1>
German Futures.............<DE/FUTEX1>   Sweden Futures/Options.....<SE/FUTEX1>
Hong Kong Futures/Options...<HK/FUTEX1>  Switzerland Futures/Options.<CH/FUTEX1>
Hungarian Futures..........<HU/FUTEX1>   Taiwan Futures/Options.....<TW/FUTEX1>
Italian Futures............<IT/FUTEX1>   United Kingdom Futures/Opts.<GB/FUTEX1>
Japanese Futures...........<JP/FUTEX1>   United States Futures/Opts..<US/FUTEX1>
Korean Futures.............<KR/FUTFX1>   Euro Futures...............<FUR/FUT1>
                                         RIC Rules Guide.............<RULES1>-7
==============================================================================
Main Guide<REUTERS>  Debt<BONDS> Equity<EQUITY> Money<MONEY> Commodities<COMMOD>
    Lost? Selective Access..<USER/HELP>     Reuters Phone Support...<PHONE/HELP>
```

```
CHICAGO BOARD OF TRADE - REUTERS SPEED GUIDE                     CBT/FUTEX3
To access information double click in the <> brackets.

Address:    141 West Jackson Boulevard, Chicago, IL 60604-2994
Tel No:     312 435 3500               Fax No.   312 341 3306

=AGRICULTURAL CONTRACTS===============NEAREST MONTH=======CONTRACT DETAILS==
Oats......................<O#O:>   <Oc1>.......................<CBT/O>
Soybeans..................<O#S:>   <Sc1>.......................<CBT/S>
Wheat.....................<O#W:>   <Wc1>.......................<CBT/W>
Soyabean Meal.............<O#SM:>  <SMc1>......................<CBT/SM>
Soyabean Oil..............<O#BO:>  <BOc1>......................<CBT/BO>
Corn......................<O#C:>   <Cc1>.......................<CBT/C>
Rough Rice................<O#RR:>  <RRc1>......................<CBT/RR>
```

```
CBOT CORN                                                            CBT/C
Contract Details, Trading Hours for the CBOT Corn Future.

CHAIN RIC           -    <O#C:>
OPTIONS RIC         -    C (See <RULES1>-7 on how to construct an Option)
UNIT OF TRADING     -    US Dollar
CONTRACT SIZE       -    5000 bushels
CONTRACT MONTHS     -    Mar(H) May(K) Jul(N) Sep(U) Dec(Z)
LAST TRADING DAY    -    Seven business days before the last business day
                         of the delivery month
FIRST NOTICE DAY    -    Last business day of month preceding the
                         delivery month
LAST NOTICE DAY     -    Next to the last business day of delivery month
DELIVERABLE GRADES  -    No.2 Yellow corn at par and substitutions at
                         differentials established by the exchange
TICK SIZE & VALUE   -    1/4 Cents per bushel  ($12.50 contract)
Daily Price Limit   -    12 cents per bushel

TRADING HOURS       -    Session 3-09:30am-13:15pm MON-FRI Open Outcry
                         Session 2-09:00pm-04:30am SUN-THU Overnight Proj A
                         All Times Local
==============================================================================
Global Futures<FUTURES>    U.S. Futures<US/FUTEX1>    CBOT Futures<CBT/FUTEX1>
    Lost? Selective Access...<USER/HELP>      Reuters Phone Support<PHONE/HELP>
```

Double-click here to see the futures prices for the chain of delivery months

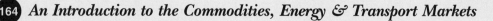

But what does all this information mean?

Typically commodity and energy futures have monthly or quarterly delivery months. However, some contracts have delivery months depending on factors such as harvest and planting months – you may need to check the contract specification if you are in doubt. It is also possible to have maturity dates out to several years but "far month" contracts are much less liquid than the "near months". This means that it is not always possible to get prices for "far months".

The price movement of a futures contract is measured in **ticks**. The **minimum price movement** for a contract is determined by the exchange. Depending on the contract and the commodity ticks vary, for example, 0.025¢/lb, 1.0¢/barrel and $1.00/tonne.

Example
The Reuters screen below displays the CBOT Corn futures price for Mar 99. As indicated in the contract specification the trading unit is 5,000 bushels and prices are quoted in $/bu – or more commonly in ¢/bu. The tick size is 0.25¢/bu. Using the contract prices from this page, the purchase of a Mar99 futures contract implies a payment of

215.25 x 5000 = $10,762.50 on delivery.

```
O#C:              CBT/      CORN           USc
Mth    Last              Bid    Ask   Size   Open 1   High    Low    Time
MAR9  ↑215¼    -2                     /      T217¼    217¾    214¾   15:31
MAY9  ↓221¼    -2                     /      T223½    223½    221    15:31
JUL9  ↑226¾    -2¼                    /      T229¼    229¼    226½   15:31
SEP9  ↓234     -1½   BBO 235½   242   8/2    T234     234     234    15:31
DEC9  ↑239½    -1¾                    /      T241¼    241½    239¼   15:31
MAR0  0T248¼         SC                /      T248¼    248¼    248¼   03:00
MAY0  PS252½   -4½                    /                              19:38
JUL0  A263           BBO       263    /                              03:00
DEC0  B250     A260  BBO 250   260   50/80                           03:57
JUL1                                  /                              :
DEC1                                  /                              :
```

Profit and Loss on a Futures Contract

In most cases the profit or loss is calculated as a simple difference and is easy to calculate as follows:

1. Calculate the difference between the prices at which the contract was opened and closed. A **positive** value represents a **profit**; a **negative** value a **loss**.

2. Multiply the value from 1. by the trading unit size

3. Multiply the value from 2. by the number of lots or contracts

$$\text{Profit/loss} = (P_{Open} - P_{Close}) \times \text{Trading unit size} \times \text{No. of contracts/lots}$$

Example
On 25th January five March LIFFE Cocoa futures contracts are bought with a price quotation of £907/tonne. On 15th February the contracts are sold with a settlement price of £928/tonne. The trading unit for the Cocoa contract is 10 tonnes.

$$
\begin{aligned}
\text{Profit or loss} &= (928 - 907) \times 10 \times 5 \\
&= \pounds 1050 \text{ profit}
\end{aligned}
$$

What Instruments Are Used in the Markets?

Relationship Between Cash and Futures Prices

For most commodities the futures price is usually **higher** than the current spot price. This is because there are costs associated with storage, freight and insurance etc which have to be covered for the futures delivery. When the futures price is higher than the spot price the situation is known as **contango**.

If a chart is drawn of spot and futures prices then as the futures expiry date is approached the plots converge. This is because the costs diminish over time and become zero at the delivery date. The difference between the futures and spot prices at any time is called the **basis**. A contango chart for a 3 month futures contract might look something like this:

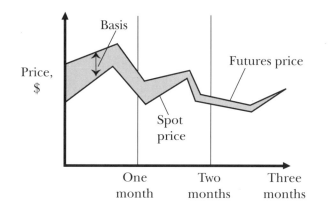

```
LME ------Officials 05-NOV-1998----
              Cash           3 Months
   CU    1597.5/1598.0    1624.0/1625.0
   SN      5580/5590         5515/5520
   PB    488.00/488.50    498.00/498.50
   ZN     951.5/952.0      970.5/971.0
   AL    1293.0/1293.5    1314.5/1315.0
   NI      4185/4190         4235/4240
   AA    1085.0/1088.0    1120.0/1121.0
```

If you look at these metal prices you will see that the futures prices for Aluminium (AL), Aluminium Alloy (AA), Zinc (ZN), Nickel (NI), Copper (CU) and Lead (PB) are all higher than the spot prices. However, the price for Tin (SN) is lower.

When the futures price is **lower** than the spot price the market is said to be in **backwardation**. Backwardation occurs in times of shortage caused by strikes, undercapacity etc but the futures price stays steady as more supplies are expected in the future.

For metals you can see at a glance whether the market prices are in backwardation (b) or contango (c) – the price differences between the cash and futures prices on the right side of the screen use the letters **b** and **c** for each metal. The difference between the prices is known as the **spread**; b and c are known as the **spread symbols**.

```
   GMT: 14:58
   Cash to 3s-
   c 27.0/26.0 c
   b    60/65    b
   c10.00/9.00 c
   c 20.0/19.0 c
   c 22.0/21.0 c
   c    65/62    c
   c 35.0/30.0 c
```

Charts of future prices over time are similar to yield curves for money market and debt market financial instruments. **Contango** markets indicate the future prices are at a **premium** to cash markets; **backwardation** markets indicate a **discount** to cash prices.

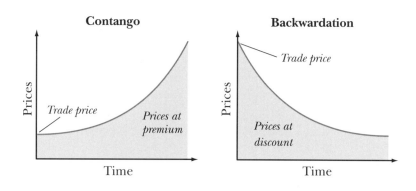

Basis is particularly important when considering commodities such as grain where the futures contract specifies delivery to an exchange such as the Chicago Board of Trade. The following example may help you to understand the importance of basis.

Example
The December futures price for corn is $2.58 per bushel and the cash price in Chicago is $2.38 per bushel. However, in Smallville, USA, the local cash price is only $2.18 – a price which reflects no transport costs, lower storage costs etc. The basis for a Smallville farmer over Chicago futures is therefore 40¢.

If the futures price remains constant but both the Chicago and Smallville cash prices rise by 2¢, then the local basis falls to 38¢. The local basis figures are illustrated in the chart below.

Local basis and basis patterns are very important to producers and are used in decisions such as:

- Accepting/rejecting cash offers for a commodity

- Whether and when to store crops

- When and in what delivery month to hedge

- When to close or lift a hedge

- When to turn an advantageous basis situation into a profit

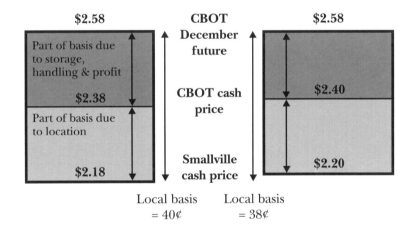

Typical Contract Quotations

Commodity and energy futures quotations are available from the financial press such as the *Financial Times* and *The Wall Street Journal* and from real-time products such as offered by Reuters. The information appears in formats similar to those following.

Financial press

Pork Bellies CME (40,000 lbs: cents /lb)

	Sett. price	Day's change	High	Low
Feb	44.050	+1.275	44.250	42.600
Mar	44.050	+0.750	44.675	43.100
May	45.700	+1.200	46.200	45.050
Jul	47.600	+1.175	47.500	46.400

Using this information, if you wish to buy a CME Pork Bellies futures contract for Jul99, then the implied contract delivery price is:

$$40,000 \times 47.600¢ = \$19,040.00$$

You can also use Reuters to find the real-time prices being traded for this contract as would appear below:

```
O#PB:          CME/    FROZEN BELLIES   USc
Mth   Last            Bid    Ask   Size   Open 1  High     Low     Time
FEB9  ↓56.100  +0.875                /    T55.400  56.950  54.325  16:16
MAR9  ↓56.400  +0.975                /    H55.750  56.925  54.800  16:16
MAY9  ↓57.950  +1.325                /    L56.900 *58.400  56.300  16:09
JUL9  ↓57.900  +0.700                /    T56.750 *58.100  56.600  15:53
AUG9  ↑58.000  +1.975                /    T56.025 *58.000  56.025  15:55
FEB0                                 /                              :
MAR0                                 /                              :
MAY0                                 /                              :
```

High Grade Copper COMEX (25,000 lbs: cents /lb)

	Sett. price	Day's change	High	Low
Jan	63.90	−0.55	64.45	63.70
Feb	64.25	−0.65	65.00	64.20
Mar	64.70	−0.70	65.45	64.20
Apr	65.15	−0.70	65.15	64.70

Using this information, if you wish to buy a COMEX High Grade Copper futures contract for Mar99, then the implied contract delivery price is:

$$25,000 \times 64.70¢ = \$16,175.00$$

You can also use Reuters to find the real-time prices being traded for this contract.

```
O#HG:          CMX/    HI/GRADE COPPER   USc
Mth   Last            Bid    Ask   Size   Open 1  High     Low     Time
JAN9  ↓65.50  -0.75                 /     T65.50  65.50  65.50  14:46
FEB9  ↓65.45  -1.00                 /     T65.70  65.70  65.45  15:14
MAR9  ↑65.85  -1.05                 /     T66.85  66.20  65.80  15:26
APR9  ↓66.40  -0.90                 /     T66.45  66.55  66.40  14:58
MAY9  ↑66.80  -0.90                 /     T66.90  66.95  66.75  15:05
JUN9  A67.55         IMQ 66.95  67.55  1/4                    13:02
JUL9  ↓67.60  -0.85                 /     T67.60  67.70  67.60  15:02
AUG9  A60.40         IMQ 67.70  60.40  1/3                    13:02
SEP9  ↓68.50  -0.65                 /     T68.50  68.50  68.50  15:06
OCT9  A69.30         IMQ 68.40  69.30  1/3                    13:02
NOV9  A69.85         IMQ 68.55  69.85  1/3                    13:02
DEC9  ↓69.60  -0.55                 /     T69.60  69.60  69.60  15:04
JANO  PS70.40  +0.55                /                         19:10
FEBO  PS70.70  +0.55                /                         19:10
MARO  PS71.05  +0.55                /                         19:10
APRO  PS71.40  +0.55                /                         19:10
MAYO  ↓71.15  -0.55                 /             71.15  71.15  15:00
JUNO  PS72.05  +0.55                /                         19:10
JULO  PS72.35  +0.55                /                         19:13
AUGO  PS72.60  +0.55                /                         19:10
SEPO  ↓72.60  -0.25                 /     T72.60  72.60  72.60  13:22
OCTO  PS73.15  +0.55                /                         19:10
NOVO  PS73.40  +0.55                /                         19:10
DECO  ↓73.00  -0.80                 /     T73.10  73.20  73.00  15:00
```

Who Uses Commodity, Energy and Freight Futures Contracts?

Hedgers

Originally futures contracts were devised so that holders of an asset – a commodity – could hedge or insure its price today for sometime in the future. Hedgers seek to transfer the risk of future price fluctuations by selling future contracts which guarantee them a future price for their asset. If the future cash price of their asset falls then they have protected themselves. However, if the future cash price rises then they have lost the opportunity to profit. Hedging offers some degree of certainty for future prices and therefore allows market players to fix prices, freight rates etc.

Hedgers are typically producers and consumers whereas speculators are typically traders who take on the risk of a futures contract for an appropriate price and the potential rewards.

The transfer of risk sought by hedgers is possible in the markets because different market players have different strategies and include:

- Hedgers with opposite risks

- Hedgers already holding positions who need to offset their positions

- Speculators with market views on likely price changes who provide the futures markets with extra liquidity

As in any futures market place for commodities, hedgers can hold **long** or **short** positions and in order to hedge their positions market players need to take an **opposite** position to the ones they hold.

It is important to understand that the principle of hedging is to maintain a neutral position. As prices in the cash market for the asset move one way, the move is compensated by an equal and opposite move in the futures' price. You can imagine the situation similar to the movement of the pans on a pair of scales.

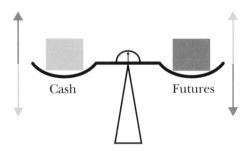

Going short futures

If a market player **holds**, or intends to hold, an asset in the cash market, then he has a **long** position. The opposite position in the futures markets means he must **go short** or **sell futures**. A **short hedge** will therefore lock in a selling price.

Going long futures

If a market player is short, or intends to go short, in the cash market, then the opposite position in the futures markets means he must **go long** or **buy futures**. A **long hedge** will therefore lock in a buying price.

What Instruments Are Used in the Markets?

Another way of considering market players using commodity, energy or freight futures contracts is to look at whether they are **buyers** or **sellers** of the contracts. In order to simplify matters the term commodity will be used to cover all the markets.

Buyers of Commodity Futures

- Wish to buy a commodity in the future and therefore **go long**.

- Expect the cash price of the commodity to **rise**. If the cash price does rise, then any losses in buying the underlying commodity in the future are offset by gains in the futures market.

The diagrams below show how the losses in the cash market are offset by gains in the futures market.

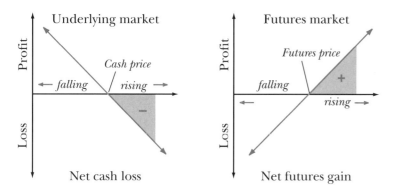

Sellers of Commodity Futures

- Wish to sell a commodity in the future and therefore **go short**.

- Expect the cash price of the commodity to **fall**. If the cash price does fall, then any losses in buying the underlying commodity in the future are offset by gains in the futures market.

The diagrams below show how the losses in the underlying instrument are offset by gains in the futures market.

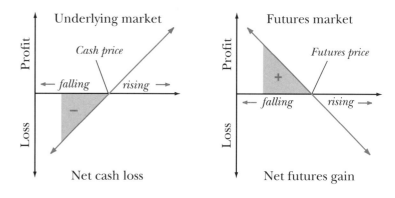

In summary:

Long Hedge	Short Hedge
• Buy futures	• Sell futures
• Protects against **rise** in cash markets	• Protects against **fall** in cash prices
• Locks in buying price	• Locks in selling price

REUTERS

These hedging positions can also be summarised in terms of buyers and sellers.

Sellers		
in the cash market...	**so in the futures market**	**Resulting hedge**
are **long** because they hold the commodity	need to be **short** or **sell** futures contracts	The positions are opposite so it protects the seller's risk in the cash market. Any cash price move **down** is offset by futures contract earnings.

Buyers		
in the cash market...	**so in the futures market**	**Resulting hedge**
are **short** because they need to buy the commodity	need to go **long** or **buy** futures contracts	The positions are opposite so it protects the buyer's risk in the cash market. Any cash price move **up** is offset by futures contract earnings.

The following examples illustrate how hedging is used by both buyers and sellers to lock in a price for a commodity.

Example 1 – Short or seller's hedge

In this case a wheat farmer is long in the cash market and needs to be short in the futures market to hedge his wheat production. In this case he sells CBOT futures contracts. The price quotation for wheat is $/bushel of wheat.

Cash	Futures
On April 1st the price of cash wheat is $3.30/bu. The farmer plants enough wheat to produce 1 million bu for sale to the Kansas silos at the end of August. Potential income = $3,300,000 **if prices remain stable.**	On April 1st the farmer sells 200 September futures contracts, each for 5,000 bu at $3.35/bu. Potential payment = $3,350,000

If at the end of August the cash price of wheat falls to $3.00/bu

Cash	Futures
The farmer sells 1 million bu of reaped grain to the Kansas silos at $3.00/bu. Income = $3,000,000	The farmer buys back the 200 contracts at $3.02/bu at a cost of $3,020,000. Since the contracts were sold for $3,350,000 the **profit** is $330,000.
Outcome: The total income is 3,000,000 + 330,000 = $3,330,000. The farmer has achieved a price of $3.33 per bu which is 3 cents more than the April price.	

If at the end of August the cash price of wheat rises to $3.50/bu

Cash	Futures
The farmer sells 1 million bu of reaped grain to the Kansas silos at $3.50/bu. Income = $3,500,000	The farmer buys back the 200 contracts at $3.55/bu at a cost of $3,550,000. Since the contracts were sold for $3,350,000 the **loss** is $200,000.

Outcome: The total income is 3,500,000 – 200,000 = $3,300,000. The farmer has achieved a price of $3.30 per bu which is the expected April price.

The farmer could let the contracts mature but in practice this is most unlikely as the farmer would have to pay the expenses of delivering the wheat to Chicago.

There is no such thing as a perfect hedge but hedging does work to offset any major losses as this example shows.

You can use the following equation to calculate the net price paid for a hedge:

Net price paid/received = Cash price ± Futures gain/loss

Just to check that the equation works – for the price fall of $3.00/bu:

$$\text{Net price received} = 3.00 + \text{gain of } 33\cent$$
$$= \$3.33$$

For the price rise to $3.50/bu:

$$\text{Net price received} = 3.50 - \text{loss of } 20\cent$$
$$= \$3.30$$

Example 2 – Long or buyer's hedge

In this case a German copper cable producer has received an order to produce a reel of cable in August. The producer stands to make a healthy profit at the current cash prices but he doesn't have sufficient warehouse capacity to buy and store the metal now. The producer also fears that the price of copper will rise soon due to labour disputes at the smelters. The producer is short in the cash market so needs to be long in the futures market to protect his position.

Cash	Futures
On May 1st the current cash price is 125¢/lb. The producer needs to buy 25,000lbs of copper for the August cable production. Potential payment = $31,250	On May 1st the producer buys a COMEX High Grade copper contract for 25,000lbs of metal at a cost of 150¢/lb. The COMEX trading months are for every month of the year. Potential payment = $37,500

Over the next 3 months there is a strike and the output from US smelters declines and the price of copper rises sharply.

Cash	Futures
On August 1st the producer buys 25,000lb of copper on the cash market and takes delivery at 205¢/lb. Cost incurred = $51,250	On August 1st the producer sells his futures contracts which now stand at 225¢/lb. The profit on the futures is therefore 225 – 150 = 75¢/lb. Payment received = $56,250

Outcome: The difference between the cash cost incurred and potential cost represents a loss of 51,250 – 31,250 = $20,000. This is offset by a profit from the futures hedge of 56,250 – 37,500 = $18,750. By hedging the producer has only made a loss of 20,000 – 18,750 = $1250. **The net price paid = 205 – 75 (futures gain) = 130¢/lb**

REUTERS

By using futures contracts, hedging removes the opportunity to profit if future cash prices rise but provides the required protection if future cash prices fall. In this respect hedging is in effect an insurance contract which locks in the future price of a commodity or financial asset.

Speculators

Speculators accept the risk that hedgers wish to transfer. Speculators have no position to protect and do not necessarily have the physical resources to make delivery of the underlying asset nor do they necessarily need to take delivery of the underlying asset. They take positions on their **expectations** of future price movements and in order to make a profit. In general they:

- **Buy** futures contracts – go long – when they expect future cash prices to **rise**

- **Sell** futures contracts – go short – when they expect future cash prices to **fall**

Speculators provide **liquidity** to the markets and without them the price protection – insurance – required by hedgers would be very expensive.

Arbitrageurs

These are traders and market-makers who deal in buying and selling futures contracts hoping to profit from **price differentials** between markets and/or exchanges.

The BIFFEX Freight Futures Contract

BIFFEX was formed in 1985 to provide a futures market for shipowners and charterers to hedge their freight risks in the **dry cargo** market up to 18 months forward. BIFFEX futures are currently traded on LIFFE.

Trading BIFFEX futures involves no supply of cargo or ships. It is a cash settled futures contract which is based on the **Baltic Freight Index, BFI**. The BFI is a measure of dry bulk freight rates for Panamax vessels (50 – 80,000 tonnes) and Capesize vessels (80,000+ tonnes). The index is simply a weighted average of rates for different worldwide dry cargoes, principally grain, coal and iron-ore. The routes, dry cargo rates and their weightings are available on electronic information services such as Reuters. Here is the Reuters BIFFEX page.

This indicates that the route is US Gulf to Antwerp/ Rotterdam/Amsterdam for a light grain cargo in a Panamax vessel and the price is 10% of the index value

```
BALTIC OCEAN FREIGHT INDEX COMPONENTS - BIFFEX                        BIFFEX1
TITLE                                    RATE    INDEX   PR.RATE  PR.INDEX
-----                                    ----    -----   -------  --------
BALTIC FREIGHT INDEX                              825               821
USG/ARA 55000 LIGHT GRAIN 10 PC         10.058   1.108    9.992     1.101
SKAW-P T/A R/V 3MLN CFT G-O-C 10 PC      6700     885     6564       867
USG/S.JAPAN 54000 HVY GRAIN 10 PC       15.117   1.094   15.142     1.096
SKAW-P VIA USG/F.EAST 3MLN CFT G-O-C 10 PC 7018   856     6986       852
USNP/S.JAPAN 54000 HVY GRAIN 10 PC       8.992   1.018    8.983     1.017
JAPAN-SK T/P R/V 3MLN CFT G-O-C 10 PC    3968     503     3911       496
HRDS NOT BALT/ROTTERDAM 110000 COAL 7.5 PC 3.400 0.698    3.408     0.700
JAPAN-SK/SKAW-P VIA USWC 3MLN CFT GC P. 10 P 4300 492     4279       489
TUBARAO/ROTTERDAM 150000 IRON ORE 7.5 PC  3.357 0.665    3.358     0.665
TUBARAO/BEILUN-BAOSHAN 140000 IRON ORE 7.5 P 4.864 0.688  4.857     0.687
R.BAY/ROTTERDAM 140000 COAL 7.5 PC        4.150 0.783    4.136     0.780

ABBREVIATIONS : HVY GRAIN - HEAVY GRAIN, SORGHUM & SOYA  P.COKE - PETROLEUM COKE
                MOP       - MURIATE OF POTASH            HRDS   - HAMPTON ROADS
                USG       - U.S. GULF                    USNP   - U.S. N PACIFIC
                USWC      - U.S. WEST COAST              SK     - SOUTH KOREA
                R.BAY     - RICHARDS BAY                 PHOS   - PHOSPHATE
                BALT      - BALTIMORE                     ARA    - ANTW-ROTT-AMST
                VANC      - VANCOUVER                     P      - PASSERO
                T/A       - TRANS-ATLANTIC               T/P    - TRANS-PACIFIC
                R/V       - ROUND VOYAGE                 MLN    - MILLION
```

The settlement price for the futures contract is calculated as an average over the last 5 trading days of the settlement month. American style options are also traded on LIFFE for BIFFEX futures contracts.

Commodity, Energy and Freight Futures Contracts in the Market Place

This section deals with a number of important matters concerning commodity, energy and freight futures which you will need to understand. In order to simplify matters the term commodity will be used to cover all the markets.

How a Commodity Futures Contract Works

By now you should be aware that once an exchange traded futures contract trade has been made the clearing house acts as counterparty to both sides of the trade. You should also be aware of the **initial** and **variation** margin system of payments and the process of **marking-to-market** which means that a futures contract is revalued at the current market price on a daily basis. Any profits and losses are paid over daily. By marking-to-market and settling all positions daily, the clearing house effectively rewrites all futures contracts at the prevailing market price. But how does the process work in practice? The following simple example illustrates variation margin payments in practice.

Example

You are a US farmer and you need to take a short hedge position on your live hogs. On 1st February 1999 you sell a CME Lean Hog April 99 futures contract with the expectation that the cash market price will fall. On 8th February 1999 you choose to close out your position and buy back the futures contract.

The contract trading unit is 40,000lbs and the Apr99 contract was sold at 37.85¢/lb. The contract was closed at 36.85¢/lb which represents a gain of 40,000 x 1.0¢ = $400.00. However, the table following shows the actual course of events.

The table shows that variation margin payments are debited/credited on a daily basis and fluctuate considerably. The overall profit is shown as $400.00 but there was a single loss of $460.00 for one particular day.

Date	Open Price, ¢	Close Price, ¢	Value of Position, $	Variation Margin, $
1.2	37.85	–	15,140	–
1.2	37.85	37.05	14,820	+320
2.2	37.05	36.85	14,740	+80
3.2	36.85	36.00	14,400	+340
4.2	36.00	37.15	14,800	−460
5.2	37.15	37.50	15,000	−140
8.2	37.50	36.85	14,700	+260
Total				+400

The process is further illustrated in the following diagrams:

On the contract date

The Seller sells a contract to the Buyer and both deposit initial margin with the Clearing house.

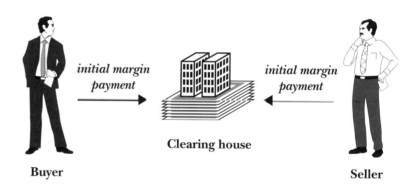

initial margin payment → Clearing house ← *initial margin payment*

Buyer · Clearing house · Seller

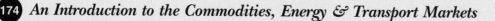

During the contract

The Seller's and the Buyer's profit and loss accounts are adjusted daily.

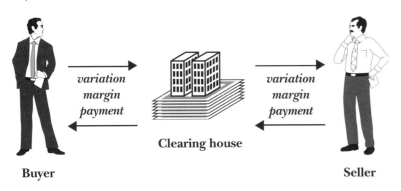

Buyer — *variation margin payment* → **Clearing house** → *variation margin payment* — **Seller**

On the delivery date or contract closure

The Seller's and the Buyer's profit and loss accounts are settled for the last time.

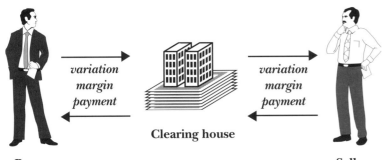

Buyer — *variation margin payment* → **Clearing house** → *variation margin payment* — **Seller**

Before moving on try this simple activity...

A seller of cocoa wishes to guarantee the price of his November crop using futures on LIFFE. As there is no November futures contract the seller has to hedge using the December contracts. Using the information here how well does the seller hedge?

Time	Action	Futures £/tonne	Cash £/tonne
Aug	Sells Dec futures	946	940
Nov	Buys Dec futures	930	920

You can check your answer over the page.

Using the information how well does the seller hedge?

To determine how well the seller has hedged all you need to do is calculate the net price received.

Net price received = Cash price + Futures gain
                     = 920 + 16
                     = £936/tonne

By hedging in this way selling the cocoa in November is only £4/tonne less than the August price – so the producer has done quite well. If he had not hedged he would have lost £20/tonne.

Commodity, Energy and Freight Futures Contracts

- A **commodity, energy** or **freight futures** contract is an **exchange traded forward transaction** with standardised conditions and specification

- Market players **buy** futures or **go long** to protect against **rising** prices in the future cash markets

- Market players **sell** futures or **go short** to protect against **falling** prices in the future cash markets

- A **short hedge** involves:

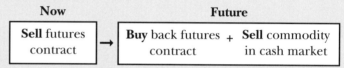

Now	Future
Sell futures contract	→	**Buy** back futures contract + **Sell** commodity in cash market

- A **long hedge** involves:

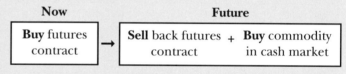

Now	Future
Buy futures contract	→	**Sell** back futures contract + **Buy** commodity in cash market

- A **clearing house** acts as **counterparty** to both the buyer and the seller of a futures contract which is **marked-to-market** on a daily basis

The following screens may help your understanding of commodity, energy and freight futures contracts and how they are used. In addition to prices it is possible to display individual contract details.

The Japanese Futures and Options Exchanges Speed Guide leads to the Tokyo Grain Exchange page, from which details about the Azuki Red Bean contracts can be obtained.

```
JAPANESE FUTURES AND OPTIONS EXCHANGES SPEED GUIDE                    JP/FUTEX1
Welcome to the Japanese Futures and Options Exchange Guide. To access
information, double click in <>. For more guidance see <USER/HELP>.

This guide lists details of all contracts traded on the following exchanges, as
well as general information about the individual exchanges:

=FUTURES & OPTIONS EXCHANGES===================================================
Tokyo Commodity Exchange (TCE).........................................<TCE/FUTEX1>
Tokyo Grain Exchange (TGE).............................................<TGE/FUTEX1>
Tokyo International Financial Futures Exchange(TIFFE)...................<TIF/FUTEX1>
Kansai Commodities Exchange............................................<KEX/FUTEX1>
Chubu Commodity Exchange...............................................<CCX/FUTEX1>
Kanmon Commodity Exchange..............................................<KCX/FUTEX1>
Yokohama Silk Exchange.................................................<YSE/FUTEX1>
Maebashi Dried Cocoon Exchange.........................................<MDC/FUTEX1>
Osaka Mercantile Exchange..............................................<OTE/FUTEX1>
Tokyo Stock Exchange (TSE).............................................<TSE/FUTEX1>
Osaka Stock Exchange (OSE).............................................<OSE/FUTEX1>

===============================================================================
```

```
O#JRB:          TOKYO REDBEAN               TGE /   JPY
Mth   Cls   hana  AM1    AM2    AM3    PM1    PM2    PM3   Sett  NetCH  Volume Time
vol:               435    349    383    454    250   1006
JAN9  12200       12190  12190  12190  12190  12190  12200 12200              63  06:13
FEB9  12020       12000  11990  11990  12000  12000  12010 12010  -10        244 06:14
MAR9  11640       11570  11580  11600  11600  11600  11630 11630  -10        319 06:16
APR9  11290       11250  11260  11300  11290  11290  11300 11300  +10        388 06:17
MAY9  11190       11190  11200  11210  11200  11200  11210 11210  +20        436 06:20
JUN9  11000       10970  11020  11000  11010  11000  11100 11100  +100      1427 06:22
```

```
TOKYO GRAIN EXCHANGE - REUTERS SPEED GUIDE                           TGE/FUTEX1
PRICES and CONTRACT DETAILS for all TGE Futures and Options contracts.

ADDRESS: Tokoku Bldg, 1-12-5 Kakigara-cho, Nihonbashi, Chuo-ku, Tokyo 103
TEL NO:  3 3668 9311

=LISTED CONTRACTS===================NEAREST MONTH========CONTRACT DETAILS==
U.S Soybeans.................<O#JAS:>  <JASc1>...................<TGE/JAS>
Azuki Red Beans..............<O#JRB:>  <JRBc1>...................<TGE/JRB>
Corn.........................<O#JCR:>  <JCRc1>...................<TGE/JCR>
Raw Sugar....................<O#JSG:>  <JSGc1>...................<TGE/JSG>
White Sugar..................<O#JWS:>  <JWSc1>...................<TGE/JWS>
Arabica Coffee...............<O#JAC:>  <JACc1>...................<TGE/JAC>
Robusta Coffee...............<O#JRC:>  <JRCc1>...................<TGE/JRC>

===============================================================================
Commodities Guide<COMMOD> Futures/Ops Guide<FUTURES> Japanese Futures<JP/FUTEX1>
```

```
AZUKI RED BEANS CONTRACT DETAILS                                       TGE/JRB
Contract Details, Trading Hours etc for the AZUKI RED BEANS FUTURE.

CHAIN RIC          -      <O#JRB:>
OPTIONS RIC        -      N/A
LOT SIZE           -      2400 kg
TICK SIZE          -      Y10 per 30 kg
CONTRACT MONTHS    -      Six Consecutive months
DELIVERY MONTHS    -      The Second last business day
LAST TRADING DAY   -      Two Business days prior to the delivery day
MIN. PRICE MOVE    -      10 Yen/30 kg

TRADING HOURS      -      Sessions:
                         AM1 - 09:00am
                         AM2 - 10:00am
                         AM3 - 11:00am
                         PM1 - 13:10pm
                         PM2 - 14:10pm
                         PM3 - 15:10pm

===============================================================================
Futures/Options Guide<FUTURES> Japanese Futures<JP/FUTEX1> TGE Guide<TGE/FUTEX1>
      Lost? Selective Access...<USER/HELP>   Reuter Phone Support...<PHONE/HELP>
```

What Instruments Are Used in the Markets?

The first screen below displays the chain of futures RICs for commodities. The second screen displays a listing of oilseed futures contracts. The third screen displays a list of Red Bean Futures and the last screen displays the Tokyo Grain Exchange Red Bean futures prices.

The top screen displays the contract specification and details of **Pulp Contracts** traded on DMLX and DM Stockholm. The middle screen displays **PULPEX** futures prices and the bottom screen displays the latest information on Exchange for Physicals (EFPs).

```
O#COMMOD-FUT     COMMODITY FUTUREExchange
RIC              Contract         ID
O#BASE-FUT       BASE METAL FUT.  RCT/
O#FIBRES-FUT     FIBRES FUTURES   RCT/
O#FINANCIAL-FUT  FINANCIAL FUTURE    /
O#FREIGHT-FUT    FREIGHT FUTURES     /
O#GRAINS-FUT     GRAINS FUTURES   RCT/
O#LIVESTOCK-FUT  LIVESTOCK FUTURES RCT/
O#OILSEEDS-FUT   OILSEEDS FUTURES RCT/
O#PRECIOUS-FUT   PRECIOUS FUTURES RCT/
O#SOFTS-FUT      SOFTS FUTURES    RCT/
```

```
O#OILSEEDS-FUT   OILSEEDS FUTURESExchange
RIC              Contract         ID
O#FLAXCHN        Flax Futures     RCT/
O#GRBEAN         Greenbean Future RCT/
O#PLMCHN         Palm Oil Futures RCT/
O#RAPECHN        Rape Futures     RCT/
O#RDBEAN         Redbean Futures  RCT/
O#SOYCHN         Soy Futures      RCT/
```

```
O#RDBEAN         Redbean Futures  Exchange
RIC              Contract         ID
O#JRB:           TOKYO REDBEAN    TGE/
O#DRB:           DCE REDBEAN      DLC/
N/A
O#JKB:           KANSAI REDBEAN      /
O#JRN:           CHUBU REDBEAN       /
O#JRK:           KANMON REDBEAN      /
O#JRB:           TOKYO REDBEAN    TGE/
```

```
O#JRB:        TOKYO REDBEAN               TGE / JPY
Mth    Cls  hana  AM1    AM2   AM3   PM1   PM2   PM3   Sett  NetCH  Volume Time
 vol:             435   349    303   454   250   1006
JAN9  12200      12190  12190 12190 12190 12190 12200 12200             63 06:13
FEB9  12020      12000  11990 11990 12000 12000 12010 12010   -10      244 06:14
MAR9  11640      11570  11580 11600 11600 11600 11630 11630   -10      319 06:16
APR9  11290      11250  11260 11300 11290 11290 11300 11300   +10      388 06:17
MAY9  11190      11190  11200 11210 11200 11200 11210 11210   +20      436 06:20
JUN9  11000      10970  11020 11000 11010 11000 11100 11100  +100     1427 06:22
```

```
PULPEX                                                         PULPEX
OMLX, London                       Official Trading Hours 13:00-16:00 (BST)
OM Stockholm, Sweden               Official Trading Hours 14:00-17:00 (CET)

===========PULP CONTRACTS===========    =========CONTRACT SPECIFICATION=======

Futures...................<O#PULP:>   PULP FUTURES
Options..................<O#PULP*.pl>  Quality : prime sheeted NBSK wood pulp
                                       Contract Size : 24 air dry metric tons
Futures settlement price....<PULPSETT> Contract Currency : US Dollars
                                       Daily Settlement Price : last traded
Bulletin board...............<PULPEY>  price on each business day
                                       PULP OPTIONS
===================================    Contract Base : one futures contract
OM Menu page.................<OM/MENU> Exercise style : european style
```

```
O#PULP:        PULPEX FUTURES      /    USD
Mth    Last   Net.Ch  Bid    Ask    Settle Open   High   Low    Volume Op.Int Time
MAR9  ↓394.00  -2.25  394.00 394.50 396.50 394.00 394.00 394.00     10    366 14:23
JUN9  ↑417.00  +0.75  413.50 417.00 417.25 417.00 417.00 417.00     15    281 14:35
SEP9  ↓340.50 -101.50 432.00 438.00 437.50 340.50 340.50 340.50      1     48 13:09
DEC9                  450.00 456.00 455.50                                  2   :
```

```
PULPEX                                                         PULPEY
OMLX, London                               OM Stockholm AB
TEL +44-171-2830678                        TEL +46-8-405 60 00

× MARKET PLACE:     PETER AKESSON
× LEGAL MATTERS:    DEREK OLIVER        ERIK RICKNELL
× DELIVERY&CLEARING: CLIFFORD LAUNDON   ULRIKA JEDENHEIM
× MARKETING :       XAVIER BRUCKERT     CLAES BETSHOLTZ


DAILY EXCHANGE FOR PHYSICAL INFORMATION:
11.12.98 12 LOT MAR 1999 PULPEX EFP REGISTERED AT 13.01
11.12.98 10 LOT JUNE 1999 PULPEX EFP REGISTERED AT 13.01
11.12.98 4 LOT SEPT 1999 PULPEX EFP REGISTERED AT 13.01
21.12.98 30 LOT MARCH 1999 PULPEX EFP REGISTERED AT 15.56
20.01.99 20 LOT MARCH 1999 PULPEX EFP REGISTERED AT 15.30
21.01.99 26 LOT JUNE 1999 PULPEX EFP REGISTERED AT 14.55
21.01.99 13 LOT SEPT 1999 PULPEX EFP REGISTERED AT 14.55
01.10.98 10 LOT DEC 1998 PULPEX EFP REGISTERED AT 15.09
23.11.98 4  LOT MAR 1999 PULPEX EFP REGISTERED AT 14.15
01.12.98 60 LOT DEC 1998 PULPEX EFP REGISTERED AT 13.35
04.12.98 16 LOT MARCH 1999 PULPEX EFP REGISTERED AT 13.01
04.12.98 24 LOT JUNE 1999 PULPEX EFP REGISTERED AT 13.01
04.12.98 48 LOT JUNE 1999 PULPEX EFP REGISTERED AT 13.01
04.12.98 26 LOT SEPT 1999 PULPEX  EFP REGISTERED AT 13.01
```

The screen on top right displays the Energy Futures Speed Guide and the screen on bottom right displays the prices of IPE Brent Guide Oil. Double clicking the contract month of MAR 9 will bring up the screen on the left which displays price information for that specific contract. The **H** in this RIC represents the month of March and the **9** is the year – 1999. A list of month codes is given below.

Month	Code	Month	Code
Jan	F	Jul	N
Feb	G	Aug	Q
Mar	H	Sep	U
Apr	J	Oct	V
May	K	Nov	X
Jun	M	Dec	Z

```
ENERGY FUTURES - REUTERS SPEED GUIDE                        ENERGY/FUT1
To access information click on codes in < > or [ ].  See also <O#ENERGY-FUT>
=FUTURES CONTRACTS CHAINS=============    =FUTURES STATISTICS=================
IPE Gasoil....................<O#LGO:>    Previous 14 Days settlements ....<SETT>
IPE Brent.....................<O#LCO:>    IPE Volumes & Open Interest..<IPESTATS>
IPE Natural Gas-Natl Bal Pt...<O#NGLN:>   Simex Volumes & Open Interest.<SIMEX06>
IPE Natural Gas-Daily.........<O#NGLD:>   NYMEX Volumes & Open Interest<NYMSTATS>
NYMEX Light Crude (WTI)........<O#CL:>    NYMEX Key previous day close...<NYMEXC>
NYMEX No.2 Heating Oil.........<O#HO:>    IPE Gasoil Opening Call .....<IPE-CALL>
NYMEX Unleaded Gasoline........<O#HU:>    CFTC Trader Commitment Reports..<1CFTD>
KCBT Natural Gas...............<O#KG:>    CFTC Reports explained .....<CFTCGUIDE>
NYMEX Liquid Propane...........<O#PN:>
SIMEX Brent ..................<O#SCO:>    =NEWS and ANALYSIS==================
NYMEX COB Electricity .........<O#EC:>    Reuters Energy News.....[CRU PROD OPEC]
NYMEX Palo Verde Electricity ..<O#EV:>    Technical Barometers........<OIL/TECH>
NYMEX Cinergy..................<O#CN:>    Energy News Directory....[ENERGY/NEWS1]
NYMEX Entergy..................<O#NT:>    IPE Energy Futures Reports........[O/L]
NYMEX Natural Gas, Henry Hub...<O#NG:>    NYMEX Energy Futures Reports......[O/N]
MGE On-Peak Electricity .......<O#BG:>    SIMEX Energy Futures Reports......[O/S]
MGE Off-Peak Electricity ......<O#BS:>
CBT TVA Electricity ...........<O#BA:>
CBT ConEd Electricity .........<O#BZ:>    Interproduct Spreads.<ENERGY/SPREAD1>-2

Derivative Guide<DERIV>      Energy Guide<ENERGY>      Continued on <ENERGY/FUT2>
  Lost?Selective Access?...<USER/HELP>    Reuters Phone Support...<PHONE/HELP>
```

```
LCOH9        BRENT CRUDE MAR9 0        IPE/   USD        20JAN99 15:37
Last       Last 1    Last 2    Last 3    Last 4    Bid       Ask
↓1066      1067      1067      1066      1067      1066      1067
Net.Chng   Cls:19JAN99 Open    High      Low       Size      Bkgrnd
-15        1081      1085      1085      1059      x         ****
Settle     Volume    Open.Int  Cnt.High  Cnt.Low   Ope.Bid   Ope.Ask
           11133     74944     1782      980       1075      1075
Cnt.Xpry   Lot.Size  Limit     Status    News      Cls.Bid   Cls.Ask
11FEB99     1000  BBL    /        /        15:14     1082      1083
```

```
O#LCO:          BRENT CRUDE    IPE/   USD
Index  1091      EFPTot 1793    PTotV 58392    Tot.V  15383    Tot.OI 244775
Mth    Last  Last1 Net  Bid   Ask   PrvSet Open  High Low  Volume EFPVol Op.Int Sett  Time
MAR9  ↓1066  1067  -15             1066  1081  1085  1085 1059  11133  1793  74944      15:37
APR9  ↓1074  1075  -11             1074  1085  1086  1091 1069  2997         48145      15:37
MAY9  ↑1090  1089  -10             1094  1100  1098  1100 1086  301          21952      15:35
JUN9  ↑1108  1107  -7              1110  1115  1113  1113 1105  151          26287      15:37
JUL9  ↓1128        -3                    1131  1128  1128 1128  4            7690       10:15
AUG9  ↓1144        -3                    1147  1144  1144 1144  6            5986       10:16
SEP9  ↓1161        -2                    1163  1161  1161 1161  1            3750       10:17
OCT9  ↓1176        -3   1170  1180  1179  1176  1176 1176  40           2995       15:26
NOV9                                      1195                            2323       16:34
DEC9  ↑1208  1207  -3   1205        1211  1210  1210 1202  750          27611      15:37
JAN0                                      1226                            866        17:16
FEB0                                      1240                            361        11:25
MAR0                                      1253                            2261       12:44
JUN0                                      1288                            5797       15:46
SEP0                                      1323                                       :
DEC0                                      1357                            5589       12:00
JUN1                                      1405                            3365       11:32
DEC1                                      1453                            4853       19:39
```

The screens below are taken from the Reuters Shipping Speed Guide. You can see the latest futures prices for the BIFFEX Ocean Freight Contracts traded on LIFFE by double-clicking the field <O#BOF>/

The top screen displays the Global Market and Public Holidays Speed Guide. The bottom screen displays the 1999 holiday dates for exchanges in France.

```
SHIPPING 2000 - REUTERS SPEED GUIDE                             BIFFEX
To access information double-click in the <> or [] brackets.

=BIFFEX INDICES======================   =HANDY & TANKER INDICES===============
Baltic Index..................<BIFFEX1>  Baltic Handy Index............<.BAHA>
Baltic Freight...................<.BAFI>  BHI Continent - Far East.......<.BACFI>
BOF US Hampton Road-ARA.........<.BFHA>  BHI Japan - N. Pacific.........<.BAJAI>
BOF Japan - S. Korea............<.BFTP>  BHI Singapore - Continent......<.BAACI>
BOF Montreal - Rotterdam........<.BFMR>  BHI Continent - NS Atlantic....<.BACAI>
BOF SKAW.........................<.BFTA>  BIT ME Gulf - Japan............<.BAGJI>
BOF KAW Gult - FE...............<.BFSE>  BIT W. Africa - US Gulf........<.BAAGI>
BOF US Gulf - ARA...............<.BFGA>  BIT W. Africa - USAC...........<.BAAUI>
BOF US Gulf - Japan............<.BFGJ>  BIT North Sea - Continent......<.BANCI>
BOF US N.Pacific - Japan........<.BFPJ>  BIT Caribbean - US Gulf........<.BACGI>
BOF Vancouver -                          BIT CPP/UNL ME Gulf - Japan...<.BACJI>
    San Diego - Rotterdam.......<.BFVR>  BIT CPP/UNL Continent - USAC...<.BACUI>
                                         BIT CPP/UNL Continent to USAC..<.BACCI>
=BIFFEX FUTURES=                          BIT ME Gulf to Continent.......<.BAGEI>
Ocean Freight Contracts........<O#BOF:>  BIT ME Gulf to Singapore.......<.BAGSI>
Nearest Month Contact Quote.....<BOFc1>  BIT Kuwait-Singapore(Crude/DPP)<.BAKSI>
Delayed (15 Minutes)..........<O#/BOF.>
                                                       MORE <BIFFEX2>
====================================================================
Main Index<REUTERS>                       Shipping Index page..<SHIPPING>
   Lost? Selective Access?..<USER/HELP>   Reuters Phone Support..<PHONE/HELP>
```

```
GLOBAL MARKET & PUBLIC HOLIDAYS - REUTERS SPEED GUIDE          HOLIDAY1
This Guide provides an overview of the key holiday information for each country.
To call up data, either type in the code within brackets or double-click on it.

=MARKET & PUBLIC HOLIDAYS BY COUNTRY===  =MARKET & PUBLIC HOLIDAYS BY COUNTRY===
Australia..................<AU/HOLIDAY>  Japan.......................<JP/HOLIDAY>
Austria....................<AT/HOLIDAY>  Latvia......................<LV/HOLIDAY>
Bahrain....................<BH/HOLIDAY>  Lithuania...................<LT/HOLIDAY>
Belgiun....................<BE/HOLIDAY>  Luxembourg..................<LU/HOLIDAY>
Brazil.....................<BR/HOLIDAY>  Malaysia....................<MY/HOLIDAY>
Dennark....................<DK/HOLIDAY>  Netherlands.................<NL/HOLIDAY>
Estonia....................<EE/HOLIDAY>  New Zealand.................<NZ/HOLIDAY>
Finland....................<FI/HOLIDAY>  Nigeria....................<NGHOLIDAY>
France.....................<FR/HOLIDAY>  Norway......................<NO/HOLIDAY>
Germany....................<DE/HOLIDAY>  Philippines.................<PH/HOLIDAY>
Ghana......................<GH/HOLIDAY>  Portugal....................<PT/HOLIDAY>
Hong Kong..................<HK/HOLIDAY>  Sweden......................<SE/HOLIDAY>
Iceland....................<IS/HOLIDAY>  Switzerland.................<CH/HOLIDAY>
Italy......................<IT/HOLIDAY>  Turkey......................<TR/HOLIDAY>
Ivory Coast................<CI/HOLIDAY>
```

```
O#BOF:          OCEAN FRGHT     LIF/    GBp
Index  825                            Tot.V     39    Tot.OI   2421
Mth    Last   Last1 Net   Bid   Ask   PrvSet Open High Low  Volume Op.Int Sett
FEB9  ↑836   835   -4   830   845    840   835  836  835    15     195
MAR9  ↑900   895   -3         910    903   895  900  885    10     209
APR9  ↑945   945   -5   925   950    950   940  945  940    14    1010
JUL9                    800   050    040                           G02
OCT9                    930          950                           373
JANO                                 940                            28
APRO                    945          970                             4
JULO                    840          840
```

```
MONEY 2000 INDEX OF KEY DISPLAYS                           FR/HOLIDAY
Listed below are the Public & Market Holidays for France

=1999 DATES=======MARKET HOLIDAY================GENERAL INFORMATION==========
Fri  01 January     New Year's Day
Fri  02 April       Good Friday
Mon  05 April       Easter Monday
Thur 13 May         Ascension Day
Mon  24 May         Whitmonday
Wed  14 July        National Day
Mon  01 November    All Saint's Day
Fri  24 December    Christmas Eve (Exchanges Open)
Fri  31 December    Saint Silvester (Exchanges Open)




Questions/Comments: Contact your local Help Desk - see <PHONE/HELP> for details
====================================================================
Main Guide <REUTERS>      Main Country Index<FRANCE>      Exchange Page<FR/EXCH1>
   Lost?Selective Access?...<USER/HELP>   Reuters Phone Support...<PHONE/HELP>
```

Futures Spreads and Strips

A **futures spread** is the difference in prices or basis between delivery months in the same or different markets. The purpose of such a spread is to profit from any change in price differential. The absolute prices of the futures contracts involved are not important – only their price difference.

A **futures strip** trade is a single transaction which locks in an average price for a future period by simultaneously opening a futures position for each contract period required. The price level of the strip is the average of the futures contract prices.

If you need an overview of futures derivatives or you need to remind yourself about derivatives in general, then you may find it useful to refer to the *Introduction to Derivatives* book (ISBN 0-471-83176-X) in this series.

Spread Trading

Spread trading is concerned with **price differentials** between cash and/or futures prices. Spread trading is not concerned with outright prices nor their price direction – up or down.

There are a number of important types of spreads which all have two common elements:

1. A spread involves at least two futures positions which are held **simultaneously**. In other words a spread involves holding a **long** position in one futures contract at the same time as holding a **short** position in another.

2. A spread is only effective if there is a **reasonably predictable relationship** between the prices of the contracts being spread. For example, the spread for the Cocoa futures contract on LIFFE for different delivery months would have a predictable relationship.

There are a number of different types of spreads used in the metals, energy, softs and grain/oilseeds markets.

Spreads can be sub-divided into the following types:

- **Intermonth** spreads, for example, May – July, July – Sept etc

- **Basis** spreads – the relationship between cash and futures prices

- **Arbitrage** – the relationship between different futures contracts

In using spread trading, a market player will purchase the cheaper or underpriced contract in his view and sell the more expensive contract. The simultaneous buying and selling of the same or similar instruments is used to profit from the price differences.

If the markets move as expected the market player profits from the change in the price relationship between the contracts rather than the more volatile movements in absolute price.

Although the LME contracts traded on base metals are forward contracts it is convenient to include these spreads here. The importance of spreads for the LME base metal contracts is discussed in more detail in the *Forward contracts* section – you may find it useful to refer to it at this stage or later.

The Reuters screen below displays the LME base metal forward contract cash to 3-month spreads.

Cash to 3-month spreads

```
LME           LONDON METAL EXCHANGE OVERVIEW          05-NOV-1998     GMT: 14:58
TIME--METAL-MMID---3n Bid/Ask MM----LME FLOOR----TIME-METAL-MMID-- Cash to 3s-
14:56  CU  =MOCC  ×1635.0/1638.0   1637.0/1638.0  13:49  CU  =WOLF  c 27.0/26.0 c
13:32  SN  =MGAA  ×  5510/5520        5520/5530   13:49  SN  =WOLF  b   60/65   b
14:52  PB  =EDFM  ×499.00/502.00   499.00/500.00  13:49  PB  =WOLF  c10.00/9.00 c
14:48  ZN  =SDUK  ×  973.0/975.0      973.0/974.0 13:49  ZN  =WOLF  c 20.0/19.0 c
14:42  AL  MSDW   ×1320.0/1323.0   1321.0/1322.0  13:49  AL  =WOLF  c 22.0/21.0 c
14:52  NI  =AMTL  ×  4275/4290         4270/4280  13:49  NI  =WOLF  c   65/62   c
13:57  AA  =AMTL  ×1120.0/1130.0   1121.0/1125.0  13:49  AA  =WOLF  c 35.0/30.0 c
13:31  CS  =WOLF     991.0/994.0
13:32  PS  =WOLF     302.0/305.0                  CURRENT SESSION: Inter-Office
Cash Date : 09-NOV-1998                           '=' denotes RING Dealing Member
3Mth Date : 05-FEB-1999                           'T' denotes LME floor trade
```

For specific LME base metals the spreads to 3-month forward prices can be displayed. Below is the page for nickel.

```
OHMNI:      NICKEL        LME/    USD      Total Stock  65562
Mth       Last         Bid      Ask        Time     Open     High     Low      Evaluation
CASH    T ↓4265.00 RING  4265    4270   RING 13:15   4330     4330    4265     E   4366.00
3MT     M  4377.5  ARON  4365    4390   ARON 16:14   4425    B4422   A4325     E   4435.00
Mth       Last         Bid      Ask        Time      Last 2     Last 3       Evaluation
C-3M    M  69     MGAA c70    c68    MGAA 12:20   M  69.5   M  69.5   P  -69.00
FEB9-3M M  48     WOLF c49    c47    WOLF 13:46   M  47     M  48     P  -46.50
MAR9-3M M  24.5   WOLF c25    c24    WOLF 13:49   M  24.5   M  23.5   P  -23.50
APR9-3M C                          :            C         C
C-FEB9  M  21.75  WOLF c22    c22    WOLF 13:49   C         M  23
FEB-MAR C         WOLF c23    c23    WOLF    :    M  23     C
MAR-APR C                                        C         C
3M-MAY9 M  21.5   BRAN c23    c20    BRAN 11:18   M  22     M  22.5   P  -22.00
3M-JUN9 M  42.5   BRAN c45    c40    BRAN 11:18   M  43     M  43.5   P  -43.00
3M-JUL9 M  68     FMAT c69    c67    FMAT 10:50   M  68.5   M  68.5   P  -68.50
3M-AUG9 M  88.5   BRAN c91    c86    BRAN 11:18   M  89     M  89.5   P  -89.00
3M-SEP9 M  108.5  BRAN c111   c106   BRAN 11:18   M  109    M  109.5  P  -109.00
3M-OCT9 M  131    BRAN c136   c132   RING 15:46   M  132    M  132.5  P  -132.00
3M-NOV9 M  151    BRAN c156   c146   BRAN 11:18   M  152    M  152.5  P  -152.00
3M-DEC9 M  171    RING c173   c166   BRAN 13:01   M  172    M  172.5  P  -172.00
3M-JAN0 M  188    BRAN c193   c183   BRAN 11:18   M  189.5  M  189    P  -189.00
3M-FEB0 M  205    BRAN c210   c200   BRAN 11:18   M  206.5  M  206    P  -206.00
3M-MAR0 M  222    BRAN c227   c217   BRAN 11:18   M  223.5  M  223    P  -223.00
3M-APR0 M  239    BRAN c244   c234   BRAN 11:18   M  240.5  M  240    P  -240.00
3M-MAY0 M  257.5  FMAT c259   c256   FMAT 10:52   M  257    M  257.5  P  -257.00
```

REUTERS

The Reuters page below shows for broken date spread quotes for all LME metals traded.

```
LME/SPREAD                                    SPREAD TRADING                                      
LONDON METAL EXCHANGE - BROKEN DATE SPREAD QUOTES TICKER              LME/SPREAD
DATE         TIME      MTL  SPREAD DATES          QUOTE / TRADE "T"
-----------  --------  ---  ----------------      ------------------
13-JAN-1999  13:04:17  MNI  CASH    -19JAN99  c   3.6 T
13-JAN-1999  13:04:13  MNI  CASH    -19JAN99  c   3.6/
13-JAN-1999  13:03:35  MNI  CASH    -19JAN99  c   3.6/
13-JAN-1999  13:03:27  MNI  CASH    -19JAN99  c   3.6/
13-JAN-1999  13:03:26  MNI  CASH    -19JAN99  c   3.6 T
13-JAN-1999  13:03:05  MNI  CASH    -19JAN99          /3.6       c
13-JAN-1999  13:02:36  MNI  17MAR99-21APR99          /23.0       c
13-JAN-1999  13:02:02  MNI  17MAR99-21APR99          /23.0       c
13-JAN-1999  12:59:28  MAL  26JAN99-3MONTHS          /6.0        c
13-JAN-1999  12:59:27  MAL  26JAN99-3MONTHS  c   6.0 T
13-JAN-1999  12:59:06  MAL  26JAN99-3MONTHS          /6.0        c
13-JAN-1999  12:59:06  MAL  26JAN99-3MONTHS  c   6.0 T
13-JAN-1999  12:59:05  MAL  26JAN99-3MONTHS          /6.0        c
13-JAN-1999  12:51:22  MZN  21APR99-20OCT99  c   35.0/34.0       c
13-JAN-1999  12:51:21  MZN  21APR99-20OCT99          /34.0       c
13-JAN-1999  12:41:27  MSN  15MAR99-17MAR99          /1.0        b
13-JAN-1999  12:33:40  MCU  17MAR99-21APR99          /8.0        c
13-JAN-1999  12:32:00  MCU  19MAY99-15DEC99  c   58.0/58.0       c
13-JAN-1999  12:31:56  MCU  19MAY99-15DEC99  c   58.0/58.0       c
13-JAN-1999  12:31:56  MCU  19MAY99-15DEC99  c   58.0/58.0       c
13-JAN-1999  12:31:52  MCU  19MAY99-15DEC99  c   58.0/
13-JAN-1999  12:31:22  MCU  20OCT99-15DEC99      14.0/
13-JAN-1999  12:17:38  MNI  17MAR99-21APR99  c   23.0/22.5       c
13-JAN-1999  12:17:37  MNI  17MAR99-21APR99          /22.5       c
13-JAN-1999  12:17:12  MNI  20JAN99-17MAR99  c   46.0/45.0       c
13-JAN-1999  12:17:11  MNI  20JAN99-17MAR99          /45.0       c
13-JAN-1999  12:11:53  MZN  CASH    -16JUN99  c   1.8/1.3         c
13-JAN-1999  12:11:50  MZN  CASH    -16JUN99          /1.3        c
13-JAN-1999  12:09:43  MPB  05FEB99-17FEB99  b   2.0/
13-JAN-1999  12:07:51  MPB  17MAR99-16JUN99  c   4.5/
13-JAN-1999  12:07:12  MPB  05FEB99-17FEB99  b   1.0/
13-JAN-1999  12:02:53  MCU  17MAR99-19MAY99          /16.0       c
13-JAN-1999  11:57:54  MAL  20JAN99-17MAR99  b   1.5/2.5         c
```

Intermonth spreads for the three important softs – coffee, cocoa and sugar – can be found on Reuters' service. The intermonth spreads are given under the **spr** columns and can be calculated easily as differences between contract prices, this screen shows **Cocoa.**

```
COCWLD                    Global Cocoa Summary              11:12
CSC   Last   Net High  Low  Mvs Spr  NYvLDN LCE  Last  Net Bid/Ask Vol Spr
MAR9 ↑1256  -17 1291 1255 149      15  113.41 MAR9↑874 -14 874 75 1060  -7
MAY9 ↓1271   25 1308 1268 498      27   98.58 MAY9↑867 -17 867 68 1935  18
JUL9 ↑1298  -26 1335 1297  62      31   99.78 JUL9↑885 -16 884 85  205  18
SEP9 ↑1329  -24 1362 1328  13      39   97.76 SEP9↑903 -16 902 03  230  24
DEC9 ↑1368  -23 1402 1359  16      38  106.15 DEC9↑927 -14 924 26  525  23
MAR0 ↓1406  -23 1440 1422   6      25  107.68 MAR0↓950 -13 948 50   71  19
MAY0  1431  -23                            MAY0↓969 -12     70   21

                   Key Foreign Exchange Rates
GBP 1.6306/1.6311  EUR 1.1269/1.1274     JPY 114.27/114.32  CHF 1.4155/1.4165
XAU 289.90/290.30  XAG 5.76 /5.79        MYR 3.7900/3.8000  AUD 0.6490/0.6500

   Cocoa News [COC]  Softs News [SOF]  Full Cocoa Index <COCOA1>
   Global Cocoa Physical Prices <O#COCOA>       Other FX Rates <FX=S>
        Have You Seen Our new speed guide page <COMMOD>.
Please click on <COFWLD> & <SUGWLD> for other Market Summaries.
```

1271 − 1256 = 15

For energy spreads you may find the page below to be useful. This page gives intermonth spreads for a range of energy futures contracts traded on NYMEX and IPE. See also OILARB at left.

```
OILARB         Energy Futures Inter-Market Spreads          10:42
      Brt/Wti Brt/Gsl       No2/Gsl Unl/No2       No2/Wti Unl/Wti  321   211
Month $/Bbl  $/Bbl   Month Cts/Gal Cts/Gal Month  $/Bbl  $/Bbl   $/Bbl $/Bbl
AUG7  1.13   4.00    JUL7  -0.60   4.05    AUG7   2.94   4.46    3.95  3.70
SEP7  1.15   4.12    AUG7  -0.21   3.60    SEP7   3.02   4.15    3.77  3.58
OCT7  1.04   4.28    SEP7  -0.19   2.70    OCT7   3.42   3.71    3.61  3.56
NOV7  0.99   4.34    OCT7  -0.30   0.70    NOV7   3.73   3.43    3.53  3.58
DEC7  1.05   4.50    NOV7  -0.87   -0.70   DEC7   3.93   3.28    3.50  3.61
JAN8  1.11   4.61    DEC7  -1.03   -1.55   JAN8   4.06   3.35    3.59  3.71
FEB8  1.03   4.51    JAN8  -1.28   -1.70   FEB8   4.08   3.54    3.72  3.81
MAR8  1.17   4.46    FEB8  -1.41   -1.30   MAR8   3.81   3.87    3.85  3.84

Help <ENERGY> More Colour Pgs <OILAXS><OILOIL><OILARB><IPEX>
  New At-the-money options chains click on <ENERGY/OPT1> or <O#ENERGY-OPT>
```

```
OILSPD          Energy Futures Inter-Month Spreads          10:43
         Wti                No2     Unl          Brent          Gasoil
Month    $/Bbl   Month    Cts/Gal Cts/Gal Month  $/Bbl   Month  $/Bbl
FEB9/MAR9 -0.14  FEB9/MAR9  -0.45  -1.30  MAR9/APR9 -0.08 FEB9/MAR9 -1.25
MAR9/APR9 -0.08  MAR9/APR9  -0.40  -3.25  APR9/MAY9 -0.16 MAR9/APR9 -1.75
APR9/MAY9 -0.14  APR9/MAY9  -0.50  -1.10  MAY9/JUN9 -0.17 APR9/MAY9 -2.25
MAY9/JUN9 -0.11  MAY9/JUN9  -0.90  -0.45  JUN9/JUL9 -0.21 MAY9/JUN9 -2.00
JUN9/JUL9 -0.20  JUN9/JUL9  -0.80  -0.40  JUL9/AUG9 -0.16 JUN9/JUL9 -1.75
JUL9/AUG9 -0.11  JUL9/AUG9  -1.45  -0.30  AUG9/SEP9 -0.17 JUL9/AUG9 -2.50
AUG9/SEP9 -0.18  AUG9/SEP9  -0.75  -0.15  SEP9/OCT9 -0.15 AUG9/SEP9 -2.75
SEP9/OCT9 -0.07  SEP9/OCT9  -0.05         OCT9/NOV9       SEP9/OCT9

Help <ENERGY> More Colour Pgs <OILAXS><OILOIL><OILARB><IPEX>
  New At-the-money options chains click on <ENERGY/OPT1> or <O#ENERGY-OPT>
```

Arbitrage or Exchange Spreads

This is where market players attempt to profit from the change in price differentials between similar contracts on two exchanges, for example, LIFFE and NYCSCE cocoa or between two products, for example, Arabica and Robusta coffee.

Exchange spreads for coffee, cocoa and sugar are available on Reuters. The exchange spreads are given in the white columns. For example, in this screen for sugar the exchange spreads for NYCSCE and LIFFE Sugar contracts are under the **NYv5** column.

Exchange spreads

In this example of NYCSCE and LIFFE sugar spreads, the LIFFE prices, which are quoted in $/tonne, have to be converted into ¢/lb, the price quotation for the NYCSCE contract, in order to calculate the exchange spreads for these similar sugar futures contracts.

Your notes

The Reuters Commodities & Energy 3000 Pro product provides a **Futures Spreads and Arbitrage Calculator** for analysis and to aid decision making for a variety of market players. The calculator provides two basic types of calculation:

- **Spread study**. This allows you to calculate the spreads between various contract months for a single futures contract, for example, IPE Brent Crude oil.

- **Arbitrage study**. This allows you to calculate the spreads between various contract months across two futures contracts, for example, across Crude oil and Heating oil. In this case the calculator allows the contract conditions to be converted into the same units for comparison purposes.

Spread Study

The **Futures Spreads and Arbitrage Calculator** page is shown at right, specifically viewing the **NYMEX Crude Oil** futures contract, **CL**. Once selected, the spreads are displayed in a matrix. A chart of the futures prices is also displayed – in this case from Mar9 to Oct9. If actually using a calculator, click on any cell of particular spread interest, for example, Apr9 to Sep9 to highlight it. Then double-click on the highlighted cell to see a chart of the differences in historic spread prices.

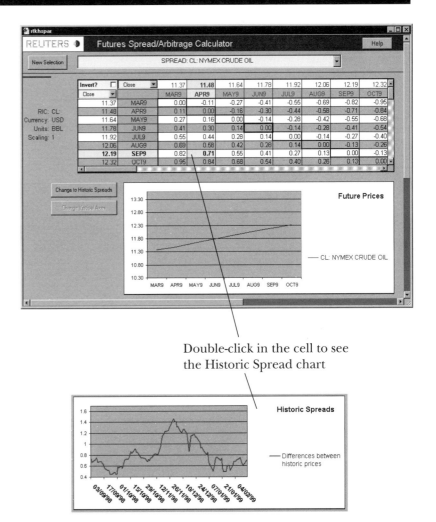

Double-click in the cell to see the Historic Spread chart

What Instruments Are Used in the Markets?

Arbitrage Study

The **Futures Spreads and Arbitrage Calculator** page is shown at right, specifically viewing the **NYMEX Crude Oil** futures contract, **CL,** and the **NYMEX Heating Oil** futures contract, **HO**. Once selected, the arbitrage spreads are displayed in a matrix. A chart of both the futures contracts prices is also displayed – in this case from Mar9 to Oct9. Click on any cell of particular spread interest, for example, Apr9 to Sep9 to highlight it. Then double-click on the highlighted cell to see a chart of the differences in historic spread prices.

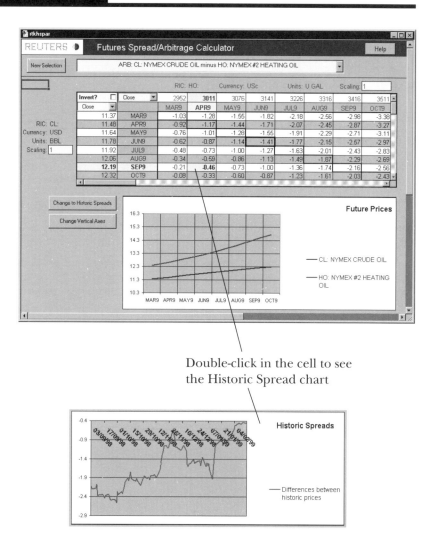

Double-click in the cell to see the Historic Spread chart

REUTERS :::

Energy Spreads

These spreads refer to those used in the energy markets **other** than time and exchange spreads discussed previously. These spreads include the following:

- **Crack spreads**

- **Spark spreads**

- **Frac spreads**

Crack spreads

Petroleum refiners need to buy crude oil in order to sell energy products produced in the **cracking** process– the principal products being unleaded gasoline and heating oil. The market prices for crude oil, unleaded gasoline and heating oil can vary widely depending on factors such as supply and demand, production economics, the weather, political events etc leaving the refiner at risk. In other words there is a **spread** between the price paid for the crude oil and the price received from the cracked products – the **crack spread**.

The crack spread depends on the **refining margin** that a refiner theoretically expects in processing crude oil. The margin is calculated by comparing the selling price of unleaded gasoline and heating oil – converted to $/barrel – with the price paid for the crude oil. If the value of the products is **greater** than the price of crude, then the cracking margin is **positive**; if the value is **less**, then the margin is **negative**.

Crack spreads always reflect the situation on the product side. For example, a **2:1:1 Crack spread** means:

> **2 barrels** of **crude oil** are used to produce **1 barrel** of **unleaded gasoline** and **1 barrel** of **heating oil**.

The gross cracking margin can be calculated as shown in the following example.

Example

Prices:

Crude oil	= $11.99/barrel
Unleaded gasoline	= 0.3635¢/gall
Heating oil	= 0.3422¢/gall

Value of products: (1 barrel = 42 gallons)

Unleaded gasoline	= 0.3635 x 42	= $15.27/barrel
Heating oil	= 0.3422 x 42	= $14.37/barrel
Total value		**= $29.64**

Cost of crude oil:

2 barrels of crude oil	= 2 x 11.99	= **$23.98**

Margin	= 29.64 – 23.98	= $5.66

Margin/barrel	= 5.66 ÷ 2	= **$2.83**

Crack spreads are used by refiners and traders whereby they simultaneously buy or sell crude oil futures and sell or buy unleaded gasoline and heating oil futures.

If crude oil prices are expected to **rise**, while product prices are expected to **fall**, a refiner **sells the crack**. If crude oil prices are expected to **fall**, while product prices are expected to **rise**, a refiner **buys the crack**.

Simultaneous action	Crude oil futures	Unleaded gasoline/ Heating oil futures
Sell the crack	Buy	Sell
Buy the crack	Sell	Buy

What Instruments Are Used in the Markets?

Spark Spreads

These are similar to crack spreads but have been developed for the **electricity** markets as an intermarket spread across electricity and natural gas. In this case the spread involves the simultaneous buying and selling of electricity and natural gas futures contracts, but why?

For power producers who use natural gas as the fuel to convert into electricity, there is a price risk between the time of buying the natural gas and that of selling the electricity. As with crack spreads there are price risks on both the buying and selling sides.

Spark spreads are only effective when natural gas is the fuel and calculations depend on the efficiency of a particular power generation station – in much the same way as refinery margins depend on individual refineries.

This efficiency is termed the **heat rate** and is a measure of the number of Btus of natural gas required to produce 1 Kwh of electricity. To match the trading units of the futures contracts better, the heat rate is expressed as the number of MMBtu of natural gas to produce 1 Mwh of electricity.

Example

The heat rate for a particular power station = 10,000.
NYMEX Natural Gas futures contract trading unit = 10,000 MMBtu
NYMEX Electricity futures contract trading unit = 736 Mwh

Therefore 1 Electricity contract equates to 0.736 Natural Gas contract – this is an approximate ratio of 4 Electricity:3 Natural Gas contracts. Heat rates can be used to establish **hedge ratios** for these spark spreads. These hedge ratios are shown in the table below.

Heat rate	Elecricity:Natural Gas contracts	Hedge ratio
8,000	5:3	0.59
10,000	4:3	0.74
12,000	9:8	0.88
13,500	1:1	0.99

Frac Spreads

In this type of energy spread processors are interested in the price of **natural gas** – the raw material – and that of **propane** – the product. Once again the spread is used to hedge price risks on both sides of the process.

The frac spread is quoted in heating value terms – $/MMBtu in order to match the trading units of the futures contracts involved. For example, one NYMEX Propane futures contract for 42,000 gallons represents about 38% of the heating value of one NYMEX Natural Gas contract with a trading unit of 10,000 MMBtu.

The two most popular ratios used for frac spreads are 3:1 or 5:2 Propane:Natural Gas futures.

The Reuters screen below displays the variety of spark and frac spreads about which a market player can obtain data.

```
INTERPRODUCT FUTURES SPREADS                                  ENERGY/SPREAD2
To access information double click on codes in < > or [ ].

=NYMEX INTER-PRODUCT SPREADS===========   =IPE INTER-PRODUCT SPREADS=============
No.2/Natural Gas NYMEX......<O#NG-HO=R>    Gasoil/Brent IPE $/Mton...<O#LGO-LCO=R>
No.2/Crude NYMEX............<O#CL-HO=R>    Gasoil/Brent IPE $/Bbl....<O#LCO-LGO=R>
Unleaded/Crude NYMEX........<O#CL-HU=R>
Unleaded/No.2 NYMEX.........<O#HU-HO=R>    =CROSS EXCHANGE SPREADS=================
Unleaded/Natural Gas NYMEX..<O#NG-HU=R>    Gasoil IPE/WTI NYMEX.......<O#LGO-CL=R>
Crude/Natural Gas NYMEX.....<O#NG-CL=R>    Gasoil IPE/Unleaded NYMEX..<O#LGU-HU=R>
2:1:1 Crack NYMEX ..........<O#CL211=R>    Gasoil IPE/No. 2 NYMEX.....<O#LGO-HO=R>
3:2:1 Crack NYMEX ..........<O#CL321=R>    Brent IPE/Unleaded NYMEX...<O#LCO-HU=R>
5:3:2 Crack NYMEX ..........<O#CL532=R>    Brent IPE/WTI NYMEX........<O#LCO-CL=R>
3:1 Frac NYMEX $/MMBTU.......<O#NG31=R>    Brent IPE/No. 2 NYMEX......<O#LCO-HO=R>
5:2 Frac NYMEX $/MMBTU.......<O#NG52=R>    Natural Gas NYMEX/KCBT .....<O#NG-KG=R>


=RELATED GUIDES=========================   =NEWS and ANALYSIS====================
Inter-Month spreads....<ENERGY/SPREAD1>    Energy Derivatives News ........[O/DRV]
Futures Index.............<ENERGY/FUT1>    All Crude and Product News ..[PROD CRU]
NYMEX Spread OPTIONS see..<ENERGY/OPT2>    Energy News Directory ...<ENERGY/NEWS1>
Exchange spreads ......<ENERGY/SPREAD3>    Energy Diary .................[O/DIARY]
                                           INSIGHT Technical Report .........[O/I]

=====================================================================================
Energy Guide<ENERGY> Derivatives Guide<DERIV>  Energy Futures Guide<ENERGY/FUT1>
     Lost?Selective Access?..<USER/HELP>        Reuters Phone Support ..<PHONE/HELP>
```

REUTERS

Strip Trading

Strip trading is used in the commodity and energy markets in order to hedge positions for several consecutive months forward.

> A **strip trade** is a single transaction which locks in an average price for several months at a time by simultaneously opening a futures position for each month required. The price level of the strip is the average of the futures contracts prices. Strip trades require margin payments in the same way as trading individual futures contracts.

A futures position in a strip is just like any other futures contract in that for any single month, the position can be:

- Liquidated by off-setting the position in the normal way

- Allowed to expire with delivery of the underlying physical commodity

- Exchanged for a physicals position

Strip trades are very important in the energy swaps markets as swaps deals are offset using exchange traded futures contracts. Within this specific market there are two types of strips used:

- A **contract strip** which has a value calculated as a **simple average** of a number of consecutive contract months. This type of strip is used in the US natural gas and electricity markets.

- A **calendar strip** which has a value calculated as a **weighted average** of a number of consecutive contract months. The weightings are determined by the number of business days prior to and after the expiration date for each month's contract. This type of strip is used in the crude oil markets such as for IPE Brent and NYMEX Light crude.

Your notes

What Instruments Are Used in the Markets?

Who Uses Futures Spreads and Strips?

Agricultural Spreads

The agricultural markets by their very nature are seasonal and subject to the effects of weather, natural disasters etc. Market players can hedge positions using spreads rather than outright futures positions. In using a spread a market player is only interested in the relationship between two futures contracts – time or exchange spreads – rather than the outright prices or market direction.

The commodities in the spread must have a reasonably predictable price relationship as has been mentioned already. This means that buying month and selling another forward tends to reduce the risk of a spread over an outright position. However, this is not always the case, especially if the spread crosses crop years. For example, the far contract price may fall, due to an expected surplus of commodity whereas the near contract may increase in value because there are reduced supplies available. The following examples illustrate typical uses of spreads in the agricultural markets.

Example – Soybean time spread
A feed manufacturer is interested in the July/November Soybean spread using CBOT futures contracts. Why is the feed producer interested in this spread? This spread is important as it represents the old-crop to new-crop price differential. In July the old-crop supplies are usually diminishing and the November prices reflect the expected harvest.

If the new-crop supplies are likely to be **low**, then as the old-crop stock levels fall, the price of July futures will **rise**. However, if the new-crop supplies look to be abundant then the effect on the spread is much less.

It is the 25th January 1999 and the producer buys a Jul/Nov CBOT Soybean futures spread contract for 5,000 bushels. The July price is 562.50¢/bu and the November price is 557.00¢/bu. The spread over the contracts on the July side is 5.5¢/bu.

By early February old-crop supplies are diminishing but the harvest is expected to be good. The price of the July contract rises to 563.00¢/bu whereas the November price falls to 551.50¢/bu. The spread is now 11.50¢/bu.

The manufacturer decides to liquidate his position by selling the position and realises a profit of 11.50 – 5.50 = 6.0¢/bu. The profit on the contract is therefore 5,000 x 6.0 = **$300.00**.

As this example shows, the outright prices of the contracts have not featured in the trade – it is the difference in prices that is important.

Example – Cocoa exchange spread
Using the below screen a commodity trader sees that the spread between Cocoa futures on the NYCSCE and LIFFE shows the potential for profit buying contracts on LIFFE and selling on NYCSCE. The contracts are both for the same trading unit of 10 tonnes, but the LIFFE contract is priced in £/tonne whereas the NYCSCE contract is for $/tonne. The spreads indicated in the page have converted the LIFFE prices into $/tonne.

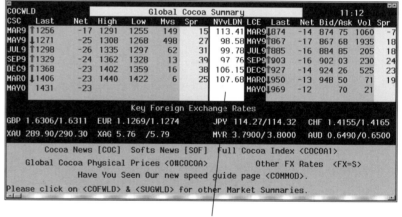

These spreads have been converted into $/tonne

REUTERS :::

Provided any foreign exchange exposure is taken into account for trading such a spread the trader can profit in the long term. But how can the trader assess the long term spread between these contracts? Using Reuters, the long term spread can be charted and used to help determine a trading strategy. The charts here show the closing prices of both Cocoa contracts on LIFFE and NYCSCE together with the interexchange spread for the period April 1993 to January 1999.

Metal Spreads and Ratios

The spread between gold and silver prices has been traded for some considerable time. More recently gold and platinum spreads have been traded but the example that follows describes the well known **Gold/Silver ratio**. This ratio is very simply calculated by dividing the price of gold/oz by that of silver/oz. In other words it represents the number of ounces of silver required to buy one ounce of gold. Using the Reuters screens below, you can obtain the gold and silver fix prices and calculate the gold/silver ratio.

From these pages you can see that the price of gold is \$292.05/oz and that of silver is \$4.995/oz. The gold/silver ratio is therefore:

$$292.05 \div 4.995 = \mathbf{58.47}$$

Over a long period of time gold and silver prices tend to move up and down together. This means that trading the gold/silver ratio can be less risky than trading outright futures contracts – it is the price difference that is important.

Gold/silver ratio trading is carried out on US exchanges such as CBOT and NYMEX where futures contracts on gold and silver can be traded simultaneously.

The gold/silver ratio is used by traders in market sectors other than commodities, for example, it is used in the FX and money markets. The ratio is influenced by a number of factors which account for the cross sector use of the spread. These factors include:

- **Economic indicators** in the US such as the balance of payments and budget deficits which both tend to increase the ratio whereas a slowdown in the economy tends to narrow the spread

- **FX markets** – as the value of the USD strengthens, the ratio tends to narrow

- **Inflation** – as this increases so does the ratio

- **Commodity prices** – as these increase due to crop failures, adverse weather conditions, disasters etc so does the ratio and as prices fall the ratio narrows

Example

The gold/silver ratio can be traded using CBOT Gold kilo and Silver 1,000oz futures contracts for the same delivery month. There are simple strategies for trading the gold/silver ratio:

1. The value of the Gold and Silver futures contracts being traded should be approximately equal

2. If the ratio is expected to **decrease**, then **sell Gold futures/buy Silver futures**

3. If the ratio is expected to **increase**, then **buy Gold futures/sell Silver futures**

Suppose a trader expects the gold/silver ratio to decrease over time. In other words he expects Silver prices to rise faster/fall slower than Gold prices. The trader could buy Silver futures outright or buy a gold/silver spread. The table below shows the advantages of the spread trade in the following circumstances:

In the future...	Gold/silver spread trade	Outright Silver futures contract
Silver prices **rise**/ Gold prices **fall**	Profit	Profit
Silver and Gold prices **rise** but Silver rise is **greater** than Gold	Profit	Profit
Silver prices **static**/ Gold prices **fall**	Profit	Break-even
Silver and Gold prices **fall** but Silver fall is **less** than Gold	Profit	Loss

So trading the gold/silver ratio provides more opportunities for profit but the trader must be accurate with his predictions for the markets.

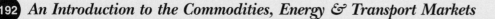

Using programs such as Reuters Graphics, the long term ratio can be charted and used to help determine a trading strategy. The charts here show the closing prices for NYMEX Gold and Silver contracts together with the gold/silver spread for the period May 1993 to January 1999.

Energy Spreads

The following example is that for a simple crack spread of unleaded gasoline/crude oil but the principle can be applied to other energy contracts and the more complicated crack, spark and frac spreads.

It is early January 1999 and a petroleum refiner is looking at the potential refinery unleaded gasoline production margin for April. Using the RT the refiner sees that unleaded gasoline prices are strong. He decides on a unleaded gasoline/crude oil spread hedge strategy which will lock in his refinery margins.

From electronic news services such as Reuters, Bloomberg and Bridge, energy spreads between contracts can be displayed.

```
INTERPRODUCT FUTURES SPREADS                                ENERGY/SPREAD2
To access information double click on codes in < > or [ ].

=NYMEX INTER-PRODUCT SPREADS===========  =IPE INTER-PRODUCT SPREADS===========
No.2/Natural Gas NYMEX......<O#NG-HO=R>  Gasoil/Brent IPE $/Mton...<O#LGO-LCO=R>
No.2/Crude NYMEX............<O#CL-HO=R>  Gasoil/Brent IPE $/Bbl....<O#LCO-LGO=R>
Unleaded/Crude NYMEX........<O#CL-HU=R>
Unleaded/No.2 NYMEX.........<O#HU-HO=R>  =CROSS EXCHANGE SPREADS===============
Unleaded/Natural Gas NYMEX..<O#NG-HU=R>  Gasoil IPE/WTI NYMEX      <O#LGO-CL=R>

O#CL-HU=R              REU/      WTI/NYUnl Sprd    USD   Status OPN
Mth          Last    Net.Ch    Close   Open    High    Low  Time
FEB9/FEB9   ↑+2.72   +0.02     +2.70   +2.53   +2.93   +2.52 15:49
MAR9/MAR9   ↓+3.11   -0.03     +3.14   +2.85   +3.40   +2.80 15:49
APR9/APR9   ↓+4.38   +0.01     +4.37   +4.44   +4.82   +4.26 15:48
MAY9/MAY9   ↑+4.73   +0.07     +4.66   +4.52   +5.01   +4.52 15:44
JUN9/JUN9   ↓+4.75   -0.07     +4.82   +5.04   +5.29   +4.71 15:47
JUL9/JUL9   ↑+4.78   -0.07     +4.85   +5.16   +5.16   +4.66 15:29
AUG9/AUG9   ↓+4.80   +0.01     +4.79   +5.24   +5.31   +4.31 15:28
SEP9/SEP9   ↑+4.68   +0.04     +4.64   +4.68   +4.72   +4.64 15:29
OCT9/OCT9   ↑+4.11   +0.08     +4.03   +3.16   +4.16   +3.11 15:42
NOV9/NOV9   ↑+3.85   +0.11     +3.74   +3.81   +3.85   +3.81 15:28
DEC9/DEC9   ↓+3.62   +0.01     +3.61   +3.63   +3.73   +3.58 15:46
JAN0/JAN0    +3.53   +0.05     +3.48   +3.53   +3.53   +3.53 15:01
                                                            19:13
                                                            19:56
                                                            18:59
```

From the Reuters screen above, the refiner sees that the Apr9/Apr9 spread is +4.38 – this means $4.38/barrel in favour of the unleaded gasoline. But how is this spread determined?

What Instruments Are Used in the Markets?

The spread between April Unleaded gasoline and Crude oil futures prices is determined as follows (1 barrel = 42 gallons):

Unleaded gasoline futures price
= 40.66¢/gall
= 40.66 x 42
= $17.08/bl

Crude oil futures price   = $12.70/bl

Unleaded gasoline/Crude oil spread = $4.38/bl

This is how the spread works in practice:

Cash	Futures
January	**January** Refiner sells crack APR spread Buys Crude oil futures @ $12.70/bl Sells Unleaded gasoline futures ($0.4066/gall) @ $17.08/bl Net spread $4.38/bl
April Buys Crude oil @ $13.20/bl Sells Unleaded gasoline ($0.4100/gall) @ $17.22/bl Net spread $4.02/bl Cash margin $4.02/bl	**April** Refiner buys crack APR spread Sells Crude oil futures @ $13.20/bl Buys Unleaded gasoline futures ($0.4100/gall) @ $17.22/bl Net spread $4.02/bl Futures gain $0.36/bl
Overall margin using spread = 4.02 + 0.36 = **$4.38/bl**	

Using the crack spread the refiner has locked in the margin decided in January.

Strips Trading

The following example is that of a strip trade for the base metal Copper. However strip trades are used quite extensively in the energy markets and the principles are the same in both the commodity and energy markets.

A US manufacturer of Copper wire has a contract with a smelter for a monthly supply of Copper cathodes based on a monthly average price when the metal is shipped.

The Copper market is currently contango and the manufacturer wants to fix the price he pays for the copper over the next 6 months. The manufacturer uses 125 tons of Copper each month. To hedge this position 100% the Manufacture will need to buy 10 COMEX High Grade Copper contracts with a trading unit of 25,000lbs/contract.

The COMEX contracts have monthly delivery dates so the manufacturer can hedge his position by buying a strip of 10 futures contracts for the next 6 months – 60 contracts in total.

The manufacturer uses his news service to display the latest prices for COMEX High Grade Copper futures.

```
O#HG:          CMX/    HI/GRADE COPPER   USc
Mth   Last                    Bid     Ask    Size
JAN9  ↑65.50   -0.75                           /
FEB9  ↓65.50   -1.00                           /
MAR9  ↑66.35   -0.60                           /
APR9  ↓66.50   -0.85                           /
MAY9  ↑67.15   -0.60                           /
JUN9  ↓67.35   -0.80                           /
JUL9  ↑68.05   -0.45                           /
AUG9  A68.90            IMQ 67.85   68.90    3/2
SEP9  A69.20            IMQ 68.45   69.20    3/2
```

The strip price for the 6 months January–June is calculated as the average of these futures prices

The manufacturer locks in the hedge price for the next 6 months – January to June 1999 – at an average price of:

$$(65.50 + 65.50 + 66.35 + 66.50 + 66.15 + 67.35) \div 6 = \textbf{66.23¢/lb}$$

If the manufacturer takes delivery of Copper from his supplier, then the futures contracts for the relevant month must be liquidated. However, the manufacturer can, if required, take delivery of the Copper if his production circumstances change.

As with any other hedge any gain or loss for a particular month's futures position will be compensated by a loss or gain in the cash market.

Futures Spreads and Strips

- A **futures spread** is the difference in prices or basis between delivery months in the same or different markets. The purpose of such a spread is to profit from any change in price differential. The absolute prices of the futures contracts involved are not important – only their price difference.

- Spreads include the following:
  - **Intermonth** and **basis**
  - **Exchange spreads** – Arbitrage spreads
  - **Energy spreads** – Crack, Spark and Frac

- A **futures strip** trade is a single transaction which locks in an average price for a future period by simultaneously opening a futures position for each contract period required. The price level of the strip is the average of the futures contract prices.

- Strips include the following:
  - **Contract strips**
  - **Calendar strips**

Using Reuters Products

The following exercises using Reuters screens may help your understanding of Futures Spreads and Strips and how they are used.

Reuters screens will show the following types of energy futures spreads:

- Intermonth spreads
- Exchange spreads
- Interproduct spreads

At right is the **Interproducts Futures Spreads Speed Guide**. Below that is **Intermonth Spreads** showing Buy/Sell prices for Brent IPE intermonth spreads. Next, from the Interproduct Futures Spreads page – and the Cross Exchange Spreads section – go to the **Brent IPE/WTI NYMEX** field to see the spreads between crude oil futures on the IPE and NYMEX. Under **IPE Inter-product Spreads** at the **Gasoil/Brent IPE $/Bbl** field **<0#LCO-LGO=R>** – to see the spreads between Gasoil and Brent futures on the IPE expressed as USD per barrel.

```
INTERPRODUCT FUTURES SPREADS - REUTERS SPEED GUIDE          ENERGY/SPREAD1
To access information double click on codes in < > or [ ].

=INTERMONTH SPREAD====================   =NEWS and ANALYSIS==================
Gasoil IPE...................<O#LGO=R>    All Energy News ..................[0]
Brent IPE....................<O#LCO=R>    Energy Derivatives News .......[0/DRV]
Gasoline IPE.................<O#LGA=R>    Energy News Directory ..<ENERGY/NEWS1>
Light Crude (WTI) NYMEX......<O#CL=R>     Energy Diary ...............[0/DIARY]
 Exchange published spreads ...<O#CL-:>   INSIGHT Technical Report ........[0/I]
No.2 Heating Oil NYMEX........<O#HO=R>
 Exchange published spreads ...<O#HO-:>   =RELATED GUIDES=====================
Unleaded Gasoline NYMEX.......<O#HU=R>    NYMEX Spread Options.....<ENERGY/OPT2>
 Exchange published spreads ...<O#HU-:>   Inter-Product spreads..<ENERGY/SPREAD2>
Natural Gas NYMEX............<O#NG=R>     Exchange spreads......<ENERGY/SPREAD3>
 Exchange published spreads ...<O#NG-:>   Spread Formulae.......<ENERGY/SPREAD4>
Brent Sinex..................<O#SCO=R>    Futures Index..........<ENERGY/FUT1>
Natural Gas KCBT.............<O#KG=R>

=CLOUR COMPOSITE DISPLAYS===============
Inter-month Spreads ..........<OILSPD>
Inter-product Arbs ...........<OILARB>
```

```
O#LCO=R         REU/    /Brent spreads    USD   Status OPN
Mth      Last   Net.Ch   Buy   Sell  Close   Open   High    Low   Time
MAY9/JUN9 B ↑+0.04  +0.02  +0.04        +0.02  +0.04  +0.04  -0.01  10:48
JUN9/JUL9 B ↑+0.05  +0.07  +0.07  +0.03 -0.02  +0.05  +0.07  +0.02  10:50
JUL9/AUG9 C ↓-0.04  -0.19  +0.05  -0.02 +0.15     0   +0.03  -0.04  10:50
AUG9/SEP9 C ↓-0.02  +0.15              -0.17  +0.01  +0.01  -0.02  10:31
SEP9/OCT9 B  0       0                    0      0      0      0   10:25
OCT9/NOV9 B ↑+0.04  -0.30              +0.34  +0.01  +0.04  +0.01  10:40
NOV9/DEC9 B ↑+0.06  +0.36              -0.30  +0.01  +0.06  +0.01  10:45
DEC9/JAN0                              +0.34                        20:02
```

These spreads are calculated by Reuters for contiguous month pairs – exchanges may list any month pairs that have been traded

```
INTERPRODUCT FUTURES SPREADS                              ENERGY/SPREAD2
To access information double click on codes in < > or [ ].

=NYMEX INTER-PRODUCT SPREADS===========   =IPE INTER-PRODUCT SPREADS=============
No.2/Natural Gas NYMEX......<O#NG-HO=R>   Gasoil/Brent IPE $/Mton...<O#LGO-LCO=R>
No.2/Crude NYMEX............<O#CL-HO=R>   Gasoil/Brent IPE $/Bbl....<O#LCO-LGO=R>
Unleaded/Crude NYMEX........<O#CL-HU=R>
Unleaded/No.2 NYMEX.........<O#HU-HO=R>   =CROSS EXCHANGE SPREADS===============
Unleaded/Natural Gas NYMEX..<O#NG-HU=R>   Gasoil IPE/WTI NYMEX.......<O#LGO-CL=R>
Crude/Natural Gas NYMEX.....<O#NG-CL=R>   Gasoil IPE/Unleaded NYMEX..<O#LGO-HU=R>
2:1:1 Crack NYMEX ..........<O#CL211=R>   Gasoil IPE/No. 2 NYMEX.....<O#LGO-HO=R>
3:2:1 Crack NYMEX ..........<O#CL321=R>   Brent IPE/Unleaded NYMEX...<O#LCO-HU=R>
5:3:2 Crack NYMEX ..........<O#CL532=R>   Brent IPE/WTI NYMEX........<O#LCO-CL=R>
3:1 Frac NYMEX $/MMBTU......<O#NG31=R>    Brent IPE/No. 2 NYMEX......<O#LCO-HO=R>
5:2 Frac NYMEX $/MMBTU......<O#NG52=R>    Natural Gas NYMEX/KCBT ....<O#NG-KG=R>

=RELATED GUIDES======================     =NEWS and ANALYSIS==================
Inter-Month spreads....<ENERGY/SPREAD1>   Energy Derivatives News ........[0/DRV]
Futures Index...........<ENERGY/FUT1>     All Crude and Product News ..[PROD CRU]
NYMEX Spread OPTIONS see..<ENERGY/OPT2>   Energy News Directory ...<ENERGY/NEWS1>
Exchange spreads ......<ENERGY/SPREAD3>   Energy Diary .................[0/DIARY]
                                          INSIGHT Technical Report .........[0/I]

Energy Guide<ENERGY> Derivatives Guide<DERIV>  Energy Futures Guide<ENERGY/FUT1>
   Lost?Selective Access?..<USER/HELP>    Reuters Phone Support ..<PHONE/HELP>
```

```
O#LCO-LGO=R      REU/    Brent/GasOil Spr  USD   Status OPN
Mth      Last   Net.Ch   Buy   Sell  Close   Open   High
MAY9/MAY9 ↑+2.72  -0.05  +2.72        +2.77  +2.88  +2.88
JUN9/JUN9 ↑+2.79  +0.02  +2.83        +2.77  +2.87  +2.89
JUL9/JUL9 ↑+3.01  +0.09              +2.92  +2.95  +3.09
AUG9/AUG9 ↑+3.15  -0.06              +3.21  +3.23  +3.23
SEP9/SEP9 ↑+3.35  +0.04              +3.31  +3.23  +3.35
OCT9/OCT9 ↑+3.58  +0.06              +3.52  +3.46  +3.58
NOV9/NOV9 ↑+3.59  -0.28              +3.87  +3.56  +3.59
DEC9/DEC9 ↑+4.00   0                +4.00  +4.04  +4.08
JAN0/JAN0
```

```
O#LCO-CL=R       REU/    Brent/WTI Spread  USD   Status OPN
Mth      Last   Net.Ch   Close   Open   High    Low   Time
MAY9/MAY9 ↑+1.73  -0.14  +1.87  +1.77  +1.84  +1.69 10:55
JUN9/JUN9 ↓+1.72  -0.14  +1.86  +1.70  +1.76  +1.68 10:55
JUL9/JUL9 ↑+1.79  +0.01  +1.78  +1.80  +1.80  +1.72 10:50
AUG9/AUG9 ↑+1.77  -0.10  +1.87  +1.75  +1.77  +1.72 10:54
SEP9/SEP9 ↑+1.59  -0.06  +1.65  +1.46  +1.59  +1.46 10:24
OCT9/OCT9 ↑+1.55  -0.05  +1.60  +1.43  +1.55  +1.43 10:25
NOV9/NOV9 ↑+1.59  -0.30  +1.89  +1.77  +1.77  +1.56 10:40
DEC9/DEC9 ↓+1.49  -0.09  +1.58  +1.44  +1.58  +1.44 10:46
JAN0/JAN0                +1.92                       19:36
```

The **Interproducts Futures Spreads Speed Guide** at right accesses spreads directly from NYMEX. From the **Light Crude (WTI) NYMEX** field see an **Intermonth Spread**. From the **Crude Versus Unleaded** field, look at the NYMEX **Inter-product Spread**.

The screen below shows how energy spreads are calculated.

```
EXPLANATION OF FUTURES SPREADS                          ENERGY/SPREAD4
To access information double click on codes in < >.

Chain        Units    FORMULA                       Click to view chain
========     =====    ==========================    ===================
LGO-HO=R     $/Tonne  LGO - (HO×3.1332)             <O#LGO-HO=R>
HO-LGO=R     Cts/Gal  (LGO/3.1332) - HO             <O#HO-LGO=R>
LCO-LGO=R    $/Bbl    (LGO/7.46) - LCO              <O#LCO-LGO=R>
LCO-HO=R     $/Bbl    (HO×0.42) - LCO               <O#LCO-HO=R>
CL-LCO=R     $/Bbl    CL-LCO                        <O#CL-LCO=R>
CL-LGO=R     $/Bbl    (LGO/7.46) - CL               <O#CL-LGO=R>
HU-HO=R      Cts/Gal  HU-HO                         <O#HU-HO=R>
CL-HO=R      $/Bbl    (HO×0.42) - CL                <O#CL-HO=R>
CL-HU=R      $/Bbl    (HU×0.42) - CL                <O#CL-HU=R>
CL211=R      $/Bbl    ((HU×0.42 + HO×0.42)/2)  - CL <O#CL211=R>
CL321=R      $/Bbl    ((HU×0.84 + HO×0.42)/3)  - CL <O#CL321=R>
NG-CL=R      $/MMTU   (CL / 5.825) - NG             <O#NG-CL=R>
Note: the units of measure of the spread is determined by the natural units of
the instrument that comes first in the code. Thus, a spread between NYMEX No.2
oil (HO) and IPE Gasoil (LGO) can be displayed in $/Tonne if entered as LGO-HO=R
or it can be displayed as Cts/Gallon if entered as HO-LGO=R. Similarly, CL-HO=R
will display in $/Bbl while HO-CL=R will display in Cts/Gallon.
=========================================================================
Energy Guide<ENERGY> Derivatives Guide<DERIV>  Energy Futures Guide<ENERGY/FUT1>
   Lost?Selective Access?..<USER/HELP>    Reuters Phone Support ..<PHONE/HELP>
```

```
INTERPRODUCT FUTURES SPREADS - REUTERS SPEED GUIDE          ENERGY/SPREAD3
To access information double click on codes in < >.

=INTERMONTH SPREAD===================  =NYMEX INTER-PRODUCT SPREADS==========
Light Crude (WTI) NYMEX........<O#CL-:>  Crude versus Unleaded .......<O#CL-HU:>
No.2 Heating Oil NYMEX.........<O#HO-:>  Crude versus Heating Oil.....<O#CL-HO:>
Unleaded Gasoline NYMEX........<O#HU-:>  Heating Oil versus Unleaded .<O#HO-HU:>
Natural Gas NYMEX..............<O#NG-:>

The above listed spread chains are updated directly from the exchange. These
may differ from the Reuters calculated spreads listed on the previous 2 pages.
Where the Reuters spreads are re-calculated with every price change on either
side of a spread, the exchange spreads display traded values from the floor.
The exchange spread chains will also list any month combinations which have
traded, whereas Reuters intermonth spreads display only contiguous month pairs.

                        =RELATED GUIDES======================
                        NYMEX Spread Options.....<ENERGY/OPT2>
                        Inter-Month spreads...<ENERGY/SPREAD1>
                        Inter-Product spreads.<ENERGY/SPREAD2>
                        Spread Formulae ......<ENERGY/SPREAD4>
```

```
O#CL-:              NYM/    CL CL Spread     USD  Status
Mth        Last     Net.Ch  Buy  Sell        Close Open   High   Low   Time
MAR9-APR9  ↓-0.06   -0.01                    -0.05 -0.05  -0.05  -0.06 04:29
MAR9-MAY9  ↑-0.13                            -0.13 -0.14  -0.13  -0.14 08:47
MAR9-JUN9  CT-0.28  +0.03                    -0.28              17:18
MAR9-AUG9  CT-0.38  +0.06                    -0.38              19:34
MAR9-AUG9  CT-0.37  +0.07                    -0.37              16:46
MAR9-SEP9  CT-0.49  +0.03                    -0.49              14:53
MAR9-OCT9  CT-0.81  +0.18                    -0.81              19:32
MAR9-DEC9  CT-1.08  +0.02                    -1.08              19:14
MAR9-JAN0  CT-1.10  -0.15                    -1.10              15:50
APR9-MAY9  CT-0.09  +0.02                    -0.09              19:46
APR9-JUN9  ↑-0.20   +0.02                    -0.22 -0.20  -0.20  -0.20 04:04
APR9-JUL9  CT-0.34  -0.07                    -0.34              18:39
APR9-OCT9  CT-0.79  -0.03                    -0.79              19:34
APR9-NOV9  CT-0.88  +0.04                    -0.88              19:56
APR9-DEC9  CT-1.05  -0.20                    -1.05              19:49
APR9-JAN0  CT-1.13  -0.15                    -1.13              17:22
MAY9-JUN9  CT-0.12  +0.01                    -0.12              19:22
MAY9-JUL9  CT-0.24  +0.01                    -0.24              20:06
MAY9-AUG9  CT-0.34  +0.01                    -0.34              12:52
MAY9-SEP9  CT-0.54  -0.04                    -0.54              19:44
MAY9-NOV9  CT-0.79  +0.41                    -0.79              17:56
MAY9-DEC9  CT-0.93                           -0.93              17:30
MAY9-APR1                                                       16:35
MAY9-DEC1  CT-3.35                           -3.35              15:10
JUN9-JUL9  CT-0.13                           -0.13              15:24
JUN9-AUG9  CT-0.26  +0.01                    -0.26              18:39
JUN9-OCT9  CT-0.54  +0.02                    -0.54              16:50
JUN9-NOV9  CT-0.68  -0.01                    -0.68              16:07
JUN9-DEC9  CT-0.83  -0.01                    -0.83              15:19
JUN9-JUN0  CT-1.50  +0.04                    -1.50              19:24
JUN9-DEC0  CT-2.22  +0.23                    -2.22              15:11
JUL9-AUG9  CT-0.14                           -0.14              18:47
```

```
O#CL-HU:            NYM/    CL HU Spread     USc  Status
Mth        Last     Net.Ch  Buy  Sell        Close Open   High   Low   Time
MAR9-FEB9  CT+2.65  +0.25                    +2.65              20:37
MAR9-MAR9  ↑+3.22   +0.02                    +3.20 +3.22  +3.22  +3.22 21:37
APR9-MAR9  CT+2.85  -0.12                    +2.85              20:32
APR9-APR9  CT+4.28  +0.01                    +4.28              15:24
MAY9-MAY9  CT+4.66  -0.01                    +4.66              16:26
JUN9-JUN9  CT+4.89  +0.09                    +4.89              19:58
JUL9-JUL9  CT+4.90  +0.10                    +4.90              16:55
AUG9-AUG9  CT+4.95  +0.05                    +4.95              18:51
OCT9-MAR9  CT+2.20                           +2.20              17:31
```

The **Futures Spreads and Arbitrage Calculator** shows a **Spread** study for a commodity futures contract the **LIFFE Cocoa** contract **LCC:**. Once the data is displayed, click on the **Change to Historic Spreads** button to display the difference between historic spreads.

Now set up an **Arbitrage** study for the spread between LIFFE Cocoa and the equivalent contract traded on NYCSCE – **CC:**. Once the data is displayed, click on the **Change Vertical Axes** button to show the price data for both futures contracts.

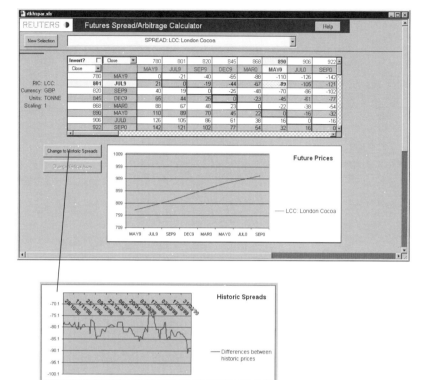

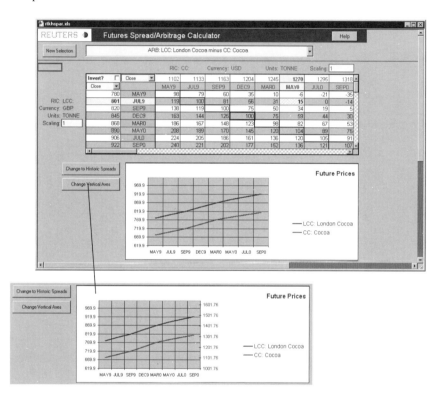

What Are the Exchange of Futures for Physicals or Swaps?

An **Exchange of Futures for Physicals (EFP)** is simply an exchange of a futures position for a physical one. EFP counterparties agree to swap cash or a physical position for an equivalent futures position or to establish opposite positions to each other in both the cash and futures markets.

An **Exchange of Futures for Swaps (EFS)** follows the same principles as those for EFPs but the instruments used are futures and swaps.

If you need an overview of futures derivatives, or you need to remind yourself about derivatives in general, then you may find it useful to refer to the *Introduction to Derivatives* book (ISBN 0-471-83176-X) in this series.

As has been mentioned previously, less than 5% of exchange traded futures contracts result in physical delivery. Most futures contracts are liquidated before the contract expires by the market player taking an equal and opposite position to that held. However, if a market player does want to take physical delivery on expiry it is possible for the exchange contract delivery specification to be varied. Under certain circumstances, rather than accepting standard delivery conditions, the buyer of the futures contract can arrange an **Alternative Delivery Procedure (ADP)** or an **EFP**.

Alternative Delivery Procedure (ADP)
For this type of delivery the buyer and the seller who have been matched by the Clearing house arrange delivery terms and conditions which are different from those specified for the futures contract. The market players have to release the Clearing house and clearing members from the contract details relating to the delivery terms and replace them with those that have been negotiated for the ADP. In other words this type of delivery is a private arrangement negotiated after the futures positions have been matched – the counterparties cannot choose with whom they are matched.

Exchange of Futures for Physicals (EFP)
This type of transaction allows market players to choose their trading partners, delivery site, grade of product to be delivered and the time of delivery. The quantity of cash commodity must be approximately equal to the quantity involved in the futures contract. The price for the EFP is agreed first and then cleared with the Clearing house. After the exchange has been notified of the transaction, the actual physical price involved in the EFP depends on the negotiated price between buyer and seller. EFPs are available for a number of commodities and energy futures contracts on worldwide exchanges such as NYMEX and IPE.

EFPs are used by market players for the following:

- To open a futures position
- To liquidate a futures position
- To transfer a futures position
- To price/cost a position for a different time of delivery
- To hedge a position and lock in prices

The following chart shows the number of EFPs for energy futures on NYMEX in 1996.

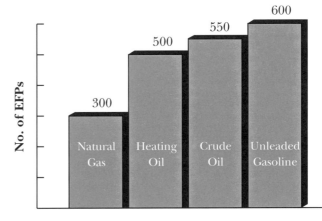

Source: NYMEX 1996

Exchanges require written documentation of EFPs. The exact terms and conditions of this documentation vary from exchange to exchange but usually form part of the general specification for a futures contract.

Most EFP documentation requires the following details:

- A statement that the EFP is be effected which will result in a change of ownership of the underlying commodity

- Date of the transaction

- Type and quantity of futures contract involved

- Price at which the EFP is to be cleared

- Clearing members involved in the transaction

Evidence of any changes in ownership of the underlying commodity, together with any payments received by the seller must be made available to the Exchange upon request. This is to satisfy the Exchange that the EFP transaction between the buyer and the seller is legitimate.

These pages on the right show energy futures specifications. The Futures Exchanges' oil contracts give details for IPE and NYMEX contracts.

New York Mercantile Exchange
NYMEX/COMEX. Two divisions, one marketplace.

futures and options home | contract specifications | | request information |

Coal Futures and Options
Contract Specifications

Trading Unit
Futures: 37,200 million British thermal units (MMBtus) of coal.
Options: One NYMEX Division coal futures contract.

Trading Hours
To be determined.

Trading Months
Futures: 18 consecutive months.
Options: To be determined.

Price Quotations
Futures and options: U.S. dollars and cents per MMBtu.

Minimum Price Fluctuation
Futures and options: $.001 per MMBtu ($37.20 per contract).

Maximum Price Fluctuation
Futures: Maximum daily price fluctuation in all but the first two months shall be $0.10 per MMBtu above or below the preceding day's settlement price. If the market settles at $0.10 above or below the previous day's settlement price, the maximum permissible fluctuation in either direction for all months during the next business session shall be $0.20. The expanded limit shall remain in effect until there are two trading days in which no month settles at the expanded limit.
In the closest two months of trading, the maximum daily price fluctuation will be $1.00, applied in two stages.
Options: No price limits.

Last Trading Day
Futures: Trading terminates on the fourth business day prior to the first day of the delivery month.
Options: Expiration occurs on the business day preceding the futures contract termination.

Exercise of Options
By a clearing member to the Exchange clearinghouse not later than 5:30 P.M., or 45 minutes after the underlying futures settlement price is posted, whichever is later, on any day up to and including options expiration.

Options Strike Prices
Twenty strike prices in increments of $0.01 per MMBtu above and below the at-the-money strike price, and the next 10 strike prices in increments of $0.05 above the highest and below the lowest one-cent increment. The at-the-money strike price is closest to the previous day's futures settlement price.

Contract Delivery Unit
The seller shall deliver 1,550 tons of coal per contract. A loading tolerance of 60 tons or 2%, whichever is greater, over the total number of contracts delivered is permitted. The MMBtus of coal is determined by multiplying the weight of the coal by the heat content of the coal as determined by testing procedures.

Delivery Location
At a delivery facility on the Ohio River between Milepost 306 and 317, or on the Big Sandy River. There will be a discount of $.004 per MMBtu below the final settlement price for any delivery to a terminal on the Big Sandy River.

Heat Content
Minimum of 12,000 Btus per pound, gross calorific value, with an analysis tolerance of 250 Btus per pound.

Ash Content
Maximum of 13.5% by weight with no analysis tolerance.

Sulfur Content
Maximum of 1.0%, measured by weight or in pounds of sulfur dioxide per MMBtu, with analysis tolerance of .05%.

Moisture Content
Surface or inherent moisture at a maximum of 10% by weight with no analysis tolerance.

Volatile Matter
Minimum of 30% gas or vapor products exclusive of moisture given off by combustion of the coal — with no analysis tolerance.

Hardness/Grindability
Minimum 41 Hardgrove Index with three point analysis tolerance below. Hardness measures how difficult it is to pulverize coal for injection into the boiler flame.

Size
Three inches topsize, nominal, with a maximum of 55% passing one-quarter-inch-square wire cloth sieve or smaller, to be determined on the basis of the primary cutter of the mechanical sampling system.

Exchange of Futures for, or in Connection with, Physicals (EFP)
The buyer or seller may exchange a futures position for a physical position of equal quantity/quality by submitting a notice to the Exchange. EFPs may be used either to initiate or liquidate a futures position. The EFP deadline is 10 A.M. (Eastern prevailing time) on the first business day following termination of trading.

Position Limits
5,000 contracts for all months combined, but not to exceed 3,500 in any one month or 200 in the last three days of trading in the spot month.

July 8, 1999

BRENT CRUDE FUTURES: Delivery mechanism

Cessation of trading
Trading shall cease at the close of business on the business day immediately preceding the 15th day prior to the first day of the delivery month, if such 15th day is a banking day in London. If the 15th day is a non-banking day in London (including Saturday), trading shall cease on the business day immediately preceding the first business day prior to the 15th day. These dates are published by the Exchange.

Delivery/settlement basis
The IPE Brent Crude futures contract is a deliverable contract based on EFP delivery with an option to cash settle against the published settlement price i.e. the Brent Index price for the day following the last trading day of the futures contract. If the contract is to be subject to the cash settlement procedure notice must be given (in accordance with LCH procedures) up to one hour after cessation of trading.

Brent Index
The Exchange issues, on a daily basis at 12 noon local time, the Brent Index which is the weighted average of the prices of all confirmed 15-day Brent deals throughout the previous trading day for the appropriate delivery month. These prices are published by the independent price reporting services used by the oil industry.

The index is calculated as an average of the following elements

1. A weighted average of first month trades in the 15-day market.

2. A weighted average of second month trades in the 15-day market plus or minus a straight average of the spread trades between the first and second months.

3. A straight average of all the assessments published in media reports.

Payment
Payment for contracts subject to the cash settlement procedure takes place through LCH within two business days of the cessation of trading.

Exchange of Futures for Physical (EFP) and Exchange of Futures for Swaps (EFS)
EFPs or EFSs may be reported to the Exchange during trading hours and registered by LCH up to one hour after the cessation of trading in the delivery month in which the EFP or EFS is traded. These allow more effective hedging opportunities for market participants with over-the-counter positions.

Law
The contract is governed by English law and includes provisions regarding force majeure, trade emergency and embargoes.

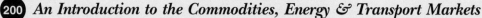

Who Uses Exchange of Futures Contracts?

Energy Markets

Although EFPs are available for many futures contracts on worldwide exchanges they are most commonly used in the energy markets. The principles and examples outlined below can be applied to EFPs on any commodity. The use of EFPs can be quite complex and the following examples illustrate the simple use of EFPs in two situations:

- To open a futures position

- To liquidate a futures position

Example – Using an EFP to open a futures position

An oil refiner has sold heating oil to a distributor at a fixed price and needs to buy in a cargo of sweet crude oil for future delivery to meet the heating oil supply to the distributor. The refiner contacts his broker who sets up a deal with an oil producer who can supply the exact feedstock required for the heating oil. The refiner thinks that the producer's price is high and needs to hedge his position. The producer also needs to hedge his position. At this stage neither the producer nor the refiner hold a futures position.

The producer agrees to sell the refiner a cargo of sweet crude oil. The price will be based on the official closing price of IPE Brent crude oil at the end of the trade date plus a differential.

The producer executes an EFP which establishes simultaneous hedges for both refiner and producer and opens a futures position. In order to execute the EFP the producer instructs his broker of the deal and provides details of the trade and the refiner's broker. The refiner's broker passes the futures contract to the producer's broker in one lot, not across the trading floor of the IPE. The transaction is registered with the IPE – the trade price is not registered but the volume of the transaction is.

The situation is summarised in the diagram and table below.

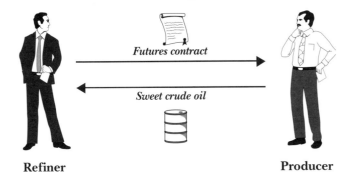

Futures contract

Sweet crude oil

Refiner   **Producer**

Refiner	Producer
• **Buys** crude oil – **long** in cash market	• **Sells** crude oil – **short** in cash market
• **Sells** EFP futures contract – **short** in futures	• **Buys** EFP futures contract – **long** in futures
• Futures position can be bought back when required	• Futures position can be sold back when required
• Final price of oil is only fixed when the futures position is liquidated	• Final price of oil is only fixed when the futures position is liquidated
• The only part of the transaction at risk is the differential paid	• The only part of the transaction at risk is the differential received
Overall The refiner has completed the physical purchase of the required type of crude oil and the position has been hedged.	**Overall** In effect the producer has exchanged crude oil for a futures position. The net position is the differential agreed.

Example – Using an EFP to liquidate a futures position
In this case a refiner needs crude oil as a feedstock but has already bought futures contracts for crude oil on NYMEX. The oil producer, who has the required feedstock, has sold futures contracts on the exchange.

Using a broker the refiner and producer agree an EFP on NYMEX based on the official closing price plus or minus a differential.

In this case both refiner and producer hold futures positions and the EFP involves identical numbers of NYMEX futures contracts for the same month.

The situation is summarised in the diagram and table below.

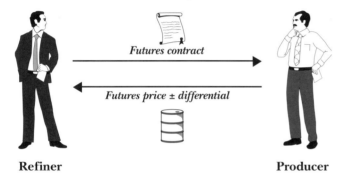

Futures contract

Futures price ± differential

Refiner   **Producer**

Refiner	Producer
• **Buys** crude oil at Futures price ± differential	• **Sells** crude oil at Futures price ± differential
• **Passes** futures contracts held to the producer – these contracts are not traded on the exchange floor	• **Buys** futures contract from the refiner
• The only part of the transaction at risk is the differential	• The only part of the transaction at risk is the differential received
Overall The refiner takes physical delivery of the crude oil and simultaneously liquidates his futures position.	**Overall** The producer sells crude oil and simultaneously liquidates his futures position.

Exchange of Futures for Swaps (EFS)
This type of transaction has been used on the IPE for Brent crude oil futures but more recently NYMEX has launched a 3-year pilot programme for EFSs in the energy markets. On NYMEX the EFS is a privately negotiated OTC swap and futures transaction which must involve futures and swap exposures in the same or related commodities. The price of the EFS is agreed between the two parties and NYMEX must be informed of the futures contracts involved in the swap and the futures price at which the transaction has to be cleared. As with EFPs , EFSs can be used to liquidate or initiate a futures position.

Exchange of Futures Contracts

- An **Exchange of Futures for Physicals (EFP)** is simply an exchange of a futures position for a physical one. EFP counterparties agree to swap cash or a physical position for an equivalent futures position or to establish opposite positions to each other in both the cash and futures markets.

- An **Exchange of Futures for Swaps (EFS)** follows the same principles as those for EFPs but the instruments used are futures and swaps.

Your notes

The top screen displays the **Contract Specification** and details of **Pulp Contracts** traded on OMLX and OM Stockholm. The bottom screen displays the latest information on Exchange For Physicals, EFPs.

These two screens display news on EFPs.

```
PULPEX                                                    PULPEX
OMLX, London              Official Trading Hours 13:00-16:00 (BST)
OM Stockholn, Sweden      Official Trading Hours 14:00-17:00 (CET)

===========PULP CONTRACTS===========  =========CONTRACT SPECIFICATION========

Futures....................<O#PULP:>   PULP FUTURES
Options..................<O#PULP*.pl>  Quality : prime sheeted NBSK wood pulp
                                       Contract Size : 24 air dry netric tons
Futures settlenent price....<PULPSETT> Contract Currency : US Dollars
                                       Daily Settlenent Price : last traded
Bulletin board...............<PULPEY>  price on each business day
                                       PULP OPTIONS
===================================== Contract Base : one futures contract
OM Menu page.................<OM/MENU> Exercise style : european style
```

```
PULPEX                                                    PULPEY
OMLX, London                     OM Stockholn AB
Warrant deli│TEL +44-171-2830678          TEL +46-8-405 60 00

===========│* MARKET PLACE:      PETER AKESSON
OMLX, The Lo│* LEGAL MATTERS:    DEREK OLIVER       ERIK RICKNELL
Derivatives │* DELIVERY&CLEARING: CLIFFORD LAUNDON  ULRIKA JEDENHEIM
107 Cannon S│* MARKETING :       XAVIER BRUCKERT    CLAES BETSHOLTZ
London EC4N │
            │
            │DAILY EXCHANGE FOR PHYSICAL INFORMATION:
            │11.12.98 12 LOT MAR 1999 PULPEX EFP REGISTERED AT 13.01
            │11.12.98 10 LOT JUNE 1999 PULPEX EFP REGISTERED AT 13.01
            │11.12.98 4 LOT SEPT 1999 PULPEX EFP REGISTERED AT 13.01
            │21.12.98 30 LOT MARCH 1999 PULPEX EFP REGISTERED AT 15.56
            │20.01.99 20 LOT MARCH 1999 PULPEX EFP REGISTERED AT 15.30
            │21.01.99 26 LOT JUNE 1999 PULPEX EFP REGISTERED AT 14.55
            │21.01.99 13 LOT SEPT 1999 PULPEX EFP REGISTERED AT 14.55
            │01.10.98 10 LOT DEC 1998 PULPEX EFP REGISTERED AT 15.09
            │23.11.98 4  LOT MAR 1999 PULPEX EFP REGISTERED AT 14.15
            │01.12.98 60 LOT DEC 1998 PULPEX EFP REGISTERED AT 13.35
            │04.12.98 16 LOT MARCH 1999 PULPEX EFP REGISTERED AT 13.01
            │04.12.98 24 LOT JUNE 1999 PULPEX EFP REGISTERED AT 13.01
            │04.12.98 48 LOT JUNE 1999 PULPEX EFP REGISTERED AT 13.01
            │04.12.98 26 LOT SEPT 1999 PULPEX  EFP REGISTERED AT 13.01
```

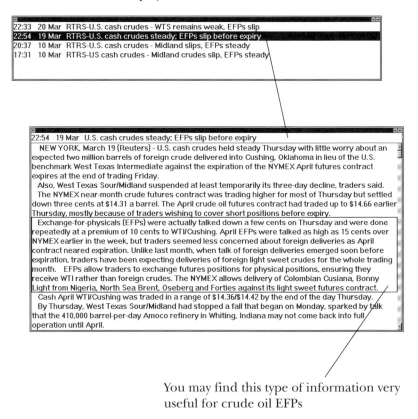

```
22:33  20 Mar  RTRS-U.S. cash crudes - WTS remains weak, EFPs slip
22:54  19 Mar  RTRS-U.S. cash crudes steady; EFPs slip before expiry
20:37  10 Mar  RTRS-U.S. cash crudes - Midland slips, EFPs steady
17:31  10 Mar  RTRS-US cash crudes - Midland crudes slip, EFPs steady
```

22:54 19 Mar U.S. cash crudes steady; EFPs slip before expiry

 NEW YORK, March 19 (Reuters) - U.S. cash crudes held steady Thursday with little worry about an expected two million barrels of foreign crude delivered into Cushing, Oklahoma in lieu of the U.S. benchmark West Texas Intermediate against the expiration of the NYMEX April futures contract expires at the end of trading Friday.
 Also, West Texas Sour/Midland suspended at least temporarily its three-day decline, traders said.
 The NYMEX near-month crude futures contract was trading higher for most of Thursday but settled down three cents at $14.31 a barrel. The April crude oil futures contract had traded up to $14.66 earlier Thursday, mostly because of traders wishing to cover short positions before expiry.
 Exchange-for-physicals (EFPs) were actually talked down a few cents on Thursday and were done repeatedly at a premium of 10 cents to WTI/Cushing. April EFPs were talked as high as 15 cents over NYMEX earlier in the week, but traders seemed less concerned about foreign deliveries as April contract neared expiration. Unlike last month, when talk of foreign deliveries emerged soon before expiration, traders have been expecting deliveries of foreign light sweet crudes for the whole trading month. EFPs allow traders to exchange futures positions for physical positions, ensuring they receive WTI rather than foreign crudes. The NYMEX allows delivery of Colombian Cusiana, Bonny Light from Nigeria, North Sea Brent, Oseberg and Forties against its light sweet futures contract.
 Cash April WTI/Cushing was traded in a range of $14.36/$14.42 by the end of the day Thursday.
 By Thursday, West Texas Sour/Midland had stopped a fall that began on Monday, sparked by talk that the 410,000 barrel-per-day Amoco refinery in Whiting, Indiana may not come back into full operation until April.

You may find this type of information very useful for crude oil EFPs

What Are Commodity or Energy Swaps?

A **commodity or energy swap** is an agreement between counterparties in which at least one set of payments involved is set by the price of the commodity/energy product or by the price of a commodity/energy index.

If you need an overview of swaps derivatives or you need to remind yourself about derivatives in general, then you may find it useful to refer to the *Introduction to Derivatives* book (ISBN 0-471-83176-X) in this series.

The most common examples of Commodity and Energy swaps involve **plain vanilla** OTC agreements for a fixed-for-floating exchange of risk. These are purely financial transactions in which **no delivery** of the physical commodity is involved.

Commodity and Energy swaps are used by many consumers and producers of commodities to hedge price rises over a long term period. For example, bread and biscuit producers hedge grain prices, whilst airlines hedge jet fuel prices.

Since the Gulf War 1990 - 1991 fixed-for-floating **energy swaps** for oil products have become increasingly more important in the derivatives markets. Producers and consumers of commodities are often linked to long term contracts to buy or sell where the delivery price is determined by an index price. This means that the price at delivery is not known until a short time beforehand or until the actual delivery date. Under these conditions there is a considerable floating price risk. The two sides of a fixed-for-floating swap are described in the table opposite.

Floating Price Side	Fixed Price Side
Many organisations have a floating price risk as they buy and sell under contract terms which are linked to an index such as Platt's prices. This means that the actual price is not known until at or near delivery.	Few market players have fixed price term deals any more. The high degree of volatility, particularly for energy products, has deterred traders in the past. Players such as market makers who do buy the fixed side of a swap will offset their risk by opposite positions in the futures or forwards markets.

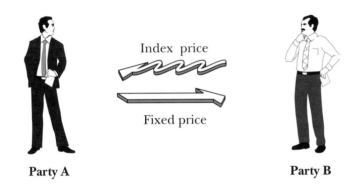

Index price

Fixed price

Party A **Party B**

A plain vanilla swap will therefore guarantee a fixed price for market players such as oil producers who have a floating price risk, regardless of the physical price when the commodity is sold.

What Instruments Are Used in the Markets?

Swaps are traded for specific time periods – typically months, quarters or years. At the end of each time period cash is exchanged between the swap buyer and the swap counterparty depending on the agreed swap price. The direction of the cash flow is as follows:

- If the index price is **lower** than the swap price, then the swap provider **pays** the difference to the swap buyer

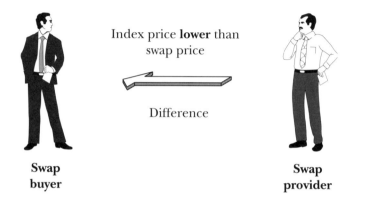

Index price **lower** than swap price

Difference

Swap buyer

Swap provider

- If the index price is **higher** than the swap price, then the swap provider **receives** the difference from the swap buyer

Index price **higher** than swap price

Difference

Swap buyer

Swap provider

But how is the swap price determined by the provider? The greater the time period involved, the greater the risk for the swap provider and the greater the need for the provider to hedge his position. The use of futures contracts **strip trades** as a means of hedging a swap transactions discussed in the *Futures Spreads and Strips* section.

In order to determine a swap price, a market maker will need to review a number of factors which will be derived from the futures strip hedge which include the following:

- **Term structure** of the futures contract to be used.

- **Correlation**. If a swap is directly related to an exchange traded futures contract such as swaps for IPE Brent crude oil, then the correlation is very high. For other swaps, for example, those for Jet fuel, the swap price is linked by a differential to exchange traded Gas oil or Heating oil futures. In these cases the correlation is not so high and the differential has to be assessed accurately. Charting price spreads using Reuters Graphics can be used to determine the differential to be applied.

- **Cost of the hedge using futures strips**. This is the most important factor. A swap provider cannot risk exposure without hedging his position particularly for long term swap trades.

In selling a swap, the provider needs to hedge his position by taking an equivalent contract position to that of the swap – by selling futures contracts. If prices fall, then the futures hedge earns a profit which will help offset the payment to the counterparty. In order to hedge the swap for the whole trade period a matching futures strip must be sold.

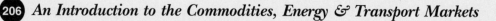

REUTERS

Two types of strips are used commonly:

- A **contract strip** which has a value calculated as a **simple average** of a number of consecutive contract months. This type of strip is used in the US Natural Gas and Electricity markets.

- A **calendar strip** which has a value calculated as a **weighted average** of a number of consecutive contract months. The weightings are determined by the number of business days prior to and after the expiration date for each month's contract. This type of strip is used in the Crude oil markets such as for IPE Brent and NYMEX Light crude.

The calculations involved in determining swap prices are quite complex and most market players use proprietary software. Reuters provides a calculator for some subscribers which displays a term structure chart of the energy futures contracts selected. The screens shown here are for Calendar strips for the NYMEX Crude Oil contract and Contract strips for the NYMEX Palo Verde Electricity contract.

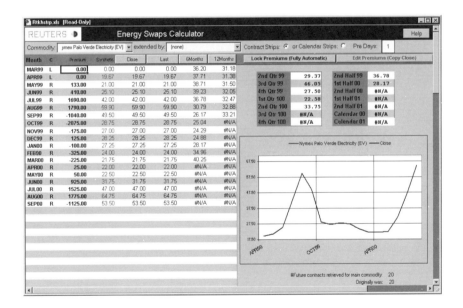

What Instruments Are Used in the Markets?

Who Uses Commodity and Energy Swaps?

Producers and Consumers

The following examples illustrate the use of swaps for energy products and commodities.

Example – a plain vanilla energy swap

 XYZ Airline needs to fix or set ticket prices for up to a year forward which are used to help predict its future revenue. Fuel prices represent approximately 35% of an airline's operating costs so any price fluctuations can seriously affect its profits if ticket prices are fixed. Also, airlines are committed usually to buy jet fuel on long term monthly delivery contracts. These contracts assure delivery but the delivery price is set based on an average monthly index price – typically Platt's prices are used.

XYZ Airline has therefore a fixed revenue from ticket sales but operating costs which can fluctuate widely. How can the airline eliminate or reduce this floating price risk?

There are a number of derivatives XYZ could transact to hedge its risk, for example, futures and options. However, an Energy swap is the most likely instrument as it provides a flexible, long term OTC contract.

Airlines often enter into swap contracts of two years maturity involving payment periods every 6 months where they either pay or receive a cash amount determined by the value of a specific Platt's index oil price. The swap contract relates to a specific amount of oil which the airline is either contracted to take physical delivery of or is bought on the spot market.

By entering into an energy swap agreement the airline effectively locks in the price of its fuel for the two year period.

This is how the swap works...

❶ The airline enters into a swap with a bank

The airline, who has the floating price risk, buys an Energy swap from the AYZ bank and agrees to pay a fixed price to the bank for a series of scheduled payments for the maturity period of the swap.

The seller of the swap, AYZ bank, agrees to pay the airline guaranteed payments based on a Platt's oil price index for each scheduled period.

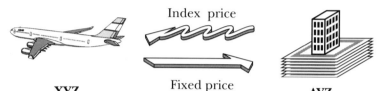

Index price

XYZ   Fixed price   AYZ

Buys oil at spot or contract price based on Platt's

❷ **Counterparties exchange payments**

The difference in payments is netted and a cash amount is paid either to the airline or to the bank.

If oil prices go down, then the airline benefits from lower spot or contract prices but they pay the difference between the fixed and floating prices to the bank.

If oil prices increase, then the airline pays more for the fuel but the bank pays the airline the difference between the fixed and floating prices. This receipt offsets the increased fuel costs.

The overall effect of the Energy swap is that the airline has fixed its costs. The following chart illustrates the process.

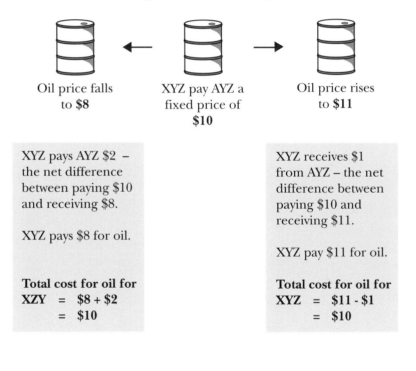

| Oil price falls to **$8** | XYZ pay AYZ a fixed price of **$10** | Oil price rises to **$11** |

| XYZ pays AYZ $2 – the net difference between paying $10 and receiving $8. XYZ pays $8 for oil. **Total cost for oil for** **XZY** = **$8 + $2** = **$10** | XYZ receives $1 from AYZ – the net difference between paying $10 and receiving $11. XYZ pay $11 for oil. **Total cost for oil for** **XYZ** = **$11 - $1** = **$10** |

Example – An industrial buyer of fuel oil

In this example the buyer has bought a swap for 10,000 tons of fuel oil per month to provide a 4-month fixed price of $86.00/ton.

- The swap agreement is for 10,000 tons per month, January to April

- The physical supply agreement is for 10,000 tons ± 5% – a standard contract clause

The following table records what happened. You should note the circumstances in which the swap buyer or seller has to pay and the monthly cost of fuel oil/ton to the buyer – the fixed price remains within 1% of the required price.

Delivery period	Jan	Feb	Mar	Apr
Price Index	85	76	88	94
Contract delivery in tons	10,000	9,500	9,900	10,300
Actual cost, $	850,000	720,200	871,200	968,200
Swap seller pays	0	0	20,000	80,000
Swap buyer pays	10,000	100,000	0	0
Final buyers cost	860,000	822,000	851,200	888,820
Cost/ton to buyer **$/ton**	**86.00**	**86.53**	**85.98**	**86.23**

In this case the hedge is not perfect but it is reasonably good. Although the cost of using the OTC swap may be more expensive than hedging with futures contracts for the industrial buyer, he does not require the services of derivatives traders nor is there a risk of taking physical delivery as the swap is cash settled. Using a swap also provides the buyer with a way of minimising basis risk which is inherent in futures trading. However, there are disadvantages in using swaps in that they are OTC transactions which involve credit risk and counterparty performance.

What Instruments Are Used in the Markets?

As with all OTC markets complete transparency is not possible but you can access swap reports and see some prices using a news service such as Reuters.

The Reuters screen below shows European oil swap trades and associated news.

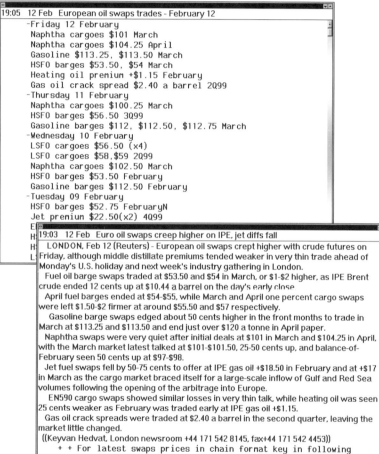

```
19:05   12 Feb  European oil swaps trades - February 12
         -Friday 12 February
         Naphtha cargoes $101 March
         Naphtha cargoes $104.25 April
         Gasoline $113.25, $113.50 March
         HSFO barges $53.50, $54 March
         Heating oil preniun +$1.15 February
         Gas oil crack spread $2.40 a barrel 2Q99
         -Thursday 11 February
         Naphtha cargoes $100.25 March
         HSFO barges $56.50 3Q99
         Gasoline barges $112, $112.50, $112.75 March
         -Wednesday 10 February
         LSFO cargoes $56.50 (x4)
         LSFO cargoes $58,$59 2Q99
         Naphtha cargoes $102.50 March
         HSFO barges $53.50 February
         Gasoline barges $112.50 February
         -Tuesday 09 February
         HSFO barges $52.75 FebruaryN
         Jet preniun $22.50(x2) 4Q99
```

```
19:03   12 Feb  Euro oil swaps creep higher on IPE, jet diffs fall
   LONDON, Feb 12 (Reuters) - European oil swaps crept higher with crude futures on
Friday, although middle distillate premiums tended weaker in very thin trade ahead of
Monday's U.S. holiday and next week's industry gathering in London.
   Fuel oil barge swaps traded at $53.50 and $54 in March, or $1-$2 higher, as IPE Brent
crude ended 12 cents up at $10.44 a barrel on the day's early close.
   April fuel barges ended at $54-$55, while March and April one percent cargo swaps
were left $1.50-$2 firmer at around $55.50 and $57 respectively.
   Gasoline barge swaps edged about 50 cents higher in the front months to trade in
March at $113.25 and $113.50 and end just over $120 a tonne in April paper.
   Naphtha swaps were very quiet after initial deals at $101 in March and $104.25 in April,
with the March market latest talked at $101-$101.50, 25-50 cents up, and balance-of-
February seen 50 cents up at $97-$98.
   Jet fuel swaps fell by 50-75 cents to offer at IPE gas oil +$18.50 in February and at +$17
in March as the cargo market braced itself for a large-scale inflow of Gulf and Red Sea
volumes following the opening of the arbitrage into Europe.
   EN590 cargo swaps showed similar losses in very thin talk, while heating oil was seen
25 cents weaker as February was traded early at IPE gas oil +$1.15.
   Gas oil crack spreads were traded at $2.40 a barrel in the second quarter, leaving the
market little changed.
   ((Keyvan Hedvat, London newsroom +44 171 542 8145, fax+44 171 542 4453))
      + + For latest swaps prices in chain format key in following
chain codes (dropping OH), followed by F3 function: + +
```

Example – A Double swap

There is an increasing use of swaps for base metals such as Copper, Aluminium and Nickel which involve an intermediary – a market-maker. This is in effect a **double swap** where the credit risk is taken on by the market maker rather than between the producer and consumer directly.

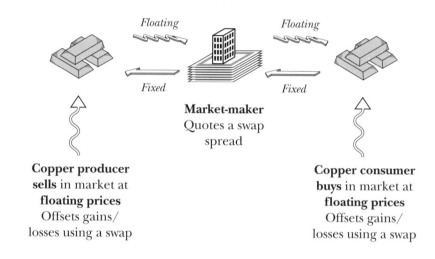

Floating   *Floating*

Fixed   *Fixed*

Market-maker
Quotes a swap spread

Copper producer sells in market at **floating prices**
Offsets gains/losses using a swap

Copper consumer buys in market at **floating prices**
Offsets gains/losses using a swap

REUTERS

Commodity and Energy Swaps

- A Commodity or Energy swap is usually a **plain vanilla** agreement which is purely financial involving **no delivery** of the physical commodity

- Market players on the **floating price** side usually buy and sell under contract terms which are linked to a commodity/ energy index such as Platt's for oil products – this means that the actual delivery price is not known until, at or near delivery

- Market players on the **fixed price** side accept the high degree of risk involved in volatile commodity and energy markets.

- Energy swap providers usually offset their risk using **futures strips** to hedge their positions

Your notes

What Instruments Are Used in the Markets?

The following screens may help your understanding of commodity and energy swaps and how they are used.

From the Reuters Energy Swaps and OTC Derivatives Speed Guide, you can access a variety of information. For example you can obtain swap prices for Brent Crude Oil Seaps, Naphtha CIF NWE and Asian "Paper", as well as contributor prices and natural gas strips prices.

```
ENERGY SWAPS AND OTC DERIVATIVES - REUTERS SPEED GUIDE        ENERGY/SWAPS1
To access information, double click on codes in < > or [ ].

=EUROPEAN SWAPS PRICES BY PRODUCT=====    =NEWS and ANALYSIS===================
Preniun Unleaded FOB ARA ..<O#PU-ARA-S>    European swap trades reported....[0/SD]
PU Crack Spread v.Brt ..<O#PU-ARA-CK-S>    European Product swaps report....[0/PS]
Naphtha CIF NWE .........<O#NAF-NWE-S>     European Crude oil swaps report..[0/CS]
Naphtha Crack Spread ..<O#NAF-NWE-CK-S>    Energy News Directory....<ENERGY/NEWS1>
Jet Fuel CIF NWE .........<O#JET-NWE-S>    INSIGHT Technical Report..........[0/I]
Jet Fuel Differentials..<O#JET-NWE-DIF>    All Energy Reports....<ENERGY/REPORTS1>
Low Sulfur Fuel FOB NWE ..<O#LFO-NWE-S>
High Sulfur Fuel FOB ARA .<O#HFO-ARA-S>
Brent Crude oil Swaps .....<O#BRT-SWAP>
Brent Crude oil CFDs .......<O#BRT-CFD>   =CONTRIBUTOR PRICES==================
Composite Page Displays.<ENERGY/SWAPS2>    Intercapital Brokers..........<ICSA>-D

=ASIAN SWAPS COVERAGE ================     =N.AMERICAN SWAPS COVERAGE BY PRODUCT==
Asian "Paper" swaps prices..<SWAPS/SG1>    Natural Gas Strips .............<PIJQ>
Asian "Paper" swaps report ......[PS/A]

Questions/Comments: Contact your local Help Desk - see <PHONE/HELP> for details.
===================================================================================
Main Index..<REUTERS>     Commodities Index..<COMMOD>    Energy Guide..<ENERGY>
   Lost?Selective Access?..<USER/HELP>    Reuters Phone Support..<PHONE/HELP>
```

```
O#NAF-NWE-S          Naphtha NWE Swap
Connodity        Del.Date       Last           Srce   Terms    Loc  Ccy Units Date
NAPHTHA-SWAP-1M  Feb          ↓ 102.50  -1.50   CIF NWE         NWE  USD TONNE 20JAN99
NAPHTHA-SWAP-2M  Mar          ↓ 105.00  -3.00   CIF NWE         NWE  USD TONNE 20JAN99
NAPHTHA-SWAP-3M  Apr          ↓ 107.00  -2.50   CIF NWE         NWE  USD TONNE 20JAN99
NAPHTHA-SWAP-4M  May          ↓ 108.50  -0.50   CIF NWE         NWE  USD TONNE 20JAN99
NAPHTHA-SWAP-1Q  2Q99         ↓ 110.36  -1.60   CIF NWE         NWE  USD TONNE 20JAN99
NAPHTHA-SWAP-2Q  3Q99         ↓ 115.61  -1.43   CIF NWE         NWE  USD TONNE 20JAN99
```

```
1306 INTERCAPITAL COMMODITY SWAPS 0171 638 1894 FAX 9209665 ICSA
NICK BLACKWELL/WILLIAM MORGAN/JOE HUTCHINSON/JOHNNY MYLNE IN LDN

            JET CIF NWE    GASOIL/BRENT   GASOIL 0.2     GASOIL EN590
                          CRACK(7.45)   CIF NWEVIPE    CIF NWEVIPE
            BID-OFF        BID-OFF        BID-OFF        BID-OFF
FEB 99      21.50-22.00    00.00-00.00   +2.00/+2.50    06.50-07.25
MAR 99      21.00-21.50    00.00-00.00   +1.25/+2.00    06.25-07.25
APR 99      19.25-20.25    00.00-00.00   +1.00/+1.75    06.75-07.25
Q2 99       19.25-19.75    02.80-02.87   +0.50/+1.50    06.25-06.75
Q3 99       21.25-22.00    03.13-03.18   +0.75/+1.50    06.25-07.25
Q4 99       24.00-24.50    03.37-03.50   +2.00/+3.00    09.50-10.50
Q1 00       25.25-25.75    03.59-03.69   +3.00/+4.25    12.00-13.00
```

```
O#BRT-SWAP           Brent Swaps
Connodity       Del.Date       Last           Srce   Terms    Loc  Ccy Units Date
BRENT-SWAP-1M   Feb          ↓ 10.72  -0.11    FOB S.VOE       EUR  USD BBL 20JAN99
BRENT-SWAP-2M   Mar          ↓ 10.83  -0.07    FOB S.VOE       EUR  USD BBL 20JAN99
BRENT-SWAP-3M   Apr          ↓ 11.00  -0.09    FOB S.VOE       EUR  USD BBL 20JAN99
BRENT-SWAP-4M   May          ↓ 11.18  -0.11    FOB S.VOE       SVoe USD BBL 20JAN99
BRENT-SWAP-5M   Jun          ↓ 11.37  -0.08    FOB            EUR  USD BBL 20JAN99
BRENT-SWAP-6M   Jul          ↓ 11.61  -0.06    FOB            EUR  USD BBL 20JAN99
BRENT-SWAP-1Q   2Q99         ↓ 11.18  -0.10    FOB S.VOE       EUR  USD BBL 20JAN99
BRENT-SWAP-2Q   3Q99         ↓ 11.69  -0.06    FOB S.VOE       EUR  USD BBL 20JAN99
BRENT-SWAP-3Q   4Q99         ↓ 12.12  -0.11
BRENT-SWAP-4Q   1Q00         ↓ 12.51  -0.11
BRENT-SWAP-5Q   2Q00         ↓ 12.85  -0.11
BRENT-SWAP-6Q   3Q00         ↓ 13.19  -0.11
BRENT-SWAP-1Y   2000         ↓ 13.02  -0.11
BRENT-SWAP-2Y   2001         ↓ 14.22  -0.11
BRENT-SWAP-3Y   2002         ↓ 15.05  -0.11
BRENT-SWAP-4Y   2003         ↓ 15.64  -0.11
BRENT-SWAP-5Y   2004         ↓ 15.97  -0.11
```

```
19:11 20JAN99   SINGAPORE PAPER SWAP PRICES        SP01047      SWAPS/SG1
Singapore oil product swaps prices:
                        Wednesday      Monday       Monday
                MTH     BUY/SELL       BUY/SELL     PROMPT PHYSICAL
Naphtha (d/b)   Feb     11.75/11.90    12.10/12.25  12.10/12.20
                Mar     11.80/11.95    12.15/12.35
Gasoline (d/b)  Feb     UNQ            UNQ          14.00/14.30
Jet/Gas oil (d/b) Feb   +1.30/+1.50    +1.50/+1.70  16.10/16.30
                Mar     +1.20/+1.40    +1.30/+1.50
                Q2 99   +0.60/+0.80    +0.60/+0.80
Gas oil (d/b)   Feb     14.50/14.60    14.70/14.80  15.10/15.40
                Mar     14.15/14.25    14.30/14.40
                Q2 99   14.10/14.30    14.50/14.70
Fuel Oil (d/t)  Feb     66.50/67.00    66.75/67.25  67.00/68.00
                Mar     65.50/66.00    66.50/67.00
                Q2 99   65.25/66.00    67.00/68.00

**Double click on the following for nore information: swaps report [PS/A]
   Singapore products cash/swaps deals [0/AS] - cash prices <PRODUCTS/SG1> -
reports [LDIS/A] [MDIS/A] [FUEL/A] - tenders <ASIA/TEND1> - stocks <TDBOILINDEX>
   Reuters Energy: speed guide <ENERGY> - news [0] - IPE crude prices <O#LCO:>
<O#LGO:> <O#CL:> <O#HO:> <O#HU:>
```

```
1552 NATURAL GAS STRIPS AND SPREADS                          PIJQ

3 MONTH            1.838        1ST/2ND MONTH     -0.015
6 MONTH            1.866        1ST/3RD MONTH     -0.025
12 MONTH           1.990
18 MONTH           2.039        CL/NG ($/MMBTU)    0.240
BALANCE CURRENT YR              HO/NG ($/MMBTU)    0.500
CALENDAR 2000      2.183        NOTE: CALENDAR
SUMMER (APR-OCT)   1.919        STRIPS CALCULATE
WINTER (NOV-MAR)   2.225        REMAINING MONTHS
CANADA (NOV-OCT)   1.959        AS EACH MONTH
1/20/99 10:53                   EXPIRES.
```

These screens display US swap prices for crude oil, unleaded gasoline and Heating oil.

```
11:00 20JAN99        US Energy Swaps        UK30507        US/SWAP/MOGAS

Time      NYMEX gasoline

Jan         35.30
Feb         36.65
Mar         39.81
Apr         40.81
May         41.51
Jun         41.91

2Q99        41.16
3Q99        41.49
4Q99        40.44
1Q00
```

```
11:02 20JAN99          US Energy Swaps                UK30507       US/SWAP/WTI
                NYMEX      Crack spreads vs      IPE     WTI v Brent
Time            Crude      Mogas    Heat oil     Brent     Spread

Jan             12.18      2.65      1.47
Feb             12.22      3.17      1.60        10.86      1.36
Mar             12.33      4.39      1.68        10.95      1.38
Apr             12.46      4.68      1.74        11.10      1.36
May             12.60      4.83      1.89        11.24      1.36
Jun             12.73      4.87      2.12        11.38      1.35

2Q99            12.60      4.79      1.91        11.24      1.36
3Q99            13.03      4.50      2.53        11.69      1.34
4Q99            13.46      3.63      3.15        12.28      1.18
1Q00            13.86                2.95        12.68      1.18
2Q00            14.20                2.59        13.02      1.18
3Q00            14.54                            13.36      1.18

1999            12.83                                        Note: All prices
2000            14.33                            13.06      1.27  in $ per barrel
2001            15.55                            14.26      1.29
2002            16.39                            15.09      1.30  Reuters contact:
2003            16.99                            15.68      1.31  San Arnold-Forster
2004            17.46                            16.01      1.45  Tel: 171 542 4984
```

```
11:01 20JAN99        US Energy Swaps        UK30507        US/SWAP/HEAT

Time      NYMEX heating oil

Jan         32.50
Feb         32.90
Mar         33.35
Apr         33.80
May         34.50
Jun         35.35

2Q99        34.55
3Q99        37.05
4Q99        39.55
1Q00        40.03
2Q00        39.97
3Q00
```

What Instruments Are Used in the Markets?

These screens are taken from the Reuters Energy Swaps Calculator.
You can access strip prices for various energy contracts here.

Your notes

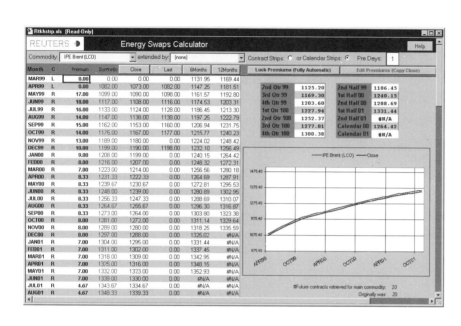

REUTERS

The diagram below indicates the availability of options on commodity and energy instruments.

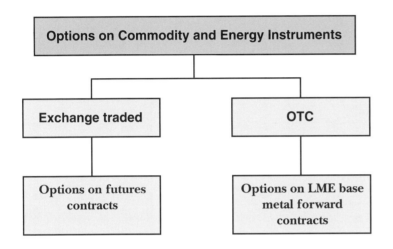

Options on Futures Contracts

A **traded** option is brought into existence by an exchange and the option contracts are cleared in the same way as futures, where the clearing house becomes counterparty to each contract.

Options are traded on exchanges such as the LIFFE, IPE, NYCSCE, CME and CBOT using an out-cry system and in some cases using automated screen-based systems thus providing 24 hours per day coverage. Most traded options are American style but some are European – you have to look at the contract conditions to confirm which style is being used.

With increasing pressures from the OTC markets, exchanges such as the NYCSCE have introduced alternative exercise style options – **Flexible Options**. These options are designed to combine the versatility of the OTC markets with the security of an exchange traded contract. In principle a Flexible Option operates in much the same way as a conventional traded option.

However, these options have been made more flexible as follows:

- **Strike price** – this can be customised as long as it is within the range listed for the current traded option

- **Exercise style** – this can be either American or European

- **Expiration date** – this can be any regular business day within certain limitations relating to the delivery period of the underlying futures contract

Exchange traded options have set expiry months which depend on the underlying futures contract. Typically the underlying contracts expire quarterly in March, June, September and December. However, many commodities have additional or slightly different months depending on matters such as crop cycles etc. Trading options using the same expiry months as the underlying futures contracts are often known as **regular options**. Some exchanges offer additional expiry months to the existing underlying futures contracts – these are known as **serial options**. In general serial options begin trading on the first business day of the **second** month preceding the expiration month. The underlying futures contract for a serial option is the **next** expiring futures contract which follows the serial month option.

This means that in addition to regular expiry months, options expire in the next three calendar months from a trade date. The diagram below illustrates serial options for a regular March option. In other words serial options can be traded for January and February expiry months.

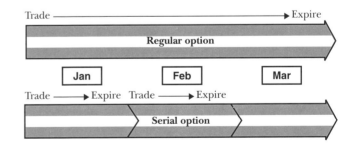

What Instruments Are Used in the Markets?

Exchange traded Commodity and Energy Options

The underlying futures contracts for commodity and energy options traded on an exchange generally are for physical delivery. Exchange traded options are standardised in terms of:

- Underlying instrument and a multiplier if necessary
- Strike prices – in general exchanges try to have a range of In-The-Money, At-The-Money and Out-of-The-Money strike prices
- Expiry dates
- Style – most exchange options are either American or European
- Premium quotations – these are dependent on the price quotation used for the underlying instrument
- Margin payments are required to be paid to the Clearing house

You may find the following chart useful as it summarises the advantages of exchange trading both futures and options on futures.

Consideration	Futures	Options
Risk	Unlimited risk on long and short positions	Defined and limited on purchase of puts and calls – unlimited on sale
Price protection	Establishes fixed price	Established floor or ceiling price protection
Margin	Required on long and short positions	No margin required for buyers – premium paid on purchase – but margin required for sellers
Hedging	Long, short, spread	Multiple hedging strategies

Exchange Contracts

There are many commodity and energy options on futures contracts on worldwide exchanges as was indicated earlier in this section. The chart below indicates a brief selection of commodity and energy options and the exchanges trading them.

Underlying	Exchange
Metals	
Copper High Grade	COMEX
Gold	COMEX, BM&F, MIDAM, CBOT
Silver	COMEX, CBOT
Platinum	COMEX
Softs	
Cocoa	LIFFE, NYCSCE
Sugar	LIFFE, NYCSCE, TGE, MATIF
Coffee	LIFFE, NYCSCE, BM&F
Grains & Livestock	
Soybean	CBOT, TGE, MIDAM
Corn	CBOT, TGE, MIDAM
Wheat	CBOT, MGE, MIDAM, SFE, KCBT, MATIF
Live cattle	BM&F, CME, MIDAM
Energy	
Crude oil	NYMEX, IPE
Unleaded gasoline	NYMEX
Natural Gas	NYMEX, KCBT
Electricity	MGE, SFE, NYMEX, CBOT, Nordpool

REUTERS :B

Typical Contract Specifications

Options contracts details vary from type-to-type and from exchange-to-exchange but the following examples taken from a LIFFE contract and a CBOT contract are typical specifications.

Option on Robusta Coffee – LIFFE	
Underlying contract	One Robusta Coffee futures contract for 5 tonnes
Premium quotations	USD/tonne
Minimum Price Fluctuation (Tick)	$1/tonne ($5)
Contract expiry	January, March, May, July, September and November
Exercise procedure	American

This is the standard contract size.

Quotes as either price per share or per index point

This is the smallest amount a contract can change value and the 'tick' size.

Option contracts are referred to by the these trading cycles

This means that contract can be exercised on or before expiry date – American

Option on Soybeans – CBOT	
Underlying contract	One Soybean futures contract for 5,000 bushels
Premium quotations	US Cents/bu
Minimum Price Fluctuation (Tick)	1/8 ¢/bu ($6.25)
Contract expiry	September, November, January, March, May, July and August
Exercise procedure	American

What Instruments Are Used in the Markets?

OTC Options on LME Base Metal Forward Contracts

The LME options offered for metals are a little different in that although the exchange guarantees the contracts, the options quoted are essentially Over-The-Counter (OTC) as they are quoted inter-office between market makers and not on the exchange floor. The options are European style and are essentially a private and confidential agreement between client and LME member. The options are always quoted as bid/ask spreads. Due to the private nature of these OTC contracts, transparency is thin. However, some options data is available on news services such as Reuters.

Shown at right is the Traded Options page, LME Index, with detail broken out for the All Metals and Copper.

```
LME/INDEX                    LME INDEX

                      ┌─────────────────┐
                      │  TRADED OPTIONS  │
                      └─────────────────┘

===MEMBER CONTRIBUTED AT-THE-MONEY OPTIONS VOLATILITES, & CALCULATED PREMIUMS===
Copper..............<MCU/IV1>-2.....All Metals, Front Month....<LME/IV1>-2
Aluniniun..........<MAL/IV1>-2.................2nd Month......<LME/IV3>-4
Zinc...............<MZN/IV1>-2.................3rd Month......<LME/IV5>-6
Nickel.............<MNI/IV1>-2.................4th Month......<LME/IV7>-8
Lead...............<MPB/IV1>-2.................5th Month......<LME/IV9>-10
Tin................<MSN/IV1>-2.................6th Month......<LME/IV11>-12
Aluniniun Alloy....<MAA/IV1>-2.................7th Month......<LME/IV13>-14

     SUMMARY DISPLAYS :--- PRICES ----- EVALUATIONS --- OPEN INTEREST
     Copper.............<LMNV>.......<MCU/VOL01>......<MCU/OPTOI>
     Aluniniun..........<LMOI>.......<MAL/VOL01>......<MAL/OPTOI>
     Zinc...............<LMOW>.......<MZN/VOL01>......<MZN/OPTOI>
     Nickel.............<LMOS>.......<MNI/VOL01>......<MNI/OPTOI>
     Lead...............<LMOQ>.......<MPB/VOL01>......<MPB/OPTOI>
     Tin................<LMPA>.......<MSN/VOL01>......<MSN/OPTOI>
     Aluniniun Alloy....<LMPI>.......<MAA/VOL01>......<MAA/OPTOI>

     DETAILED DISPLAYS :--- INDEX -------- PRICES ------ VOLUME & OPEN INT
     Copper.............<MCU/OPT>....<MCU/OPTO1>-27..<MCU/OPTOI01>-27
     Aluniniun..........<MAL/OPT>....<MAL/OPTO1>-27..<MAL/OPTOI01>-27
     Zinc...............<MZN/OPT>....<MZN/OPTO1>-27..<MZN/OPTOI01>-27
     Nickel.............<MNI/OPT>....<MNI/OPTO1>-27..<MNI/OPTOI01>-27
     Lead...............<MPB/OPT>....<MPB/OPTO1>-15..<MPB/OPTOI01>-15
     Tin................<MSN/OPT>....<MSN/OPTO1>-15..<MSN/OPTOI01>-15
     Aluniniun Alloy....<MAA/OPT>....<MAA/OPTO1>-15..<MAA/OPTOI01>-15
```

```
LONDON METAL EXCHANGE - COPPER OPT    - JANUARY 1999      MCU/OPTO1

TOTAL COPPER VOLUMES -      09DEC98 | Open Interest (c/p) - 08DEC98   6480/5431
(ALL CONTRACTS)     call    put   | Volume (c/p)   - 08DEC98     1278/475
Prev Day (Official)  1950   1565  |
Total to Morning                  |
Total to Afternoon                |
Total Daily                       |
----------------------------------|------------------------------------------
TRADE PRICES - 08DEC98            | PROVISIONAL / FINAL EVALUATIONS - 08DEC98
Trade  Strike  Matched Trades     |   Strike   Volatilities  Final Preniums
Time   Price   call    put        |   Price    Prov. Final   call     put
18:30  1525           46.00       | -5
18:30  1525           45.00       | -4
18:08  1525           44.00       | -3
17:37  1550   10.50               | -2
17:34  1550   10.00               | -1
17:15  1475           20.50       | ATM 1500=  16.25  16.25   24.43   30 15
17:13  1525   17.75               | +1
16:35  1525   17.25               | +2
16:35  1525   17.00               | +3
16:32  1525   17.46               | +4
12:57  1475           16.01       | +5

Eve Eval Sunn..<MCU/VOL01>  Trd Report Sunn..<MCU/TRD01>  OI Sunn..<MCU/OPTOI01>
```

```
LME - REAL-TIME INDICATIVE AT-THE-MONEY OPTION PREMIUMS        LME/IV2
JAN-99           CONTRACT
METAL  | TIME  FUT PRC ATM SP | CALL PREMIUM DELTA | PUT PREMIUM   DELTA
~~~~~  | ~~~~  ~~~~~~~ ~~~~~  | ~~~~~~~~~~~~ ~~~~~  | ~~~~~~~~~~~~  ~~~~~
COPPER | 09:40 1506.00  1500= |  28.68/31.97  0.54 |  22.72/26.00  -0.45
TIN    | 09:09 5318.00  5300= |  70.59/87.99  0.54 |  52 70/70.10  -0.45
LEAD   | 09:50 518.50   525=  |  11.33/13.16  0.44 |  17.79/19.62  -0.55
ZINC   | 11:11 988.00   1000= |  11.10/13.20  0.40 |  23.03/25.13  -0.60
ALUMIN | 09:40 1270.00  1275= |  14.40/18.57  0.46 |  19.37/23.54  -0.53
NICKEL | 09:40 3794.00  3800= | 101.29/126.29 0.50 | 107.26/132.26 -0.49
AL.ALY |       1067.75  1075= |  13.11/15.47  0.44 |  20.32/22.68  -0.55

          PROVISIONAL(P) / FINAL(E) CLOSE VALUES : 08DEC98
METAL  | ATM STK | CALL PREMIUM  PUT PREMIUM | CLS VOLATILITY QTE
~~~~~  | ~~~~~~~ | ~~~~~~~~~~~  ~~~~~~~~~~~  | ~~~~~~~~~~~~~~~~~~~
COPPER |  1500=  | E  24.43     E  30.15     | E  16.25
TIN    |  5300=  | E  77.58     E  73.60     | E  12.75
LEAD   |  525=   | E  11.26     E  21.45     | E  27.25
ZINC   |  975=   | E  19.97     E  15.24     | E  16.02
ALUMIN |  1275=  | E  17.09     E  24.54     | E  14.50
NICKEL |  3800=  | E 106.00     E 136.32     | E  28.50
AL.ALY |  1075=  | E  13.52     E  22.72     | E  14.83

ATM Volatilities...<LME/IV3>  LME Options...<LME/OPT1>  LME Futures...<LME/FUT1>
```

The LME also trades Asian or **Traded Average Price Options (TAPOs)** for copper and aluminium base metals. A TAPO reflects more closely the needs of a volatile market place where the strike prices for options are based on a Monthly Average Settlement Price (MASP). A TAPO cannot be exercised early so it is like a European option in this respect. A TAPO is exercised automatically if it is In-The-Money and the buyer or seller receives the difference between the contract strike price and the MASP. Details on TAPOs can be found on Reuters.

From the Reuters LME Index is the TAPOs – Traded Average Price Options section at right. Below that is the premiums and volatilities page for copper.

This page gives the call and put premiums for strike prices together with price **volatilities**. Can you remember what option volatilities are and their significance in options trading? You may need to refer to the *Introduction to Derivatives* book, *Section 3* at this stage.

```
LME/INDEX                        LME INDEX

              ┌─────────────────────────────────────────┐
              │  TAPOs - TRADED AVERAGE PRICE OPTIONS     │
              └─────────────────────────────────────────┘

         COPPER                    |          ALUMINIUM
         ======                    |          =========
SUMMARY DISPLAYS :-                | SUMMARY DISPLAYS :-
Premiums & Volatilities....<MCU/SUM01> | Premiums & Volatilities....<MAL/SUM01>
Notional Average Prices....<MCU/SUM02> | Notional Average Prices....<MAL/SUM02>
Open Interest.............<MCU/SUM03> | Open Interest.............<MAL/SUM03>
                                   |
DETAILED DISPLAYS :-               | DETAILED DISPLAYS :-
Index................<MCU/TAPO>    | Index................<MAL/TAPO>
Price Information....<MCU/TAP001>-2B | Price Information....<MAL/TAP001>-2B
Volume & Open Int....<MCU/TAP00I01>-2B | Volume & Open Int....<MAL/TAP00I01>-2B
```

```
19:15 11DEC98                              UK13891         MCU/SUM01
          LONDON METAL EXCHANGE - TRADED AVERAGE PRICE OPTIONS (TAPOS)
AT-THE-MONEY INDICATIVE OPTION CLOSING PREMIUMS & VOLATILITIES  - COPPER

MONTH STRIKE  VOL    CALL    PUT    MONTH STRIKE  VOL    CALL    PUT
================================================================================
DEC98 1450   15.64   25.74   0.75   FEB00 1550   17.43  109.87  109.66
JAN99 1450   16.18   33.94  22.22   MAR00 1550   17.39  115.27  110.68
FEB99 1475   19.34   43.43  47.87   APR00 1550   17.21  119.25  111.36
MAR99 1475   19.34   57.03  54.25   MAY00 1550   17.21  124.11  112.84
APR99 1475   19.20   69.65  58.48   JUN00 1575   17.21  118.00  126.95
MAY99 1500   19.02   68.82  74.44   JUL00 1575   17.04  121.56  127.11
JUN99 1500   18.77   78.18  76.06   AUG00 1575   17.04  125.98  128.13
JUL99 1500   18.59   87.17  77.71   SEP00 1575   17.04  130.25  129.39
AUG99 1525   18.43   84.34  92.04   OCT00 1575   16.93  133.86  129.66
SEP99 1525   18.32   92.40  93.05   NOV00 1575   16.93  138.10  130.55
OCT99 1525   17.96   98.07  93.07   DEC00 1575   16.93  141.82  131.59
NOV99 1525   17.93  105.22  94.83   JAN01 1600   16.86  134.85  144.70
DEC99 1550   17.86  100.42 108.76   FEB01 1600   16.86  138.03  145.88
JAN00 1550   17.43  104.24 108.30   MAR01 1600   16.86  141.20  146.75

                        Copper monthly notional average prices <MCU/SUM02>
================================================================================
Base Summary..<METAL/SUM>    Metals Index..<METAL1>     LME Options <LME/OPT1>
```

What Instruments Are Used in the Markets?

Who Uses Commodity and Energy Options?

Buyers/Sellers

There are a number of reasons that market players buy and sell commodity or energy options on futures instruments. Buyers and sellers use options in order to:

- Hedge

- Speculate

- Participate in arbitrage

Hedgers

Market players use options as a risk management tool in much the same way as they use futures contracts to protect a position. However, options have benefits over futures contracts. For example, the holder or buyer of an option buys protection against price risk whilst retaining the right to benefit from any favourable price movements in the underlying instrument.

Producers

These are naturally long in the underlying instrument. If they sell a call this means the producer has the obligation to sell the underlying that he holds if the option is exercised. What benefit is this to the producer? If the market price for the underlying remains static or falls, then the holder will not exercise the option at expiry. The producer thus profits from the premium received. However, if prices rise and the option is exercised at expiry, then the producer loses on the option because he has to sell the underlying at a lower price than the current higher price.

Consumers

These are naturally short in the underlying instrument. If they sell a put this means the consumer has the obligation to buy the underlying if the option is exercised. What benefit is this to the consumer? If the market price for the underlying remains static or rises, then the holder will not exercise the option and the consumer profits from the premium received. If the market price falls, then the holder will exercise the option at expiry and the consumer will be obliged to buy the underlying.

The rights and obligations of Call and Put options, from the point of view of sellers and buyers, are summarised in the chart below.

Who?	Call	Put
Buyer	• Right to buy • Pays premium • Losses limited to premium payments • Gains can be limitless • Expectation of rising prices	• Right to sell • Pays premium • Losses limited to premium payments • Gains can be limitless • Expectation of falling prices
Seller	• Obligation to sell if the buyer decides to buy • Collects premium • Gains limited to premium payments • Losses can be limitless • Expectation of neutral/ falling prices	• Obligation to buy if the buyer decides to sell • Collects premium • Gains limited to premium payments • Losses can be limitless • Expectation of neutral/ rising prices

REUTERS :

Speculators

These market players buy and sell options and take on the risk that hedgers wish to insure against. Speculators use their market knowledge to predict future prices for instruments and set up option trading strategies to profit from their views. These activities are obviously not without risks! Why should a trader use an option rather than a futures contract? The following example illustrates a situation in which an option is more beneficial than a futures contract.

Example

A speculator oil trader is checking news on energy products on his news service such as Reuters and sees that oilfield workers in a particular producer country have gone on strike. He suspects that NYMEX Crude oil prices will rise and so buys one lot of the near month futures contract – he buys one lot of 1000 barrels at $19.00 per barrel. The next day his prediction is proven correct and the price of a barrel of NYMEX Crude oil has risen to $22.00. The trader closes out his futures position with a profit of 1000 x $3.00 = $3000.

The trader who buys an option is able to limit his loss to the amount of the premium paid, in return for potentially unlimited profit. The seller of an option assumes the risk that the option buyer wishes to avoid. The seller has assumed potentially unlimited loss in return for a fixed reward, so must be able to utilise risk management techniques to practically limit potential loss. Option sellers tend to be professional speculators, like banks, with sufficient expertise and capital to benefit from markets' volatility.

But supposing the day after buying the futures contract it had been announced that another oil producer was about to increase production figures dramatically with a resulting fall in prices to $16.00 per barrel? In this case the trader would have lost heavily – $3000 – because of the futures contract obligations.

The speculator still has the same objective – to maximise profit and minimise loss, but what can the trader do?

This time the trader uses a call option and buys the right to buy a futures contract at a strike price of $19.00 per barrel and pays a premium of $0.50 per barrel.

If the trader's view is correct and the price rises to $22.00 per barrel, then on exercise of the option, he buys the futures contract at $19.00 and immediately sells it in the markets at $22.00 per barrel. The trader's profit is now the futures profit less the premium paid which is 3000 – 500 = $2500. This is not as much profit as using the futures contract but it still a reasonable amount.

If the prices fall to $16.00 per barrel, then the trader does not exercise the option and walks away from the deal. The trader's loss in this case is a modest $500.

Arbitrageurs

These market players provide liquidity to the options markets by taking advantage of price differences by simultaneously buying/selling similar options and/or underlying instruments with a view to profit.

Exchange traded Contracts

The chart below indicates the buyers and sellers of options on commodity and energy futures contracts and the rights to the respective underlying instruments if the options are exercised.

Option on futures contract	Buyer/holder has right to:	On exercise Seller/writer has obligation to:
Call	**Buy** underlying futures Go long	**Sell** underlying futures Go short
Put	**Sell** underlying futures Go short	**Buy** underlying futures Go long

The following chart describes the same information as given above but in a slightly different way and describes the way market players might use the different types of options.

Option type:	On exercise:	Use
Long put	**Right** to **sell** underlying commodity or energy futures contract	Protect from a **fall** in underlying cash market prices
Short put	**Obligation** to **buy** underlying commodity or energy futures contract	To earn extra revenue in a neutral or bearish market
Long call	**Right** to **buy** underlying commodity or energy futures contract	Protect from a **rise** in underlying cash market prices
Short call	**Obligation** to **sell** underlying commodity or energy futures contract	To earn extra revenue in a neutral or bearish market

It is important to remember that options are traded independently and separately from the underlying instruments. Long puts and long calls are often used as hedges whereas short puts and short calls are more speculative in their use.

It is also important to remember that when selling calls or puts the writer may take a **covered** or **uncovered – naked** – position. A covered position is when the writer possesses the underlying instrument, for example, shares, or has sufficient funds or other instruments available to cover his or her position if the option is exercised. A naked position is when the writer does **not** have the resources to cover the position and is therefore taking a considerable risk.

The Balanced Hedge

Balanced hedging combines the use of both futures and options on futures contracts to achieve the desired risk strategy. If a hedge is poorly placed it can expose the hedger to more risk than the original unprotected position.

If consumers need protection against upward price movements, then they can:

1. Buy futures contracts

2. Buy call options on futures

3. Sell put options on futures

4. Use a balanced combination of 1,2 and 3

If producers need protection against declining price movements, then they can:

1. Sell futures contracts

2. Buy put options on futures

3. Sell call options on futures

4. Use a balanced combination of 1,2 and 3

Your notes

Options on Commodity and Energy Futures Contracts in the Market Place

This section deals with typical contract quotations, how options are traded and how premiums are calculated for the exchange traded options on commodity and energy futures and forward contracts.

Typical Exchange traded Option on Equity Quotations

Commodity and energy option quotations are available from the financial press such as the *Financial Times* and *The Wall Street Journal* and from electronic news services such as Reuters. The information appears in a similar style to those in the following examples.

Financial press – Option on a softs commodity futures contract

Contract trading unit

Contract price quote

Cocoa (NYCSCE) 10 tonnes; $ per tonne

Strike price	Calls - Settle			Puts - Settle		
	Mar	Apr	May	Mar	Apr	May
1200	121	155	158	1	3	6
1250	72	109	117	2	7	14
1300	29	69	80	9	36	30
1350	9	38	50	40	64	48

Expiry dates

Strike prices of futures contracts in $ per tonne

How much will the premium be for an April1250 Call? In other words how much does it cost for the right to buy a 10 tonnes cocoa contract on or before the April expiry date at a strike price of $1250 per ton?

Using the data, which can be found in the financial press, the premium for this contract is $109/tonne.

So for a 10 ton contract the cost is 10 x 109 = $1090.00

The Reuters screens below show the Call and Put premiums for all strike prices on the May 1999 expiry month.

```
O#COMMOD-OPTS      Exchange    All Strikes
RIC                ID          Contract
O#BASE-OPT         RCT/        Base Metal Opts
O#FIBRES-OPT       RCT/        Fibres Options
O#FINANCIAL-OPT    RCT/        Financial Opts
O#GRAINS-OPT       RCT/        Grains Options
O#LIVESTOCK-OPT    RCT/        Livestock Opts
O#OILSEEDS-OPT     RCT/        Oilseeds Optio
O#PRECIOUS-OPT     RCT/        Precious Optic
O#SOFTS-OPT        RCT/        Softs Options
```

```
O#SOFTS-OPT        Exchange    Softs Options
RIC                ID          Contract
O#COCOPT           RCT/        Cocoa Options
O#COFOPT           RCT/        Coffee Options
O#OJOPT            RCT/        Orange Options
                               Sugar Options
```

```
O#COCOPT           Exchange    Cocoa Options
RIC                ID          Contract
O#LCC+             LIF/        LONDON COCOA
O#CC+              /           CSC COCOA
```

```
O#CC+              Exchange    CSC COCOA
RIC                ID          Contract
O#CCJ9+            CSC/        COCOA OPTIONS
O#CCK9+            CSC/        COCOA OPTIONS
O#CCN9+            CSC/        COCOA OPTIONS
O#CCU9+            CSC/        COCOA OPTIONS
O#CCZ9+            CSC/        COCOA OPTIONS
O#CCHO+            CSC/        COCOA OPTIONS
```

```
COCOA OPTIONS   CSC/    USD CCK9      CSC/    LT 1314    +13        H1319      L1304
Strike  Last              Bid    Ask    Size   Open 1  High    Low   Time
110   C  PS201   +29                    /                              19:22
110   P  PS1     -1                     /                              19:26
115   C  PS152   +29                    /                              19:22
115   P  PS2     -1                     /                              19:26
120   C  PS103   +27                    /                              19:22
120   P  PS3     -3                     /                              19:26
125   C  15      -54                    /       5       5       5     13:46
125   P  15      -4                     /       5       5       5     13:46
130   C  A31     +6             31      /       30      30      30    14:00
130   P  PS23    -20                    /                              19:26
135   C  11      +3                     /       11      11      11    14:04
135   P  PS56    -28                    /                              19:26
140   C  PS5     +2                     /                              19:22
140   P  PS103   -28                    /                              19:26
145   C  PS1                            /                              19:22
145   P  PS149   -30                    /                              19:26
150   C  PS1                            /                              19:22
150   P  PS199   -30                    /                              19:26
155   C  PS1                            /                              19:22
```

Reuters Commodities & Energy Pro 3000 – Options Calculator

This Reuters application helps users assess and analyse exchange traded options and to monitor implied volatility sensitivity.

The user will need to have the **Calculator** tab to the front. In the **Commodity Item** field the user types in the RIC required – in this case it is for the **LIFFE Robusta Coffee** contract **LKD**. The **Options** and **Futures Contract** months default to the nearest month contracts for both instruments but the user can change them as necessary from the drop down lists. In the centre of the screen, under the **Strikes** column, the **At-The-Money, ATM** price is highlighted. **Calls** and **Put** premiums and other data are displayed either side of the strike prices. The **sensitivities** for both Calls and Puts default to **Delta** but can be changed to the Greek required from the drop down lists.

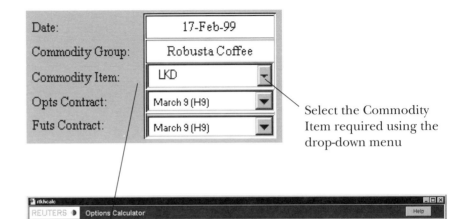

Date:	17-Feb-99
Commodity Group:	Robusta Coffee
Commodity Item:	LKD
Opts Contract:	March 9 (H9)
Futs Contract:	March 9 (H9)

Select the Commodity Item required using the drop-down menu

Gamma

Change to the Greek required using this drop-down menu

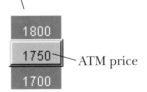

| 1800 |
| 1750 |
| 1700 |

ATM price

What Instruments Are Used in the Markets?

Financial press – Option on an energy futures contract

Contract trading unit

Contract price quote

Brent Crude (IPE) 1,000 net barrels; $ per bl

Strike price	Calls - Settle			Puts - Settle		
	Mar	Apr	May	Mar	Apr	May
1000	1.06	1.36	1.61	.06	.27	.37
1050	.64	1.07	1.27	.14	.42	.54
1100	.31	.74	.98	.30	.64	.76
1150	.17	.52	.76	.66	.92	1.04

Expiry dates

Strike prices of futures contracts in $ per barrel, for example 1000 = $10.00

How much will the premium be for a May1100 Put? In other words how much does it cost for the right to sell a 1,000 barrels of Brent crude oil contract on or before the May expiry date at a strike price of $11.00 per barrel?

Using the data, which can be found in the financial press, the premium for this contract is $0.76 or 76¢ per barrel.

So for a 1,000 barrel contract the cost is 1000 x 0.76 = $760.00.

These Reuters screens show the call and put premiums for all strike prices on the April 1999 expiry month.

O#ENERGY-OPT	Energy Options	Exchange
RIC	Contract	ID
O#ENERGY-OPTS	All Strikes	RCT/
O#ENERGY-ATM	At the Money	RCT/

O#ENERGY-OPTS	All Strikes	Exchange
RIC	Contract	ID
O#CL+	NYM CRUDEOIL-L	/
O#HO+	NYM HEAT OIL	/
O#HU+	NYM GAS UNLEAD	/
O#HC+	HO/CL CRACK	NYM/
O#UC+	NYM HU/CL CRACK	/
O#NG+	NYM NATURAL GAS	/
O#NP+	NYM PERM NT GAS	/
O#NC+	CDN NAT GAS	/
O#EC+	NYM CA/ORG ELEC	/
O#EV+	NYM PALO VERDE	/
O#KG+	KBT WESTERN GAS	/
O#LCO+	BRENT CRUDE	IPE/
O#LGO+	GAS OIL	IPE/

O#LCO+	Exchange	BRENT CRUDE
RIC	ID	Contract
O#LCOJ9+	IPE/	CRUDE OIL
O#LCOK9+	IPE/	CRUDE OIL
O#LCOM9+	IPE/	CRUDE OIL
O#LCON9+	IPE/	CRUDE OIL
O#LCOQ9+	IPE/	CRUDE OIL
O#LCOU9+	IPE/	CRUDE OIL

BRENT CRUDE APR9	IPE USD	LCOJ9x IPE	LT↑	1003 14:50 H 1006	Div	
			Net	-2	L 990	

Strike	Call	Ask	Bid	Close	Vol	Time	OI		Put	Ask	Bid	Close
950				75		:		↑	22	27	21	20
1000		41	35	45		:						40
1050		24	18	26		:	210			80	75	71
1100	↓ 10			14	200	14:00	125					109
1150	↓ 5			7	200	14:00	1980					152
1200				3		:	1100					198
1250				2		:	75					247
1300				1		:						296
1350				1		:	710					345
1400				1		:	200					395
1450				1		:	250					445
1500				1		:						495
1550				1		:						545
1600				1		:						595
1650				1		:						645
1700				1		:	400					695
1750				1		:						745

Reuters Commodities & Energy Pro 3000 – Options Calculator

The user has the **Calculator** tab to the front and in the **Commodity Item** field types in the RIC required – in this case it is for the **IPE Brent Crude** contract **LCO**. The **Options** and **Futures Contract** months default to the nearest month contracts for both instruments but you can change them as necessary from the drop down lists. In the centre of the screen, under the **Strikes** column, the **At-The-Money, ATM** price is highlighted. **Calls** and **Put** premiums and other data are displayed either side of the strike prices. The **sensitivities** for both Calls and Puts default to **Delta** but can be changed to the Greek required from the drop down lists.

How an Exchange traded Option Contract Works

Exchange traded options on commodity and energy instruments are traded in a similar way to exchange traded futures contracts in that margin payments are required by the Clearing house. Initial margin is payable by the appropriate party at the time of the trade.

The price of an option is marked-to-market every day that the option is open and the resulting profits/losses are credited/debited to both counterparty margin accounts.

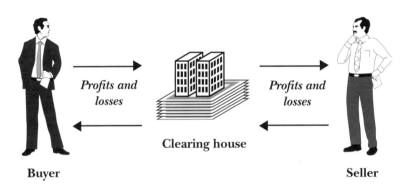

Buyer   *Profits and losses*   **Clearing house**   *Profits and losses*   **Seller**

If an option on a commodity or energy futures contract is exercised, then the **underlying commodity** or **energy product** is physically delivered or received.

A simple way of calculating the profit/loss on an option is to use the following equation.

$$\text{Profit/loss} =$$
$$(\text{Premium}_{\text{Exercise}} - \text{Premium}_{\text{Start}}) \times \text{Unit of trading} \times \text{No. of contracts}$$

Options Calculator screen

Date:	13-Apr-99	Calc Method:	American B&S		Futures Bid:	1498.00	Strike:	1.00
Commodity Group:	IPE Brent Crude	ATM:	1500		Futures Ask:	1500.00	Premium:	1.00
Commodity Item:	LCO	Ric Code:	LCO1500F9		Futures Last:	1499.00	Step:	50.00
Opts Contract:	June 9 (M9)	Opts Expiry:	11-May-99		Futures Close:	1481.00	Interest Rate:	4.92
Puts Contract:	July T (QT)	Puts Expiry:	15-Apr-99		20-Days Hist Vol:	36.93	Auto ATM Calc	Manual

| | | CALLS | | | | | | STRIKES | | PUTS | | | | | | | |
Gamma	Delta	Imp Vol	Volz	Bid	Ask	Theo Val	Close		Close	Theo Val	Ask	Bid	Volz	Imp Vol	Delta	Gamma
0.001	0.081	41.48	0.00	0.00	0.00	0.00	6.00	1750	286.00	0.00	0.00	0.00	0.00	56.16	-0.840	0.001
0.001	0.125	41.29	0.00	7.00	14.00	0.00	10.00	1700	240.00	0.00	0.00	0.00	0.00	53.17	-0.806	0.001
0.002	0.185	40.89	0.00	12.00	18.00	0.00	16.00	1650	196.00	0.00	0.00	0.00	0.00	50.86	-0.758	0.002
0.002	0.263	40.48	0.00	24.00	30.00	0.00	25.00	1600	155.00	0.00	0.00	0.00	0.00	48.73	-0.693	0.002
0.002	0.359	39.43	0.00	0.00	0.00	0.00	37.00	1550	117.00	0.00	0.00	0.00	0.00	46.71	-0.613	0.002
0.003	0.473	38.42	0.00	53.00	61.00	0.00	54.00	1500	84.00	0.00	0.00	0.00	0.00	45.22	-0.516	0.002
0.003	0.602	36.77	0.00	0.00	0.00	0.00	76.00	1450	56.00	0.00	0.00	0.00	0.00	43.65	-0.407	0.002
0.002	0.735	35.07	0.00	0.00	0.00	0.00	105.00	1400	35.00	0.00	30.00	25.00	0.00	42.82	-0.297	0.002
0.002	0.862	31.95	0.00	0.00	0.00	0.00	140.00	1350	20.00	0.00	21.00	0.00	0.00	42.17	-0.197	0.002
0.000	0.000	0.00	0.00	0.00	0.00	0.00	180.00	1300	10.00	0.00	14.00	0.00	0.00	41.28	-0.116	0.001
0.000	0.000	0.00	0.00	0.00	0.00	0.00	224.00	1250	4.00	0.00	0.00	0.00	0.00	39.79	-0.055	0.001

Calculator / Zero Curve / Deposits / Futures History / Smile Curve / Profit & Loss / Decay Chart /

What Instruments Are Used in the Markets?

Example – Buying a call to set a cap

It is January and a fleet user of unleaded gasoline is worried that prices may rise by March. March NYMEX unleaded futures are currently trading at 32¢/gallon. The fleet user could buy these futures contracts to lock in the a price of 32¢/gallon but if prices fall, then he may be paying considerably in excess of spot prices in the future.

The fleet user decides to **buy** a March **Call** option on the NYMEX futures unleaded gasoline contract with a strike price of 32¢/gallon. This option has a premium of 2.0¢/gallon.

In March the spot price of gasoline has risen to 50¢/gallon and the fleet user exercises the option. This means that the fleet user has the right to buy the underlying futures contract and take delivery of gasoline at 32¢/gallon. The overall cost of the gasoline is therefore the cost of the futures plus the premium –

$$32 + 2 = 34¢/\text{gallon}$$

The result is a reasonable hedge and a cap has effectively been set on the future price of the gasoline.

However, if the spot price of gasoline had fallen to 28¢/gallon, then the right to buy the futures contract at 32¢/gallon has no value. The fleet user allows the option position to expire with the loss of the premium paid. The overall cost of the gasoline in this case is therefore the spot cost plus the premium –

$$28 + 2 = 30¢/\text{gallon}$$

Once again this is a reasonable hedge. Even though the fleet user is paying slightly more than the spot price his position has been effectively protected.

Example – Buying a put to set a floor

It is January and an oil refiner is worried that prices of unleaded gasoline may fall by March. March NYMEX unleaded futures are currently trading at 32¢/gallon. The refiner could buy these futures contracts to lock in the a price of 32¢/gallon but he would like to be able to earn extra revenue if prices were to rise unexpectedly.

The fleet user decides to **buy** a March **Put** option on the NYMEX futures unleaded gasoline contract with a strike price of 32¢/gallon. This option has a premium of 2.0¢/gallon.

In March the spot price of gasoline has fallen to 28¢/gallon and the refiner exercises the option. This means that the refiner has the right to sell the underlying futures contract and make delivery of gasoline at 32¢/gallon. The overall selling price of the gasoline is therefore the price received for the futures less the premium –

$$32 - 2 = 30¢/\text{gallon}$$

The result is a reasonable hedge and a floor has effectively been set on the future price of the gasoline.

However, if the spot price of gasoline had risen to 50¢/gallon, then the right to sell the futures contract at 32¢/gallon has no value. The refiner allows the option position to expire with the loss of the premium paid. The overall price received for the gasoline in this case is therefore the spot cost less the premium –

$$50 - 2 = 48¢/\text{gallon}$$

Once again this is a reasonable hedge. Even though the refiner receives slightly less than the spot price his position has been effectively protected.

REUTERS :B

OTC Options on LME Base Metal Forward Contracts

Traded options were introduced on the LME in 1987. These options use the underlying forward contracts and are therefore available against monthly prompt dates out to 27 months. Although these options are administered by the exchange and the LME guarantees particular strike prices, they are in essence OTC instruments quoted inter-office between market makers.

The options are quoted as bid/ask spreads with strike price increments of $25 until $1750, then $50 until $4950, then $100 over $5000.

Options are traded on all the base metals including Aluminium Alloy and are used by market players in much the same way as are exchange traded options.

As these traded options are OTC in nature, prices are not reported in the financial press. However, information on LME options can be found from the **LME/INDEX** page via Reuters, as shown earlier. In addition a number of LME ring Dealers such as Rudolf Wolff contribute prices.

The Reuters screens at right show the **Rudolf Wolff Indicated Metal Options Menu Page**. Also shown are the **aluminium** and **tin** fields displaying the current bid and ask price indications for calls and puts for different months for aluminium and tin options from this ring dealer.

```
09:36 15FEB99          LON METAL OPTIONS       UK38342          DELTA
               RUDOLF WOLFF & CO LTD RING DEALING MEMBER OF THE LME
     LONDON 0171-836-1368  HAMBURG 040-320220  NY 212-370-5115  TOKYO 003-322-20171
                       OPTIONS DIRECT LINE 0171-836-1368

                       INDICATED METAL OPTIONS MENU PAGE.
                       ×××××××××××××××××××××××××××××××××

         ALUMINIUM    COPPER      NICKEL      LEAD       TIN         ZINC
         <ALOPT1>    <CUOPT1>    <NIOPT1>   <PBOPT1>   <SNOPT1>    <ZNOPT1>

     AVERAGE RATE/ASIAN OPTION INDICATIONS ON PAGE 4 OF RESPECTIVE METAL.

                     VOLATILITIES           DISCLAIMER
                       <OPTVOL>            <RWDISCLAIM>


              ×××××××××××××××××××××××××××××××××××××××××××××××××
              CALL THE OPTIONS DESK IN LONDON OR YOUR NEAREST
                 RUDOLF WOLFF OFFICE FOR CURRENT QUOTES
              ×××××××××××××××××××××××××××××××××××××××××××××××××
```

```
12:01 15FEB99          LON METAL OPTIONS       UK38342          ALOPT1
               RUDOLF WOLFF & CO LTD RING DEALING MEMBER OF THE LME
                     ALUMINIUM OPTIONS CURRENT INDICATIONS

CALL  MARCH      DIFF: -12.50          APRIL    DIFF: -4.00           3 MONTH
         BID    ASK   DELTA  THETA      BID    ASK   DELTA  THETA  INDICATION
1175   28.00  31.00   0.68   0.71     45.00  48.00   0.65   0.39  BID 1207.5
1200   14.00  17.00   0.46   0.79     30.75  33.75   0.53   0.42  ASK 1208
1225    5.25   8.25   0.26   0.65     19.75  22.75   0.40   0.42
1250    1.00   4.00   0.12   0.40     11.75  14.75   0.29   0.37
1275    0.00   3.00   0.04   0.18      6.50   9.50   0.19   0.30
1300    0.00
1325    0.00
1350    0.00

PUT   MARCH
         BID
1050    0.00
1075    0.00
1100    0.00
1125    0.00
1150    1.75
1175    7.75
1200   18.75
1225   35.00
```

```
11:55 15FEB99          LON METAL OPTIONS       UK38342          SNOPT1
               RUDOLF WOLFF & CO LTD RING DEALING MEMBER OF THE LME
                        TIN OPTIONS CURRENT INDICATIONS

CALL  MARCH      DIFF: 22.00           APRIL    DIFF: 10.00           3 MONTH
         BID    ASK   DELTA  THETA      BID    ASK   DELTA  THETA  INDICATION
5000  168.00 188.00   0.86   1.51    197.00 217.00   0.71   1.35  BID 5140
5100   91.00 111.00   0.67   2.54    134.00 154.00   0.58   1.57  ASK 5150
5200   38.00  58.00   0.42   2.76     85.00 105.00   0.45   1.61
5300    8.00  28.00   0.21   2.01     49.00  69.00   0.32   1.46
5400    0.00  15.00   0.08   1.00     24.00  44.00   0.21   1.19
5500    0.00  15.00   0.02   0.35      9.00  29.00   0.13   0.87
5600    0.00  15.00   0.00   0.09      0.00  20.00   0.07   0.58  MENUS
5700    0.00  15.00   0.00   0.02      0.00  15.00   0.04   0.35  <DELTA>

PUT   MARCH      DIFF: 22.00           APRIL    DIFF: 10.00
         BID    ASK   DELTA  THETA      BID    ASK   DELTA  THETA  VOLATILITY
4500    0.00  15.00   0.00   0.00      0.00  15.00  -0.01   0.09  <OPTVOL>
4600    0.00  15.00   0.00   0.00      0.00  15.00  -0.02   0.20
4700    0.00  15.00   0.00   0.02      0.00  16.00  -0.05   0.41
4800    0.00  15.00  -0.01   0.14      4.00  24.00  -0.10   0.71  NEXT
4900    0.00  15.00  -0.04   0.60     18.00  38.00  -0.18   1.06  <SNOPT2>
5000    1.00  21.00  -0.14   1.55     43.00  63.00  -0.28   1.38
5100   24.00  44.00  -0.33   2.55     80.00 100.00  -0.41   1.58  PREVIOUS
5200   70.00  90.00  -0.58   2.76    130.00 150.00  -0.55   1.60  <PBOPT4>
```

What Instruments Are Used in the Markets?

More recently the LME has introduced **Asian** or **Traded Average Price Options (TAPOs)** for Copper and Aluminium. A TAPO reflects more closely the needs of a volatile market place where the strike prices for options are based on a Monthly Average Settlement Price, MASP. A TAPO cannot be exercised early so it is like a European option in this respect. A TAPO is exercised automatically if it is In-The-Money and the buyer or seller receives the difference between the contract strike price and the MASP. TAPOs information can be found on the Reuters screens below.

The notional average prices for settlement are shown below for Aluminium TAPOs.

```
LME/INDEX                    LME INDEX

        ╔════════════════════════════════════════╗
        ║    TAPOs - TRADED AVERAGE PRICE OPTIONS ║
        ╚════════════════════════════════════════╝

            COPPER           |        ALUMINIUM
            ======           |        =========
SUMMARY DISPLAYS :-          | SUMMARY DISPLAYS :-
Premiums & Volatilities....<MCU/SUM01> | Premiums & Volatilities....<MAL/SUM01>
Notional Average Prices....<MCU/SUM02> | Notional Average Prices....<MAL/SUM02>
Open Interest..............<MCU/SUM03> | Open Interest..............<MAL/SUM03>

DETAILED DISPLAYS :-         | DETAILED DISPLAYS :-
Index...............<MCU/TAPO>         | Index...............<MAL/TAPO>
Price Information....<MCU/TAPO01>-28   | Price Information....<MAL/TAPO01>-28
Volume & Open Int....<MCU/TAPOOI01>-28 | Volume & Open Int....<MAL/TAPOOI01>-28
```

```
07:44 15FEB99                                          UK13891        MAL/SUM02
         LONDON METAL EXCHANGE - TRADED AVERAGE PRICE OPTIONS (TAPOS)
The following represents the notional average prices of LME ALUMINIUM 27 months
forward. For the current month, it is the arithmetic average of Official
Settlement Prices for dates already published (see <SETTMAL1>) and the Evening
Evaluations (see <LMES>) for those still to be fixed. All forward months are
derived by interpolation of the Evening Evaluations.

     MONTH   AVERAGE        MONTH   AVERAGE        MONTH   AVERAGE
     ===================================================================
     FEB99   1200.15        DEC99   1269.05        OCT00   1323.62
     MAR99   1201.80        JAN00   1275.04        NOV00   1328.92
     APR99   1210.23        FEB00   1281.01        DEC00   1333.32
     MAY99   1216.92        MAR00   1287.06        JAN01   1338.69
     JUN99   1224.98        APR00   1291.96        FEB01   1343.07
     JUL99   1231.97        MAY00   1297.63        MAR01   1348.13
     AUG99   1239.79        JUN00   1302.79        APR01   1353.57
     SEP99   1247.88        JUL00   1308.43        MAY01   1359.00
     OCT99   1254.56        AUG00   1313.74
     NOV99   1261.92        SEP00   1318.41  FEB99 Avg to Date : 1206.10

                             Aluminium traded average price options <MAL/SUM01>
     ===================================================================
Base Summary..<METAL/SUM>      Metals Index..<METAL1>      LME Futures <LME/FUT1>
```

```
07:44 15FEB99                                          UK13891        MAL/SUM01
         LONDON METAL EXCHANGE - TRADED AVERAGE PRICE OPTIONS (TAPOS)
AT-THE-MONEY INDICATIVE OPTION CLOSING PREMIUMS & VOLATILITIES   -  ALUMINIUM

MONTH  STRIKE  VOL   CALL    PUT    MONTH  STRIKE  VOL    CALL    PUT
========================================================================

FEB99  1200   17.78   5.21   5.06   APR00  1300  14.79   73.78   81.35
MAR99  1200   17.70  23.73  21.94   MAY00  1300  14.79   78.93   81.15
APR99  1200   17.33  38.03  27.90   JUN00  1300  14.79   83.76   81.16
MAY99  1225   17.20  36.89  44.86   JUL00  1300  14.50   87.21   79.38
JUN99  1225   16.80  45.89  45.91   AUG00  1325  14.50   81.11   91.53
JUL99  1225   16.50  53.91  47.09   SEP00  1325  14.50   85.37   91.44
AUG99  1250   16.20  50.25  60.19   OCT00  1325  14.40   89.21   90.48
SEP99  1250   16.05  57.84  59.90   NOV00  1325  14.40   93.61   90.03
OCT99  1250   15.73  63.79  59.38   DEC00  1325  14.40   97.52   89.96
NOV99  1250   15.73  71.21  59.74   JAN01  1350  14.29   90.77  101.00
DEC99  1275   15.73  66.60  72.30   FEB01  1350  14.29   94.45  100.69
JAN00  1275   15.00  69.63  69.59   MAR01  1350  14.29   98.40  100.08
FEB00  1275   15.00  75.22  69.51   APR01  1350  14.29  102.62   99.43
MAR00  1275   15.00  80.94  69.54   MAY01  1350  14.29  106.73   98.73

                      Aluminium monthly notional average prices <MAL/SUM02>
========================================================================
Base Summary..<METAL/SUM>      Metals Index..<METAL1>      LME Options <LME/OPT1>
```

REUTERS :▣

Example – A TAPO used as a hedge

A copper smelter needs to sell its production output at an average price of at least $1450.00/tonne. The copper market has been particularly volatile recently and the smelter would like to hedge its position but also take advantage of any cash price increases in the next 6 months.

It is January and the smelter contacts its broker to buy June TAPO Puts with a strike price of $1600 – the premium for this option is $132.38. This means the smelter has the right to sell the underlying forward contract on exercise. This hedge locks in a minimum price of $1600.00 – 132.28 = $1467.62/tonne. The forward price for June delivery is $1486.00/tonne.

At the end of June the LME announces a Monthly Average Settlement Price, MASP of $1716.00. The TAPO is not automatically exercised as it is Out-The-Money. The smelter sells its copper at $1716.00/tonne in the cash market – after deducting the cost of the premium the net profit is:

$$\$1716.00 - 132.28 = \mathbf{\$1583.62/tonne}$$

The smelter has been able to take advantage of a cash price increase whilst hedging the required position of $1450.00/tonne.

However, if at the end of June the MASP for copper had fallen to $1416.00/tonne, then the TAPO would have been exercised automatically as it is In-The-Money. The smelter would receive the difference between the strike price and the MASP:

$$\$1600.00 - 1416.00 = \$184.00/tonne$$

If the original premium is deducted from this gain, then the net profit on the TAPO is $184.00 – 134.28 = $51.62/tonne. The smelter sells the copper at the MASP of $1416.00/tonne to which the net option profit is added:

$$\$1416.00 + 51.62 = \mathbf{\$1462.62/tonne}$$

In this case, when cash prices fall, the hedge is reasonable for the average production price required of $1450.00/tonne.

	LME	Cash
Price rise in future		
	January Buy Jun 1600 TAPO Put Premium @ $132.28/tonne **June** Option expires OTM	 **June** Smelter sells in cash market @ $1716.00/tonne
	Profit/loss = –$132.28/tonne	**Profit/loss** = +1716.00 – 132.28 +1583.62
Net price received for Copper = $1583.62/tonne		
Price fall in future		
	January Buy Jun 1600 TAPO Put Premium @ $132.28/tonne **June** ITM option exercised @ $1416.00/tonne	 **June** Smelter sells in cash market @ $1416.00/tonne
	TAPO **Profit/loss** = 1600 – 1416 = +$184.00/tonne **Net Profit/loss** = 184.00 – 132.28 = $51.62/tonne	**Profit/loss** = +1416.00 + 51.62 +1467.62
Net price received for Copper = $1467.62/tonne		

Trading Strategies for Options

There are many strategies available in the options markets – some are quite complex and have colourful names.

The various strategies are usually represented diagrammatically as **break-even graphs** which show the potential for making a profit. The diagrams use the break-even point as the basis for the diagram where

Break-even point   =   Strike price ± premium

The most basic buy /sell strategies for puts and calls are illustrated using profit/loss charts in the following examples. You may find it useful to refer to option strategies in general described in the *Introduction to Derivatives* book in this series.

Depending on whether the market player is a buyer or seller of a call or put, gains or losses either have ceiling values or are limitless. The following examples apply to options on commodities and energy futures contracts.

Buying a Call option – Long Call

Buyers of call options seek to profit from any future price rises but do not want to lock in a firm price by buying futures contracts. In the case of buying a call – a long call – a producer typically has a bullish view of the market but is still hesitant that prices may fall thus reducing the cost of his raw materials.

Example

An oil refiner thinks that the current price of crude oil at $10.00/barrel will increase in the future. Therefore the refiner buys an IPE Brent Crude oil $11.00 Call with a premium of $1.00/barrel.

At expiry the profit/loss chart for the Long Call looks like this:

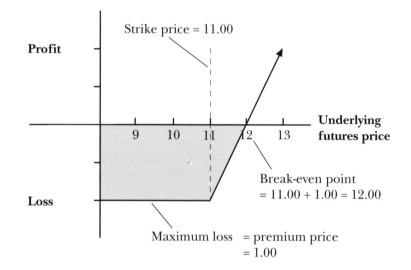

Futures price	Outcome
> 12.00	Profit increases and is unlimited as futures price rises
12.00	Break-even point
11.00 – 12.00	Loss which decreases as futures price increases
< 11.00	Loss is limited to a maximum of the premium price

Buying a Put option – Long Put

In buying a put a market player takes the opposite view to that in buying a call. In other words the buyer of a put – a long put – expects future cash prices to fall. However, the market player still would like to protect himself against price rises. If prices do rise, then the put buyer's loss is limited to the cost of the premium.

Example

In the US a copper smelter is concerned that the future spot price for his metal will fall but there is a chance that prices could rise. The smelter would like to hedge his position and take advantage of any future price rises.

The COMEX High Grade Copper futures contract for December is currently trading at 64¢/lb. The smelter decides to buy a COMEX Dec Put with a strike price of 62¢/lb which has a premium of 4.00¢/lb.

At expiry the profit/loss chart for the Long Put looks like this:

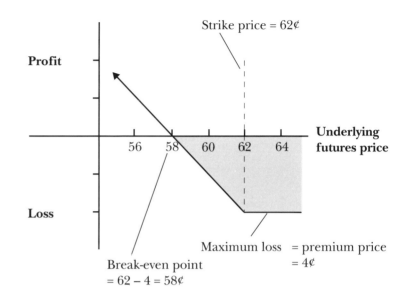

Market price	Outcome
> 62¢	Maximum loss is equal to the premium
62 – 58¢	Loss decreases as underlying share price falls
58¢	Break-even point
< 58¢	Profit increases as underlying share price falls and is unlimited

Before moving on see if you can sketch the profit/loss charts for a Short Call and a Short Put.

You may also like to comment on who might use these options and why.

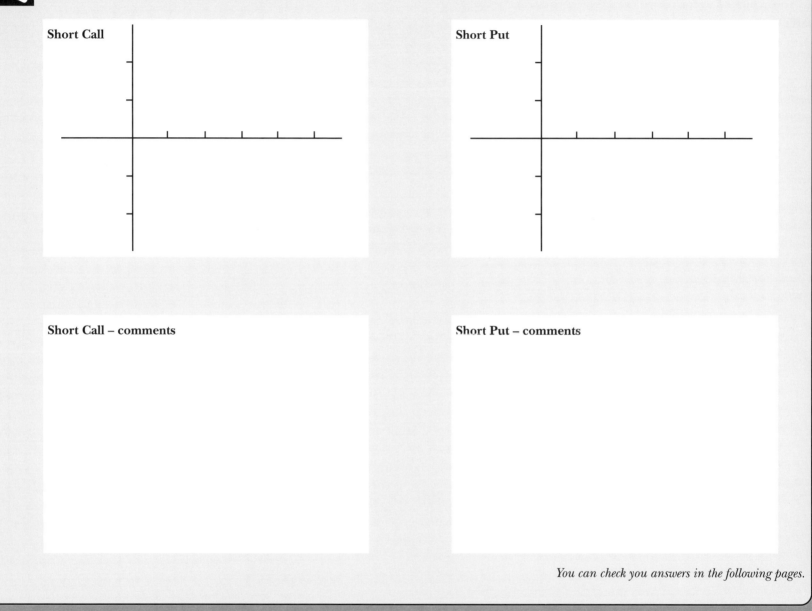

Short Call

Short Put

Short Call – comments

Short Put – comments

You can check you answers in the following pages.

Selling a Call option – Short Call

In selling or writing an option a market player receives the premium from the buyer. If the producer of a commodity expects that prices will remain steady or fall slightly in the future, then writing an option can provide extra revenue when the commodity is sold in the cash market.

Option writers who hold a commodity do not expect the option to be exercised. If the option does expire worthless, then the writer retains the full amount of premium. However, if the option is exercised, then losses to the writer can be limitless. In many cases market players write call options for the following reasons:

- To earn extra revenue

- To reduce the cost of holding the commodity

- To hedge, partially, a fall in prices

Example

It is November and a Cocoa producer is looking at the NYCSCE March Cocoa futures contract which is trading at $1300/tonne. The producer's view is that this price will remain static for several months. He decides to sell a March 1300 Call which has a premium of $30.00/ tonne. The underlying futures contract for this option is for 10 tonnes of Cocoa. Therefore, each contract the producer writes will receive a premium of 10 x 30 = $300.

At expiry the profit/loss chart for the Short Call looks like this:

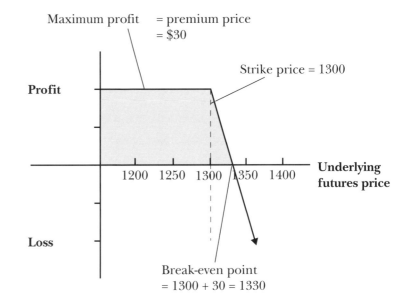

Market price	Outcome
> 1330	Loss increases as market price increases and is unlimited
1330	Break-even point
1300 – 1330	Profit increases as market price decreases
< 1300	Maximum profit is equal to the premium

Selling a Put option – Short Put

The writer of a put takes the opposite market view to that of the call writer. In other words the market player expects prices will remain steady or rise slightly. The writer of a put is limited to a maximum earned income equal to the value of the premium. If the market player felt that future prices were definitely likely to rise, then he would probably buy futures contracts or buy a call option. The market player does not expect the option to be exercised. If exercise does take place, then the market player has to take delivery of a commodity at a higher price than the cash market and therefore makes a loss. If prices remain static or rise slightly, then the market player earns extra premium revenue.

Example

A food manufacturer uses substantial quantities of sugar and may write put options in order to reduce the cost of future sugar purchases.

It is December and the manufacturer sees that the NYCSCE March Sugar futures contract price is 6.70¢/lb. The manufacturer's view is that sugar prices will remain static for several months and decides to sell a March 700 Put which has a premium of 0.32¢/lb. The underlying futures contract is for 112,000lb of sugar. Therefore each contract the manufacturer writes represents an income of 112,000 x 0.32 = $358.40. Providing the option is not exercised, the effective future price of sugar is the cash price less the premium received.

At expiry the profit/loss chart for the Short Put looks like this:

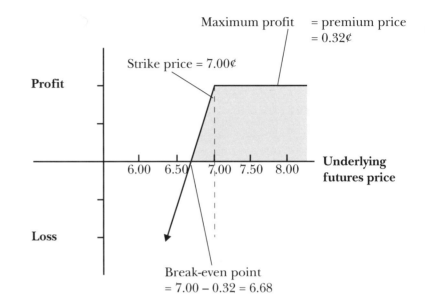

Market price	Outcome
> 7.00	Maximum profit is equal to the premium
6.68 – 7.00	Profit increases as market price increases
6.68	Break-even point
< 6.68	Loss increases as market price decreases and is unlimited

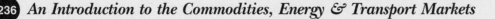

Options on Commodity and Energy Instruments

- Options on commodity and energy instruments are traded on exchanges and OTC for LME forward contracts – if exercised both types of option are settled by **physical delivery** of the underlying

- For options on commodity and energy instruments the **buyer** or **holder** of a **call/put** has the **right** to **sell/buy** the **underlying instrument** if the option is exercised

- For options on commodity and energy instruments the **seller** or **writer** of a **call/put** has the **obligation** to **sell/buy** the **underlying instrument** if the option is exercised

- Options on commodity and energy instruments are usually **American** or **European style** but exchange traded **Asian (Average Price)** and **flexible** options have been introduced more recently

- Premium quotations on commodity and energy instruments options are expressed as values which are related to the underlying futures prices

Your notes

What Instruments Are Used in the Markets?

The following illustrations of Reuters screens may help your understanding of commodity and energy options and how they are used.

The screen on top right is the Reuters Energy Options Speed Guide from which information about the various options can be accessed. The screen on bottom right displays the option months for the various contracts. The screen below displays the option prices for a particular option month.

```
CRUDE OIL OPTION NYM/    USD CLK9      NYM/   LT B15.53   A15.58   H15.74
Strike  Last            Bid   Ask   Size   Open 1  High   Low   Time
12    C PS3.75   +0.38                /                          21:00
12    P PS0.02                        /                          20:25
12.5  C PS3.26   +0.38                /                          19:41
12.5  P PS0.03                        /                          20:25
13    C PS2.77   +0.36                /                          18:05
13    P PS0.04   -0.02                /                          20:25
13.5  C PS2.29   +0.34                /                          17:07
13.5  P PS0.06   -0.04                /                          20:25
14    C PS1.85   +0.30                /                          18:04
14    P PS0.11   -0.08                /                          20:25
14.5  C PS1.44   +0.25                /                          20:17
14.5  P PS0.20   -0.13                /                          20:25
15    C PS1.08   +0.27                /                          20:17
15    P  A0.45            0.45   /6                              04:10
15.5  C PS0.77   +0.16                /                          20:04
15.5  P PS0.53   -0.22                /                          20:25
16    C  A0.65            0.65   /10                             04:10
16    P PS0.78   -0.27                /                          20:06
16.5  C PS0.35   +0.08                /                          20:23
16.5  P PS1.11   -0.30                /                          21:00
17    C PS0.23   +0.05                /                          20:24
17    P PS1.48   -2.73                /                          20:26
17.5  C PS0.15   +0.03                /                          20:24
```

```
ENERGY OPTIONS - REUTERS SPEED GUIDE                        ENERGY/OPT1
Price Information for Energy Options. Double click on the codes in < > or [ ]

=NYMEX OPTIONS=============SPEED GUIDE= ==Full Chains=== ==Near Money Chains==
Light Crude Oil (WTI).....<ENERGY/OPT2>  ....<O#CL+>.....  ....<O#CL++>.........
Heating Oil...............<ENERGY/OPT2>  ....<O#HO+>.....  ....<O#HO++>.........
Unleaded Gasoline.........<ENERGY/OPT2>  ....<O#HU+>.....  ....<O#HU++>.........
Heat Crack Spreads........<ENERGY/OPT2>  ....<O#HC+>.....  ....<O#HC++>.........
Unleaded Crack Spreads....<ENERGY/OPT2>  ....<O#UC+>.....  ....<O#UC++>.........
Henry Hub Natural Gas.....<ENERGY/OPT3>  ....<O#NG+>.....  ....<O#NG++>.........
Pernian Natural Gas.......<ENERGY/OPT3>  ....<O#NP+>.....  ....<O#NP++>.........
Alberta Natural Gas.......<ENERGY/OPT3>  ....<O#NC+>.....  ....<O#NC++>.........
COB Electricity...........<ENERGY/OPT4>  ....<O#EC+>.....  ....<O#EC++>.........
Palo Verde Electricity....<ENERGY/OPT4>  ....<O#EV+>.....  ....<O#EV++>.........

=KCBT OPTIONS========================
Western Natural Gas.......<ENERGY/OPT3>  ....<O#KG+>.....  ....<O#KG++>.........

=IPE OPTIONS=========================
Brent Oil.................<ENERGY/OPT5>  ....<O#LCO+>.....  ....<O#LCO++>........
Gas Oil...................<ENERGY/OPT5>  ....<O#LGO+>.....  ....<O#LGO++>........
                Energy News and Reports..<ENERGY/NEWS1>
=====================================================================
Main Index<REUTERS>          Energy Guide<ENERGY>       Contd on <ENERGY/OPT2>
   Lost?Selective Access? <USER/HELP>    Reuters Phone  Support <PHONE/HELP>
```

```
ENERGY OPTIONS - REUTERS SPEED GUIDE                        ENERGY/OPT2
To access information, double click on the codes in < >.

==== NYMEX OPTIONS CONTRACTS ========             ===== CRACK SPREADS ====
============ CRUDE OIL === UNLEADED === HEATING OIL == UNLEADED = HEATING OIL=
January 99.... <O#CLF9+> ... <O#HUF9+> ... <O#HOF9+> ... <O#UCF9+> ... <O#HCF9+>
Febuary 99.... <O#CLG9+> ... <O#HUG9+> ... <O#HOG9+> ... <O#UCG9+> ... <O#HCG9+>
March 99...... <O#CLH9+> ... <O#HUH9+> ... <O#HOH9+> ... <O#UCH9+> ... <O#HCH9+>
April 99...... <O#CLJ9+> ... <O#HUJ9+> ... <O#HOJ9+> ... <O#UCJ9+> ... <O#HCJ9+>
May 99........ <O#CLK9+> ... <O#HUK9+> ... <O#HOK9+> ... <O#UCK9+> ... <O#HCK9+>
June 99....... <O#CLM9+> ... <O#HUM9+> ... <O#HOM9+> ... <O#UCM9+> ... <O#HCM9+>
July 99....... <O#CLN9+> ... <O#HUN9+> ... <O#HON9+> ... <O#UCN9+> ... <O#HCN9+>
August 99..... <O#CLQ9+> ... <O#HUQ9+> ... <O#HOQ9+> ... <O#UCQ9+> ... <O#HCQ9+>
September 99.. <O#CLU9+> ... <O#HUU9+> ... <O#HOU9+> ... <O#UCU9+> ... <O#HCU9+>
October 99.... <O#CLV9+> ... <O#HUV9+> ... <O#HOV9+> ... <O#UCV9+> ... <O#HCV9+>
November 99... <O#CLX9+> ... <O#HUX9+> ... <O#HOX9+> ... <O#UCX9+> ... <O#HCX9+>
December 99... <O#CLZ9+> ... <O#HUZ9+> ... <O#HOZ9+> ... <O#UCZ9+> ... <O#HCZ9+>
January 2000.. <O#CLF0+> ... <O#HUF0+> ... <O#HOF0+> ... <O#UCF0+> ... <O#HCF0+>
Febuary 2000.. <O#CLG0+> ... <O#HUG0+> ... <O#HOG0+> ... <O#UCG0+> ... <O#HCG0+>

See also "RIC Rules Guide" on how to retrieve Options chains ........<RULES1>-7
=====================================================================
  NYMEX Natural Gas Options <ENERGY/OPT3>      Electricity Options <ENERGY/OPT4>
     Lost? Selective Access?..<USER/HELP>         Reuter Support..<PHONE/HELP>
```

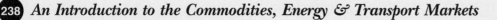

These Reuters screens show increasing detail about ATM Oilseed Contracts. Starting with the screen in the far upper right corner, the user goes from the general oilseed category, to the soya and rapeseed categories, to detail about the May 9 contract for each.

Begin here to see the various ATM commodity options.

O#COMMOD-ATM	Exchange	At the Money
RIC	ID	Contract
O#BASE-ATM	RCT/	Base Metal ATMs
O#FIBRES-ATM	RCT/	Fibres ATMs
O#FINANCIAL-ATM	RCT/	Financial ATMS
O#GRAINS-ATM	RCT/	Grains ATMs
O#LIVESTOCK-ATM	RCT/	Livestock ATM
O#OILSEEDS-ATM	RCT/	Oilseeds ATMs
O#PRECIOUS-ATM	RCT/	Precious ATMs
O#SOFTS-ATM	RCT/	Softs ATMs

O#OILSEEDS-ATM	Exchange	Oilseeds ATMs
RIC	ID	Contract
O#FLAXATM	RCT/	Flax ATMs
O#RAPEATM	RCT/	Rape ATMs
O#SOYATM	RCT/	Soy ATMs

O#RAPEATM	Exchange	Rape ATMs
RIC	ID	Contract
O#RS++	/	WPG CANOLA

O#SOYATM	Exchange	Soy ATMs
RIC	ID	Contract
O#S++	/	CBT SOYBEANS
O#XS++	/	MAC SOYABEANS
O#JAS++	TGE/	TOKYO SOYBEAN
O#SM++	/	CBT SOYBEAN
O#BO++	/	CBT SOYBEAN OIL

O#RS++	Exchange	WPG CANOLA
RIC	ID	Contract
O#RSc1++	/	MAY9
O#RSc2++	/	JUL9
O#RSc3++	/	AUG9
O#RSc4++	/	NOV9
O#RSc5++	/	JAN0

O#S++	Exchange	CBT SOYBEANS
RIC	ID	Contract
O#Sc1++	/	MAY9
O#Sc2++	/	JUN9
O#Sc3++	/	JUL9
O#Sc4++	/	AUG9
O#Sc5++	/	SEP9
O#Sc6++	/	NOV9
O#Sc7++	/	JAN0
O#Sc8++	/	MAR0
O#Sc9++	/	MAY0
O#Sc10+		

CANOLA May9 / CAD RSK9×WPG/ LT↑340.2 19:15 H342.1 L332.5

Strike	Mth	Calls	Bid	Ask	Volume	Time	Puts	Bid	Ask	Volume	Time
270	MAY9					:					:
280	MAY9					:					15:43
290	MAY9					:					16:21
300	MAY9					18:39			1.0		19:18
310	MAY9					17:24			1.5		18:14
320	MAY9	20.0				19:02			2.0		17:33
330	MAY9	11.0	12.0			18:46		3.5	3.6		18:05
340	MAY9	↑6.0	7.0	8.0	1	17:20	↓9.0	5.0	8.0	1	16:34
350	MAY9	↑4.0	3.0	4.0	1	19:07	9.0	15.0			:
360	MAY9	0.2				16:54					17:29
370	MAY9					17:44					17:28
380	MAY9					17:49					15:47
390	MAY9					17:26					18:23
400	MAY9					18:31					19:18
410	MAY9					16:11					:

SOYBEANS May9 / USc SK9×CBT/ LT↓497½ 10:06 H498¾ L497½

Strike	Mth	Calls	Bid	Ask	Volume	Time	Puts	Bid	Ask	Volume	Time
325	MAY9					16:07					:
350	MAY9					19:00					18:13
375	MAY9					16:04					15:32
400	MAY9					19:13					18:04
425	MAY9					15:55					18:04
450	MAY9	↓48				04:10					18:34
475	MAY9					19:13					19:14
500	MAY9	11½	12			19:14					19:14
525	MAY9					19:15					19:14
550	MAY9		2½			19:11					18:16
575	MAY9		1			17:19					15:40
600	MAY9		0½			19:14					15:32
625	MAY9		0½			18:06					18:53
650	MAY9					16:00					16:23
675	MAY9					16:15					18:34

Begin with the screen at right, showing the LME Option volumes for a specific day. The screen directly below is the index page for copper options, from which the user can obtain greater detail about premiums, volatilities and total volumes.

```
O#LME-OPTS-VOL              LME OPTIONS VOLS

                Today's Volumes : 22MAR99 18:00   Previous Day's Official Volumes

                Calls    Puts     Total          Calls    Puts     Total
COPPER          6430     1801     8231           6520     1801     8321
TIN
LEAD
ZINC                     800      800                     800      800
ALUMINIUM       15221    4528     19749          15221    4528     19749
AL. ALLOY
NICKEL          30       256      286            30       256      286
```

```
LME - REAL-TIME INDICATIVE AT-THE-MONEY OPTION PREMIUMS            MCU/IV2
Copper                    Current 3 Mth Forward :1460.0 1463.0    at 11:20
MONTH | TIME   FUT PRC  ATM SP | CALL PREMIUM   DELTA | PUT PREMIUM    DELTA
~~~~~ | ~~~~   ~~~~~~~  ~~~~~~ | ~~~~~~~~~~~~   ~~~~~ | ~~~~~~~~~~~   ~~~~~
APR-99 | 10:49  1450.25  1450= |  29.33/34.00    0.51 |  29.08/33.75  -0.49
MAY-99 | 11:11  1452.75  1450= |  46.25/49.69    0.52 |  43.52/46.96  -0.47
JUN-99 | 10:46  1463.50  1475= |  52.63/56.45    0.49 |  64.01/67.82  -0.50
JUL-99 | 10:46  1470.00  1475= |  66.09/70.76    0.51 |  71.02/75.68  -0.48
AUG-99 | 10:46  1477.00  1475= |  77.03/82.26    0.52 |  75.07/80.30  -0.46
SEP-99 | 10:46  1483.50  1475= |  85.78/91.52    0.53 |  77.47/83.21  -0.44
OCT-99 |             =         /                       |              /

       PROVISIONAL(P) / FINAL(E) CLOSE VALUES : 22MAR99
MONTH | ATM STK | CALL PREMIUM  PUT PREMIUM | CLS VOLATILITY
~~~~~ |         |  ~~~~~~~~~~~   ~~~~~~~~~~~ |  ~~~~~~~~~~~~~
APR-99 |
MAY-99 |
JUN-99 |
JUL-99 |
AUG-99 |
SEP-99 |
OCT-99 |
ATM Vola
```

```
09:30 23MAR99                                                   MCU/VOLO1
            LONDON METAL EXCHANGE SUMMARY
AT-THE-MONEY INDICATIVE OPTION CLOSING PREMIUMS & VOLATILITIES - COPPER

MONTH STRIKE  VOL    CALL    PUT     MONTH STRIKE  VOL    CALL    PUT
=====================================================================
APR99  1375   18.50  21.90   20.41   JUN00  1475   19.11  114.24  117.29
MAY99  1375   21.00  44.94   35.01   JUL00  1475   18.57  116.02  115.32
JUN99  1400   21.00  47.91   54.84   AUG00  1475   18.57  120.95  116.53
JUL99  1400   21.00  62.78   62.04   SEP00  1475   18.54  126.11  118.24
AUG99  1400   20.98  73.93   66.09   OCT00  1475   18.18  128.12  117.05
SEP99  1425   20.80  72.22   81.51   NOV00  1500   18.18  121.63  130.81
OCT99  1425   20.75  83.64   84.86   DEC00  1500   18.18  126.13  132.53
```

```
LME - TRADED OPTIONS INDEX, COPPER                               MCU/OPT
=====================================================================
** ATM Volatilities................<MCU/IV1>   **
** ATM Premiums.....................<MCU/IV2>   **
** Open Interest Summary............<MCU/OPTOI> **
** Closing Premiums & Volatilities...<MCU/VOLO1> **
** Matched Trade Reports Summary ...<MCU/TRDO1> **
Month   Summary     Op Int Detail    Month  Summary      Op Int Detail
-----   -------     -------------    -----  -------      -------------
APR99 <MCU/OPT01> <MCU/OPTOI01>      JUN00 <MCU/OPT15> <MCU/OPTOI15>
MAY99 <MCU/OPT02> <MCU/OPTOI02>      JUL00 <MCU/OPT16> <MCU/OPTOI16>
JUN99 <MCU/OPT03> <MCU/OPTOI03>      AUG00 <MCU/OPT17> <MCU/OPTOI17>
JUL99 <MCU/OPT04> <MCU/OPTOI04>      SEP00 <MCU/OPT18> <MCU/OPTOI18>
AUG99 <MCU/OPT05> <MCU/OPTOI05>      OCT00 <MCU/OPT19> <MCU/OPTOI19>
SEP99 <MCU/OPT06> <MCU/OPTOI06>      NOV00 <MCU/OPT20> <MCU/OPTOI20>
OCT99 <MCU/OPT07> <MCU/OPTOI07>      DEC00 <MCU/OPT21> <MCU/OPTOI21>
NOV99 <MCU/OPT08> <MCU/OPTOI08>      JAN01 <MCU/OPT22> <MCU/OPTOI22>
DEC99 <MCU/OPT09> <MCU/OPTOI09>      FEB01 <MCU/OPT23> <MCU/OPTOI23>
JAN00 <MCU/OPT10> <MCU/OPTOI10>      MAR01 <MCU/OPT24> <MCU/OPTOI24>
FEB00 <MCU/OPT11> <MCU/OPTOI11>      APR01 <MCU/OPT25> <MCU/OPTOI25>
MAR00 <MCU/OPT12> <MCU/OPTOI12>      MAY01 <MCU/OPT26> <MCU/OPTOI26>
APR00 <MCU/OPT13> <MCU/OPTOI13>      JUN01 <MCU/OPT27> <MCU/OPTOI27>
MAY00 <MCU/OPT14> <MCU/OPTOI14>            <MCU/OPT28> <MCU/OPTOI28>

TAPOs Index...<MCU/TAPO>   LME Index...<LME/INDEX>   Metals Guide...<METAL1>
```

```
LONDON METAL EXCHANGE - COPPER OPT      - APRIL 1999              MCU/OPT01

TOTAL COPPER VOLUMES -       23MAR99 | Open Interest (c/p) - 22MAR99  6442/3438
(ALL CONTRACTS)          call  put   | Volume (c/p)   - 22MAR99       591/55
Prev Day (Official)      6520  1801  |
Total to Morning                     |
Total to Afternoon                   |
Total Daily                          |
====================================================================
TRADE PRICES - 23MAR99               | PROVISIONAL / FINAL EVALUATIONS - 22MAR99
Trade   Strike    Matched Trades     |    Strike   Volatilities   Final Premiums
Time    Price      call    put       |    Price    Prov. Final    call    put
08:06   1475       16.00             | -5
                                     | -4
                                     | -3
                                     | -2
                                     | -1
                                     | ATM 1375=  18.50 18.50     21.90   20.41
                                     | +1
                                     | +2
                                     | +3
                                     | +4
                                     | +5
====================================================================
Eve Eval Summ..<MCU/VOLO1>  Trd Report Summ..<MCU/TRDO1>  OI Summ..<MCU/OPTOI>
```

The Reuters Options Calculator at right enables you to quickly determine pricing. With the calculator tab to the front of the screen, you would designate a commodity in the designated field (in this case, **LKD** for the LIFFE Robusta Coffee contract) to view displays for Bid/Ask, Puts/Calls to see changes in the values for the Greeks.

Then, by changing the **Commodity Item** to **LCO** for **IPE Brent Crude** contract, you can request and view the **Smile Curve**.

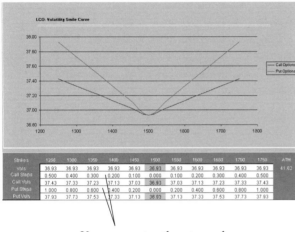

You can enter the step values required here to define the smile curve

Commodity item

Note the differences in the Greek values for Bid/Ask prices compared with those for Close prices

London International Financial Futures and Options Exchange

Futures	Contract Unit	Price basis	Option
No. 7 Cocoa	10 tonnes	GBP/tonne	✔
Robusta Coffee	5 tonnes	USD/tonne	✔
No. 5 White sugar	50 tonnes	USD/tonne	✔
No. 7 Premium white sugar	50 long tons	USD/ton	✘
Potato	20 tonnes	GBP/tonne	✔
Wheat	100 tonnes	GBP/tonne	✔
Barley	100 tonnes	GBP/tonne	✔
BIFFEX	Baltic Freight Index	10 USD per Index Point	✔

Tel No: +44 (171) 623 0444

www.liffe.com

Chicago Board of Trade

Futures	Contract Unit	Price basis	Option
Corn	5,000 bu	US cents/bu	✔
Oats	5,000 bu	US cents/bu	✔
Rough rice	2,000 cwt	US cents/cwt	✔
Soybeans	5,000 bu	US cents/bu	✔
Soybean oil	60,000 lb	US cents/lb	✔
Wheat	5,000 bu	US cents/bu	✔
Gold	1 kg	USD/troy oz	✘
Silver	1,000 troy oz	USD/troy oz	✔
TVA Hub Electricity	1,680 Mwh	USD/Mwh	✔

Tel No:+1 (312) 435 3500

www.cbot.com

The Singapore Exchange

Futures	Contract Unit	Price basis	Option
Gold	100 troy oz	USD/troy oz	✘
Heavy fuel oil	100 tonnes	USD/tonne	✘
Brent crude oil	1,000 bls	USD/bl	✘

Tel No: +65 236 8888

www.simex.com.sg

Tokyo Grain Exchange

Futures	Contract Unit	Price basis	Option
Red Bean	80 bags	JPY/bag	✘
Corn	100,000 kg	JPY/1000 kg	✔
Raw sugar	50,000 kg	JPY/1000 kg	✔
US Soybean	30,000 kg	JPY/1000 kg	✔
Arabica coffee	3,450 kg	JPY/69kg	✘
Robusta coffee	5,000 kg	JPY/100 kg	✘

Tel No: +81 (3) 3668 9321

www.tge.or.jp

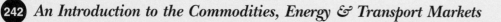

Minneapolis Grain Exchange 🇺🇸

Futures	Contract Unit	Price basis	Option
White shrimp	5,000 lb	US cents/lb	✔
Black Tiger shrimp	5,000 lb	US cents/lb	✔
Hard Red Spring wheat	5,000 bu	US cents/bu	✔
Soft White wheat	5,000 bu	US cents/bu	✔
Durum wheat	5,000 bu	US cents/bu	✔
Twin-Cities Electricity	736 Mwh	USD/Mwh	✔

Tel No: +1 (612) 338 6212   www.mgex.com

Sydney Futures Exchange 🇦🇺

Futures	Contract Unit	Price basis	Option
Wool	2,500 kg	AUS cents/kg	✖
Wheat	50 tonnes	A$/tonne	✔
NSW Electricity	500 Mwh	Price x 500	✔
Victorian Electricity	500 Mwh	Price x 500	✔

Tel No: +61 (2) 256 0555   www.sfe.com.au

TOCOM Tokyo Commodity Exchange ⬤

Futures	Contract Unit	Price basis	Option
Gold	1 kg	JPY/g	✖
Silver	60 kg	JPY/g	✖
Platinum	500 g	JPY/g	✖
Aluminium	10 tonnes	JPY/g	✖
Cotton yarn	1,814.36 kg	JPY/kg	✖
Rubber	5,000 kg	JPY/kg	✖
Wool yarn	5,000 kg	JPY/kg	✖

Tel No: +81 (3) 3661 9191   www.tocom.or.jp

Bolsa de Mercadorias & Futuros

Futures	Contract Unit	Price basis	Option
Arabica coffee	100 bags	USD/bag	✔
Robusta coffee	100 bags	USD/bag	✖
Soybean	450 x 60 kg	USD/60 kg	✖
Live cattle	330 arrobas	USD/arroba	✔
Cotton	10,000 lbs	USD/lb	✖
Crystal sugar	270 Bags	USD/Bag	✖
Corn	450 x 60 kg	USD/60 kg	✖
Gold	1000 g	USD/g	✔

Tel No: +55 11 232 5454   www.bmf.com.br

What Instruments Are Used in the Markets?

New York Mercantile Exchange

Futures	Contract Unit	Price basis	Option
Gulf Coast unleaded gasoline	1,000 bls	USD/bl	✔
Heating oil	1,000 bls	USD/bl	✔
Light sweet crude oil	1,000 bls	USD/bl	✔
Henry Hub Natural Gas	10,000 MMBtu	USD/MMBtu	✔
Propane	1,000 bls	USD/bl	✖
Sour crude oil	1,000 bls	USD/bl	✔
Palo Verde Electricity	736 Mwh	USD/Mwh	✔
Cinergy & Entergy Electricity	736 Mwh	USD/Mwh	✔
Permian Basin Natural Gas	10,000 MMBtu	USD/MMBtu	✔

Tel No: +1 (212) 748 3000   www.nymex.com

Commodity Exchange of New York

Futures	Contract Unit	Price basis	Option
Copper (High Grade)	25,000 lb	US cents/lb	✔
Gold	100 troy oz	USD/troy oz	✔
Silver	5,000 troy oz	USD/troy oz	✔
Platinum	50 troy oz	USD/troy oz	✔
Palladium	100 troy oz	USD/troy oz	✖

Tel No: +1 (212) 748 3000   www.nymex.com

New York Coffee, Sugar and Cocoa Exchange

Futures	Contract Unit	Price basis	Option
Sugar No.11	112,000 lb	US cents/lb	✔
Sugar No.14	112,000 lb	US cents/lb	✖
White sugar	50 tonnes	USD/tonne	✖
Arabica Coffee C	37,500 lb	US cents/lb	✔
Cocoa	10 tonnes	USD/tonne	✔
Cheddar cheese	10,500 lb	US cents/lb	✔
Milk	50,000 lb	US cents/cwt	✔
Butter	10,000 lb	US cents/lb	✔

Tel No: +1 (212) 742 6000   www.nybot.com

Shanghai Metal Exchange

Futures	Contract Unit	Price basis	Option
Copper	5 tonnes	Yuan/tonne	✖
Aluminium	5 tonnes	Yuan/tonne	✖
Lead	5 tonnes	Yuan/tonne	✖
Zinc	5 tonnes	Yuan/tonne	✖
Tin	2 tonnes	Yuan/tonne	✖
Nickel	3 tonnes	Yuan/tonne	✖

Tel No: +86 (021) 244 6688   www.shme.com

Chicago Mercantile Exchange

Futures	Contract Unit	Price basis	Option
Live cattle	40,000 lb	US cents/lb	✔
Feeder cattle	50,000 lb	US cents/lb	✔
Lean hogs	40,000 lb	US cents/lb	✔
Frozen pork bellies	40,000 lb	US cents/lb	✔
Non-fat dry milk	44,000 lb	US cents/lb	✔
Butter	40,000 lb	US cents/lb	✔
Cheddar cheese	40,000 lb	US cents/lb	✔
Dry whey	44,000 lb	US cents/lb	✔
Random length lumber	80,000 ft	USD/1000 ft	✔

Tel No: +1 (312) 930 1000   www.cme.com

London Metal Exchange

Futures	Contract Unit	Price basis	Option
Copper	25 tonnes	USD/tonne	OTC
Aluminium	25 tonnes	USD/tonne	OTC
Aluminium Alloy	20 tonnes	USD/tonne	OTC
Nickel	6 tonnes	USD/tonne	OTC
Zinc	25 tonnes	USD/tonne	OTC
Tin	5 tonnes	USD/tonne	OTC
Lead	25 tonnes	USD/tonne	OTC

Tel No: +44 (171)264 5555   www.lme.co.uk

New York Cotton Exchange

NYCE
COTTON · CITRUS · FINEX · NYFE

Futures	Contract Unit	Price basis	Option
Cotton	50,000 lb	US cents/lb	✔
Orange juice -Frozen concentrate	15,000 lb	US cents/lb	✔

Tel No: +1 (212) 742 5050   www.nybot.com

Kansas City Board of Trade

Futures	Contract Unit	Price basis	Option
Hard Red Winter wheat	5,000 bu	USD/bu	✔
Western Natural Gas	10,000 MMBtu	USD/MMBtu	✔

Tel No: +1 (816) 753 7500   www.kcbt.com

What Instruments Are Used in the Markets?

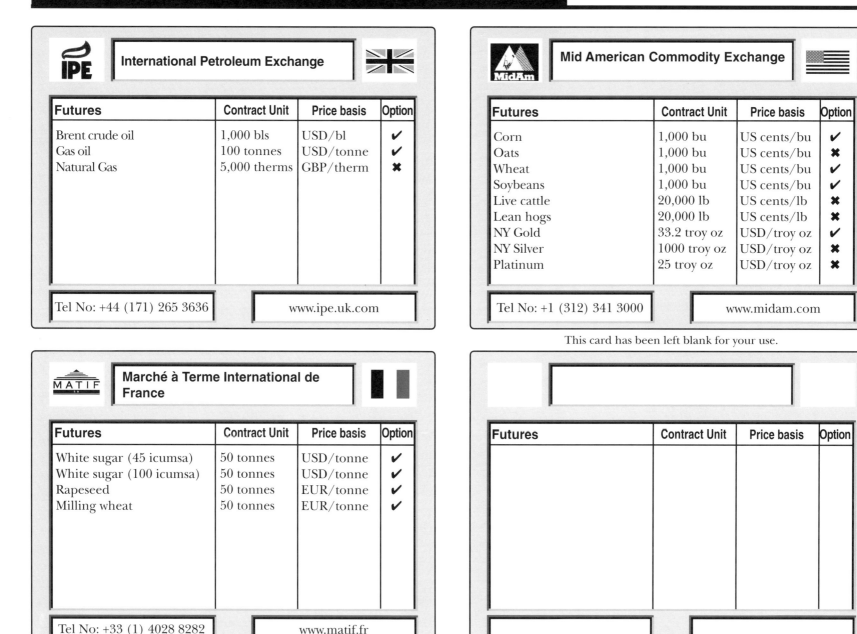

IPE — International Petroleum Exchange 🇬🇧

Futures	Contract Unit	Price basis	Option
Brent crude oil	1,000 bls	USD/bl	✔
Gas oil	100 tonnes	USD/tonne	✔
Natural Gas	5,000 therms	GBP/therm	✘

Tel No: +44 (171) 265 3636   www.ipe.uk.com

MidAm — Mid American Commodity Exchange 🇺🇸

Futures	Contract Unit	Price basis	Option
Corn	1,000 bu	US cents/bu	✔
Oats	1,000 bu	US cents/bu	✘
Wheat	1,000 bu	US cents/bu	✔
Soybeans	1,000 bu	US cents/bu	✔
Live cattle	20,000 lb	US cents/lb	✘
Lean hogs	20,000 lb	US cents/lb	✘
NY Gold	33.2 troy oz	USD/troy oz	✔
NY Silver	1000 troy oz	USD/troy oz	✘
Platinum	25 troy oz	USD/troy oz	✘

Tel No: +1 (312) 341 3000   www.midam.com

This card has been left blank for your use.

MATIF — Marché à Terme International de France

Futures	Contract Unit	Price basis	Option
White sugar (45 icumsa)	50 tonnes	USD/tonne	✔
White sugar (100 icumsa)	50 tonnes	USD/tonne	✔
Rapeseed	50 tonnes	EUR/tonne	✔
Milling wheat	50 tonnes	EUR/tonne	✔

Tel No: +33 (1) 4028 8282   www.matif.fr

Futures	Contract Unit	Price basis	Option

This chart shows the futures contracts available on worldwide exchanges for commodities in general.

	CBOT	CME	NYMEX	COMEX	CSCE	KCBT	MACE	MGE	NYCE	LIFFE	LME	IPE	MATIF	TGE	TCE	B&MF	SFE	SGX	SICOM	WCE	WTB	OMLX	SHME	Nordpool	NZFOE
Corn	✔						✔						✔	✔											
Oats	✔						✔													✔					
Soybean	✔						✔						✔	✔											
Wheat	✔					✔	✔	✔		✔			✔							✔					
Rice	✔																								
Milk		✔		✔																					
Butter		✔		✔																					
Wool														✔			✔								
Cotton									✔					✔	✔										
Orange juice									✔																
Coffee					✔					✔			✔		✔			✔							
Cocoa					✔					✔															
Sugar					✔					✔		✔	✔		✔										
Live cattle		✔					✔								✔										
Lean hogs/pigs		✔					✔													✔					
Pork bellies		✔																							
Lumber/pulp		✔																				✔			
Crude oil			✔									✔						✔							
Unleaded gasoline			✔																						
Heating oil/Gas oil			✔									✔						✔							
Natural Gas			✔			✔						✔													
Electricity	✔		✔					✔									✔							✔	✔
Copper				✔							✔												✔		
Aluminium											✔				✔								✔		
Nickel											✔												✔		
Lead											✔												✔		
Zinc											✔												✔		
Tin											✔												✔		
Gold	✔			✔			✔							✔	✔			✔							
Silver	✔			✔			✔								✔										
Platinum				✔			✔								✔										
Palladium				✔																					

Summary

You have now finished the third section of the book and you should have a clear understanding of the following:

- Spot, cash and physical delivery contracts used in the commodity, energy and transport markets

- The forward contracts used in the commodity, energy and transport markets

- The derivatives used in the commodity, energy and transport markets

As you have probably realised by now, the commodity, energy and transport markets are innovative and market participants are constantly seeking to provide new ways of hedging, speculating or offsetting their risks. The instruments that have been described here are not an exhaustive list and you will probably encounter variations or types not discussed. However, you should find most of the important types of contracts and their derivatives have been covered.

As a check on your understanding you should try the Quick Quiz Questions which follow. You may also find the Overview section to be a helpful learning tool.

Your notes

REUTERS

Quick Quiz Questions

1. Why do commodities/energy traders operate in the futures markets?

2. Who are the risk takers in the futures markets?

3. Do the specifications for futures contracts for the same commodity vary from different exchanges?

4. Some LME metal prices have the letters b and c beside them. What do these letters stand for and can you define the terms?

5. What are the main differences between forwards and futures contracts?

6. What is the main difference between a futures contract and an option on a futures contract for a particular commodity?

7. What factors influence premiums for an option?

8. Which of the following conditions does a futures contract specify?

    ❏ a) Contract asset
    ❏ b) Delivery date
    ❏ c) Delivery price
    ❏ d) Standard specification

9. If you place an order for a futures contract, when will you be required to pay initial margin?

    ❏ a) At expiry of the contract
    ❏ b) Only if you buy a contract
    ❏ c) At the time of trading the contract
    ❏ d) Only if you sell a contract

10. A trader buys 8 Brent crude oil futures on the IPE at $10.53 and sells after a rally at $11.52. If the contract size is 1000 barrels and the tick size is 0.01, what is the trader's loss or profit?

    ❏ a) $9,900 profit
    ❏ b) $7,920 profit
    ❏ c) $990 profit
    ❏ d) $990 loss

11. A speculator buys 1 lot of Coffee futures on LIFFE at $1,872/tonne. He closes his position with a loss of $125/tonne. If the tick value is $1 and the contract size is 5 tonnes, at what price has the speculator closed out?

    ❏ a) $2,497
    ❏ b) $1,997
    ❏ c) $1,747
    ❏ d) $1,247

12. A Cocoa producer sells Cocoa futures on the NYCSCE for $1,310/tonne in March. In May he buys the futures back at $1,350/tonne and sells his Cocoa in the cash market at $1,250/tonne. What is the producers net profit for his Cocoa/tonne?

    ❏ a) $1,210
    ❏ b) $1,290
    ❏ c) $1,350
    ❏ d) $1,390

13. In the Tin market there is a backwardation of $47 to the 3-month forward price. If the 3-month forward price is $5,525/tonne, what is the current cash price?

    ❏ a) $5,478
    ❏ b) $5,500
    ❏ c) $5,547
    ❏ d) $5,572

14. If a market player is hedging his or her position, then the market player:

    ❏ a) Holds only a futures position
    ❏ b) Holds only a cash position
    ❏ c) Holds a futures position the same as the cash position
    ❏ d) Holds a futures position opposite to the cash position

15. On which of the following exchanges are Copper futures contracts traded?

    ❏ a) LME
    ❏ b) NYCSCE
    ❏ c) NYMEX
    ❏ d) SFE

16. Which of the following statements describes a call option?

- ❑ a) The other side of a put option transaction
- ❑ b) The right to buy an underlying security in the future
- ❑ c) The right to sell an underlying security in the future
- ❑ d) The obligation to buy an underlying security in the future

17. Which of the following statements is/are true? An in-the-money call option has a –

- ❑ a) Future price greater than its strike price
- ❑ b) Future price less than its strike price
- ❑ c) Intrinsic value
- ❑ d) Time value only

18. Which of the following statements are true for a commodity option traded on an exchange?

- ❑ a) The buyer has the right, but not the obligation, to buy the underlying instrument on exercise
- ❑ b) The premium is payable when the trade is made
- ❑ c) The option can be exercised at any price set by the buyer
- ❑ d) The buyer has the right, but not the obligation, to sell the underlying instrument on exercise

19. Which of the following statements are true for an American style option? The holder can exercise the option

- ❑ a) Only if the strike price is above the exercise price
- ❑ b) An option with premiums paid in US Dollars
- ❑ c) Only on the expiry date
- ❑ d) At any time up to and including the expiry date

20. A broker buys call options on an exchange for a client. Which one of the following is the ultimate counterparty for the client?

- ❑ a) Broker
- ❑ b) Exchange clearing member
- ❑ c) Exchange clearing house
- ❑ d) Option writer

21. Which of the following strategies could a market player adopt if he thought that share prices were likely to fall considerably in the future.

- ❑ a) Short Put
- ❑ b) Long Put
- ❑ c) Short Call
- ❑ d) Long Call

22. The current price of cocoa is $1,320/tonne. A producer decides to buy a Call option with an exercise price of $1,300 and a premium of $29. What is the break-even point price for this option?

- ❑ a) $1,271
- ❑ b) $1,320
- ❑ c) $1,329
- ❑ d) $1,349

23. An investor decides to buy 3 Coffee March100 Call options on the NYCSCE. The premium is 4.80¢/lb and the contract size is 37,500lb of coffee. How much premium has to be paid?

- ❑ a) $1,800
- ❑ b) $5,400
- ❑ c) $18,000
- ❑ d) $54,000

You can check your answers on page 253.

Overview

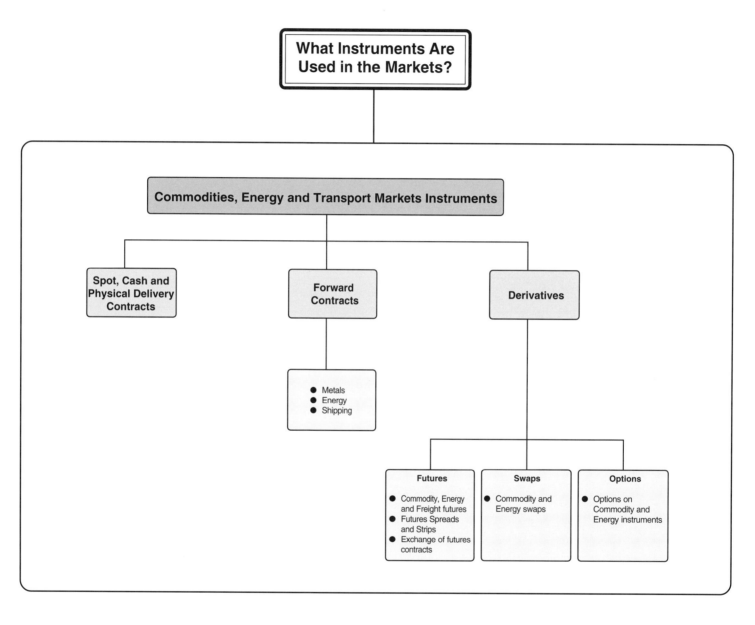

Quick Quiz Answers

1. *Why do commodities/energy traders operate in the futures markets?*
   The traders need to hedge their position against risk depending on whether they need to buy or sell. They may also speculate in the markets for profit.

2. *Who are the risk takers in the futures markets?*
   Speculators – they have no position to protect and therefore buy and sell purely for profit.

3. *Do the specifications for futures contracts for the same commodity vary from different exchanges?*
   Yes. Each exchange sets its own specification as to quality, contract unit, price basis etc for the commodities/energy products it trades.

4. *Some LME metal prices have the letters b and c beside them. What do these letters stand for and can you define the terms?*
   b = **Backwardation**: This is when the futures price for the commodity is at a discount to its spot or cash price.

   c = **Contango**: This is when the futures price is at a premium to its spot or cash price.

5. *What are the main differences between forwards and futures contracts?*
   Although both contracts involve transactions for the delivery of a specified quantity and quality of commodity at a future date, the main difference is that a forwards contract is not traded on an exchange. Forward contracts are private and negotiated between the parties with no standardised conditions, no exchange guarantees and no margin payments are involved. Futures contracts are standardised contracts traded on an exchange floor, which are guaranteed and reported by the exchange, and which involve margin payments.

6. *What is the main difference between a futures contract and an option on a futures contract for a particular commodity?*
   Options on futures contracts again concern transactions to be settled at some time in the future. The emphasis is on the **right** of the option holder to buy (call option) or sell (put option) a futures contract – there is **no obligation** to buy or sell as there is in a futures contract.

7. *What factors influence premiums for an option?*
   There are four main factors:
   - The option strike price
   - Underlying futures contract price
   - Option expiry date
   - Volatility of the underlying futures contract. In general the higher the volatility the higher the option premium.

                         ✔ or ✖

8. a), b) and d) ❑ ❑ ❑

9. c) ❑

10. b) ❑

11. c) ❑

12. a) ❑

13. d) ❑

14. d) ❑ ❑

15. a) and c) ❑ ❑

	✔ or ✘
16. b)	❑
17. a) and c)	❑
	❑
18. a) and b)	❑
	❑
19. d)	❑
20. c)	❑
21. b)	❑
22. c)	❑
23. b)	❑

How well did you score? You should have managed to get most of these questions correct.

Your notes

Further Resources

Books

The Penguin International Dictionary of Finance
Graham Bannock & William Manser, Penguin, 2nd Edition 1995
ISBN   0 14 051279 9

Wolff's Guide to the London Metal Exchange
Rudolff Wolff & Co Limited, Metal Bulletin Books

Publications

Reuters
- Coverage of the London Metal Exchange
  Version 1.01, October 1998

Chicago Mercantile Exchange
- Commoditiy Futures and Options: Facts and Resources
- Risk Management Guide for Agricultural Lenders
- Introduction to Livestock and Meat Fundamentals

Chicago Board Options Exchange
- Trading in Futures: An Introduction for Speculators
- Introduction to Hedging with Futures and Options
- Options as an investment tool
- CBOT Agricultural Option Strategies Menu
- Trading Agricultural Option Volatility: A Step-by-Step Approach
- Gold/Silver Ratio Spread

London International Financial Futures and Options Exchange
- An Introduction to Commodity Options
- LIFFE Options Strategies: A quick reference guide

International Petroleum Exchange
- Natural Gas futures
- A proposal to reduce CO_2 emissions in the European Union
  through the introduction of an emissions trading programme

Drewry Shipping Consultants Ltd
- Shipping Futures and Derivatives – From BIFFEX to Forward
  Freight Agreements (FFAs) and beyond. September 1997

New York Coffee, Sugar and Cocoa Exchange
- Understanding Options on Futures
- Flexible Options

New York Mercantile Exchange
- A Guide to Energy Hedging
- A Guide to Metals Hedging
- Crack Spread Options
- Options Strategies
- Glossary of Terms

Swiss Bank Corporation
- Options: The fundamentals. ISBN 0 9641112 0 9

London Metal Exchange
- TAPOs – Traded Average Price Options

Internet

RFT Web Site
- **http://www.wiley.rft.reuters.com**
This is the series' companion web site where additional quiz
questions, updated screens and other information can be found.

World Bank
- **http://www.worldbank.org**

Standard & Poor's Platt's
- **http://www.platts.com**

Exchanges

Refer to the back of this book for a listing of worldwide exchanges'
contact information and web sites.

Your notes

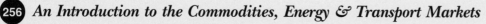

This section of the book should take between one and two hours of study time. You may not take as long as this or it may take a little longer – remember your learning is individual to you.

'Then five minutes of what looks like total confusion and mayhem unfolds, as the whole Market is engulfed in a cauldron of noise, waving hands, and frantic business.'

A Dealer's Life by Martin Hayes, Senior Metal Correspondent, Reuters Ltd, The Ringsider, p16, October 1998

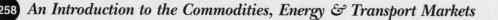

Introduction

By now you should have some understanding of why the markets exist, how the markets operate and what instruments are traded. You should also be clear on who the market players are in the individual commodities, energy and transport markets. In most of these markets brokers act as intermediaries between counterparties and do not usually deal on their own account but earn commissions on the deals they arrange. However, in some markets it is possible for a market player to be both market maker and broker.

This section is concerned with *how* trading takes place in the commodities, energy and transport markets and the regulation of these markets. As you will see the use of automated electronic trading systems is becoming increasingly more important in these markets which operate 24 hours per day. It is also important to understand that in the commodities and energy markets, although the contracts traded are usually concerned with the physical delivery of an agricultural crop, barrels of oil, ingots of metal etc, most trading is carried out in the derivatives markets where delivery of the underlying is unusual. In other words, trading in the spot and cash markets accounts for a small proportion of market activity and by its nature is OTC and private.

Before moving on, try the activity opposite.

What are bid and ask prices quoted for contracts? Write down your descriptions here.

You can check you answer over the page.

Before moving on check your answers to the previous activity.

> **R** You probably didn't have too much trouble with this one!
>
> The **Bid** price – the lower value – is the price the market-maker is prepared to **buy** at. You sell to the market-maker who pays you for the commodity.
>
> The **Ask** price – the higher one– is the price the market-maker is prepared to **sell** at. You buy from the market-maker who charges you for the commodity.

There have been many important changes in the way worldwide exchanges trade since 1996 – in particular with the use of electronic trading. Some of the more recent developments are discussed here.

Exchange traded Contracts

Many of the exchange traded futures originated with the needs of producers and consumers of cash crops, mining, livestock etc. For example, the Chicago Board of Trade (CBOT) was established in 1848 to help farmers hedge the risk in grain cash transactions while the LME was founded in 1877 as a market place for trading important metals in the industrial revolution in England.

The exchanges provided a way in which producers could hedge their risk and processors could protect their requirements for a particular commodity against price rises. For example, livestock farmers can sell futures contracts on the CME to guarantee prices whilst the US meat packers such as Conagra and IBP Inc buy futures.

On certain exchanges, such as the LME, exchange members act as market makers to fix prices. When requested for a quote they must provide a two-way bid/ask price.

Open Outcry

Trading on an exchange using open outcry and hand signals makes the exchange floor a noisy, crowded and colourful place. Exchange trading is described in more detail in the *Introduction to Derivatives* book.

In general, exchanges comprise members who lease a **seat** or trading permit. Such a seat allows a member to trade on the exchange floor in areas known as **pits** or **rings**. Different pits or rings specialise in different futures and options contracts. Traders must be qualified by the exchange to trade on the floor and they are not allowed to deal directly with the public. The intermediaries between traders and the public are brokers.

Some exchange floors, for example the IPE, are quite small only involving a few pits; others are large, for example, the CME which covers 70,000 square feet on two floors.

Many of the exchanges also operate automated matching or electronic trading systems for out-of-hours floor trading periods. For example, on CBOT the system is known as Project A and on IPE the system is ETS. These trading systems have the same trading rules as those for pit trading regarding margin payments, settlement etc. There are three characteristics of an automated matching system:

- Users send their bids and offers to a central matching system
- The bids and offers are distributed to all other market participants
- The system identifies possible trades based on price, size, redit and any other rules relevant to the market

This method of using predominately open outcry supplemented by out-of-hours electronic trading is rapidly disappearing on some exchanges, being replaced by automated electronic trading.

Electronic Trading

Automated matching or electronic systems which once supplemented open outcry pit trading out-of-hours are now rapidly becoming an integral way in which exchange trading takes place. On some exchanges such as MATIF, open outcry has been replaced completely by electronic trading. But why should this be?

There are a number of reasons which have contributed to the dramatic changes taking place in the way exchanges trade – particularly on European exchanges. Some of the more important reasons include the following;

- **Increasing competition** from the cash and OTC derivatives markets. Many market players trade simultaneously on exchanges and in the OTC markets and are constantly looking at ways of reducing costs while operating with maximum flexibility.

- The improved **availability and access to high speed communications networks** means that electronic systems cut across product and institutional markets.

- For a variety of political and economic reasons many exchanges have either entered or are considering **strategic alliances/partnerships/mergers** with other exchanges and/or brokers in order to create a single trading platform and reduce clearing and marketing costs. Some exchanges operate Mutual Offset Systems for specific contracts, for example, the Brent Crude oil futures contract can be offset on SIMEX and vice versa.

Automated matching systems comprise three components:

1. Computer terminals where orders are placed and trade confirmations are received
2. A host computer that processes trades
3. A network that links the terminals to the host computer

On many exchanges electronic trading takes place using a system of rules for the host computer to match bid and offer orders. Each exchange has its own rules which typically relate to matters such as order size, type of order and time of order. If the exchange Clearing house is also connected to the host computer, then trades can be cleared electronically. The following diagram shows a typical electronic trading system.

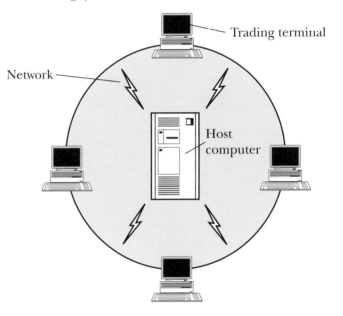

The effectiveness of any trading system, open outcry or electronic, can be measured as its ability to create market liquidity and to minimise the costs of trading.

Market players in the futures and options markets need to be able to buy and sell contracts quickly for a fair price. On an exchange trading floor liquidity is provided by traders who are constantly available for trading even when activity is slow. Traders using electronic systems can shift their activity to where trading is most active very quickly.

In some cases, for large and complex trades in particular, floor trading may offer the best method of trading as the traders can interact immediately with each other. However, it is probably only a matter of time before improved software solutions become available for large and complex electronic trades.

Electronic systems can reduce the costs of trading in that less labour and time are required for trading. Also electronic systems do not involve large buildings with pits for trading. The following chart summarises the trading differences between open outcry and electronic trading systems.

Trading	Open Outcry	Electronic
Main suppliers of liquidity	Floor traders	Large institutions and market-makers
Main costs	Trading floor and back office activities	Hardware, software and network costs
Main sources of information	Floor traders see what is going on	Order book and outside news
Operating efficiency	Relatively high investment of labour and time	Quick, accurate and transparent
Possible sources of trading errors or misconduct	Lack of precise trade records and floor traders are known to each other	Manipulation of orders prior to and on entry

Another important advantage of electronic systems is the feasibility of alliances and mergers which may affect the competitiveness of an exchange. For example, in 1998 futures trading for the Bund contract on LIFFE was severely affected by the merger of the Deutsche Termin Börse (DTB) and the Swiss Options and Financial Futures Exchange (SOFFEX). This merger was called **Eurex** and the new exchange traded electronically. Eurex also established the **Euro Alliance** which formed strategic alliances with MATIF and MONEP – both electronic exchanges – and CBOT which uses some electronic trading. The activities of Eurex have forced LIFFE into a commitment to become an electronic exchange as soon as possible in order to compete.

The Reuters screen below shows Eurex data.

```
10:09 15FEB99                EUREX              GE65200            EUREX
                     X-pand into the Future

FOR FUNCTIONAL HELP PLS CALL                      TECHNICAL HELPDESK
     STOCKS        ++49 69 2101 1210                 ++49 69 2101 1200
     INDEX         ++49 69 2101 1220
   INTEREST RATE   ++49 69 2101 1240
     CLEARING      ++49 69 2101 1250

                  T A B L E   O F   C O N T E N T S
NEW TRADING SERIES 1/3   <EUREX02>   SMI-CAP.FACTOR + NO. OF SHARES  <EUREX17>
NEW TRADING SERIES 2/3   <EUREX03>   GENERAL ASS./DIVIDEND DATES 1/3 <EUREX18>
NEW TRADING SERIES 3/3   <EUREX04>   GENERAL ASS./DIVIDEND DATES 2/3 <EUREX19>
BLOCKTRADE ME
BLOCKTRADE ME│12:38 08MAR99           EUREX              GE65200         EUREX11
BASISTRADE ME│               X-pand into the Future
BASISTRADE ME│
EMERGENCY 1/2│        F I N A L   S E T T L E M E N T   V A L U E S
EMERGENCY 2/2│
FINAL SETTLEM│CAPITAL MARKET PRODUCTS   MONEY MARKET PRODUCTS   INDEX PRODUCTS
NOTIFICATION/│
LAST TRADING │BUND MAR99 = 114.68    LIB1 NOV = 96.485    FDAX DEC = 4693.56
TRADING FEES │BOBL MAR99 = 108.54    LIB3 NOV = 96.360    ODAX FEB = 4843.14
CAP. ADJ./ADJ│SHAZ MAR99 = 104.88                         FMDX DEC = 3912.86
CAP. ADJ./ADJ│                       FEU1 FEB = 96.875    FVDX DEC = 38.21
             │                       FEU3 FEB = 96.900
             │CONF MAR99 = 129.36    FLI3 FEB = 96.905    FSMI DEC = 6982.8
             │COMI MAR99 = 114.03                         OSMI FEB = 6992.2
             │                                            FESX DEC = 3130.54
             │FGBS MAR =  104.88                          OESX FEB = 3373.96
             │FGBM MAR =  108.54                          FSTX DEC = 3161.07
             │FGBL MAR =  114.68                          OSTX FEB = 3358.10
             │FGBX MAR =  114.55


             │<EUREX10>              <EUREX>              <EUREX12>
```

Also announced in 1998 was the merger of the New York Coffee, Sugar and Cocoa Exchange with the New York Cotton Exchange to form the New York Board of Trade (NYBT).

However, the introduction of electronic trading is not without its pitfalls! The article opposite was written by Reuters correspondent, David Clarke, from the Paris Newsroom.

Sell in haste, repent at leisure. The potential pitfalls of electronic trading were graphically illustrated on Thursday when a contract on French derivatives exchange MATIF SA plunged more than a point and a half in seconds and then bounced back.

Traders said a trader placed a sell order for 10,000 10-year French government bond futures at market, when the price was 105.10, about 15 minutes before the close. A MATIF spokeswoman confirmed the amounts and timing but declined to say which institution had placed the sell order.

With relatively low volume being traded at the time of the order, the price of the contract kept falling until buy orders could be found to match all the contracts on offer.

After trading in a narrow range for most of the day, the 10-year bond future slumped from 105.10 to 103.61 – the so-called limit-down price which halts trading to prevent excessively large price swings.

"The contract lost a point and a half in seconds," said one trader in Paris.

Market sources speculated that the trader who put in the large sell order had punched in more zeroes for the volume than intended. Talk in the market was that the unfortunate seller had tried to stem the slump by yanking his machine's plug from its socket.

The contract quickly bounced back to 105, allowing those who had bought on the way down to make a profit, and left the initial seller looking at an unexpected loss.

As one tick is worth 50 francs, 10,000 contracts sold at 149 basis points below the market price could have resulted in a maximum loss of 74,500,000 francs. However, it was not clear how many contracts of the sell order were actually sold, nor at what price.

Commodities Markets

The **physical** or **cash** markets represent huge worldwide trading marketplaces without which futures markets would not be required for hedging or speculating. The term **spot** market is also used for physical markets but beware – sometimes futures traders use the term spot to indicate the first contract month!

For centuries **auction** or **sales rooms** in trading ports were where merchants bought and sold commodities. For example, auctions for commodities such as tea shipped from India and China were first held in London in 1679. The method of selling tea at this time was rather bizarre in that it was sold 'by the candle'. This meant that when an inch of candle had burned the auctioneer set the price! By the 1830s tea auctions took place in the grand settings of Plantation House, London, and could take up to six days to complete. Improvements in communications, transport and technology have all contributed to the demise of many commodity auction rooms. Many commodities are now traded actively on the Internet and many large consumers buy direct from plantation owners. The last tea auction took place in London in June 1998 but a chest of Ceylon tea was sold at a record £555 per kilo.

St. Katharine Docks

Opened in 1828 the St. Katharine Docks in London were purpose built for warehousing valuable commodities such as ivory, shells, sugar, marble, wines, spices, rubber and feathers. In order to construct the docks some 11,000 people were 'displaced' and the church of St. Katharine was demolished – hence the name given to the docks. As trade to London increased so did the dock size and in 1852 the Ivory House was added. This building was specifically designed for the storage of elephant tusks and was well ventilated to cope with the smell! The Ivory House still exists but many of the old warehouses have gone. However, there are still links with commodity trading as the IPE and the LIFFE exchange floor for commodities – the former London Commodity Exchange – operate on sites once occupied by warehouses.

Most physical trades involve actual delivery of the commodity and are often negotiated directly by phone, fax or telex between buyers and sellers, although sometimes a broker is involved. As the trade is direct both parties have to understand all the contract conditions concerning quality, quantity, delivery conditions, taxes, costs etc. This is very important as there is no guarantee of performance as with exchange contracts. Each market has its own time period for spot trades. For example, New York Gasoline Spot deliveries are for 2–3 days, whereas Dated Brent deliveries are for 15 days.

In a **forward trade** the contract is for delivery of the commodity to take place sometime in the future which is usually specified by the market. The time period may be historical as in the case of the LME where the standard forward contract time is 3 months – why 3 months?. When the LME was established this was the time it took shipments from South America to reach London. In the case of Brent oil the forward contract is for 15 days.

One of the more interesting commodity exchanges trading derivatives contracts is the London Metal Exchange, LME. The methods of trading the base metal forward contracts and options on metals differs considerably from other commodities exchanges trading futures and options contracts. As with many other exchanges the LME is currently considering the introduction of electronic trading. As the LME is a unique commodity exchange its operations are discussed in a little more detail here.

London Metal Exchange

The LME was established in 1877 at the height of the industrial revolution for trading metals including pig-iron. Today the exchange deals only with base or non-ferrous metals. The exchange has about 100 members over 90% of whom are wholly or part-owned by overseas organisations.

The LME is an unusual exchange in that it provides both a physical and futures and options market in the same place. In some respects the LME is also like the FX market with both spot and forward prices quoted by brokers.

Modern telecommunications systems have enabled the LME to become an international 24 hour market with members and associate members being able to trade any time they wish. The exchange traded contracts are cleared through the London Clearing House (LCH) which guarantees the terms of the contract for both buyers and sellers. Approximately 80% of LME trades now occur 'off-exchange'.

The LME is not a conventional futures market but provides forward - dated contracts which are very similar to futures contracts. The published LME contracts are settled in US dollars, although the exchange permits settlement in deutschemarks, sterling and yen.

The LME trading day has changed little since the exchange was founded. Only **Ring Dealing Members** of the LME are allowed to trade directly on the exchange floor.

Originally open out-cry trading was conducted around a chalk circle which had been drawn on the floor to denote the "ring". Today the traders sit on 36 red leather chairs arranged in a circle, slightly sunken into the floor, so all the seats face each other. This arrangement ensures that no trader has an advantage over another during trading.

Clients channel their business via the member brokers onto the floor of the exchange.

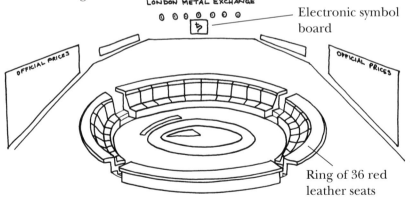

Electronic symbol board

Ring of 36 red leather seats

Around the 36 seats is a wooden bar and outside the circles of blue and green floor covering are booths for the traders. A bell rings to start each 5 minute trading session at which point traders take their seats and communicate their deals with each other by shouting across the ring – trading in copper can be particularly noisy. Each metal being traded is indicated by a symbol on an electronic board – although each metal has specific trading times. The symbols for the seven metals contracts traded on the exchange are given below.

Copper — During the trading sessions member firm clerks etc stand at the wooden circular bar around the ring and relay information back to their booths using hand signals.

Aluminium — Although the exchange operates for 24 hours per day, activity on the floor is limited to short bursts of trading lasting five minutes each known as **rings**. Each ring is metal specific and each metal has two rings in a morning session and two again in an afternoon session. After the 14 morning rings (seven metals traded twice over) the **LME official prices** are generally calculated and quoted from the mid-point of the close of the second morning ring. These official prices are displayed on two large boards either side of the ring.

Nickel

Zinc — The LME official prices act as the daily settlement prices and are used by buyers and sellers for long term contract pricing and by the LCH for calculating daily margin requirements. A cash settlement price is also published by the LME and is the official ask price on a cash contract.

Tin

Lead — The morning ring sessions are of particular interest in the Asian time zone for exchanges such as the Shanghai Metal Exchange and the Shenzen Metal Exchange. The afternoon rings are watched by customers in the US who are interested in the New York COMEX prices. Consequently the LME provides an international pricing mechanism.

Aluminium Alloy

When the LME was first established trading could only take place during the rings. However, sometimes traders did not complete a trade before the closing bell was rung. In these cases the trading continued outside the exchange building, on the pavement **kerb**. In the 1900s **kerb dealing** or **kerb trading**, as it had become known, became so rowdy that the police had to intervene and from thereafter unofficial kerb trading was permitted in the exchange after the official morning rings.

Also outside the ring sessions the Ring Dealing Members and Associate Members are permitted to trade LME contracts inter-office and quote prices for any delivery date.

While the market place operates, in theory, for 24 hours daily, a typical trading day runs from 07.00–19.00 London time, catering for Asian business at the morning ring sessions and for US needs after the afternoon sessions.

The Reuters screens at right show who the LME market markers are and trading times.

```
LME/BROKER                    LME BROKERS

Market      | 3M &  |        **** F O R W A R D S ****
Makers      | spreads| Cu    Al    Zn    Ni    Pb    Sn    AA

AIG International | <AIGI> |
Amalganated Metals | <AMTL> | <AMTM> <AMTN> <AMTA> <AMTB> <AMTD> <AMTE> <AMTC>
J Aron (Goldman S) | <ARON> |
Barclays          | <BARC> | <BMLA> <BMLB> <BMLC> <BMLD> <BMLF> <BMLE>
Billiton          | <BILL> | <BILI> <BILJ> <BILK>
Brandeis          | <BIBL> | <BRND> <BRNE> <BRNF> <BRNG>
                  |        | <BIBC> <BIBA> <BIBE> <BIBE>
Carr Futures      | <CFLM> |
Chase Manhattan   | <CHSA> |
Credit Lyonnais   | <CLRS> | <CLRT> <CLRU>
Deutsche Sharps   | <DSML> | <DSMM> <DSMN> <DSMO>
```

```
LME/BROKER                    LME BROKERS

Metdist       | <MDTL> |        <MDTM>
Mitsui Bussan | <MBUA> | <MBUB> <MBUC> <MBUD>
Morgan Stanley| <MSDW> |
NM Rothschild | <NMRS> |
PruBache (HK) | <BHHK> |
PruBache (Ldn)| <PBBL> | <PBBM> <PBBN> <PBBO> <PBBQ> <PBBR> <PBBS>
Refco         | <REFO> | <RF1B> <RF1D> <RF1F> <RF1H>
Rudolf Wolff  | <WLFA> | [Also see page <WLFZ>]
              | <WLFB> |
ScotiaMocatta Bank | <MCLO> | <MCLP> <MCLQ> <MCLR> <MCLN> <MCLS>
Sogenin       | <SGME> | <SGMF> <SGMG> <SGMH>
Standard Bank | <SBNK> |
Sucden        | <SDUK> |
Triland       | <TRIL> | <TRIM> <TRIN> <TRIO>
```

```
The London Metal Exchange   Trading Times                    LME/TIMES1

=================== LME MORNING TRADING TIMES ===========================
London Inter-office Trading:        07:00 - 11:45

                  Aluminium Alloy:   11:45 - 11:50
                  Tin:               11:50 - 11:55
                  Primary Aluminium: 11:55 - 12:00
                  Copper:            12:00 - 12:05
                  Lead:              12:05 - 12:10
                  Zinc:              12:10 - 12:15
                  Nickel:            12:15 - 12:20
                  INTERVAL
                  Copper:            12:30 - 12:35   (Officials)
                  INTERVAL
                  Tin:               12:40 - 12:45   (Officials)
                  Lead:              12:45 - 12:50   (Officials)
                  Zinc:              12:50 - 12:55   (Officials)
                  Primary Aluminium: 12:55 - 13:00   (Officials)
                  Nickel:            13:00 - 13:05   (Officials)
                  Aluminium Alloy:   13:05 - 13:10   (Officials)
                  KERB:              13:10 - 13:30   (Officials)
```

Energy Markets

Oil and Oil Products

Prior to OPEC and the introduction of the futures markets, the oil markets were totally under the control of the major oil companies – the Seven Sisters. The OPEC producers, other national oil companies and refiners have taken over or replaced the role formerly held by the oil companies and are active in the markets. This is a result of producers having refining plants, sometimes at source, in order to increase their share of the oil products markets.

Government agencies and large industrial organisations, for example, Dow Chemicals, BASF and ICI are players in the markets as a way of ensuring feed stocks for their products and reducing their exposure to third parties.

Oil traders, in particular speculators, have grown in number from the late 1970s and are active players in the spot physical markets. Many of the companies such as Marc Rich, Cargill, Vitol are refiners also in their own right.

The players described above are active in the spot physical and forward markets where, in most cases, physical delivery is contracted. In the forward markets cash settlement is also used rather than taking physical delivery of the oil.

Participants in the derivative futures and options markets are mainly the players already described who are hedging risks or speculating on the markets. However, as physical delivery rarely takes place, exchange traded futures and options are also used by banks, commodity houses, fund managers and private individuals.

The physical markets are not transparent – individual contract prices are not declared – which means that Reuters editorial staff, price clerks and reporters are in constant daily contact with the market players to gather indicative prices. **Platt's** report these prices, and through historical links are often regarded as the price benchmark.

Before moving on, look at the information available to players from **Platt's** via the Reuters screens below. Shown are the Platt's Main Speed Guide, Global Alert, World Crude Assessment and Dated Brent Indications.

```
                                                          PLATTS
PLATT'S MAIN SPEED GUIDE:This guide will help you find Platt's news and data. To
see itens, most users can double-click on the codes in <> or [] brackets. For
more help with this guide, double click here on <USER/HELP> or key in USER/HELP.

PLATT'S MAIN SERVICES                    PLATT'S GLOBAL ALERT ADD-ONS
Platt's Global Alert        <PGAINDEX>   Bunker Add-on           <PGBINDEX>
Platt's Marine Alert        <PGMINDEX>   Tanker Add-on           <PGTINDEX>
Platt's Metal
Platt's Petro
Inside FERC's
McGraw-Hill's
```

```
                                                          PGAINDEX
Platt's Global Alert Main Speed Guide

European Marketscan ............[nPLEUSCAN]  Crudeoil Marketwire .....[nPLCRUDE]
News ====================================    Crude ==============================
Platt's oil news, deals and connent ..[PGA]  Crude oil speed guide ....<PGACRDA>
Notifications of Platt's assessments ..[PGA]  Spot crude deals ..........[PGA003]
Platt's news, non-market .......[PLTN\-PGA]  World crude assessments ...<PGA012>
Crude news, deals and connent ........[CRU]  US crude assessments ...<PGA171>
Products news, deals and connent ....[PROD]  Pacific rin assessments ...<PGA165>
OPEC news......................[OPEC]        Hourly Brent/WTI .........<PGA162>
US refinery turnarounds...........<PGA049>   Brent/Dubai spreads ........<PGA164>
European refinery turnarounds.....<PGA206>   Dated Brent indications ...<PGA578>
Asian refinery turnarounds.<PGA283><PGA284>  Crude market connent ......[PGA013]
```

```
17:01 16DEC98            PLATT'S              UK34448      PGA012
12--Platt's Crude Oil Assessments - 16Dec98
16Dec98/459 pn EST/2159 GMT
Brent(JAN)  +11.22-11.25+   Dubai(FEB) +11.25-11.30+
Brent(FEB)  +11.34-11.36+   Dubai(MAR) +11.34-11.42+
Brent(MAR)  +11.52-11.56+   Dubai(APR) +11.42-11.53+
Brent(Dtd)  +10.79-10.
Forties     +11.04-11.
Ekofisk     +10.94-11.
Statfjord   +10.98-11.
Oseberg     +11.07-11.
Flotta      +10.18-10.
Forcados    +10.58-10.
Bonny Light +10.63-10.
Qua Ibo     +10.69-10.
See pages 171,280 for
         --
```

```
08:02 17DEC98                  PLATT'S              UK34448     PGA578
578--Latest Dated Brent Indications -- 13:02 GMT
17Dec98    Feb Brent        Differential    Dated Brent
1300 GMT  11.22-11.24       -0.55/-0.50     10.67-10.74
1200 GMT  11.19-11.21       -0.55/-0.50     10.64-10.71
1100 GMT  11.08-11.10       -0.55/-0.50     10.53-10.60
1000 GMT  11.08-11.10       -0.55/-0.50     10.53-10.60
--------------------16Dec98-------------------
1700 GMT  11.32-11.34       -0.66/-0.64     10.66-10.70
1600 GMT  11.24-11.26       -0.66/-0.64     10.58-10.62
1500 GMT  11.15-11.17       -0.66/-0.64     10.49-10.53
1300 GMT  11.02-11.04       -0.66/-0.64     10.36-10.40
1200 GMT  10.95-10.97       -0.66/-0.64     10.29-10.33
1100 GMT  11.05-11.07       -0.66/-0.64     10.39-10.43
1000 GMT  11.11-11.13       -0.66/-0.64     10.45-10.49
                 --Platt's Global Alert--
```

Electricity

Within the world energy markets the commodity electricity commands a huge market with a value in excess of $250 billion for 1997 and it is still growing. This market in electricity is relatively new being created by the deregulation of state or public utilities, particularly in Europe and in the US.

Deregulation has brought large wholesale markets involving spot, forward and more recently derivative contracts. However, market players in the generation, wholesale supply and consumption of power are now more exposed to risk than when power prices and supply were controlled and more predictable.

Electricity is known as a flow commodity because it cannot be stored in the conventional sense. Commodities such as crude oil are known as cash and carry because once bought they can be stored.

As a flow commodity, electricity is not easy to price as the variables involved are numerous and can be quite unpredictable. The following is a list of some of the more important variables electricity prices are subject to:

- Demand which is determined by time of use

- Geographic location of generation

- Source of power generation – coal, natural gas, oil, nuclear, hydroelectric etc

- Unpredictable price rises and falls

- Seasonal demand for power

- Dependence on power transmission facilities available

- Unpredictable weather conditions

In the spot markets electricity is bought in units of Mega Watt hours (MWh). In a single day the price can vary considerably with the time of use as illustrated here:

- 06.00 $34.20 per MWh
- 13.00 $900.00 per MWh
- 21.00 $21.00 per MWh

Source: PJM OIS for 21st July 1998

Another important cash market is the forward market which is known as the **day-ahead** or **next-day** market. For these forward electricity contracts power generators analyse predicted usage, watch the weather and make decisions about meeting consumers power requirements for the next day. Typically forward transactions involve blocks of 50 MWh of power. However, the next-day markets can be very volatile and unpredictable as illustrated here:

In June 1998 the US Mid West was subjected to scorching hot weather. This fact combined with a series of scheduled and unscheduled close downs of power generation plants resulted in a serious imbalance between power demand and supply. This imbalance was reflected in the next-day markets. The following Cinergy electricity forward prices for a seven day period in June demonstrate the dramatic rise and fall in prices:

	$/MWh
23/06/98	173.5
24/06/98	346.4
25/06/98	523.6
26/06/98	2461.1
27/06/98	78.8
28/06/98	100.0
29/06/98	1703.8

It is important to recognise that in this forward market every next-day contract is unique.

Your notes

The risks for market players in the electricity markets has predictably lead to the introduction of OTC and exchange traded derivative contracts. Producers and consumers of this commodity need to hedge their risks and speculators provide liquidity in the markets.

There are now several exchanges worldwide trading electricity futures and options on futures contracts. These contracts specify a particular geographical delivery point for an amount of power to be delivered daily during the on-peak hours for a contract month. The original NYMEX electricity futures were based on US West Coast cash market activity for 2MWh of power per on-peak hour. For power generation a working day has 16 on-peak hours, a working week has 5 working days and the maximum number of working days in a month is 23. Therefore the NYMEX futures contracts were set for delivery of up to:

$$2 \ \times \ 16 \ \times 23 \ = 736 \ \text{MWh}$$

Other exchange traded electricity futures contracts have different delivery amounts but are calculated in a similar way.

Before moving on, review the Reuters screens on the next page with information about the electricity spot and next-day prices.

The screen at the right shows McGraw-Hills' electricity alert speed guide, from which you can see details about recent deals, news and contracts.

```
MCGRAW-HILL'S ELECTRICITY ALERT SPEED GUIDE                    PEAINDEX

News ==================================  Into ConEd forward markets.....<PEA526>
Electricity news headlines.....<PEA010>  Mid-Columbia forward markets ..<PEA527>
                                         Into TVA forward markets.......<PEA528>
Real-time Spot Deals ==================  ERCOT forward markets .........<PEA529>
Heard in the markets...........<PEA700>
                                         Price Indexes =====================
Daily Market Commentary ===============  Weekly index/range ............<PEA500>
Northeast commentary ..........<PEA300>  Monthly index/range............<PEA510>
Western commentary ............<PEA350>  Daily on-peak indexes .........<PEA505>
Midwestern commentary .........<PEA400>  Daily off-peak indexes ........<PEA507>
Southern commentary ...........<PEA450>  Dow Jones COB index ...........<PEA100>
Futures commentary.............<PEA950>
                                         Methodology =======================
Forward Prices ========================  Price methodology..............<PEA005>
COB forward markets............<PEA520>
Palo Verde forward markets.....<PEA521>  Miscellaneous =====================
PJM forward markets............<PEA522>  More Electricity Alert Pages <PEAINDX2>
New England forward markets....<PEA523>  Reuters Energy Speed Guide ....<ENERGY>
Into Cinergy forward markets...<PEA524>  Copyright Notice & Disclaimer .<PLATTS>
Into Entergy forward markets...<PEA525>
```

```
15:53 16DEC98              PLATT'S              UK34448           PEA521
521--Palo Verde Forward Markets
Washington (EPP)-
In $/MWh updated as of Dec. 14
Contract       Transacted    Bid/Ask        Deal
Bal. Dec.      16 Dec                        27.00-28.50
Bal. Dec.      15 Dec                        25.25
Bal. Dec.      14 Dec                        24.50-25.00
Bal. Dec.      11 Dec                        25.00-25.25
Bal. Dec.      10 Dec                        25.25-26.00
January        14 Dec                        25.25
January        11 Dec                        24.75
January        10 Dec                        24.50
Dec/Jan99      17 Nov                        28.85
1Q99           17 Nov                        27.25
3Q99            1 Dec                        52.50
3Q99           20 Nov                        56.00-61.50
```

```
10:00 17DEC98             PLATT'S              UK34448           PEA700
700--Heard in the markets 4: PJM west Thurs-for-Fri $22.50
17Dec98/957 am EST/1457 GMT
Dec17: PJM western hub Thursday-for-Friday sold at $22.50/MWh
Dec17: PJM western hub 2-by-16 weekend on-peak deal sold for
$18/MWh
Dec17: PJM pool loads projected daily high is 35,800 MW
Dec17: PJM pool dispatch rate is $22/MWh with loads of 32,500
MW; no transmission constraints
(16Dec98)
Dec16: Balance-of--December prices at COB and Mid-C spiked to
$30/MWh on a forecast revision calling for frigid temperatures
in the Northwest next week
Dec16: PJM balance of month falls to deals at $22 and
$22.25/MWh as forward curve softens
Dec16: PJM forwards fall with Jan/Feb99 down to $26.65/MWh,
Begins <PEA700--McGraw-Hill's Electricity Alert-- Cont <PEA701>
```

Shipping Markets

There are three parties associated with these markets:

- Shipowners

- Charterers who are normally the cargo owners

- Ship brokers

Collectively shipowners and charterers are known as the **principals**. Principals may be:

- Dedicated vessel owners, for example, Onassis, Chandris and Stena

- Industrial or oil companies, for example, Shell, BP, Dow Chemicals, BASF

- Governments or utilities

The broker acts as an intermediary between principals to **fix** a vessel with a cargo. Once the broker has fixed the contract, the legal contract – the **charter party** – is drawn up, issued and signed by the principals. The broker also has the responsibility of ensuring that all operational matters are communicated correctly, for example, voyage order, letters of indemnity, freight invoices etc. Brokers can act in a number of ways. These include:

- Providing independent services. Because the tonnage of cargo shipped worldwide is very large an individual principal will use a broker as it is the most efficient and economic way to fix a contract. Thus independent brokers provide principals with a service which would be too expensive for the individual principals and it is cost effective because the brokers feed the same information to different clients. A broker may communicate information to a valued client 10-15 times daily. Brokers earn their income as a commission from successfully fixing a contract.

- Working for a charterer

- Broking exclusive tonnage for an owner such as a major oil company

- Broking for principals within one country or area. This is the traditional way of broking but with the advent of improved telecommunications and services it is not uncommon for brokers to act cross-border.

Brokers spend the majority of their time researching the market for relevant information. The types of information the broker requires are outlined here:

Ship Positions
- Are the ships contracted? - Are the ships likely to be freed from their current contracts? - Are the ships likely to be delayed? - Are the ships negotiating for another cargo?
Cargo Status
- Who has control of the cargo? - Will that party want a vessel or will the cargo be sold on? - Will the cargo be withdrawn from the market? - Who is likely to require a vessel?
Rates
- What rates are being paid at the moment? - What is the trend? - Are there any special circumstances affecting current rates?

Trading in the Commodities, Energy & Transport Markets

In addition brokers will find out about port conditions and general market intelligence collected from port agents, other brokers and freight forwarders. The broker is also on the look out for 'spot' opportunities which could, for example, make the transport of a particular commodity to a particular location attractive. Most brokers use databases to make their matching of cargoes to vessel sizes easier.

The role of the ship broker is similar to that of an estate agent and the process is outlined opposite.

Some ship owners have their own broking operations – owners' brokers – as do certain oil companies – charterers' brokers. Although these operations are subsidiaries of principals they also engage in competitive broking in the open market place.

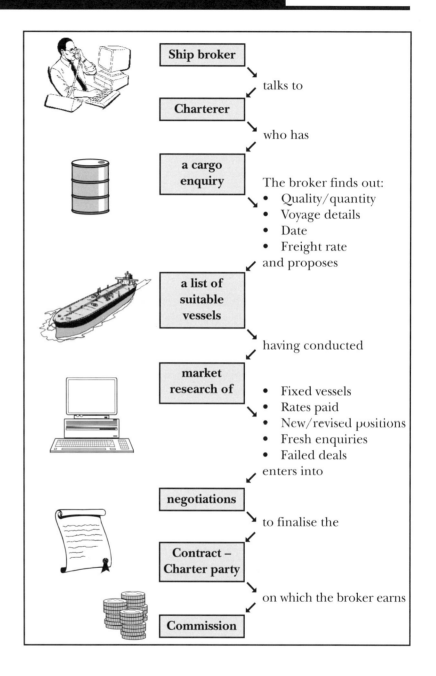

Ship broker

talks to

Charterer

who has

a cargo enquiry

The broker finds out:
- Quality/quantity
- Voyage details
- Date
- Freight rate

and proposes

a list of suitable vessels

having conducted

market research of

- Fixed vessels
- Rates paid
- New/revised positions
- Fresh enquiries
- Failed deals

enters into

negotiations

to finalise the

Contract – Charter party

on which the broker earns

Commission

Shipping Communications

The importance of communications, in terms of both speed and breadth, for ship brokers is probably obvious from the preceding description of their roles. Brokers need to communicate constantly with owners of vessels requiring cargoes, charterers requiring vessels and with other brokers.

Information is exchanged by one of the following means:

- **Face-to-face**. This is generally for public relations only – business is seldom conducted in this way.

- **Telephone**. This is the prime medium for conducting negotiations, carrying out market research, obtaining cargo quotes and for maintaining PR.

- **Telex**. Because of its accepted legal status under Maritime law as 'best admissible evidence', telex is used for initial offers, recaps of contractual terms – charter parties – voyage orders, letters of indemnity, invoices and other legally sensitive communications.

- **Fax**. For speed and cost effectiveness fax is used for documents of lesser legal significance, vessel positions, cargo enquiries, fixture reports, market information and lengthy specialist contract clauses.

- **E-mail**. A cost effective way of using computer networks to send and receive written information.

- **Network datacommunications systems**. Systems such as Internet mail provide a high-speed, cost effective communications. It is probably only a matter of time before hard-copy print outs from these systems gain legal acceptance. This type of system is very attractive to both brokers and principals as communications in general ar expensive – for many brokers it is the single biggest expense after salaries!

Options for shipping communications					
Need	**Face-to-face**	**Phone**	**Telex**	**Fax**	**E-mail**
PR	✔	✔			✔
Cargo quotation		✔			✔
Negotiations		✔			✔
Market information		✔		✔	✔
Offers			✔		✔
Vessel positions		✔	✔	✔	✔
Enquiries		✔	✔	✔	✔
Fixtures		✔	✔	✔	✔
Contractual			✔		✔

Regulation of the Markets

Many exchanges originally operated from public meeting places such as coffee houses as no formal exchange building existed. In such circumstances there were few rules and the activities of the market players often involved overspeculation, fraud and deception.

Gradually exchanges became more formalised and were located in permanent, purpose-built premises. The exchanges also introduced their own rules and regulations which were administered on a self-regulatory basis. More recently many worldwide government agencies and international bodies have been created to oversee the activities and regulate the different financial and commodity markets.

The purpose of regulation is to ensure the financial security of participants and counterparties and ensure standardisation of procedures. In particular market regulation aims to:

- Protect investors – especially individual investors

- Allow markets to function smoothly and efficiently

- Minimise the impact of adverse market movements on the economy at large

- Foster competitive practices

- Prevent unfair practices

Most regulatory bodies share these broad aims.

Domestic Regulatory Bodies

In most countries the government has a range of bodies to regulate the markets. Central banks such as the Federal Reserve Bank in the US and the Bank of England in the UK have certain direct responsibilities for regulating the primary market, whereas regulations governing secondary market activities are the responsibility of a variety of government agencies.

In the US the **Securities and Exchange Commission (SEC)** is the principal regulatory authority. Under the US Securities Exchange Act of 1934, the Fed is obliged to regulate the margin requirements in securities and futures markets. The Fed limits the amount of credit that may be provided by securities brokers and dealers and the system is regulated by the SEC. However, the SEC operates with the following organisations to ensure the markets are fair and run smoothly:

- The **Commodity Futures Trading Commission (CFTC)** which regulates trading in futures and options

- The exchanges such as NYMEX, CBOT, CME etc which are self-regulating

Commodity Futures Trading Commission (CFTC)

The US federal government established this agency in 1974 giving it authority to regulate commodities futures and related trading in the US. The commission comprises five commissioners, one of whom acts as chairman. The primary functions of the CFTC are to encourage competitiveness, efficiency, market and trading practice integrity, fairness and to ensure the economic soundness of the US commodities futures markets.

Before an exchange can list a futures or options on futures contract it has to be approved by the CFTC. The commission is responsible for the registration of firms and individuals who handle customer accounts or give trading advice. The commission also approves and oversees rule enforcement on all the appropriate US exchanges.

Before moving on, you can find out more about the type of information reported by the CFTC using the Reuters screens here.

From the CFTC Guide Page at right, you can pull the Futures Commitment of Traders Report, with supporting details.

```
CFTCGUIDE                      CFTC Guide

The index pages for the COT Reports are displayed on pages 1CFTC-4CFTC. Pages
<1CFTC> and <2CFTC> contain the Futures only reports for the current week and
prior week respectively, while pages <3CFTC> and <4CFTC> contain the combined
Futures and Options reports for the current and prior weeks.

           <1CFTC> Futures only report - Current week
           <2CFTC> Futures only report - Previous week
           <3CFTC> Futures & Options report - Current week
           <4CFTC> Futures & Options report - Previous week

COT reports summarise data on the open interest for markets in which five or
more traders hold positions equal to or above the reporting levels established
by the Commission. The reports summarise weekly data for release every two
weeks: on Friday for the futures only and on Monday for the combined futures and
options, unless otherwise noted in the CFTC schedule below.

               1998 COT Reports Release Dates
```

```
CFTC FUTURES COMMITMENT OF TRADERS REPORT: CURRENT WEEK                   1CFTC

CONTRACT                PAGE            CONTRACT              PAGE

CBT  WHEAT            <1CFTF>           CBT  CORN            <1CFTG>
CBT  OATS             <1CFTH>           CBT  ROUGH RICE      <1CFTI>
CBT  SOYBEANS         <1CFTJ>           CBT  SOYBEAN OIL     <1CFTK>
CBT  SOYBEAN MEAL     <1CFTL>           CBT  DOW JONES INDUS <1CFTM>
CBT  U.S. TREASURY B  <1CFTN>           CBT  2-YEAR U.S. TRE <1CFTO>
CBT  10-YEAR U.S. TR  <1CFTP>           CBT  5-YEAR U.S. TRE <1CFTQ>
CBT  30-DAY FEDERAL   <1CFTR>           CBT  MUNICIPAL BOND  <1CFTS>
CME  LEAN HOGS        <1CFTT>           CME  PORK BELLIES    <1CFTU>
CME  LIVE CATTLE      <1CFTV>           CME  FEEDER CATTLE   <1CFTW>
CME  MILK             <1CFTX>           CME  CANADIAN DOLLAR <1CFTY>
CME  SWISS FRANC      <1CFTZ>           CME  DEUTSCHE MARK   <1CFUA>
CME  POUND STERLING   <1CFUB>           CME  JAPANESE YEN    <1CFUC>
CME  AUSTRALIAN DOLL  <1CFUD>           CME  RUSSIAN RUBLE   <1CFUE>
CME  MEXICAN PESO     <1CFUF>           CME  BRAZILIAN REAL  <1CFUG>
CME  E-MINI S&P 500   <1CFUH>           CME  S&P 500 BARRA G <1CFUI>
CME  S&P 500 BARRA V  <1CFUJ>           CME  S&P 500 STOCK I <1CFUK>
CME  S&P 400 MIDCAP   <1CFUL>           CME  NASDAQ-100 STOC <1CFUM>
CME  RUSSEL 2000 STO  <1CFUN>           CME  NIKKEI STOCK AV <1CFUO>

            NEXT PAGE <1CFTD>                     PREVIOUS WEEK <2CFTC>
```

```
CFTC FUTURES COMMITMENT OF TRADERS REPORT: CURRENT WEEK                   1CFTD

CONTRACT                PAGE            CONTRACT              PAGE

CME  13-WEEK U.S. TR  <1CFUP>           CME  1-MONTH LIBOR R <1CFUQ>
CME  3-MONTH EURODOL  <1CFUR>           CME  3-MO EURO CANAD <1CFUS>
CME  3-MO. EUROYEN    <1CFUT>           CME  GOLDMAN-SACHS C <1CFUU>
CME  RANDOM LENGTH L  <1CFUV>           KCB  WHEAT           <1CFUW>
KCB  STOCK INDEX FUT  <1CFUX>           MCE  U.S. TREASURY B <1CFUY>
MGE  WHEAT            <1CFUZ>           CMX  STOCK INDEX FUT <1CFVA>
CMX  SILVER           <1CFVB>           CMX  COPPER-GRADE #1 <1CFVC>
CMX  GOLD             <1CFVD>           CSC  BFP MILK        <1CFVE>
CSC  COCOA            <1CFVF>           CSC  SUGAR NO. 11    <1CFVG>
CSC  SUGAR NO. 14     <1CFVH>           CSC  COFFEE C        <1CFVI>
NYC  COTTON NO. 2     <1CFVJ>           NYC  FRZN CONCENTRAT <1CFVK>
NYC  SFRANK/DMARK CR  <1CFVL>           NYC  YEN/MARK CROSSR <1CFVM>
NYC  SWEDISH KRONA/D  <1CFVN>           NYC  ITAL. LIRA/MARK <1CFVO>
NYC  DMARK/POUND CRO  <1CFVP>           NYC  U.S. DOLLAR IND <1CFVQ>
NYF  HIGH TEC
NYM  NO. 2 HE
NYM  ELECTRIC
NYM  ELECTRIC

       NEX
```

```
CFTC FUTURES COMMITMENT OF TRADERS REPORT: CSC  COFFEE C             1CFVI
COFFEE C - COFFEE, SUGAR & COCOA EXCHANGE
          REPORTABLE POSITIONS AS OF 12/01/98          |
-------------------------------------------------------| NONREPORTABLE
     NON-COMMERCIAL    |    COMMERCIAL   |    TOTAL     |   POSITIONS
----------------------|-----------------|--------------|----------------
 LONG  | SHORT |SPREADING| LONG  | SHORT | LONG  | SHORT | LONG  | SHORT
------------------------------------------------------------------------
(CONTRACTS OF 37,500 POUNDS)                    OPEN INTEREST:    28,717
COMMITMENTS
  4,743   3,091   1,356  13,086  18,019  19,185  22,466   9,532   6,251
CHANGES FROM 11/24/98 (CHANGE IN OPEN INTEREST:   -179)
     54     -78    -150     370     452     274     224    -453    -403
PERCENT OF OPEN INTEREST FOR EACH CATEGORY OF TRADERS
   16.5    10.8     4.7    45.6    62.7    66.8    78.2    33.2    21.8
NUMBER OF TRADERS IN EACH CATEGORY (TOTAL TRADERS:     120)
     23      15       5      57      46      83      64

        CURRENT WEEK INDEX <1CFTC>       PREVIOUS WEEK INDEX <2CFTC>
```

In the UK the **Financial Services Authority (FSA)** formerly known as the **Securities and Investment Board (SIB)** exercises regulation of the financial markets on behalf of HM Treasury. The change took place in 1997 and over a staged period the FSA will extend its powers and it will acquire regulatory and registration functions currently operated by a number of bodies including the **Securities and Futures Authority (SFA)**. This is a **Self-Regulatory Organisation (SRO)**, which is responsible for markets in securities, futures and options, commodities and currencies together with the activities of brokers and dealers.

The FSA also operates with **Recognised Investment Exchanges (RIEs)**, such as the LME, IPE and LIFFE. The current regulatory structure in the UK is illustrated in the chart below.

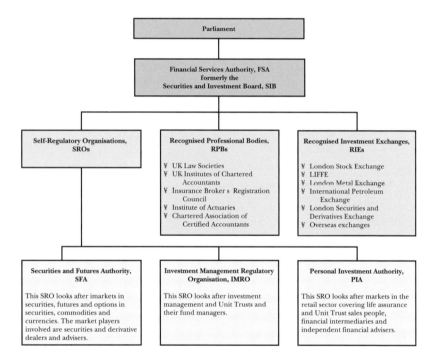

Securities and Futures Authority (SFA)

Currently the role of the SFA is:

- To help protect private and professional investors from financial loss

- To provide effective regulation to help the markets to operate

The SFA authorises individual member firms of an RIE to operate businesses in securities in the UK. The SFA has some 1300 member firms and the exchanges in which they operate are listed in the chart under RIEs. The RIEs provide the market place for authorised members to trade. The SFA's regulatory process is in four parts:

- **Authorisation**. This is the initial vetting of a firm to ensure that it is suitable to be permitted to conduct investment business.

- **Monitoring**. All members are required to provide a wide range of financial and other information for SFA teams of inspectors who make routine visits to check compliance with the rules.

- **Investigation**. This occurs when the SFA suspect the rules have been broken or that they receive external reports of irregularities.

- **Prosecution**. If the SFA investigators feel that there has been a serious breach of the rules then the case is referred to the relevant body, for example the DTI or police. If the judgement goes against the firm the SFA can give a warning, impose a fine, issue a temporary stop trading order or expel the firm from the SFA. The latter has the effect of de-authorising the firm so they would no longer to allowed to trade on an RIE.

The Markets

The markets also regulate their own activities to a certain extent. Worldwide exchanges have their own rules and procedures which members must adhere to.

Although specific details differ slightly from exchange to exchange, in general members must demonstrate that they have the following:

- Adequate financial resources

- Proper conduct of business rules

- Proper and liquid markets in products

- Procedures for recording transactions

- Effective monitoring and enforcement of rules

- Proper arrangements for clearing and performance of contracts

The last requirement is generally fulfilled by a clearing house, for example, the **London Clearing House (LCH)** and the **Board of Trade Clearing Corporation (BOTCC)**.

Although the roles of specific clearing houses may differ in detail, in general their specific function in the derivatives market for which they operate is to:

- Maintain a record of all open contracts

- Hold margin payments

- Carry out settlement and delivery of underlying You have now finished the last section of the workbook and you should have a clear understanding of the trading in the commodities, energy and transport markets including:

- The importance in electronic trading in the derivatives markets

- Trading spot, forward and derivative contracts in the commodities, energy and shipping markets

- Regulation of the markets

The clearing house safeguards the interests of the market players, enables contracts to be traded more or less free from counterparty risk, and promotes market integrity.

Exchange members have to meet the conditions of both a clearing house and the domestic regulatory body in order to be authorised. The main criterion is that a member organisation must maintain sufficient resources at all times to meet its obligations.

However, the system of regulation and supervision can only minimise risks **not** eliminate them. This was clearly demonstrated by the Baring Bros Bank collapse in February 1995, when over $800m was lost in the derivatives market.

Summary

You have now finished the last section of the book and you should have a clear understanding of trading in the commodities, energy and transport markets including:

- The importance in electronic trading in the derivatives markets

- Trading spot, forward and derivative contracts in the commodities, energy and shipping markets

- Regulation of the markets

As a check on your understanding you should try the Quick Quiz Questions on the next page. You may also find the Overview section to be a helpful learning tool.

Your notes

Quick Quiz Questions

1. Prior to OPEC and the introduction of energy futures markets, who effectively controlled the oil markets?

2. In addition to commodities and energy market producers and consumers, what other players operate in the Commodities and Energy derivatives markets?

3. Who are the three parties associated with the shipping markets?

4. What does the term 'kerb dealing' mean?

5. In the UK and US, what government organisations are responsible for the regulation of commodities derivatives trading?

You can check your answers on page 281.

Overview

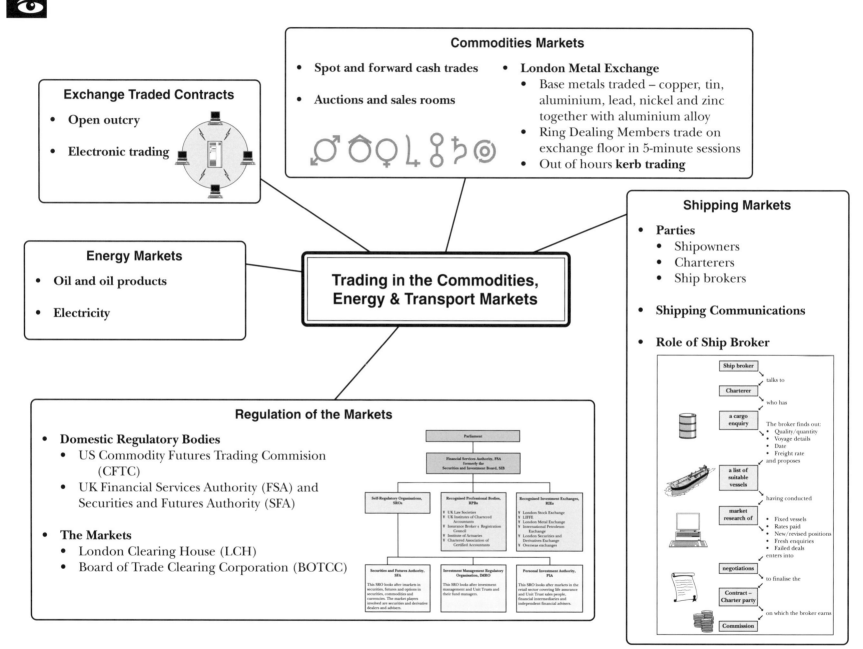

Exchange Traded Contracts

- Open outcry
- Electronic trading

Commodities Markets

- Spot and forward cash trades
- Auctions and sales rooms

- London Metal Exchange
  - Base metals traded – copper, tin, aluminium, lead, nickel and zinc together with aluminium alloy
  - Ring Dealing Members trade on exchange floor in 5-minute sessions
  - Out of hours **kerb trading**

Energy Markets

- Oil and oil products
- Electricity

Trading in the Commodities, Energy & Transport Markets

Shipping Markets

- **Parties**
  - Shipowners
  - Charterers
  - Ship brokers

- **Shipping Communications**

- **Role of Ship Broker**

Regulation of the Markets

- **Domestic Regulatory Bodies**
  - US Commodity Futures Trading Commision (CFTC)
  - UK Financial Services Authority (FSA) and Securities and Futures Authority (SFA)

- **The Markets**
  - London Clearing House (LCH)
  - Board of Trade Clearing Corporation (BOTCC)

Quick Quiz Answers

1. *Prior to OPEC and the introduction of energy futures markets, who effectively controlled the oil markets?*

   Prior to OPEC and the introduction of energy futures the oil markets were under the control of the major oil companies. These companies were known as the Seven Sisters – BP, Exxon, Gulf, Mobil, Royal Dutch/Shell, Chevron and Texaco.

2. *In addition to commodities and energy market producers and consumers, what other players operate in the Commodities and Energy derivatives markets?*

   As no physical delivery has to take place, exchange traded futures and options are also used by banks, fund managers and private individuals.

3. *Who are the three parties associated with the shipping markets?*

   The shipowners, charterers and the shipbrokers – the 'middle men'.

4. *What does the term 'kerb dealing' mean?*

   Kerb dealing originates from the times when trading carried on outside an exchange, on the pavement kerb, after the closing bell had been rung. In the 1900s kerb dealing became a rowdy affair, frequently requiring police intervention. Kerb dealing now signifies trading which takes place outside official market hours and which is permitted in the exchange.

5. *In the UK and US, what government organisations are responsible for the regulation of commodities derivatives trading?*

   In the US it is the Commodity Futures Trading Commission (CFTC).

   In the UK the Financial Services Authority (FSA) exercises overall regulation of the financial markets via a number organisations such as the Securities and Futures Authority (SFA).

Further Resources

Publications

Chicago Mercantile Exchange
- The Merc at Work: A Guide to the Chicago Mercantile Exchange
- CME: A World Marketplace
- The Financial Safeguard System of the Chicago Mercantile Exchange

Chicago Board of Trade
- Action in the marketplace

Financial Services Authority
- Financial Services Authority: an outline

New York Mercantile Exchange
- Safeguards and Standards

Internet

RFT Web Site
- **http://www.wiley-rft.reuters.com**

This is the series' companion web site where additional quiz questions, updated screens and other information can be found.

Exchanges

Refer to the back of this book for a listing of worldwide exchanges' contact information and web sites.

Your notes

Glossary of Commodities, Energy and Transport Terms

The following terms have been compiled from the main text to provide for easy reference.

15-Day Brent
Forward oil cargo loading after the Dated Brent.

A

Agricultural Commodity
Materials such as coffee, cocoa, sugar, grains, soya, corn, rubber and cotton.

Alternative Delivery Procedures (ADP)
Buyers and sellers may jointly agree to deliver a commodity using different standards, conditions, methods or locations of delivery. When the standard conditions of a futures contract are thus altered and it results in a physical contract, the clearinghouse guarantees are forfeited.

B

Backwardation
Describes when the futures price is lower than the spot price or at a discount to the cash price.

Bareboat (Demise)
Shipowner provides only the boat.

Base Metals
Aluminium, Zinc, Copper, Tin, Nickel, and Lead are the six most actively traded base metals.

Basis
The difference between the futures and spot prices at any one time.

Bill of Lading
A bearer document representing a commodity in transit that can be bought, sold or transferred. Presentation of the bill of lading allows its holder to collect the commodity.

Brent Crude
Serves as the price benchmark for other crude oils. Brent crude is a blend of crude oils from the Brent and Ninian systems and is a light sweet crude.

Bunker
Fuel required for all aspects of a vessel's operations. A vessel stops at a port for "bunkering," or refueling.

C

Cash Market/Cash Settlement
The physical markets in which buying and selling is settled with cash.

Charterer
Owner of a cargo wanting to transport the commodity by ship.

Charter Party
The written contractual agreement that fixes a vessel, the terms agreed upon between buyer and seller.

Clean Products
Refined oil products.

Coffee
Ranked second only to oil in international trade. The two types of coffee are Arabica and Robusta. Coffee ranks as the world's most popular beverage.

Commodity
Basic raw material.

Commodity or Energy Swap
Agreement between counterparties in which at least one set of payments involved is set by the price of the commodity/energy product or by the price of a commodity/energy index.

Commodity Market
Market dealing with the buying and selling of raw materials

Consecutive Voyage Charter
Shipowner hires out vessel for a series of consecutive voyages for the charterer.

Contango
Describes when a futures price is higher than the spot price or at a premium to the spot price.

Contract for Affreightment
Also known as a lump-sum contract. The shipowner agrees to perform a given number of voyages to carry a specified cargo for a given rate usually between two locations for a defined period.

Cost Insurance Freight (CIF)
Describes a sale in which the buyer pays a unit price that includes the FOB value plus all costs of insurance and transportation.

Cracking
Using pressure and heat to produce a lighter product from crude oil.

Crack Spread
The difference between the price paid for the crude oil and the price received from the cracked products.

Covered Position
During an options transaction, the writer possesses the underlying instrument or sufficient cash, to cover his or her position if the option is exercised.

Crude Oil
Brown to black liquid petroleum extracted from the earth.

Crush Margin
The profit margin calculated by subtracting the cost of soybeans from the sum of soybean oil and meal prices. The crush margin is used as a hedging device.

D

Dated Brent
Oil cargo loading within a designated 15-day period.

Dead Weight Tonnage (dwt)
Tanker size measured by cargo and fuel capacity.

Demurrage
Time in excess of laytime, the time allowed for loading and discharging a vessel, the cost of which is usually incorporated into the charter fee.

Dirty Products
Crude oil products.

Displacement Size
Tanker size based on tonnage of water displacement (sum of cargo and vessel weight).

E

Exchange based (or Physical) Markets
Buying and selling of an actual commodity with settlement in cash.

Exchange of Futures for Physicals (EFPs)
A transaction in which a position in the futures market is exchanged for an equivalent position in the physical market, by either reversing one's position or taking an equal and opposite position to each other in the cash and futures markets.

Ex store
Same as in store (simplest physical delivery in which seller is responsible for delivery to the agreed upon warehouse) plus the seller prepays storekeeper for loading onto the buyer's transport.

EXW (Ex-works)
The seller makes the goods ready for pickup on his premises by the buyer and the buyer takes responsibility for loading, customs and the costs and risks of transport.

Fix, Fixture
To match cargo with a vessel for transport.

Flat (or Straight) Price
Spot price quoted in dollar and cents value (not versus a future contract).

Forward Contract
A cash transaction in which the buyer and seller agree upon delivery of a specified quality and quantity of a commodity on a specified future date. A price may be agreed upon in advance or at the time of delivery.

Forward Freight Agreement (FFA)
Contract between a buyer and seller for an agreed freight or hire date, for a specific cargo or type of vessel, for an agreed BFI rate, for an agreed rate in the future against the relevant index route rate.

Forward Price
Spot or cash price plus cost of carry.

Fractional Distilling (topping)
The process of evaporation and condensation during refinery distillation that separates crude oil into various products that differ by weight and/or volatility.

Free Along Side (FAS)
The seller's obligations cease when he brings the cargo along side the ship, that is, does not have to load the cargo.

Free On Board (FOB)
Once a seller has loaded a bulk commodity over a ship's rail at a named port of shipment, the seller has fulfilled its obligations.

Futures Contract
A firm contractual agreement between a buyer and seller for a specified asset on a fixed date in the future. The contract price will vary according to the market place, but it is fixed when the trade is made. The contract also has a standard specification so both parties know exactly what is being traded.

Futures Spread
The difference in prices or basis between delivery months in the same or different markets. The purpose of such a spread is to profit from any change in price differential. The absolute prices of the futures contracts involved are not important — only their price difference.

Futures Strip
A single transaction that locks in an average price for a future period simultaneously opening a futures position for each contract period required. The price level of the strip is the average of the futures contract prices.

G

Gas Separation
Natural gas is separated from crude oil at well head.

Go Long
Buy a contract expecting its price to rise; upon its sale prior to the expiry date, you make a profit if you sell at a higher price than when you bought the contract.

Go Short
Sell a contract expecting its price to fall; upon its purchase prior to the expiry date, you purchase more cheaply.

Grains and Oilseeds
Category of commodities including cereals, fibres, meal, livestock, soya and oilseeds.

H

Hard Commodities
Materials such as non-ferrous and precious metals.

Hedging
Using a financial transaction to offset risk.

I

Indication (Price Indication)
Bid and offer quotes that appear on news providers by market makers. Indications are only estimates of actual prices; market players must contact the buyer or seller for a "firm" or actual price quote.

In store
Simplest form of physical delivery often used for base metals, cocoa and coffee, in which the seller is responsible for delivery of the commodity to the agreed upon warehouse.

L

Laytime
The time allowed for loading and discharging a vessel, the cost of which is usually incorporated into the charter fee.

Lump-Sum Contract
Also known as a Contract for Affreightment. The shipowner agrees to perform a given number of voyages of a specified cargo for a given rate usually between two locations for a defined period.

M

Margin Payment
The amount a naked options writer is required to deposit and maintain to cover a position; the margin requirement is calculated daily.

Mark-to-Market
Price of contract is calculated at the close of exchange trading.

Metals
Category of commodities including base, precious and strategic/minor metals.

Minimum Price Movement
Contract price change as determined by an exchange.

N

Netback
An assigned value of a crude oil determined by product yield, local market price, refinery costs and transport costs.

O

OBO
Ore, Bulk and Oil carrier.

OTC (Over-the-Counter or Open) Market
Market in which the commodity is sold for cash and delivered immediately.

Official (or posted) Price
Crude oil's price as preset by a supply agreement between producers and refiners.

Official Selling Price (OSP)
The formula used by a national oil company to price crude oil. The formula is typically based on a benchmark oil price or average of benchmarks with a differential applied.

Official Settlement
Bid and offer prices published by most exchanges and used for daily margin payments and contract settlement. Used for cash settlements and by market players in spot markets to price contracts. Used only as a price guide.

Offset Hedge
Use a LME forward contract to protect a market player from the risks involved in a physical transaction. Need to know if market is in contango or backwardation at time of hedge as this affects profit potential.

Open (Over-the-Counter) Market
Market in which the commodity is sold for cash and delivered immediately.

P

Paper Market
An exchange, acting as the counterparty, provides competitive market for trading hard and physical commodities futures transactions. The futures contracts have standardised terms.

Physical (or Exchange based) Market/Physical Settlement
Buying and selling of an actual commodity with settlement in cash.

Pit
Area on an exchange floor designated for the trading of a certain commodity.

Posted (or official) Price
Crude oil's price as preset by a supply agreement between producers and refiners.

Profit Margin
Used as a key indicator of a refinery's product level. Calculated by subtracting the cost of crude oil and operations costs from gross profit value (GPV).

Prompt Date
Delivery date for a contract versus the date on which the contract price is quoted.

Price Fix Hedge
Used by a buyer or seller to lock in an attractive forward price level for a base metal traded on the LME. Used to remove any marketplace volatility by fixing the price of buyer's or seller's raw materials at the same time allowing them to make a profit on their activities.

R

Refining
Four-step conversion process through which crude oil is made into products usable by consumers.

Refining Margin
Margin determined by comparing the selling price of unleaded gasoline and heating oil — converted to US$/barrel — with the price paid for crude oil. If the value of the product is more than the price of the crude, then the crack margin is positive; if the value of the product is less than the price of the crude, then the margin is negative.

RoRo
Roll-on, roll-off vessel.

S

Ship Broker
Party who acts as an intermediary between a ship owner and a charterer (owner of cargo).

Ship Owner
Party who owns a ship used for the transport of a commodity.

Spot (or cash) Market
Goods are sold for cash and delivered immediately.

Spread
The difference between the cash and futures prices.

Glossary of Commodities, Energy and Transport Terms

Strip Trade
A single transaction which locks in an average price for several months at a time by simultaneously opening a futures position for each month required. The price level of the strip is the average of the futures contract prices. Strip trades require margin payments in the same way as trading individual futures contracts.

Softs
Category of commodities including coffee, cocoa, sugar, rubber, pepper, tea and citrus fruits.

T

Tanker FFA
Contract to fix a wet freight rate on a predetermined route, at or over a mutually agreed time.

Tender
Invitation to bid to buy or sell a product.

Tick
Increments by which a futures contract's price movement is measured.

Time Charter by Demise
Charterer hires a vessel for a specific period of time and provides for all costs.

Time Charter Non-Demise
The shipowner handles all aspects of the ship's operation and charges the charterer.

Tonnage Exchange
Shipowners exchange vessels for logistic reasons.

Turnaround
The scheduled or unscheduled closing of an oil refinery for repairs.

U

ULCC (Ultra Large Crude Carrier)
Tanker with a capacity of up to 300,000 tonnes unladen.

Uncovered (Naked) Position
During an options transaction, the writer does not possess the underlying instrument or sufficient cash, to cover his or her position if the option is exercised.

Unladen
Weight of vessel without cargo.

V

VLCC (Very Large Crude Carrier)
Tanker with a capacity of up to 550,000 tonnes unladen.

W

Weather Derivatives
Underlying instrument is a weather index or variable. Option contracts are available for specific locations and calendar periods based on Heating Degree Days (HDD — average temperatures below 65) and Cooling Degree Days (CDD — average temperatures above 65). Contract trading size is 100 X CME HDD or CDD index.

Weight (of a shipment)
Weight equals density times volume.

Worldscale (WS) Worldscale Tanker Nominal Freight Scale
A benchmark rate used by shipowners and charterers to determine fixture rates. The standard — WS 100 - or standard rate, is based on a 75,000 tonne tanker and enables one to derive the specific cost of a cargo based on a per tonne rate.

Directory of Futures & Options Exchanges

courtesy of Numa Financial Systems Ltd

The following directory is taken from the Numa Directory of Futures & Options Exchanges which can be found on the internet at the URL address, http://www.numa.com/ref/exchange.htm. The Publisher will not be responsible for any inaccuracies found in the listing below. Kindly address any queries to Numa Financial Systems Ltd via their home page at http//www.numa.com.

Argentina

Buenos Aires Stock Exchange
(Bolsa de Comercio de Buenos Aires)
Sarmiento 299, Buenos Aires
Tel: +54 1 313 3334
Fax: +54 1 312 9332
Email: cau@sba.com.ar
URL: http://www.merval.sba.com.ar

Merfox
(Mercados de Futuros y Opciones SA)
Samiento 299, 4/460, Buenos Aires
Tel: +54 1 313 4522
Fax: +54 1 313 4472

Buenos Aires Cereal Exchange
(Bolsa de Cereales de Buenos Aires)
Avenida Corrientes 127, Buenos Aires
Tel: +54 1 311 9540
Fax: +54 1 311 9540
Email: bolcerc@datamarkets.com.ar

Buenos Aires Futures Market
(Mercado a Termino de Buenos Aires SA)
Bouchard 454, 5to Piso, Buenos Aires
Tel: +54 1 311 47 16
Fax: +54 1 312 47 16

Rosario Futures Exchange
(Mercado a Termino de Rosario)
Cordoba 1402, Pcia Santa Fe, Rosario
Tel: +54 41 21 50 93
Fax: +54 41 21 50 97
Email: termino@bcr.com.ar

Rosario Stock Exchange
(Mercado de Valores de Rosario SA)
Cordoba Esquina Corrientes, Pcia Santa Fe, Rosario
Tel: +54 41 21 34 70
Fax: +54 41 24 10 19
Email: titulos@bcr.com.ar

Rosario Board of Trade
(Bolsa de Comercio de Rosario)
Cordoba 1402, Pcia Santa Fe, Rosario
Tel: +54 41 21 50 93
Fax: +54 41 21 50 97
Email: titulos@bcr.com.ar

La Plata Stock Exchange
(Bolsa de Comercio de La Plata)
Calle 48, No. 515, 1900 La Plata, Buenos Aires
Tel: +54 21 21 47 73
Fax: +54 21 25 50 33

Mendoza Stock Exchange
(Bolsa de Comercio de Mendoza)
Paseo Sarmiento 199, Mendoza
Tel: +54 61 20 23 59
Fax: +54 61 20 40 50

Cordoba Stock Exchange
(Bolsa de Comercio de Cordoba)
Rosario de Santa Fe 231, 1 Piso, Cordoba
Tel: +54 51 22 4230
Fax: +54 51 22 6550
Email: bolsacba@nt.com.ar

Mercado Abierto Electronico SA
(Mercado Abierto Electronico SA)
25 de Mayo 565, 4 Piso, Buenos Aires
Tel: +54 1 312 8060
Fax: +54 1 313 1445

Armenia

Yerevan Stock Exchange
22 Sarian Street, Yerevan Centre
Tel: +374 2 525 801
Fax: +374 2 151 548

Australia

Australian Stock Exchange
Exchange Centre, 20 Bond Street, Sydney
Tel: +61 29 227 0000
Fax: +61 29 235 0056
Email: info@asx.com.au
URL: http://www.asx.com.au

Sydney Futures Exchange
SFE
30-32 Grosvenor Street, Sydney
Tel: +61 29 256 0555
Fax: +61 29 256 0666
Email: sfe@hutch.com.au
URL: http://www.sfe.com.au

Austria

Austrian Futures & Options Exchange
(Osterreichische Termin Und Optionenborse)
OTOB
Strauchgasse 1-3, PO Box 192, Vienna
Tel: +43 1 531 65 0
Fax: +43 1 532 97 40
Email: contactperson@otob.ada.at
URL: http://www.wtab.at

Vienna Stock Exchange
(Wiener Borse)
Wipplingerstrasse 34, Vienna
Tel: +43 1 53 499
Fax: +43 1 535 68 57
Email: communications@vienna-stock-exchange.at
URL: http://www.wtab.at

Bahrain

Bahrain Stock Exchange
P.O. Box 3203, Manama
Tel: +973 261260
Fax: +973 256362
Email: bse@bahrainstock.com
URL: http://www.bahrainstock.com

Bangladesh

Dhaka Stock Exchange
Stock Exchange Building, 9E & 9F, Motijheel C/A, Dhaka
Tel: +880 2 956 4601
Fax: +880 2 956 4727
Email: info@dse.bdnet.net

Barbados

Securities Exchange of Barbados
5th Floor, Central Bank Building, Church Village, St Michael
Tel: +1809/1246 246 436 9871
Fax: +1809/1246 246 429 8942
Email: sebd@caribf.com

Belgium

Brussels Stock Exchange
(Societe de la Bourse de Valeurs Mobilieres de Bruxelles)
Palais de la Bourse, Brussels
Tel: +32 2 509 12 11
Fax: +32 2 509 12 12
Email: dan.maerten@pophost.eunet.be
URL: http://www.stockexchange.be

European Association of Securities Dealers Automated Quotation
EASDAQ
Rue des Colonies, 56 box 15, 1000 Brussels
Tel: +32 2 227 6520
Fax: +32 2 227 6567
Email: easdaq@tornado.be
URL: http://www.easdaq.be/

Belgian Futures & Options Exchange
BELFOX
Palais de la Bourse, Rue Henri Mausstraat, 2, Brussels
Tel: +32 2 512 80 40
Fax: +32 2 513 83 42
Email: marketing@belfox.be
URL: http://www.belfox.be

Antwerp Stock Exchange
(Effectenbeurs van Antwerpen)
Korte Klarenstraat 1, Antwerp
Tel: +32 3 233 80 16
Fax: +32 3 232 57 37

Bermuda

Bermuda Stock Exchange
BSE
Email: info@bse.com
URL: http://www.bsx.com

Bolivia

Bolivian Stock Exchange
(Bolsa Boliviana de Valores SA)
Av. 16 de Julio No 1525, Edif Mutual La Paz, 3er Piso, Casillia 12521, La Paz
Tel: +591 2 39 29 11
Fax: +591 2 35 23 08
Email: bbvsalp@wara.bolnet.bo
URL: http://bolsa-valores-bolivia.com

Botswana

Botswana Stock Exchange
5th Floor, Barclays House, Khama Crescent, Gaborone
Tel: +267 357900
Fax: +267 357901
Email: bse@info.bw

Brazil

Far-South Stock Exchange
(Bolsa de Valores do Extremo Sul)
Rua dos Andradas, 1234-8 Andar, Porte Alegre
Tel: +55 51 224 3600
Fax: +55 51 227 4359

Santos Stock Exchange
(Bolsa de Valores de Santos)
Rua XV de Novembro, 111, Santos
Tel: +55 132 191 5119
Fax: +55 132 19 1800

Regional Stock Exchange
(Bolsa de Valores regional)
Avenida Dom Manuel, 1020, Fortaleza
Tel: +55 85 231 6466
Fax: +55 85 231 6888

Parana Stock Exchange
(Bolsa de Valores do Parana)
Rua Marechal Deodoro, 344-6 Andar, Curitiba
Tel: +55 41 222 5191
Fax: +55 41 223 6203

Minas, Espirito Santo, Brasilia Stock Exchange
(Blsa de Valores Minas, Espirito Santo, Brasilia)
Rua dos Carijos, 126-3 Andar, Belo Horizonte
Tel: +55 31 219 9000
Fax: +55 21 273 1202

Rio de Janeiro Stock Exchange
(Bolsa de Valores de Rio de Janeiro)
Praca XV de Novembro No 20, Rio de Janeiro
Tel: +55 21 271 1001
Fax: +55 21 221 2151
Email: info@bvrj.com.br
URL: http://www.bvrj.com.br

Sao Paolo Stock Exchange
(Bolsa de Valores de Sao Paolo)
Rua XV de Novembro 275, Sao Paolo
Tel: +55 11 233 2000
Fax: +55 11 233 2099
Email: bovespa@bovespa.com.br
URL: http://www.bovespa.com.br

Bahia, Sergipe, Alagoas Stock Exchange
(Bolsa de Valores Bahia, Sergipe, Alagoas)
Rua Conselheiro Dantas, 29-Comercio, Salvador
Tel: +55 71 242 3844
Fax: +55 71 242 5753

Brazilian Futures Exchange
(Bolsa Brasileira de Futuros)
Praca XV de Novembro, 20, 5th Floor, Rio de Janeiro
Tel: +55 21 271 1086
Fax: +55 21 224 5718
Email: bbf@bbf.com.br

The Commodities & Futures Exchange
(Bolsa de Mercadoris & Futuros)
BM&F
Praca Antonio Prado, 48, Sao Paulo
Tel: +55 11 232 5454
Fax: +55 11 239 3531
Email: webmaster@bmf.com.br
URL: http://www.bmf.com.br

Pernambuco and Paraiba Stock Exchange
(Bolsa de Valores de Pernambuco e Paraiba)
Avenida Alfredo Lisboa, 505, Recife
Tel: +55 81 224 8277
Fax: +55 81 224 8412

Bulgaria

Bulgarian Stock Exchange
1 Macedonia Square, Sofia
Tel: +359 2 81 57 11
Fax: +359 2 87 55 66
Email: bse@bg400.bg
URL: http://www.online.bg/bse

Canada

Montreal Exchange
(Bourse de Montreal)
ME
The Stock Exchange Tower, 800 Square Victoria, C.P. 61, Montreal
Tel: +1 514 871 2424
Fax: +1 514 871 3531
Email: info@me.org
URL: http://www.me.org

Vancouver Stock Exchange
VSE
Stock Exchange Tower, 609 Granville Street, Vancouver
Tel: +1 604 689 3334
Fax: +1 604 688 6051
Email: information@vse.ca
URL: http://www.vse.ca

Winnipeg Stock Exchange
620 - One Lombard Place, Winnipeg
Tel: +1 204 987 7070
Fax: +1 204 987 7079
Email: vcatalan@io.uwinnipef.ca

Alberta Stock Exchange
21st Floor, 300 Fifth Avenue SW, Calgary
Tel: +1 403 974 7400
Fax: +1 403 237 0450

Toronto Stock Exchange
TSE
The Exchange Tower, 2 First Canadian Place, Toronto
Tel: +1 416 947 4700
Fax: +1 416 947 4662
Email: skee@tse.com
URL: http://www.tse.com

Winnipeg Commodity Exchange
WCE
500 Commodity Exchange Tower, 360 Main St., Winnipeg
Tel: +1 204 925 5000
Fax: +1 204 943 5448
Email: wce@wce.mb.ca
URL: http://www.wce.mb.ca

Toronto Futures Exchange
TFE
The Exchange Tower, 2 First Canadian Place, Toronto
Tel: +1 416 947 4487
Fax: +1 416 947 4272

Cayman Islands

Cayman Islands Stock Exchange
CSX
4th Floor, Elizabethan Square, P.O Box 2408 G.T., Grand Cayman
Tel: +1345 945 6060
Fax: +1345 945 6061
Email: CSX@CSX.COM.KY
URL: http://www.csx.com.ky/

Chile

Santiago Stock Exchange
(Bolsa de Comercio de Santiago)
La Bolsa 64, Casilla 123-D, Santiago
Tel: +56 2 698 2001
Fax: +56 2 672 8046
Email: ahucke@comercio.bolsantiago.cl
URL: http://www.bolsantiago.cl

Bolsa Electronica de Chile
Huerfanos 770, Piso 14, Santiago
Tel: +56 2 639 4699
Fax: +56 2 639 9015
Email: info@bolchile.cl
URL: http://www.bolchile.cl

China

Wuhan Securities Exchange Centre
WSEC
2nd Floor, Jianghchen Hotel, Wuhan
Tel: +86 27 588 4115
Fax: +86 27 588 6038

China Zhengzhou Commodity Exchange
CZCE
20 Huanyuan Road, Zhengzhou
Tel: +86 371 594 44 54
Fax: +86 371 554 54 24

Shanghai Cereals and Oils Exchange
199 Shangcheng Road, Pudong New District, Shanghai
Tel: +86 21 5831 1111
Fax: +86 21 5831 9308
Email: liangzhu@public.sta.net.cn

China -Commodity Futures Exchange, Inc of Hainan
CCFE
Huaneng Building, 36 Datong Road, Haikou, Hainan Province
Tel: +86 898 670 01 07
Fax: +86 898 670 00 99
Email: ccfehn@public.hk.hq.cn

Guandong United Futures Exchange
JingXing Hotel, 91 LinHe West Road, Guangzhou
Tel: +86 20 8755 2109
Fax: +86 20 8755 1654

Shenzhen Mercantile Exchange
1/F Bock B, Zhongjian Overseas Decoration , Hua Fu Road, Shenzhen
Tel: +86 755 3343 502
Fax: +86 755 3343 505

Shanghai Stock Exchange
15 Huang Pu Road, Shanghai
Tel: +86 216 306 8888
Fax: +86 216 306 3076

Beijing Commodity Exchange
BCE
311 Chenyun Building, No. 8 Beichen East Road, Chaoyang District, Beijing
Tel: +86 1 492 4956
Fax: +86 1 499 3365
Email: sunli@intra.cnfm.co.cn

Shenzhen Stock Exchange
203 Shangbu Industrial Area, Shenzhen
Tel: +86 755 320 3431
Fax: +86 755 320 3505

Colombia

Bogota Stock Exchange
BSE
Carrera 8, No. 13-82 Pisos 4-9, Apartado Aereo 3584, Santafe de Bogota
Tel: +57 243 6501
Fax: +57 281 3170
Email: bolbogot@bolsabogota.com.co
URL: http://www.bolsabogota.com.co

Medellin Stock Exchange
(Bolsa de Medellin SA)
Apartado Aereo 3535, Medellin
Tel: +57 4 260 3000
Fax: +57 4 251 1981
Email: 104551.1310@compuserve.com

Occidente Stock Exchange
(Bolsa de Occidente SA)
Calle 10, No. 4-40 Piso 13, Cali
Tel: +57 28 817 022
Fax: +57 28 816 720
Email: bolsaocc@cali.cetcol.net.co
URL: http://www.bolsadeoccidente.com.co

Costa Rica

National Stock Exchange
(Bolsa Nacional de Valores, SA)
BNV
Calle Central, Avenida 1, San Jose
Tel: +506 256 1180
Fax: +506 255 0131

Cote D'Ivoire (Ivory Coast)

Abidjan Stock Exchange
(Bourse des Valeurs d'Abidjan)
Avenue Marchand, BP 1878 01, Abidjan 01
Tel: +225 21 57 83
Fax: +225 22 16 57

Croatia (Hrvatska)

Zagreb Stock Exchange
(Zagrebacka Burza)
Ksaver 208, Zagreb
Tel: +385 1 428 455
Fax: +385 1 420 293
Email: zeljko.kardum@zse.hr
URL: http://www.zse.hr

Cyprus

Cyprus Stock Exchange
CSE
54 Griva Dhigeni Avenue, Silvex House, Nicosia
Tel: +357 2 368 782
Fax: +357 2 368 790
Email: cyse@zenon.logos.cy.net

Czech Republic

Prague Stock Exchange
PSE
Rybna 14, Prague 1
Tel: +42 2 2183 2116
Fax: +42 2 2183 3040
Email: marketing@pse.vol.cz
URL: http://www.pse.cz

Denmark

Copenhagen Stock Exchange & FUTOP
(Kobenhavns Fondsbors)
Nikolaj Plads 6, PO Box 1040, Copenhagen K
Tel: +45 33 93 33 66
Fax: +45 33 12 86 13
Email: kfpost@xcse.dk
URL: http://www.xcse.dk

Ecuador

Quito Stock Exchange
(Bolsa de Valores de Quito CC)
Av Amazonas 540 y Carrion, 8vo Piso
Tel: +593 2 526 805
Fax: +593 2 500 942
Email: bovalqui@ecnet.ec
URL: http://www.ccbvq.com

Guayaquil Stock Exchange
(Bolsa de Valores de Guayaquil, CC)
Av. 9 de Octubre, 110 y Pinchina, Guayaquil
Tel: +593 4 561 519
Fax: +593 4 561 871
Email: bvg@bvg.fin.ec
URL: http://www.bvg.fin.ec

Egypt

Alexandria Stock Exchange
11 Talaat Harp Street, Alexandria
Tel: +20 3 483 7966
Fax: +20 3 482 3039

Cairo Stock Exchange
4(A) El Cherifeen Street, Cairo
Tel: +20 2 392 1402
Fax: +20 2 392 8526

El Salvador

El Salvador Stock Exchange
(Mercado de Valores de El Salvador, SA de CV)
6 Piso, Edificio La Centroamericana, Alameda Roosevelt No 3107,
San Salvador
Tel: +503 298 4244
Fax: +503 223 2898
Email: ggbolsa@gbm.net

Estonia

Tallinn Stock Exchange
Ravala 6, Tallinn
Tel: +372 64 08 840
Fax: +372 64 08 801
Email : tse@depo.ee
URL: http://www.tse.ee

Finland

Helsinki Stock Exchange
HSE
Fabianinkatu 14, Helsinki
Tel: +358 9 173 301
Fax: +358 9 173 30399
Email : mika.bjorklund@hex.fi
URL: http://www.hse.fi

Finnish Options Exchange
(Suomen Optioporssi Oy)
FOEX
Erottajankatu 11, Helsinki
Tel: +358 9 680 3410
Fax: +358 9 604 442
Email : info@foex.fi
URL: http://www.foex.fi

Finnish Options Market
SOM
Keskuskatu 7, Helsinki
Tel: +358 9 13 1211
Fax: +358 9 13 121211
Email : webmaster@hex.fi
URL: http://www.som.fi

France

Paris Stock Exchange
(Bourse de Paris)
39 rue Cambon, Paris
Tel: +33 1 49 27 10 00
Fax: +33 1 49 27 13 71
Email: 100432.201@compuserve.com

MONEP
(Marche des Options Negociables de Paris)
MONEP
39, rue Cambon, Paris
Tel: +33 1 49 27 18 00
Fax: +33 1 9 27 18 23
URL: http://www.monep.fr

MATIF
(Marche a Terme International de France)
MATIF
176 rue Montmartre, Paris
Tel: +33 33 1 40 28 82 82
Fax: +33 33 1 40 28 80 01
Email : larrede@matif.fr
URL: http://www.matif.fr

Germany

Stuttgart Stock Exchange
(Baden-Wurttembergische Wertpapierborse zu Stuttgart)
Konigstrasse 28, Stuttgart
Tel: +49 7 11 29 01 83
Fax: +49 7 11 22 68 11 9

Hanover Stock Exchange
(Niedersachsische Borse zu Hanover)
Rathenaustrasse 2, Hanover
Tel: +49 5 11 32 76 61
Fax: +49 5 11 32 49 15

Dusseldorf Stock Exchange
(Rheinisch-Westfalische Borse zu Dusseldorf)
Ernst-Schneider-Platz 1, Dusseldorf
Tel: +49 2 11 13 89 0
Fax: +49 2 11 13 32 87

Berlin Stock Exchange
(Berliner Wertpapierborse)
Fasanenstrasse 85, Berlin
Tel: +49 30 31 10 91 0
Fax: +49 30 31 10 91 79

German Stock Exchange
(Deutsche Borse AG)
FWB
Borsenplatz 4, Frankfurt-am-Main
Tel: +49 69 21 01 0
Fax: +49 69 21 01 2005
URL: http://www.exchange.de

Hamburg Stock Exchange
(Hanseatische Wertpapierborse Hamburg)
Schauenburgerstrasse 49, Hamburg
Tel: +49 40 36 13 02 0
Fax: +49 40 36 13 02 23
Email: wertpapierboerse.hamburg@t-online.de

Deutsche Terminborse
DTB
Boersenplatz 4, Frankfurt-am-Main
Tel: +49 69 21 01 0
Fax: +49 69 21 01 2005
URL: http://www.exchange.de

Bavarian Stock Exchange
(Bayerische Borse)
Lenbachplatz 2(A), Munich
Tel: +49 89 54 90 45 0
Fax: +49 89 54 90 45 32
Email: bayboerse@t-online.de
URL: http://www.bayerischeboerse.de

Bremen Stock Exchange
(Bremer Wertpapierborse)
Obernstrasse 2-12, Bremen
Tel: +49 4 21 32 12 82
Fax: +49 4 21 32 31 23

Ghana

Ghana Stock Exchange
5th Floor, Cedi House, Liberia Road, PO Box 1849, Accra
Tel: +233 21 669 908
Fax: +233 21 669 913
Email : stockex@ncs.com.gh
URL: http://ourworld.compuserve.com/homepages/khaganu/
stockex.htm

Greece

Athens Stock Exchange
ASE
10 Sophocleous Street, Athens
Tel: +30 1 32 10 424
Fax: +30 1 32 13 938
Email: mailto:aik@hol.gr
URL: http://www.ase.gr

Honduras

Honduran Stock Exchange
(Bolsa Hondurena de Valores, SA)
1er Piso Edificio Martinez Val, 3a Ave 2a Calle SO, San Pedro Sula
Tel: +504 53 44 10
Fax: +504 53 44 80
Email: bhvsps@simon.intertel.hn

Hong Kong

Hong Kong Futures Exchange Ltd
HKFE
5/F, Asia Pacific Finance Tower, Citibank Plaza, 3 Garden Road
Tel: +852 2842 9333
Fax: +852 2810 5089
Email: prm@hfke.com
URL: http://www.hkfe.com

Hong Kong Stock Exchange
SEHK
1st Floor, One and Two Exchange Square, Central
Tel: +852 2522 1122
Fax: +852 2810 4475
Email: info@sehk.com.hk
URL: http://www.sehk.com.hk

Chinese Gold and Silver Exchange Society
Gold and Silver Commercial Bui, 12-18 Mercer Street
Tel: +852 544 1945
Fax: +852 854 0869

Hungary

Budapest Stock Exchange
Deak Ferenc utca 5, Budapest
Tel: +36 1 117 5226
Fax: +36 1 118 1737
URL: http://www.fornax.hu/fmon

Budapest Commodity Exchange
BCE
POB 495, Budapest
Tel: +36 1 269 8571
Fax: +36 1 269 8575
Email: bce@bce-bat.com
URL: http://www.bce-bat.com

Iceland

Iceland Stock Exchange
Kalkofnsvegur 1, Reykjavik
Tel: +354 569 9775
Fax: +354 569 9777
Email: gw@vi.is

India

Cochin Stock Exchange
38/1431 Kaloor Road Extension, PO Box 3529, Emakulam, Cochin
Tel: +91 484 369 020
Fax: +91 484 370 471

Bangalore Stock Exchange
Stock Exchange Towers, 51, 1st Cross, JC Road, Bangalore
Tel: +91 80 299 5234
Fax: +91 80 22 55 48

The OTC Exchange of India
OTCEI
92 Maker Towers F, Cuffe Parade, Bombay
Tel: +91 22 21 88 164
Fax: +91 22 21 88 012
Email: otc.otcindia@gems.vsnl.net.in

Jaipur Stock Exchange
Rajasthan Chamber Bhawan, MI Road, Jaipur
Tel: +91 141 56 49 62
Fax: +91 141 56 35 17

The Stock Exchange ñ Ahmedabad
Kamdhenu Complex, Ambawadi, Ahmedabad
Tel: +91 79 644 67 33
Fax: +91 79 21 40 117
Email: supvsr@08asxe

Delhi Stock Exchange
3&4/4B Asaf Ali Road, New Delhi
Tel: +91 11 327 90 00
Fax: +91 11 327 13 02

Madhya Pradesh Stock Exchange
3rd Floor, Rajani Bhawan, Opp High Court, MG Road, Indore
Tel: +91 731 432 841
Fax: +91 731 432 849

Magadh Stock Exchange
Industry House, Suinha Library Road,
Patna
Tel: +91 612 223 644

Pune Stock Exchange
Shivleela Chambers, 752 Sadashiv Peth, Kumethekar Road, Pune
Tel: +91 212 441 679

The Stock Exchange, Mumbai
Phiroze Jeejeebhoy Towers, Dalal Street, Bombay
Tel: +91 22 265 5860
Fax: +91 22 265 8121
URL: http://www.nseindia.com

Uttar Pradesh Stock Exchange
Padam Towers, 14/113 Civil Lines, Kanpur
Tel: +91 512 293 115
Fax: +91 512 293 175

Bhubaneswar Stock Exchange Association
A-22 Falcon House, Jharapara, Cuttack Road, Bhubaneswar
Tel: +91 674 482 340
Fax: +91 674 482 283

Calcutta Stock Exchange
7 Lyons Range, Calcutta
Tel: +91 33 209 366

Coimbatore Stock Exchange
Chamber Towers, 8/732 Avanashi Road, Coimbatore
Tel: +91 422 215 100
Fax: +91 422 213 947

Madras Stock Exchange
Exchange Building, PO Box 183, 11 Second Line Beach, Madras
Tel: +91 44 510 845
Fax: +91 44 524 4897

Ludhiana Stock Exchange
Lajpat Rai Market, Near Clock Tower, Ludhiana
Tel: +91 161 39318

Kanara Stock Exchange
4th Floor, Ranbhavan Complex, Koialbail, Mangalore
Tel: +91 824 32606

Hyderabad Stock Exchange
3-6-275 Himayatnagar, Hyderabad
Tel: +91 842 23 1985

Gauhati Stock Exchange
Saraf Building, Annex, AT Road, Gauhati
Tel: +91 361 336 67
Fax: +91 361 543 272

Indonesia

Jakarta Stock Exchange
(PT Bursa Efek Jakarta)
Jakarta Stock Exchange Building, 13th Floor, JI Jenderal Sudiman,
Kav 52-53, Jakarta
Tel: +62 21 515 0515
Fax: +62 21 515 0330
Email: webmaster@jsx.co.id
URL: http://www.jsx.co.id

Surabaya Stock Exchange
(PT Bursa Efek Surabaya)
5th Floor, Gedung Madan Pemuda, 27-31 Jalan Pemuda, Surabaya
Tel: +62 21 526 6210
Fax: +62 21 526 6219
Email: heslpdesk@bes.co.id
URL: http://www.bes.co.id

Indonesian Commodity Exchange Board
(Badan Pelaksana Bursa Komoditi)
Gedung Bursa, Jalan Medan Merdeka Selatan 14, 4th Floor, Jakarta
Pusat
Tel: +62 21 344 1921
Fax: +62 21 3480 4426

Capital Market Supervisory Agency
(Baden Pelaksana Pasar Modal)
BAPEPAM
Jakarta Stock Exchange Building, 13th Floor, JI Jenderal Sudiman,
Kav 52-53, Jakarta
Tel: +62 21 515 1288
Fax: +62 21 515 1283
Email: bapepam@indoexchange.com
URL: http://www.indoexchange.com/bapepam

Iran

Tehran Stock Exchange
228 Hafez Avenue, Tehran
Tel: +98 21 670 309
Fax: +98 21 672 524
Email: stock@neda.net
URL: http://www.neda.net/tse

Ireland

Irish Stock Exchange
28 Anglesea Street, Dublin 2
Tel: +353 1 677 8808
Fax: +353 1 677 6045

Irish Futures & Options Exchange
IFOX
Segrave House, Earlsfort Terrace, Dublin 2
Tel: +353 1 676 7413
Fax: +353 1 661 4645

Israel

Tel Aviv Stock Exchange Ltd
TASE
54 Ahad Haam Street, Tel Aviv
Tel: +972 3 567 7411
Fax: +972 3 510 5379
Email: etti@tase.co.il
URL: http://www.tase.co.il

Italy

Italian Financial Futures Market
(Mercato Italiano Futures)
MIF
Piazza del Gesu' 49, Rome
Tel: +39 6 676 7514
Fax: +39 6 676 7250

Italian Stock Exchange
(Consiglio de Borsa)
Piazza degli Affari, 6, Milan
Tel: +39 2 724 261
Fax: +39 2 864 64 323
Email: postoffice@borsaitalia.it
URL: http://www.borsaitalia.it

Italian Derivatives Market
IDEM
Piazza Affari 6, Milan
Tel: +39 2 72 42 61
Fax: +39 2 72 00 43 33
Email: postoffice@borsaitalia.it
URL: http://www.borsaitalia.it

Jamaica

Jamaica Stock Exchange
40 Harbour Street, PO Box 1084, Kingston
Tel: +1809 809 922 0806
Fax: +1809 809 922 6966
Email: jse@infochan.com
URL: http://www.jamstockex.com

Japan

Tokyo Commodity Exchange
(Tokyo Kogyoin Torihikijo)
TOCOM
10-8 Nihonbashi, Horidome-cho, Chuo-ku, 1-chome, Tokyo
Tel: +81 3 3661 9191
Fax: +81 3 3661 7568

Japan Securities Dealing Association
(Nihon Shokengyo Kyokai)
Tojyo Shoken Building, 5-8 Kayaba-cho, 1-chome, Nihonbashi, Tokyo
Tel: +81 3 3667 8451
Fax: +81 3 3666 8009

Osaka Textile Exchange
(Osaka Seni Torihikijo)
2-5-28 Kyutaro-machi, Chuo-ku, Osaka
Tel: +81 6 253 0031
Fax: +81 6 253 0034

Tokyo Stock Exchange
(Tokyo Shoken Torihikijo)
TSE
2-1 Nihombashi-Kabuto-Cho, Chuo-ku, Tokyo
Tel: +81 3 3666 0141
Fax: +81 3 3663 0625
URL: http://www.tse.or.jp

Kobe Raw Silk Exchange
(Kobe Kiito Torihiksho)
KSE
126 Higashimachi, Chuo-ku, Kobe
Tel: +81 78 331 7141
Fax: +81 78 331 7145

Kobe Rubber Exchange
(Kobe Gomu Torihiksho)
KRE
49 Harima-cho, Chuo-ku, Kobe
Tel: +81 78 331 4211
Fax: +81 78 332 1622

Nagoya Stock Exchange
(Nagoya Shoken Torihikijo)
NSE
3-17 Sakae, 3-chome, Naka-ku, Nagoya
Tel: +81 81 52 262 3172
Fax: +81 81 52 241 1527
Email: nse@po.iijnet.or.jp
URL: http://www.iijnet.or.jp/nse-jp/

Nagoya Textile Exchange
2-15 Nishiki 3 Chome, Naka-ku, Naka-ku, Nagoya
Tel: +81 52 951 2171
Fax: +81 52 961 6407

Osaka Securities Exchange
(Osaka Shoken Torihikijo)
OSE
8-16, Kitahama, 1-chome, Chuo-ku, Osaka
Tel: +81 6 229 8643
Fax: +81 6 231 2639
Email: osakaexc@po.iijnet.or.jp
URL: http://www.ose.or.jp

Tokyo Grain Exchange
(Tokyo Kokumotsu Shohin Torihikijo)
TGE
1-12-5 Nihonbashi, Kakigara-cho, 1-Chome, Chuo-ku, Tokyo
Tel: +81 3 3668 9321
Fax: +81 3 3661 4564
Email: webmas@tge.or.jp
URL: http://www.tge.or.jp

Tokyo International Financial Futures Exchange
TIFFE
1-3-1 Marunouchi, Chiyoda-ku, Tokyo
Tel: +81 3 5223 2400
Fax: +81 3 5223 2450
URL: http://www.tiffe.or.jp

Hiroshima Stock Exchange
KANEX
14-18 Kanayama-cho, Naka-ku, Hiroshima
Tel: +81 82 541 1121
Fax: +81 82 541 1128

Fukuoka Stock Exchange
KANEX
2-14-2 Tenjin, Chuo-ku, Fukuoka
Tel: +81 92 741 8231
Fax: +81 92 713 1540

Niigata Securities Exchange
(Niigata Shoken Torihikijo)
1245 Hachiban-cho, Kamiokawame-don, Niigata
Tel: +81 25 222 4181
Fax: +81 25 222 4551

Sapporo Securities Exchange
(Sapporo Shoken Torihikijo)
5-14-1 Nishi-minami, I-jo, Chuo-ku, Sapporo
Tel: +81 11 241 6171
Fax: +81 11 251 0840

Kammon Commodity Exchange
(Kammon Shohin Torihikijo)
1-5 Nabe-cho, Shimonoseki
Tel: +81 832 31 1313
Fax: +81 832 23 1947

Kyoto Stock Exchange
KANEX
66 Tachiurinishi-machi, Higashinotoin-higashiiru, Shijo-dori,
Shimogyo-ku, Kyoto
Tel: +81 75 221 1171
Fax: +81 75 221 8356

Maebashi Dried Cocoa Exchange
(Maebashi Kanken Torihikijo)
1-49-1 Furuichi-machi, Maebashi
Tel: +81 272 52 1401
Fax: +81 272 51 8270

Cubu Commodity Exchange
3-2-15 Nishiki, Naka-ku, Nagoya
Tel: +81 52 951 2170
Fax: +81 52 961 1044

Yokohama Raw Silk Exchange
(Yokohama Kiito Torihikijo)
Silk Centre, 1 Yamashita-cho, Naka-ku, Yokohama
Tel: +81 45 641 1341
Fax: +81 45 641 1346

Kansai Agricultural Commodities Exchange
KANEX
1-10-14 Awaza, Nishi-ku, Osaka
Tel: +81 6 531 7931
Fax: +81 6 541 9343
Email: kex-1@kanex.or.jp
URL: http://www.kanex.or.jp

Jordan

Amman Financial Market
PO Box 8802, Ammam
Tel: +962 6 607171
Fax: +962 6 686830
Email: afm@go.com.jo
URL: http://accessme.com/AFM/

Kenya

Nairobi Stock Exchange
PO Box 43633, Nairobi
Tel: +254 2 230692
Fax: +254 2 224200
Email: nse@acc.or.ke

Korea (South)

Korea Stock Exchange
KSE
33 Yoido-dong, Youngdeungpo-gu, Seoul
Tel: +82 2 3774 9000
Fax: +82 2 786 0263
Email: world@www.kse.or.kr
URL: http://www.kse.or.kr

Kuwait

Kuwait Stock Exchange
PO Box 22235, Safat, Kuwait
Tel: +965 242 3130
Fax: +965 242 0779

Latvia

Riga Stock Exchange
Doma Iaukums 6, Riga
Tel: +7 212 431
Fax: +7 229 411
Email: rfb@mail.bkc.lv
URL: http://www.rfb.lv

Lithuania

National Stock Exchange of Lithuania
Ukmerges St 41, Vilnius
Tel: +370 2 72 14 07
Fax: +370 2 742 894
Email: office@nse.lt
URL: http://www.nse.lt

Luxembourg

Luxembourg Stock Exchange
(Societe Anonyme de la Bourse de Luxembourg)
11 Avenue de la Porte-Neuve
Tel: +352 47 79 36-1
Fax: +352 47 32 98
Email: info@bourse.lu
URL: http://www.bourse.lu

Macedonia

Macedonia Stock Exchange
MSE
Tel: +389 91 122 055
Fax: +389 91 122 069
Email: mse@unet.com.mk
URL: http://www.mse.org.mk

Malaysia

Kuala Lumpur Commodity Exchange
KLCE
4th Floor, Citypoint, Komplex Dayabumi, Jalan Sulta Hishamuddin,
Kuala Lumpur
Tel: +60 3 293 6822
Fax: +60 3 274 2215
Email: klce@po.jaring.my
URL: http://www.klce.com.my

Kuala Lumpur Stock Exchange
KLSE
4th Floor, Exchange Square, Off Jalan Semantan, Damansara
Heights, Kuala Lumpur
Tel: +60 3 254 64 33
Fax: +60 3 255 74 63
Email: webmaster@klse.com.my
URL: http://www.klse.com.my

The Kuala Lumpur Options & Financial Futures Exchange
KLOFFE
10th Floor, Wisma Chase Perdana, Damansara Heights, Jalan
Semantan, Kuala Lumpur
Tel: +60 3 253 8199
Fax: +60 3 255 3207
Email: kloffe@kloffe.com.my
URL: http://www.kloffe.com.my

Malaysia Monetary Exchange BHD
4th Floor, City Point, PO Box 11260, Dayabumi Complex, Jalan
Sultan Hishmuddin, Kuala Lumpur
Email: mme@po.jaring.my
URL: http://www.jaring.my/mme

Malta

Malta Stock Exchange
27 Pietro Floriani Street, Floriana, Valletta 14
Tel: +356 244 0515
Fax: +356 244 071
Email: borza@maltanet.omnes.net

Mauritius

Mauritius Stock Exchange
Stock Exchange Commission, 9th Floor, SICOM Building, Sir
Celicourt Anselme Street, Port Louis
Tel: +230 208 8735
Fax: +230 208 8676
Email: svtradha@intnet.mu
URL: http://lynx.intnet.mu/sem/

Mexico

Mexican Stock Exchange
(Bolsa Mexicana de Valores, SA de CV)
Paseo de la Reforma 255, Colonia Cuauhtemoc, Mexico DF
Tel: +52 5 726 66 00
Fax: +52 5 705 47 98
Email: cinform@bmv.com.mx
URL: http://www.bmv.com.mx

Morocco

Casablanca Stock Exchange
(Societe de la Bourse des Valeurs de Casablanca)
98 Boulevard Mohammed V, Casablanca
Tel: +212 2 27 93 54
Fax: +212 2 20 03 65

Namibia

Namibian Stock Exchange
Kaiserkrone Centre 11, O Box 2401, Windhoek
Tel: +264 61 227 647
Fax: +264 61 248 531
Email: tminney@nse.com.na
URL: http://www.nse.com.na

Netherlands

Financiele Termijnmarkt Amsterdam NV
FTA
Nes 49, Amsterdam
Tel: +31 20 550 4555
Fax: +31 20 624 5416

AEX-Stock Exchange
AEX
Beursplein 5, PO Box 19163, Amsterdam
Tel: +31 20 550 4444
Fax: +31 20 550 4950
URL: http://www.aex.nl/

AEX-Agricultural Futures Exchange
Beursplein 5, PO Box 19163, Amsterdam
Tel: +31 20 550 4444
Fax: +31 20 623 9949

AEX-Options Exchange
AEX
Beursplein 5, PO Box 19163, Amsterdam
Tel: +31 20 550 4444
Fax: +31 20 550 4950
URL: http://www.aex-optiebeurs.ase.nl

New Zealand

New Zealand Futures & Options Exchange Ltd
NZFOE
10th Level, Stock Exchange Cen, 191 Queen Street, Auckland 1
Tel: +64 9 309 8308
Fax: +64 9 309 8817
Email: info@nzfoe.co.nz
URL: http://www.nzfoe.co.nz

New Zealand Stock Exchange
NZSE
8th Floor Caltex Tower, 286-292 Lambton Quay, Wellington
Tel: +64 4 4727 599
Fax: +64 4 4731 470
Email: info@nzse.org.nz
URL: http://www.nzse.co.nz

Nicaragua

Nicaraguan Stock Exchange
(BOLSA DE VALORES DE NICARAGUA, S.A.)
Centro Financiero Banic, 1er Piso, Km. 5 1/2 Carretera Masaya
Email: info@bolsanic.com
URL: http://bolsanic.com/

Nigeria

Nigerian Stock Exchange
Stock Exchange House, 8th & 9th Floors, 2/4 Customs Street, Lagos
Tel: +234 1 266 0287
Fax: +234 1 266 8724
Email: alile@nse.ngra.com

Norway

Oslo Stock Exchange
(Oslo Bors)
OSLO
P.O. Box 460, Sentrum, Oslo
Tel: +47 22 34 17 00
Fax: +47 22 41 65 90
Email: informasjonsavdelingen@ose.telemax.no
URL: http://www.ose.no

Oman

Muscat Securities Market
Po Box 3265, Ruwi
Tel: +968 702 665
Fax: +968 702 691

Pakistan

Islamabad Stock Exchange
Stock Exchange Building, 101-E Fazal-ul-Haq Road, Blue Area,
Islamabad
Tel: +92 51 27 50 45
Fax: +92 51 27 50 44
Email: ise@paknet1.ptc.pk

Karachi Stock Exchange
Stock Exchange Building, Stock Exchange Road, Karachi
Tel: +92 21 2425502
Fax: +92 21 241 0825
URL: http://www.kse.org

Lahore Stock Exchange
PO Box 1315, 19 Khayaban e Aiwan e Iqbal, Lahore
Tel: |92 42 636 8000
Fax: +92 42 636 8484

Panama

Panama Stock Exchange
(Bolsa de Valores de Panama, SA)
Calle Elvira Mendex y Calle 52, Edif Valarino, Planta Baja
Tel: +507 2 69 1966
Fax: +507 2 69 2457
URL: http://www.urraca.com/bvp/

Paraguay

Ascuncon Stock Exchange
(Bolsa de Valores y Productos de Ascuncion)
Estrella 540, Ascuncion
Tel: +595 21 442 445
Fax: +595 21 442 446
Email: bolsapya@pla.net.py
URL: http://www.pla.net.py/bvpasa

Peru

Lima Stock Exchange
(La Bolsa de Valores de Lima)
Pasaje Acuna 191, Lima
Tel: +51 1 426 79 39
Fax: +51 1 426 76 50
Email: web_team@bvl.com.pe
URL: http://www.bvl.com.pe

Philippines

Philippine Stock Exchange
Philippine Stock Exchange Cent, Tektite Road, Ortigas Centre, Pasig
Tel: +63 2 636 01 22
Fax: +63 2 634 51 13
Email: pse@mnl.sequel.net
URL: http://www.pse.com.ph

Manila International Futures Exchange
MIFE
7/F Producer's Bank Centre, Paseo de Roxas, Makati
Tel: +63 2 818 5496
Fax: +63 2 818 5529

Poland

Warsaw Stock Exchange
Gielda papierow, Wartosciowych w Warszawie SA,
Ul Nowy Swiat 6/12, Warsaw
Tel: +48 22 628 32 32
Fax: +48 22 628 17 54
Email: gielda@kp.atm.com.pl

Portugal

Oporto Derivatives Exchange
(Bolsa de Derivados do Oporto)
BDP
Av. da Boavista 3433, Oporto
Tel: +351 2 618 58 58
Fax: +351 2 618 56 66

Lisbon Stock Exchange
(Bolsa de Valores de Lisboa)
BVL
Edificio da Bolsa, Rua Soeiro Pereira Gomes, Lisbon
Tel: +351 1 790 99 04
Fax: +351 1 795 20 21
Email: webmaster@bvl.pt
URL: http://www.bvl.pt

Romania

Bucharest Stock Exchange
BSE
Doamnei no. 8, Bucharest
Email: bse@delos.ro
URL: http://www.delos.ro/bse/

Romanian Commodities Exchange
(Bursa Romana de Marfuri SA)
Piata Presei nr 1, Sector 1, Bucharest
Tel: +40 223 21 69
Fax: +40 223 21 67

Russian Federation

Moscow Interbank Currency Exchange
MICEX
21/1, Sadovaya-Spasskay, Moscow
Tel: +7 095 705 9627
Fax: +7 095 705 9622
Email: inmicex@micex.com
URL: http://www.micex.com/

Russian Exchange
RCRME
Myasnitskaya ul 26, Moscow
Tel: +7 095 262 06 53
Fax: +7 095 262 57 57
Email: assa@vc-rtsb.msk.ru
URL: http://www.re.ru

Moscow Commodity Exchange
Pavilion No. 4, Russian Exhibition Centre, Moscow
Tel: +7 095 187 83 07
Fax: +7 095 187 9982

St Petersburg Futures Exchange
SPBFE
274 Ligovski av., St Petersburg
Tel: +7 812 294 15 12
Fax: +7 812 327 93 88
Email: seva@spbfe.futures.ru

Siberian Stock Exchange
PO box 233, Frunze St 5, Novosibirsk
Tel: +7 38 32 21 06 90
Fax: +7 38 32 21 06 90
Email: sibex@sse.nsk.su

Moscow Central Stock Exchange
9(B) Bolshaya Maryinskaya Stre, Moscow
Tel: +7 095 229 88 82
Fax: +7 0995 202 06 67

Moscow International Stock Exchange
MISE
Slavyanskaya Pl 4, Bld 2, Moscow
Tel: +7 095 923 33 39
Fax: +7 095 923 33 39

National Association of Securities Market Participants
(NAUF)
Floor 2, Building 5, Chayanova Street 15, Moscow
Tel: +7 095 705 90
Fax: +7 095 976 42 36
Email: naufor@rtsnet.ru
URL: http://www.rtsnet.ru

Vladivostock Stock Exchange
VSE
21 Zhertv Revolyutsii Str, Vladivostock
Tel: +7 4232 22 78 87
Fax: +7 4232 22 80 09

St Petersburg Stock Exchange
SPSE
274 Ligovsky pr, St Petersburg
Tel: +7 812 296 10 80
Fax: +7 812 296 10 80
Email: root@lse.spb.su

Saudi Arabia

Saudi Arabian Monetary Authority
SAMA
PO Box 2992, Riyadh
Tel: +966 1 466 2300
Fax: +966 1 466 3223

Singapore

Singapore Commodity Exchange Ltd
SICOM
111 North Bridge Road, #23-04/, Peninsula Plaza
Tel: +65 338 5600
Fax: +65 338 9116
Email: sicom@pacific.net.sg

Stock Exchange of Singapore
No. 26-01/08, 20 Cecil Street, The Exchange
Tel: +65 535 3788
Fax: +65 535 6994
Email: webmaster@ses.com.sg
URL: http://www.ses.com.sg

Singapore International Monetary Exchange Ltd
SIMEX
1 Raffles Place, No. 07-00, OUB Centre
Tel: +65 535 7382
Fax: +65 535 7282
Email: simex@pacific.net.sg
URL: http://www.simex.com.sg

Slovak Republic

Bratislava Stock Exchange
(Burza cenny ch papierov v Bratislave)
BSSE
Vysoka 17, Bratislava
Tel: +42 7 5036 102
Fax: +42 7 5036 103
Email: kunikova@bsse.sk
URL: http://www.bsse.sk

Slovenia

Commodity Exchange of Ljubljana
Smartinskal 52, PO Box 85, Ljubljana
Tel: +386 61 18 55 100
Fax: +386 61 18 55 101
Email: infos@bb-lj.si
URL: http://www.eunet.si/commercial/bbl/bbl-ein.html

Ljubljana Stock Exchange, Inc
LJSE
Sovenska cesta 56, Lbujljana
Tel: +386 61 171 02 11
Fax: +386 61 171 02 13
Email: info@jse.si
URL: http://www.ljse.si

South Africa

Johannesburg Stock Exchange
JSE
17 Diagonal Street, Johannesburg
Tel: +27 11 377 2200
Fax: +27 11 834 3937
Email: r&d@jse.co.za
URL: http://www.jse.co.za

South African Futures Exchange
SAFEX
105 Central Street, Houghton Estate 2198, Johannesburg
Tel: +27 11 728 5960
Fax: +27 11 728 5970
Email: jani@icon.co.za
URL: http://www.safex.co.za

Spain

Citrus Fruit and Commodity Market of Valencia
(Futuros de Citricos y Mercaderias de Valencia)
2, 4 Libreros, Valencia
Tel: +34 6 387 01 88
Fax: +34 6 394 36 30
Email: futuros@super.medusa.es

Spanish Options Exchange
(MEFF Renta Variable)
MEFF RV
Torre Picasso, Planta 26, Madrid
Tel: +34 1 585 0800
Fax: +34 1 571 9542
Email: mefrv@meffrv.es
URL: http://www.meffrv.es

Spanish Financial Futures Market
(MEFF Renta Fija)
MEFF RF
Via Laietana, 58, Barcelona
Tel: +34 3 412 1128
Fax: +34 3 268 4769
Email: marketing@meff.es
URL: http://www.meff.es

Madrid Stock Exchange
(Bolsa de Madrid)
Plaza de la Lealtad 1, Madrid
Tel: +34 1 589 26 00
Fax: +34 1 531 22 90
Email: internacional@bolsamadrid.es
URL: http://www.bolsamadrid.es

Barcelona Stock Exchange
Paseo Isabel II No 1, Barcelona
Tel: +34 3 401 35 55
Fax: +34 3 401 38 59
Email: agiralt@borsabcn.es
URL: http://www.borsabcn.es

Bilbao Stock Exchange
(Sociedad Rectora de la Bolsa de Valoes de Bilbao)
Jose Maria Olabarri 1, Bilbao
Tel: +34 4 423 74 00
Fax: +34 4 424 46 20
Email: bolsabilbao@sarenet.es
URL: http://www.bolsabilbao.es

Valencia Stock Exchange
(Sociedad Rectora de la Bolsa de Valoes de Valencia)
Libreros 2 y 4, Valencia
Tel: +34 6 387 01 00
Fax: +34 6 387 01 14

Sri Lanka

Colombo Stock Exchange
CSE
04-01 West Bloc, World Trade Centre, Echelon Square, Colombo 1
Tel: +94 1 44 65 81
Fax: +94 1 44 52 79
Email: cse@sri.lanka.net
URL: http://www.lanka.net/cse/

Swaziland

Swaziland Stock Market
Swaziland Stockbrokers Ltd, 2nd Floor Dlan'ubeka House, Walker
St, Mbabane
Tel: +268 46163
Fax: +268 44132
URL: http://mbendi.co.za/exsw.htm

Sweden

The Swedish Futures and Options Market
(OM Stockholm AB)
OMS
Box 16305, Brunkebergstorg 2, Stockholm
Tel: +46 8 700 0600
Fax: +46 8 723 1092
URL: http://www.omgroup.com

Stockholm Stock Exchange Ltd
(Stockholm Fondbors AB)
Kallargrand 2, Stockholm
Tel: +46 8 613 88 00
Fax: +46 8 10 81 10
Email: info@xsse.se
URL: http://www.xsse.se

Switzerland

Swiss Options & Financial Futures Exchange AG
SOFFEX
Selnaustrasse 32, Zurich
Tel: +41 1 229 2111
Fax: +41 1 229 2233
Email: webmaster@swx.ch
URL: http://www.bourse.ch

Swiss Exchange
SWX
Selnaustrasse 32, Zurich
Tel: +41 1 229 21 11
Fax: +41 1 229 22 33
URL: http://www.bourse.ch

Taiwan

Taiwan Stock Exchange
Floors 2-10, City Building, 85 Yen Ping Road South, Taipei
Tel: +886 2 311 4020
Fax: +886 2 375 3669
Email: intl-aff@tse.com.tw
URL: http://www.tse.com.tw

Thailand

The Stock Exchange of Thailand
SET
2nd Floor, Tower 1, 132 Sindhorn Building, Wireless Road, Bangkok
Tel: +66 2 254 0960
Fax: +66 2 263 2746
Email: webmaster@set.or.th
URL: http://www.set.or.th

Trinidad and Tobago

Trinidad and Tobago Stock Exchange
65 Independence Street, Port of Spain
Tel: +1809 809 625 5108
Fax: +1809 809 623 0089

Tunisia

Tunis Stock Exchange
(Bourse des Valeurs Mobilieres de Tunis)
Centre Babel - Bloc E, Rue Jean-Jacques Rousseau, Montplaisir, Tunis
Tel: +216 1 780 288
Fax: +216 1 789 189

Turkey

Istanbul Stock Exchange
(Istanbul Menkul Kiymetler Borasi)
ISE
Istinye, Istanbul
Tel: +90 212 298 21 00
Fax: +90 212 298 25 00
Email: info@ise.org
URL: http://www.ise.org

United Kingdom

The London Securities and Derivatives Exchange
OMLX
107 Cannon Street, London
Tel: +44 171 283 0678
Fax: +44 171 815 8508
Email: petter.made@omgroup.com
URL: http://www.omgroup.com/

International Petroleum Exchange of London Ltd
IPE
International House, 1 St. Katharine's Way, London
Tel: +44 171 481 0643
Fax: +44 l7l 481 8485
Email: busdev@ipe.uk.com
URL: http://www.ipe.uk.com

London International Futures & Options Exchange
LIFFE
Cannon Bridge, London
Tel: +44 171 623 0444
Fax: +44 171 588 3624
Email: exchange@liffe.com
URL: http://www.liffe.com

London Metal Exchange
LME
56 Leadenhall Street, London
Tel: +44 171 264 5555
Fax: +44 171 680 0505
Email: lsnow@lmetal.netkonect.co.uk
URL: http://www.lme.co.uk

The Baltic Exchange
Tel: +44 171 623 5501
Fax: +44 171 369 1622
Email: enquiries@balticexchange.co.uk
URL:http://www.balticexchange.co.uk

London Stock Exchange
LSE
Old Broad Street, London
Tel: +44 171 797 1000
Fax: +44 171 374 0504

Tradepoint Investment Exchange
35 King Street, London
Tel: +44 171 240 8000
Fax: +44 171 240 1900
Email: g171@dial.pipex.com
URL: http://www.tradepoint.co.uk

London Commodity Exchange
LCE
1 Commodity Quay, St. Katharine Docks, London
Tel: +44 171 481 2080
Fax: +44 171 702 9923
URL: http://www.liffe.com

United States

New York Stock Exchange
NYSE
11 Wall Street, New York
Tel: +1 212 656 3000
Fax: +1 212 656 5557
URL: http://www.nyse.com

Minneapolis Grain Exchange
MGE
400 S. Fourth St., Minneapolis
Tel: +1 612 338 6216
Fax: +1 612 339 1155
Email: mgex@ix.netcom.com
URL: http://www.mgex.com

Philadelphia Stock Exchange
PHLX
1900 Market Street, Philadelphia
Tel: +1 215 496 5000
Fax: +1 215 496 5653
URL: http://www.phlx.com

Kansas City Board of Trade
KCBT
4800 Main St., Suite 303, Kansas City
Tel: +1 816 753 7500
Fax: +1 816 753 3944
Email: kcbt@kcbt.com
URL: http://www.kcbt.com

Chicago Board Options Exchange
CBOE
400 S. LaSalle Street, Chicago
Tel: +1 312 786 5600
Fax: +1 312 786 7409
Email: investor_services@cboe.com
URL: http://www.cboe.com

Chicago Board of Trade
CBOT
141 West Jackson Boulevard, Chicago
Tel: +1 312 435 3500
Fax: +1 312 341 3306
Email: comments@cbot.com
URL: http://www.cbt.com

New York Mercantile Exchange
NYMEX
4 World Trade Center, New York
Tel: +1 212 938 222
Fax: +1 212 938 2985
Email: marketing@nymex.com
URL: http://www.nymex.com

Chicago Stock Exchange
CHX
One Financial Place, 440 S. LaSalle St, Chicago
Tel: +1 312 663 222
Fax: +1 312 773 2396
Email: marketing@chiacgostockex.com
URL: http://www.chicagostockex.com

MidAmerica Commodity Exchange
MIDAM
141 W. Jackson Boulevard, Chicago
Tel: +1 313 341 3000
Fax: +1 312 341 3027
Email: comments@cbot.com
URL: http://www.midam.com

Philadelphia Board of Trade
1900 Market Street, Philadelphia
Tel: +1 215 496 5357
Fax: +1 215 496 5653

The Cincinnati Stock Exchange
400 South LaSalle Street, Chicago
Tel: +1 312 786 8803
Fax: +1 312 939 7239

Boston Stock Exchange, Inc
BSE
38th Floor, One Boston Place, Boston
Tel: +1 617 723 9500
Fax: +1 617 523 6603
URL: http://www.bostonstock.com

Nasdaq Stock Market
1735 K Street NW, Washington DC
Tel: +1 202 728 8000
Fax: +1 202 293 6260
Email: fedback@nasdaq.com
URL: http://www.nasdaq.com

American Stock Exchange
AMEX
86 Trinity Place, New York
Tel: +1 212 306 1000
Fax: +1 212 306 1802
Email: jstcphan@amex.com
URL: http://www.amex.com

New York Cotton Exchange
NYCE
4 World Trade Center, New York
Tel: +1 212 938 2702
Fax: +1 212 488 8135
URL: http://www.nyce.com

Pacific Stock Exchange, Inc
PSE
301 Pine Street, San Francisco
Tel: +1 415 393 4000
Fax: +1 415 393 4202
URL: http://www.pacificex.com

Chicago Mercantile Exchange
CME
30 S. Wacker Drive, Chicago
Tel: +1 312 930 1000
Fax: +1 312 930 3439
Email: info@cme.com
URL: http://www.cme.com

Coffee, Sugar & Cocoa Exchange Inc.
CSCE
4 World Trade Center, New York
Tel: +1 212 938 2800
Fax: +1 212 524 9863
Email: csce@ix.netcom.com
URL: http://www.csce.com

Venezuela

Maracaibo Stock Exchange
(Bolsa de Valores de Maracaibo)
Calle 96, Esq Con Avda 5, Edificio
Banco Central de Vene, Piso 9, Maracaibo
Tel: +58 61 225 482
Fax: +58 61 227 663

Venezuela Electronic Stock Exchange
(de Venezuela)
C·mara de Comercio de Valencia, Edif. C·mara de Comercio, Av.
BolÌvar, Valencia, Edo. Carabobo, Apartado 151
Tel: +58 57.5109
Fax: +58 57.5147
Email: set@venezuelastock.com
URL: http://www.venezuelastock.com

Caracas Stock Exchange
(Bolsa de Valores de Caracas)
Edificio Atrium, Piso 1 Calle Sorocaima, Urbanizacion, El Rosal,
Caracas
Tel: +58 2 905 5511
Fax: +58 2 905 5814
Email: anafin@true.net
URL: http://www.caracasstock.com

Yugoslavia

Belgrade Stock Exchange
(Beogradska Berza)
Omladinskih 1, 3rd Floor, PO Box 214, Belgrade
Tel: +381 11 19 84 77
Fax: +381 11 13 82 42
Email: beyu@eunet.yu

Zimbabwe

Zimbabwe Stock Exchange
5th Floor, Southampton House, Union Avenue, Harare
Tel: +263 4 736 861
Fax: +263 4 791 045

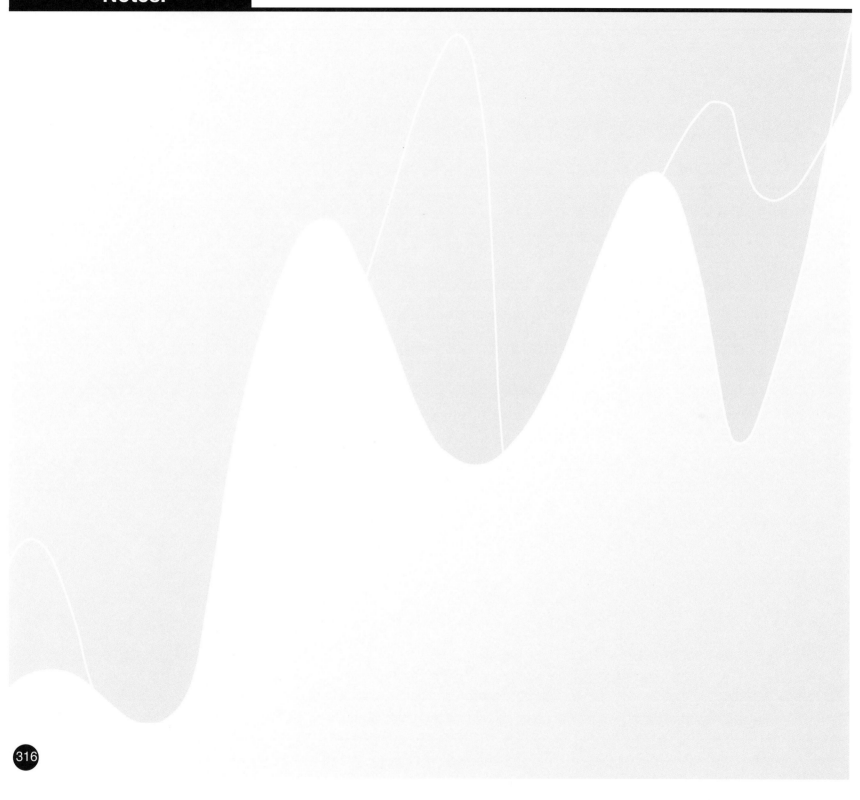